MCSA/MCSE: Exchange Server 2003 Implem[illegible]tion and Management Study Guide

Implementing and Managing Microsoft Exchange Server [illegible]

OBJECTIVE	[illegible]ER
INSTALLING, CONFIGURING, AND TROUBLESHOOTING EXCHANGE SERVER 2003	
Prepare the environment for deployment of Exchange Server 2003	3
Install, configure, and troubleshoot Exchange Server	3, 8
Install, configure, and troubleshoot Exchange Server 2003 in a clustered environment	3, 4
Upgrade from Exchange Server 5.5 to Exchange Server 2003	11
Migrate from other messaging systems to Exchange Server 2003	11, 12
Use the Migration Wizard to migrate from other messaging systems	
Migrate from other Exchange organizations	
Configure and troubleshoot Exchange Server 2003 for coexistence with other Exchange organizations	8, 11, 12, 13
Configure and troubleshoot Exchange Server 2003 for coexistence with other messaging systems	8, 13
Configure and troubleshoot Exchange Server 2003 for interoperability with other SMTP messaging systems	8, 13
MANAGING, MONITORING, AND TROUBLESHOOTING EXCHANGE SERVER COMPUTERS	
Manage, monitor, and troubleshoot server health	10
Manage, monitor, and troubleshoot data storage	9, 14
Manage, monitor, and troubleshoot Exchange Server clusters	4
Perform and troubleshoot backups and recovery	14
Remove an Exchange Server computer from the organization	14

SYBEX

OBJECTIVE	CHAPTER
MANAGING, MONITORING, AND TROUBLESHOOTING THE EXCHANGE ORGANIZATION	
Manage and troubleshoot public folders	6
Manage and troubleshoot virtual servers	4
Manage and troubleshoot front-end and back-end servers	4
Manage and troubleshoot connectivity	7
Monitor, manage, and troubleshoot infrastructure performance	10
MANAGING SECURITY IN THE EXCHANGE ENVIRONMENT	
Manage and troubleshoot connectivity across firewalls	15
Manage audit settings and audit logs	15
Manage and troubleshoot permissions	10, 15
Manage and troubleshoot encryption and digital signatures	15
Detect and respond to security threats	15
MANAGING RECIPIENT OBJECTS AND ADDRESS LISTS	
Manage recipient policies	10
Manage user objects	5
Manage distribution and security groups	5
Manage contacts	5
Manage address lists	5
MANAGING AND MONITORING TECHNOLOGIES THAT SUPPORT EXCHANGE SERVER 2003	
Diagnose problems arising from host resolution protocols	15
Diagnose problems arising from Active Directory issues	15
Diagnose network connectivity problems	15

Exam objectives are subject to change at any time without prior notice and at Microsoft's sole discretion. Please visit Microsoft's Training & Certification Web site (`www.microsoft.com/trainingandservices`) for the most current listing of exam objectives.

MCSA/MCSE: Exchange Server 2003 Implementation and Management

Study Guide

MCSA/MCSE: Exchange Server 2003 Implementation and Management Study Guide

Will Schmied

and James Chellis

San Francisco • London

Associate Publisher: Neil Edde
Acquisitions and Developmental Editor: Maureen Adams
Production Editor: Susan Berge
Technical Editors: Chris N. Crane, James F. Kelly
Copyeditor: Linda S. Recktenwald
Compositor: Laurie Stewart, Happenstance Type-O-Rama
CD Coordinator: Dan Mummert
CD Technician: Kevin Ly
Proofreaders: Laurie O'Connell, Nancy Riddiough
Indexer: Ted Laux
Book Designers: Bill Gibson, Judy Fung
Cover Designer: Archer Design
Cover Photograph: Photodisc and Victor Arre

Library of Congress Card Number: 2004104103

ISBN: 0-7821-4338-5

Manufactured in the United States of America

10 9 8 7 6 5 4 3 2

To Our Valued Readers:

Thank you for looking to Sybex for your Microsoft certification exam prep needs. We at Sybex are proud of the reputation we've established for providing certification candidates with the practical knowledge and skills needed to succeed in the highly competitive IT marketplace. Sybex is proud to have helped thousands of Microsoft certification candidates prepare for their exams over the years, and we are excited about the opportunity to continue to provide computer and networking professionals with the skills they'll need to succeed in the highly competitive IT industry.

With its rollout of Windows 2003 MCSA and MCSE tracks, and the new Messaging and Security Specializations, Microsoft has raised the bar for IT certifications yet again. The new programs better reflect the skill set demanded of IT administrators in today's marketplace and offer candidates a clearer structure for acquiring the skills necessary to advance their careers.

The authors and editors have worked hard to ensure that the Study Guide you hold in your hand is comprehensive, in-depth, and pedagogically sound. We're confident that this book will exceed the demanding standards of the certification marketplace and help you, the Microsoft certification candidate, succeed in your endeavors.

As always, your feedback is important to us. If you believe you've identified an error in the book, please send a detailed e-mail to support@sybex.com. And if you have general comments or suggestions, feel free to drop me a line directly at nedde@sybex.com. At Sybex we're continually striving to meet the needs of individuals preparing for certification exams.

Good luck in the pursuit of your Microsoft certification!

Neil Edde
Associate Publisher—Certification
Sybex, Inc.

Software License Agreement: Terms and Conditions

The media and/or any online materials accompanying this book that are available now or in the future contain programs and/or text files (the "Software") to be used in connection with the book. SYBEX hereby grants to you a license to use the Software, subject to the terms that follow. Your purchase, acceptance, or use of the Software will constitute your acceptance of such terms.

The Software compilation is the property of SYBEX unless otherwise indicated and is protected by copyright to SYBEX or other copyright owner(s) as indicated in the media files (the "Owner(s)"). You are hereby granted a single-user license to use the Software for your personal, noncommercial use only. You may not reproduce, sell, distribute, publish, circulate, or commercially exploit the Software, or any portion thereof, without the written consent of SYBEX and the specific copyright owner(s) of any component software included on this media.

In the event that the Software or components include specific license requirements or end-user agreements, statements of condition, disclaimers, limitations or warranties ("End-User License"), those End-User Licenses supersede the terms and conditions herein as to that particular Software component. Your purchase, acceptance, or use of the Software will constitute your acceptance of such End-User Licenses.

By purchase, use or acceptance of the Software you further agree to comply with all export laws and regulations of the United States as such laws and regulations may exist from time to time.

Software Support

Components of the supplemental Software and any offers associated with them may be supported by the specific Owner(s) of that material, but they are not supported by SYBEX. Information regarding any available support may be obtained from the Owner(s) using the information provided in the appropriate read.me files or listed elsewhere on the media.

Should the manufacturer(s) or other Owner(s) cease to offer support or decline to honor any offer, SYBEX bears no responsibility. This notice concerning support for the Software is provided for your information only. SYBEX is not the agent or principal of the Owner(s), and SYBEX is in no way responsible for providing any support for the Software, nor is it liable or responsible for any support provided, or not provided, by the Owner(s).

Warranty

SYBEX warrants the enclosed media to be free of physical defects for a period of ninety (90) days after purchase. The Software is not available from SYBEX in any other form or media than that enclosed herein or posted to www.sybex.com. If you discover a defect in the media during this warranty period, you may obtain a replacement of identical format at no charge by sending the defective media, postage prepaid, with proof of purchase to:

SYBEX Inc.
Product Support Department
1151 Marina Village Parkway
Alameda, CA 94501
Web: http://www.sybex.com

After the 90-day period, you can obtain replacement media of identical format by sending us the defective disk, proof of purchase, and a check or money order for $10, payable to SYBEX.

Disclaimer

SYBEX makes no warranty or representation, either expressed or implied, with respect to the Software or its contents, quality, performance, merchantability, or fitness for a particular purpose. In no event will SYBEX, its distributors, or dealers be liable to you or any other party for direct, indirect, special, incidental, consequential, or other damages arising out of the use of or inability to use the Software or its contents even if advised of the possibility of such damage. In the event that the Software includes an online update feature, SYBEX further disclaims any obligation to provide this feature for any specific duration other than the initial posting.

The exclusion of implied warranties is not permitted by some states. Therefore, the above exclusion may not apply to you. This warranty provides you with specific legal rights; there may be other rights that you may have that vary from state to state. The pricing of the book with the Software by SYBEX reflects the allocation of risk and limitations on liability contained in this agreement of Terms and Conditions.

Shareware Distribution

This Software may contain various programs that are distributed as shareware. Copyright laws apply to both shareware and ordinary commercial software, and the copyright Owner(s) retains all rights. If you try a shareware program and continue using it, you are expected to register it. Individual programs differ on details of trial periods, registration, and payment. Please observe the requirements stated in appropriate files.

Copy Protection

The Software in whole or in part may or may not be copy-protected or encrypted. However, in all cases, reselling or redistributing these files without authorization is expressly forbidden except as specifically provided for by the Owner(s) therein.

For my family: with you all things are possible.
—Will Schmied

Acknowledgments

Thanks to James for giving me the opportunity to work with the great team at Sybex!

—Will Schmied

Contents at a Glance

Contents

Table of Exercises

Introduction

Microsoft's new Microsoft Certified Systems Engineer (MCSE) track for Windows Server 2003 is the premier certification for computer industry professionals. Covering the core technologies around which Microsoft's future will be built, the new MCSE certification is a powerful credential for career advancement.

This book has been developed to give you the critical skills and knowledge you need to prepare for the Exchange Server 2003 elective requirements of the new MCSE certification program for Windows Server 2003. You will find the information you need to acquire a solid understanding of Exchange Server 2003's tools and concepts, to prepare for Exam 70-284: Implementing and Managing Microsoft Exchange Server 2003, and to progress toward MCSE certification.

Why Become Certified in Exchange Server 2003?

As the computer network industry grows in both size and complexity, the need for *proven* ability is increasing. Companies rely on certifications to verify the skills of prospective employees and contractors.

Whether you are just getting started or are ready to move ahead in the computer industry, the knowledge, skills, and credentials you have are your most valuable assets. Microsoft has developed its Microsoft Certified Professional (MCP) program to give you credentials that verify your ability to work with Microsoft products, including Exchange Server 2003, effectively and professionally.

Over the next few years, thousands of companies around the world will use Exchange Server 2003 as their central messaging and collaboration system. This will generate an enormous need for qualified consultants and personnel to design, deploy, and support Exchange Server 2003 networks.

Is This Book for You?

If you want to acquire a solid foundation in Exchange Server 2003, this book is for you. You'll find clear explanations of the fundamental concepts you need to grasp.

If your goal is to prepare for the exam by learning how to use and manage the new operating system, this book is for you. It will help you to achieve the high level of professional competency you need to succeed in this field.

If you want to become certified as an MCSE, this book is definitely for you. However, if you just want to attempt to pass the exam without really understanding Exchange Server 2003, this book is *not* for you. This book is written for those who want to acquire hands-on skills and in-depth knowledge of Exchange Server 2003.

What Does This Book Cover?

Think of this book as your complete guide to administering Exchange Server 2003. It begins by covering basic concepts, such as the fundamentals of messaging services and the architecture behind Exchange Server 2003. Each chapter teaches you how to perform important tasks, including the following:

- Installing and upgrading to Exchange Server 2003
- Creating and managing recipients and public folders
- Configuring storage, routing, and administration in an Exchange organization
- Configuring client applications and Internet protocols
- Using Exchange Server 2003's advanced security components

Throughout the book, you will be guided through hands-on exercises, which give you practical experience for each exam objective. At the end of each chapter, you'll find a summary of the topics covered in the chapter. Finally, each chapter concludes with 20 review questions that test your knowledge of the information covered and provides thorough explanations of the answers. Many more questions, as well as multimedia demonstrations of the hands-on exercises, are included on the CD that accompanies this book, as explained in the "What's on the CD?" section at the end of this Introduction.

The topics covered in this book map directly to Microsoft's official exam objectives. Each exam objective is covered completely.

How Do You Become an MCSA or MCSE?

Attaining MCSE certification has always been a challenge. However, in the past, individuals could acquire detailed exam information—even most of the exam questions—from online "brain dumps" and third-party "cram" books or software products. For the new MCSE exams, this simply will not be the case.

To avoid the "paper-MCSE syndrome" (a devaluation of the MCSE certification because unqualified individuals manage to pass the exams), Microsoft has taken strong steps to protect the security and integrity of the new MCSE track. Prospective MCSEs will need to complete a course of study that provides not only detailed knowledge of a wide range of topics but true skills derived from working with Windows Server 2003 and related software products.

In the new MCSE program, Microsoft is heavily emphasizing hands-on skills. Microsoft has stated that "Nearly half of the core required exams' content demands that the candidate have troubleshooting skills acquired through hands-on experience and working knowledge."

The MCSA certification track is relatively new and was designed and implemented from its beginning using the same methods and standards of learning as the older MCSE certification track.

Fortunately, if you are willing to dedicate time and effort with Windows Server 2003, you can prepare for the exams by using the proper tools. If you work through this book and the other books in this series, you should meet the exam requirements successfully.

This book is a part of a complete series of MCSA and MCSE Study Guides, published by Sybex, that covers the core and elective requirements you need to complete your MCSA or MCSE track. Titles include the following:

- *MCSA/MCSE: Windows Server 2003 Environment Management and Maintenance Study Guide (70-290)*
- *MCSA/MCSE: Windows Server 2003 Network Infrastructure Implementation, Management, and Maintenance Study Guide (70-291)*
- *MCSE: Windows Server 2003 Network Infrastructure Planning and Maintenance Study Guide (70-293)*
- *MCSE: Windows Server 2003 Active Directory Planning, Implementation, and Maintenance Study Guide (70-294)*
- *MCSA/MCSE: Windows 2000 Professional Study Guide, Second Edition (70-210)*
- *MCSA/MCSE: Windows XP Professional Study Guide, Second Edition (70-270)*
- *MCSA/MCSE: Windows Server 2003 Upgrade Study Guide (70-292 and 70-296)*

Exam Requirements

Successful candidates must pass a minimum set of exams that measure technical proficiency and expertise:

- Candidates for MCSE certification must pass seven exams, including four core networking system exams, one core operating system exam, one core design exam, and one elective exam. The following table shows the exams that a new certification candidate must pass.

  All of these exams are required:

Exam #	Topic	Requirement Met
70-290	Managing and Maintaining a Microsoft Windows Server 2003 Environment	Core (networking system)
70-291	Implementing, Managing, and Maintaining a Microsoft Windows Server 2003 Network Infrastructure	Core (networking system)

Exam #	Topic	Requirement Met
70-293	Planning and Maintaining a Microsoft Windows Server 2003 Network Infrastructure	Core (networking system)
70-294	Planning, Implementing, and Maintaining a Microsoft Windows Server 2003 Active Directory Infrastructure	Core (networking system)

One of these exams is required:

Exam #	Topic	Requirement Met
70-270	Installing, Configuring, and Administering Microsoft Windows XP Professional	Core (operating system)
70-210	Installing, Configuring, and Administering Microsoft Windows 2000 Professional	Core (operating system)

One of these exams is required:

Exam #	Topic	Requirement Met
70-297	Designing a Microsoft Windows Server 2003 Active Directory and Network Infrastructure	Core (design)
70-298	Designing Security for a Microsoft Windows Server 2003 Network	Core (design)

One of these exams is required:

Exam #	Topic	Requirement Met
70-284	Implementing and Managing Microsoft Exchange Server 2003	Elective
Any other current MCSE elective listed on the MCSE on Windows Server 2003 page	Various	Elective

- Candidates for MCSA certification must pass four exams, including two core networking system exams, one core operating system exam, and one elective exam. The following table shows the exams that a new certification candidate must pass.

  All of these exams are required:

Exam #	Topic	Requirement Met
70-290	Managing and Maintaining a Microsoft Windows Server 2003 Environment	Core (networking system)
70-291	Implementing, Managing, and Maintaining a Microsoft Windows Server 2003 Network Infrastructure	Core (networking system)

  One of these exams is required:

Exam #	Topic	Requirement Met
70-270	Installing, Configuring, and Administering Microsoft Windows XP Professional	Core (operating system)
70-210	Installing, Configuring, and Administering Microsoft Windows 2000 Professional	Core (operating system)

  One of these exams is required:

Exam #	Topic	Requirement Met
70-284	Implementing and Managing Microsoft Exchange Server 2003	Elective
Any other current MCSE elective listed on the MCSE on Windows Server 2003 page	Various	Elective

For a more detailed description of the Microsoft certification programs, including a list of current MCSE and MCSA electives, check Microsoft's Learning website at `www.microsoft.com/learning/mcp/`.

The Exchange Server 2003 Exam

The Exchange Server 2003 exam covers concepts and skills required for administering Exchange Server 2003, emphasizing the following areas:

- Standards and terminology
- Planning
- Implementation
- Troubleshooting

This exam can be quite specific regarding Exchange Server 2003, and it can be particular about how administrative tasks are performed. It also focuses on fundamental concepts relating to Exchange Server 2003's operation as an enterprise messaging system. Careful study of this book, along with hands-on experience, will help you prepare for this exam.

Microsoft provides exam objectives to give you a very general overview of possible areas of coverage of the Microsoft exams. However, exam objectives are subject to change at any time without prior notice and at Microsoft's sole discretion. Please visit Microsoft's Learning website (`www.microsoft.com/learning/exams/70-284.asp`) for the most current exam objectives listing.

Types of Exam Questions

In the previous tracks, the formats of the MCSE exams were fairly straightforward, consisting almost entirely of multiple-choice questions appearing in a few different sets. Prior to taking an exam, you knew how many questions you would see and what type of questions would appear. If you had purchased the right third-party exam preparation products, you could even be quite familiar with the pool of questions you might be asked. As mentioned earlier, all of this is changing.

In an effort to both refine the testing process and protect the quality of its certifications, Microsoft has introduced some new exam elements. You will not know in advance which type of format you will see on your exam. These innovations make the exams more challenging, and they make it much more difficult for someone to pass an exam after simply "cramming" for it.

Microsoft will be accomplishing its goal of protecting the exams by regularly adding and removing exam questions, limiting the number of questions that any individual sees in a beta exam, and adding new exam elements.

Exam questions come in many forms in the new MCP exams, so let's examine these forms now.

Active Screen

The active screen question, seen in Figure 1, tests your working knowledge of the product by presenting you with a dialog box and requiring you to configure or change one or more options in order to successfully answer the question. You may need to select or deselect options, use drop-down menus, or drag text elements into text areas within the dialog box to meet the requirements of the question. Note that not every element you see in the dialog box will be active for you to interact with—use this to your advantage in weeding out actions that you do not need to perform.

Build List and Reorder

The build list and reorder question type, seen in Figure 2, has been used in MCP exams for quite some time but has been refined a bit for the new MCSE on Windows Server 2003 track. When presented with a build list and reorder type of question, you will be required to create a list, in the correct order, that represents the steps required to complete the stated problem.

Create a Tree

The create a tree question type, seen in Figure 3, has also been used previously in the MCP exams but has also been refined for the new certification tracks. When presented with a create a tree question, you are being asked to drag source nodes into the answer tree area in their correct location in order to successfully answer the question.

FIGURE 1 The active screen question format

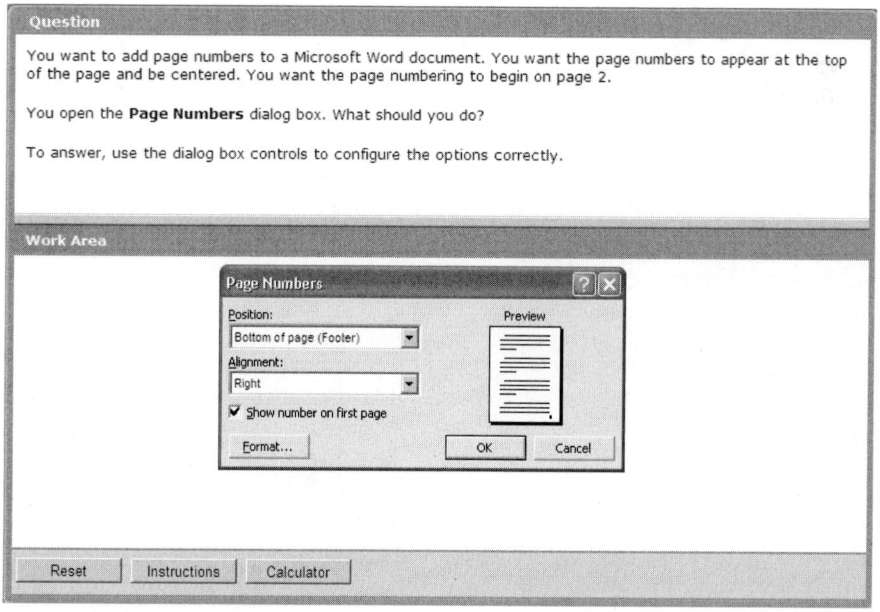

FIGURE 2 The build list and reorder question format

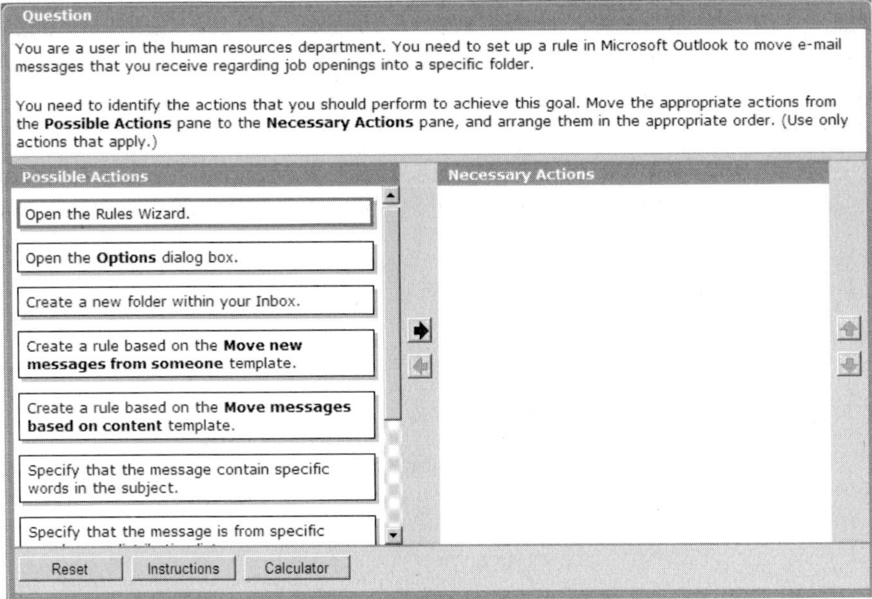

Question
You are a user in the human resources department. You need to set up a rule in Microsoft Outlook to move e-mail messages that you receive regarding job openings into a specific folder.
You need to identify the actions that you should perform to achieve this goal. Move the appropriate actions from the Possible Actions pane to the Necessary Actions pane, and arrange them in the appropriate order. (Use only actions that apply.)
Possible Actions
Open the Rules Wizard.
Open the Options dialog box.
Create a new folder within your Inbox.
Create a rule based on the Move new messages from someone template.
Create a rule based on the Move messages based on content template.
Specify that the message contain specific words in the subject.
Specify that the message is from specific
Necessary Actions
Reset
Instructions
Calculator

FIGURE 3 The create a tree question format

Question

You are a user in the finance department. You are creating documents that will be used in the company's annual report, and you need to determine the best program to use to create the documents. You need to identify the program in which you should perform each task. Move the appropriate tasks to the corresponding program. (Use only tasks that apply. Use tasks only once.)

List Area

- Create a letter to shareholders.
- Create a mission and vision statement.
- Create an organization chart.
- Create the financial statements.

Work Area

- Access
- Excel
- Outlook
- PowerPoint
- Visio
- Word

Reset | Instructions | Calculator

Drag and Drop

One of the new question types in the MCSE on the Windows Server 2003 track, the drag and drop question, seen in Figure 4, requires you to drag source objects into the correct target area in order to successfully answer the question.

Hot Area

The hot area question type, seen in Figure 5, asks you to select one or more areas of a graphic to correctly answer the question. You will be able to easily see where in the graphic the selectable options exist.

Multiple Choice

The multiple choice question is the old standby when it comes to certification exams. Not much has changed when it comes to this question type. You can expect questions that require one correct answer and/or multiple correct answers. In some instances you will be told specifically how many choices to make; in others you will not. Microsoft has made this question more difficult, however, by increasing the amount of information that you must sift through in order to successfully answer the question correctly.

The questions throughout this study guide and on the accompanying CD are presented in the same multiple-choice format that you will see on the exam.

FIGURE 4 The drag and drop question format

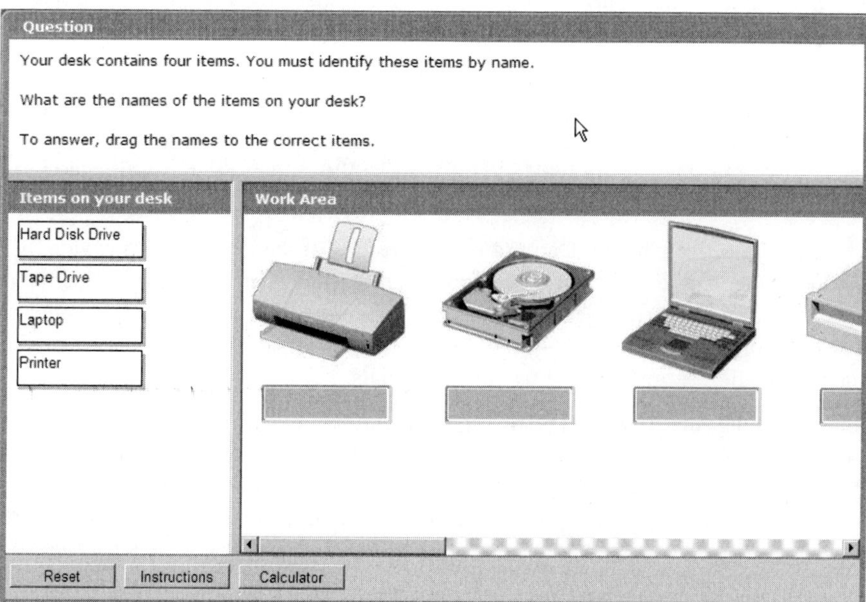

FIGURE 5 The hot area question format

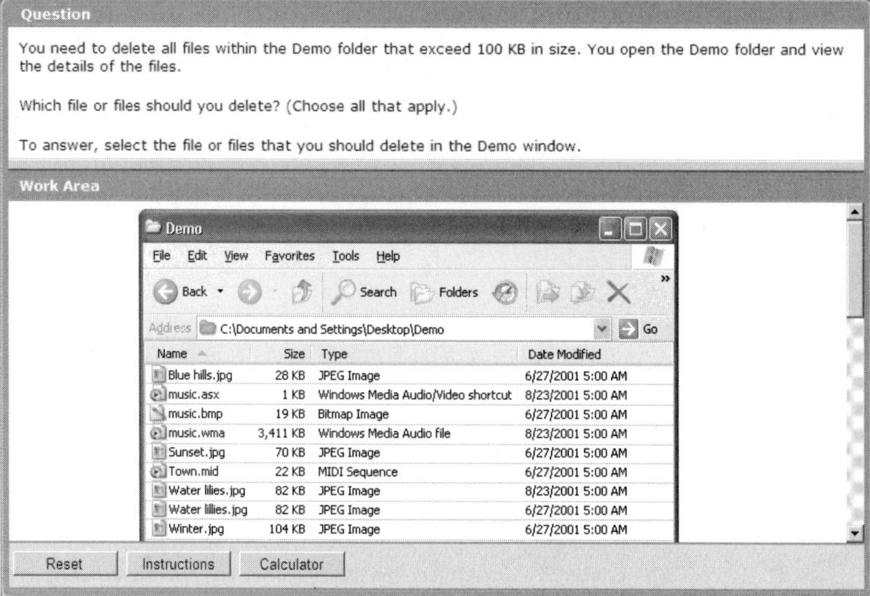

Exam Question Development

Microsoft follows an exam-development process consisting of eight mandatory phases. The process takes an average of seven months and involves more than 150 specific steps. The MCP exam development consists of the following phases:

Phase 1: Job Analysis Phase 1 is an analysis of all of the tasks that make up a specific job function, based on tasks performed by people who are currently performing that job function. This phase also identifies the knowledge, skills, and abilities that relate specifically to the performance area to be certified.

Phase 2: Objective Domain Definition The results of the job analysis provide the framework used to develop objectives. The development of objectives involves translating the job-function tasks into a comprehensive set of more specific and measurable knowledge, skills, and abilities. The resulting list of objectives—the *objective domain*—is the basis for the development of both the certification exams and the training materials.

Phase 3: Blueprint Survey The final objective domain is transformed into a blueprint survey in which contributors are asked to rate each objective. These contributors may be past MCP candidates, appropriately skilled exam development volunteers, or Microsoft employees. Based on the contributors' input, the objectives are prioritized and weighted. The actual exam items are written according to the prioritized objectives. Contributors are queried about how they spend their time on the job. If a contributor doesn't spend an adequate amount of time actually performing the specified job function, his or her data is eliminated from the analysis. The blueprint survey phase helps determine which objectives to measure, as well as the appropriate number and types of items to include on the exam.

Phase 4: Item Development A pool of items is developed to measure the blueprinted objective domain. The number and types of items to be written are based on the results of the blueprint survey.

Phase 5: Alpha Review and Item Revision During this phase, a panel of technical and job-function experts reviews each item for technical accuracy and then answers each item, reaching a consensus on all technical issues. Once the items have been verified as technically accurate, they are edited to ensure that they are expressed in the clearest language possible.

Phase 6: Beta Exam The reviewed and edited items are collected into beta exams. Based on the responses of all beta participants, Microsoft performs a statistical analysis to verify the validity of the exam items and to determine which items will be used in the certification exam. Once the analysis has been completed, the items are distributed into multiple parallel forms, or *versions*, of the final certification exam.

Phase 7: Item Selection and Cut-Score Setting The results of the beta exams are analyzed to determine which items should be included in the certification exam based on many factors, including item difficulty and relevance. During this phase, a panel of job-function experts determines the *cut score* (minimum passing score) for the exams. The cut score differs from exam to exam because it is based on an item-by-item determination of the percentage of candidates who answered the item correctly and who would be expected to answer the item correctly.

Phase 8: Live Exam As the final phase, the exams are given to candidates. MCP exams are administered by Sylvan Prometric and Virtual University Enterprises (VUE).

Microsoft will regularly add and remove questions from the exams. This is called item *seeding*. It is part of the effort to make it more difficult for individuals to merely memorize exam questions passed along by previous test-takers.

Tips for Taking the Exchange Server 2003 Exam

Here are some general tips for taking the exam successfully:

- Arrive early at the exam center so you can relax and review your study materials. During your final review, you can look over tables and lists of exam-related information.
- Read the questions carefully. Don't be tempted to jump to an early conclusion. Make sure you know *exactly* what the question is asking.

- Answer all questions.
- Use a process of elimination to get rid of the obviously incorrect answers first on questions that you're not sure about. This method will improve your odds of selecting the correct answer if you need to make an educated guess.

Exam Registration

You may take the exams at any of more than 1,000 Authorized Prometric Testing Centers (APTCs) and VUE Testing Centers around the world. For the location of a testing center near you, call Sylvan Prometric at 800-755-EXAM (755-3926), or call VUE at 888-837-8616. Outside the United States and Canada, contact your local Sylvan Prometric or VUE registration center.

You should determine the number of the exam you want to take and then register with the Sylvan Prometric or VUE registration center nearest to you. At this point, you will be asked for advance payment for the exam. The exams are $125 each. Exams must be taken within one year of payment. You can schedule exams up to six weeks in advance or as late as one working day prior to the date of the exam. You can cancel or reschedule your exam if you contact the center at least two working days prior to the exam. Same-day registration is available in some locations, subject to space availability. Where same-day registration is available, you must register a minimum of two hours before test time.

You may also register for your exams online at www.2test.com or www.vue.com.

When you schedule the exam, you will be provided with instructions regarding appointment and cancellation procedures, ID requirements, and information about the testing center location. In addition, you will receive a registration and payment confirmation letter from Sylvan Prometric or VUE.

Microsoft requires certification candidates to accept the terms of a Non-Disclosure Agreement before taking certification exams.

What's on the CD?

With this new book in our best-selling MCSE Study Guide series, we are including quite an array of training resources. On the CD are numerous simulations, practice exams, and flashcards to help you study for the exam. Also included are the entire contents of the book. These resources are described in the following sections.

The Sybex E-book for Exchange Server 2003

Many people like the convenience of being able to carry their whole study guide on a CD. They also like being able to search the text to find specific information quickly and easily. For these reasons, we have included the entire contents of this study guide on a CD, in PDF format. We've also included Adobe Acrobat Reader, which provides the interface for the contents, as well as the search capabilities.

Sybex WinSim Exchange 2003

We developed the WinSim Exchange 2003 product to allow you to get some hands-on practice with the skills you need to know to pass the exam. The product provides both video files and hands-on experience with key features of Exchange Server 2003. Built around the exercises in this study guide, WinSim Exchange 2003 can give you the knowledge and hands-on skills that are invaluable for understanding Exchange Server 2003 (and passing the exam). A sample screen from the product is shown below.

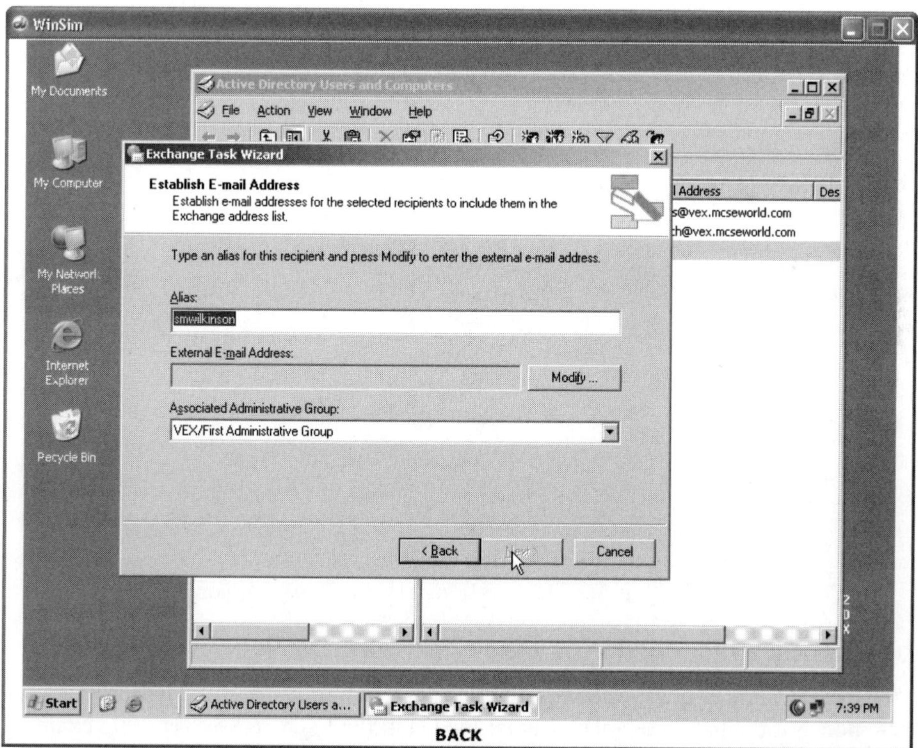

The Sybex MCSE Test Engine

This is a collection of multiple-choice questions that will help you prepare for your exam. There are three sets of questions:

- Two bonus exams designed to simulate the actual live exam.
- All the questions from the Study Guide, presented in a test engine for your review. You can review questions by objective or take a random test.
- The assessment test.

Here is a sample screen from the Sybex MCSE Test Engine:

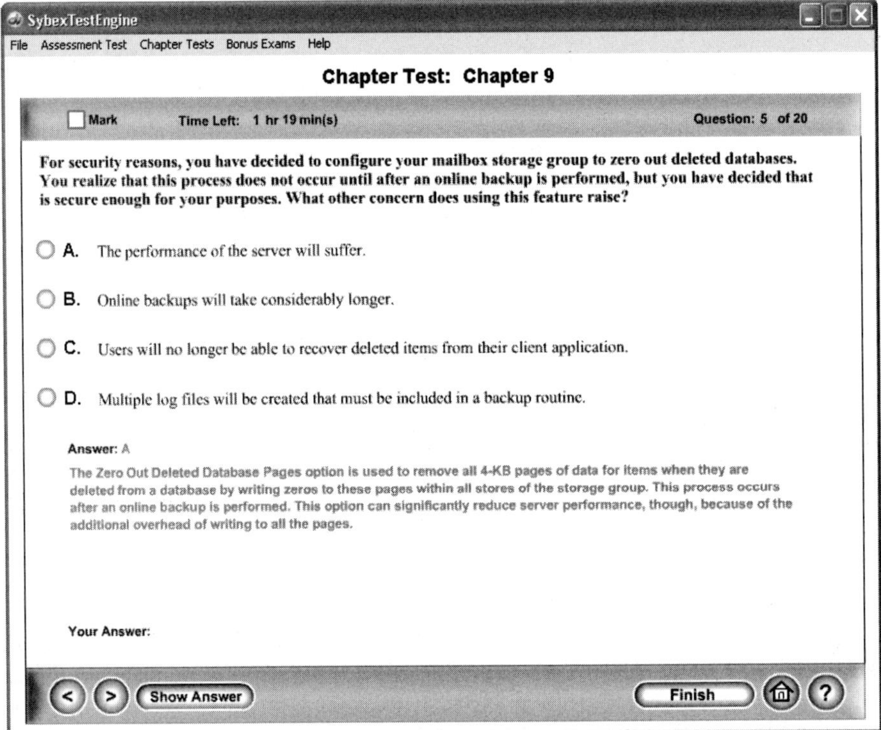

SybexTestEngine
File Assessment Test Chapter Tests Bonus Exams Help
Chapter Test: Chapter 9
Mark
Time Left: 1 hr 19 min(s)
Question: 5 of 20
For security reasons, you have decided to configure your mailbox storage group to zero out deleted databases. You realize that this process does not occur until after an online backup is performed, but you have decided that is secure enough for your purposes. What other concern does using this feature raise?
A. The performance of the server will suffer.
B. Online backups will take considerably longer.
C. Users will no longer be able to recover deleted items from their client application.
D. Multiple log files will be created that must be included in a backup routine.
Answer: A
The Zero Out Deleted Database Pages option is used to remove all 4-KB pages of data for items when they are deleted from a database by writing zeros to these pages within all stores of the storage group. This process occurs after an online backup is performed. This option can significantly reduce server performance, though, because of the additional overhead of writing to all the pages.
Your Answer:
Show Answer
Finish

Sybex MCSE Flashcards for PCs and Palm Devices

The "flashcard" style of question offers an effective way to quickly and efficiently test your understanding of the fundamental concepts covered in the Exchange Server 2003 exam. The Sybex MCSE Flashcards set consists of approximately 150 questions presented in a special engine developed specifically for this Study Guide series. Here's what the Sybex MCSE Flashcards interface looks like:

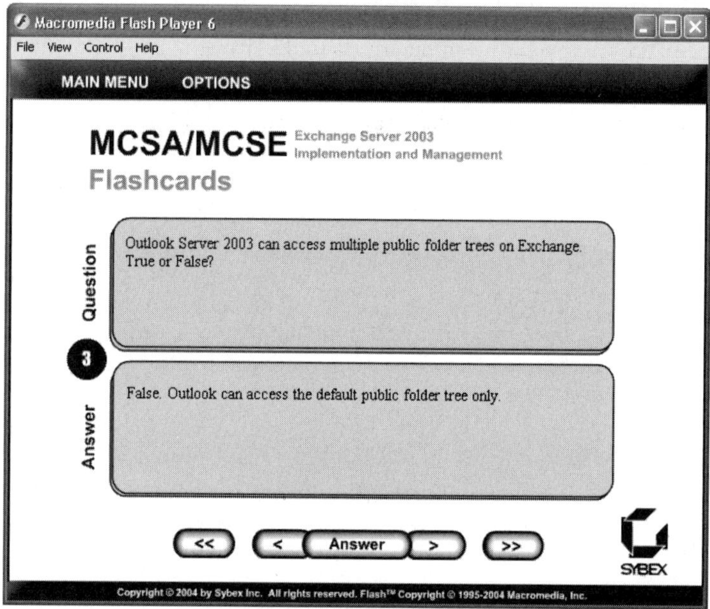

How Do You Use This Book?

This book can provide a solid foundation for the serious effort of preparing for the Exchange Server 2003 exam. To best benefit from this book, you may wish to use the following study method:

1. Study each chapter carefully. Do your best to fully understand the information.
2. Complete all hands-on exercises in the chapter, referring back to the text as necessary so that you understand each step you take. If you do not have access to a lab environment in which you can complete the exercises, install and work with the exercises available in the WinSim Exchange 2003 software included with this Study Guide.
3. Answer the review questions at the end of each chapter. If you would prefer to answer the questions in a timed and graded format, install the Sybex Test Engine from the CD that accompanies this book and answer the chapter questions there instead of in the book.
4. Note the questions you did not understand, and study the corresponding sections of the book again.

5. Make sure you complete the entire book.
6. Before taking the exam, go through the training resources included on the CD that accompanies this book. Try the adaptive version that is included with the Sybex Test Engine. Review and sharpen your knowledge with the MCSE Flashcards.

In order to complete the exercises in this book, you'll need to have access to at least one machine running Windows Server 2003 Enterprise Edition and preferably two such machines networked together. You will also need access to Exchange Server 2003 Enterprise Edition, of which you can order a trial version through Microsoft. Some exercises may require you to have administrative access or to be part of an Active Directory domain. If possible, we strongly recommend that you do not install Exchange on a network that is actually connected to your production network, because the interaction with other Exchange servers on the network and with Active Directory could produce unwanted results.

To learn all of the material covered in this book, you will need to study regularly and with discipline. Try to set aside the same time every day to study and select a comfortable and quiet place in which to do it. If you work hard, you will be surprised at how quickly you learn this material. Good luck!

Contacts and Resources

To find out more about Microsoft Education and Certification materials and programs, to register with Sylvan Prometric or VUE, or to get other useful information, check the following resources:

Microsoft Learning Home Page `www.microsoft.com/learning`

This website provides information about the MCP program and exams. You can also get information on related Microsoft products.

Prometric `www.2test.com`

(800) 755-EXAM

Contact Sylvan Prometric to register to take an MCP exam at any of more than 800 Prometric Testing Centers around the world.

Virtual University Enterprises (VUE) `www.vue.com`

(888) 837-8616

Contact the VUE registration center to register to take an MCP exam at one of the VUE Testing Centers.

Assessment Test

1. You are testing Exchange Server 2003 to determine whether it is worth upgrading to. You have just finished installing an Exchange server and are exploring the directories in which the files were created when you come across two files named `PUB.EDB` and `PUB.STM`. You recognize from earlier versions of Exchange Server that the `PUB.EDB` file is the database for your public folders. What is the `PUB.STM` file used for?

   A. Allowing web access to the public folders

   B. Storing information about the folders that are compatible with earlier versions of Exchange Server

   C. Storing certain types of media files in their native format

   D. Providing a backup of the `PUB.EDB` file

2. You have installed multiple public folder trees in your organization. Which of the following clients will be able to access the default public folder tree and all of the additional trees? (Choose all that apply.)

   A. Outlook

   B. A web browser

   C. An Office application

   D. A generic POP3 client

3. You are the administrator of a large Exchange organization and have been given the task of creating a connector between two routing groups. You have the following requirements:

   - Use the simplest connector possible in terms of configuration and maintenance.
   - Configure multiple bridgehead servers.
   - Assign a low cost to this connector so that is it more likely to be used than other connectors between the same routing groups.
   - Have servers issue authentication before sending any mail.

   You implement the following solution:

   Install a Routing Group Connector between the two routing groups.

   Which of the requirements does the proposed solution meet? (Choose all that apply.)

   A. Use the simplest connector possible in terms of configuration and maintenance.

   B. Configure multiple bridgehead servers.

   C. Assign a low cost to this connector so that is it more likely to be used than other connectors between the same routing groups.

   D. Have servers issue authentication before sending any mail.

4. You are the Exchange administrator for a large network and are about to install the first Exchange server in the organization. Before you do that, however, you must run the ForestPrep utility to prepare your forest. To which of the following groups must you belong in order to run the ForestPrep utility? (Choose all that apply.)

   A. Server Admins

   B. Domain Admins

   C. Schema Admins

   D. Enterprise Admins

5. You have five computers on which you are considering installing Exchange Server 2003 as a testing environment. Which of the following systems meet the requirements for installing Exchange Server 2003? (Choose all that apply.)

   A. Pentium 90, 64 MB RAM, 500 MB disk space

   B. Pentium 133, 64 MB RAM, 2500 MB disk space

   C. Pentium II 450, 256 MB RAM, 1000 MB disk space

   D. Pentium II 400, 512 MB RAM, 200 MB disk space

   E. Pentium III 500, 256 MB RAM, 2000 MB disk space

6. You have three Exchange 2000 Server computers at Service Pack 3 that are running Windows 2000 Advanced Server Service Pack 2. What do you need to update before you can upgrade these servers to Exchange Server 2003? (Choose all that apply.)

   A. You will need to update the Windows 2000 Advanced Server installations to Service Pack 3.

   B. You will need to update the Windows 2000 Advanced Server installations to Service Pack 4.

   C. You will need to update the Exchange 2000 Server installations to Service Pack 4.

   D. You will need to update the current Active Directory schema using the ForestPrep utility.

7. Which of the following MAPI components is a replaceable component that communicates with the server side of the messaging system?

   A. Client Application Layer

   B. MAPI subsystem

   C. Common Mail Call

   D. MAPI service provider

8. Your company has hired an outside agency to provide accounting services. Many of your employees need to e-mail messages to people in this agency using the Internet. You want to set it up so that the people in the agency appear in the Exchange Global Address List. What type of recipient object do you need to configure for each person in the outside agency?

   A. Mailbox

   B. Mail-enabled user

   C. Contact

   D. A mailbox with a foreign owner

9. Your organization has three routing groups: RG1, RG2, and RG3. Each group consists of three Exchange servers configured with about 500 users each. RG1 and RG2 are connected with a 256-KB wide area network (WAN). RG2 and RG3 are connected with a switched 56-KB connection. RG1 is not directly connected to RG3. You have created a public folder that contains 600 MB of data. Users in RG1 and RG3 need access to the folder throughout the day. Users in RG2 need only occasional access. The folder data is updated on a daily basis. On what servers should replicas be placed?

   A. On every server

   B. On one server in each routing group

   C. On every server in RG1 and RG3

   D. Only on the server where the public folder was originally created

   E. Only on domain controllers

10. You are the administrator of a large network running Lotus Notes. As part of a plan for moving to Exchange Server 2003, you have just installed the first Exchange Server 2003 server and created a new Exchange organization. You would like to gradually migrate users from the Lotus Notes system and allow users of both systems to exchange messages during the migration. In order to do this, first you must set up a way for the two systems to communicate. What component of Exchange Server 2003 would you use?

    A. Migration kit

    B. Connector

    C. Import/Export tool

    D. None of the above

11. You have three Exchange 2000 Server computers at Service Pack 3 that are running Windows 2000 Advanced Server Service Pack 2. What Exchange 2000 Server components do you need to remove before you can upgrade these servers to Exchange Server 2003? (Choose all that apply.)

    A. Exchange Chat

    B. Key Management Service

    C. SMTP connectors

    D. MS Mail connector

12. How can Exchange Server 2003 routing groups be connected to one another? (Choose all that apply.)

    A. Using Routing Group Connectors

    B. Using SMTP Connectors

    C. Using X.400 Connectors

    D. Using Calendar connectors

13. You are running a mixed-mode organization that contains a number of Exchange Server 2003 and Exchange Server 5.5 servers in several different sites. How do Exchange 5.*x* servers in different sites exchange directory information?

    A. Using e-mail messages

    B. Using MAPI

    C. Using RPCs

    D. Using LDAP

14. Which of the following objects can an administrative group hold? (Choose all that apply.)

    A. Servers

    B. Routing groups

    C. Recipients container

    D. System policy containers

    E. Tools container

15. You are creating an Active/Active Exchange Server 2003 cluster. How many total storage groups should you place in this cluster for best performance?

    A. Two

    B. Three

    C. Four

    D. Five

16. You are planning your company's Exchange Server 2003 deployment and are deciding how to group servers into routing groups. Which of the following criteria must servers meet to be in the same routing group? (Choose all that apply.)

    A. All servers must be in the same forest.

    B. All servers must be in the same domain tree.

    C. All servers must be in the same domain.

    D. All servers must be capable of supporting SMTP connectivity.

    E. All servers must be in the same administrative group.

    F. All servers must be capable of supporting high-speed connectivity.

17. You have configured four storage groups on your Exchange server. One group holds five mailbox stores and no public stores. The other two groups are configured with two public stores each and no mailbox stores. The final group has one mailbox store and one public store. How many sets of transaction logs are maintained on the server?

    A. One

    B. Four

    C. Six

    D. Seven

    E. Nine

18. You have just configured your Exchange server for IMAP4 client access. IMAP4 clients can be authenticated with either Basic or Basic with SSL authentication. The administrator of your firewall informs you that the firewall will allow traffic from SMTP (port 25), IMAP4 (port 143), and HTTP (port 80). What additional traffic must the firewall be configured to allow for your Exchange server IMAP4 configuration to be used?

    A. 993

    B. 995

    C. 137

    D. 135

19. You are the administrator of a large Exchange organization. Recently, you have become aware that users on the Internet have been using an SMTP server that you configured outside your firewall to relay messages not bound for your organization. How can you stop this?

    A. Use the Relay setting on the SMTP virtual server object's Access property page.

    B. Use the Inbound Security settings on the SMTP virtual server object's Advanced property page.

    C. Use the Authentication setting on the SMTP virtual server object's Access property page.

    D. Configure the Relay settings for the SMTP Connector object.

20. What type of policy will you need to configure to limit mailbox store size?

    A. Recipient policy

    B. Storage policy

    C. Mailbox store policy

    D. Server policy

21. Management would like for you to configure the Exchange Server 2003 organization at your company so that users can access their mailboxes and other Exchange-based folders over the Internet. You have decided that the easiest way to do this would be for the users to be able to connect with a web browser. Which of the following components work together to allow web browsers to access an Exchange server? (Choose all that apply.)

   A. Internet Information Services

   B. Outlook Browser Access

   C. Outlook Web Access

   D. Exchange Web Server

22. Which of the following types of Windows authentication are used in a network operating at the Windows 2000 native domain functional level? (Choose all that apply.)

   A. Kerberos v3

   B. Kerberos v5

   C. NTLM

   D. Basic

   E. Basic over SSL

23. Which of the following permissions would you assign to an object if you wanted an administrator to be able to view the contents of a container in System Manager but not access the object's properties?

   A. Read

   B. Write

   C. Read Properties

   D. List Contents

   E. Read Contents

24. You have just received a message encrypted using a public-key encryption system. What key will be used to decrypt the message?

   A. The sender's public encryption key

   B. The sender's private encryption key

   C. Your public encryption key

   D. Your private encryption key

25. A user named Mary is the owner of a public folder. Mary leaves your company, and the former administrator deletes her user account. As the current administrator, you now need to modify the permissions on the public folder. What will you have to do?

   A. Create a new account with the same user information as the deleted account.

   B. Restore a backup tape of the server that was created before the user was deleted.

   C. Designate your account as the owner of the folder.

   D. Create a new public folder and move the contents of the old folder to it.

26. Which of the following tools provides a way to log the operation statistics of a computer's resources over time?

    A. Performance snap-in

    B. Computer Management

    C. Monitoring and Status

    D. Task Manager

27. Several of your users routinely travel with their portable Windows XP Professional computers. When they travel, they use Outlook 2003 to access your Exchange organization via POP3. All messages they send or receive during this time are stored in a PST file. When the users get back, they import any required message items back into their Exchange mailboxes. One of these users has called you from a remote job site complaining that she cannot access her PST file. What tool should you tell her to use to try to fix the problem?

    A. PST Integrity Checker

    B. PST Repair Tool

    C. Outlook Repair Tool

    D. Inbox Repair Tool

28. You are taking a long-overdue vacation and want system notifications regarding public folders to be sent to one of your assistants while you are away. What permission would you assign the assistant on each of the folders?

    A. Folder Owner

    B. Folder Manager

    C. Folder Contact

    D. Folder Notification

29. Your Windows Active Directory forest consists of two domain trees. The first tree consists of a single root-level domain and four child domains of that root domain. The second tree consists only of a single root domain. You plan to install Exchange Server 2003 servers in both root domains and in one child domain of the first root domain. How many times would you need to run the DomainPrep utility?

    A. One

    B. Two

    C. Three

    D. Six

30. Which Exchange role allows the user to add, delete, and rename objects but not modify permissions on objects?

    A. Exchange Full Administrator

    B. Exchange Administrator

    C. Exchange View-Only Administrator

    D. Exchange Read-Only Administrator

31. You have been directed to create a highly available Outlook Web Access solution for your employees. Over 3,000 of your company's 4,000 employees routinely travel and need access to the Exchange organization. You've decided to implement a front-end/back-end solution using an Active/Passive cluster on the back end and a Network Load Balancing cluster on the front end. How many nodes will your Active/Passive cluster be able to have if you use Exchange Server 2003 Enterprise Edition on Windows Server 2003 Enterprise Edition?

    A. Minimum of one, maximum of four

    B. Minimum of two, maximum of six

    C. Minimum of two, maximum of eight

    D. Minimum of one, maximum of two

32. You are the Exchange administrator for an organization that is currently running Exchange Server 5.5. You are going to upgrade to Exchange Server 2003 but plan to do so in stages. During this time, your organization must operate in mixed mode. Which of the following are limitations of working in a mixed-mode organization? (Choose all that apply.)

    A. Administrative groups and Exchange Server 5.5 sites must be mapped on a one-to-one basis.

    B. Routing groups and Exchange Server 5.5 sites must be mapped on a one-to-one basis.

    C. You can create only one administrative group for your Exchange 2000 organization, and all Exchange Server 5.5 sites must be contained in that group.

    D. You can create only one routing group for your Exchange Server 2003 organization, and all Exchange Server 5.5 sites must be contained in that group.

33. For security reasons, you have decided to configure your mailbox storage group to zero out deleted databases. When does this process occur?

    A. During routing information store maintenance

    B. Every four hours by default, but you can change this setting

    C. Once per day by default, but you can change this setting

    D. After an online backup is performed

34. Which of the following constructs is used to track the set of root Certificate Authorities whose certificates can be trusted in a domain?

    A. Certificate Revocation List

    B. Certificate Trust List

    C. Certificate Authority List

    D. Root CA List

35. You have an Exchange server that contains four storage groups. The first storage group contains a single mailbox store that consumes 20 GB of disk space. The second storage group contains two mailbox stores that consume 10 GB of disk space each. The third storage group holds a single public store that consumes 10 GB of disk space. The fourth storage group holds a mailbox store that consumes 15 GB of disk space. You want to enable full-text indexing on all of these stores. How much total disk space should the stores consume after indexing is complete?

    A. 55 GB

    B. 60.5 GB

    C. 66 GB

    D. 71.5 GB

    E. 82.5 GB

36. You are the Exchange administrator for a large mixed-mode organization that is gradually upgrading to Exchange Server 2003. You are about to decommission one of your Exchange 5.5 servers and need to move all of the mailboxes on that server to a single mailbox store on one of your Exchange Server 2003 servers. You connect to the Exchange 5.5 server using Exchange Administrator and try to move the mailboxes, but during the process you get an error, and the operation fails. What is the likely problem?

    A. You cannot use Exchange Administrator to move mailboxes from Exchange 5.5 to Exchange Server 2003.

    B. You must first configure a temporary one-way connection agreement between the Exchange 5.5 server and the Exchange Server 2003 server.

    C. The mailbox store must be dismounted before this operation can take place.

    D. The mailbox store is not empty.

37. Which of the following backup types would cause the archive bit for a file that is backed up to be set to the on position? (Choose all that apply.)

    A. Normal

    B. Copy

    C. Incremental

    D. Differential

    E. None of these

38. You are configuring a connector between two routing groups that are in different buildings. You have a dedicated, high-speed link between the buildings but have decided to create a routing group for each building anyway. You would like to use a connector that is fairly easy to set up and configure, but you also need the connector to support TLS encryption. What type of connector would you choose?

    A. Routing Group Connector

    B. Site Connector

    C. X.400 Connector

    D. SMTP Connector

39. Which of the following statements are true concerning an offline backup? (Choose all that apply.)

    A. File corruption is checked by using checksums.

    B. Purged transaction logs are not cleared from the server.

    C. The database must be dismounted.

    D. Users experience no interruption in mailbox store access.

40. You have just configured your Exchange server for HTTP client access. Your company has a front-end server running outside the company firewall that can accept the HTTP client requests. This server authenticates HTTP clients with either Basic (Clear-Text) or Basic over SSL. The firewall currently allows traffic via SMTP (port 25) and POP3 (port 110). Which additional ports must be opened on the firewall to allow clients to connect using HTTP? (Choose all that apply.)

    A. 80

    B. 135

    C. 443

    D. 2890

    E. 3268

Answers to Assessment Test

1. C. An Exchange Server 2003 database represents two physical database files: a rich-text (.EDB) file and a streaming media (.STM) file. The rich-text file holds messages and works much like the database files in previous versions of Exchange Server. The streaming media file has been added to provide native support for many types of streaming media, including voice, audio, and video. See Chapter 2 for more information.

2. B, C. MAPI clients, such as Outlook, can access only the default public folder tree in an organization. Clients that can directly access the file system, such as Office applications, web browsers, and Windows Explorer, can access multiple public folder trees. POP3 clients have no mechanism for accessing public folders at all. See Chapter 6 for more information.

3. A, B, C. The Routing Group Connector (RGC) is preferred for connecting routing groups, because it is robust and simple to configure and maintain. It allows the use of multiple bridgehead servers and cost assignment. Only the SMTP Connector can issue authentication before sending mail, specify TLS encryption, and remove mail from queues on remote servers. See Chapter 8 for more information.

4. C, D. In order to run the ForestPrep utility, a user must belong to both the Schema Admins and Enterprise Admins global groups. The user must also belong to the local Administrators group on the computer on which the utility is actually run. See Chapter 3 for more information.

5. C, E. Exchange Server 2003 requires a *minimum* of a Pentium 133, 256 MB RAM, and 500 MB disk space. See Chapter 3 for more information.

6. A, D. Before you can upgrade an existing Exchange 2000 Server, both Exchange 2000 Server and Windows 2000 Server must have at least Service Pack 3 (or later) installed. In addition, before you can install the first Exchange Server 2003 computer, you must run the Exchange Server 2003 ForestPrep and DomainPrep utilities to prepare the schema and the domains for the new Exchange Server 2003 installations. See Chapter 12 for more information.

7. D. MAPI service providers are replaceable components that communicate with the server side of the messaging system. There are three types of service providers: address book providers, message store providers, and message transport providers. See Chapter 7 for more information.

8. C. A contact holds the address of a non-Exchange mail recipient. Contacts are made visible in the Global Address List. See Chapter 5 for more information.

9. B. There is really no need to have replicas configured on multiple servers in each routing group. However, because of the slow link speed between routing groups (especially RG2 and RG3), it is important that at least one server in each routing group have a replica. Since there is more available bandwidth at night, and since the public folder data is not time-critical, you could also schedule replication to occur only at night. See Chapter 8 for more information.

10. B. Connectors provide a way to connect Exchange servers in different routing groups and a way to connect Exchange organizations to external messaging systems. The Lotus Notes connector is one of the connectors supplied with Exchange Server 2003. Once the connector is configured, you will be able to have both messaging systems coexist with each other and eventually perform the migration to Exchange Server 2003. See Chapter 13 for more information.

11. A, B, D. Before you can upgrade an Exchange 2000 Server to Exchange Server 2003, you must remove the following unsupported components:

- Microsoft Mobile Information Server
- Instant Messaging
- Exchange Chat
- Exchange 2000 Conferencing Server
- Key Management Service
- The cc:Mail connector
- The MS Mail connector

See Chapter 12 for more information.

12. A, B, C. Exchange Server 2003 routing groups can be connected using the easy-to-configure Routing Group Connector or the multipurpose SMTP or X.400 Connectors. See Chapter 8 for more information.

13. A. All Exchange 5.*x* servers in the same site automatically replicate directory information using RPCs. Replication of directory information between Exchange 5.*x* servers in different sites must be configured manually and occurs by sending e-mail messages over whatever connector is used to connect the sites. See Chapter 11 for more information.

14. A, B, D. Administrative groups can contain servers, routing groups, public folder trees, and system policies. See Chapter 8 for more information.

15. C. Since all resources on a failed node in an Active/Active cluster have only one possible server to failover to, you should not configure more than four total storage groups on an Active/Active cluster. See Chapter 4 for more information.

16. A, D. In order to be in the same routing group, all servers must have reliable, permanent, and direct network connectivity that supports SMTP. They must also belong to the same Active Directory forest and be able to connect to a routing group master. See Chapter 8 for more information.

17. B. Only one transaction log set is maintained for each storage group. See Chapter 9 for more information.

18. A. IMAP4 uses TCP port 143. If Secure Sockets Layer (SSL) is being used to create an encrypted authentication channel, port 993 is used instead. See Chapter 7 for more information.

19. A. By default, an SMTP virtual server will accept messages from any host but will relay only messages sent from authorized clients. This allows clients in your domain using POP3 or IMAP4 clients to send SMTP messages using the SMTP virtual host. If you want to configure your SMTP virtual server to act as a smart host for relay messages coming in from other domains, you can configure the specific clients to relay messages by using this button. See Chapter 13 for more information.

20. C. A mailbox store policy can be used to configure mailbox size limits. See Chapter 10 for more information.

21. A, C. Internet Information Services is a web server service built into Windows Server 2003 that provides the Internet protocol support for Exchange Server 2003. Outlook Web Access is a component that allows IIS to access the Web Store and then present information to Web browsers in HTML format. See Chapter 2 for more information.

22. B, D, E. The Basic (Clear-Text) and Basic over SSL authentication methods may be used on any type of network. The third method available is Integrated Windows authentication. When operating at the Windows 2000 native mixed-domain functional level, Integrated Windows authentication uses the NTLM protocol supported by Windows NT 4.0. When running in native mode, Integrated Windows authentication used Kerberos v5. See Chapter 15 for more information.

23. D. The List Contents permission lets a user view the contents of a container object but not access its properties. See Chapter 10 for more information.

24. D. The recipient's public key is used to encrypt a message, and the recipient's private key is used to decrypt the message. See Chapter 15 for more information.

25. C. An administrator has the permission to change the owner of a folder. Once the administrator takes ownership of the folder, they can then perform administrative tasks, such as adding rules and installing forms. See Chapter 6 for more information.

26. A. The Performance snap-in lets you create a log of the performance of certain resources over time and then use that log to chart results. Other tools on this list also provide some performance data, but none allow for logging. See Chapter 10 for more information.

27. D. The Inbox Repair Tool (`SCANPST.EXE`) tests and repairs a personal folder store (*.PST). It scans for bad blocks and attempts to rebuild them. If a PST file is corrupted beyond repair, this program will try to evacuate the good blocks of data and remove the corrupted blocks. This program does not need to be run unless there are operational problems with personal folders. See Chapter 10 for more information.

28. C. A person with the Folder Contact permissions can receive e-mail notifications relating to a folder. Notifications include replication conflicts, folder design conflicts, and storage limit notifications. See Chapter 6 for more information.

29. C. DomainPrep is a tool used to prepare each domain in which Exchange will be installed. The tool is run using the `/domainprep` switch for the `SETUP.EXE` program. See Chapter 3 for more information.

30. B. The *Exchange Administrator role* gives the same full administrative capability as the Exchange Full Administrator role but does not give administrators permission to modify permissions for objects. See Chapter 10 for more information.

31. C. An Active/Passive cluster using Exchange Server 2003 Enterprise Edition on Windows Server 2003 Enterprise Edition can have a maximum of eight nodes. You must have at least two nodes in the cluster. See Chapter 4 for more information.

32. A. Exchange Server 5.5 sites are mapped directly to Exchange Server 2003 Server administrative groups and vice versa. This gives you less flexibility in setting up administrative groups than when working in native mode. See Chapter 11 for more information.

33. D. The Zero Out Deleted Database Pages option is used to remove all 4-KB pages of data for items when they are deleted from a database by writing zeros to these pages within all stores of the storage group. This process occurs after an online backup is performed. This option can significantly reduce server performance, though, because of the additional overhead of writing to all the pages. See Chapter 9 for more information.

34. B. The *Certificate Trust List (CTL)* for a domain holds the set of root CAs whose certificates can be trusted. Trust in root CAs can be set by policy or by managing the CTL directly. See Chapter 15 for more information.

35. C. An indexed store requires about 20 percent more disk space than a non-indexed store. Before indexing, the combined space consumed by the stores was 55 GB. Following indexing, this would increase by 20 percent, making the combined space consumed 66 GB. See Chapter 9 for more information.

36. A. Moving mailboxes from Exchange 5.5 to Exchange Server 2003 with Exchange Administrator is not supported. You must use the Exchange Task Wizard, which is accessed from the Active Directory Users and Computers console. See Chapter 11 for more information.

37. E. No backup type sets the archive bit to on. When a file is created or modified, the archive bit is set to on. When some types of backups run, the archive bit is set to off, which indicates that the file has been backed up. The normal and incremental backup types set the archive bit to off so that the same files will not be backed up in subsequent backups unless the files change. See Chapter 14 for more information.

38. D. The Routing Group Connector is the fastest and simplest to set up. However, only the SMTP Connector offers the ability to use authentication and encryption of the connection. See Chapter 8 for more information.

39. B, C. An offline backup requires that you first dismount the database to be backed up, thus making it unavailable for user access. Besides taking the database out of use, offline backups also do not purge committed transaction logs after the backup has completed. In addition, no automatic checksum error checking is performed during an offline backup. You will need to use the `eesutil` utility to check the offline backup for corruption after it has been completed. See Chapter 14 for more information.

40. A, E. Since the front-end server is outside the firewall, it can already accept HTTP and HTTP over SSL connections. The front-end server must be able to look up information from the Global Catalog server using port 3268 and transfer information with the back-end server using port 80. Therefore those two ports must be opened on the firewall. See Chapter 15 for more information.

Chapter 1

Introduction to Microsoft Exchange

Microsoft Exchange Server 2003 is the server portion of a rather powerful client/server enterprise messaging system. "Great," you say, "but what does that mean?" This chapter introduces the capabilities of Exchange Server 2003 and sets the stage for the rest of the book by dissecting the phrase "client/server enterprise messaging system." First, this chapter introduces messaging systems—what they are and what they are used for on modern networks. Second, it examines several different computing models and shows how Exchange Server fits into the client/server model. Third, it answers the question "what does it take to be an enterprise-level system?" Finally, this chapter discusses the major industry standards on which Microsoft Exchange is based.

Messaging Systems

An enterprise needs information in order to get work done. For this reason, electronic messaging has become a mission-critical function in most organizations. While electronic mail (*e-mail*) is still the core ingredient of any messaging system, other applications are becoming more popular. Messaging can be divided into the following categories:

- E-mail
- Groupware
- Other messaging applications, such as real-time chat applications

Each of these categories, and how Exchange addresses them, is briefly discussed in the following text.

Due to the multiple functionality of some of the client programs, a single program could fit into more than one of the categories listed. For example, Microsoft Outlook includes e-mail functions and groupware functions such as group scheduling.

E-mail

An e-mail program allows a user to create, send, read, store, and manipulate electronic messages and attachments. E-mail is an example of *push-style* communication, meaning that the sender initiates the communication. Because of the importance of e-mail in the overall communication of organizations, e-mail client programs have evolved from merely creating and sending text messages into multifeatured programs.

Microsoft also has server components that enable standard Internet clients to be Exchange e-mail clients. Those Internet clients include the following:

- Web browsers through the Outlook Web Access component
- Internet e-mail programs with the Post Office Protocol, version 3 (POP3)
- Internet e-mail programs with Internet Message Access Protocol, version 4 (IMAP4) support

Figure 1.1 illustrates these e-mail client applications.

FIGURE 1.1 E-mail clients to Exchange Server

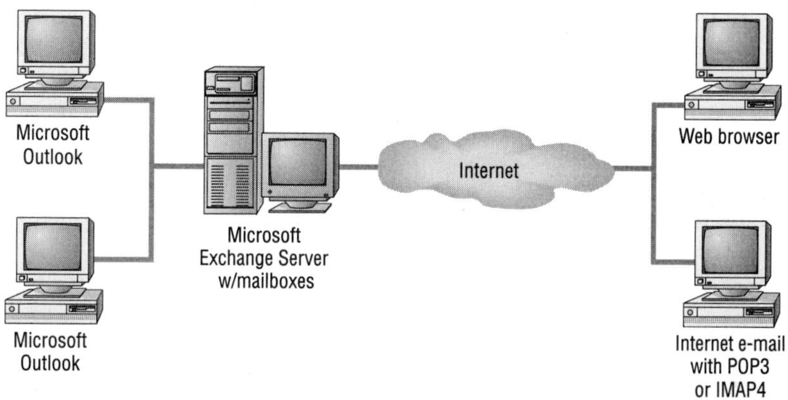

Microsoft Office Outlook 2003

Outlook 2003 is an e-mail client that ships with Exchange Server 2003 and Microsoft Office 2003 as a stand-alone product. Outlook is referred to as a desktop information manager because it is more than just an e-mail client. It also performs such tasks as calendaring, scheduling, and task and contact management. Outlook is intended to be a central program for management of data of all types.

Microsoft Outlook includes a vast feature set, some of which are listed here:

Universal inbox (mailbox) This central storage area can hold not only e-mail messages but other data such as word processing documents, spreadsheet files, faxes, electronic forms, and even voicemail files.

Two terms refer to a user's mailbox: mailbox and inbox. The most common usage in this book will be mailbox. This is our primary term for two reasons. One, Microsoft divides a mailbox into folders, one of which is labeled the Inbox. Using the term inbox for only the folder helps prevent confusion. The other reason is that the server-based storage area for a user's messages is also called a mailbox.

Hierarchical data storage Outlook organizes the client's *mailbox* into several default folders: Deleted Items, Drafts, Inbox, Junk E-mail, Outbox, and Sent Items. Users can also create their own folders, thereby personalizing the organization of their data.

Customized views Users have the ability to determine what and how data is presented to them on their screens. Messages can be ordered by sender, date, priority, subject, and other properties.

Search tool Users can search and retrieve messages in their mailboxes using a variety of search criteria, such as sender, date, and subject.

Rich-text message content Historically, most e-mail content was simple text. Outlook enables the creation of rich-text message content that can include multiple fonts, sizes, colors, alignments, and other formatting controls. In addition, Outlook provides for the safe display of HTML mail if desired.

Microsoft Word as message editor Even though Outlook includes a rich message editor, it can also be configured to use Microsoft Word as its message editor. This ability provides access to many of the standard Word features, such as tables, embedded pictures, and linked objects, right inside the e-mail message.

Compound messages and drag-and-drop editing Outlook is *OLE 2 (Object Linking and Embedding)* compliant and, therefore, allows the creation of compound documents. For example, a user could drag and drop a group of cells from a spreadsheet into Outlook.

Secure messages *Digital signatures* and message *encryption* are advanced security features built into Outlook.

Cache mode A new feature in Outlook 2003 allows users to operate in cache mode, whereby they have the benefits of both online mode and offline mode simultaneously. When Outlook first connects to the user's Exchange mailbox during a session, the contents of the mailbox are synchronized to an offline folder file on the local computer. Outlook then connects to the Exchange server periodically to check for updates and synchronizes the local offline folder and sends any outgoing messages. Should the client lose connectivity to the Exchange server, the user can continue to work normally until connectivity has been restored.

Offline mode Because more and more employees spend part of their workday outside the office, special features allow users to create folders on their local computers that synchronize with folders on an Exchange server when the local computer is connected to a network. When the computer is not connected, the folders that have been synchronized are available and users can create, work with, and send messages. Sent messages are placed in the Outbox and are actually delivered the next time the offline folders are synchronized.

Delegated access Some users need to allow other users to access their mailbox. For example, a manager might want a secretary to read meeting request messages in order to handle the manager's schedule. In many mail systems, this would be accomplished by having the secretary log on as the manager. This creates an obvious security problem. Exchange and Outlook solve this problem by allowing the manager to grant the secretary limited permission to access the manager's mailbox. This permission can be restricted to certain folders. The secretary can also be granted permission to send messages on behalf of the manager or even send messages as the manager, using the Send As feature.

Voting Outlook supports the ability to add voting buttons in the header of a mail message and to collect the responses. This allows surveys to be conducted through e-mail.

Auto Create Outlook can automatically convert one Outlook item into another. For example, a mail message may contain an action item that the user can simply drag and drop into the Task folder. Outlook would automatically convert the mail message into a task.

Recover deleted items Users of Outlook can recover deleted items in a mailbox or public folder for a certain amount of time determined by the Exchange administrator.

Block junk e-mail Outlook now provides an enhanced junk e-mail filtering system that can effectively keep junk e-mail out of your Inbox.

Block unwanted attachments Users of Outlook can prevent unwanted, and often bulky, attachments from taking up mailbox space. E-mail messages and files are blocked from people who have not been placed on a user's Safe Senders List, allowing the user to examine the message and determine whether they wish to receive the message and any attached files.

These are just some of the e-mail features of Outlook. This client program and others are discussed further in Chapter 7, "Configuring Client Access."

Web Browsers

Exchange Server 2003 includes a component named *Outlook Web Access (OWA)* that runs in conjunction with Microsoft *Internet Information Server (IIS)*. OWA enables web browsers to access Exchange resources such as mailboxes and public folders. Any standard web browser can be used, such as Microsoft Internet Explorer or Netscape Navigator, though only Internet Explorer 5 or later supports some of the advanced features that OWA provides. This Exchange functionality permits users of other operating system platforms, such as Unix or IBM's OS/2, to also be Exchange clients. Chapter 7 covers the Exchange components required for web browser clients.

One of the new improvements in Outlook Web Access in Exchange Server 2003 is the ability to choose between the basic experience or the premium experience, which is supported only by Internet Explorer version 5 and later.

Internet E-mail Programs with POP3

Exchange has built-in support for the *Post Office Protocol, version 3 (POP3)*. POP enables mail clients to retrieve mail messages stored on a remote mail server. Exchange's support for this protocol allows Internet e-mail programs that support POP3, such as Outlook Express, to access their Exchange mailbox and download their messages. Chapter 7 covers POP3 in the Exchange environment.

Exchange also has built-in support for the *Internet Message Access Protocol, version 4 (IMAP4)*. IMAP is similar to POP in that it is a mail retrieval protocol. But IMAP has more features than POP, such as the ability to select the messages to download rather than having to download all new messages. Outlook Express is also an IMAP client that can be used with Exchange Server 2003. Chapter 7 provides further details on IMAP4.

Groupware

A simple definition of *groupware* is any application (the *ware* in *groupware*) that allows groups to store and share information. That is a very broad definition and one that includes applications such as e-mail and electronic forms. And indeed, as you will see, these applications are important ingredients in groupware. However, the emphasis in groupware is on collaboration—not merely sending an item, but enabling many people to cooperatively use that item. Outlook incorporates many groupware functions, such as the ability to share a calendar, schedule, task list, and contact list.

Another example of groupware is folder-based applications. These applications utilize public folders. A *public folder* is a special storage area for group access. Various types of information can be contained in a public folder, such as documents, spreadsheets, graphics, e-mail messages, forms, and many other types of information. Along with storing information, a public folder can be assigned security, so that only selected users or groups can access the public folder. Other features such as views and rules can also be assigned to a public folder. Using a simple folder-based application, a Sales department could place all of their sales letters in a specified public folder for the department. Only the employees in the Sales department would be given permission to access this public folder.

Folder-based applications can also utilize electronic forms. A specific electronic form or set of forms can be associated with a public folder. Users can fill out and post the form to the public folder. Other users can then access the public folder and view the posted information. An example of this type of application is a discussion-and-response application. A product manager could create a public folder for discussion about a product under development. That manager could also create customized electronic forms that people could use to enter their comments and that they could then send, through e-mail, to the public folder. The product manager and product developers could then access the public folder to read the comments. It is even possible to set up customized views of the content in the public folder in order to view only data on a specific topic. A marketing person, for example, might want to see only comments related to the possible market for the product.

Folder-based applications are examples of *pull-style* communication, because users go to the information and decide what is relevant to them. See Chapter 6, "Using Public Folders," for more on the topic of public folders. Figure 1.2 illustrates folder-based applications.

Other Messaging Applications

Along with e-mail, electronic forms, and groupware, there are many other types of messaging applications. Exchange provides an open platform that encourages the integration of other types of applications, including the following:

Workflow While Exchange includes some basic workflow capabilities, some third-party workflow solutions that work with Exchange are also available. An example of a workflow application would be Streem Center from Streem Communications.

Fax Fax software can be integrated with the Exchange clients so that e-mail and faxes can be sent and received from the same location, as well as share the same address book. An example of a fax application would be FAXMaker from GFI Software.

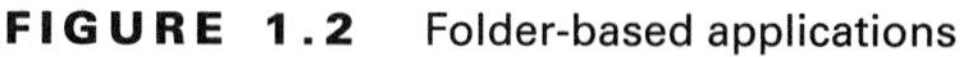

FIGURE 1.2 Folder-based applications

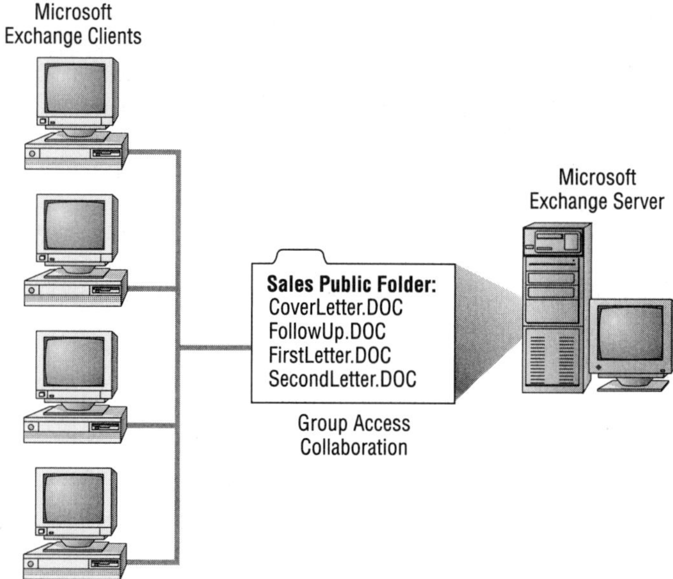

Voicemail There are various voicemail products that integrate with Exchange and store their messages in an Exchange mailbox. An example of a voicemail application would be Avaya Unified Messenger from Avaya.

Custom applications Through its installable file system, public folders, wide support of Internet protocols, and support of scripting, Exchange Server 2003 also serves as a wonderful platform for the creation of custom business applications.

Computing Models

Microsoft Exchange uses a client/server computing model to implement its messaging system. To better understand the client/server model, two other models are discussed briefly to provide a context for the client/server model. In all, the three models discussed in this section are:

- Mainframe computing
- Shared-file computing
- Client/server computing

Mainframe Computing

Mainframe computing consists of a powerful host computer, such as a mainframe computer or minicomputer, and numerous input-output devices attached to the host, such as terminals, printers, and personal computers running terminal emulation software. The advantages of this architecture are its powerful, centralized processing, administration, and backup. These features permit a large number of users on systems built according to this model. The disadvantages are that these features incur high costs, that personal computing power and applications are not leveraged, and that most of these systems have a proprietary architecture. Examples of messaging systems that use this type of model are IBM PROFS (Professional Office System) and OfficeVision.

Figure 1.3 illustrates the host-based computing model.

FIGURE 1.3 Host-based computing model

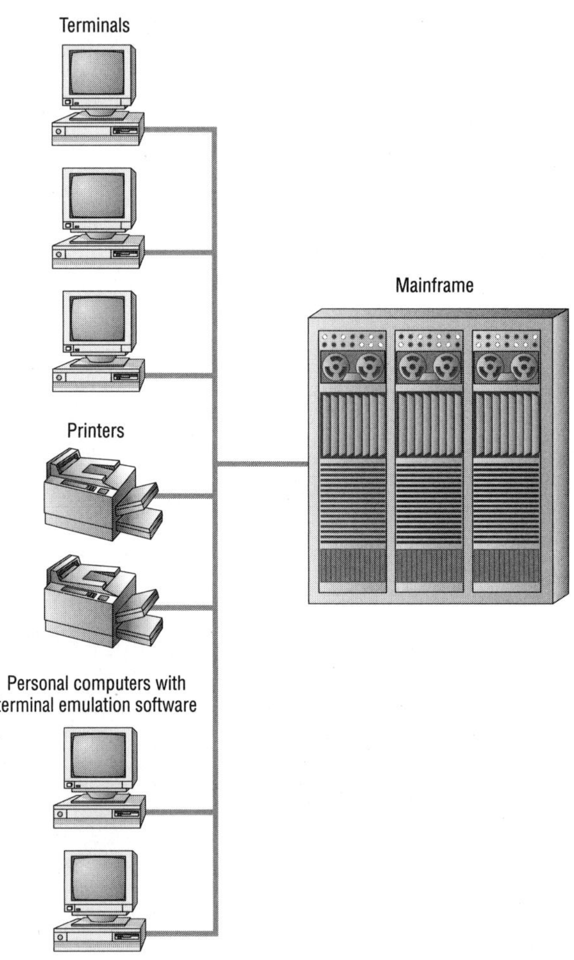

Shared-file Computing

This network computing model works in a local area network (LAN) context. At least one computer is used as a server computer to store files. Users, working on their own networked personal computers, access and share the files on the server computer. Microsoft Mail is a messaging system that uses this type of architecture.

Using this model, a *shared-file messaging system* has active clients and passive servers. Each mail user is assigned a mailbox. A mailbox is actually a directory on the server where mail messages are placed. The server software is passive in that its main task is to store mail messages. The client software is said to be active because it performs almost all mail activities. Along with the normal mail activities of creating and reading mail, the client software is also responsible for depositing mail in the correct recipient mailboxes and checking its own mailbox for new mail (this is referred to as *polling*).

This model could be compared to a postal system where people must take their outgoing mail to the post office and place it in the respective recipients' mail slots and also visit the post office to check their mail slots for any new mail. The primary duty of the post office is to store the mail. This is analogous to the shared-file messaging system in that the people (clients) are active and the post office (server) is passive.

The advantages of shared-file messaging systems include the following:

Minimal server requirements Because the server has a passive role, it does not need to run on a high-end hardware platform.

Minimal server configuration in a single-server environment Because the server is mainly a storage location, it does not need a lot of configuration.

The disadvantages of shared-file messaging systems include the following:

Limited security Because the client software is responsible for sending mail to a recipient's mailbox, each client must have write permissions on each mail directory. Each client must also have read permissions on the entire mail directory structure in order to read forwarded or copied messages. From a security standpoint, this is considered an excessive level of permissions.

Increased network traffic The periodic client polling of mailboxes for new mail increases network traffic.

Increased client load The active clients do almost all of the processing work.

Limited scalability These systems cannot accommodate large numbers of users because of the shared-file model. Users must access common files that can be opened by only one process at a time.

Single point of failure A single mail server in this type of arrangement becomes a single point of failure for clients seeking to access its services.

Figure 1.4 illustrates a shared-file messaging system.

FIGURE 1.4 Shared-file messaging system

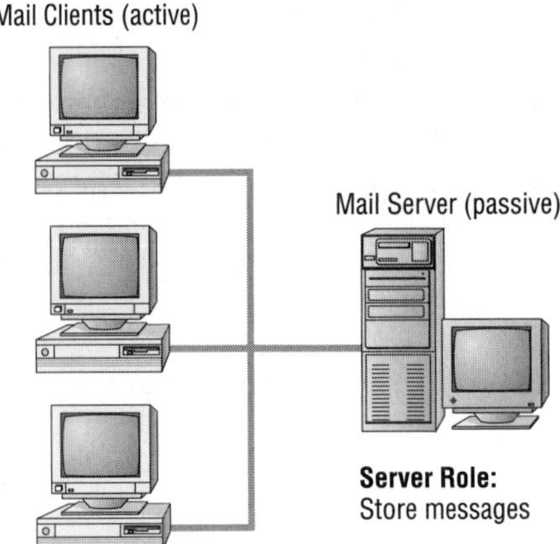
Mail Clients (active)
Mail Server (passive)
Server Role:
Store messages
Client Role:
– Poll mail directory for new mail
– Read mail (necessitates read permission over entire mail directory structure)
– Create mail
– Send mail (necessitates write permission over entire mail directory structure)

Client/Server Computing

In *client/server messaging*, a task is divided between the client processes and server processes. Each side works to accomplish specific parts of the task. The two processes are usually running on separate computers and are communicating over a network. The communication is in the form of requests and replies passed back and forth through messages.

The client side includes a user's personal computer or workstation and client software. The client software provides the interface for the user to employ when manipulating data and making requests to and receiving replies from the server. The processing power to carry out those tasks is provided by the client's computer.

The server side includes the server computer and server software. The server software receives and processes client requests, provides storage capabilities, implements security, provides for administrative functions, and performs many more duties. The server's processor, or processors, powers these functions.

When this model is applied to a mail system, both the client side and the server side are active participants. Mail activities are divided between the two sides in a way that takes advantage of both parties. The client software enables users to initiate mail activities such as creating, sending, reading, storing, and forwarding mail and attachments.

The server software also has an active role. Some of its tasks are implementing security, placing messages in mailboxes (as opposed to the client software doing it), notifying clients of new mail (which eliminates the need for clients to poll their mailboxes), and performing specified actions on mail, such as applying rules, rerouting messages, and many other tasks. Many of the mail activities that are initiated by the client software are actually implemented on the server. For example, when a client initiates the reading of a message, the client software sends a read request to the server where the message physically resides. The server software receives this request, processes it (for example, checks security to see if this user is permitted to read this message), and then sends the message to the client. The user can then use the client software and processor to manipulate the message (edit the message, for example). This illustrates how both sides are active.

In this model, the software running on the client machine is frequently referred to as the front-end program, while the software running on the server is referred to as the back-end program.

Exchange Server 2003 now supports front-end and back-end servers, a designation that allows an Exchange administrator to balance the various loads placed on Exchange servers among multiple computers. This concept is discussed in detail in Chapter 2, "Microsoft Exchange Architecture," and Chapter 7. Do not confuse front- and back-end programs with front- and back-end servers.

The advantages of the client/server model include the following:

Distributed computer processing The computer processing power of both the client and server machines is utilized. The client processor handles the end-user mail activities, such as creating, reading, and manipulating mail, while the server processor (or processors) handles the security, routing, and special handling of mail. This spreads the processing load over a multitude of client processors, while still utilizing the powerful processing of the server machine.

Tight security The server software is responsible for the security of the mail system. The server software is the entity that actually places messages in mailboxes. The clients therefore do not need permissions to all mailboxes. This creates a much more secure mail system.

Reduced network traffic Because the server software informs clients of new mail, the client software does not have to poll the server, thus reducing network traffic.

Scalable The term *scalable* relates to the ability to grow easily. A client/server mail system can scale to any size organization.

The primary disadvantage of the client/server model is the following:

Increased server hardware requirements Because the server has an active role in the messaging environment, there are greater requirements for the server hardware platform. This should not be seen as much of a disadvantage in light of scalability, central administration, backup, and other advantages.

Figure 1.5 illustrates the client/server mail system.

FIGURE 1.5 Client/server mail system

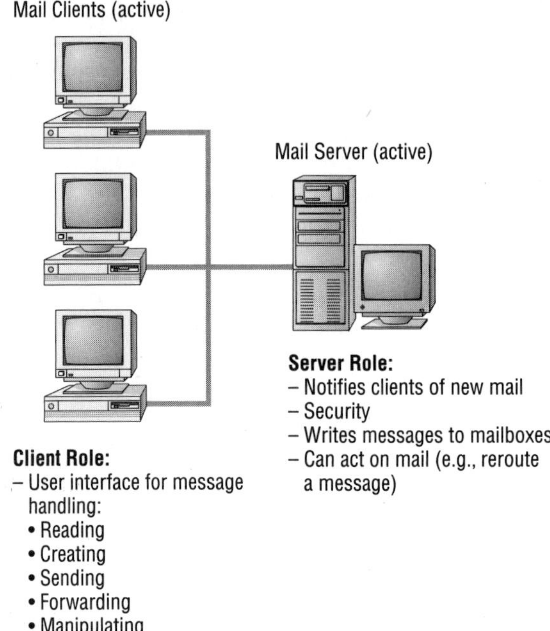

Exchange is a client/server messaging system. The Exchange Server 2003 software runs as a series of services on a Windows Server 2003 or Windows 2000 Server computer. It provides server-side messaging functions for the client applications.

So far, you have learned what features make up Exchange Server 2003 and how the system is implemented, namely the client/server model. Now we need to turn our attention to the context or scale in which Exchange can be implemented.

Enterprise-Quality Features

Microsoft Exchange Server 2003 actually comes in two editions. The first is the Standard Edition (or, simply, Microsoft Exchange Server 2003), which is targeted for use by small- to medium-sized businesses. The other edition is Microsoft Server 2003 Enterprise Edition. It is designed to be an enterprise messaging system, meaning one that is more scalable and includes features meant for larger organizations. Table 1.1 details the key specifications of both Microsoft Exchange Server 2003 Standard Edition and Microsoft Exchange Server 2003 Enterprise Edition.

TABLE 1.1 Exchange Server 2003 Version Comparison

Feature	Standard Edition	Enterprise Edition
Maximum database size	Limited to 16 GB	Limited only by hardware
Number of regular storage groups supported	One	Four
Supports the recovery storage group (above the regular storage groups)	Yes	Yes
Number of databases per storage group	Two	Five
Supports clustering	No	Yes
Supports front-end and back-end server configuration	Yes	Yes
Supports Volume Shadow Copy	Yes	Yes
X.400 connector	Not included	Included

For Exchange to be an enterprise messaging system, a large number of technologies had to be included or leveraged from other products (such as Microsoft Windows Server 2003). This section briefly discusses the technologies that make Exchange a true enterprise messaging system. Those technologies fall into six categories:

- Enterprise-quality application platform
- Scalability
- Interoperability
- Performance
- Administration
- Reliability

Enterprise-Quality Application Platform

Before a determination can be made as to whether or not a product can scale to the size an organization needs, it must be determined that the product can do the things it needs to do. Exchange provides the necessary application platform to meet the requirements of almost any organization. The following are some of the elements of the Exchange application platform:

Supports a large number of messaging services E-mail, electronic forms, groupware, and add-on products for faxing, paging, videoconferencing, voicemailing, and many other services are supported.

Supports a large number of client platforms There is client software that runs on MS-DOS, Windows 3.*x*, Windows 95, Windows 98, Windows NT, Windows 2000, Windows XP, Windows Server 2003, Apple Macintosh, Unix, and IBM OS/2, as well as virtually every other operating system available today.

Provides open architecture/extensibility Exchange is based on an open architecture, meaning that the specifications of many of its protocols are available in the public domain. Examples of published protocols include the *Messaging Application Programming Interface* (*MAPI*), Internet protocols, and various Comite Consultatif International Telegraphique et Telephonique (CCITT) protocols. Developers can use this openness to create additional applications and programs that work with or extend Exchange. That is what is meant by extensible. One example of the way Microsoft encourages this is by including a single-user version of the Microsoft Visual InterDev product with Exchange Server. Developers can use Visual InterDev to create web-based applications that enable web clients to access Exchange resources.

Based on industry standards The Exchange protocols, along with being open and extensible, are based on industry standards (protocols can be open and extensible but not based on industry standards). The MAPI protocol is considered an industry standard. Some of the industry standard Internet and CCITT protocols used in Exchange are as follows:

> **Internet mail** *Simple Mail Transfer Protocol* (*SMTP*), Post Office Protocol, version 3 (POP3), and Internet Message Access Protocol, version 4 (IMAP4). See Chapter 7.
>
> **Internet directory access** *Lightweight Directory Access Protocol* (*LDAP*). See Chapter 7.
>
> **Internet news services** *Network News Transfer Protocol* (*NNTP*). See Chapter 7.
>
> **Internet management** *Simple Network Management Protocol* (*SNMP*). See Chapter 10, "Administration and Maintenance."
>
> **Internet security** *Secure MIME (S/MIME)*, Secure Sockets Layer, version 3 (SSL), and Simple Authentication and Security Layer (SASL).
>
> **Internet web protocols** *HyperText Transfer Protocol* (*HTTP*) and HyperText Markup Language (HTML). See Chapter 7.
>
> **CCITT message transfer** Comit Consultatif International Telegraphique et Telephonique (International Telegraph and Telephone Consultative Committee): X.400. See the section "Industry Standards" later in this chapter.
>
> **CCITT directory** X.500. See the section "Industry Standards" later in this chapter.

Security features Using the Internet security protocols listed above, along with other protocols, Exchange can provide advanced security features. For example, messages can be sent with a digital signature to confirm the identity of the sender, and message content can be encrypted to prevent unauthorized viewing. Exchange Server 2003 supports many of the most popular encryption algorithms today, including 3DES and SHA. Chapter 15, "Securing Exchange Server 2003," discusses the protocols and administration of advanced security in Exchange. Further security features, and ones that are leveraged from Microsoft Windows Server 2003, include:

Mandatory logon A user must have a domain account and password to log on to a Windows Server 2003 or a Windows 2000 Server domain.

Discretionary access control An Exchange administrator can use Windows Server 2003 or Windows 2000 Server security to control access to Exchange resources. For example, one administrator could have permission to manage particular Exchange servers or features but not others.

Auditing Windows Server 2003 or Windows 2000 Server can be configured to monitor and record certain events. This can help diagnose security events. The audit information is written to the Windows Event Log.

Scalability

Once a product has been determined to accomplish the types of things you need to get done, then you must find out if it can do them on the scale you need. Exchange is extremely scalable due to the following features:

Software scalable Exchange can be implemented with a single Exchange server, or dozens of servers, depending on the messaging requirements. Even with multiple Exchange servers, a single enterprise messaging system exists. This is due to the Exchange features that enable communication between servers. This functionality permits Exchange to scale from single-server to multiple-server implementations. Microsoft itself uses Exchange for its worldwide messaging system.

Hardware scalable Scalability is also evidenced by the maximum hardware specifications that Exchange can utilize.

CPUs Scalable from 1 to 64 processors, depending on the operating system in use.

RAM Maximum addressable by Exchange is 4 GB.

Disk storage Storage is limited only by hardware capacity. The Standard Edition of Microsoft Exchange Server 2003 has a 16-GB storage limit on each of the Exchange databases. The Enterprise edition has no limit on the databases.

Interoperability

For a product to fit into an enterprise, it might need to work with an existing messaging system. This is called interoperability or *coexistence*. An organization might need to move all of its existing messaging data to a new messaging product. This is called a *migration*. Exchange addresses both of these issues.

To interoperate with various non-Exchange systems, referred to as foreign systems, Microsoft had to write special software programs called *connectors*. Connectors are similar to translators that understand both Exchange and the foreign system and translate between them. Third-party companies have also written similar programs. Microsoft refers to these programs as gateways. Messaging systems that Exchange can interoperate with include the following:

- Internet mail
- X.400 mail systems
- Lotus Notes
- Novell GroupWise
- Digital Equipment Corporation (DEC) All-IN-1
- Verimation MEMO

Exchange Server 2003 ships with connectors for Internet mail, Lotus Notes, and Novell GroupWise systems. Connectivity to other systems, such as DEC ALL-IN-1 or Verimation MEMO, is provided through third-party gateway products.

For Exchange to interoperate with some of the previous systems, third-party software is required. Chapter 13, "Connecting with Other Messaging Systems," discusses interoperability in more detail.

Exchange Server 2003 can perform a migration from the following messaging systems:

- Microsoft Mail
- Microsoft Exchange
- Lotus cc:Mail
- Lotus Notes
- GroupWise 4.*x*
- GroupWise 5.*x*
- Internet Directory LDAP via ADSI
- Internet IMAP4 mail

If you have other messaging systems in place, such as Verimation MEMO, you will need to migrate them to Exchange 2000 Server first and then upgrade them to Exchange Server 2003. Alternatively, you may find a third-party conversion utility that can be used for this task.

Performance

A messaging system requires adequate performance to be used on an enterprise scale. Exchange meets that requirement by being a 32-bit, multithreaded program running on a high-performance operating system, Microsoft Windows Server 2003 or Windows 2000 Server. Many features are built into the Exchange System Manager to help optimize server performance.

Administration

An important element of any enterprise application is the ability to effectively and efficiently administer it. Exchange meets this need by including powerful administration programs, one of which is the *Exchange System Manager* snap-in for the Microsoft Management Console (MMC). This program provides a single point of administration for an entire Exchange organization. Exchange servers anywhere in the enterprise can be managed from this program, as well as such activities as configuring a server, managing connections to foreign systems, and monitoring services centrally.

Along with its own administrative utilities, Exchange can leverage the administrative capabilities of the Windows Server 2003 or Windows 2000 Server operating system. Exchange integrates with Windows utilities such as Performance Monitor and Event Viewer. Another powerful administration feature in Exchange Server 2003 involves Active Directory. Exchange-related user features (such as mailbox properties) are now managed using the Active Directory Computers and Users utility—the same tool used by Windows administrators to manage users and groups.

Exchange Server 2003 also supports the Simple Network Management Protocol (SNMP). This enables third-party SNMP monitor programs to collect various management information about an Exchange server, such as the performance information gathered by Performance Monitor. The topic of Exchange Server administration is covered in Chapter 10.

Reliability

Because of the importance of a messaging system to an enterprise, it must be reliable. Exchange provides reliability through the following ways:

Transaction log files Data that is to be written to an Exchange database is first written to these log files (which can be done very fast). The data is later written to the appropriate database, which takes longer because of the structured nature of a database. If, for whatever reason, a server has an unintended shutdown, data that has not been written to the database is not lost; it can be automatically reconstructed from the transaction log files. Chapter 2 and Chapter 14, "Backup and Recovery," discuss this topic further.

Windows Backup utility When Exchange is installed, it adds extensions to the Windows Backup utility, allowing that program to back up Exchange information.

Replicas Exchange can be configured to have multiple copies, called replicas, of a single public folder on different servers. This prevents a single point of failure in terms of data access and provides quicker access by putting folders on servers closer to the users in an organization.

Intelligent message routing This feature allows multiple routes to a destination, thereby preventing a single point of failure for message delivery.

Windows Server fault tolerance Exchange takes advantage of the many fault-tolerant features of the Windows Server 2003 and Windows 2000 Server operating systems, such as disk mirroring and disk striping with parity. Exchange Server 2003 Enterprise Edition also supports Active/Passive and Active/Active clustering, which provides fault tolerance in the event of a server malfunction. If one server fails, another server can take its place, thereby providing uninterrupted service to users.

Industry Standards

Microsoft Exchange is based on industry standard technologies, ensuring an open architecture and, therefore, extensibility (i.e., the ability to easily add on to the product). An adequate understanding of the standards used in Exchange will help in utilizing it. This section presents a brief explanation of the following standards:

- Messaging Application Programming Interface (MAPI)
- The Remote Procedure Call (RPC) protocol
- X.400
- X.500

The Internet standards are also very important in Exchange, and they will be discussed in Chapter 2 and Chapter 7.

Messaging Application Programming Interface (MAPI)

To understand MAPI, you must first understand what an application programming interface is. At the code level, a program's functions are invoked through specific instructions. The collection of those instructions is referred to as an *application programming interface* (*API*). That phrase is appropriate because the API allows a programmer to interface with the functions of a program. For example, if a program has the ability to read a message, there is a specific API instruction, also called a function call, that can invoke that ability. If two programs need to interact, they must do so with an API they both understand. For example, if program A sends the instruction `Read_Message 4` to program B, but program B understands only the instruction `Message_4_Read`, then the instruction will not be understood. Humans can use slightly different grammar and still understand one another, but computers are not that forgiving.

In the past, many client/server messaging products had their own APIs for the client/server interaction. If someone wrote a client program, it would work only with the messaging system whose API it used. If a user needed to connect to multiple messaging systems, multiple client programs were needed. See Figure 1.6.

FIGURE 1.6 Multiple messaging APIs require multiple programs.

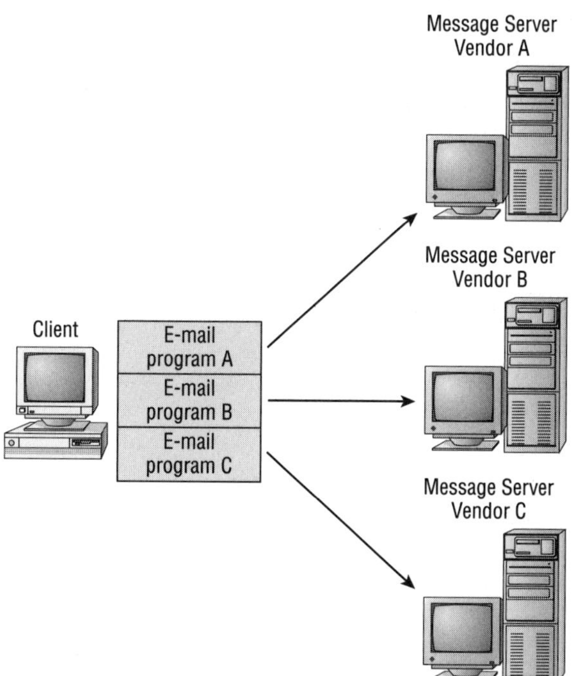

Microsoft decided to remedy that situation by creating a standard messaging architecture, referred to as the Messaging API (MAPI). MAPI accomplishes two broad goals. One, it provides a standard API for client/server messaging interaction. This role makes MAPI a type of middleware, meaning that it stands in the middle between clients and servers. Some authors refer to middleware as the slash (/) between the words *client* and *server*. MAPI makes it possible for a single-client application to access different messaging servers. See Figure 1.7 for an illustration.

The second broad goal of MAPI is to provide a standard set of services to client messaging applications. These services include address books, message storage, and transport mechanisms. Even when using different types of MAPI applications, such as e-mail, fax, and voicemail, a user can access a single address book (a universal address book) and store different data types in the same folder (a universal inbox). The transport mechanisms relate to a single client application that can connect to different messaging systems. A single MAPI e-mail application can access an Exchange server, a Microsoft Mail post office, an Internet mail server, and others.

Although MAPI includes individual API instructions, it most often communicates those instructions in an object-oriented manner. An object is a container; in this context, it functions as a container of API instructions. The Microsoft specification for object-oriented programming is called the Component Object Model (COM). MAPI, OLE, ActiveX, and other technologies are part of the COM standard.

FIGURE 1.7 Accessing different messaging servers through MAPI

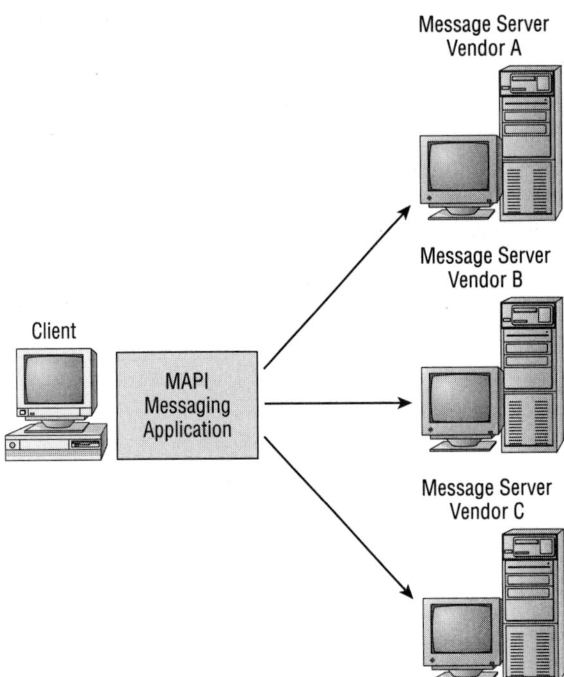

The original version of MAPI (called Simple MAPI) was developed by Microsoft. But in the subsequent version (MAPI 1), Microsoft worked with over 100 different vendors to develop an industry standard. Microsoft has also turned over the vast majority of the MAPI specification to standards organizations, while still taking a leadership role by including the core MAPI component with its Windows operating systems.

While MAPI deals with instructions, the next section discusses the protocols that enable those instructions to be passed between clients and servers.

Procedure Calls

You now know the instruction standard used by the Exchange client/server messaging applications, namely MAPI. But client/server applications are divided across physical machines. When a client issues a read instruction for a message, that message could be on the server. The server could understand that instruction and could send the message, but the instruction has to get to the server and the message has to get back to the client. MAPI does not handle those procedures. From MAPI's perspective, the physical distinction of the client and the server does not exist; it is transparent. Microsoft uses the Remote Procedure Call (RPC) protocol to pass instructions and data between machines. Before discussing the RPC protocol, we will first define what a procedure call is and then discuss the two types of procedure calls, local and remote.

In Exchange Server 5.5 and earlier, servers in the same Exchange site relied on RPCs to transfer messages and directory information between them. Exchange Server 2003 and Exchange 2000 Server use SMTP to exchange this information between servers. You'll learn more about this in Chapter 2.

Procedure calls handle the transfer of instructions and data between a program and a processor or processors. When a program issues an instruction, that instruction is passed to the processor for execution, and the results of the execution are passed back to the program. Now, let's look at the two main types of procedure calls.

Local Procedure Calls

When a program issues an instruction that is executed on the same computer as the program executing the instruction, the procedure is referred to as a *local procedure call*. When Exchange Server components perform activities on that server, they issue instructions that are executed by that server's CPU or CPUs. That is an example of a local procedure call. Exchange uses a Microsoft protocol called the Local Procedure Call (LPC) to implement this mechanism.

Remote Procedure Calls

A *remote procedure call* is similar to a local procedure call in that it relates to the transfer of instructions and data between a program and processor. But unlike a local procedure call, a remote procedure call enables an instruction issued on one computer to be sent over the network to another computer for execution, with the results being sent back to the first computer. The computer making the instruction and the computer performing the execution are remote from each other. The transfer of instructions and data between the computers is totally transparent to the original program and to the user. To the program issuing the instruction, all of its instructions appear to be locally executed. Remote procedure calls are a key ingredient in distributed processing and client/server computing.

The RPC mechanism permits the optimization of performance by assigning different computers to do specific tasks. For example, some programs require lots of processor power, memory, or storage or all three. It would be impractical to give every computer running these applications the necessary levels of resources. But one specialized computer could be given, for example, four processors, 1 GB of RAM, and 200 GB of storage. Clients could use those resources through the RPC mechanism.

Because the request/reply aspect of RPC is intended to be transparent to the client program and user, the speed of network communication is a factor. The computers involved in an RPC session need to have a high-speed permanent link between them, such as a local area network (LAN) or a high-speed wide area network (WAN).

Exchange uses remote procedure calls in many of its communications. The protocol that Exchange uses to implement remote procedure calls is called the Remote Procedure Call (RPC) protocol. This protocol is discussed in the following section.

Remote Procedure Call (RPC) Protocol

The Remote Procedure Call protocol is based on a protocol created by the standards group Open Software Foundation (OSF) and is part of the OSF's Distributed Computing Environment (DCE) protocol suite. Microsoft includes the RPC protocol with their Windows Server 2003 and Windows 2000 Server operating systems. In older versions of Exchange (Exchange 5.5 and earlier), servers within an Exchange site transferred messages between themselves using RPCs. In Exchange Server 2003 (and Exchange 2000 Server), this functionality has been largely taken over by SMTP. RPCs are still used to communicate with Exchange 5.5 servers, but SMTP is now used for all communications between newer Exchange servers inside and outside the boundaries of a routing group.

When a user chooses to read a message, the client program issues a MAPI instruction (`MAPIReadMail`). The RPC protocol on the client transfers this instruction to the Exchange server where the message physically resides. This is called a request. The RPC protocol on the server receives this request, has it executed, and sends the message back to the client's screen. This is called a reply. RPC clients make requests, and RPC servers make replies. RPC is sometimes referred to as a request/reply protocol. RPCs are also used in some Exchange server-to-server communications. Figure 1.8 illustrates the RPC mechanism.

FIGURE 1.8 The Remote Procedure Call protocol

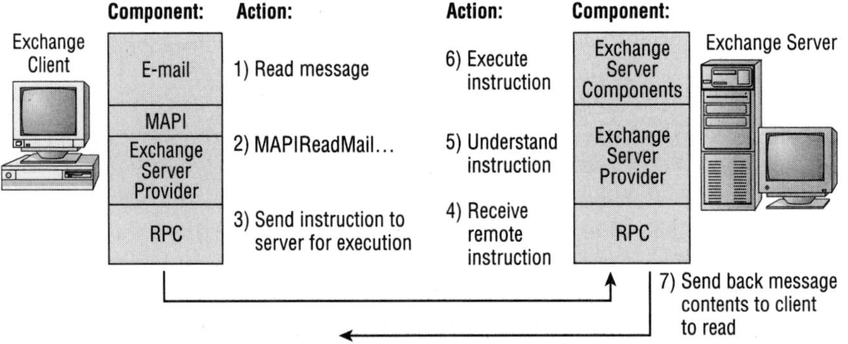

Note that being an RPC client or server doesn't really have anything to do with being a messaging client or server. In the example in Figure 1.8, the messaging client is also the RPC client, but an RPC client is really just the computer that issued the RPC. Exchange servers often communicate information between themselves using RPCs. The computer that initiates the connection request is the RPC client, and the computer that receives the request is the RPC server.

CCITT X.400

For most of the history of electronic messaging in the private sector, there were no widely accepted messaging standards. Different messaging products used vastly different messaging protocols. This made interoperability between different systems difficult and costly, sometimes impossible. To address this situation, different standards organizations began to develop what they hoped would become internationally recognized messaging standards. One of those standards organizations was the Comite Consultatif International Telegraphique et Telephonique (CCITT). This is translated in English as the International Telegraph and Telephone Consultative Committee. One of the standards they developed was the *X.400* Message Handling System (MHS) standard. Exchange uses some of the technologies of the X.400 standard.

The CCITT is now a subdelegation of the International Telegraph Union (ITU), which is an agency of the United Nations. The State Department is the voting member from the United States.

The different versions of the X.400 standard are referred to by the year they were officially published and by a specified color. Versions to date are as follows:

- 1984 "Red Book"
- 1988 "Blue Book"
- 1992 "White Book"

The Message Handling System (MHS) discussed in this section is not the same standard as the Novell-related Message Handling System (MHS).

X.400 is a set of standards that relates to the exchange of electronic messages (messages can be e-mail, fax, voicemail, telex, etc.). The goal of X.400 is to enable the creation of a global electronic messaging network. Just as you can make a telephone call from almost anywhere in the world to almost anywhere in the world, X.400 hopes to make that a reality for electronic messaging. X.400 defines only application-level protocols and relies on other standards for the physical transportation of data (e.g., X.25 and others).

X.400 Addressing: Originator/Recipient Address

Try to imagine what the American telephone system would be like if different parts of the country used different numbering schemes: different number lengths, different placement of the area code, etc. Obviously that would lead to a lot of complexity and problems; hence a standard numbering scheme exists. Electronic messaging also needs a standard addressing scheme to avoid the same sort of chaos.

You might think that you could simply list people's names in alphabetical order. But there are many problems with that scheme. The addressing scheme needs to be able to potentially scale to the entire world's population. An alphabetical list would be quite long. There is also the problem of what constitutes a last name; different countries have different methods (e.g., Anwar el-Sadat, Willem de Kooning). A truly global addressing scheme needs to be totally unambiguous.

The addressing scheme that X.400 uses is called the Originator/Recipient Address (O/R Address). It is similar to a postal address in that it uses a hierarchical format. While a postal address hierarchy is country, zip code, state, city, street, and recipient's name, the O/R Address hierarchy consists of countries, communication providers (such as AT&T), companies or organizations, and other categories. Figure 1.9 and Table 1.2 present some of these categories, called fields.

The O/R Address specifies an unambiguous path to where the recipient is located in the X.400 network (it does not specify a path the message might take, only the path to where the recipient is located).

In actual practice, this addressing scheme is not as standardized as Table 1.2 makes it seem, nor is it used in the standardized way. Although the address fields have always been specified, the order in which to write them was not specified until 1993. Consequently, you will see them written in different ways. Some X.400 implementations have modified the standard.

X.400 Message Format: Interpersonal Messaging (IPM)

X.400 also specifies the protocols for formatting messages. The most common one is called Interpersonal Messaging (IPM) and is used for e-mail messages. There are other protocols for other types of messaging, such as Electronic Data Interchange (EDI).

TABLE 1.2 X.400 Originator/Recipient Address Example

Field	Abbreviation/Example	Description
Country code	c=US	Country
Administrative Management Domain (ADMD)	a=MCI	The third-party networking system used (e.g., AT&T, MCI, Sprint, etc.)
Private Management Domain (PRMD)	p=WidgetNet	Subscriber to the ADMD (company name)
Organization	o=Widget	Name of company or organization
Surname	s=Wilson	Last name
Given name	g=Jay	First name

FIGURE 1.9 X.400 Originator/Recipient Address example

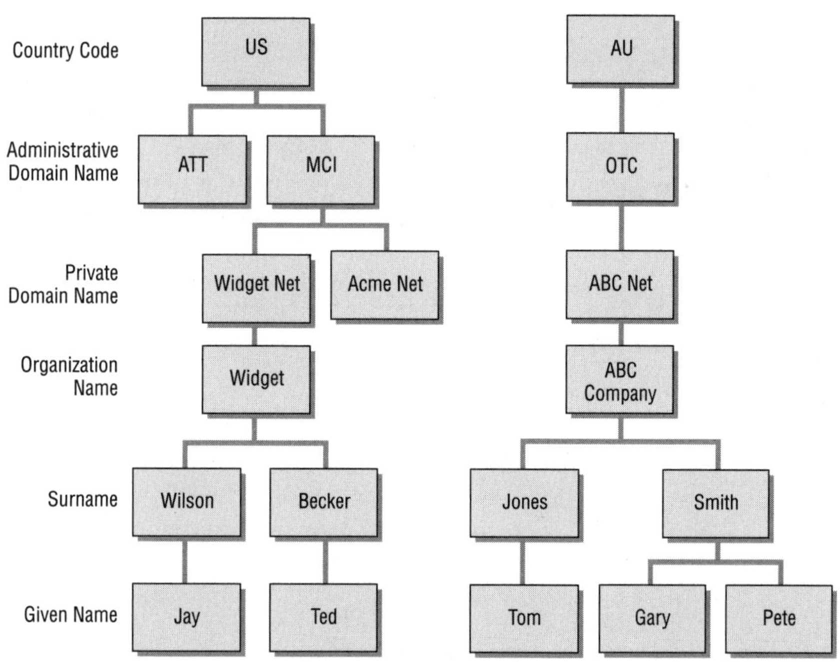

X.400 Message Routing: Message Transfer Agent (MTA)

Another very important X.400 protocol is Message Transfer Agent (MTA). MTA is the protocol that runs in the message routing machines (i.e., routers). MTA is like a local post office in that it receives and routes messages to their ultimate destinations. And just like a postal system (a snail-mail system), electronic messages can go through several MTAs before they arrive at their ultimate destinations. This type of delivery method is called store and forward. An MTA machine receives a message, stores it so it can calculate its next route, and then forwards it to either another MTA machine or its ultimate destination. This method eliminates the need for the sender's application and the recipient's application to perform any simultaneous actions in order to exchange data. A sender's message is simply packaged with all the necessary addressing information and is sent to the next store-and-forward MTA machine (i.e., router). That MTA can route it to the next MTA, and so on, until it reaches its final destination.

Other X.400 Information

While the X.400 standard does not define the protocols for the physical transportation of messages, it does specify what other standards it can use. They include the following OSI (Open Systems Interconnection) protocols:

- TP0/X.25

- TP4 (CLNP)
- TP0/RPC 1006 to TCP/IP

TP stands for Transport Protocol.

Third-party X.400 networks that can be subscribed to include AT&T Mail, AT&T EasyLink, MCI Mail, Sprintmail, Atlas 400 (France), Envoy 100 (Canada), Telebox 400 (Germany), and Telecom Australia. Microsoft Exchange is an X.400 messaging product.

Exchange Server 2003 does not support the TP4 protocol, unlike previous versions of Exchange.

CCITT X.500

The CCITT X.500 standard defines the protocols for a global directory service. A directory service is a database of information on resources. Resources can be user accounts, user groups, mailboxes, printers, fax machines, and many other items. These resources are officially referred to as objects. The information about an object, such as a mailbox, can include the owner of the mailbox and the owner's title, phone number, fax number, as well as many other types of information. The information about an object is referred to as its properties or attributes. A directory enables objects and their properties to be made available to users and administrators.

The directory's importance cannot be overstated. To use a telephone analogy, imagine the current global telephone system without telephone directories. The technology to make a call would be in place, but you would have a hard time locating a person's number to call. The creation of global electronic yellow pages could go a long way toward solving the "I know it's out there, I just can't find it" problem.

To create a directory service, X.500 addresses two main areas:

Directory structure How resources should be organized

Directory access How one is able to read, query, and modify a directory

X.500 Directory Structure

The X.500 directory structure is hierarchical, which facilitates a logical organization of information. Figure 1.10 illustrates the X.500 directory structure, and Table 1.3 explains it.

The X.500 terminology for the structure of a directory is the Directory Information Tree (DIT). The term for the information in the directory is Directory Information Base (DIB).

FIGURE 1.10 X.500 directory structure example

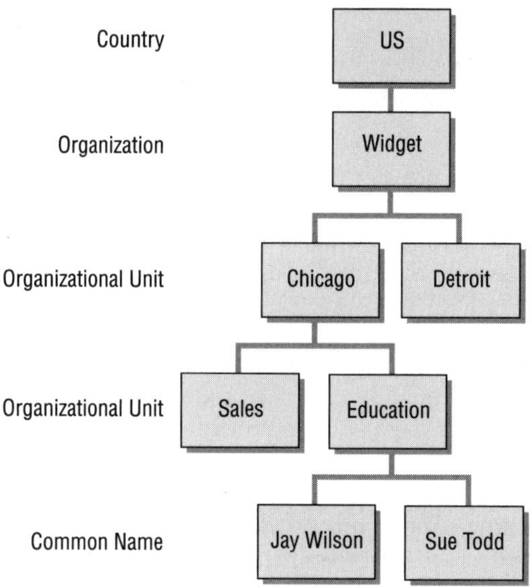

TABLE 1.3 Descriptions of X.500 Objects

X.500 Object	Abbreviation/Example	Description
Country	c=US	Country of the organization
Organization	o=Widget	Name of the organization
Organizational unit	ou=Chicago	Subcategory of the organization
	ou=Detroit	
Organizational unit	ou=Sales	Subcategories under the ou=Chicago
	ou=Education	
Common name	cn=JayWilson	Name of a specific resource (username, fax name, printer name, etc.)

To communicate the location of an object in the directory hierarchy, list the path to that object, starting at the top and moving down. This is called a Distinguished Name (DN). The DN of the example in Figure 1.10 is as follows:

c=US; o=Widget; ou=Chicago; ou=Education; cn=JayWilson

The differences between an X.500 address, the Distinguished Name (DN), and an X.400 address are due to their different purposes. A DN is the location of an object in the directory, whereas the X.400 address is the location of an object in a messaging system. Getting back to the telephone analogy, a DN is the location of a person in the phone book, and an X.400 address is where they are in the physical telephone system. This is illustrated by the fact that an X.400 address can include information about third-party messaging networks that are used to physically deliver a message, some examples being AT&T, MCI, and Sprint.

The 1988 release of X.400 incorporated the use of a DN address instead of, or along with, an O/R address. Some implementations of X.400 also incorporated some of the X.500 fields, such as ou=*x* and cn=*x*.

A directory also puts a more natural interface on network resources. Many communication objects have long numeric identifiers that are hard to remember. A directory allows objects to be presented to users by a natural descriptive term. The directory then maps the descriptive term to the numeric identifier.

X.500 has a 1988 version and a 1993 version.

Directory Access

Having a directory is only half the equation. Users and administrators must also be able to access it to read, query, and write to it. A user might query the directory for a printer on the fourth floor in the Sales department, and the directory could respond with the needed information about the printer. Other issues that must be addressed are security (e.g., who can access an object and modify its properties) and directory replication (a true global directory would need to be on more than one machine). These issues are addressed by directory access protocols.

The standard access protocol in the X.500 recommendations is the Directory Access Protocol (DAP). DAP is considered more of a model than a real-world protocol. This is because DAP is very computer-resource intense (i.e., heavy) on client machines, and the few implementations of it are proprietary. But a newer access protocol that is getting a lot of attention today is the Lightweight Directory Access Protocol (LDAP). LDAP is an Internet protocol derived from the X.500 DAP. One of the reasons LDAP is called lightweight is because it requires fewer computer resources on the client. While LDAP is an Internet protocol, it is designed to enable access to an X.500-type directory. Almost every major software vendor has pledged support for LDAP.

Summary

The Exchange product is a powerful client/server enterprise messaging product.

The types of applications in an Exchange environment are as follows:

- Electronic mail (e-mail)
- Groupware
- Other applications, such as fax, paging, and voicemail

The network computing model that Exchange uses to implement its messaging system is the client/server model. This model utilizes the computing power of both client computers and server computers.

Exchange was designed for enterprise-wide implementations and, consequently, meets the following requirements:

- Enterprise-quality application services
- Scalability
- Interoperability
- Performance
- Administration
- Reliability

The following industry standards are used by Exchange:

- Messaging Application Programming Interface (MAPI)
- Internet protocols (e.g., SMTP, POP3, IMAP4, LDAP, SNMP, and others)
- Remote Procedure Call (RPC)
- X.400
- X.500

Exam Essentials

Know the features and limitations of Exchange Server 2003. Remember that the two different versions of Exchange Server 2003 have very different capabilities and limitations. Exchange Server 2003 Standard Edition is limited to one storage group plus the recovery storage group with a limit of two databases (16 GB maximum in size) in that storage group. Clustering is not supported in Standard Edition, although a front-end/back-end configuration is. Exchange Server 2003 Enterprise Edition allows four regular storage groups plus the recovery storage group on each server. Each storage group can have up to five databases of unlimited size (limited only by hardware configuration). The Enterprise Edition does provide support for clustering, the X.400 connector and front-end/back-end configurations.

Know the available migration paths to Exchange Server 2003. As with most things, the migration paths to Exchange Server 2003 have changed from those in Exchange 2000 Server. Keep in mind these available migration paths using the Exchange Migration Wizard: Microsoft Mail, Microsoft Exchange, Lotus cc:Mail, Lotus Notes, GroupWise 4.*x*, GroupWise 5.*x*, Internet Directory LDAP via ADSI, and Internet IMAP4 mail.

Don't forget about X.500. As you will see the more you work with Windows Server 2003 and Exchange Server 2003, everything in Active Directory is based on the X.500 standard. If you can't already break down a distinguished name into its component parts by looking at it, you should look again at what makes up X.500.

RPC is key. In previous versions of Exchange, message transport between local Exchange servers occurred via RPC. Exchange 2000 Server and Exchange Server 2003 use SMTP for local message transport but still provide RPC for backward compatibility with Exchange 5.5 servers. Of course, the Outlook client still uses RPCs to interact with the Exchange servers. Keep an open eye later in the book, in Chapter 7, when we discuss the new RPC over HTTP feature of Exchange Server 2003 and Office Outlook 2003.

Review Questions

1. In Exchange Server 2003 Enterprise Edition, how many total storage groups can each server hold?

   A. One

   B. Two

   C. Three

   D. Four

   E. Five

2. You are evaluating client applications for use with Exchange Server 2003. Many of your users need to be able to have offline access to all their mail folders and address books. Which of the following clients provide this? (Choose all that apply.)

   A. Outlook 2003

   B. POP3 clients

   C. IMAP4 clients

   D. Web browsers via Outlook Web Access

3. What is the name of the mechanism used when two Exchange components on the same machine pass instructions and data?

   A. Remote procedure call

   B. Remote instruction call

   C. Local instruction call

   D. Local procedure call

4. Which of the following operating systems can be used to run client applications that let users access Exchange Server 2003 computers? (Choose all that apply.)

   A. Windows 3.*x*

   B. Windows 98

   C. Windows 2000

   D. Macintosh

   E. Unix

   F. OS/2

5. What new feature of Exchange Server 2003 and Outlook 2003 allows clients to work from a local copy of their Exchange mailbox while still periodically connecting to the Exchange server?

   A. Cache mode

   B. Online mode

   C. Connected mode

   D. Offline mode

6. You are preparing a report on the features of Exchange Server 2003 for your manager. Which of the following would you list as features that are available in Exchange Server 2003 Enterprise Edition that are not available in the Standard Edition? (Choose all that apply.)

   A. Multiple databases per server

   B. Volume Shadow Copy support

   C. Front-end and back-end server support

   D. Clustering support

7. What does Exchange Server 2003 use to speed up the writing of data into the database?

   A. Hyper-threading

   B. Symmetric multi-processing (SMP)

   C. Multithreading

   D. Transaction logs

8. Which of the following protocols can be used to *retrieve* messages from Exchange Server 2003? (Choose all that apply.)

   A. LDAP

   B. PNP

   C. PPP

   D. POP3

9. In the X.500 Distinguished Name c=US; o=Widget; ou=Chicago; ou=Education; cn=JayWilson, what is the name of the organization?

   A. US

   B. Widget

   C. Chicago

   D. Education

   E. JayWilson

10. Which Outlook feature enables e-mail content to include multiple format types, such as fonts, sizes, and colors?

    A. WordPerfect

    B. This software cannot do this.

    C. Richman message content

    D. Rich-text message content

11. Which of the following components work together to allow web browsers to access an Exchange server? (Choose two.)

    A. Internet Information Services

    B. Outlook Browser Access

    C. Outlook Web Access

    D. Exchange Web Server

12. You are the manager of a large Exchange organization. Recently, you began to suspect that someone was attempting to log on to resources without permission. You enabled auditing on your servers to keep track of suspicious activity. Which utility would you use to view the audited information?

    A. Exchange System Manager

    B. Active Directory Users and Computers

    C. Computer Management

    D. Security Manager

    E. Windows Event Log

13. You are a consultant who has been hired by the Arbor Shoes Company. Some time ago, their network administrator set up a messaging system. The administrator has left the company, and the company now wants you to help them decide whether to keep the existing system or move to Exchange Server 2003. In either case, you will need to train someone how to manage the system. A person at the company describes the messaging system to you in the following way: There is one server on their network that functions as the mail server. Whenever a new person needs a mailbox, the administrator creates a new folder and assigns it permissions. Then, the client application must be pointed to that folder. What type of messaging system do you suspect the company is running?

    A. Client/server messaging system

    B. Shared-file messaging system

    C. Mainframe messaging system

    D. Host-based messaging system

14. You have created a set of public folders on one of six Exchange servers. Since their creation, the public folders have become an important resource in your organization, and you are concerned that having all of the folders on one server creates a single point of failure; should that server fail, no one will have access to the folders. What is the simplest way to remedy this situation?

    A. Back the public folders up hourly so that you can quickly restore them to another server if necessary.

    B. Configure two of the servers as a cluster.

    C. Configure replicas of the public folder on another Exchange server.

15. You are currently making recommendations for the purchase of Exchange Server 2003 software. You expect that the size of your databases on several servers will run around 25 GB. Which edition of Exchange 2000 would you need for these servers?

    A. Exchange Server 2003

    B. Exchange Server 2003 Advanced Edition

    C. Exchange Server 2003 Enterprise Edition

    D. Exchange Server 2003 Datacenter Edition

16. In X.500, which of the following constructs describes the location of an object in a directory?

    A. Distinguished Name

    B. X.500 Address

    C. Organizational unit

    D. Common name

17. Your company is currently running Microsoft Mail, a shared-file messaging system. You have been trying to convince your manager to move to Exchange Server 2003. In telling your manager about the features of client/server messaging systems, which of the following features would you *not* include?

    A. Distributed processing

    B. Tight security

    C. Passive client application

    D. Reduced network traffic

18. Which of the following is an Internet management protocol supported by Exchange Server 2003?

    A. SNMP

    B. SMTP

    C. MMX

    D. MID

19. Which of the following protocols are used by web browsers? (Choose all that apply.)

    A. HTTP

    B. HTML

    C. SNMP

    D. SMTP

20. Which of the following is the X.400 component whose primary responsibility is to receive and route messages to their ultimate destination?

    A. Message Routing Agent

    B. Message Transfer Agent

    C. Message Handling Agent

    D. Message Delivery Agent

Answers to Review Questions

1. E. Exchange Server 2003 Enterprise Edition can support four production storage groups and a fifth storage group, called the recovery storage group, which can be used to perform quicker restorations of databases to the server. Exchange Server 2003 Standard Edition can support only one production storage group and also the recovery storage group, for a total of two storage groups.

2. A. Only Outlook 2003 and some previous versions of Outlook provide support for using folders and address books offline.

3. D. A local procedure call is an instruction passed between two components on the same computer. A remote procedure call is passed between two components on different computers that are linked via a permanent high-speed network.

4. A, B, C, D, E, F. Any operating system that can run a web browser (and there is one available for every OS out there) or a POP3 or IMAP4 client can access Exchange Server 2003 as long as Exchange is configured correctly.

5. A. Outlook 2003 allows users to operate in cache mode, whereby they have the benefits of both online mode and offline mode simultaneously. When Outlook first connects to the user's Exchange mailbox during a session, the contents of the mailbox are synchronized to an offline folder file on the local computer. Outlook then connects to the Exchange server periodically to check for updates and synchronizes the local offline folder and sends any outgoing messages. Should the client lose connectivity to the Exchange server, the user can continue to work normally until connectivity has been restored.

6. A, C, D. Volume Shadow Copy support is available in the Standard Edition of Exchange Server 2003. All of the other features listed require Exchange Server 2003 Enterprise Edition.

7. D. Data that is to be written to an Exchange database is first written to these log files (which can be done very fast). The data is later written to the appropriate database, which takes longer because of the structured nature of a database. If, for whatever reason, a server has an unintended shutdown, data that has not been written to the database is not lost; it can be automatically reconstructed from the transaction log files.

8. D. POP3 is a message retrieval protocol. LDAP is a directory access protocol. PPP is a remote access protocol.

9. B. In the X.500 Distinguished Name c=US; o=Widget; ou=Chicago; ou=Education; cn=JayWilson, Widget is the name of the organization. The country is US, the organizational units are Chicago and Education, and the common name is JayWilson.

10. D. Outlook enables the creation of rich-text message content that can include multiple fonts, sizes, colors, alignments, and other formatting controls.

11. A, C. Internet Information Services is a web server service built into Windows Server 2003 and provides the Internet protocol support for Exchange Server 2003. Outlook Web Access is a component that allows IIS to access the Web Store and then present information to web browsers in HTML format.

12. E. Windows Server 2003 and Windows 2000 Server can be configured to monitor and record certain events. This can help diagnose security events. The audit information is written to the Windows Event Log.

13. B. A shared-file messaging system is one in which a passive server is basically configured with a set of shared folders. Client applications are configured to regularly poll the shared folders to see if new mail has been deposited there.

14. C. Exchange Server 2003 allows you to configure replicas of public folders on multiple servers.

15. C. Exchange Server 2003 Standard Edition has a 16-GB limit on the size that a database can reach. Exchange Server 2003 Enterprise Edition does not have this limit. There is no such edition as Exchange Server 2003 Advanced Edition or Datacenter Edition.

16. A. In X.500, the Distinguished Name (DN) describes the location of an object in the X.500 directory.

17. C. In a shared-file messaging system, servers are relatively passive, and clients perform almost all active messaging functions. Even though the server in a client/server system plays a much more active role, the client is still by no means passive.

18. A. Simple Network Management Protocol (SNMP) is a TCP/IP-based management protocol supported by Exchange Server 2003 in the form of the MADMAN MIB, an information base of manageable Exchange components.

19. A, B. HTTP is the protocol used to define how messages are sent between a web browser and a web server. HTML is the markup language that a web browser uses to determine how a page should be displayed in the browser window.

20. B. The Message Transfer Agent (MTA) is the protocol that runs in the message routing machines (i.e., routers). An MTA machine receives a message, stores it so it can calculate its next route, and then forwards it to either another MTA machine or its ultimate destination.

Chapter 2 Microsoft Exchange Architecture

An *architecture* is the structure of something. When applied to a software product, an architecture is a description of the software components of the product, what they are, what they do, and how they relate to each other. In Exchange, examples of these components are the Information Store service that manages the databases of messages on a server and the System Attendant service that performs routine maintenance on a server. Part of what software components do is create and manage objects (i.e., resources) such as servers, mailboxes, public folders, and address books. How those objects are structured or organized is also part of software architecture.

There are many practical benefits to understanding the architecture of Microsoft Exchange. Such knowledge will aid a person in designing, installing, administering, and troubleshooting an Exchange system. For example, understanding component functionality will assist you in deciding what optional components, if any, to choose during an installation. Troubleshooting can frequently benefit from a good understanding of architecture; just understanding some error messages requires such knowledge. This chapter provides you with a good conceptual background of the topics covered in the remainder of the book.

In this chapter, we will address the following issues:

- The Windows Server 2003 Active Directory and its integration with Exchange Server 2003
- Information storage on an Exchange server
- Message flow in the Exchange environment

Active Directory

The *Active Directory* is one of the most important parts of Windows Server 2003 networking. Although a full discussion of Active Directory is outside the scope of this book, the nature of Exchange Server 2003's tight integration with Active Directory warrants a brief discussion of the technology itself and an examination of how it affects the Exchange environment.

To learn more about Active Directory, start by checking out the Windows Server 2003 product documentation. It provides an overview of the technology and illustrates many of the benefits of using Active Directory. If you are interested in going past the basics, take a look at *Active Directory for Microsoft Windows Server 2003 Technical Reference*, by Mike Mulcare and Stan Reimer (MS Press, 2003).

Active Directory in Windows Server 2003

To understand Active Directory, it is first necessary to understand what a *directory* is. Put simply, a directory contains a hierarchy that stores information about objects in a system.

A directory service is the service that manages the directory and makes it available to users on the network. Active Directory stores information about objects on a Windows Server 2003 network and makes this information easy for administrators and users to find and use. Active Directory uses a structured data store as the basis for a hierarchical organization of directory information.

You can use Active Directory to design a directory structure tailored to your organization's administrative needs. For example, you can scale Active Directory from a single computer to a single network or to many networks. Active Directory can include every object, server, and domain in a network.

What makes Active Directory so powerful, and so scalable, is that it separates the logical structure of the Windows Server 2003 domain hierarchy from the physical structure of the network itself.

Logical Components

In Exchange 5.5 Server and prior versions, resources were organized separately in Windows and Exchange. Now, the organization you set up in Windows Server 2003 and the organization you set up in Exchange Server 2003 are the same. (The same goes for Windows 2000 and Exchange 2000 as well.) In fact, the Active Directory Users and Computers tool (whose use is covered in Chapter 5, "Creating and Managing Exchange Recipients") is now used to configure and manage Windows users and Exchange-related user features, such as mailbox storage and protocol use. This requires a shift in thinking from previous versions of Exchange, where the duties of Windows and Exchange administrators were more clearly separated. Now, it is often advantageous to have one user administrator manage all aspects of user configuration. In Active Directory, the domain hierarchy is organized using a number of constructs to make administration simpler and more logical. These logical constructs, which are described in the following subsections, allow you to define and group resources so that they can be located and administered by name rather than by physical location.

Objects

An *object* is the basic unit in Active Directory. It is a distinct named set of *attributes* that represents something concrete, such as a user, printer, computer, or application. Attributes are the characteristics of the object; for example, a computer is an object, and its attributes include its name and location, among other things. A user is also an object. In Exchange, a user's attributes include the user's first name, last name, and e-mail address. User attributes also include Exchange-related features, such as whether the object can receive e-mail, the formatting of e-mail it receives, and the location where it can receive e-mail.

Organizational Units

An *organizational unit* (OU) is a container in which you can place objects such as user accounts, groups, computers, printers, applications, file shares, and other organizational units. You can use organizational units to hold groups of objects, such as users and printers, and you can assign specific permissions to them. An organizational unit cannot contain objects from other domains and is the smallest unit to which you can assign or delegate administrative authority. Organizational units are provided strictly for administrative purposes and convenience. They are transparent to the end user, but can be extremely useful to an administrator when segmenting users and computers within an organization.

You can use organizational units to create containers within a domain that represent the hierarchical, logical structures within your organization. This enables you to manage how accounts and resources are configured and used.

Organizational units can also be used to create departmental or geographical boundaries. In addition, they can be used to delegate administrative authority over particular tasks to particular users. For instance, you can create an OU for all your printers and then assign full control over the printers to your printer administrator.

Domains

A *domain* is a group of computers and other resources that are part of a network and share a common directory database. A domain is organized in levels and is administered as a unit with common rules and procedures. All objects and organizational units exist within a domain.

You create a domain by installing the first domain controller inside it. A domain controller is simply a Windows Server 2003 computer that has Active Directory enabled on it. Once a server has been installed, you can use the Active Directory Wizard to install Active Directory. In order to install Active Directory on the first server on a network, that server must have access to a server running DNS (Domain Name Service). If it does not, you'll be given the chance to install and configure DNS during Active Directory installation.

A domain can exist in one of four possible domain functional levels as outlined in the following list:

- *Windows 2000 mixed.* The default domain functional level all new domain controllers are installed in allows for Windows NT 4.0 backup domain controllers (BDCs), Windows 2000 Server domain controllers, and Windows Server 2003 domain controllers. Local and global groups are supported, but universal groups are not. Global catalog servers are supported.
- *Windows 2000 native.* The minimum domain functional level at which universal groups become available, along with several other Active Directory features; allows for Windows 2000 Server and Windows Server 2003 domain controllers only.
- *Windows Server 2003 interim.* Supports only Windows NT 4.0 and Windows Server 2003 domain controllers. The domains in a forest are raised to this functional level; the forest level has been increased to interim.
- *Windows Server 2003.* The highest domain functional level available, it provides all new features and functionality and allows for only Windows Server 2003 domain controllers.

The mixed mode and native mode you might have been used to when using Windows 2000 Server have been replaced by the domain and forest functional levels in Windows Server 2003. Note, however, that the Windows 2000 mixed mode is similar to the Windows 2000 mixed functional level and that the Windows 2000 native mode is similar to the Windows Server 2003 functional level.

The move from a lower functional level to a higher one is irreversible, so take care to ensure that all older (Windows NT 4.0 or Windows 2000 Server) domain controllers have been retired or upgraded before changing the functional level.

Domain Trees

A *domain tree* is a hierarchical arrangement of one or more Windows Active Directory domains that share a common namespace. *Domain Name Service (DNS)* domain names represent the tree structure. The first domain in a tree is called the *root domain*. For example, a company named Widgets (that has the Internet domain name widgets.com) might use the root domain widgets.com in its primary domain tree. Additional domains in the tree under the root domain are called *child domains*. For example, the domain hsv.widgets.com would be a child domain of the widgets.com domain. Figure 2.1 shows an example of a domain tree.

FIGURE 2.1 A domain tree is a hierarchical grouping of one or more domains.

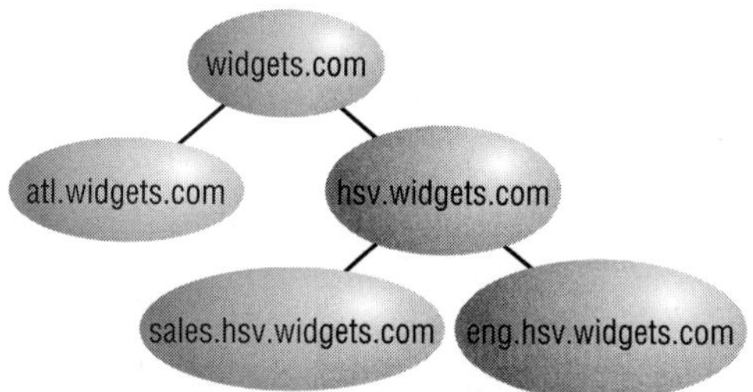

Domains establish trust relationships with one another that allow objects in a trusted domain to access resources in a trusting domain. Windows Server 2003 and Active Directory support transitive, two-way trusts between domains. When a child domain is created, a trust relationship is automatically configured between that child domain and the parent domain. This trust is two-way, meaning that resource access requests can flow from either domain to the other. The trust is also transitive, meaning that any domains trusted by one domain are automatically trusted by the other domain. For example, in Figure 2.1, consider the three domains named widgets.com, hsv.widgets.com, and sales.hsv.widgets.com. When hsv .widgets.com was created as a child domain of widgets.com, a two-way trust was formed between the two. When sales.hsv.widgets.com was created as a child of hsv.widgets.com, another trust was formed between those two domains. Though no explicit trust relationship was ever defined directly between the sales.hsv.widgets.com and widgets.com domains, the two domains trust each other anyway because of the transitive nature of trust relationships.

Domain Forests

A *domain forest* is a group of one or more domain trees that do not form a contiguous namespace but may share a common schema and global catalog. There is always at least one forest on the network, and it is created when the first Active Directory–enabled computer (domain controller) on a network is installed. This first domain in a forest is called the *forest root domain* and is special because it is really the basis for naming the entire forest. It cannot be removed from the forest without removing the entire forest itself. Finally, no other domain can ever be created above the forest root domain in the forest domain hierarchy. Figure 2.2 shows an example of a domain forest with multiple domain trees.

FIGURE 2.2 A domain forest consists of one or more domain trees.

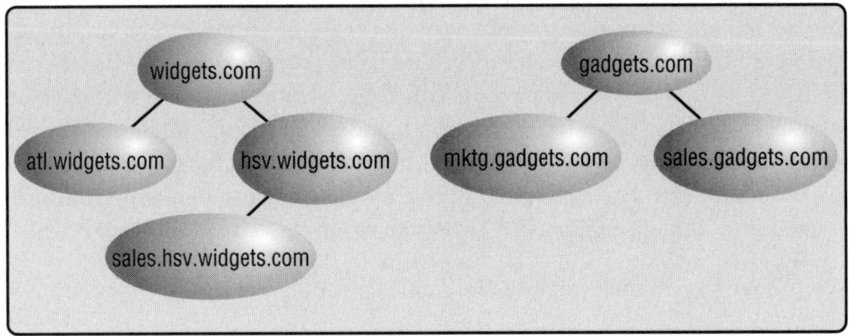

A forest is the outermost boundary of Active Directory; the directory cannot be larger than the forest. You can create multiple forests and then create trust relationships between specific domains in those forests; this would let you grant access to resources and accounts that are outside a particular forest. However, an Exchange organization cannot span multiple forests.

Physical Components

The physical side of Active Directory is primarily represented by domain controllers and sites. These enable organizations to optimize replication traffic across their networks and to assist client workstations in finding the closest domain controller to validate logon credentials.

Domain Controllers

Every domain must have at least one *domain controller*, a computer running Windows Server 2003 that validates user network access and manages Active Directory. To create a domain controller, all you have to do is install Active Directory on a Windows Server 2003 computer. During this process, you have the option of creating a new domain or joining an existing domain. If you create a new domain, you also have the option of creating or joining an existing domain tree or forest. A domain controller stores a complete copy of all Active Directory information for that domain, manages changes to that information, and replicates those changes to other domain controllers in the same domain. Schema and infrastructure configuration information is replicated between all domain controllers in a forest.

In previous versions of Windows, a distinction was drawn between primary and backup domain controllers. In Windows Server 2003 and Windows 2000 Server, all domain controllers are considered peers, and each holds a complete copy of Active Directory.

Global Catalog

In a single-domain environment, users can rely on Active Directory for the domain to provide all of the necessary information about the resources on the network. In a multi-domain environment, however, users often need to access resources outside of their domain—resources that may be more difficult to find. For this, a *global catalog* is used to hold information about all objects in a forest. The global catalog enables users and applications to find objects in an Active Directory domain tree if the user or application knows one or more attributes of the target object.

Through the replication process, Active Directory automatically generates the contents of the global catalog from the domain controllers in the directory. The global catalog holds a partial replica of Active Directory. Even though every object is listed in the global catalog, only a limited set of attributes for those objects is replicated in it. The attributes listed for each object in the global catalog are defined in the schema. A base set of attributes is replicated to the global catalog, but you can specify additional attributes to meet the needs of your organization.

By default, there is only one global catalog in the entire forest, and that is the first domain controller installed in the first domain of the first tree. All others must be configured manually. We recommend adding a second global catalog for backup and load balancing. Furthermore, each domain should have at least one global catalog to provide for more efficient Active Directory searches and network logons.

Windows Server 2003 Sites

A Windows Server 2003 site is a group of computers that exist on one or more IP subnets. Computers within a site must be connected by a fast, reliable network connection. Using *Windows sites* helps maximize network efficiency and provide fault tolerance. Windows sites also help clients find the closest domain controller to validate logon credentials.

In versions of Exchange Server prior to Exchange 2000 Server, the concept of a site was used to identify a group of Exchange servers that shared a permanent, high-bandwidth connection and also represented an administrative boundary in Exchange. The concept of Windows sites is unrelated to the use of sites in earlier versions of Exchange. Exchange Server 2003 (and Exchange 2000 Server) has replaced the concept of Exchange sites with routing groups and administrative groups. Routing groups are used to define groups of Exchange servers that share a reliable (but not necessarily high-bandwidth) connection. Administrative groups are used to define administrative boundaries within an Exchange environment.

Exchange Server 2003 makes extensive use of Active Directory information on global catalog servers. For efficient communication, Exchange Server 2003 requires direct access to a global catalog server in your LAN.

Sites are created using the Active Directory Sites and Services tool. No direct relationship exists between Windows domains and sites, so a single domain can span multiple sites and a single site can span multiple domains.

Schema

A *schema* represents the structure of a database system—the tables and fields in that database and how the tables and fields are related to one another. The Active Directory information is also represented by a schema. All objects that can be stored in Active Directory are defined in the schema.

Installing Active Directory on the first domain controller in a network creates a schema that contains definitions of commonly used objects and attributes. The schema also defines objects and attributes that Active Directory uses internally. When Exchange Server 2003 is installed, Exchange setup extends the schema to support information that Exchange needs. Updates to the schema require replication of the schema across the forest and also to all domain controllers in the forest. For more information about how Exchange updates the schema, see Chapter 3, "Installing Microsoft Exchange Server 2003."

Active Directory and Exchange Server 2003

In versions of Exchange Server prior to Exchange 2000 Server, Exchange maintained a directory of its own through a service known as the Directory Service. On each Exchange server, the Directory Service maintained a copy of the directory in a database file on the Exchange server and took care of replicating changes in the directory to other Exchange servers. In Exchange Server 2003, the Directory Service has been removed altogether. Exchange is now totally reliant on Active Directory to provide its directory services.

This new reliance caused a shift in the way that the Exchange directory is maintained. This first section examines the effects that boundaries of a forest place on Exchange. It then looks at the interaction of DNS in an Exchange organization. Finally, it looks at the differences in directory replication now that Exchange itself no longer handles the directory information or uses the Active Directory Connector to exchange data with previous versions of Exchange Server.

Forests

By default, the global catalog shows only objects within a single Windows Server 2003 forest, so an Exchange organization must be within the boundaries of a forest. This is different from earlier versions of Windows NT and Exchange 5.5. In previous versions, an Exchange organization could span domains that did not trust one another because Exchange 5.5 did not rely so much on the underlying security structure of Windows NT. With Active Directory and Exchange Server 2003, the security structure is integrated, which means that a single Exchange organization cannot span multiple forests, but can span multiple domains within a single forest.

Domain Name Service (DNS)

In previous versions of Windows NT, the *Windows Internet Name Service* (WINS) was the primary provider of name resolution within an organization because it provided dynamic publishing and full names to network address mapping. DNS was really only required for organizations that needed Internet connectivity, though it was usually a recommended practice to use DNS with earlier versions of Exchange Server as well. Windows Server 2003 relies almost exclusively on DNS because it provides maximum interoperability with Internet technologies. In order for Exchange Server 2003 to function, a DNS service must be running in your organization. Outlook Web Access, SMTP connectivity, and Internet connectivity all rely on DNS.

Active Directory is often called a *namespace*, which is similar to the directory service in earlier versions of Exchange and means any bounded area in which a given name can be resolved. The DNS name creates a namespace for a tree or forest, such as widgets.com. All child domains of widgets .com, such as sales.widgets.com, share the root namespace. In Exchange Server 2003, Active Directory forms a namespace in which the name of an object in the directory can be resolved to the object. All domains that have a common root domain form a *contiguous namespace*. This means that the domain name of a child domain is the child domain name appended to the name of the parent domain.

In Windows Server 2003 domains using DNS, a domain name such as hsv.widgets.com does not affect the e-mail addresses for Exchange users created in that domain. Although a user's logon name might be user@hsv.widgets.com, you control how e-mail addresses are generated using recipient policies in System Manager and Active Directory Users and Computers.

Directory Replication

In versions of Exchange Server prior to Exchange 2000 Server, the directory was a part of Exchange, and replication of that directory was handled by Exchange Server. When attributes of directory objects changed, the entire object was replicated throughout the organization.

Now, all directory functions have been passed to Active Directory, which replicates at the attribute level instead of the object level. This means that if a change is made to an attribute, only that attribute (and not the entire object) is replicated to other domain controllers in the domain, resulting in less network traffic and more efficient use of server resources.

Active Directory Connector (ADC)

Exchange Server 2003 supports coexistence with Exchange 5.5 through the Active Directory Connector. For organizations using earlier versions of Exchange, this is a critical component in upgrading to Exchange Server 2003.

Because Exchange Server 2003 uses Active Directory as its directory service, directory information is managed in one location. The Active Directory Connector is a Windows service that synchronizes the Exchange 5.5 directory with Active Directory. This allows you to administer your directory from Active Directory or the Exchange 5.5 directory service. You can also use ADC to migrate objects from the Exchange directory service to Active Directory. For more information on configuring Exchange Server 2003 to work with Exchange 5.5, see Chapter 11, "Coexisting with and Migrating from Exchange 5.5."

Information Storage

In Exchange Server 2003, a service named the *Information Store* is responsible for data storage and management. It supports access by MAPI clients and by numerous Internet protocols via Internet Information Server. It also supports access through application programming interfaces (APIs) such as Collaboration Data Objects (CDO), ActiveX Data Objects (ADO), and the Active Directory Services Interface (ADSI). What all of this means is that the Exchange Information Store has become much more than a place where messages and data are stored. It has become a single repository in which an entire network of users and applications can store and manage information of just about any type. Since it holds all types of data and provides such varied access methods, Microsoft describes the Information Store in Server 2003 as the *Web Store*.

With this new version of Exchange, the support and management of protocols have been passed from the Exchange software itself to Internet Information Server. Separating the protocols from the storage system and providing other features, such as an Installable File System, front-end/back-end servers, and clustering support, have allowed Exchange Server 2003 to become much more robust and scalable than previous versions of Exchange.

Web Storage System

The Exchange Server 2003 Web Store combines features of the Web, the file system, and Exchange Server 2003 into a single, unified system for storing and accessing information. The Web Store serves as the sole repository for managing diverse types of information within a single infrastructure. In addition, almost every resource in the Web Store is now addressable through a solitary *Uniform Resource Identifier (URI)* location, commonly referred to a *Uniform Resource Locator (URL)*.

It is important to understand that the Web Store is not so much a specific entity or technology as it is a concept of how Exchange information is stored and used. As in previous versions of Exchange, information is still stored in databases and still managed by a service named the Information Store. Sometimes the storage system as a whole is called the Information Store, sometimes the Web Store. Both of these terms refer to the same system, but you may find them used in different situations based on context. For example, in the product documentation, Microsoft likes to call it the Web Store when they are pointing out new, web-related features. New features such as supporting multiple databases per server that can be grouped into storage groups makes Exchange all the more powerful. The Web Store moniker is really just a way to get across the idea that the information databases of Exchange can be used for more than just storing e-mail messages. They can be used to store almost any kind of information or document, and they can be accessed not only by e-mail clients but by web browsers and custom applications as well.

Exchange Databases

An Exchange Server 2003 database is actually a logical entity that represents two physical database files, a *rich-text (EDB) file* and a *streaming media (STM) file*. For example, a single mailbox database might consist of the files `priv1.edb` and `priv1.stm`. Each database incorporates both files, and Exchange Server 2003 treats them as a single unit. Furthermore, the reported Information Store size will be the combination of both the rich-text store and the native content store along with the transaction logs, which have the extension `.log`. Both types of data are stored in an *Extensible Storage Engine (ESE)* database format.

The rich-text file holds messages and works much like the database files in previous versions of Exchange Server. The streaming media file has been added to provide native support for many types of streaming media, including voice, audio, video, and others. To do this, the streaming media file is designed to store files as *Multipurpose Internet Mail Extensions (MIME)* content, a specification for formatting non-ASCII messages so that they can be sent over the Internet. This means that multimedia content can be delivered to the Exchange server using non-MAPI protocols in the media's native format, stored, and then passed along to clients without ever having to be converted into a MAPI-acceptable format. This minimizes the time needed to deliver the files to the client and thereby helps to reduce network traffic and also eliminates the risk of introducing errors into the media during a conversion process.

Multiple Databases and Storage Groups

Exchange Server 2003 provides support for multiple databases and *storage groups* on a single server. As outlined earlier in Chapter 1, "Introduction to Microsoft Exchange," Exchange Server 2003 Enterprise Edition allows up to five databases per storage group and up to four production storage groups per server. Each database must exist inside a storage group.

Although each instance of a database runs under the same *Web Storage System* process, you can mount or dismount individual databases on the fly. This means that you can take one database down for maintenance while others continue to service client requests. Also, each database is checked for consistency when the Web Storage System process starts. Should one database be unable to mount, other databases remain unaffected and will mount normally.

Each storage group is represented by a single instance of the ESE and shares a single set of transaction log files. Whenever a transaction occurs on an Exchange server, the responsible service first records the transaction in a *transaction log*. Using transaction logs allows for faster completion of the transaction than if the service had to immediately commit the transaction to a database, because the transaction log structure is much simpler than the database structure. Data is written to these log files sequentially as transactions occur. Regular database maintenance routines commit changes in the logs to the actual databases later, when system processes are idle. Consequently, the most current state of an Exchange service is represented by the EDB database and STM database, plus the current log files.

The *checkpoint files* are used to keep track of transactions that are committed to the database from a transaction log. Using checkpoint files ensures that transactions cannot be committed to a database more than once. Checkpoint files are named `edb.chk` and reside in the same directories as their log files and databases. Those transaction logs that have been committed to the database are cleared during a database backup (discussed further in Chapter 14, "Backup and Recovery") or by circular logging if configured (discussed further in Chapter 9, "Configuring the Information Store").

The use of multiple databases and storage groups allows you to plan your organization's data storage by classifying various types of data or assigning separate databases to more important users. You can learn more about using multiple databases and storage groups in Chapter 9.

Public Folders

Public folders provide centralized storage of just about any type of data that is meant to be accessed by multiple users in an organization. The primary use of public folders is to serve as a sort of discussion forum, allowing users to post and reply to messages in a setting where conversations are threaded by subject. However, public folders can also be used for much more, including the storage of Microsoft Office documents, administrative messages generated by Exchange Server, and even as the basis for advanced workflow applications.

Like other databases in Exchange, a public folder is actually composed of two database files—a rich-text file and a streaming content file. The addition of the streaming content file means that websites can actually be hosted from within a public folder. The HTML, Active Server Pages (ASP), or ASP.NET files reside in the streaming file of the public folder store and are accessible from any web browser using simple URLs. Also, because Exchange stores the websites, pages in the sites can make use of Exchange-specific functionality such as calendars and messaging.

Also like other databases, Exchange Server 2003 supports the storage of multiple public folder stores on a single Exchange server. In addition, Exchange Server 2003 supports multiple public folder trees in an organization.

In versions of Exchange Server prior to Exchange 2000 Server, it was only possible to have one *public folder tree*, a hierarchy that forms the boundaries of the entire set of public folders available in the organization. Now, you can create multiple public folder trees and thus multiple sets of public folders. There is one caveat, however. When Exchange Server 2003 is installed, a default public folder tree, named All Public Folders, is created. This tree is accessible by all MAPI, IMAP4, NNTP (Network News Transfer Protocol), and web clients. Additional public folder trees will be available only to NNTP and HTTP clients. Additional trees are not accessible by any MAPI clients such as Office Outlook 2003. Additional trees such as these are intended for use as file repositories for groups or projects.

Learn more about the structure, creation, and management of public folders in Chapter 6, "Using Public Folders."

Internet Information Services

One of the great strengths of Exchange Server 2003 lies in the way it supports standard Internet protocols for message transfer. In previous versions of Exchange, the Exchange Server software itself provided and managed the Internet protocols. Now, the responsibility of managing protocol support has been passed entirely to *Internet Information Services (IIS)*, a built-in component of Windows Server 2003. All Exchange Server 2003 protocols are hosted within the IIS process. When Exchange Server 2003 is installed, it enhances the SMTP service built into IIS with a more robust version capable of handling the demanding Exchange routing environment.

Exchange Server 2003 subsystems, such as protocols and storage, can now be placed on separate servers to improve scalability. For this to work, a fast, reliable method of exchanging information between IIS and the Exchange storage system, the Web Store, is needed. This need is met by a component named the *Exchange Interprocess Communication Layer (ExIPC)*. ExIPC is basically a high-performance queue that allows IIS and the Web Store to exchange data. Figure 2.3 illustrates the basic Exchange architecture.

The Information Store (a process named `store.exe`) is the Exchange service that manages the Information Store on an Exchange server. One instance of `store.exe` runs for each storage group on a server. `store.exe` manages processes such as store replication; maintains the ESE databases; and provides protocol stubs, interfaces that allow the ExIPC to transfer data between the IIS (a process named `inetinfo.exe`) and the Information Store. As you can see in Figure 2.3, a protocol stub exists for each protocol handled by IIS. The queuing process used by ExIPC is asynchronous, meaning that Exchange is able to allocate memory immediately after one portion of a process finishes.

FIGURE 2.3 Exchange Server 2003 architecture

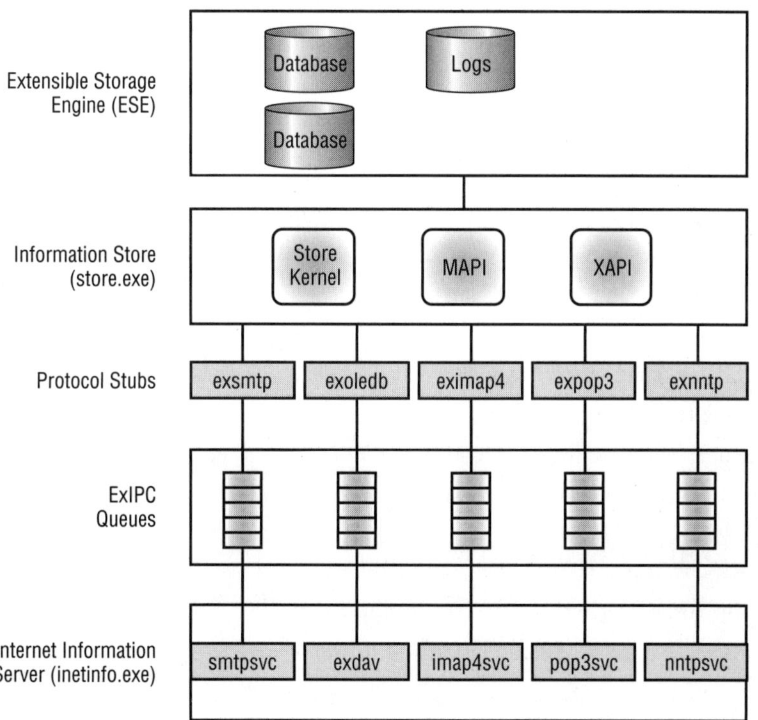

Installable File System

The *Installable File System (IFS)* permits normal network client redirectors, such as Exchange, to share folders and items. This is a means of exposing the Exchange Information Store to users and applications on the network. Because your local computer can assign, or map, a drive letter to these resources, standard applications such as Windows Explorer and the Office 2003 suite can access resources in the Exchange Store. A user could, for example, map a drive letter to their mailbox or open a public folder from within Microsoft Word. The primary benefit of the IFS is that it allows clients to access Exchange data with no special software other than standard operating system components.

In Exchange 2000 Server, installation of the Exchange server created an M: drive that served as the portal into the Exchange Store for Windows applications. By default, the M: drive was shared using the share name `BackOfficeStorage`. This is no longer the case in clean or upgrade installations of Exchange Server 2003. This change was brought about to prevent file-level corruption through direct file access from virus scanning and backup/restoration operations. The Exchange Information Store can still be connected to at `\BackOfficeStorage`.

Front-End/Back-End Servers

Since Exchange Server 2003 separates its databases from the client access protocols (now managed by IIS), there is now a distinction between store management and protocol management. Exchange now allows administrators to configure *front-end servers* that handle client access and *back-end servers* that handle the databases themselves. The front-end server becomes the point of contact for all client applications.

MAPI clients must connect directly to a back-end server and cannot use a front-end server, but other types of clients (POP3, IMAP4, etc.) can. Clients that can connect to a front-end server do so using the following process:

1. The client connects to the front-end server and makes a request using a particular protocol.
2. The front-end server relays the request to the back-end server using the same protocol used by the client.
3. The back-end server returns the requested data.
4. The front-end server returns the data to the client.

This arrangement provides load balancing for servers and also creates a unified namespace for clients.

Clustering

An Exchange Server 2003 *cluster* consists of between two and eight connected computers referred to as *nodes*. These nodes share a common storage device, such as a RAID-5 array. Exchange Server 2003 can operate in either *active/active clustering* or *active/passive clustering*.

This provides a redundant hardware solution, since clients can connect to any *node* in the cluster rather than to just one computer. Clustering also provides fault tolerance. Should one node in the cluster fail, the Microsoft Clustering Service (MSCS) restarts or moves the services on the failed node to a functional node in the cluster. During scheduled maintenance of a node, an administrator can also manually move services to other nodes, thus reducing or eliminating any client downtime.

When active/active clustering is used, one instance of the clustered resource runs on each of the nodes in the cluster. Exchange Server 2003 supports active/active clustering using two nodes only. If one of the nodes fails, the instance of the clustered resource is transferred to the other node. Although it might seem that using active/active clustering is economical in that it allows you to always use your available servers, it has the disadvantage of not being nearly as reliable or scalable as active/passive clustering.

The preferred type of clustering is active/passive clustering, in which one or more nodes of the cluster is online providing service to clients and one or more nodes of the cluster is online and available to pick any resources from failed active servers. When one of the active nodes fails, the resources that were running on that node are failed over to the passive node. The passive node then changes its state to active and begins to service client requests. The downside to this clustering model is that the passive nodes may not be used for any other purpose during normal operations because they must remain absolutely available should a failover situation occur. In addition, all of the nodes must be configured identically to ensure that when failover occurs, no performance loss is experienced.

The number of nodes in your cluster is dependent upon the operating system on which the Exchange Server 2003 computer is installed. Active/passive clustering in Exchange Server 2003 is limited to two nodes when Exchange is installed on Windows 2000 Advanced Server Service Pack 4 (or later), four nodes when Exchange is installed on Windows 2000 Datacenter Server Service Pack 4 (or later), and eight nodes when Exchange is installed on Windows Server 2003 Enterprise Edition or Windows Server 2003 Datacenter Server Edition.

Full-Text Indexing

The Information Store creates and manages indexes for common fields using the *Microsoft Search Service*. In previous versions of Exchange, searches were conducted on every item in every folder, resulting in long search times for larger databases. With *full-text indexing*, every word in all mailboxes and public folders is indexed, making searches much faster and more accurate. The service can index all messages, attachments, Microsoft Office documents, HTML files, text files, and even PDF files. Users can also search on document properties of many types of data, including properties such as author, file size, and modification dates.

All searches are passed through Exchange Server 2003, which is responsible for handling security. If users do not have permissions to access particular objects, they are not allowed to bypass this using the Search Service.

An indexed database usually requires around 20 percent more available drive space than a nonindexed database, so you should allow for this when planning your Exchange server hardware. As an example, a 10-GB database that has full-text indexing configured will require an additional 2 GB or so of disk space for the index. You should also be aware that indexing large databases can be quite time-consuming. Because indexes are created for each database, creating multiple databases can often make the indexing process easier.

You'll learn more about how to configure indexing in Chapter 9.

Message Flow

The flow of messages between components of an Exchange environment can be complicated. As an administrator, it would serve you well to learn how messages flow from one place (a sender) to another place (a recipient) in that environment. On a single Exchange server, component communication is relatively simple. As servers are added and grouped together into routing groups, this communication grows more complex. This section provides an introduction to the Exchange components involved in message flow and then examines the actual flow of messages in different situations.

Routing Architecture

Before we can look at the process of message flow in Exchange, it is first necessary to become familiar with some of the basic components that play a part in the routing of a message. Specifically, we will examine SMTP, the protocol used to transfer most messages in Exchange, routing groups that are used to define the routing topology of an organization, and connectors that are used to connect routing groups to one another and provide a way to transfer messages outside an Exchange organization altogether.

SMTP

SMTP is the native transport protocol in Exchange Server 2003 used to route messages within and between routing groups. In versions of Exchange Server prior to Exchange 2000 Server, a component named the *Message Transfer Agent (MTA)* used a protocol named X.400 to provide most routing functions. The MTA and X.400 still exist in Exchange Server 2003 but are now used only to provide communications with Exchange Server 5.5 and with foreign messaging systems using the X.400 protocol. SMTP has replaced X.400 over the past few years as the standard messaging protocol throughout the world, and so it has found acceptance in Exchange Server 2003 as the protocol of choice.

IIS handles SMTP and transfers information with Exchange via the ExIPC service that you learned about earlier in this chapter. The basic SMTP support in IIS is extended in a number of ways when Exchange Server 2003 is installed:

- A secondary store driver, `drviis.dll`, is added that provides message pickup and drop-off using ExIPC.
- An enhanced routing engine is installed that adds link-state information—nearly instant information about the state of links to other servers.

- Additional command verbs are added that support the exchange of link-state information with other servers.

The adoption of SMTP provides a great advantage to Exchange Server 2003. In versions of Exchange Server prior to Exchange 2000 Server, servers were divided into Exchange sites that served as both routing and administrative boundaries. Within a site, communications between servers took place using *remote procedure calls (RPCs)*, a method for invoking services on a remote computer. While RPCs are effective for message transport, they require full-time, relatively high-bandwidth connections between computers. This means that Exchange sites could really only span groups of computers that were connected by high-speed networking.

SMTP offers an advantage over RPCs: SMTP does not require a high-performance network connection. This and the elimination of Exchange sites in Exchange Server 2003 have led to much greater flexibility in the deployment of servers. Exchange Server 2003 supports routing groups, which are groups of servers connected by a permanent connection, and administrative groups, which group servers and components according to administrative needs. The result of all this is that administrative needs can now be balanced with topology requirements in the deployment of Exchange servers.

Routing Groups

A *routing group* is a collection of servers with full-time, reliable connectivity. Topologically, a routing group is similar to the Exchange site used in previous versions of Exchange Server but, unlike the site, it imposes no administrative restrictions. Within a routing group, all messages are transferred directly between servers using SMTP. If you have a single Exchange server or if all your Exchange servers are connected over full-time, reliable connections, there will probably not be much reason for you to create more than one routing group. In fact, unless you create a second routing group, the fact that a routing group even exists is not evident in the Exchange System Manager. When a second routing group is added, the Routing Groups container appears in System Manager, and servers are grouped according to the routing group to which they belong.

There are several reasons why you may choose to set up multiple routing groups in your organization, such as the following:

- Many Exchange servers do not have full-time, reliable, and direct SMTP connectivity to one another. This may be the case if your organization spans large geographic distances.
- You must control the path that messages travel between servers. You can create a routing group boundary to force computers in one group to use a single bridgehead server (BHS) to send messages to another group.

You can learn more about using routing groups in Chapter 8, "Building Administrative and Routing Groups."

Connectors

Communications between servers in different routing groups and with foreign messaging systems outside the Exchange organization are established using *connectors*. You'll learn more about configuring and managing connectors in Chapter 8, but a brief introduction is useful here.

Three types of connectors can be used to connect routing groups to one another:

- Routing Group Connector
- SMTP Connector
- X.400 Connector

Routing Group Connector

The *Routing Group Connector* is the preferred method of connecting two routing groups in the same organization; it is fast, reliable, and the simplest to configure (since it has the fewest settings). SMTP is the native protocol used by the Routing Group Connector, and the connector consults Exchange Server's link-state table for routing information.

The Routing Group Connector is a unidirectional connection that goes from one server to another. Therefore, when you configure a Routing Group Connector, you'll need to create two connectors to form a logical bidirectional link between the two routing groups. However, to reduce administrative effort, you can autoconfigure the other side of a Routing Group Connector when installing the first end of the connector just like a Site Connector in Exchange Server 5.5.

A *bridgehead server* is a server that is designated to pass messages from one routing group to another, as shown in Figure 2.4. The Routing Group Connector offers a level of fault tolerance by allowing multiple source and destination bridgehead servers. Bridgehead servers can be used in one of three ways:

- No bridgehead server is designated, and all of the servers in the routing group function as bridgehead servers for message transmission.
- One bridgehead server is designated, and all mail destined for other routing groups flows through that one server. This gives the administrator great control over messaging configuration.
- Multiple bridgehead servers are used, and all mail flows through one of these designated servers. This configuration offers the advantages of load balancing and fault tolerance. Should one bridgehead server be unavailable for message transport, another will be available.

  Routing Group Connectors offer administrators the ability to control connection schedules, message priority, and message size limits.

SMTP Connector

Although the Routing Group Connector uses SMTP as its native transport mechanism, Exchange Server 2003 also provides an *SMTP Connector* that can be used to link routing groups. There are three reasons why you might want to use an SMTP Connector instead of a Routing Group Connector:

- The SMTP Connector is more configurable than the Routing Group Connector and thereby offers the ability to more finely tune the connection. The SMTP Connector also offers the ability to issue authentication before sending mail, specifying TLS encryption and removing mail from queues on remote servers.

- The SMTP Connector always has to use SMTP. When you are connecting an Exchange Server 2003 with an Exchange 5.5 server, the Routing Group Connector uses RPCs to communicate because it has no way of knowing whether the Exchange 5.5 server is configured to use SMTP, which was provided through the Internet Mail Service in previous versions of Exchange. There is no way to force the Routing Group Connector to use SMTP, so an SMTP Connector may be used instead.
- The SMTP Connector is also capable of connecting independent Exchange forests within an organization so that messages can be transferred.

Another advantage of the SMTP Connector is that it can be used to connect an Exchange organization to the Internet or to a foreign (non-Exchange) messaging system that uses SMTP.

When connected to the Internet, the SMTP Connector uses a smart host or mail exchange (MX) record in DNS for next-hop routing. When configured internally between two routing groups, this connector will relay link-state information between routing groups but will still depend on the MX records in DNS for next-hop information.

X.400 Connector

The *X.400 Connector* can be used to link Exchange routing groups and also to link an Exchange organization to a foreign, X.400-based messaging system. X.400 Connectors are useful for linking routing groups when there is very little bandwidth (less than 16 Kbps) available between servers or when X.400 is the only connectivity available. When linking routing groups with the X.400 Connector, a single server in each group must be designated as the bridgehead server. You must set up multiple X.400 Connectors between multiple servers in each routing group to gain a load-balancing feature. Note that you can also install a Routing Group Connector alongside an X.400 Connector.

FIGURE 2.4 Bridgehead servers are responsible for transferring messages between routing groups.

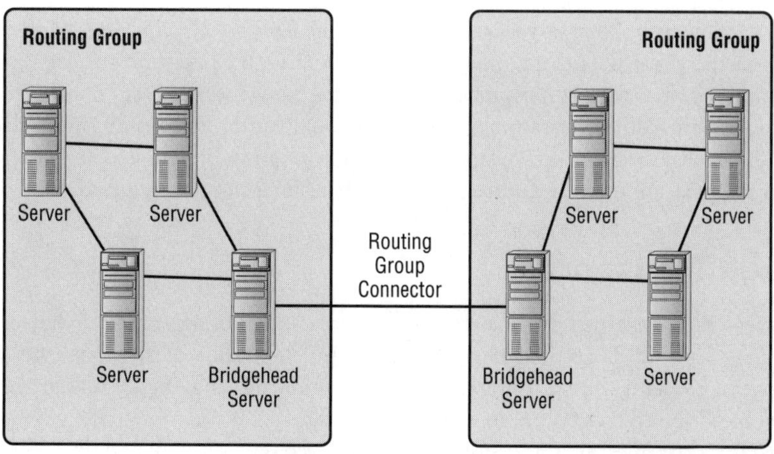

Link State Algorithm

Whenever multiple routing groups are connected, the connections over which messages are transferred are referred to as links. Every *link* can exist in one of two states: up (available) or down (unavailable). In addition, every link is assigned a value that represents the cost of using that link relative to other available links. By default, the cost of any connector created is 1, but cost can range from 1 to 100, with lower number values being the preferred routes. You can configure the cost of connectors in your organization to create a bias for certain routes.

Exchange Server 2003 uses link-state tables to provide all servers in the system with information that lets the servers determine whether any given link is functioning. The link-state information also lets servers determine the best route to send a given message based on the total cost of all connectors a route will use. For example, a route that crossed two connectors whose individual costs were 2 (for a total cost of 4) would be favored over a route that crossed two connectors with individual costs of 3 (for a total cost of 6). Connectors that are in a down state are never considered. The information in these link-state tables is based on a protocol named the *Link State Algorithm.*

Support for the Link State Algorithm was first introduced in Exchange 2000 Server, though it has been around for many years elsewhere. In fact, it forms the foundation of the *Open Shortest Path First (OSPF)* protocol that is used extensively by routers today. Exchange Server 2003 still incorporates routes and costs but relies heavily on link-state information to route messages between routing groups.

The Link State Algorithm propagates the state of the messaging system in almost real time to all servers in the organization. There are several advantages to this:

- Each Exchange server can make the best routing decision before sending a message downstream where a link might be down.
- Message ping-pong is eliminated, because alternate route information is also propagated and considered in the routing calculations.
- Message looping is eliminated.

In each routing group, one server is designated as the *Routing Group Master* and will become the bridgehead server to the other routing group. By default, the first server added to a particular routing group becomes that group's master. When one bridgehead server connects to another bridgehead server in a different routing group and link-state information is exchanged, this is done with SMTP. The Routing Group Master holds the information of who is up or down and propagates that information to each Routing Group Master in each routing group.

Message Transport

All good messaging systems rely on a strong transport and routing engine to deliver messages, and Exchange Server 2003 is no different. A solid understanding of how messages are transferred between Exchange Server components is essential to managing a reliable organization and to troubleshooting any failure in message transfer.

For the most part, messages are submitted to an Exchange server using the SMTP protocol. These messages may come from a client within the Exchange system or from an outside system such as the Internet. Though messages may also be submitted to the Exchange server via direct submission from a client using IFS or via the MTA from a foreign system, we will concern ourselves here with the SMTP process.

Here's the basic procedure that occurs when a client submits a message to the Exchange server (see Figure 2.5):

1. An SMTP client opens a connection on the SMTP Service.
2. The IIS process on the SMTP Service responds.
3. After negotiation, the SMTP process receives and processes the message.
4. The SMTP process hands the message to an advanced queuing engine, which places it into a Pre-Categorizer queue.
5. A *Categorizer* resolves the sender and recipient for the message, expanding any distribution lists as needed and resolving all recipients in the list. In previous versions of Exchange Server, this task was performed by the MTA.
6. Next, the advanced queuing engine passes the message to the routing engine, which parses the message against its Domain Mapping and Configuration table. The routing engine checks Active Directory and decides whether the message is destined for the local store or a remote server. If destined for a remote server, a *Destination Message queue* is created for the message as a temporary queue from which the SMTP service can read the message and pass it along.

FIGURE 2.5 A client submits a message to an Exchange server using SMTP.

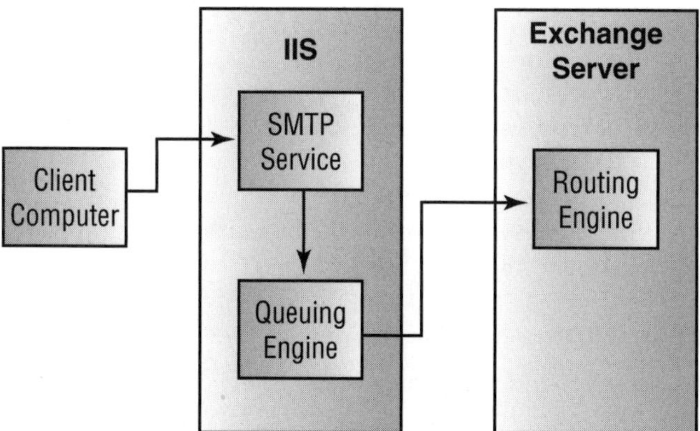

Once the message has been submitted, the routing engine decides where the message is supposed to go. In all, Exchange Server 2003 messages can get from a sender to a recipient in one of four contexts. A message can be sent as follows:

- From a sender to a recipient on the same server. This may be the case when two users have mailboxes on the same server and transfer messages between them, when a user posts a message to a public folder that exists on the same server, or when an Exchange Server component delivers a message to a local recipient.

- Between different servers in the same routing group.
- Between different routing groups.
- From a sender in the Exchange organization to a user on a foreign messaging system outside the Exchange organization.

On the Same Server

If the message is destined for the local store, it is placed in the Local Delivery queue, and the `store.exe` process reads the message out of the queue and writes it to the local database. Thereafter, the message is associated with the destination mailbox, and the user is notified that new mail has arrived. This is the simplest of the message transport contexts.

Between Servers in the Same Routing Group

Messages routed between servers in the same routing group use SMTP as their transport. The steps involved in routing a message between two servers in the same group are slightly more complicated than on a single server:

1. Since the message is not intended for local delivery, the message is passed to the routing engine.
2. Once in the routing engine, the message is parsed against the Domain Mapping and Configuration table and then placed in the outgoing SMTP queue for the destination server.
3. The sending server looks up the recipient's home directory in Active Directory, conducts a DNS lookup for the MX record associated with the destination server on which the recipient's mailbox is stored, and then creates a TCP connection to that server.
4. The message is transmitted to the destination server.
5. Once the destination server receives the message, it processes it in different ways depending on the destination of the message. If it determines that the message goes to a recipient in its local store, it follows the procedure discussed in the previous section. If it determines that the message goes to a different server or outside the organization, the above process is repeated to route the message to the correct server.

Between Routing Groups

Messages routed between servers in multiple groups incur the use of a bridgehead server at each end of the connector. The steps involved in routing messages between servers in different routing groups are as follows (see Figure 2.6, where the solid line represents the flow of messages and the dashed line represents queries):

1. Since the message is not intended for local delivery, the message is passed to the routing engine.
2. The routing group information is gathered from the configuration naming context of Active Directory.
3. The link-state information is consulted to determine the best routing path.

4. The message is passed to the bridgehead server.
5. The bridgehead server passes the message to the destination bridgehead server in the other routing group.
6. The receiving bridgehead server passes the message to the destination server in its group.
7. The message is brought into the destination server via the SMTP service and placed in the Local Delivery queue.
8. The message is taken out of the queue by the `store.exe` process and associated with the recipient's inbox.

FIGURE 2.6 Routing messages between routing groups

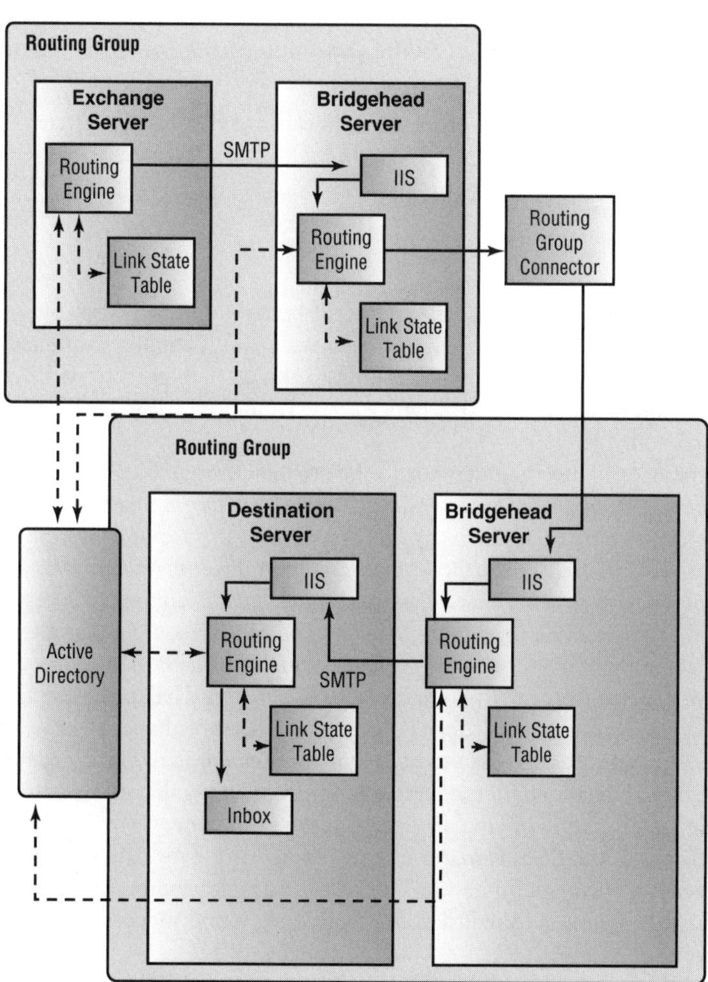

Outside the Exchange Organization

Message delivery outside of the Exchange organization is similar to delivery to another routing group in that a connector must be used to pass the message. Here are the steps involved in routing to another e-mail system:

1. Since the message is not intended for local delivery, the message is passed to the routing engine.
2. The routing group information is gathered from the configuration-naming context of Active Directory.
3. The link-state information is consulted to determine the best routing path. In this case, the path must end with the connector to the foreign system.
4. The routing server then either sends the message over the appropriate connector to the foreign system or, if the connector is in a different routing group, sends the message to that routing group.
5. The message is passed over the appropriate connector to the foreign system.

Summary

The better you understand how the system works, the better you'll be able to plan a viable network and troubleshoot that network when problems occur. This chapter examined three basic aspects of Exchange Server 2003 architecture: how Exchange is integrated with Active Directory, how information is stored on an Exchange server, and how messages flow within an Exchange organization.

At the top of the Active Directory hierarchy is the domain forest, which represents the outside boundary that any Exchange organization can reach. A domain tree is a hierarchical arrangement of domains that share a common namespace. The first domain in a tree is called the root domain. Domains added under this are called child domains. Within the domain tree, domains establish trust relationships with one another that allow objects in a trusted domain to access resources in a trusting domain. A domain is a group of computers and other resources that are part of a network and share a common directory database. Each domain contains at least one domain controller. Multiple domain controllers per domain can be used for load balancing and fault tolerance.

When Exchange is installed, many objects, such as users, are enhanced with Exchange-related features. A global catalog is used to hold information about all of the objects in a forest. Objects can be grouped into containers called organizational units that allow administrators to effectively manage large groups of similar objects at the same time.

In Exchange Server 2003, the Information Store is responsible for data storage and management. It supports access through numerous Internet and application programming protocols. This Information Store is also referred to as the Web Store, a nod to its support for web-based protocols and access.

SMTP is the native transport protocol in Exchange Server 2003, and it's used to route messages within and between routing groups. Internet Information Services (IIS) handles the SMTP protocol and transfers information with Exchange via the ExIPC service.

Multiple servers in an Exchange Server 2003 organization are grouped in routing groups. Servers within a routing group must share full-time reliable connectivity. Different routing groups are linked to one another using one of three types of connectors: the Routing Group Connector, which is the easiest to set up; the SMTP connector, which can be fine-tuned a bit more than the Routing Group Connector; and the X.400 Connector, which is used for very low-bandwidth connections.

Exam Essentials

Understand Active Directory. While this book is not trying to prepare you for an exam related to Active Directory design, support, or administration, it is absolutely imperative that you understand how Active Directory is designed and functions. With Exchange being completely Active Directory–integrated and aware, all administrative functions related to users and mailboxes are tied into Active Directory. To that end, ensure that you have a good understanding of both the logical and physical structure of Active Directory. In addition, you should be aware of, and understand, the various domain functional levels that are available in Windows Server 2003 and how they will impact your overall network.

Understand the Exchange database structure. Although only two core files make up the database portion of an Exchange database, there are actually several critical files that are part of an Exchange Server database—you must know them all. The rich-text (EDB) file and the streaming media (STM) file are the actual database files. However, there exists a checkpoint file and one or more transaction log files that must be considered part of the Exchange Server database in order for it to be complete. The transaction logs are used as a temporary storage location for transactions that have not yet been committed to the database files because writing to the database files is a much more time-consuming evolution than writing to the transaction logs. The checkpoint file is used to keep track of transactions that are committed to the database from a transaction log. Using checkpoint files ensures that transactions cannot be committed to a database more than once.

Know the difference between the versions of Active Directory Connector. Recall that the Active Directory Connector that Windows includes by default is designed to allow Windows Active Directory domains to interact with Windows NT 4.0 domain controllers. Exchange Server 2003 installs its own special (upgraded) version of the Active Directory Connector that allows for the interoperation of (and eventual migration from) Exchange Server 5.5 computers. These two different versions of the Active Directory Connector should not be confused.

Understand basic message routing. It is helpful, both in preparing for this exam and in the day-to-day administration of Exchange Server 2003, to understand the various message routing processes that may take place. Recall that there are four basic message routing scenarios:

- From a sender to a recipient on the same server. This may be the case when two users have mailboxes on the same server and transfer messages between them, when a user posts a message to a public folder that exists on the same server, or when an Exchange Server component delivers a message to a local recipient.
- Between different servers in the same routing group.
- Between different routing groups.
- From a sender in the Exchange organization to a user on a foreign messaging system outside the Exchange organization.

You should ensure that you understand the specifics of each message routing scenario.

Review Questions

1. You are currently running in the Windows 2000 mixed domain functional level and are considering making the switch to the Windows 2000 native domain functional level. Which of the following would be valid concerns to take into account before making the switch? (Choose all that apply.)

   A. The switch is irreversible.

   B. If you later decide to switch back to the Windows 2000 mixed domain functional level, all object configuration will be lost.

   C. Exchange Server 5.5 cannot be run in a Windows 2000 native domain functional level environment.

   D. You must upgrade or retire all Windows NT 4.0 domain controllers.

2. Which of the following statements is true of domains in a single domain tree?

   A. Domains are not configured with trust relationships by default.

   B. Domains are automatically configured with one-way trust relationships flowing from parent domains to child domains.

   C. Domains are automatically configured with two-way nontransitive trusts.

   D. Domains are automatically configured with two-way transitive trusts.

3. What is the relationship between a Windows Server 2003 site and an Exchange site?

   A. The terms are used interchangeably.

   B. There must be a one-to-one mapping of Windows Server 2003 sites and Exchange sites.

   C. A Windows Server 2003 site can span multiple Exchange sites.

   D. An Exchange site can span multiple Windows Server 2003 sites.

   E. There is no relationship between Exchange sites and Windows Server 2003 sites.

4. A hierarchical arrangement of one or more Windows Server 2003 domains that share a common namespace is referred to as a:

   A. Windows Server 2003 site

   B. Domain site

   C. Domain tree

   D. Domain forest

5. You have just installed the first Windows Server 2003 server on your network and want to make it a domain controller. How would you do this?

   A. The first Windows Server 2003 server is automatically made a domain controller.

   B. Install Active Directory on the computer.

   C. Install DNS on the computer.

   D. Install the Schema on the computer.

6. Which of the following statements is true?

   A. An organizational unit cannot contain objects from other domains.

   B. An organizational unit can contain objects only from other trusted domains.

   C. An organizational unit can contain objects only from other domains in the same domain tree.

   D. An organizational unit can contain objects only from other domains in the same domain forest.

7. What service is the primary provider of name resolution on a Windows Server 2003 network?

   A. X.400

   B. DNS

   C. WINS

   D. SMTP

8. Which of the following tasks can the Active Directory Connector be used for? (Choose all that apply.)

   A. Connecting the Active Directory information on a Windows Server 2003 server to the security database on a Windows NT 4 server

   B. Connecting the Exchange-related Active Directory information on a Windows Server 2003 server to an Exchange 5.5 directory service

   C. Migrating objects from an Exchange 5.5 directory service to Active Directory

   D. Synchronizing the Active Directory between Windows Server 2003 domain controllers

9. You are backing up the database files created by Exchange and come across two files named `pub.edb` and `pub.stm`. You recognize that the `pub.edb` file is the database for your public folders. What is the `pub.stm` file used for?

   A. Maintaining a log of transactions made to the `pub.edb` file

   B. Storing information about the folders that are compatible with earlier versions of Exchange Server

   C. Storing certain types of media files in their native format

   D. Providing a backup of the `pub.edb` file

10. What is the maximum number of databases that can exist on a single Exchange server?

    A. 5

    B. 6

    C. 10

    D. 20

11. You are performing a backup of an Exchange private Information Store that uses the default store name and need to make sure that you back up all of the necessary files for that store. Which of the following files compose the Exchange Server 2003 message database? (Choose all that apply.)

    A. `priv.edb`

    B. `priv.dat`

    C. `priv.stm`

    D. `edb.chk`

    E. `edb.log`

12. You have installed multiple public folder trees in your organization. Which of the following clients would be able to access only the default public folder tree and none of the additional trees?

    A. Office Outlook 2003

    B. A web browser

    C. An Office 2003 application

    D. A generic POP3 client

13. Which of the following technologies permits normal network client redirectors, such as Exchange, to share folders and items?

    A. Installable File System

    B. SMTP

    C. Clustering

    D. Exchange Interprocess Communication Layer

14. You are configuring a Windows Server 2003 active/passive cluster to run your main Exchange mail servers and are planning to use Windows Server 2003 Enterprise Edition. How many nodes will you be able to configure in the active/passive cluster?

    A. 2

    B. 4

    C. 8

    D. 10

15. Which of the following represent the Microsoft Exchange Information Store service?

 A. `store.exe`

 B. `inetinfo.exe`

 C. `mad.exe`

 D. `explorer.exe`

16. You are configuring a connector between two routing groups and want to have servers issue authentication before sending any mail. Which connector allows this?

 A. Routing Group Connector

 B. SMTP Connector

 C. X.400 Connector

 D. Active Directory Connector

17. Which of the following connector types can use multiple bridgehead servers? (Choose all that apply.)

 A. Routing Group Connector

 B. SMTP Connector

 C. X.400 Connector

 D. TCP Connector

18. Your organization consists of two routing groups linked by a very slow link (you average around 8 Kbps). Which type of connector is best for supporting this type of link?

 A. Routing Group Connector

 B. SMTP Connector

 C. X.400 Connector

 D. TCP Connector

19. What primary advantage does SMTP offer over RPCs for connectivity between servers within a routing group?

 A. SMTP is faster.

 B. SMTP does not require full-time connectivity.

 C. SMTP does not require high-speed connectivity.

 D. SMTP does not require reliable connectivity.

20. What two constructs in Exchange Server 2003 replace the Exchange 5.5 site? (Choose all that apply.)

A. Windows Server 2003 sites

B. Routing groups

C. Administrative groups

D. Organizational units

Answers to Review Questions

1. A, D. The switch to the Windows 2000 native domain functional level is a one-time, one-way switch and is irreversible. Once you have switched to the Windows 2000 native domain functional level, you will no longer be able to have Windows NT 4.0 domain controllers within the organization.

2. D. Windows Server 2003 (along with Windows 2000 Server) and Active Directory support transitive two-way trusts between domains. When a child domain is created, a trust relationship is automatically configured between that child domain and the parent domain. This trust is two-way, meaning that resource access requests can flow from either domain to the other.

3. E. Exchange sites are a construct from Exchange 5.5 that defined administrative and routing boundaries. Sites are no longer used in Exchange Server 2003. Windows Server 2003 sites are groups of computers on the same IP subnet.

4. C. A domain tree is a hierarchical arrangement of one or more Windows Active Directory domains that share a common namespace. Domain Name Service (DNS) domain names represent the tree structure. The first domain in a tree is called the root domain.

5. B. To create a domain controller, all you have to do is install the Active Directory service on it. During this process, you have the option of creating a new domain or joining an existing domain. If you create a new domain, you also have the option of creating or joining an existing domain tree or forest.

6. A. An organizational unit is a container in which you can place objects such as user accounts, groups, computers, printers, applications, file shares, and other organizational units. An organizational unit cannot contain objects from other domains and is the smallest unit you can assign or delegate administrative authority to. Organizational units are provided strictly for administrative purposes and convenience.

7. B. DNS is the primary provider of name resolution for Windows Server 2003–based networks. In fact, the Windows Server 2003 domain structure is based on DNS structure, and Active Directory requires that DNS be used.

8. B, C. The Active Directory Connector is a Windows Server 2003 service that synchronizes the Exchange 5.5 directory with Active Directory. This allows you to administer your directory from Active Directory or the Exchange 5.5 directory service. You can also use ADC to migrate objects from the Exchange directory service to Active Directory.

9. C. An Exchange Server 2003 database is actually a logical entity that represents two physical database files, a rich-text (EDB) file and a streaming media (STM) file. The rich-text file holds messages and works much like the database files in previous versions of Exchange Server. The streaming media file has been added to provide native support for many types of streaming media, including voice, audio, video, and others.

10. D. Exchange allows up to five databases per storage group and up to four production storage groups per server. Each database must exist inside a storage group. The recovery storage group is not taken into consideration when examining the number of databases a server can hold.

11. A, C, D, E. The most current state of any Exchange store is the EDB database, the STM database, the current log file, and the current checkpoint file.

12. A. MAPI clients, such as Outlook, can access only the default public folder tree in an organization. Clients that can directly access the file system, such as Office applications, web browsers, and Windows Explorer, can access multiple public folder trees. POP3 clients cannot access public folders at all.

13. A. This is a means of exposing the Exchange Information Store to users and applications on the network. Because your local computer can assign, or map, a drive letter to these resources, standard applications such as Windows Explorer and Office 2003 can access resources in the Exchange Store.

14. C. Windows Server 2003 Enterprise Edition and Windows Server 2003 Datacenter Server Edition both support up to eight nodes in an active/passive cluster. Windows 2000 Advanced Server supports two nodes in an active/passive cluster. Windows 2000 Datacenter Server supports up to four nodes an active/passive cluster.

15. A. The Information Store (a process named `store.exe`) is the Exchange service that manages the Information Store on an Exchange server. One instance of `store.exe` runs for each storage group on a server. `store.exe` manages processes such as store replication; maintains the ESE databases; and provides protocol stubs, interfaces that allow the ExIPC to transfer data between the IIS (a process named `inetinfo.exe`). `explorer.exe` is the Windows shell and `mad.exe` is the service used by the Microsoft Exchange System Attendant.

16. B. The SMTP Connector is more configurable than the Routing Group Connector and thereby offers the ability to more finely tune the connection. The SMTP Connector offers the ability to issue authentication before sending mail, specifying TLS encryption and removing mail from queues on remote servers.

17. A, B. Both the Routing Group Connector and SMTP Connector can be configured to use multiple source and destination bridgehead servers. The X.400 Connector can support only one bridgehead server. There is no such thing as a TCP Connector.

18. C. X.400 Connectors are useful for linking routing groups when there is very little bandwidth (less than 16 Kbps) available between servers or when X.400 is the only connectivity available.

19. C. SMTP does not require a high-performance network connection. This and the elimination of Exchange sites in Exchange Server 2003 have led to much greater flexibility in the deployment of servers.

20. B, C. Exchange Server 2003 has replaced the concept of Exchange 5.5 sites with routing groups and administrative groups. Routing groups are used to define groups of Exchange servers that share a reliable (but not necessarily high-bandwidth) connection. Administrative groups are used to define administrative boundaries.

Installing Microsoft Exchange Server 2003

MICROSOFT EXAM OBJECTIVES COVERED IN THIS CHAPTER:

- ✓ Prepare the environment for deployment of Exchange Server 2003
- ✓ Install, configure, and troubleshoot Exchange Server 2003
- ✓ Install, configure, and troubleshoot Exchange Server 2003 in a clustered environment
- ✓ Configure and troubleshoot hardware profiles

Because Exchange Server 2003 is a Microsoft Windows Server 2003 application, the installation process is pretty straightforward. However, there are still some issues that need to be addressed in a careful manner. In this chapter, you will learn the necessary steps to install Microsoft Exchange Server 2003. The main subjects of this chapter are as follows:

- Exchange Server 2003: Standard Edition vs. Enterprise Edition
- Pre-installation considerations
- Installing Exchange Server 2003
- Upgrading from Exchange 2000 Server to Exchange Server 2003
- Installing Exchange Server on a cluster
- Post-installation considerations
- Troubleshooting a Microsoft Exchange installation

Exchange Server 2003: Standard Edition vs. Enterprise Edition

Microsoft Exchange Server 2003 is available in two editions: a *Standard Edition*, which is simply called Exchange Server 2003, and an *Enterprise Edition*. The main difference between them is the advanced features supported in the Enterprise Edition.

Standard Edition Features

The Standard Edition includes the following features:

- Basic messaging functionality
- Microsoft Exchange Web Storage System
- Connectors for Lotus Notes and Novell GroupWise
- Distributed (front-end/back-end) configuration of servers
- Support for Volume Shadow Copy

- Usage of the Recovery Storage Group
- Support for Outlook Mobile Access (OMA) and Outlook Web Access (OWA)

Additional Enterprise Edition Features

The Enterprise edition includes all of the features of the Standard edition and adds the following:

- No limit on database size (the Standard Edition is limited to 16 GB).
- Allows up to five databases per storage group (the Standard Edition allows only for up to two databases per storage group).
- Up to four production storage groups per server (the Standard Edition supports only one per server).
- Active/Active and Active/Passive clustering support.
- The X.400 connector is included.

Pre-installation Considerations

You must address several important issues before installing Exchange Server. Having the correct information and making the right decisions about these issues will go a long way toward ensuring a successful installation. The following pre-installation issues are covered in this section:

- Verifying system requirements
- Windows Active Directory domain user accounts related to the Exchange installation
- Licensing issues
- Verifying that Windows services are installed and running
- Running diagnostics tests on domain controllers and the network
- Preparing Active Directory
- Other pre-installation steps

Verifying System Requirements

This section lists the minimum requirements for the computer system upon which Exchange is to be installed. These minimums are valid when you install only the core components. Using additional Exchange components, and depending on your particular performance demands, could require more resources than the following minimum requirements.

Hardware Requirements

The minimum and recommended hardware requirements for installing Exchange are detailed in Table 3.1.

TABLE 3.1 Exchange Server 2003 Hardware Requirements

Item	Minimum	Recommended
CPU	133 MHz Pentium or comparable	733 MHz Pentium or comparable
RAM	256 MB	512 MB
Disk space	500 MB available on the Exchange drive, 200 MB available on the system drive	Space as required, with the databases kept on fault-tolerant drive sets
Drives	CD-ROM for installation	CD-ROM for installation
Video display	VGA or better	VGA or better

The Microsoft Exchange Server software comes on a CD. If the machine intended to be the Exchange server has no CD-ROM drive, the administrator can copy the necessary files from the CD to a shared hard disk or share a CD-ROM drive on another machine.

Software Requirements

The software requirements for an Exchange installation are listed below:

Operating system Microsoft Windows Server 2003 Standard Edition, Enterprise Edition, or Datacenter Edition. Windows 2000 Server, Advanced Server, or Datacenter Server with at least Windows 2000 Service Pack 3.

Active Directory All domain controllers and global catalog servers that Exchange Server 2003 will contact must be running Windows Server 2003 or Windows 2000 Server 2000 Service Pack 3 or higher. The Exchange server must have access to domain controllers and global catalog servers that are located in the same Active Directory site as the Exchange server.

DNS At least one DNS server must be available that meets the needs of Active Directory. Multiple DNS servers are recommended in larger environments.

TCP/IP	Transmission Control Protocol/Internet Protocol (TCP/IP) is required on all Exchange servers and on all clients that need to access Exchange Server.
IIS	Internet Information Services, along with its WWW, NNTP, and SMTP subcomponents, must be installed on any server on which Exchange Server 2003 will be installed.
File system	The volumes to hold the Exchange application files and Exchange database and log files should all be formatted with the NTFS file system.

Windows Active Directory User Accounts Related to the Exchange Installation

Because of Exchange Server 2003's involvement with Active Directory, its installation involves a number of Windows Active Directory user and group security accounts. Following are some of the more pertinent accounts:

Schema Admins	Members of this group have the rights and permissions necessary to modify the schema of Active Directory. To run the ForestPrep tool (described later in this chapter) that modifies the schema for Exchange Server 2003, you must belong to the Schema Admins group, the Enterprise Admins group, and the local Administrators group on the computer on which you actually run the tool.
Enterprise Admins	Members of this group have the rights and permissions necessary to administer any domain in a forest. To run the ForestPrep tool, you must be a member of the Enterprise Admins group, the Schema Admins group, and the local Administrators group on the computer running the tool.
Domain Admins	Members of this group have the rights and permissions necessary to administer any computer or resource in a domain. You must be a member of this group in order to run the DomainPrep tool (also discussed later in this chapter) that prepares each domain for Exchange Server 2003 installation.
Administrators	Members of this local group are given the rights necessary to administer a local computer and install software on it. To install Exchange Server 2003 on a Windows Server 2003 or Windows 2000 Server, you must be a member of this group. This level of privileges is needed because, during installation, services will be started and files will be copied to the `\<winnt_root>\SYSTEM32` directory.

Exchange Domain Servers	Along with the Exchange Enterprise Servers local group, this global security group provides Exchange servers with the permissions necessary to access one another and perform necessary Exchange functions. All Exchange servers are placed into the Exchange Domain Servers group, and this group is placed into the Exchange Enterprise Servers local group on each Exchange computer.
Exchange Enterprise Servers	See the description of the Exchange Domain Servers group above.
Site Services Account	Exchange Server 5.5 services use this account to log on to the Windows system and carry out their functions.

Licensing Issues

Licensing issues relate to matters of legality (specifically, the number of servers Exchange can be installed on and the number of clients that can access a server). Three main licenses pertain to the various Microsoft Exchange product packages:

- Server License
- Client Access License (CAL)
- Client License

Server License

The basic *Server License* provides the legal right to install and operate Microsoft Exchange Server 2003 on a single-server machine. In addition, the Exchange System Manager Microsoft Management Console snap-in (the primary utility used to administer an Exchange organization) can be installed on additional machines without additional licenses.

Since many licensing policies can change over time, always check for the latest policy to ensure your compliance. You can find the licensing policies for Exchange Server 2003 at `www.microsoft.com/exchange/howtobuy/enterprise.asp`.

Client Access License (CAL)

A *Client Access License (CAL)* gives a user the legal right to access an Exchange server. An organization designates the number of CALs it needs when a Microsoft Exchange server is purchased. Each CAL provides one user the legal right to access the Exchange server. Any client software that has the ability to be a client to Microsoft Exchange Server is legally required to have a CAL purchased for it. Microsoft Exchange Server 2003 uses a per-seat licensing mode, which means that each client accessing the server must possess a valid CAL.

Client Access Licenses are *not* included in any version of Microsoft Windows or Microsoft Office. For example, the version of Office Outlook 2003 that comes with Microsoft Office 2003 requires, by law, that a separate CAL be purchased before accessing an Exchange server.

Client License

In addition to having a CAL, each piece of client software must also be licensed for use on the client computer. This means that each piece of client software, such as Office Outlook 2003, needs its own license to be legally installed on the client computer plus a CAL to legally connect to an Exchange server.

Verifying Windows Services

The Exchange Server 2003 setup process has been made easier and more error-proof than ever before. As part of this improved setup process, you are prompted to verify and install, as required, those key services that are required to support the installation of Exchange Server 2003. Before Exchange Server 2003 can be installed on a server, the NNTP, SMTP, and WWW services must be installed and running on the server. If the server is Windows Server 2003, then ASP.NET must also be installed.

The steps to verify Windows services, perform network diagnostics, and run ForestPrep and DomainPrep are all part of the normal installation sequence for a new Exchange Server 2003 organization. All of these steps are accessible from the Exchange Server Deployment Tools page, as you'll see later in Exercise 3.2.

Exercise 3.1 outlines the steps that you will need to perform to install and enable the required services.

EXERCISE 3.1

Installing and Enabling Required Services

1. Open the Add or Remove Programs applet, located in the Control Panel.
2. Click the Add/Remove Windows Components button.
3. On the Windows Components dialog box, select the Application Server option and click the Details button.

EXERCISE 3.1 *(continued)*

4. On the Application Server dialog box, shown below, select the ASP.NET option.

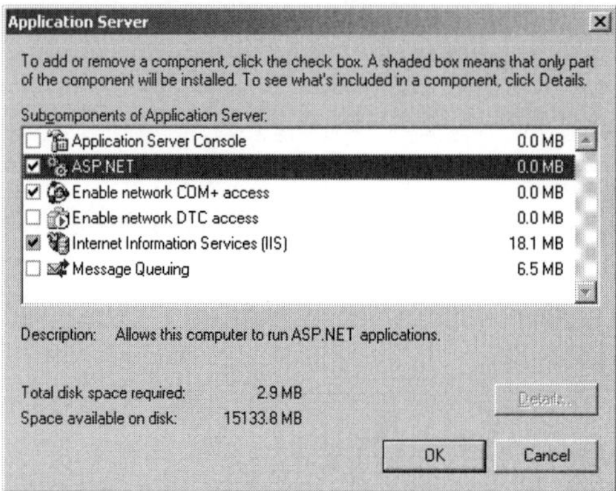

5. Select the Internet Information Services (IIS) option and click the Details button.

6. On the Internet Information Services (IIS) dialog box, shown below, select the NNTP Service, the SMTP Service, and the World Wide Web Service.

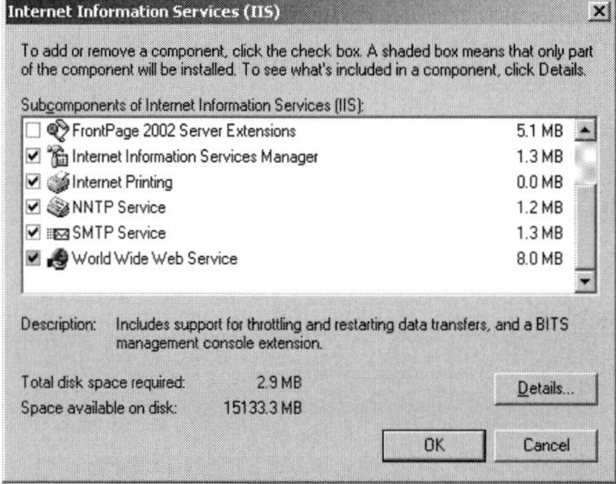

7. Click OK to close the Internet Information Services (IIS) dialog box.

8. Click OK to close the Application Server dialog box.

9. Back at the Windows Components dialog box, click Next to continue.

10. Click Finish when prompted.

EXERCISE 3.1 *(continued)*

11. To enable ASP.NET, open the Internet Information Services (IIS) console located in the Administrative Tools folder.
12. Expand the nodes to locate the Web Service Extensions node.
13. In the right-hand pane of the console, select the ASP.NET option and click the Allow button.

You can verify that services are running by opening the Services console located in the Administrative Tools folder.

Performing Diagnostics Testing

In an effort to prevent problems that often occur from difficulties connecting to domain controllers and other network hosts, the Exchange Server 2003 setup process includes steps to run DCDiag and NetDiag to perform diagnostics on domain controllers and the network, respectively.

The Exchange Server Deployment Tools make it easy for you perform these tests as long as you have your Windows Server 2003 CD available. You will simply need to install the Windows Support Tools from the Support folder on the Windows Server 2003 CD and then run these two diagnostics tools. Although they are run during the normal Exchange Server setup process, locating and correcting any problems now will make the actual installation an easier one.

Preparing Active Directory

Before installing the first Exchange server in an organization, you may need to prepare the forest and each domain into which Exchange will be installed. For these tasks, you will use two tools provided with the Exchange installation software: *ForestPrep* and *DomainPrep*. ForestPrep must be run once in a forest. It extends the Active Directory schema with the objects necessary to run Exchange Server 2003. DomainPrep must be run in each domain to identify the domain's address list server and to create special domain accounts that Exchange needs in order to run properly.

Though this seems like a complicated installation routine, it does provide a significant advantage. Many networks separate the administrative responsibilities of domain management, schema management, and Exchange management. For example, one group may be in charge of administering the schema and the primary domains of the forest, another may be in charge of managing the child domains, and still another group will manage Exchange.

These additional setup tools provide the ability for separate administrators to perform their necessary part of the Exchange installation and simplify the Exchange deployment. For example, the group in charge of managing the schema will have the permissions required to run the ForestPrep tool to extend the schema. Domain administrators will have the permissions required to use the DomainPrep tool that modifies domains. Once these tasks are done, Exchange administrators can install and manage Exchange without having to be given permissions for the other preparation tasks.

If a single administrator or group runs the network and has all the appropriate permissions (or if there is only one domain in your forest), the installation of Exchange is simplified. If the account with which you install the first Exchange server belongs to the Schema Admins, Enterprise Admins, and Administrators groups for the local computer, you do not need to manually run ForestPrep or DomainPrep since you will run them during the normal Exchange setup process.

Preparing a Windows Active Directory Forest

In order to run the ForestPrep tool, you must belong to the Schema Admins and Enterprise Admins security groups. In addition, you must belong to the local Administrators group on the server on which Exchange will be installed. If you are not a member of these groups, the appropriate administrator will have to run the ForestPrep tool before you can install Exchange Server 2003.

When ForestPrep is run, it performs several tasks:

- It extends the Active Directory schema with Exchange-related information.
- It creates the organization object in Active Directory.
- If the forest contains no existing versions of Exchange Server, ForestPrep prompts you for an Exchange organization name and then creates the organization object in the Active Directory. If the forest contains a previous version of Exchange Server 5.5, ForestPrep creates the organization object in the Active Directory based on information in the Exchange Server 5.5 organization. The organization is at the top of the Exchange hierarchy. This case-sensitive field can be up to 64 characters in length. The organization name is associated with every object in the Exchange directory, such as mailboxes, public folders, and distribution lists. The organization name cannot be modified after installation.
- It assigns the Exchange Full Administrator role to the account that you specify. This account or group has the authority to install and manage Exchange 2003 Server on any computer throughout the forest. This account or group also can delegate additional Exchange Full Administrator permissions after the first server is installed.

Exercise 3.2 outlines the steps for running ForestPrep in a forest that does not have a previous version of Exchange running. The process to prepare a forest and domain for Exchange Server 2003 coexistence with Exchange Server 5.5 is lengthier and will be discussed later in Chapter 11, "Coexisting with and Migrating from Exchange 5.5."

EXERCISE 3.2

Running ForestPrep in a Forest with No Previous Versions of Exchange

1. Insert the Microsoft Exchange Server CD into the server's CD-ROM drive. If your CD-ROM drive is set to automatically run CDs, this will automatically open the Welcome to Exchange Server 2003 Setup page, as shown below. If not, browse to the location of your CD-ROM and double-click the `setup.exe` file.

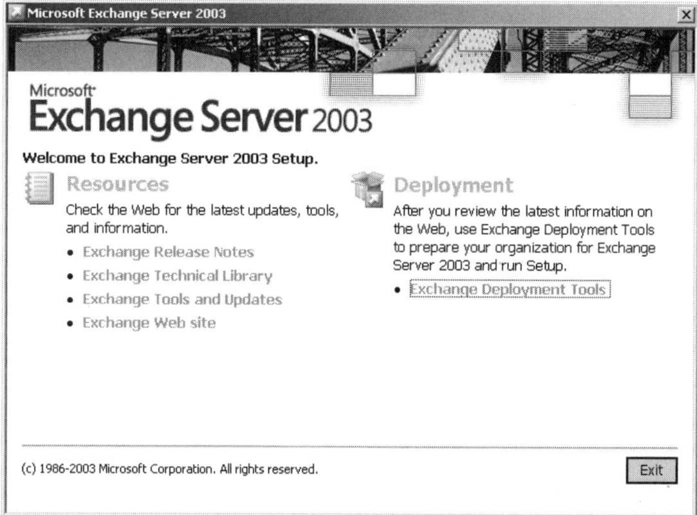

2. Click the Exchange Deployment Tools link.

3. On the Welcome to the Exchange Server Deployment Tools page shown below, click the Deploy The First Exchange 2003 Server link.

EXERCISE 3.2 *(continued)*

4. On the Deploy the First Exchange Server 2003 page, shown below, click the New Exchange 2003 Installation link.

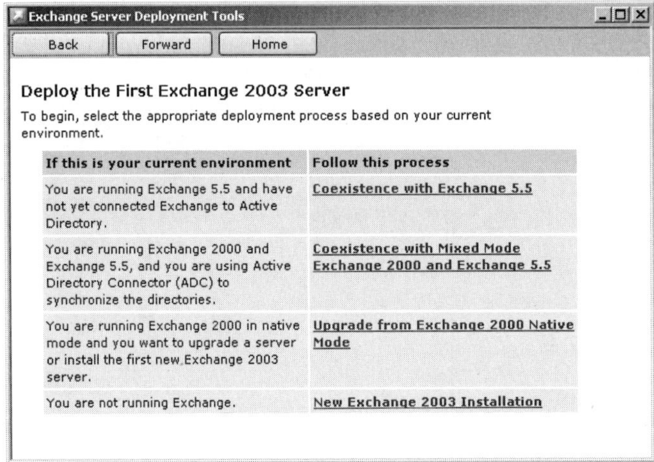

5. Scroll down the Exchange Server Deployment Tools page, shown below, until you locate item 6, Run ForestPrep. Click the Run ForestPrep Now link.

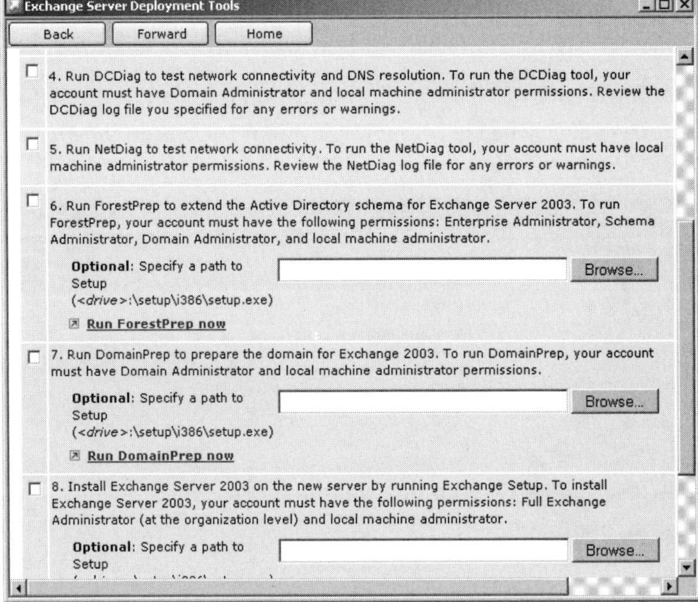

EXERCISE 3.2 *(continued)*

6. When prompted, agree to the EULA, and then click Next to continue.
7. Enter your 25-digit CD key, and click Next to continue.
8. On the Component Selection dialog box, shown below, note that ForestPrep has been selected. Click Next to begin the forest preparation process.

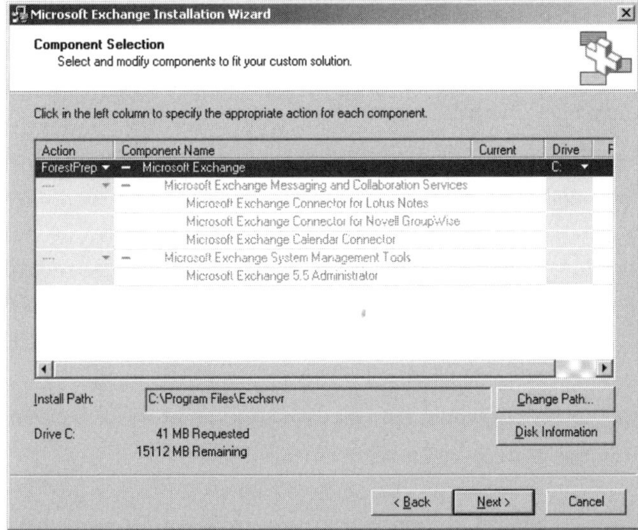

9. On the Microsoft Exchange Server Administrator Account dialog box, type the name of the user who will be responsible for administering Exchange, and click Next. The account must be entered in the format of **`domain\account`**. This account is assigned the Exchange Full Administrator role and will have the permissions to install Exchange Server 2003 and to create other types of Exchange administrator accounts.
10. Next, ForestPrep begins to update the schema and may prompt you with a dialog to verify the update. If it does, click OK to go on.
11. Once the schema is updated (and this can take quite a long time, depending on the size of your forest), the Completion screen appears. Click Finish.

You can also start the ForestPrep process from the command line by entering the command `d:\setup\i386\setup.exe /forestprep` where volume D represents the correct location of the Exchange Server 2003 installation files.

Preparing a Windows Active Directory Domain

Once you have prepared the Windows Active Directory forest using ForestPrep, you must also prepare each domain in the forest that will run Exchange Server 2003 using DomainPrep. In addition, you must run DomainPrep in the forest root domain and each domain that will contain Exchange Server 2003 mailbox-enabled objects or that has users or groups that will manage Exchange Server 2003 computers.

To run DomainPrep, you must be a member of the Domain Admins group for that domain and the Administrators group on the local computer where you will be running DomainPrep. DomainPrep performs the following tasks:

- Creates the Exchange Domain Servers global group
- Creates the Exchange Enterprise Servers local group
- Adds the Exchange Domain Servers group to the Exchange Enterprise Servers group
- Creates the Exchange System Objects container, which is used for mail-enabled public folders
- Sets permissions for the Exchange Enterprise Servers group at the root of the domain, so that the Recipient Update Service has the appropriate access to process recipient objects
- Adds the local Exchange Domain Servers group to the Pre–Windows 2000 Compatible Access group
- Grants permissions for Exchange Server 2003 administrators and servers

Exercise 3.3 outlines the steps for running DomainPrep.

EXERCISE 3.3

Running DomainPrep

1. Insert the Microsoft Exchange Server CD into the server's CD-ROM drive. If your CD-ROM drive is set to automatically run CDs, this will automatically open the Welcome to Exchange Server 2003 Setup page, as seen previously in Exercise 3.2. If not, browse to the location of your CD-ROM and double-click the `setup.exe` file.
2. Click the Exchange Deployment Tools link.
3. On the Welcome to the Exchange Server Deployment Tools page shown in the previous exercise, click the Deploy The First Exchange 2003 Server link.
4. On the Deploy the First Exchange Server 2003 page, click the New Exchange 2003 Installation link.
5. Scroll down the Exchange Server Deployment Tools page until you locate item 7, Run DomainPrep. Click the Run DomainPrep Now link.

EXERCISE 3.3 *(continued)*

6. When prompted, agree to the EULA, and click Next to continue.
7. Enter your 25-digit CD key, and click Next to continue.
8. On the Component Selection dialog box note that DomainPrep has been selected. Click Next to begin the domain preparation process.
9. On the Completion screen, click Finish.

You can also start the DomainPrep process from the command line by entering the command `d:\setup\i386\setup.exe /domainprep` where volume D represents the correct location of the Exchange Server 2003 installation files.

Other Pre-installation Steps

Prior to installing the Exchange Server software, you should consider these additional steps:

- Verify that the Windows Server 2003 domain controllers and global catalog servers are operational.
- Close any messaging-aware applications.
- Verify that Microsoft Clustering Service is installed and properly configured if you will be installing Exchange in that environment.

Installing Exchange Server

This section explains several installation scenarios and component options and then walks you through an actual installation of the first server in an organization. So boot up your Windows Server 2003 computer, grab your Exchange Server 2003 CD, and get ready.

There are four basic contexts in which Exchange Server 2003 can be installed:

- As the Exchange Server 2003 computer in an organization
- As a subsequent Exchange Server 2003 installation
- As an upgrade from Exchange 2000 Server to Exchange Server 2003
- As a coexistence with or migration from Exchange Server 5.5 to Exchange Server 2003

In addition to these four contexts, this section also covers installing Exchange on a cluster.

We will examine the installation and management of Exchange Server 2003 computers for coexistence with and migration from Exchange Server 5.5 in Chapter 11.

Installing the First Exchange Server

Installing the first Exchange Server 2003 in an organization is a fairly important task. If you have already run (or had someone else run) the ForestPrep and DomainPrep tools, then the Active Directory and Windows domains are all ready for the Exchange installation.

If you are a member of the Schema Admins, Enterprise Admins, and local Administrators groups, you can forgo running the ForestPrep tool; it is possible to update the schema during the setup of the initial Exchange Server. In addition, if you are installing into a single domain environment, you can forgo running the DomainPrep tool. *Be warned, though: If you install Exchange without running the ForestPrep tool into a forest where no version of Exchange already exists, Setup creates an organization based on the name of the domain.*

When installing the first Exchange server, you will be prompted to enter information on the following topics:

Name of the directory for installation The default directory location and name are `C:\Program Files\Exchsrvr`, but this can be modified by the installer.

CD Key The Setup program will present you with a dialog box requesting the CD Key or Product ID (PID) number. The CD Key is a unique 25-digit number found on the back of the Exchange Server CD case.

Choosing Installation Components

You can initiate Exchange Server Setup by using either the graphical Welcome to Exchange Server 2003 Setup page that loads if auto-play is enabled or alternatively by executing the `setup.exe` command, which is located on the Exchange Server CD in the `\Setup\I386\` directory.

You can perform the installation from a network share if desired.

When Setup runs, it checks for a current installation of Exchange on that machine. If it finds one, it goes into maintenance mode and lets you add or remove components and reinstall or remove all components.

If Setup does not find a current installation, it prompts you for the specific components to install, as seen previously in the final screen shown in Exercise 3.2.

There are two main categories of components available under the main Microsoft Exchange entry:

- Microsoft Exchange Messaging and Collaboration Services, which includes the basic Exchange routing engine and optional subcomponents for the various available messaging connectors
- Microsoft Exchange System Management Tools, which includes the System Manager snap-in for managing Exchange and a single optional subcomponent—the Exchange 5.5 Administrator tool for managing Exchange 5.5 servers

In addition, there are three installation types that you can choose using the drop-down menu (under the Action heading) to the left of the Microsoft Exchange component at the top of the component list:

- *Typical*, which installs the Messaging and Collaboration Services and the System Management Tools components but none of their subcomponents
- *Minimum*, which installs only the Messaging and Collaboration Services component itself
- *Custom*, which you can use to select individually only the components you want

When you install Exchange Server 2003 into a forest where no version of Exchange already exists, Setup creates a default routing group, named First Routing Group, and a default administrative group, named First Administrative Group. If you want to create groups with more imaginative (or useful) names, run the ForestPrep and DomainPrep tools as normal. Then, perform an installation of Exchange Server 2003, but select only the Microsoft Exchange System management Tools to be installed. Using this console, you can then create routing and administrative groups before you ever deploy your first actual Exchange server.

Performing an Installation

Exercise 3.4 provides the actual steps to install Microsoft Exchange Server 2003. This exercise assumes that you have already used both the ForestPrep and DomainPrep tools and that you are installing the first Exchange server in an organization.

Remember that Setup will run ForestPrep and DomainPrep for you if they have not already been performed and you have all of the required permissions on your user account.

Please review the system requirements needed by your lab computer to perform these exercises. Those requirements are found in the introduction of this book in the section "How to Use This Book."

EXERCISE 3.4

Installing Microsoft Exchange 2000 Server

1. Insert the Microsoft Exchange Server CD into the server's CD-ROM drive. If your CD-ROM drive is set to automatically run CDs, this will automatically open the Welcome to Exchange Server 2003 Setup page as seen previously in Exercise 3.2. If not, browse to the location of your CD-ROM and double-click the `setup.exe` file.
2. Click the Exchange Deployment Tools link.
3. On the Welcome to the Exchange Server Deployment Tools page, click the Deploy The First Exchange 2003 Server link.
4. On the Deploy the First Exchange Server 2003 page, click the New Exchange 2003 Installation link.
5. Scroll down the Exchange Server Deployment Tools page until you locate item 8, Install Exchange Server 2003. Click the Run Setup Now link.
6. When prompted, agree to the EULA, and click Next to continue.
7. Enter your 25-digit CD key, and click Next to continue.
8. The Component Selection page lists the installation options, as well as the option to choose the directory into which Exchange Server will be installed. This latter option is accessed through the Change Path button. For this exercise, we will assume that the installation directory is the default, `C:\Program Files\Exchsrvr`. The installation option we will use for this exercise is the Typical option, which includes the messaging components and management tools. If you would like to see the individual components that can be selected, choose the Custom option from the drop-down menu to the left of the first item in the list, Microsoft Exchange. You can then choose whether to install each individual option using that option's drop-down menu. Once you've made all of your decisions, click Next to go on.
9. A Licensing screen appears, explaining the need for you to purchase Client Access Licenses before clients can access this Exchange server. Exchange Server 2003 supports only the per-seat licensing mode. Once you have read and agreed to this licensing, click the I Agree That I Have Read And Will Be Bound By The License Agreements For This Product option, and then click Next.

EXERCISE 3.4 *(continued)*

10. The Installation Summary dialog box appears, asking you to confirm your installation choices. You can use the Back button to change any settings you have made. When you are satisfied with your choices, click Next to install Exchange Server 2003.

11. The installation process can take some time. When it is done, a Congratulations screen appears, informing you that the installation is complete. Click the Finish button.

After the initial setup, you can add and remove individual components by running the Setup program again using the same procedure as outlined above. You can also access the Setup program using the Windows Add or Remove Programs Control Panel applet.

Installing Subsequent Exchange Servers

There are many reasons to add additional Exchange servers to an organization. The primary reasons are performance, capacity and scaling, and fault tolerance. Each is briefly discussed below.

Performance An organization could place certain Exchange services on additional Exchange servers, dedicating those servers to those functions. Examples are as follows:

Public and/or private information stores These databases could be located on an additional Exchange server dedicated to performing as a mailbox server or public folder server.

Connector software The same principle relates to running connector software on a dedicated Exchange server.

Capacity and scaling If the physical limits of a particular system are being approached, Exchange services and their related physical resources (e.g., disk space) can be spread out among multiple Exchange servers. This issue also relates to performance problems.

Fault tolerance through redundancy Many Exchange services and resources are replicated throughout an Exchange organization. This redundancy implements a built-in level of fault tolerance. For example, all the Exchange servers within a site share the same directory information through replication. If one particular Exchange server is taken offline, its directory information is automatically updated by another Exchange server through the replication mechanism when it comes back online.

The actual process of adding a subsequent Exchange server to an existing organization is nearly identical to installing the first server. The only difference is when you have defined more than one administrative or routing group in your organization (as detailed in Chapter 8, "Building Administrative and Routing Groups"). In this case, you will see two extra dialog boxes while using the Installation Wizard. The first lets you choose the administrative group you want the new server to be a part of. The second dialog box, shown in Figure 3.1, lets you choose a routing group within the chosen administrative group that the server should be a part of. If you have not configured more than one administrative or routing group, you will see neither of these screens, and the installation will be identical to installing the first server.

FIGURE 3.1 Choosing a routing group for a subsequent installation

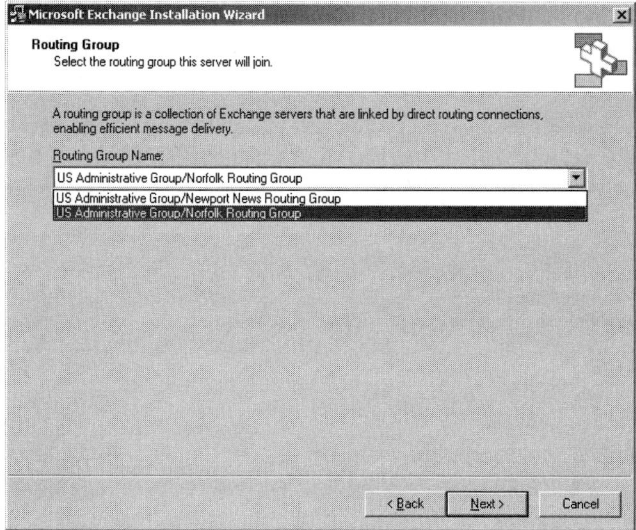

Upgrading from Exchange 2000 Server

Exchange Server 2003 supports upgrades only for servers that are running Exchange 2000 Server with Service Pack 3 or later installed. If you are currently running a previous version of Exchange Server, you can either upgrade it to Exchange 2000 Server with Service Pack 3 to support an upgrade to Exchange Server 2003 or upgrade it to Exchange 5.5 Server with Service Pack 3 for a co-existence/migration scenario, as discussed later in Chapter 11.

The process to upgrade an Exchange Server 2003 Service Pack 3 computer to Exchange Server 2003 is a fairly simple once you've met all of the prerequisites. You should ensure that you understand the following points before attempting to upgrade your Exchange 2000 Server:

- The server must be running Windows 2000 Service Pack 3 or higher or Windows Server 2003.
- The Exchange 2000 Server installation must not have any of these components installed (you must uninstall them before upgrading):
  - Microsoft Mobile Information Server components
  - Exchange 2000 Conferencing Server

- The Instant Messaging service
- The Exchange Chat service
- The Key Management service
- The cc:Mail connector
- The MS Mail connector

If you need to continue using any of these components and services, you will not be able to upgrade that server to Exchange Server 2003.

- If you use a front-end/back-end Exchange server arrangement (discussed more in Chapter 4, "Creating and Managing Exchange Clusters," and Chapter 7, "Configuring Client Access"), you must upgrade *all* of your front-end servers before starting to upgrade any of your back-end servers.
- You can upgrade only the same language version of Exchange. For example, you cannot use the French language version of Exchange Server 2003 to upgrade a German language version of Exchange 2000 Server.
- The Exchange 2000 Server organization must be operating in native mode.

For more information about Exchange 2000 Server to Exchange Server 2003 upgrade considerations, be sure to see Knowledge Base article 822942, located at `http://support.microsoft.com/default.aspx?scid=kb;en-us;822942`.

Once all of these requirements are in place, upgrading to Exchange 2000 Server is not too difficult.

Before undertaking an upgrade, you should always perform a complete backup of your current installation. If something goes drastically wrong with the upgrade, you can then go back to your previous installation.

Performing the Exchange 2000 Server Upgrade

Once you've met all of the requirements to upgrade your Exchange 2000 Server native mode servers to Exchange Server 2003, the actual upgrade process is very similar to that of installing a new Exchange Server 2003 computer.

The basic sequence of steps you must perform, as instructed by the Exchange Server Deployment Tools Upgrade From Exchange 2000 Native Mode option, is as follows:

1. Verify that the required services are installed and running as discussed earlier.

2. Run the DCDiag and NetDiag tools to gather diagnostics data on your domain controllers and network.
3. Run ForestPrep to extend the Active Directory schema for Exchange Server 2003.
4. Run DomainPrep to prepare the required domains for Exchange Server 2003.
5. Upgrade the Exchange 2000 Server computer by running the Exchange Setup application and selecting Upgrade on the Component Selection dialog box. The user account you are using must have Full Exchange Administrator permissions and must be a member of the local Administrators group on the server.

Installing Exchange Server 2003 on Clustered Servers

As stated earlier in this chapter, the Enterprise Edition of Exchange Server 2003 is designed to work with the *Microsoft Clustering Service*. Clustering groups servers logically into an interdependent system, called a *cluster*, for the purpose of fault tolerance. This cluster appears as a single server to clients and applications. In the event of a failure on one system, the Clustering Service moves the affected services to a functioning node in the cluster. Previously Exchange 5.5 supported only Active/Passive clustering, in which only one node of a cluster was active at a time, and Exchange 2000 Server supported only Active/Active clustering, in which all nodes function simultaneously. Exchange Server 2003 supports both Active/Active clustering with two nodes and Active/Passive clustering with between two and eight nodes. Server clusters allow you to enable *resource groups* that are not bound to a specific computer and can fail over to another node. Exchange considers each resource group as a separate instance of Exchange, called a *virtual server*.

Each resource group in a cluster running Exchange must share the following resources:

- IP address
- Network name
- A physical disk or disk system, such as RAID5
- Exchange System Attendant service

Obviously, there is a lot more to clustering than a single chapter can go into. For more detailed information on Exchange clustering, see Chapter 4.

In order to run Exchange with the Microsoft Clustering Service, you must be running Windows Server 2003 Enterprise Edition, Windows Server 2003 Datacenter Edition, Windows 2000 Advanced Server, or Windows 2000 Datacenter Server. The number of nodes you can have in the Exchange Server 2003 cluster is limited by the operating system the server is running:

- You are limited to two nodes when installing on Windows 2000 Advanced Server SP4.
- You are limited to four nodes when installing on Windows 2000 Datacenter Server SP4.
- You can have up to eight nodes when installing on Windows Server 2003 Enterprise Edition or Windows Server 2003 Datacenter Server Edition.

When installing Exchange Server 2003 into a cluster, it must be completely installed on one node before being installed on another node. In addition, you must install Exchange on each node using the same user account that you used to install the Clustering Service. You must also install Exchange on the same drive letter and directory on all nodes. Finally, you must install the same Exchange components on all nodes. We will examine the installation and management of Exchange clusters in more detail in Chapter 4.

Post-installation Considerations

This section discusses some of the results of the Exchange installation. During the installation of Exchange, the activities of `setup.exe` include creating Exchange services, creating an Exchange directory structure, copying files to that directory structure, creating share points to the directory structure, and adding keys and values to the Windows Registry. Knowing the results of these activities is helpful for the Exchange administrator, especially in troubleshooting situations (which will be discussed later in this chapter).

Exchange Services

After a successful installation of Exchange Server 2003, you can verify that the required services are installed. When you examine the Services console, you should see the following new Exchange services listed:

- Microsoft Exchange Event
- Microsoft Exchange IMAP4
- Microsoft Exchange Information Store
- Microsoft Exchange Management
- Microsoft Exchange MTA Stacks
- Microsoft Exchange POP3
- Microsoft Exchange Routing Engine
- Microsoft Exchange Site Replication Service
- Microsoft Exchange System Attendant

Not all of the services listed will be configured for an automatic startup. For example, until you configure and start using POP3, it will remain in a disabled state. In addition, you may have other services installed depending on the type of installation you have performed.

Default Directory and File Structure for Exchange

The default root directory for Exchange is `\Program Files\Exchsrvr`. Setup creates subdirectories under that root directory and copies Exchange files to those subdirectories. Table 3.2 is a listing of the default Exchange subdirectories under the root and the type of files in those subdirectories.

TABLE 3.2 Default Exchange Directories and Their Contents

Folder	Contents
`ADDRESS`	This directory contains subdirectories with program files (DLLs) that can be used to generate foreign addresses for Exchange recipients. When an Exchange server uses a connector or gateway to create interoperability with a foreign system, the System Attendant component automatically generates a foreign address for each Exchange recipient. This foreign address, also referred to as a proxy address or simply an e-mail address, is what the users of the foreign mail system see and where they send mail. The program files in the subdirectories can generate these proxy addresses. The complete installation downloads files for the following foreign mail systems: Lotus cc:Mail, Microsoft Mail, Novell GroupWise, Lotus Notes, Internet mail (SMTP), and X.400 mail.
`BIN`	This directory contains many of the files that are the components and services of Microsoft Exchange Server.
`CONNDATA`	This directory contains subdirectories that hold the files that are the Microsoft connectors. The complete installation downloads files for the following connectors: the Microsoft GroupWise Connector, the Microsoft Schedule+ Free/Busy Connector, and the Lotus Notes Connector.
`ExchangeServer_`*`computername`*	This directory is named using the NetBIOS name of the computer and holds miscellaneous files for global Exchange support.
`exchweb`	This directory holds files for Outlook Web Access.
`Computername.log`	This directory holds log files for message tracking.
`Mailroot`	This directory holds working directories for message transfer.

TABLE 3.2 Default Exchange Directories and Their Contents *(continued)*

Folder	Contents
MDBDATA	This directory is one of the most important on your server, because it contains the Information Store database. This database is composed of the following files: the Private Information Stores (EDB and STM), which are the server-based storage of mailboxes; the Public Information Stores (EDB and STM), which are the server-based storage of public folder data; and the database transaction log files (LOG), which are the files to which data is initially written in order to provide for faster performance and fault tolerance.
MTADATA	This directory holds the files that make up and relate to the Message Transfer Agent (MTA).
OMA	This directory holds files for Outlook Mobile Access.
RES	This directory holds files that contain message strings used when Exchange logs events to the Windows Event Log.
SCHEMA	This directory holds the XML files that support the Exchange extension of the Active Directory Schema.
SRSDATA	This directory holds Site Replication Service–related data.

Share Points and Permissions for Exchange Directories

Table 3.3 lists the Exchange directories that are shared on the network, with the specified share names and permissions, assuming that Exchange was installed on the C: drive.

TABLE 3.3 Microsoft Exchange Network Shares and Permissions

Folder	Shared As	Permissions
C:\EXCHSRVR\ADDRESS	Address	Administrators group: Full Control Everyone group: Read
C:\EXCHSRVR\RES	Resource$	Administrators group: Full Control Everyone group: Read
C:\EXCHSRVR\ *COMPUTERNAME.LOG*	*COMPUTERNAME.LOG*	Administrators group: Full Control

Exchange Entries in the Windows Registry

During installation, Setup creates entries in the Windows Registry. Some of these entries are mentioned here.

Registry information about the presence of the Exchange application on a machine, as well as the directory location of the installation, is found in the following Registry location:

```
HKEY_LOCAL_MACHINE
   \SOFTWARE
      \Microsoft
         \Exchange
            \Setup
```

The following Registry location records the settings for the various Event Logs created by the different Exchange components:

```
HKEY_LOCAL_MACHINE
   \SYSTEM
      \CurrentControlSet
         \Services
            \EventLog
               \Application
                  \<Exchange components>
```

The Exchange component settings are stored in the Registry at the following location:

```
\HKEY_LOCAL_MACHINE
   \SYSTEM
      \CurrentControlSet
         \Services
            \<Exchange component>
```

License settings for Exchange are stored in the following location:

```
\HKEY_LOCAL_MACHINE
   \SYSTEM
      \CurrentControlSet
         \Services
            \LicenseInfo
               \MSExchangeIS
```

Although these Registry locations are good to know, don't expect to be tested on them during your exam.

Exchange System Manager

One powerful feature of Microsoft Exchange is the ability to centrally administer an entire Exchange organization. This is accomplished through a snap-in for the Microsoft Management Console named *Exchange System Manager* (see Figure 3.2). This snap-in can run on any Windows 2000, Windows XP Professional, or Windows Server 2003 computer on the Exchange network. From this single point, an administrator can administer all the Exchange servers in an organization. This is sometimes referred to as single-seat administration.

FIGURE 3.2 The Exchange System Manager

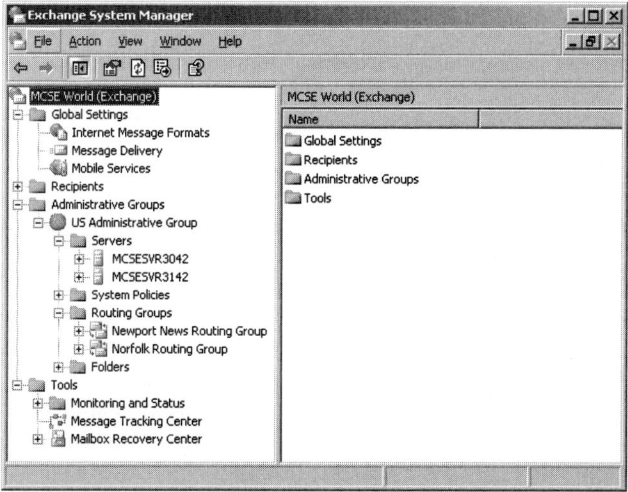

The actual snap-in file for System Manager is `Exchange System Manager.msc` and is stored in the `\EXCHSRVR\BIN` directory. While the Exchange Setup program can install the snap-in on the Exchange Server machine, the administrator will probably also want the Exchange System Manager on their workstation. Installing the Exchange System Manager onto a computer also installs a new version of the Windows Backup utility and extensions to the Active Directory Users and Computers and Performance Monitor programs. These changes enable those programs to work with Exchange Server 2003.

Deploying Exchange Server 2003 in a Large Organization

You are the lead network administrator for a large manufacturing corporation that has 45 geographical locations within North America. In the past, your company has never had a real company-wide network that spanned all locations and linked all users and resources together. You have just completed the installation of a new Windows Server 2003 Active Directory network that provides one unified network to all users and all locations within your organization.

Your network consists of a single Active Directory forest and five domains under the root domain named canada.manufacturing.com, mexico.manufacturing.com, west.manufacturing.com, central.manufacturing.com, and east.manufacturing.com.

The root domain of manufacturing.com contains no user accounts or member servers. You have two assistant administrators for each of the five child domains that have Domain Admins permissions for their applicable child domain. Only your user account has the Enterprise Admins and Schema Admins permissions configured. As well, only your user account has the Domain Admins permissions for the root domain. You have local administrative access on the servers in the root domain, and your assistant administrators have local administrative access on all computers and servers in their child domain. Your office is located within the east.manufacturing.com child domain.

To facilitate the process of installing Exchange Server 2003 on six Windows Server 2003 computers in each child domain, you have provided network shares in each child domain that contain the installation source files. As well, you have run the ForestPrep portion of the Exchange Setup program to extend the Active Directory Schema to support the installation of Exchange Server 2003.

After ForestPrep has been run, your domain user account now has Exchange Full Administrator permissions. In order to allow your assistant administrators to perform the installation of Exchange Server 2003 in their respective domains, you will need to delegate the Full Administrator permissions to their domain user accounts. Before you can perform this delegation, however, you must install the first Exchange Server 2003 computer in one of the child domains. In order to perform this installation, you instruct one of the assistant network administrators in the east.manufacturing.com domain to run the DomainPrep command to prepare that domain for the installation of Exchange Server 2003. After DomainPrep has been run, you can install the first Exchange Server 2003 computer and delegate the Exchange Full Administrator permission to the rest of your assistant administrators. You may, however, want to consider installing the Exchange System Manager first to create and customize your Administrative Group and Routing Group structure for the Exchange organization.

Once your assistant administrators have been delegated the Exchange Full Administrator permission, they may begin to install the 29 other Exchange Server 2003 computers using the installation source files located on their local network shares. As you can see, the Exchange installation process can be quite lengthy and complicated in a large network environment; however, careful planning and execution can lead to first-time success.

Troubleshooting an Exchange Installation

If any problems arise during an Exchange installation, there are several areas you may want to investigate first. Should you run into installation problems, you should begin your troubleshooting efforts by checking the following:

Make sure that you have installed Internet Information Services (IIS) and the necessary protocol support. IIS is no longer automatically installed on a clean installation of Windows Server 2003. You will need to install IIS and the required services and components of IIS as discussed earlier in this chapter.

Make sure that you have installed Windows 2000 Service Pack 3. Installing Exchange Server 2003 on a Windows 2000 Server computer requires that Windows 2000 Service Pack 3 or later has been installed first. Without SP3 or later installed, the installation of Exchange Server 2003 will fail.

Determine that you have the appropriate permissions to install the software. In order to install Exchange Server 2003, you must have local Administrators permission on the server on which you want to install. In order to run the ForestPrep tool, you must be a member of the Enterprise Admins and Schema Admins groups and the local Administrators group on the computer on which you run the utility. In order to run DomainPrep, you must be a member of the Domain Admins group and the local Administrators group on the computer on which you run the utility.

Verify that you have properly prepared the forest and domain. In order to install Exchange Server 2003 in all but the simplest single-domain situation, the ForestPrep tool may need to be run once in the forest, and the DomainPrep tool may need to be run in each domain in which Exchange Server 2003 will be installed.

Make sure that you have established share permissions. Make sure the necessary Exchange directories are shared if other servers are having problems connecting to the Exchange server after installation.

Observe the Exchange Server boot process for alert messages and to ensure that all necessary services have been started. If there are any problems with the Exchange server boot process, alert messages can be sent to the console and/or written to the Windows Event Log. You may also want to check that all the necessary Exchange services have been started. This can be done by going to Administrative Tools and Services or to a command prompt and executing `NET START`. Some Exchange services are dependent on other Windows services being started. If the dependent service is not started, the Exchange service will not start.

Use the Setup Log to determine problems that the Exchange Setup program may have logged. While Setup is running, it creates a log of what it is attempting. This log file, called `Exchange Server Setup Progress.log`, is stored in the root directory of the drive on which Exchange is installed. If you run into problems during installation, the log file can help you find out what part of the installation failed or, at least, where in the installation process the failure occurred.

Summary

Although installing Microsoft Exchange Server is a straightforward process, there are still some important concepts for you to understand. One of the most important phases of an installation is pre-installation. Before starting the actual installation, you must make sure that the minimum requirements for Exchange are met. You must obtain the proper licenses to ensure compliance with legal issues. Because Exchange utilizes user accounts from Active Directory, Exchange Server 2003 is tightly integrated with Active Directory. Before Exchange can be installed, you will need to ensure that the required IIS services and components are installed and running. To avoid problems during the setup process, you should use the DCDiag and NetDiag tools to test your network's connectivity. Finally, you must prepare the Active Directory forest by running ForestPrep (or by having someone with the appropriate permissions do so) and prepare each domain that will host Exchange Server 2003 by running DomainPrep.

Exchange installation happens in one of four contexts: as the first server in an organization, as a subsequent server, as an upgrade, or for a coexistence/migration. During the first or a subsequent installation, you will select the various components that make up an Exchange server. Upgrades can be performed from Exchange Server 2003 Service Pack 3 computers that are operating in Exchange native mode. If Exchange Server 5.5 is being used in your organization, you will need to coexist with and/or migrate to Exchange Server 2003. There are three types of installation options:

Typical This option installs the Exchange Server software, the basic Messaging and Collaboration components, and the System Manager snap-in program. It does not include the additional connectors.

Custom This option lets you choose exactly which components should be installed.

Minimum This option installs only the Exchange Server software and the basic Messaging and Collaboration components.

After an Exchange Server installation, you should know the directory structure that Setup has created. The default directory name for the installation is `Program Files\Exchsrvr`. Setup also creates network shares and modifies the Windows Registry.

Exam Essentials

Understand ForestPrep and DomainPrep. If you're working in single-domain forest, you may likely never need to work with ForestPrep and DomainPrep. Even if this is case, you should not neglect to learn what these powerful setup tools do and what permissions are required to use them. Consider the example of a very large, geographically dispersed network where multiple administrators at various levels work together to manage and maintain the network—in this situation ForestPrep and DomainPrep are invaluable tools that can assist in getting Exchange Server 2003 installed by splitting the installation tasks up according to domain group permissions that have been assigned.

Remember which groups interact with Exchange. Several different domain and local groups interact with Exchange before, during, and after the installation of Exchange is complete. You should keep in mind the basic functions and responsibilities of each of these groups.

Know the limitations on upgrading from Exchange 2000 Server. Recall that Exchange Server 2003 does not support the following Exchange 2000 Server services and components; thus they must be removed before upgrading an Exchange 2000 Server computer:

- Microsoft Mobile Information Server components
- Exchange 2000 Conferencing Server
- The Instant Messaging service
- The Exchange Chat service
- The Key Management service
- The cc:Mail connector
- The MS Mail connector

Remember the requirements to install Exchange Server 2003. Exchange Server 2003 can be installed on a Windows Server 2003 computer or a Windows 2000 Server Service Pack 3 or later computer. All domain controllers and global catalog servers that the Exchange Server 2003 computer will communicate with must be at least Windows 2000 Server SP3. The hardware requirements listed previously in Table 3.1 are minimums and will likely yield the minimum acceptable performance if used in a production environment.

Review Questions

1. One of your company's locations contains an Exchange server with 25 users, each using Microsoft Outlook. You have purchased 25 Client Access Licenses. The company hires 10 new employees who will connect to the site remotely. Five of the new users will be using POP3 applications, and five will be using HTTP applications. How many additional Client Access Licenses must you purchase?

   A. 0

   B. 2

   C. 5

   D. 6

   E. 10

   F. 12

2. You are the Exchange administrator for a large network. You do not have the appropriate permissions to update the Active Directory Schema on your network, so you must get another administrator to do this before you can install Exchange Server 2003. To which of the following groups must that person belong in order to run the ForestPrep utility? (Choose all that apply.)

   A. Server Admins

   B. Domain Admins

   C. Schema Admins

   D. Enterprise Admins

3. You have two Exchange Server 2003 computers that provide all messaging access for your 250 network users. If all 250 of your users connect to the Exchange server using Office Outlook 2003 and Outlook Web Access, how many CALs do you need to have?

   A. 1

   B. 2

   C. 250

   D. 500

4. Your company is running a messaging system that consists of four Exchange 2000 Servers running on Windows 2000 Advanced Server. Which of the following steps must you take in order to upgrade all of your servers to Exchange Server 2003? (Choose all that apply.)

   A. Upgrade all servers to Windows 2000 Server Service Pack 3.

   B. Upgrade all servers to Exchange 2000 Server Service Pack 2.

   C. Upgrade all servers to Windows 2000 Server Service Pack 2.

   D. Install the Active Directory Connector on all servers.

   E. Install Windows Server 2003 on all servers.

   F. Upgrade all servers to Exchange 2000 Server Service Pack 3.

   G. Place all Exchange 2000 Servers in Exchange native mode.

5. You have four computers on which you are considering installing Exchange Server 2003 as a testing environment. Which of the following systems would you have to upgrade before installing Exchange Server 2003? (Choose all that apply.)

   A. Pentium 90 MHz, 256 MB RAM, 750 MB disk space

   B. Pentium II 450 MHz, 256 MB RAM, 2500 MB disk space

   C. Pentium III 933 MHz, 256 MB RAM, 1000 MB disk space

   D. Pentium II 400, 512 MB RAM, 250 MB disk space

6. You have just finished an installation of Exchange Server 2003 and have restarted the computer. When the computer restarts, you get a message saying that several services were unable to start. You verify this fact using the Event Viewer and then determine that none of the Exchange services are running. Which file would you use to see the details of the Exchange installation?

   A. `Exchange Server Setup Progress.txt`

   B. `Exchange Server Setup Progress.log`

   C. `Exchange Server Setup Log.txt`

   D. `Exchange Server Error.log`

7. Your network consists of a single Active Directory forest with three domains: one root domain and two child domains. If Exchange Server is to be installed in only one of the two child domains and not at all in the root domain, how many times must you run the ForestPrep tool?

   A. None

   B. One time

   C. Two times

   D. Three times

8. You are configuring a custom Microsoft Management Console snap-in for an assistant administrator who will be taking care of certain Exchange tasks for you. You would like to configure the System Manager snap-in so that the assistant can run it on their personal workstation instead of giving them access to the Exchange server. What file from the Exchange server would you need to install on the workstation?

   A. `\EXCHSRVR\BIN\Exchange System Manager.msc`

   B. `\EXCHSRVR\BIN\System Manager.mmc`

   C. `\EXCHSRVR\Exchange System Manager.msc`

   D. `\EXCHSRVR\BIN\Exchadmin.msc`

9. Your network consists of a single Active Directory forest with three domains: one root domain and two child domains. If Exchange Server is to be installed in only one of the two child domains and not at all in the root domain, how many times (minimum) must you run the DomainPrep tool?

   A. None

   B. One time

   C. Two times

   D. Three times

10. You are the network administrator for a large importing company. You are preparing to implement a new Exchange Server 2003 organization for your corporate network. You would like to be able to organize your Exchange organization before installing the first actual Exchange Server 2003 computer. Which of the following steps are required to allow you to perform this task? (Choose all that apply.)

    A. Run the ForestPrep tool.

    B. Install the Exchange System Manager.

    C. Run the DomainPrep tool in all domains.

    D. Install the Windows Server 2003 support tools.

    E. Run the DomainPrep tool in the root domain of the forest.

11. Your Windows Active Directory forest consists of a single domain tree. That tree consists of a single root-level domain and four child domains of that root domain. You are about to prepare the root-level domain for an Exchange Server 2003 installation. Which of the following commands would you use?

    A. `forestprep.exe`

    B. `forestprep.exe /setup`

    C. `setup.exe /domainprep`

    D. `setup.exe /domain`

12. Which of the following features are included in a Typical setup of Exchange Server 2003? (Choose all that apply.)

 A. Exchange System Manager

 B. The Novell GroupWise connector

 C. The core Messaging and Collaboration Services files

 D. The Exchange 5.5 Administrator

13. You are preparing to install Exchange Server 2003 on a computer running Windows 2000 Server Service Pack 4. Which of the following components of Internet Information Services should you make sure are installed prior to installing Exchange Server 2003? (Choose all that apply.)

 A. SMTP

 B. WWW

 C. FTP

 D. NNTP

14. You are planning to create a Windows 2000 cluster on which to install Exchange Server 2003. Which of the following is a requirement for Exchange Server 2003 to work with the Microsoft Clustering Service? (Choose all that apply.)

 A. The purchase of a 1,000-user license

 B. Microsoft Windows 2000 Advanced Server or Datacenter Server

 C. The purchase of the optional Windows 2000 Clustering Server

 D. The Enterprise Edition of Exchange Server 2003

15. You are preparing to upgrade an Exchange 2000 Server computer to Exchange Server 2003. Which of the following conditions must be met before this upgrade can take place? (Choose all that apply.)

 A. The server must be running Windows Server 2003.

 B. The Exchange Key Management service must be removed.

 C. The Exchange Chat service must be removed.

 D. The SMTP Service must be removed.

16. What is different about installing the second and subsequent Exchange Server 2003 computers into an existing Exchange organization as compared to the installation of the first Exchange Server 2003 computer? (Choose all that apply.)

 A. You will not be asked for your 25-digit CD key.

 B. You will be able to select the administrative group that the server should be a part of.

 C. You will be able to select the routing group that the server should be a part of.

 D. You will be able to designate additional Exchange Full Administrators.

17. Your Windows Active Directory forest consists of a single domain tree. That tree consists of a single root-level domain and 14 child domains of that root domain. You are about to prepare the forest itself for an Exchange Server 2003 installation. Which of the following commands would you use?

    A. `setup.exe /forest`

    B. `forestprep.exe /setup`

    C. `forestprep.exe`

    D. `setup.exe /forestprep`

18. You have been directed to create an Active/Passive cluster of four Exchange Server 2003 computers. Which operating systems will you be able to use on the servers to perform this task? (Choose all that apply.)

    A. Windows Server 2003

    B. Windows 2000 Advanced Server

    C. Windows Server 2003 Enterprise Edition

    D. Windows 2000 Datacenter Server

19. Exchange Server 2003 supports which of the following types of clustering? (Choose all that apply.)

    A. Active/Active

    B. Active/Passive

    C. Passive/Passive

    D. Unified

20. With which of the following resources must each resource group in a cluster running Exchange Server 2003 be configured? (Choose all that apply.)

    A. IP address

    B. A physical disk drive

    C. Exchange System Attendant Service

    D. Exchange Message Transfer Agent Service

    E. System Manager Console

Answers to Review Questions

1. E. Every user who connects to the Exchange server will need a Client Access License, no matter what client software is used to connect.

2. C, D. In order to run the DomainPrep utility, a user must belong to both the Schema Admins and Enterprise Admins global groups. The user must also belong to the local Administrators group on the computer on which the utility is actually run.

3. C. Exchange Server 2003 is licensed in the per-seat mode, meaning that each client that accesses the server must have a valid CAL. Since you have a total of 250 clients, you need to have 250 CALs for your organization, even if the clients access the Exchange server in more than one way, such as Outlook or Outlook Web Access.

4. A, F, G. In order to upgrade Exchange 2000 Server computers to Exchange Server 2003 computers, the Exchange organization must be operating in Exchange native mode. In addition, all Windows 2000 Server installations and Exchange 2000 Server installations must be updated with Windows 2000 Service Pack 2 and Exchange 2000 Server Service Pack 3, respectively. There is no need to upgrade to or install Windows Server 2003 on the computers for the upgrade as long as all domain controllers and global catalog servers are running Windows 2000 Server SP3 at the minimum. The Active Directory Connector is used for coexistence with and migration from Exchange Server 5.5.

5. A, D. Exchange Server requires a minimum of a Pentium 133 MHz processor, 256 MB RAM, and 500 MB of disk space available on the Exchange drive (with 200 MB available on the system drive).

6. B. While Setup is running, it creates a log of what it is attempting. This log file, called `Exchange Server Setup Progress.log`, is stored in the root directory of the drive on which Exchange is installed.

7. B. You must run the ForestPrep tool one time, and one time only, for each Active Directory forest that will have Exchange Server 2003 installed into it.

8. A. The actual snap-in file for System Manager is `Exchange System Manager.msc` and is stored in the `\EXCHSRVR\BIN` directory.

9. C. Once the Windows Active Directory forest is prepared using ForestPrep, each domain in the forest that will run Exchange Server 2003 must also be prepared using DomainPrep. In addition, the forest root domain and each domain that will contain Exchange Server 2003 mailbox-enabled objects or that has users or groups that will manage Exchange Server 2003 computers must have DomainPrep run in it.

10. A, B, E. By running the ForestPrep and DomainPrep tools on the root domain, you can install the Exchange System Manager and create administrative groups and routing groups before the first Exchange Server 2003 computer is ever installed. This allows you to create the organization ahead of time and then simply install your Exchange servers and place them as desired, saving time and headache later.

11. C. Use DomainPrep to prepare each domain in which Exchange will be installed. The tool is run using the `/domainprep` switch for the `setup.exe` program.

12. A, C. A Typical installation installs the Messaging and Collaboration Services and the System Management Tools components but none of their subcomponents. You can install connectors or the Exchange 5.5 Administrator using a Custom installation.

13. A, B, D. The NNTP Service, the SMTP Service, and the World Wide Web Service must be installed before attempting to install Exchange Server 2003. If these protocols are not installed, the Exchange Setup program will terminate.

14. B, D. The Enterprise Edition of Exchange Server 2003 is designed to work with the Microsoft Clustering Service that is available in Windows 2000 Advanced Server, Windows 2000 Datacenter Server, Windows Server 2003 Enterprise Edition, and Windows Server 2003 Datacenter Edition.

15. B, C. Exchange Server 2003 does not support the following Exchange 2000 Server services and components, thus they must be removed before upgrading an Exchange 2000 Server computer:

    - Microsoft Mobile Information Server components
    - Exchange 2000 Conferencing Server
    - The Instant Messaging service
    - The Exchange Chat service
    - The Key Management service
    - The cc:Mail connector
    - The MS Mail connector

    There is no need to upgrade the server to Windows Server 2003; however, you will need to ensure that the server is updated to at least Windows Server 2000 Service Pack 3. The SMTP Service is required by Exchange Server 2003, as well as Exchange 2000 Server, for proper operation.

16. B, C. The process of adding a subsequent Exchange server to an existing organization is nearly identical to installing the first server. The only difference is when you have defined more than one administrative or routing group in your organization. In this case, you will see two extra dialog boxes while using the Installation Wizard. The first lets you choose the administrative group you want the new server to be a part of. The second dialog box lets you choose a routing group within the chosen administrative group that the server should be a part of. If you have not configured more than one administrative or routing group, you will see neither of these screens, and the installation will be identical to installing the first server.

17. D. Use ForestPrep to prepare the forest by extending the Active Directory Schema for Exchange Server. The tool is run using the `/forestprep` switch for the `setup.exe` program.

18. C, D. In order to run Exchange with Microsoft Clustering Service, you must be running Windows Server 2003 Enterprise Edition, Windows Server 2003 Datacenter Edition, Windows 2000 Advanced Server, or Windows 2000 Datacenter Server. The number of nodes you can have in the Exchange Server 2003 cluster is limited by the operating system the server is running:

- You are limited to two nodes when installing on Windows 2000 Advanced Server SP4.
- You are limited to four nodes when installing on Windows 2000 Datacenter Server SP4.
- You can have up to eight nodes when installing on Windows Server 2003 Enterprise Edition or Windows Server 2003 Datacenter Server Edition.

19. A, B. Exchange 5.5 supported only Active/Passive clustering, in which only one node of a cluster was active at a time. Exchange 2000 Server supported only Active/Active clustering, in which all nodes functioned simultaneously. Exchange Server 2003 supports both types of clustering and allows for up to eight cluster nodes when using Windows Server 2003 Enterprise Edition or Windows Server 2003 Datacenter Edition.

20. A, B, C. Each resource group in a cluster running Exchange must contain an IP address, a network name, a physical disk drive, and the Exchange System Attendant Service.

Chapter 4

Creating and Managing Exchange Clusters

MICROSOFT EXAM OBJECTIVES COVERED IN THIS CHAPTER:

- ✓ **Install, configure, and troubleshoot Exchange Server 2003 in a clustered environment**
- ✓ **Manage, monitor, and troubleshoot Exchange Server clusters**
- ✓ **Manage and troubleshoot front-end and back-end servers**
- ✓ **Manage and troubleshoot virtual servers**

In smaller organizations, you might have an Exchange organization consisting of one or two Exchange servers that have mailboxes split across them. Should one of your Exchange servers stop functioning, the users with mailboxes on the affected server are unable to access their mailboxes until you either correct the problem or restore the latest backup set to another server and place it in operation as a replacement server. This type of downtime might be acceptable in organizations with very small budgets or where e-mail is not considered a mission-critical service. But what about those organizations that rely on e-mail as a mission-critical service and cannot tolerate these types of outages? In cases such as this, Exchange can be installed in clusters. A cluster is a collection of independent servers that work together as a large collective group, providing redundancy and reliability in the event that an operating server should stop responding to client requests or otherwise experience a failure.

In this chapter, we will examine the types of clustering available in Exchange Server 2003, the process of creating and managing Exchange clusters, and also configuring Exchange servers in a front-end/back-end arrangement.

Clustering Concepts

Clustering is not a feature of Exchange Server 2003 itself but instead a feature provided by the operating system: Windows 2000 Server or Windows Server 2003. Exchange, however, is clustering aware, meaning that it can recognize that is being installed into a cluster and will configure itself appropriately during the installation to support operation in this environment. Before we get any further into working with Exchange clusters, we need to first step back and examine the types of clustering available in Windows Server 2003 and then discuss basic clustering models and terminology. This will lead the way into creating and managing Exchange clusters later in this chapter.

Clustering Methods

Windows Server 2003 provides support for two different clustering methods: Network Load Balancing and the Microsoft Clustering Service. Each of these methods has different purposes and, as you might expect, different hardware requirements.

Network Load Balancing

Network Load Balancing (NLB) is the simpler of the two clustering methods to understand, and thus we will examine it first. Network Load Balancing is installed on all participating members as an additional network interface driver that uses a mathematical algorithm to equally distribute incoming requests to all members of the NLB cluster. Other than having two network interfaces installed in each NLB cluster member, there are no special hardware requirements to implement Network Load Balancing. Incoming client requests are assigned to cluster members based on their current loading level but can be modified through the use of filtering and an affinity for applications that require session state data to be maintained, such as an e-commerce application that uses cookies to place items in a shopping cart for purchase.

Having two network interfaces installed is actually more of a "best practice" than a requirement. It is possible, but not recommended, to install and operate a Network Load Balancing cluster using only one network interface per server.

The members of the NLB cluster are kept aware of one another's existence (and thus their operational state) by the use of a special communication among members that is referred to as a *heartbeat*. If a cluster member stops sending out heartbeat messages for a specified period of time, it is assumed to no longer be responding to client requests, and thus a process known as *convergence* occurs. During the process of convergence, the remaining cluster members determine who is still available and distribute incoming requests accordingly. In Network Load Balancing, heartbeats are used only to track whether a server is responding to the heartbeat—it may not be able to respond to client requests, but if it still sends out a heartbeat, the cluster will consider it active and available.

Because all members of an NLB cluster are considered to be equal to one another, a client's initial connection may be made to any available cluster member. This sort of arrangement works very well for services such as websites, FTP servers, and VPN servers but does not work well when clients must connect to a specific Exchange server that hosts their mailboxes. Members of NLB clusters do not require any specialized storage devices, nor do they need to be members of a domain in order to be configured as part of the NLB cluster. Windows Server 2003 provides for up to 32 nodes in a Network Load Balancing cluster. Exchange Server 2003, however, does not support operation on a Network Load Balancing cluster.

So if Exchange Server 2003 cannot be installed onto an NLB cluster, why even discuss it here? The answer is simple. Even though you cannot install Exchange itself onto a Network Load Balancing cluster, you will likely use NLB clusters to implement your front-end Outlook Web Access servers that run IIS and Exchange. We will examine this topic more fully later in the chapter.

Microsoft Clustering Service

The *Microsoft Clustering Service* (MSCS) is the second clustering method available in Windows Server 2003, and it is the only one that Exchange Server 2003 supports. MSCS provides for highly available server solutions through a process known as *failover*. An MSCS cluster consists of two more nodes (members) that are configured such that upon the failure of one node, any of the remaining cluster nodes can transfer the failed node's resources to itself, thus keeping the resources available for client access. During this time, clients will see little, if any, interruption in service as the resources failover from the nonresponsive node to a remaining functional node.

Much the same as Network Load Balanced clusters, MSCS clusters rely on a heartbeat to keep all cluster members apprised of the current status of every other member. Unlike Network Load Balancing, however, the Microsoft Clustering Service is service aware, meaning that it can monitor individual services on a member, not just the member as an overall entity. You will see how this comes into play when we examine creating Exchange virtual servers later in this chapter. Also, unlike Network Load Balancing, clustering using MSCS has very high hardware requirements, including the use of a shared storage device to which all nodes have equal access. Clustering using MSCS is especially useful in applications that use large database files, such as Exchange Server or SQL Server, where it is impossible for more than one node to have the database open at a time. Hence, when a member of an MSCS cluster fails, the resources on that failed member are immediately transferred to another (operating) member of the cluster through the failover process.

Clusters using the Microsoft Clustering Service can be created in one of two clustering modes: Active/Active and Active/Passive. When using Exchange Server 2003 on Windows Server 2003 Enterprise Edition or Datacenter Edition, you can create up to eight-node Active/Passive clusters. When creating an Active/Active Exchange Server 2003 cluster, you can have only two nodes. We will examine these two clustering modes shortly, but before we get to that we need to examine some basic clustering terminology that will make the rest of this discussion easier to follow.

Active/Passive clustering in Exchange Server 2003 is limited to two nodes when installing on Windows 2000 Advanced Server Service Pack 4, four nodes when installing on Windows 2000 Datacenter Server Service Pack 4, and eight nodes when installing on Windows Server 2003 or Windows Server 2003 Datacenter Server Edition.

Clustering Terminology

It seems that everything related to the field of information technology has its own special set of acronyms and buzzwords that you must understand in order to work with, and discuss, the specific technology at hand. Clustering is no different, and it is perhaps one of the more esoteric fields when it comes to terms you must understand. A thorough understanding of the following basic clustering terms will serve you well through the rest of this chapter and in your duties as an Exchange administrator. It probably won't hurt too much for the exam experience either.

Cluster A *cluster* is a group of two or more servers that act together as a single, larger resource.

Cluster resource A *cluster resource* is a service or property, such as a storage device, an IP address, or the Exchange System Attendant service, that is defined, monitored, and managed by the cluster service.

Virtual server A *virtual server* is an instance of the application running on a cluster node (Exchange Server 2003 in this case) that uses a set of cluster resources. Virtual servers may also be referred to as cluster resource groups.

Failover Failover is the process of moving resources off a cluster node that has failed to another cluster node. If any of the cluster resources on an active node becomes unresponsive or unavailable for a period of time exceeding the configured threshold, failover will occur.

Failback *Failback* is the process of cluster resources moving back to their preferred node after the preferred node has resumed active membership in the cluster.

Node A *node* is an individual member of a cluster, otherwise referred to as a cluster node, cluster member, member, or cluster server.

Quorum disk A *quorum disk* is the disk set that contains definitive cluster configuration data. All members of an MSCS cluster must have continuous, reliable access to the data that is contained on a quorum disk. Information contained on the quorum disk includes data about the nodes that are participating in the cluster, the applications and resources that are defined within the cluster, and the current status of each member, application, and resource. Quorum disks represent one of the specialized hardware requirements of clusters and are typically placed on a large shared storage device.

Clustering Modes

Recall from our earlier discussion that clustering uses a group of between two and eight servers, all tied to a common shared storage device to create a highly available solution for clients. Clustering considers applications, services, IP addresses, and hardware devices to all be resources that it monitors to determine the health status of the cluster and its members. When a problem with a resource is first noted, the Microsoft Clustering Service will first attempt to correct the problem on that cluster node. An example of this might be attempting to restart a service that has stopped. If the problem with the resource cannot be corrected within a specific amount of time, the clustering service will fail the resource, take the affected virtual server offline, and then move it to another functioning node in the cluster. After the move, the clustering service will restart the virtual server so that it can begin servicing client requests on the new node.

Windows Server 2003 and Exchange Server 2003 support two different clustering modes, as discussed next.

Active/Passive Clustering

When *Active/Passive clustering* is used, a cluster can contain between two and eight nodes. At least one node must be active and at least one node must be passive. You can have any other combination as well, such as a six-node Active/Passive cluster that has four active nodes and two passive nodes. The active nodes are online actively providing the clustered resources to clients. The passive nodes must sit idle, not being used to provide services of any kind to clients. Should an active node need to be failed, the clustering service can then transfer the virtual server from the failed node to the previously passive node. The passive node's operational state is changed to active, and it can now begin to service client requests for the clustered resource. Since any passive node may have to pick up the load of any active node, all active and passive nodes in the cluster should be configured identically both in hardware and software. As you will see in our discussion of Active/Active clustering next, the Active/Passive clustering mode is the preferred mode of operation for Exchange Server clusters.

One of the hardest selling points when it comes to Active/Passive clustering is that people often see the passive nodes as a wasteful expenditure. The passive nodes in an Active/Passive cluster cannot be used to provide any services to network clients while in their passive state. They must simply sit idly by and wait for the clustering service to failover one or more virtual servers to them.

Active/Active Clustering

When *Active/Active clustering* is used, each node in the cluster runs one instance of the clustered service. Should a failure of the clustered service occur, that instance is transferred to the other active node. Although you will be able to use both nodes of the cluster in Active/Active mode, you are limited in how many storage groups and Exchange mailboxes each node can host.

A single Exchange Server 2003 Enterprise Edition server is limited to a maximum of four storage groups. Should one of the nodes fail, the single remaining node will now have to be tasked with providing all of the storage from both of the nodes. If one node had three storage groups and the second node had two storage groups, one storage group would not be able to be started on the remaining operational node should one node fail. In addition to these restrictions, the nodes in an Active/Active cluster may have only 1,900 active mailboxes each, which is several thousand fewer than an Exchange server might typically be able to hold.

Cluster Models

After determining the cluster mode that you will use, you still have more choices ahead of you. The Microsoft Clustering Service offers you three different clustering models to choose from. The clustering model you choose dictates the storage requirements and configuration of your new cluster, so you will want to choose wisely and only after giving it adequate thought and planning. We will examine each of the three available models next.

In all reality, you will not be alone when it comes time to plan your hardware requirements and resources for a cluster. In most cases, your hardware vendor will have specific hardware and software packages to recommend depending on your needs and your budget. It is all but unheard of to create your own "white-box" cluster solutions; rather they typically come from a reputable vendor.

Single Node Cluster

The *single node cluster* is the simplest cluster model to implement. This model has one cluster node that uses either local storage or an external storage device, as depicted in Figure 4.1. Although this model does not offer all of the benefits of the single quorum cluster, discussed next, it should not be overlooked because it does still provide some benefits to the organization interested in clustering Exchange Server 2003.

FIGURE 4.1 The single node cluster

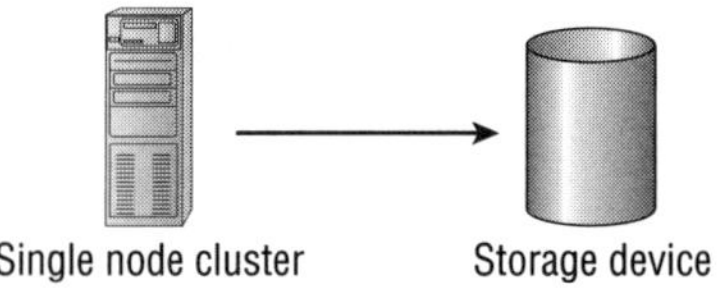

Although you'd never want to use a single node cluster model to provide highly available Exchange resources to clients, it can be used to develop and test cluster processes and procedures for an organization. The single node cluster still retains clustering ability to attempt to restart failed services; thus it mimics a production cluster in this way. You may also consider creating a single node cluster using an external storage device as a means to prestage for a larger cluster solution. You will simply need to join the additional nodes to the existing cluster and configure the desired policies for the cluster.

Don't expect to ever use a single node cluster except for testing and development purposes.

Single Quorum Cluster

The *single quorum cluster*, seen in Figure 4.2, is the standard clustering model that comes to mind when most people think of clustering. In the single quorum model, all nodes are attached to the external shared storage device. All cluster configuration data is kept on this storage device; thus all cluster nodes have access to the quorum data. The single quorum model is used to create Active/Active and Active/Passive clusters that are located in a single location, such as within a single server room.

FIGURE 4.2 The single quorum cluster

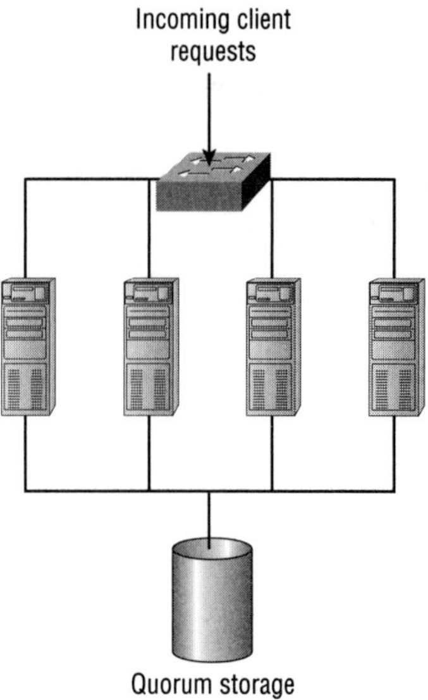

Majority Node Set Cluster

The *majority node set cluster* model, seen in Figure 4.3, is a new high-end clustering model first available in Windows Server 2003 that allows for two or more cluster nodes to be configured so that multiple storage devices can be used. The cluster configuration data is kept on all disks across the cluster, and the Microsoft Clustering Service is responsible for keeping this data up-to-date. Although this model has the advantage of being able to locate cluster nodes in different geographical locations, it is a very complex and costly model to implement.

FIGURE 4.3 The majority node set cluster

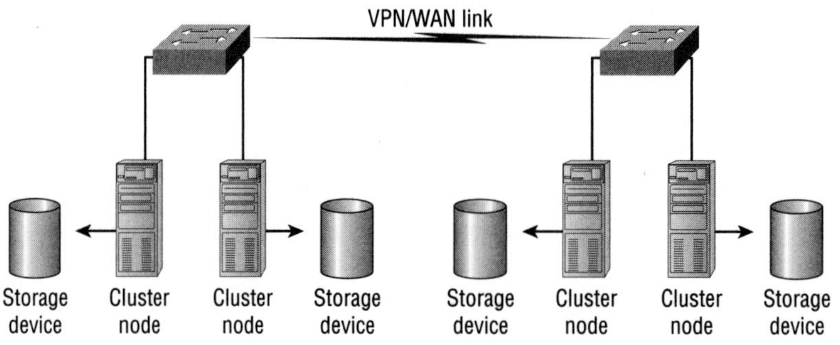

Majority node cluster sets are likely the future of advanced clustering; however, they are not right for everyone. A maximum of two well-connected (500 ms or less latency) sites can be used to create a majority node set. As well, Microsoft currently recommends that you implement majority node set clustering only in very specific instances and only with close support provided by your original equipment manufacturer, independent software vendor, or independent hardware vendor.

Don't get wrapped around the axle with the majority node set cluster—you're unlikely to ever see it on this exam or in use for an Exchange cluster.

Cluster Operation Modes

Having gotten this far into the discussion about clustering, there is one more item you must consider when preparing to implement a clustered solution: what mode of cluster operation you wish to use.

The modes apply only when you are using a single quorum cluster or a majority node set cluster.

When discussing cluster operation modes, you're really talking about how cluster nodes will react when a failover situation occurs, i.e., how the node will failover to an available cluster node. The four modes of cluster operation that you can choose from are the following:

We will discuss preferred owners and possible owners more when we configure virtual servers later in this chapter.

Failover pair When the *failover pair* is configured, resources are configured to failover between two specific cluster nodes. This is accomplished by listing only these two specific nodes in the Possible Owners list for the resources of concern. This mode of operation could be used in either Active/Active or Active/Passive clustering.

Hot standby When *hot standby* is configured, a passive node can take on the resources of any failed active node. Hot standby is really just another term for Active/Passive, as discussed earlier in this section. You configure for hot standby through a combination of using the Preferred Owners list and the Possible Owners list. The preferred node is configured in the Preferred Owners list and designated as the node that will run the application or service under normal conditions. The spare (hot standby) node is configured in the Possible Owners list. As an example, in a six-node Active/Passive cluster, two of the active nodes might point to one passive node as a possible owner and the other two active nodes might point to the other passive node as a possible owner.

Failover ring The *failover ring* mode, also referred to as Active/Active as discussed previously, has each node in the cluster running an instance of the application or resource being clustered. When one node fails, the clustered resource is moved to the next node in the sequence. In Exchange clusters, this mode of operation is not useful because these resources have nowhere else to failover to but the single remaining node in a two-node Active/Active cluster.

Random failover When *random failover* is configured, the clustered resource will be randomly failed over to an available cluster node. The random failover mode is configured by providing an empty Preferred Owners list for each virtual server.

Failover Policies

A failover policy is what the cluster service uses to determine how to react when a clustered resource is unavailable. A failover policy consists of three items:

- A list of preferred nodes. This list designates the order in which the resource should be failed over to other remaining nodes in the cluster.
- Failover threshold and timing. You can configure the clustering service to immediately failover the resource if the resource fails or to first attempt to restart it a specific number of times within a specified amount of time.
- Failback time constraints. Because it might not always be in your best interests to have resources failing back to their original nodes automatically, you can configure how and when failback is to occur.

Creating and Monitoring Exchange Clusters

The process to create any clustered resource, including an Exchange cluster, is a lengthy one, but one that can be completed effectively if you have prepared adequately ahead of time. The following list represents the basic, high-level steps that you must complete to create an Exchange Server 2003 cluster.

The remaining discussion in this chapter assumes that you will be creating a single quorum cluster, which is the most widely used type at the current time.

1. Procure the required servers and storage device, making sure that all hardware is listed on the Hardware Compatibility List, located at `www.microsoft.com/whdc/hcl/`.

2. Install and configure the hardware as directed by the hardware vendor.
3. Install Windows Server 2003 Enterprise Edition or Datacenter Edition on each server that will be part of the cluster.
4. Join all servers that will be part of the cluster to the domain.
5. Use the Windows Components Wizard to install the required services on each server, as discussed in Exercise 3.1.
6. Configure the servers to support the shared storage device per the hardware vendor's instructions.
7. Configure the two network interfaces in each server to connect to the two different networks required. One network interface in each server will be part of the private network that is used for administrative traffic among cluster nodes, including the heartbeat. The other network interface will be part of the publicly accessible network that will service incoming client requests. These two networks should be on different subnets and not connected to each other in any way. Figure 4.4 provides a simplified illustration of how this will look.
8. Prepare the Active Directory forest for the Exchange installation as discussed in Exercise 3.2.
9. Prepare the Active Directory domain into which the cluster will be installed, as well as any other domains that will have Exchange users or Exchange administrators, as discussed in Exercise 3.3.
10. Create a domain user account using Active Directory Users and Computers that will be used by the MSCS. The password on this account should be configured to never expire, although you can go back later and change the password as required by your organization's security policies. This account will be used when the cluster is created and will be given special cluster-related rights.

FIGURE 4.4 Two networks are used for a cluster.

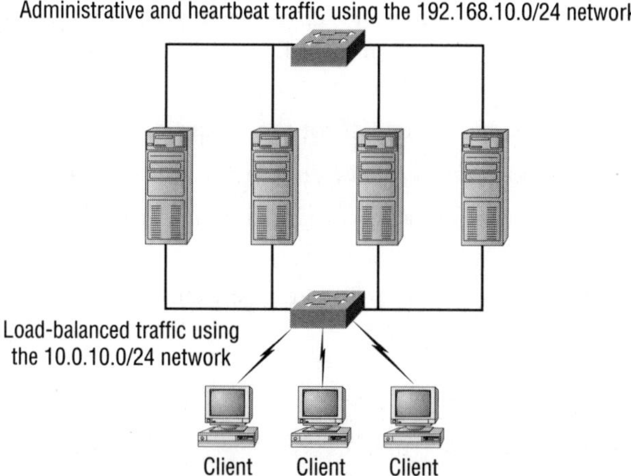

11. Verify that the cluster service is running on each server that will be a member of the cluster by opening the Cluster Administrator (located in the Administrative Tools folder). The cluster service must be operational before installing Exchange onto any server that will be a part of the cluster.
12. Create the first member of the cluster, as discussed later in Exercise 4.1.
13. Add the remaining servers to the cluster, as discussed later in Exercise 4.2.
14. Install the Microsoft Distributed Transaction Coordinator as a cluster resource, as discussed later in Exercise 4.3.
15. Completely install Exchange Server 2003 on the first node, as discussed in Exercise 3.4.
16. Grant the cluster service account you created in Step 10 the Exchange Full Administrator permission, as discussed later in Exercise 4.4.
17. Install Exchange Server 2003 on each of the remaining cluster nodes, as discussed previously in Exercise 3.4.
18. Create an Exchange virtual server on each active cluster node, as discussed later in Exercise 4.5.

With that high-level examination of the Exchange cluster creation process out of the way, we can now move forward into the more detailed subprocesses that are involved.

Creating a Cluster

Once you've gotten to this point, you've undoubtedly done your homework and are well prepared to create the cluster for your Exchange Server 2003 installation. As a last-minute checklist, be sure you have answers for the following questions:

- Which quorum model will you be using?
- Do you have a standard configuration and operating procedure for your shared storage device?
- Have you set aside the required IP addresses and hardware required to create the subnets for your private and public networks? (Each of these IP addresses should be statically configured.)
- Have you acquired the required static IP address for the cluster as a whole?
- Have you determined the NetBIOS cluster name? (This must be 15 characters or less.)
- Have you determined the failover and failback policies that you will need for your clustered resource?

Exercise 4.1 walks through the required steps to create a new cluster.

EXERCISE 4.1

Creating a New Cluster

1. On the first node, open the Cluster Administrator by selecting Start ➢ All Programs ➢ Administrative Tools ➢ Cluster Administrator. You should see the Open Connection to Cluster dialog box.

2. If you do not see this dialog box, click the File menu and select Open Connection.
3. From the Action drop-down, select Create New Cluster and then click OK. The New Server Cluster Wizard opens.
4. Click Next to dismiss the opening page of the New Server Cluster Wizard.
5. On the Cluster Name and Domain page, seen below, select the domain that the cluster will belong to. The default selection is the domain in which the cluster is located. You will also need to enter a NetBIOS-friendly cluster name in the Cluster Name box. Click Next.

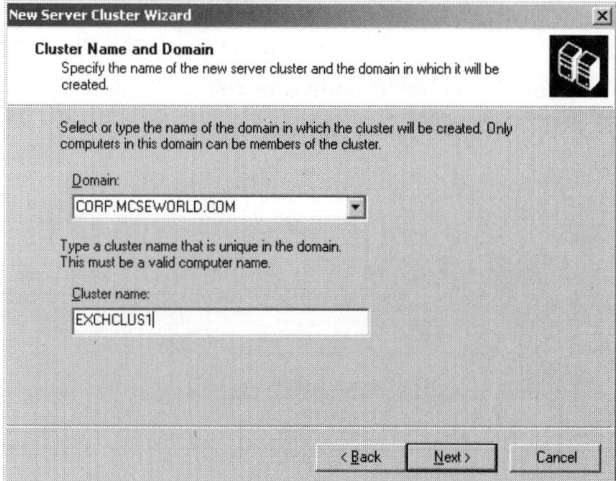

EXERCISE 4.1 *(continued)*

6. In the Select Computer page, seen below, select the server that will be the first node of the new cluster. By default, this is the computer on which you are performing the process. Click Next.

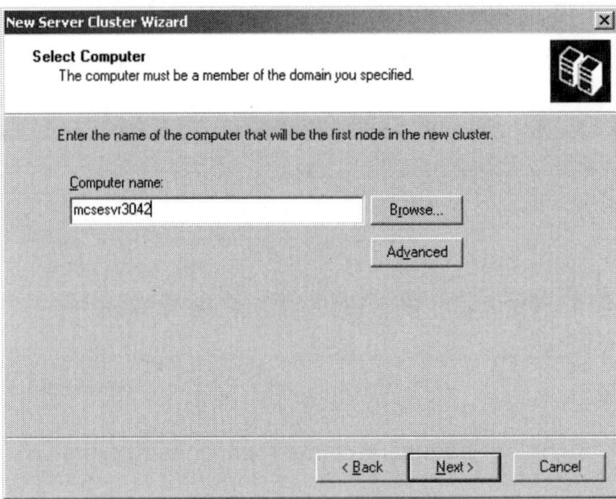

7. The Analyzing Configuration page will appear, and the analysis process will run for a short period of time. When the process is done you may see an output similar to that shown below. Cautions indicate areas you may wish to investigate and correct if required. Warnings prevent the creation of the cluster. Click Next after viewing the output.

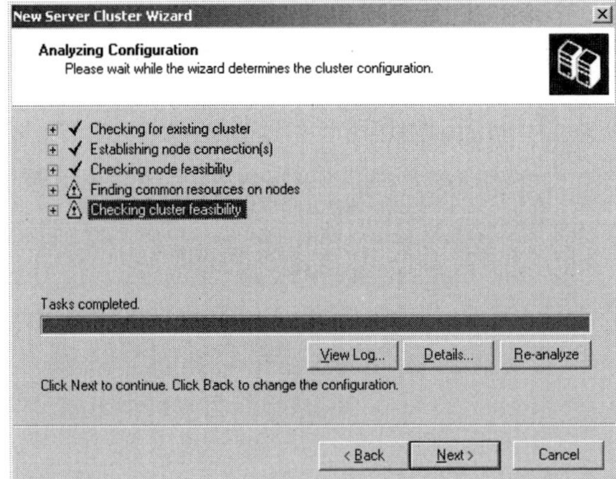

EXERCISE 4.1 *(continued)*

Note: The analysis results shown here are consistent with the cluster creation process on a server that does not have an external shared storage device.

8. On the IP Address page, enter the IP address that is being assigned to the cluster itself. Click Next.

9. On the Cluster Service Account page, enter the credentials for the domain user account that you created previously to act as the cluster service account. Click Next.

10. On the Proposed Cluster Configuration page, you will be able to review the proposed configuration. Clicking the Quorum button will allow you change the type of quorum being used, if applicable. Click Next to create the cluster.

11. Click Finish to complete the New Server Cluster Wizard. You will see your new single node cluster in the Cluster Administrator.

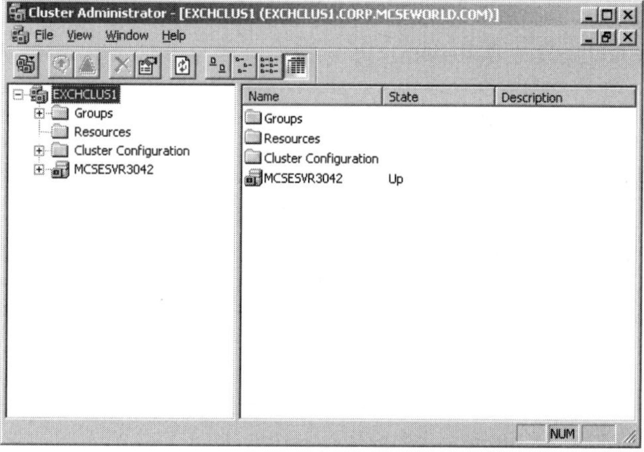

That's all there is to creating a new cluster and the first node in the cluster. Congratulations! Now it's time to move on to adding additional nodes to the cluster. Exercise 4.2 shows the required steps to add a new node to an existing cluster.

EXERCISE 4.2

Adding Nodes to an Existing Cluster

1. If it is not already open, open the Cluster Administrator. If the cluster does not appear in the Cluster Administrator, choose File ➢ Open Connection and supply the required information to connect to the cluster.

2. Right-click the cluster name in the Cluster Administrator and select New ➢ Node from the context menu.

3. Click Next to dismiss the opening page of the Add Nodes Wizard.

4. On the Select Computers page, seen below, enter the names of the rest of the servers that are to be added to the cluster. Click Next.

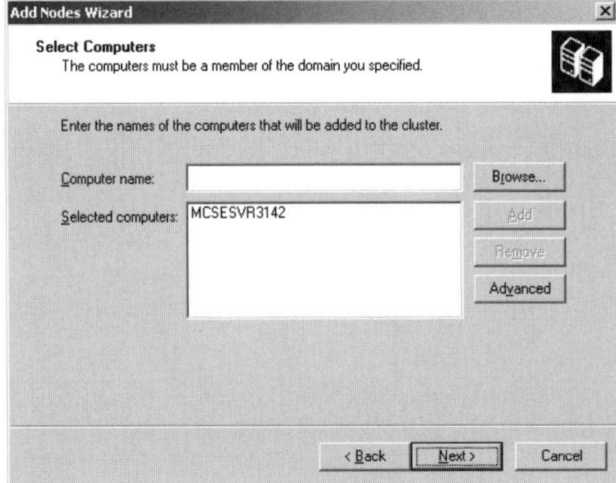

5. The Analyzing Configuration page will appear, and the analysis process will run for a short period of time. Click Next after viewing the output.

6. On the Cluster Service Account page, enter the credentials for the domain user account that you created previously to act as the cluster service account. Click Next.

7. On the Proposed Cluster Configuration page, you will be able to review the proposed configuration. Click Next.

8. The Adding Nodes to the Cluster dialog box appears, detailing the status of the node addition. Click Next.

9. Click Finish to complete the Add Nodes Wizard.

Configuring the Exchange Cluster

After the cluster has been created and all nodes added, you are ready to begin installing Exchange Server 2003 on all nodes. Before you can do this, however, you must install the Microsoft Distributed Transaction Coordinator. Exercise 4.3 outlines the required steps to install the MSDTC.

EXERCISE 4.3

Installing the Microsoft Distributed Transaction Coordinator

1. If it is not already open, open the Cluster Administrator. If the cluster does not appear in the Cluster Administrator, choose File ➢ Open Connection and supply the required information to connect to the cluster.

2. Expand the Groups container and right-click the Cluster Group item. Select New ➢ Resource from the context menu.

3. The New Resource dialog box opens, as seen below. Enter a name and description for the new resource. Select Distributed Transaction Coordinator from the Resource Type drop-down list and click Next.

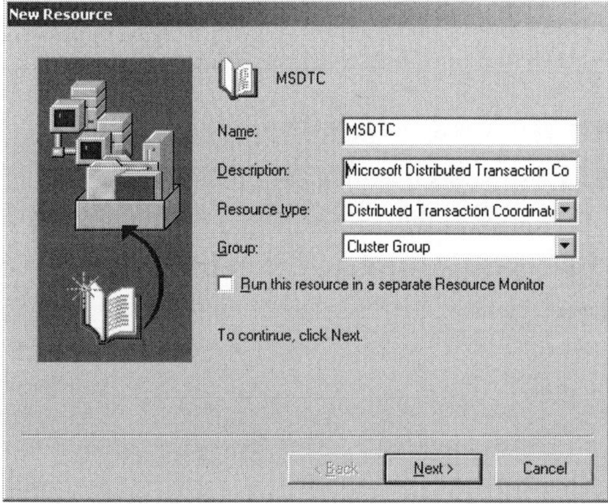

4. On the Possible Owners page, select the first server in the node and click Next.

5. On the Dependencies page, select the cluster name and disk resource. Click Next.

6. Click Finish.

7. After the MSDTC resource appears in the Cluster Administrator, right-click it and select Bring Online.

After you've created the MSDTC resource, you can install Exchange Server 2003 on the first node in the cluster, as discussed previously in Exercise 3.4. Once you have done this, complete the steps in Exercise 4.4 to grant the cluster service account the Exchange Full Administrator permission.

You can now install Exchange Server 2003 on the remaining cluster nodes, one at a time, following the procedure discussed in Exercise 4.4. Once you've completed this step, you are ready to complete the Exchange cluster creation process by creating the Exchange virtual servers and associated resources. An Exchange virtual server consists of the following additional resources that, all together, make up a cluster resource group:

- An IP address resource
- A network name resource
- A disk resource
- An Exchange 2003 System Attendant resource

EXERCISE 4.4

Granting the Exchange Full Administrator Permission

1. Open the Exchange System Manager.
2. Right-click the organization name and select Delegate Control from the context menu. The Exchange Administration Delegation Wizard opens.
3. Click Next to dismiss the opening page of the wizard.
4. On the Users or Groups page, seen below, click the Add button to locate and grant the cluster service account the Exchange Full Administrator permission. Click Next.

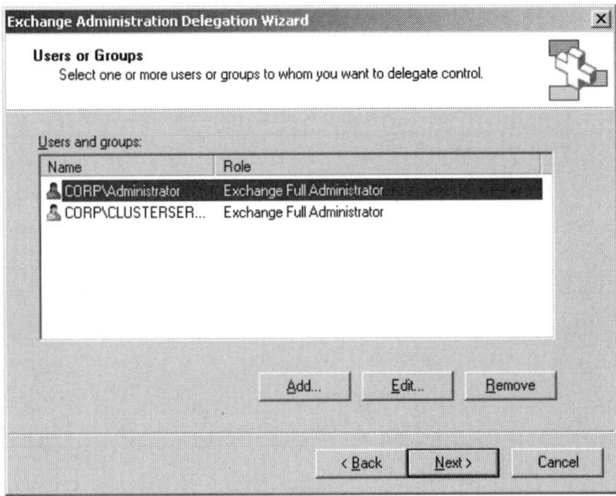

5. Click Finish to complete the Exchange Administration Delegation Wizard.

Exercise 4.5 walks you through the required steps to create the Exchange virtual server and its related resources.

EXERCISE 4.5

Creating the Exchange Virtual Server and Related Resources

1. If it is not already open, open the Cluster Administrator. If the cluster does not appear in the Cluster Administrator, choose File ➢ Open Connection and supply the required information to connect to the cluster.

2. Right-click the Groups container and select New ➢ Group from the context menu. The New Group dialog box, seen below, opens. Enter the name and description and click Next.

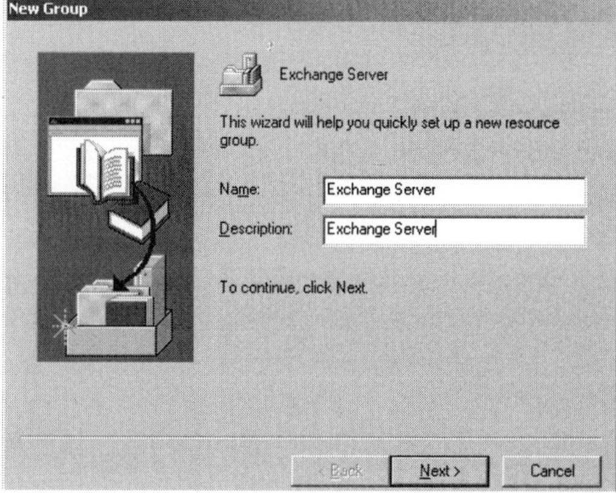

3. On the Preferred Owners page, verify that no cluster nodes are listed in the Preferred Owners list and click Next.

4. Click Finish. The new virtual server (also known as a cluster resource group) will be displayed under the Groups container, as seen below.

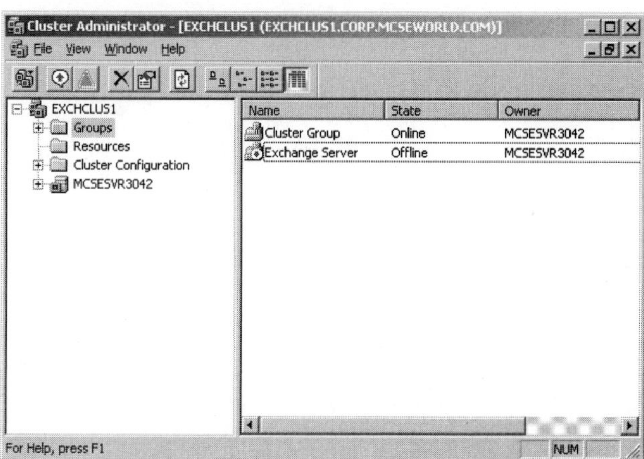

EXERCISE 4.5 *(continued)*

5. To create the IP address resource, right-click the newly created virtual server and select New ➢ Resource. The New Resource page opens.

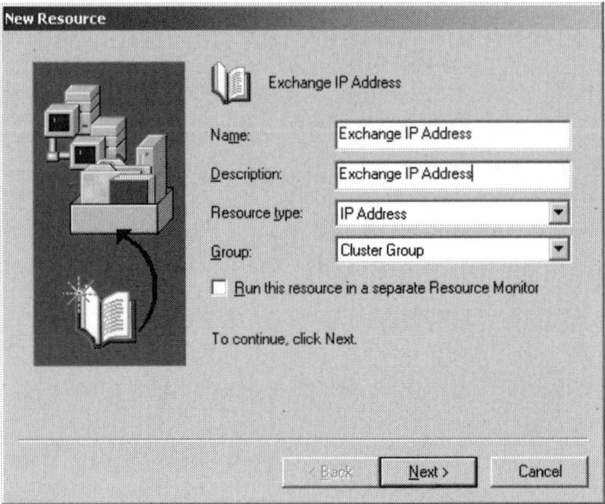

6. Enter a name and description for the resource. Select the IP Address option from the Resource Type drop-down and make sure the correct group is selected. Click Next.

7. On the Possible Owners page, ensure that the first server in the node is listed in the Possible Owners list and click Next.

8. On the Dependencies page, ensure that no resources are listed in the Resource Dependencies list and click Next.

9. On the TCP/IP Address Parameters page, enter the statically assigned IP address and subnet mask that will be used as the IP address of the Exchange virtual server. This IP address, as with any other IP address, must be unique within your cluster and your network. Click Finish.

10. To create the network name resource, right-click the virtual server again and select New ➢ Resource from the context menu.

EXERCISE 4.5 *(continued)*

11. On the New Resource page, enter the name and description. Select the Network Name option from the Resource Type drop-down and make sure the correct group is selected, as seen below. Click Next.

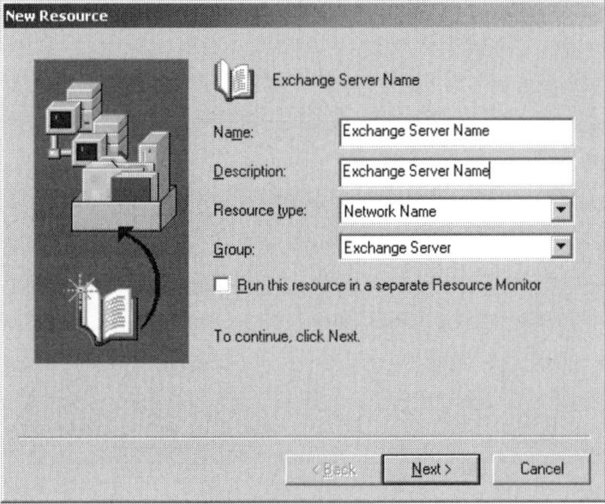

12. On the Possible Owners page, ensure that the first server in the node is listed in the Possible Owners list and click Next.

13. On the Dependencies page, ensure that the Exchange IP Address resource is listed in the Resource Dependencies list, as seen below, and click Next.

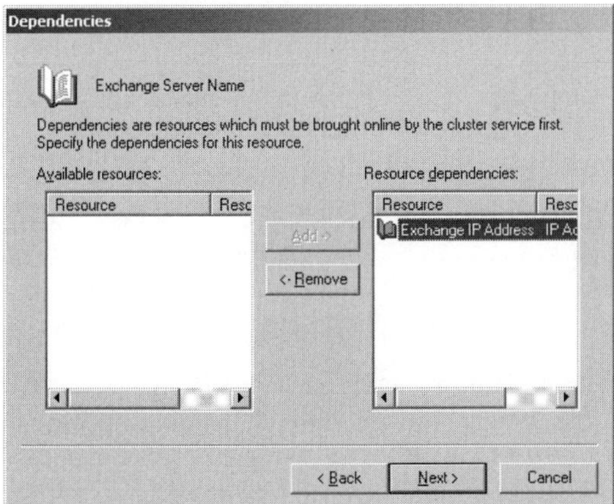

EXERCISE 4.5 ***(continued)***

14. On the Network Name Parameters page, seen below, enter a NetBIOS-friendly name and click Finish.

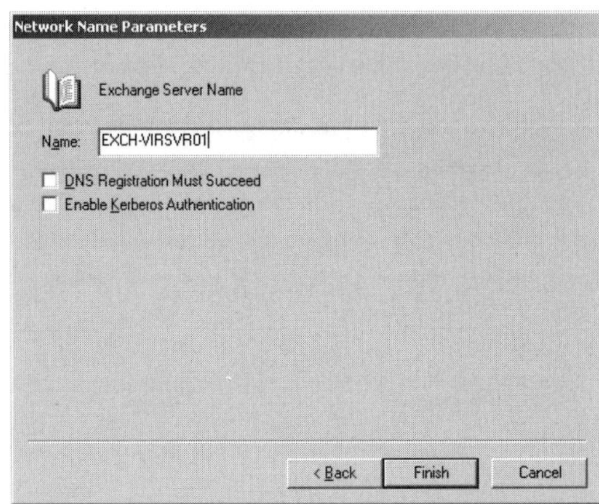

15. To create the disk resource, right-click the virtual server again and select New ➢ Resource from the context menu.

16. On the New Resource page, enter the name and description. Select the Physical Disk option from the Resource Type drop-down, and make sure the correct group is selected. Click Next.

    You will need a SCSI or Fibre Channel disk in order to be able to configure the Physical Disk resource.

17. On the Possible Owners page, ensure that the first server in the node is listed in the Possible Owners list and click Next.

18. On the Dependencies page, ensure that no resources are listed in the Resource Dependencies list and click Next.

19. On the Disk Parameters page, select the desired disk. Click Finish.

20. Right-click the virtual server and select Bring Online from the context menu. Notice that the status icon of the virtual server changes briefly to Online Pending and then to Online.

21. Right-click the virtual server and select New ➢ Resource to create the Exchange System Attendant resource.

22. On the New Resource page, enter the name and description. Select the Microsoft Exchange System Attendant option from the Resource Type drop-down, and make sure the correct group is selected. Click Next.

EXERCISE 4.5 *(continued)*

23. On the Possible Owners page, ensure that the first server in the node is listed in the Possible Owners list and click Next.
24. On the Dependencies page, ensure that the Network Name and Physical Disk resources are listed under the Resource Dependencies list and click Next.
25. On the Data Directory page, verify that the data directory location points to the physical disk resource that has been assigned to this Exchange virtual server. This is the location that will be used by this Exchange virtual server to store the transaction log files, public folder store files, and mailbox store files.
26. Click Finish.
27. Bring the Exchange virtual server back online again.

After you've completed the steps in Exercise 4.5, you will need to repeat the same process on each node that will be in an active state within the cluster.

Monitoring Exchange Clusters

Once you've gone through all of the work to create and configure your Exchange cluster, you'll undoubtedly want to perform some monitoring on it to ensure proper operation. For Active/Passive clusters, no real special monitoring need be performed over and above that for any other Exchange Server 2003 computer. For Active/Active clusters, you will want to pay special attention to the following two items that can indicate problems, both currently and in the future. If you monitor either, or both, of these conditions routinely occurring for periods of time greater than 10 minutes, you will need to move mailboxes off the servers:

- The number of concurrent users accessing their mailboxes exceeds 1,900.
- The CPU load directly attributable to users accessing their mailboxes exceeds 40 percent.

By their very nature, clusters are designed to be reliable and redundant in their operations. In most cases, you may never even notice a problem until a failover occurs. Should a node experience failover, you will want to examine the Event Logs immediately to try to locate any clues to the cause of the event.

Configuring Front-End/Back-End Servers

The mobile workforce is growing as each year goes by. It's commonplace now for employees to want to make connections to the corporate network using portable computers, 802.11 wireless devices, and even cellular telephones. To that end, Exchange Server 2003 ships with an improved version of Outlook Web Access (OWA) and a new included feature in Outlook Mobile Access (OMA). Although OWA and OMA could serve as a primary means of connecting to your Exchange organization, in most cases, it will be your remote and traveling users who will take advantage of these services. We'll be examining Outlook Web Access later in Chapter 7, "Configuring Client Access," but for now it's enough to understand what its basic purpose is and how it factors into the discussion at hand.

The primary purpose of Outlook Web Access might be something similar to this: to enable remote access to the Exchange organization using industry-standard protocols and applications. In its most basic form, Outlook Web Access is nothing more than an HTTP connection using any recent browser to an Exchange/IIS server that has been configured to pass traffic back to an Exchange server. To increase security, you can (and should) configure an IIS server certificate, thus requiring the use of SSL. Once SSL encryption has been implemented, you can implement Basic authentication of users over the SSL connection. All recent browsers, no matter which operating system, support SSL and thus make ideal candidates for an OWA session.

With this basic description of the process in hand, you should be starting to see inherent security issues that can arise when using OWA. It's never considered good practice to have secured or unsecured Internet HTTP connections coming directly into your internal protected network. After all, you place your web servers outside at least one firewall, separating them from the rest of your corporate network...don't you? You will do the same with OWA servers as well, thus configuring Exchange and Outlook Web Access in what we will refer to from here on out as a front-end/back-end (FE/BE) arrangement, as illustrated in Figure 4.5.

By looking at the portion of the network shown in Figure 4.5, you can start to determine for which protocols, and thus for which ports, you will need to provide access at the internal and external firewalls. Table 4.1 lists some of the more common ports associated with an Exchange messaging organization that may be using a front-end/back-end configuration.

FIGURE 4.5 A basic front-end/back-end arrangement

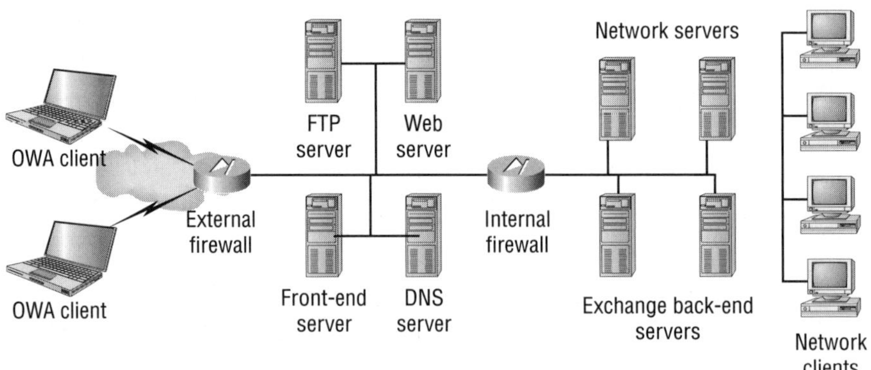

TABLE 4.1 The Common Exchange Ports

Port	Function	External Firewall	Internal Firewall
25	SMTP	Open **	Open **
53	DNS	Open	Open
80	HTTP	Open **	Open **
88	Kerberos authentication	Closed	Open
110	POP3	Open **	Open **
119	NNTP	Open **	Open **
143	IMAP4	Open **	Open **
135	RPC port mapping	Closed	Open
389	LDAP to domain controller	Closed	Open
443	HTTP over SSL	Open **	Open **
563	NNTP over SSL	Open **	Open **
993	IMAP4 over SSL	Open **	Open **
995	POP3 over SSL	Open **	Open **
3268	LDAP to global catalog	Closed	Open
1024-65535	RPC service ports (can be manually assigned to a specific port using a Registry modification)	Closed	Open

Items marked by a double asterisk (**) should be opened only if that specific type of traffic needs to be passed through the particular firewall. It is recommended that SSL be used to secure all inbound connections to your organization as much of the time as possible since all common messaging protocols support SSL.

Now that you understand the basic premise of, and reason for, a front-end/back-end server arrangement, let's look at the tasks you'll need to perform in order to implement a secure front-end/back-end messaging infrastructure for your clients.

Outlook Web Access, when configured to use SSL, provides a secure and robust messaging experience for users using Internet Explorer 5.01 and later that almost exactly mimics the experience a user would have when connecting to an Exchange Server using Outlook 2003. As an alternative to OWA, you may wish to consider implementing RPC over HTTP for remote users using Outlook 2003, as discussed in Chapter 7.

Configuring Front-End Servers

The basic process to create a front-end/back-end server arrangement is actually pretty simple if you break it down into some basic steps. You first need to determine whether you will be clustering the back-end servers or network load-balancing (recommended) the front-end servers. This decision should be made before you go any further. After this, you only need to install the Exchange servers as previously discussed in Chapter 3 and earlier in this chapter. There is no extra configuration required on the back-end servers above and beyond that of configuring Exchange itself.

Front-end servers require additional configuration but nothing extraordinarily difficult. The first change you will need to make is to configure the front-end servers to act as front-end servers—in other words, let them know that they will be contacting other back-end mailbox and public folder servers instead of actually hosting mailboxes and public folders. This configuration is done from the server Properties dialog box by selecting the This Is A Front-End Server option, as seen in Figure 4.6.

When you close the server Properties dialog box, you will be presented with a warning dialog telling you to restart the Exchange server to complete the configuration change. As well, you will be prompted to install an IIS server certificate so that you can use SSL-secured connections on the server. Once the Exchange server has restarted, you should install the requested IIS server certificate. We will examine server certificates later in Chapter 15, "Securing Exchange Server 2003."

Front-end servers communicate with back-end servers using TCP port 80—and only TCP port 80. You will not be able to use SSL on port 443 to secure this connection; thus you are highly encouraged to implement an IPSec policy between your front-end servers and back-end servers. You should also IPSec-secure traffic between domain controllers/global catalog servers and your front-end servers.

For more information about configuring and implementing IPSec policies on your network, see Chapter 6, "Deploying Network Services," from the Windows Server 2003 Deployment Kit at `www.microsoft.com/technet/prodtechnol/windowsserver2003/proddocs/deployguide/dnsbj_ips_overview.asp`.

FIGURE 4.6 Configuring a front-end server

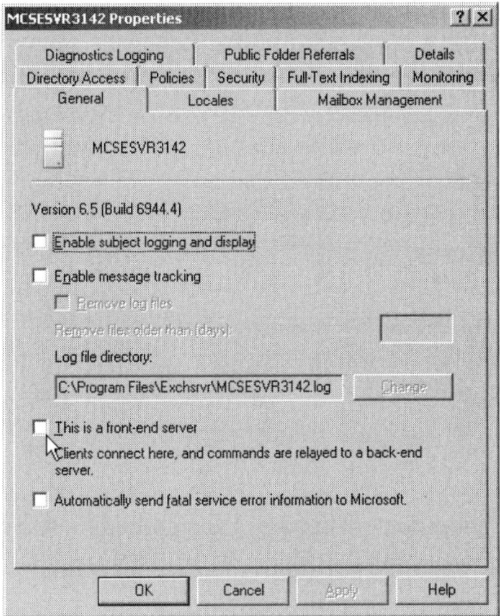

Securing Front-End Server Services

There are several services that are available by default on an Exchange Server 2003 computer that have no reason to be available on a front-end server. By reducing any unnecessarily running services, you can quickly reduce the attack vector for the server, making your entire organization a little safer. The following services can safely be disabled on your front-end Exchange servers:

- Microsoft Exchange Management
- Microsoft Exchange MTA stacks
- Microsoft Exchange Routing Engine

To disable unnecessary services on your front-end servers, perform the steps discussed in Exercise 4.6.

For even greater security on your front-end servers, and any other server that is located in a screened subnet, see the Windows Server 2003 Security Guide, located at `www.microsoft.com/technet/security/prodtech/win2003/w2003hg/sgch00.asp`. Chapter 11 of the guide contains information about bastion hosts and includes preconfigured security templates that you may find useful in your organization.

EXERCISE 4.6

Disabling Services on Front-End Servers

1. Open the Services console, located in the Administrative Tools folder.
2. Stop the following Exchange-related services:

   Microsoft Exchange Information Store

   Microsoft Exchange Management

   Microsoft Exchange MTA stacks

   Microsoft Exchange Routing Engine

   Microsoft Exchange System Attendant

   World Wide Web Publishing Service
3. Configure the Microsoft Exchange Management, Microsoft Exchange MTA stacks, and Microsoft Exchange Routing Engine services for a startup type of Disabled.
4. Restart the Microsoft Exchange Information Store, Microsoft Exchange System Attendant, and World Wide Web Publishing Service services.
5. Close the Services console.

Summary

Exchange Server 2003 computers can be clustered to provide a highly available solution in environments demanding near 100 percent messaging system uptime. Clustering is not a feature of Exchange Server 2003 itself but instead a feature provided by the operating system: Windows 2000 Server or Windows Server 2003. Exchange, however, is clustering aware, meaning that it can recognize that it is being installed into a cluster and will configure itself appropriately during the installation to support operation in this environment.

Windows Server 2003 provides support for two different clustering methods: Network Load Balancing and the Microsoft Clustering Service. Each of these methods has different purposes and, as you might expect, different hardware requirements.

Network Load Balancing is installed on all participating members as an additional network interface driver that uses a mathematical algorithm to equally distribute incoming requests to all members of the NLB cluster. Incoming client requests are assigned to cluster members based on their current loading level but can be modified through the use of filtering and an affinity for applications that require session state data to be maintained, such as an e-commerce application that uses cookies to place items in a shopping cart for purchase.

The Microsoft Clustering Service is the second clustering method available in Windows Server 2003 and the only one that Exchange Server 2003 supports. MSCS provides for highly available server solutions through a process known as failover. An MSCS cluster consists of two more nodes (members) that are configured such that upon the failure of one node, any of the remaining cluster nodes can transfer the failed node's resources to itself, thus keeping the resources available for client access. During this time, clients will see little, if any, interruption in service as the resources failover from the nonresponsive node to a remaining functional node.

Clusters using the Microsoft Clustering Service can be created in one of two clustering modes: Active/Active and Active/Passive. When using Exchange Server 2003 on Windows Server 2003 Enterprise Edition or Datacenter Edition, you can create up to eight-node Active/Passive clusters.

When Active/Passive clustering is used, a cluster can contain between two and eight nodes. At least one node must be active and at least one node must be passive. You can have any other combination as well, as long as you meet these minimum requirements. Due to its flexibility and lack of restriction, the Active/Passive clustering mode is the preferred mode of operation for Exchange Server clusters.

When Active/Active clustering is used, each node in the cluster runs one instance of the clustered service. Should a failure of the clustered service occur, that instance is transferred to the other active node. Although you will be able to use both nodes of the cluster in Active/Active mode, you are limited in how many storage groups and Exchange mailboxes each node can host because a single Exchange server can hold only four production storage groups. In addition to this restriction, the nodes in an Active/Active cluster can have only 1,900 active mailboxes each, which is several thousand less than an Exchange server might typically be able to hold.

You should deploy your Exchange servers in a front-end/back-end configuration for increased security and greater flexibility. The front-end servers, which are located in your screened subnet, provide only a secure connection point for those users located on the Internet to connect to your Exchange organization. SSL is used to secure the traffic in this connection. Front-end servers then pass information back and forth between back-end servers and clients. Therefore, clients never directly connect to a back-end server, which is located in your private, protected network. IPSec can be used to secure the connections between the front-end servers and back-end servers, domain controllers, and global catalog servers for further security. Front-end servers can also be set up in a Network Load Balancing cluster for improved availability.

Exam Essentials

Understand the clustering methods. The majority of this chapter has focused on clustering using the Microsoft Clustering Service, but you will need to have read the introductory sections pertaining to both of the clustering methods available in Windows Server 2003. Although you will be deploying only Exchange servers on MSCS clusters, you may need to deploy front-end Exchange servers in an NLB cluster as part of your front-end/back-end solution. Be aware of the perks and drawbacks of each clustering method.

Understand the clustering modes. In previous versions of Exchange, only one clustering mode or the other was fully supported. In Exchange Server 2003, you now have the choice to create either Active/Active or Active/Passive clusters. Ensure that you understand the specific requirements and limitations of each clustering mode.

Understand the limitations on Active/Active cluster nodes. Active/Passive clustering is the preferred method of deploying Exchange Server 2003 clusters. You will want to remember why this is so and what limitations are imposed on Active/Active clusters.

Know how to secure a front-end server. Several services that are, by default, running on any Exchange server can (and should) be safely disabled on any front-end server you configure. Ensure that you understand how this process is completed and which specific services you can safely disable to secure a front-end server. As well, understand the security methods that can be used to secure traffic from a client to a front-end server and from the front-end server to other hosts inside the protected, internal network.

Review Questions

1. You have been directed to implement a highly available solution for your Exchange Server 2003 organization using Active/Active clustering. All of your Exchange servers are running Exchange Server 2003 Enterprise Edition on Windows Server 2003 Enterprise Edition. In this clustering mode, what is the minimum and maximum number of Exchange servers you will be able to have as a part of your cluster?

   A. Two, four

   B. Two, eight

   C. One, eight

   D. Two, two

2. You have been directed to implement a highly available solution for your Exchange Server 2003 organization using Active/Active clustering. All of your Exchange servers are running Exchange Server 2003 Enterprise Edition on Windows Server 2003 Enterprise Edition. In this clustering mode, how many mailboxes are you limited to on each Exchange server?

   A. 1,400

   B. 1,800

   C. 1,900

   D. 2,400

3. You are completing the configuration on a new front-end server that is to be placed in your organization's screened subnet. Your remote and traveling employees will use this front-end server to create secure connections to Outlook Web Access. This server will join a DNS server that will be placed in the screened subnet at the same time. Which ports, at the minimum, will you need to ensure are open on the external firewall separating your screened subnet from the Internet? (Choose all that apply.)

   A. 80

   B. 389

   C. 53

   D. 443

4. You are completing the configuration on a new front-end server that is to be placed in your organization's screened subnet. Your remote and traveling employees will use this front-end server to create secure connections to Outlook Web Access. You want to further secure this new front-end server by disabling any unnecessary Exchange-related services. Which services can you safely disable on this front-end server? (Choose all that apply.)

   A. Microsoft Exchange Information Store
   B. Microsoft Exchange Management
   C. Microsoft ExchangeMTA stacks
   D. Microsoft ExchangeRouting Engine
   E. Microsoft Exchange System Attendant
   F. World Wide Web Publishing Service

5. You have been directed to implement a highly available solution for your Exchange Server 2003 organization using Active/Passive clustering. All of your Exchange servers are running Exchange Server 2003 Enterprise Edition on Windows Server 2003 Enterprise Edition. In this clustering mode, what is the minimum and maximum number of Exchange servers you will be able to have as a part of your cluster?

   A. Two, four
   B. Two, eight
   C. One, eight
   D. Two, two

6. You have just completed the installation of Exchange Server 2003 on all four of the nodes in your Active/Passive cluster. Which of the following items will you need to configure on each of the Active nodes? (Choose all that apply.)

   A. An IP address resource
   B. A disk resource
   C. An Exchange System Attendant resource
   D. A network name resource

7. You have just completed the installation and configuration of Exchange Server 2003 on both nodes of an Active/Active cluster. Each node hosts three storage groups. Each storage group contains 600 users. If one of these nodes should fail, what will happen to its three storage groups?

   A. All three will failover to the other node.
   B. None of them will failover to the other node.
   C. Only two of them will failover to the other node.
   D. Only one of them will failover to the other node.

8. You want to configure a six-node Active/Passive Exchange cluster. What minimum version of Exchange Server 2003 and Windows will you require to accomplish this? (Choose the two correct answers.)

A. Exchange Server 2003 Enterprise Edition

B. Exchange Server 2003 Standard Edition

C. Windows 2000 Server Datacenter Server Edition

D. Windows Server 2003 Enterprise Edition

E. Windows Server 2003 Datacenter Edition

9. You have just completed the implementation of a front-end/back-end Exchange server arrangement. Clients are allowed to make only SSL-secured HTTP connections to the front-end server. You need to secure the communications between the front-end and back-end servers. What method will you use?

A. SSL

B. Kerberos v5

C. NTLM v2

D. IPSec

10. While monitoring your Active/Active Exchange Server 2003 cluster, what specific additional items (above and beyond normal server monitoring) should you be watching to determine whether the servers are potentially overloaded?

A. The number of concurrent mailbox connections

B. The disk utilization directly attributable to users accessing their mailboxes

C. The CPU utilization directly attributable to users accessing their mailboxes

D. The number of non-delivery reports being generated

11. You have been directed to implement a highly available solution for your Exchange Server 2003 organization using Active/Passive clustering. All of your Exchange servers are running Exchange Server 2003 Enterprise Edition on Windows 2000 Advanced Server. In this clustering mode, what is the minimum and maximum number of Exchange servers you will be able to have as a part of your cluster?

A. Two, four

B. Two, eight

C. One, eight

D. Two, two

12. You have just completed the installation and configuration of Exchange Server 2003 on all nodes of a six-node Active/Passive cluster. Four nodes in the cluster are active and the remaining two nodes are passive. Each node hosts three storage groups. Each storage group contains 600 users. If one of these active nodes should fail, what will happen to its three storage groups?

    A. All three will failover to the other node.

    B. None of them will failover to the other node.

    C. Only two of them will failover to the other node.

    D. Only one of them will failover to the other node.

13. You have just completed the installation and configuration of Exchange Server 2003 on all nodes of a six-node Active/Passive cluster. Four nodes in the cluster are active and the remaining two nodes are passive. How many total instances of the Exchange System Attendant resource will you need to create to properly configure this cluster?

    A. One

    B. Two

    C. Four

    D. Six

14. What do cluster nodes use to determine the operational status of other cluster nodes?

    A. A ping sweep

    B. A ping

    C. A heartbeat

    D. A pulse

15. What major advantage does clustering with the Microsoft Clustering Service (MSCS) have over Network Load Balancing?

    A. MSCS clusters can have more nodes.

    B. MSCS clusters are less expensive to create and maintain.

    C. MSCS clusters are service aware.

    D. MSCS clusters are server aware.

16. You have been directed to implement a highly available solution for your Exchange Server 2003 organization using Active/Passive clustering. All of your Exchange servers are running Exchange Server 2003 Enterprise Edition on Windows 2000 Datacenter Server. In this clustering mode, what is the minimum and maximum number of Exchange servers you will be able to have as a part of your cluster?

    A. Two, four

    B. Two, eight

    C. One, eight

    D. Two, two

17. Which cluster operation mode is essentially just another name for Active/Passive clustering?
    A. Failover pair
    B. Hot standby
    C. Failover ring
    D. Random failover

18. Which cluster operation mode is essentially just another name for Active/Active clustering?
    A. Failover pair
    B. Hot standby
    C. Failover ring
    D. Random failover

19. Which cluster model will you be unable to use to create an Active/Passive Exchange server cluster with four active nodes and two passive nodes?
    A. Single node cluster
    B. Single quorum cluster
    C. Majority node set cluster

20. When creating the NetBIOS name for a new cluster, what is the maximum number of characters long that the name can be?
    A. 12
    B. 13
    C. 15
    D. 16

Answers to Review Questions

1. D. When Active/Active clustering is used, you can have two and only two nodes in the Exchange cluster.

2. C. In an Active/Active cluster, you must not place more than 1,900 mailboxes on each node. This is done to prevent an overloaded situation on the single remaining node in the event that a failover action would occur.

3. C, D. The minimum ports you must open are port 53 for DNS and port 443 for HTTP over SSL. You should never open port 389 on an external firewall. Port 80 will not be needed for unsecured HTTP connections unless you are planning on placing a public web server in the screened subnet as well.

4. B, C, D. You can safely disable the Microsoft Exchange Management, Microsoft Exchange MTA stacks, and Microsoft Exchange Routing Engine services on a front-end server for increased security.

5. B. When Active/Passive clustering is configured on Windows Server 2003 Enterprise Edition or Windows Server 2003 Datacenter Edition, you must have a minimum of two nodes with a maximum of eight nodes.

6. A, B, C, D. To properly and completely configure the active node of an Active/Passive cluster, you will need to create an IP address resource, a disk resource, an Exchange System Attendant resource, and a network name resource.

7. D. A single Exchange server can hold only four production storage groups. Thus, when Active/Active clustering is used it is highly recommended that each node hold only two storage groups. Two of the storage groups on the failed node will not be available to clients.

8. A, D. You will need Exchange Server 2003 Enterprise Edition in order to create Exchange clusters. In addition, only Windows Server 2003 Enterprise Edition or Datacenter Edition can support clusters larger than four nodes.

9. D. Front-end servers communicate only on port 80 to back-end servers; thus using SSL is not an option. NTLM v2 and Kerberos v5 are network authentication methods.

10. A, C. You should monitor Active/Active cluster servers for CPU utilization above 40 percent or concurrent mailbox sessions above 1,900 and over 10 minutes long. These items are in addition to the normal monitoring that you would perform on any Exchange server.

11. D. When Active/Passive clustering is configured on Windows 2000 Advanced Server, you are limited to two nodes total. You must have a minimum of two nodes with a maximum of two nodes.

12. A. In the Active/Passive mode, the passive node will be able to assume the complete load that the failed active node previously carried; thus all three storage groups will be able to successfully failover to the passive node.

13. C. You will need one instance for each of the active nodes. To properly and completely configure the active node of an Active/Passive cluster, you will need to create an IP address resource, a disk resource, an Exchange System Attendant resource, and a network name resource.

14. C. Cluster nodes are kept aware of one another's existence (and thus their operational state) by the use of a special communication among members that is referred to as a heartbeat.

15. C. The advantage offered by MSCS clustering is that it is service aware, meaning that it can monitor individual services on a node, not just the status of the node overall.

16. A. When Active/Passive clustering is configured on Windows 2000 Datacenter Server, you are limited to four nodes total. You must have a minimum of two nodes with a maximum of four nodes.

17. B. When hot standby is configured, a passive node can take on the resources of any failed active node. Hot standby is really just another term for Active/Passive. You configure for hot standby through a combination of the Preferred Owners list and the Possible Owners list.

18. C. The failover ring mode, also referred to as Active/Active mode, has each node in the cluster running an instance of the application or resource being clustered. When one node fails, the clustered resource is moved to the next node in the sequence. In Exchange clusters, this mode of operation is not useful because these resources have nowhere else to failover to but the single remaining node in a two-node Active/Active cluster.

19. A. A single node cluster model cannot be used to provide highly available Exchange resources to clients. It can, however, be used to develop and test cluster processes and procedures for an organization. The single node cluster still retains clustering ability to attempt to restart failed services; thus it mimics a production cluster in this way.

20. C. NetBIOS names are limited to 15 characters in length.

Creating and Managing Exchange Recipients

MICROSOFT EXAM OBJECTIVES COVERED IN THIS CHAPTER:

- ✓ Manage user objects
- ✓ Manage distribution and security groups
- ✓ Manage contacts
- ✓ Manage address lists

One of an administrator's most important tasks is to create and configure Exchange *recipients*. A recipient is an object in Active Directory that references a resource that can receive a message. The resource might be a mailbox in a private Information Store, such as in the case of a user, or a public folder in the public Information Store that is shared by many users. No matter where an actual resource exists, though, a recipient object is always created in the Active Directory.

In this chapter, we will discuss the types of Exchange recipients, their creation, and their properties. Exchange has four basic types of recipients:

Users A *user* is an Active Directory object that typically represents a person who uses the network. Once Exchange is installed and updates the schema, each user in the Active Directory can be mailbox-enabled, mail-enabled, or neither. A *mailbox-enabled user* has an associated mailbox in a private Information Store on an Exchange server. Each user's *mailbox* is a private storage area that allows an individual user to send, receive, and store messages. A *mail-enabled user* is one who has an e-mail address but does not have a mailbox on an Exchange server. These users send and receive e-mail by using an external ISP.

Groups A *group* in Active Directory is like a container to which you can assign certain permissions and rights. You can then place users (and other groups) into that group, and they automatically inherit the group's permissions and rights. Exchange uses the concept of mail-enabled groups to form distribution lists. Messages sent to a group are redirected and sent to each member of the group. These groups allow users to send messages to multiple recipients without having to address each recipient individually.

Contacts A *contact* is a pointer object that refers to an e-mail address for a non-Exchange recipient. Contacts are most often used for connecting your organization to foreign messaging systems, such as Microsoft Mail, Lotus cc:Mail, or the Internet. As an administrator, you would create contacts so that frequently used e-mail addresses are available in the Global Address List (GAL) as real names. This makes it easier to send mail because users do not need to guess at cryptic e-mail addresses.

Public folders A *public folder* is like a public mailbox. It is a container for information to be shared among a group of people. Public folders can contain e-mail messages, forms, word-processing documents, spreadsheet files, and files of many other formats. Public folders can also be configured to send information to other recipients.

The rest of this chapter discusses the creation and configuration of these four recipient objects, as well as related management tasks.

Users

In previous versions of Exchange, such as Exchange Server 5.5, both the tool used to create user accounts (User Manager for Domains) and the tool used to administer Exchange (Exchange Administrator) could be used to create and manage mailboxes. This has changed in Exchange Server 2003. Now, one tool, named Active Directory Users and Computers, is used to create and manage mail-related user properties. Although the concept of the mailbox as a physical area of storage on an Exchange server is still valid, the concept of a mailbox as a recipient object in the Exchange directory no longer is. Now, there are only user objects in the Active Directory. Property pages of the user object are now used to configure Exchange-related properties.

This tying together of user accounts and mailbox properties means that Exchange administrators and Windows administrators will now have to work more closely than ever before. Though many Exchange administrators who have worked with Exchange Server 5.5 may hate the idea of giving up control of mailbox administration, this is usually what happens. Since all of the user-related functions of mailbox management are now accessed through Active Directory Users and Computers, it makes sense to have one account administrator handle all of the user-management details.

Exchange Server 2003 supports two mail configurations for a user: mailbox-enabled and mail-enabled. The creation and management of each type are discussed in the following sections.

Mailbox-Enabled Users

Every user in an organization needs access to an Exchange-based mailbox in order to send and receive messages using the Exchange server. One of the principal administrative tasks in Exchange is the creation and management of these mailboxes. In Exchange Server 2003, a user with an associated mailbox is called a mailbox-enabled user. Mailbox-enabled users are able to send and receive messages, as well as store messages on an Exchange server.

Creating a Mailbox-Enabled User

When the Active Directory forest is prepared for Exchange Server 2003, a number of important changes are made. One is that the Active Directory schema is updated with attributes for objects that relate to Exchange. Another important change is that the Active Directory Users and Computers snap-in is updated with extensions that allow the automatic creation of mailboxes whenever users are created. It is also easy to create mailboxes for existing users. Exercise 5.1 outlines the steps for creating a new user and an associated mailbox using Active Directory Users and Computers. Exercise 5.2 outlines the steps for creating a mailbox for an existing user. Both exercises assume that Exchange Server 2003 has previously been installed in the domain.

EXERCISE 5.1

Creating a New User and Mailbox

1. Choose Start ➢ Programs ➢ Administrative Tools ➢ Active Directory Users and Computers.
2. From the Action menu, point to New, and select User.
3. On the New Object – User screen, seen below, fill in the information for the new user. This includes the user's full name and logon name. When you have finished, click Next.

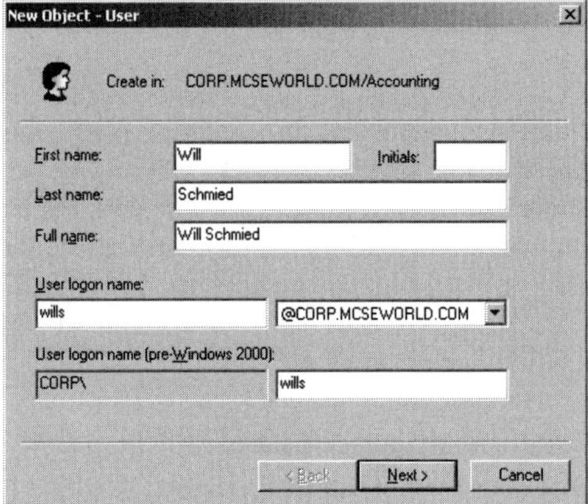

4. On the next screen, enter and verify the user's password, and set any password restrictions you want, as seen below. When you have finished, click Next.

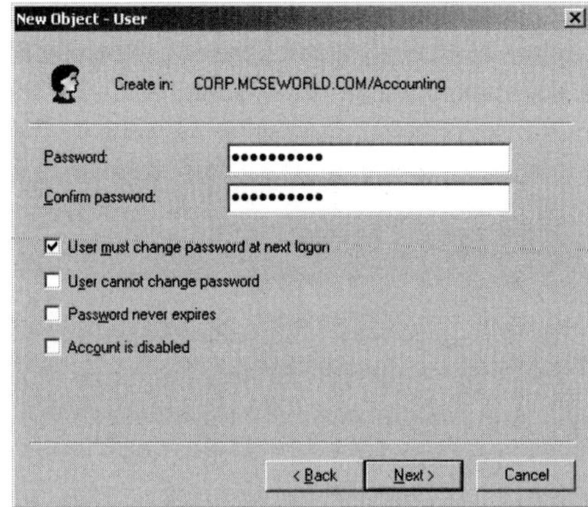

EXERCISE 5.1 *(continued)*

5. Next, you are given the opportunity to create an Exchange mailbox for the user. To do so, first make sure the Create An Exchange Mailbox option is selected, as seen below.

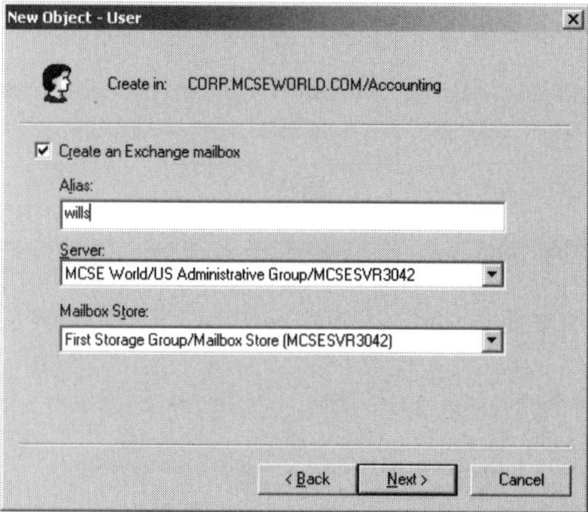

6. An *alias* is suggested based on the logon name that you chose for the user. The alias is an alternate means of addressing a user that is used by foreign messaging systems that may not be able to handle a full display name. You can change this if you have a specific policy in place for creating aliases, or you can leave it at the Windows default.

7. By default, the first Exchange server is selected as the server on which the mailbox should be created. Use the drop-down menu to change this if you want to create the mailbox on a different server.

8. Also by default, the first storage group on the selected server is chosen for you. Use the drop-down menu to alter that choice if desired. Once you have made your selections, click Next to go on.

9. A summary screen is now displayed asking you to confirm your choices. If you want to change any of the settings, you can use the Back button to do so. Once you are satisfied with your choices, click Finish to exit the wizard, create the new user object in the Active Directory, and create the new mailbox on the selected Exchange server.

EXERCISE 5.2

Creating a Mailbox for an Existing User

1. Choose Start ➢ Programs ➢ Administrative Tools ➢ Active Directory Users And Computers.
2. In the Tree pane on the left, click the Users container.
3. In the Results pane on the right, find and select the user object for which you want to create a mailbox.
4. From the Action menu, select Exchange Tasks.
5. Click Next to bypass the Welcome screen of the wizard.
6. On the Available Tasks screen, seen below, make sure that Create Mailbox is selected, and click Next.

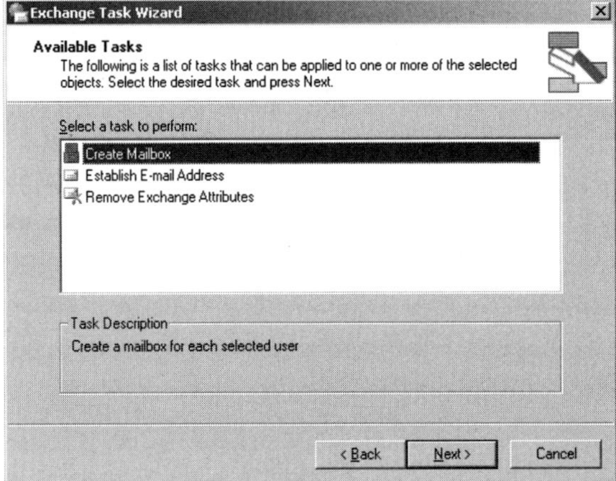

7. On the Create Mailbox screen, make sure that the alias, server, and storage group selections are all appropriate, and then click Next.
8. A summary screen is now displayed asking you to confirm your choices. If you want to change any of the settings, you can use the Back button to do so. Once you are satisfied with your choices, click Next to create the mailbox.
9. After the mailbox has been completed, click Finish to exit the wizard.

Configuring Mailbox Properties

A user object, like all objects, has properties. Those properties are configured and viewed through property pages and the individual attributes on those property pages. Mailbox properties are configured using several Exchange-related property pages of the user object. The property pages of a user object are accessed in one of two ways. With the user highlighted, you can use the Properties command on the Action menu to access the property pages. A quicker way is simply to double-click the user object.

Many of the attributes that you can configure are straightforward and do not warrant much explanation (e.g., phone number). This section describes several of the property pages that pertain to the Exchange organization and the important individual attributes.

The terms *properties* and *attributes* are used interchangeably in this chapter.

General Page

The General page, shown in Figure 5.1, records general information about the user object. The first name, middle initial, and last name that you enter are used to generate a display name, which is the name of the recipient as it appears in the Active Directory Users and Computers window. The rest of the information on this page is used to further identify the recipient. All of this information is available to users when they browse the Global Address List from their e-mail client.

FIGURE 5.1 The General page of a mailbox

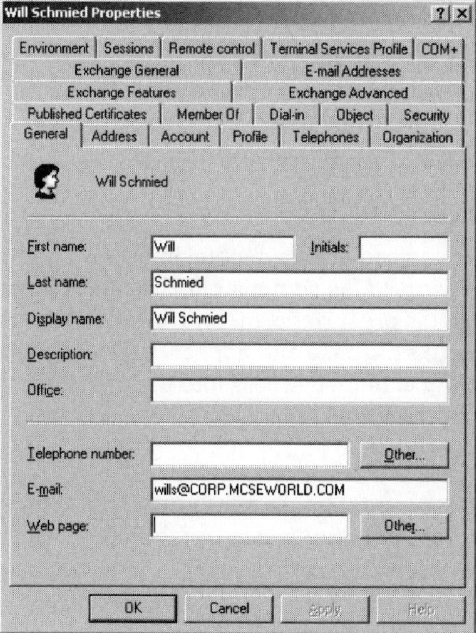

Organization Page

The Organization page contains fields for recording the organization information for the user, the name of the user's manager, and the people who report to the user. These people are referred to as *direct reports*. All of these fields are optional. All the information configured on this property page is also available in the Global Address List.

Address and Telephones Pages

The Address and Telephones pages contain information on addresses and phone numbers, as well as a place for free-form notes about the user. All of this information is also available in the Global Address List.

Exchange General Page

The Exchange General page, shown in Figure 5.2, is used to configure general properties governing the Exchange mailbox associated with the user. The mailbox store that the user belongs to is displayed but cannot be changed. The alias is an alternate means of addressing a user that is used by foreign messaging systems that may not be able to handle a full display name.

You will also find three buttons on this page that lead to more important settings: Delivery Restrictions, Delivery Options, and Storage Limits.

DELIVERY RESTRICTIONS

The Delivery Restrictions dialog box, seen in Figure 5.3, contains information regarding from whom this mailbox will accept or reject messages. The default is to accept messages from everyone. In addition, you can configure size restrictions on incoming and outgoing messages on the mailbox.

DELIVERY OPTIONS

The Delivery Options dialog box, seen in Figure 5.4, specifies a list of users who can send mail "on behalf of" this mailbox user. It also allows mail sent to this mailbox to be rerouted to another mailbox, referred to as an *alternate recipient*. You can configure the alternate recipient to receive mail instead of the original mailbox or along with the original mailbox.

Send On Behalf Of permission can also be helpful in troubleshooting. If you assign this permission to yourself, as administrator, it allows you to test messages from any recipient in the organization. However, you should always use test mailboxes created for this purpose and not actual user mailboxes. Many users would consider having extended access into their e-mail an intrusion.

STORAGE LIMITS

The Storage Limits dialog box, seen in Figure 5.5, lets you set two parameters: *storage limits* and *deleted item retention time*. Storage limits refer to the limit placed on the size to which a mailbox can grow and what happens when that limit is crossed. By default, the Information Store (IS) settings will be used. However, this can be overridden. If it is overridden, you can set values (in kilobytes) for when warnings will be issued, when sending messages will be prohibited, and when sending and receiving messages will be prohibited.

FIGURE 5.2 The Delivery Restrictions dialog box

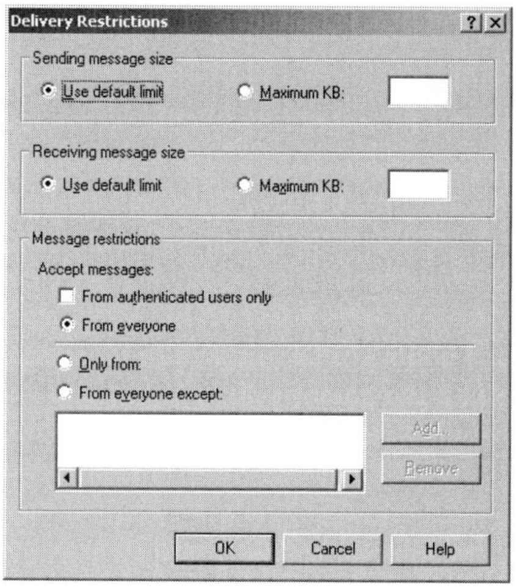

FIGURE 5.3 The Delivery Options dialog box

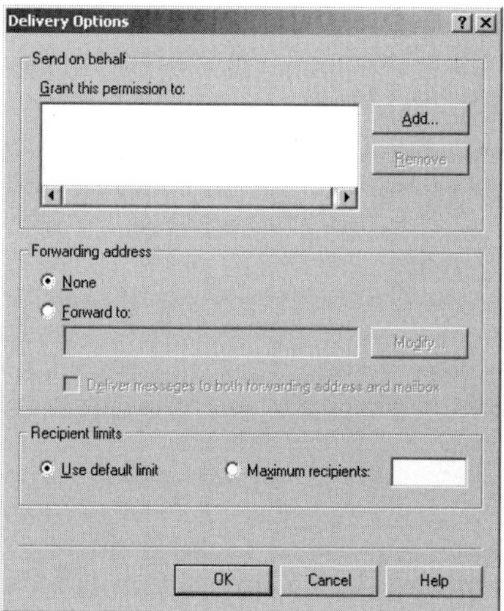

The deleted item retention feature enables mailbox users to retrieve deleted items. But to prevent excessive build-up of deleted items, Exchange allows you to set a retention time for deleted items. You can configure that length of time through this setting or at the IS object. The IS default value will be used, but you can configure a mailbox to override that setting by specifying the number of days for deleted item retention. You can also configure a mailbox to keep deleted items (i.e., not permanently deleted) until the mailbox has been backed up.

FIGURE 5.4 The Storage Limits dialog box

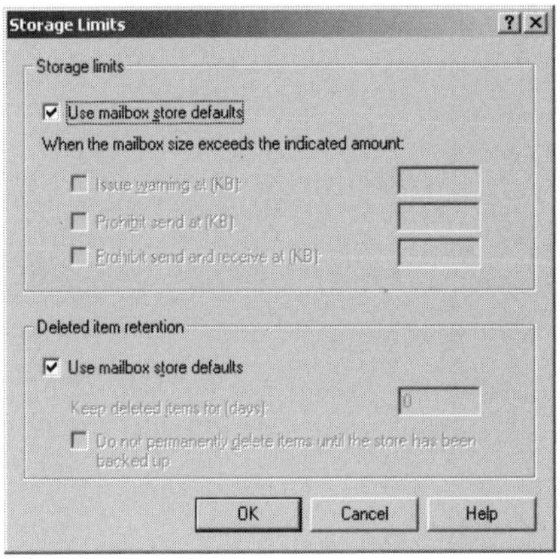

FIGURE 5.5 The Exchange General page of a mailbox

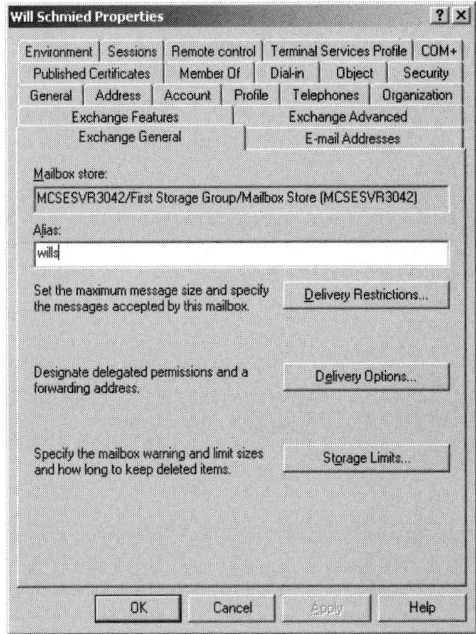

E-mail Addresses Page

Each time an Exchange mailbox is created, a number of non-Exchange mail addresses, also called *foreign mail addresses* or *proxy addresses*, are automatically generated for that Exchange mailbox. This allows Exchange mailboxes to be prepared to receive mail from foreign mail systems. The E-mail Addresses page, seen in Figure 5.6, lets you configure these addresses.

Microsoft Exchange can generate foreign addresses for the following systems, although by default it creates only X.400 and SMTP foreign addresses:

- Custom address
- X.400 address
- Microsoft Mail address
- SMTP address
- cc:Mail address
- Lotus Notes address
- Novell GroupWise address

Exchange Features Page

The Exchange Features page, shown in Figure 5.7, lets you enable and disable advanced Exchange features for an individual mailbox. Such features include Outlook Mobile Access features, Outlook Web Access, and the ability to connect to the Exchange organization using various e-mail protocols.

Exchange Advanced Page

The Exchange Advanced page, shown in Figure 5.8, lets you configure a number of miscellaneous features that the Exchange designers decided were advanced for one reason or another.

The *simple display name* is an alternate name for the mailbox. It appears when, for some reason, the full display name cannot. This situation often occurs when multiple language versions of System Manager are used on the same network.

FIGURE 5.6 The E-mail Addresses page

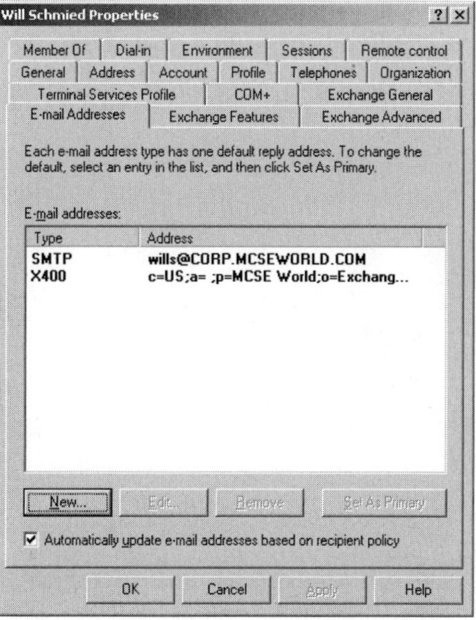

FIGURE 5.7 The Exchange Features page

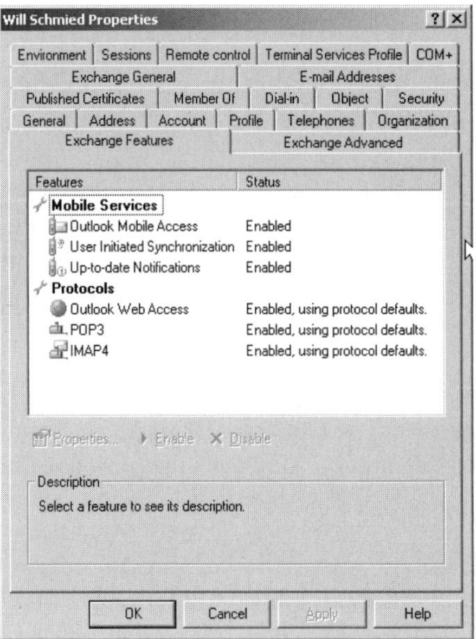

FIGURE 5.8 The Exchange Advanced page

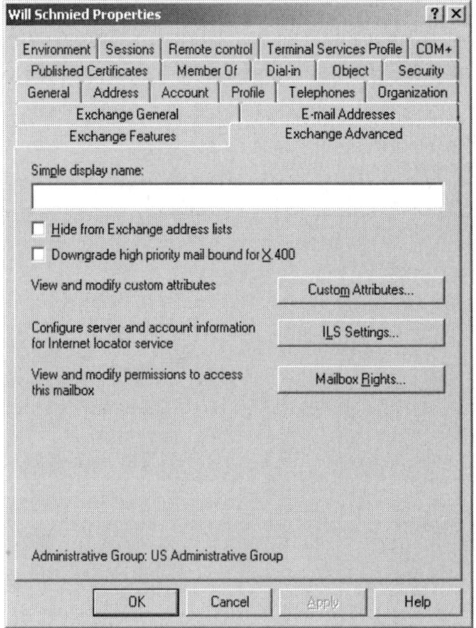

By default, all recipients except public folders are visible to users via the Global Address List. You can use the Hide From Exchange Address Lists option to hide a mailbox from that list or other lists created in System Manager. The mailbox will still be able to receive mail; it just will not be included in address lists.

If you select the Downgrade High Priority Mail Bound For X.400 option, the current mailbox cannot send high-priority messages to X.400 systems. If a high-priority message is sent, it will automatically be downgraded to normal priority.

In addition to the attributes just mentioned, three buttons lead to separate dialog boxes with more configuration options: Custom Attributes, ILS Settings, and Mailbox Rights.

CUSTOM ATTRIBUTES

The Custom Attributes page lets you enter information about a mailbox in 15 custom fields. These fields can be used for any information that you need to include that isn't available on the other property pages. For example, if your company uses a special employee identification numbering system, you could create a custom field for that number. These fields are available to users in the Global Address List only if they are using a special template that displays them or if they perform a specific LDAP query. By default, these fields are labeled extensionAttribute1 through extensionAttribute15, but they can be customized to suit your needs. Just select a field, and click Edit to enter a new value.

ILS SETTINGS

Two fields on this page allow you to specify the server name of a Microsoft Internet Locator Service (ILS) and the account name (ILS account) for this mailbox. This is applicable if your network is using Microsoft NetMeeting for online meetings.

MAILBOX RIGHTS

This page allows you to view and configure the permissions that users and groups have for this mailbox. It should be noted that you could assign multiple users as the owners of a mailbox. This is useful when you want to create a mailbox that will be used by a group of people, such as a Help Desk department. A single mailbox could be created, and all users of that department could be made an owner of that mailbox.

You can modify the particular rights of any user in the list by selecting the user and modifying the Allow and Deny check boxes beside the individual mailbox rights. Some of the more common rights that you can assign here are:

The Delete Mailbox Storage right Allows a user to delete the actual mailbox from the Information Store. This right is given only to administrators by default.

The Read Permissions right Lets the user read mail in the mailbox. You could use this right alone to allow a user to read another user's mail but not send, change, or delete messages.

The Change Permissions right Allows a user to delete or modify items in the primary user's mailbox.

The Take Ownership right Allows a user to become the owner of a mailbox. By default, only administrators are given this permission.

The Full Mailbox Access right Allows a user to access a mailbox and read and delete messages. It also allows the user to send messages using the mailbox.

Security Page

The Security page, seen in Figure 5.9, lets you configure security options for the Active Directory object (in this case, a user account), including the Send As option. Previously this was configured using the Mailbox Rights page.

In order to see the Security page of the user account, you will need to have enabled the Advanced Features view in Active Directory Users and Computers. You can do this by selecting the Advanced Features option located on the View menu of the Active Directory Users and Computers console.

Member Of Page

This page specifies the distribution groups of which this mailbox is a member. Not only can you manage a group from a user's properties, but you can also manage a group from the group's properties. For more information on distribution lists, see the section "Groups" later in this chapter.

Mail-Enabled Users

A mail-enabled user is simply a user who has an e-mail address but not a mailbox on an Exchange server. This means that the user can receive e-mail through their custom address but cannot send mail using the Exchange system. You cannot mail-enable a user during account creation. The only way to create a mail-enabled user is first to create a new user that is not mailbox-enabled and then to enable mail for that user. Exercise 5.3 outlines the steps for mail-enabling a user.

FIGURE 5.9 The Security page

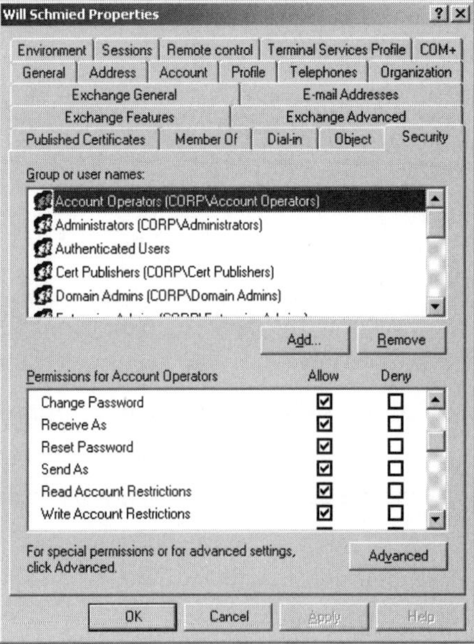

EXERCISE 5.3

Creating a Mail-Enabled User

1. Click Start, point to Programs, point to Administrative Tools, and select Active Directory Users And Computers.
2. In the tree pane on the left, click the Users container.
3. In the right pane, find and select the user object for which you want to enable mail.
4. From the Action menu, select Exchange Tasks.
5. Click Next to dismiss the opening page of the Exchange Task Wizard.
6. Select the Establish E-mail Address option from the list, as seen below, and click Next.

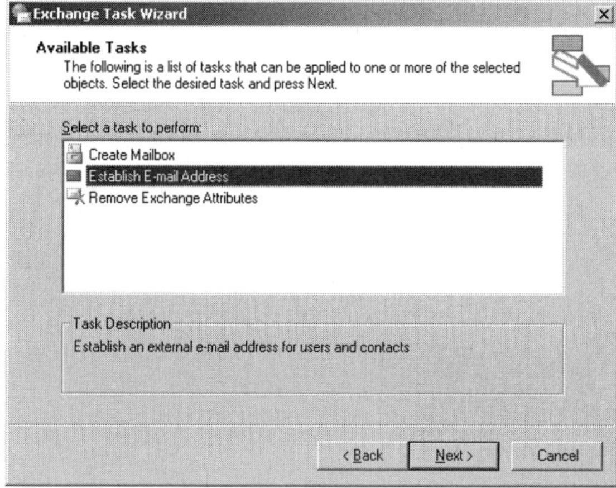

7. On the Establish E-mail Address page, seen below, enter the desired alias for the user and then click the Modify button to create an e-mail address for the mail-enabled user.

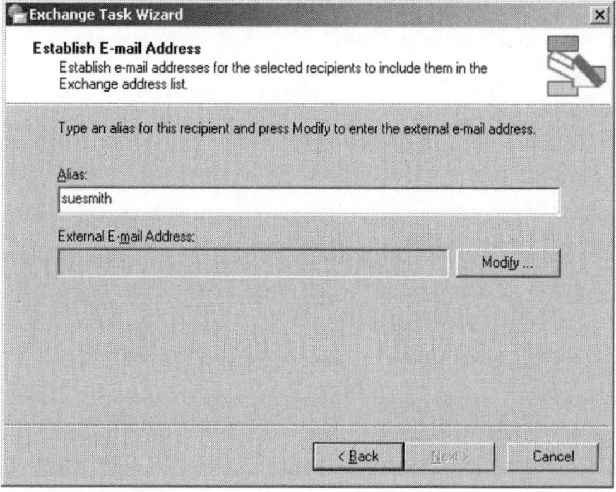

EXERCISE 5.3 *(continued)*

8. The New E-mail Address dialog appears, as seen below, with a list of address types. From this list, select the type of e-mail address you want to create for the user, and click OK. For this exercise, we will create an SMTP e-mail address.

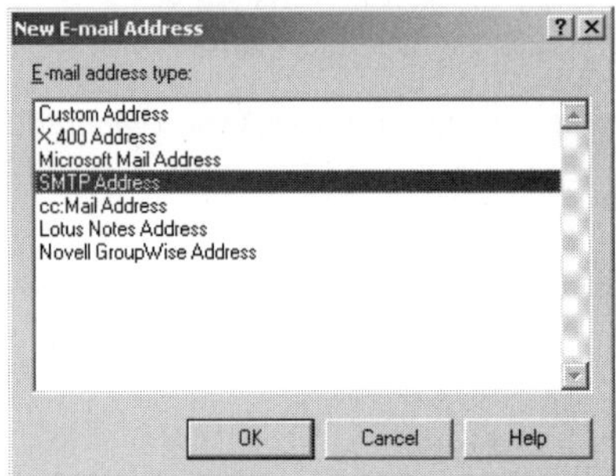

9. The Internet Address Properties dialog opens, as seen below. On the General tab of the dialog, enter the e-mail address for the user.

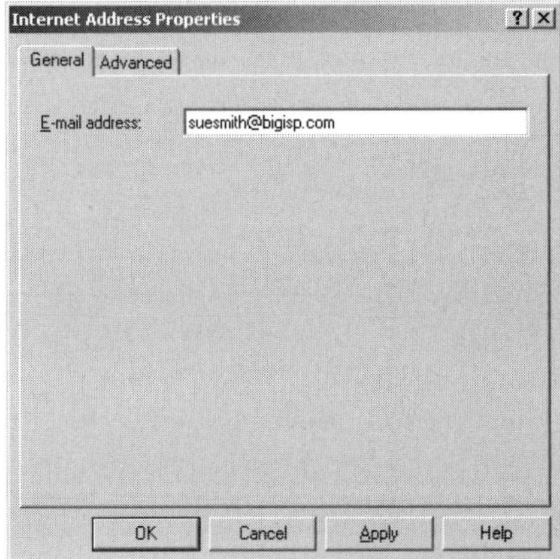

EXERCISE 5.3 *(continued)*

10. You can configure advanced settings by switching to the Advanced tab, seen below. If desired you can override the Internet Mail Service default settings for the user by checking the Override Internet Mail Service Settings For This Recipient box and configuring your own message format settings. When you have finished, click OK.

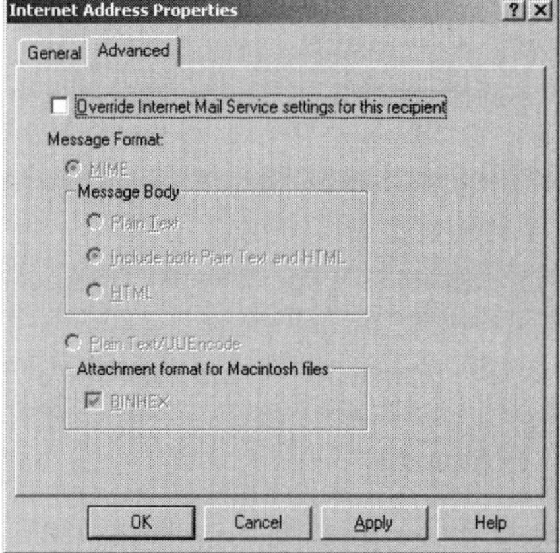

11. You are now returned to the Exchange Task Wizard, and the new e-mail address appears in the appropriate field. Click Next to go on.

12. The Exchange Task Wizard will now mail-enable the user. When the process has completed you will be presented with a summary page. Click Finish to exit the wizard.

Once you enable mail for a user following this procedure, you can configure the mail settings in the same way you would for a mailbox-enabled user.

Microsoft has introduced a new type of user object in Exchange Server 2003. The InetOrgPerson object is used to improve compatibility between Exchange Server 2003 and those directory services that use the InetOrgPerson object. You can learn more about the InetOrgPerson object at `www.faqs.org/rfcs/rfc2798.html`.

Groups

In Windows Server 2003, a group is an Active Directory object that can hold users and other groups. In the case of security groups, permissions can be assigned to a group and are inherited by all of the objects in that group. This makes the group a valuable Windows security construct. Exchange Server 2003 also uses the group for another purpose. A group can be made mail-enabled and then populated with other mail- or mailbox-enabled recipients to make a distribution list, a term you may be familiar with from earlier versions of Exchange Server. A group can contain users, contacts, public folders, and even other groups. When a message is sent to a mail-enabled group, the list of members is extracted, and the message is sent to each member of the list individually. Groups are visible in the Global Address List if they are configured properly to be mail-enabled.

Windows Server 2003 supports two distinct types of groups. A security group can be assigned permissions and rights and be mail-enabled. A distribution group can only be mail-enabled.

Group Types and Scopes

Before we can begin any discussion on creating and managing groups, a discussion on group types and group scopes is necessary. You will need to have a good understanding of how the two different group types and three different group scopes work before you can effectively use groups in your Exchange organization.

Group Types

As mentioned previously, there are two types of groups within Active Directory: security groups and distribution groups. The names of these groups are fairly descriptive in regard to their usage.

Security groups Security groups, as the name implies, are used primarily to configure and assign security settings for those user and group objects placed within the group. An administrator can configure the desired rights and permissions on the group, and these settings will then automatically be applied to all group members without the need to manually configure the settings on the individual objects. As you can see, this is a benefit from both an administrative point of view (less work to be done) and from an accuracy point of view (fewer chances of configuring individual object permissions incorrectly). Security groups can also be mail-enabled if desired, therefore allowing their mailbox-enabled and mail-enabled members to receive all messages that are sent to the security group.

Distribution groups Distribution groups, as their name implies, are used only for sending messages to a large number of objects without having to manually select each user, group, or contact. You can place all members of a specific department or geographical location into a distribution group and then send one message to the group that will be distributed to all members. Since distribution groups are not access control list (ACL)–enabled as security groups are, you cannot assign user rights or permissions to them.

You can change a distribution group into a security group at any time with no loss in functionality. However, changing a security group into a distribution group will result in the rights and permissions that have been configured on that group being lost. You will be warned of this fact when attempting to make the change.

Group Scopes

Within Active Directory, three different group scopes exist. The scope of the group determines who may be members of the group from an Active Directory standpoint. From an Exchange standpoint, the group scope determines who will be able to determine group membership when multiple domains exist within the organization.

Domain local groups The membership of domain local groups is not published to the global catalog servers in the organization, thus preventing Exchange users from being able to determine the group membership of mail-enabled domain local groups outside the domain in which their user account is located. In most cases, if your organization consists of multiple domains, then you may opt to not use domain local groups for Exchange distribution purposes. The membership of domain local groups is dependent on the domain functional level of the domain but typically can include accounts from any domain in the forest.

Global groups The membership of global groups is also not published to the global catalog servers in the organization. In most cases, if your organization consists of multiple domains, then you may opt to not use global groups for Exchange distribution purposes. The membership of global groups is dependent on the domain functional level of the domain but typically can include only accounts from the same domain in the forest as the group was created in.

Universal groups Only universal groups have their membership information published to the global catalog servers in the organization. This then allows Exchange users that are located in any domain in the forest to be able to determine the group membership of any group in the forest, regardless of the domain it has been created in. The ability to create, and therefore use, universal groups is dependent on the domain functional level of the domain in that they can be created only when the domain functional level is at Windows 2000 native or Windows Server 2003. If your organization is capable of using universal groups, you'll want to consider their usage for Exchange distribution groups, especially when creating query-based distribution groups, as discussed later in this chapter. Universal groups can contain members from any domain in the forest.

There is a lot more to be said about group scopes, including how the domain functional level impacts your ability to work with the different scopes. You can find more information about group scopes by searching the Windows Server 2003 help files for "Group Scopes" or by visiting this website: www.microsoft.com/technet/prodtechnol/windowsserver2003/proddocs/standard/sag_ADgroups_3groupscopes.asp.

Creating a Group

Creating and configuring a new group object is very simple. Exercise 5.4 outlines the steps involved.

EXERCISE 5.4

Creating a New Group in Active Directory

1. Choose Start ➢ Programs ➢ Administrative Tools ➢ Active Directory Users and Computers.
2. From the Action menu, point to New, and select Group.
3. The New Object - Group dialog box opens, as seen below. In the Group Name field, type a name that represents the members of the group you are creating. Notice that Windows automatically fills in a pre–Windows 2000–compatible group name for you.

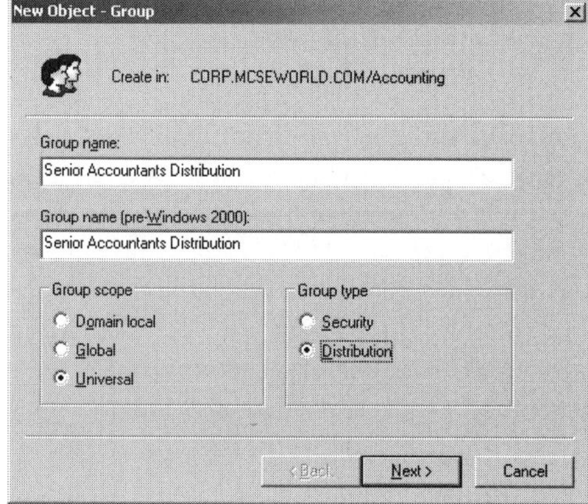

EXERCISE 5.4 *(continued)*

4. Next, you must choose a group scope. This determines at what level the group will be available in Active Directory—local, global, or universal. If you are going to create a simple distribution group (shown in the next step), it is usually best to make the group universal in scope so that it will be available throughout the organization. Otherwise, you may find that the group is limited by domain boundaries. Note that a domain must be running in the Windows 2000 native or Windows Sever 2003 domain functional level to support universal groups.
5. Next, you must define a group type. This determines whether the group is for security or distribution purposes. A *security group* can be made mail-enabled and used for distribution purposes. Recall that security groups can also be assigned permissions and made part of access control lists (ACLs) for resources. A *distribution group* is used for e-mail purposes only and cannot be used for security purposes. Security groups can be later converted into distribution groups, with a loss of all configured ACL entries. Likewise, distribution groups can later be converted into security groups if desired.
6. Click Next to go on.
7. Select the Create An Exchange E-mail Address option.
8. If you want, you can change the alias name or the administrative group to which the new group belongs. When you have finished, click Next to go on.
9. The final page summarizes the setup. Click Finish to create the new group.

Properties of a Distribution Group

Once you have created a new group, you will configure it the same way you configure other objects—with property pages. Three Exchange-related property pages connected with distribution groups need to be explained: Members, Managed By, and Exchange Advanced.

Members Page

The Members property page lists every member of the group. Use the Add button to access the Active Directory list, from which you can add new members to the group. Use the Remove button to remove selected members.

Managed By Page

The Managed By property page, shown in Figure 5.10, lets you assign an owner whose job it is to manage the group's membership. By default, the administrator who creates the group is the owner, but you can designate any user, group, or contact in the GAL as the owner. If you give ownership to another user, that user can use Outlook to modify the group's membership and does not need access to Active Directory Users and Computers. You can relieve yourself of a great deal of work by specifying the owners of a group. As groups grow larger, they can consume a considerable amount of management time.

Exchange Advanced Page

The Exchange Advanced property page, shown in Figure 5.11, holds several configuration items that may be familiar to you, such as Simple Display Name and a Custom Attributes button.

FIGURE 5.10 Using the Managed By page to let other users manage a group

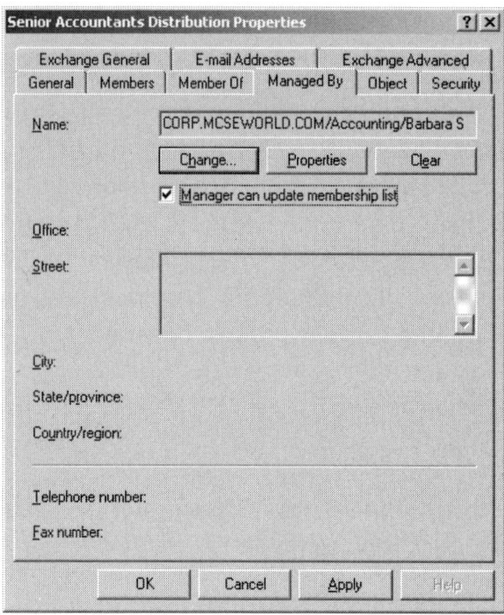

FIGURE 5.11 Setting advanced group properties with the Exchange Advanced page

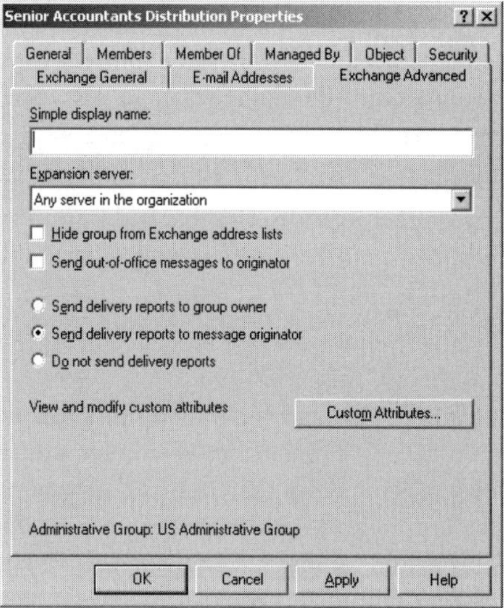

You can, however, also configure several options that are particular to distribution lists. They are as follows:

Expansion Server Whenever a message is sent to a group, the group must be expanded so that the message can be sent to each member of the group. A categorizer performs this expansion. The default choice is Any Server In The Organization. This choice means that the home server of the user sending the message always expands the group. You can also designate a specific server to handle the expansion of the group. The choice of a dedicated expansion server is a good one if you have a large group. In this case, expansion could consume a great amount of server resources, which can compromise performance for busy servers.

We will discuss the creation and administration of administrative groups and routing groups in Chapter 8, "Building Administrative and Routing Groups."

Real World Scenario

Configuring Expansion Servers

What's the big deal about using expansion servers? Why do you even need to bother thinking about them? Consider the fact that expansion of messages sent to larger distribution groups occurs by default on the first Exchange server that handles the message—the Exchange server that houses the mailbox of the user who originally sent the message. This may not be a desirable situation when that mailbox server is already highly loaded just by providing mailbox access to your network. What if you had 25 distribution groups that each had over 500 members? Would you want a mailbox server to be used to expand these messages? Probably not—and thus the need for an expansion server.

In larger organizations, you may want to give some serious consideration to designating one or more Exchange servers in each routing group to be an expansion server. Expansion servers should not contain any mailbox stores but can be public folder servers or even bridgehead servers for that routing group. By using these servers as expansion servers, you remove the additional overhead of expanding messages sent to distribution groups from your already taxed mailbox servers.

Sounds great doesn't it? Well before you run out and configure a specific expansion server for all of your distribution groups, you need to be aware of the ramifications of doing so. By configuring an expansion server for a distribution group you are effectively creating a single point of failure (SPOF) for that distribution group. Should the designated expansion server be unavailable for any reason, the message will not be expanded and none of the group's members will receive the message.

Hide Group From Exchange Address Lists If you enable this option, the group is not visible in the GAL.

Send Out-Of-Office Messages To Originator Users of Exchange clients can configure rules that enable the clients to automatically reply to messages received while the users are away from their office. When this option is enabled, users who send messages to groups can receive those automatic out-of-office messages from members of the list. For particularly large groups, it's best not to allow out-of-office messages to be delivered because of the excess network traffic they generate.

Send Delivery Reports To Group Owner If you enable this option, notification is sent to the owner of the group whenever an error occurs during the delivery of a message to the group or to one of its members. Note that this option is unavailable if the group has not been assigned an owner.

Send Delivery Reports To Message Originator If you enable this option, error notifications are also sent to the user who sent a message to the group.

Do Not Send Delivery Reports If you enable this option, error notifications will not be sent.

Custom Attributes Just as you can configure up to 15 custom attributes for a mailbox, you can configure up to 15 custom attributes for a distribution group as well.

Query-Based Distribution Groups

Among the new features in Exchange Server 2003 is the *query-based distribution group*. One of the biggest problems with using distribution groups in the past has been the amount of work and time that it can take to maintain an accurate and up-to-date group membership. Query-based distribution groups aim to correct that problem. As the name implies, a query-based distribution group is a mail-enabled distribution group that has its membership defined by the results of an LDAP query that is made against the content of Active Directory.

The obvious advantage to using a query-based distribution is that it provides a way to dynamically configure the membership of a group from all Exchange recipients based on a configured LDAP query. You can create a query, for example, that might limit the membership of a group to those users who are part of the Accounting department of your organization. By that same logic, you could also create a query-based distribution group that specifies membership is to be limited to those users, contacts, and distribution groups that are located in a specific building or in a specific geographical area (such as a state or city) within your organization. By being able to quickly create, and change, the queries used to create these groups you save time and energy over maintaining larger standard distribution groups. As well, query-based distribution groups are much more accurate in their group membership because all the work is done by the results of the query you create.

As you might suspect by now, there is a trade-off to the power and flexibility that query-based distribution groups provide. This trade-off comes in the form of increased loading on your global catalog servers. Each time an e-mail is sent to a query-based distribution group, the LDAP query you have configured must be run against the global catalog to determine the membership of the group.

To make use of query-based distribution groups, your network should be using Windows Server 2003 global catalog servers and Exchange Server 2003 or Exchange 2000 Server at Service Pack 3. If you still have any remaining Windows 2000 Server global catalog servers, don't despair; you can still use query-based distribution groups as long as you modify the Registry on your Exchange 2000 Servers to accommodate them. You can perform this Registry modification as detailed in Exercise 5.5.

EXERCISE 5.5

Modifying Exchange 2000 Servers for Query-Based Distribution Groups

1. On the Exchange 2000 Server, open the Registry Editor by clicking Start ➤ Run and entering **regedit**.
2. Locate the following Registry key: `HKEY_LOCAL_MACHINE\SYSTEM\CurrentControlSet\Services\SMTPSVC\Parameters`
3. Once you have located and expanded this key, you will need to create a new DWORD for it. In the right-hand pane of the Registry Editor, right-click and select New ➤ DWORD Value from the context menu.
4. For the DWORD name, enter **DynamicDLPageSize**.
5. To modify the data in the new DWORD, right-click it and select Modify from the context menu. Select the Decimal option and enter the value **31** in the Value Data area.
6. Click OK to accept the changes.
7. Close the Registry Editor.

When you are ready to create a query-based distribution group, you can do so by completing the process detailed in Exercise 5.6.

EXERCISE 5.6

Creating a Query-Based Distribution Group

1. Choose Start ➤ Programs ➤ Administrative Tools ➤ Active Directory Users and Computers.
2. From the Action menu, point to New, and select Query-Based Distribution Group.
3. The New Object – Query-Based Distribution Group dialog box opens, as seen below. Enter the name for the new group and its e-mail alias, and then click Next.

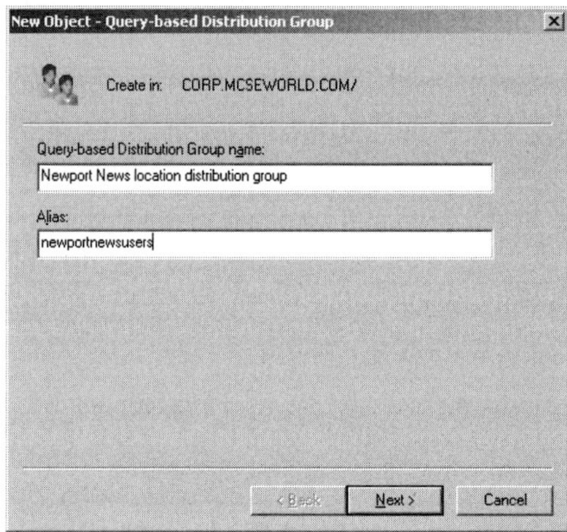

4. On the next page, seen below, you will be able to select the Active Directory container against which you want the query to be run. To change the default value, click the Change button and select the new container.

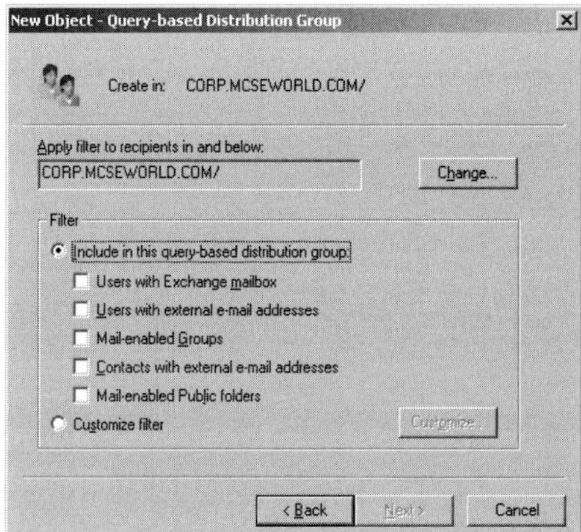

EXERCISE 5.6 *(continued)*

5. The next step is to create the filter, or LDAP query, that will be used to determine the group membership. Several preconfigured options exist, as you saw previously. In most cases, however, you will want to select the Customize Filter option and then build a custom filter by clicking the Customize button. You can see how we might select from all available Exchange recipients that are located in the city of Newport News. Be aware, however, that not all attributes of an object are replicated to the global catalog. A list of the attributes that are not replicated, and thus not suitable for use in the filter of a query-based distribution group, follows this exercise.

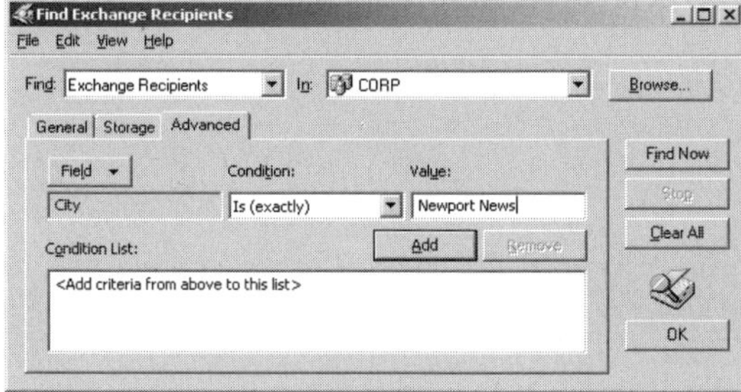

6. When you have finished creating your filter, click the OK button to close the Find Exchange Recipients dialog box.

7. Click Next on the New Object - Query-based Distribution Group dialog box to continue. You will be presented with a summary of the query you have created.

8. Click the Finish button to create the new query-based distribution group.

9. To see the results your query returned, you can use the Preview tab of the group's properties. Right-click the new query-based distribution group and select Properties from the context menu. Switch to the Preview tab, seen below, to see the results of the filter query.

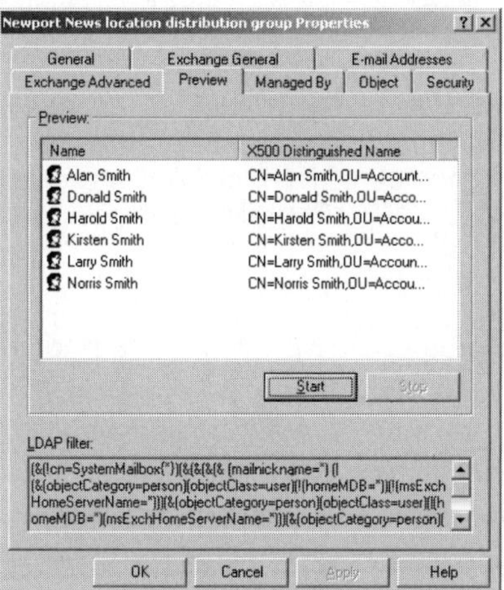

As mentioned in Exercise 5.6, there are several object attributes that are not replicated to the global catalog and are thus not suitable for use in the creation of a filter for a query-based distribution group. The following list presents these attributes:

- Assistant
- Comment
- Direct reports
- Division
- E-mail address (other)
- Employee ID
- Generational suffix
- Home address
- Home drive
- Home folder
- ILS settings
- International ISDN number
- International ISDN number (others)
- Logon workstations
- Member of
- Middle name
- Teletex number
- Teletex number (others)
- Title

Although you might be tempted to create the LDAP query by hand, don't give it serious consideration unless you are very familiar with this operation. The simple query we created in Exercise 5.6 that looked just for Exchange objects with a city of Newport News produced the following result:

```
(&(!cn=SystemMailbox{*})(&(&(&(& (mailnickname=*) (| (&(objectCategory=person)
(objectClass=user)(!(homeMDB=*))(!(msExchHomeServerName=*)))(&(objectCategory=
person)(objectClass=user)(|(homeMDB=*)(msExchHomeServerName=*)))(&(objectCategory
=person)(objectClass=contact))(objectCategory=group)(objectCategory=publicFolder
)(objectCategory=msExchDynamicDistributionList)
)))(objectCategory=user)(l=Newport News))))
```

As you can imagine, adding in other filter items would quickly result in a very complicated query string. Should the LDAP query you are using for a query-based distribution group have bad formatting or not be in the proper LDAP syntax, a user who sends an e-mail message to that group will receive a code 5.2.4 nondelivery report (NDR). On the other hand, should the query be formatted properly but return no Exchange objects, no NDR will be generated because the query-based distribution group functioned as it was properly configured—thus demonstrating the importance of checking group membership using the Preview tab.

Contacts

A contact is a pointer object that holds the address of a non-Exchange mail recipient. Contacts are made visible in the Global Address List and, therefore, permit Exchange clients to send messages to non-Exchange mail users. This functionality assumes that the necessary connector or gateway is in place between the Exchange system and the foreign system, such as the Internet Mail SMTP Connector for sending and receiving mail from the Internet.

Creating a Contact

Like other objects, contacts are created using the Active Directory Users and Computers tool. When creating a contact, you must be prepared to select the type of e-mail address to create and to enter the foreign e-mail address. The standard options for the types of foreign addresses are as follows:

- Custom address
- X.400 address
- Microsoft Mail address
- SMTP address
- cc:Mail address
- Lotus Notes address
- Novell GroupWise address

Exercise 5.7 walks you through the creation of this type of recipient.

EXERCISE 5.7

Creating a Contact

1. Choose Start ➢ Programs ➢ Administrative Tools ➢ Active Directory Users And Computers.
2. From the Action menu, point to New, and select Contact.
3. Enter the full name and display name of the user for whom you want to create a contact object, and then click Next.
4. Make sure the alias is correct, and then click Modify.
5. From the list of address types in the New E-mail Address dialog that appears, select the type of e-mail address you want to create for the user, and click OK.
6. On the General page of the Internet Address Properties dialog that opens, enter the e-mail address for the user.
7. Click Next to go on.
8. A summary screen is then displayed asking you to confirm your choices. If you want to change any of the settings, you can use the Back button to do so. Once you are satisfied with your choices, click Finish to create the new contact object.

Properties of a Contact

The properties of a contact are very similar to those of a standard Exchange mailbox. The main difference is that the attributes dealing directly with the capabilities or restrictions of a mailbox are not available. For example, you cannot set storage limits on a contact since there is no storage on the Exchange server to limit. In addition, you cannot configure protocol settings for a contact.

Public Folder Recipients

A public folder is a sharable container of information. It is a recipient object because, in addition to being able to view information in it, users can send information to it.

Like mailboxes, public folders are created and stored on a specific home server. But because users on different servers and in different sites could need access to that public folder, you can configure public folders to be copied automatically to other Exchange servers. This is called *replication*, and each copy of the same public folder is called a *replica*.

While the other recipients are created from Active Directory Users and Computers, public folders are created and managed using either a Microsoft Exchange client application (such as Outlook) or through the Exchange System Manager snap-in. All properties of a public folder are available for management within System Manager, and many are also available using an Exchange client. This allows users to take over much of the management of public folders.

The creation and configuration of public folders is covered in detail in Chapter 6, "Using Public Folders."

Basic Management of Recipient Objects

Even after they have been created, recipient objects still require care from administrators. Some of the basic management activities are as follows:

- Using templates for recipient creation
- Filtering a recipient
- Finding a recipient
- Moving a mailbox
- Using address lists

Each of these activities is covered briefly in the following discussions.

Using Templates for Recipient Creation

A *template* is a pattern that can be used to more efficiently create something—in this case, a recipient object. A template recipient, or multiple template recipients, can be created with the desired default values. These default values can then be used when creating actual recipient objects.

Any object can be used as a template. A simple method is to create an object, such as a user, that holds all of the default attribute settings you desire. Once the template is created, use it by highlighting it and then selecting the Copy command from the Action menu of the Active Directory Users and Computers tool. The New Object Wizard will open, just as when you create a new object, except that all of the default information configured in the template will already appear in the new object. The exception is that no matter what type of template object you use, the first name, last name, display name, alias name, directory name, and e-mail address are not copied to the new recipient objects created from the template.

When you create a recipient to use as a template, you probably will want to hide the recipient from the address book using the template's Exchange Advanced property page. This way, users won't be able to view it in the GAL. You will always be able to see it in Active Directory Users and Computers, though. You should also name your template in such a way that it is both easy to find and easy to distinguish from regular recipients. For example, you might name all of your templates with an underscore (_) at the beginning so that they all appear at the top of the list.

Filtering a Recipient

By default, all types of recipients are shown in Active Directory Users and Computers, including public folders. You can filter that view with the View menu so that only select types of recipients are shown. Filtering your recipient view can be useful if you are looking for a specific recipient and the list based on recipient type is not very long, or if you need to select all the recipients of a certain type.

In addition to using the View menu, you can also apply more advanced filters that let you view sets of objects according to selected attribute settings. To apply a filter, select a container holding Exchange recipients in Active Directory Users and Computers (such as Users), and choose Filter Options from the View menu. This opens the Filter Options dialog shown in Figure 5.12.

The default setting is to view recipients of all types. Click the Show Only The Following Types Of Objects option, and check the types of recipients you want to view. When you click OK, only those types of recipients are displayed in the Users container. The Filter Options dialog also lets you specify how many recipients should be displayed per folder.

The filter options you set apply to the entire Active Directory hierarchy, not just the Users container. This means that if you set the filter to show only users and groups, for example, no computers will show up in your Computers folder until you reset the filter.

FIGURE 5.12 Filtering recipients

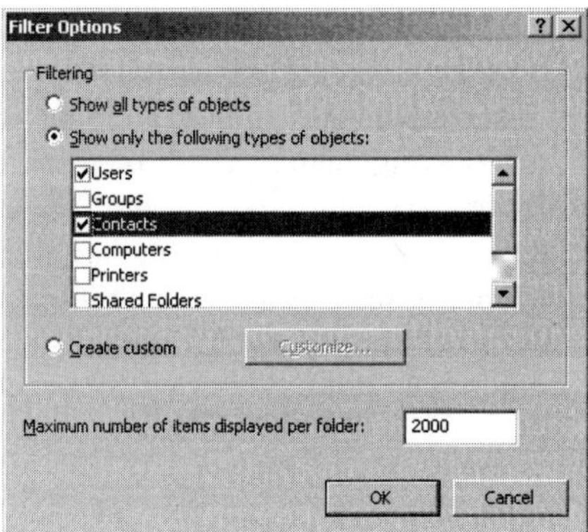

Finding a Recipient

Active Directory Users and Computers provides a recipient search tool with sophisticated search criteria. Open this tool by selecting the Find command in the Action menu. This command opens the Find Users, Contacts, and Groups window, shown in Figure 5.13.

FIGURE 5.13 Finding a recipient

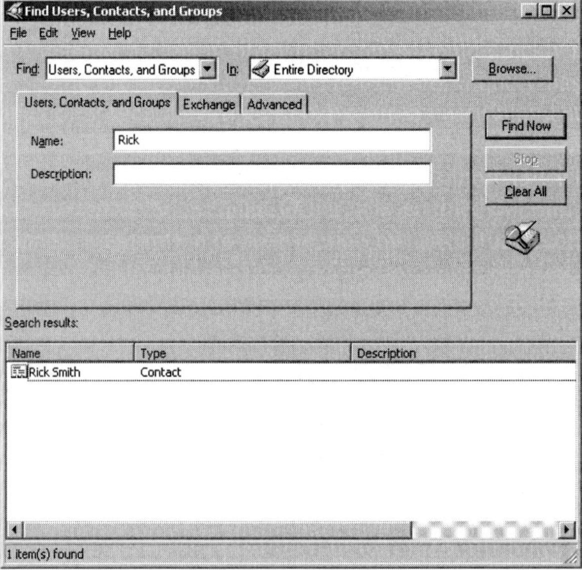

Use the Find field to specify what types of objects you want to find. The default is to find users, contacts, and groups. Use the In field to specify the container in which you want to perform the search. The default is to search in the Users container. Enter any part of a name or description, and click Find Now to begin the search. The Find window expands to display the results. You can manipulate objects in the Find window just as you would in the main Active Directory Users and Computers window by right-clicking them to access their shortcut menus.

There are also a few advanced options you can use to narrow your search. The Exchange tab in the Find window lets you specify that you want to view only Exchange recipients in your search results and even lets you set the specific types of recipients you want displayed.

Moving a Mailbox

Physically, mailboxes and their contents reside on their home server. Mailboxes can be moved to other servers or to other mailbox stores on the same server. This is done through Active Directory Users and Computers. Simply highlight the user whose mailbox you want to move, and select the Exchange Tasks command from the Action menu. On the first screen, select the Move Mailbox option. The Exchange Task Wizard will then step you through choosing a new server and storage group for the mailbox, as seen in Figure 5.14. When you finish the wizard, the mailbox is moved.

FIGURE 5.14 Moving a mailbox to a different server

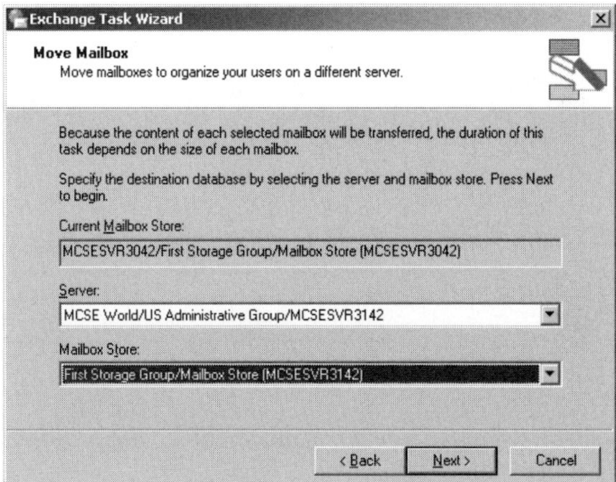

When you move a mailbox, the size of the mailbox can increase. When a message is sent to multiple recipients in the same storage group, Exchange stores only one copy of the message on the server and gives all the recipients on that server a pointer to that single copy. This is called *single-instance storage*. But when a mailbox is moved outside the storage group, the single-instance storage for that mailbox is lost in the new location because each message must be copied there. For example, suppose 10 mailboxes take up 55 MB of disk space in the Private Information Store. Each mailbox has five messages of 1 MB and a pointer to five single-instance messages of 1 MB. If those 10 mailboxes were moved to another server, the single-instance storage would be lost, and each mailbox would have 10 MB of storage. The Private Information Store on the new server would increase by 100 MB.

Mailboxes might be moved for several reasons:

- To balance the load between servers
- To move mailboxes to a server that is on the same local area network as the mailbox owners
- To take a server down for maintenance reasons and still allow users access to their mailboxes

Because groups and contacts are primarily logical entities, they are not tied to any one specific Exchange server. You can move these objects into different containers within the Active Directory organization if needed.

Using Address Lists

Users on your network normally search for other users using the Global Address List (GAL), which contains all messaging recipients in an organization. If your network contains a large number of recipients, searching through the GAL for a specific recipient can become a daunting task. Fortunately, you can configure your own address lists that limit the scope of recipients included in the list.

Default Address Lists

Exchange Server 2003 comes with several default address lists built in. When a user opens their address list in a client application, they can choose which address list to view. Table 5.1 shows the default address lists.

TABLE 5.1 Default Address Lists in Exchange Server 2003

Address List	Contains
All Contacts	All mail-enabled contacts in the organization.
All Groups	All mail-enabled groups in the organization. These include both security and distribution groups.
All Users	All mailbox-enabled and mail-enabled users in the organization.
Public Folders	All mail-enabled public folders in the organization that are not hidden from the address list.
Default Global Address List	All recipients in the organization.

Custom Address Lists

Exchange Server 2003 also lets you create your own custom address lists based on most of the fields available on recipient objects. For example, you could create an address list that showed only the users based in a certain city or in a certain department. Address lists are created in the Recipients container in System Manager, as shown in Figure 5.15.

FIGURE 5.15 Viewing address lists in System Manager

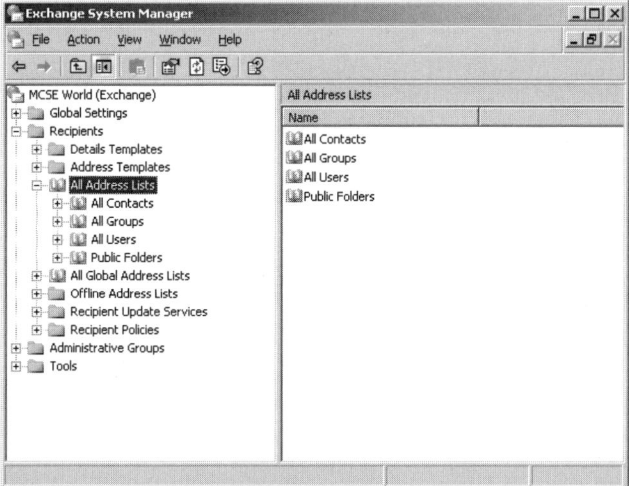

All address lists must be created inside other address lists. To create a top-level address list, create it inside the All Address Lists list. Since address lists can be nested, you can get pretty sophisticated in creating an address list structure. For example, suppose that you wanted your users to be able to quickly locate your corporate executives. You might first create an address list called Corporate Executives. Under that you could then create additional address lists named Board Members, Executive Secretaries, and Vice Presidents. Under these lists you could go even further by creating lists for geographical location. Figure 5.16 shows a hierarchy like this example. You could alternatively create address lists that are nested by state, city, and building if you desired.

Nesting address lists also provides a way to hide address lists from users. You can deny access to an address list by denying the user the Open Address List permission on the list's Security property page. However, this only prevents the user from viewing the contents of the list, not from viewing the list itself. The way around this is to create an empty address list and deny the Open Address List permission on that list. Name this list whatever you like. Then, create any address lists you want to be hidden from view inside this address list.

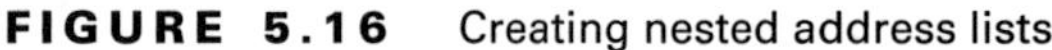

FIGURE 5.16 Creating nested address lists

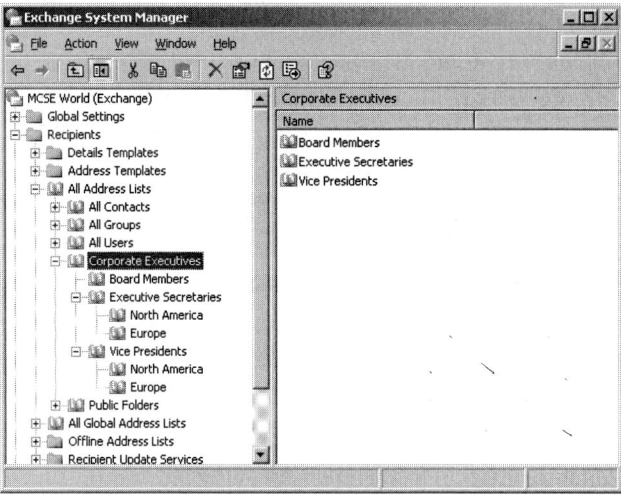

When you create a new address list, a dialog box opens that lets you name the list and set up filter rules that define the recipients contained in the list. You can set up the filter rules when you create the list or go back and do it later by opening the property pages for the list. When we are creating a nest of address lists, we often find it helpful to go ahead and create the structure by simply creating and naming the lists and then going back later to set up the filter rules.

You create filter rules using an interface much like the one used for finding recipients in Active Directory that we discussed earlier in the chapter (see Figure 5.17). Use the General tab of this dialog box to choose the types of recipients you want included on the list. Use the Storage tab to specify the server on which mailboxes or public folders are stored. Use the Advanced tab to restrict membership on the list by selecting criteria for specific fields for a recipient, such as their city, department, or any custom attribute.

FIGURE 5.17 Setting up filter rules for an address list

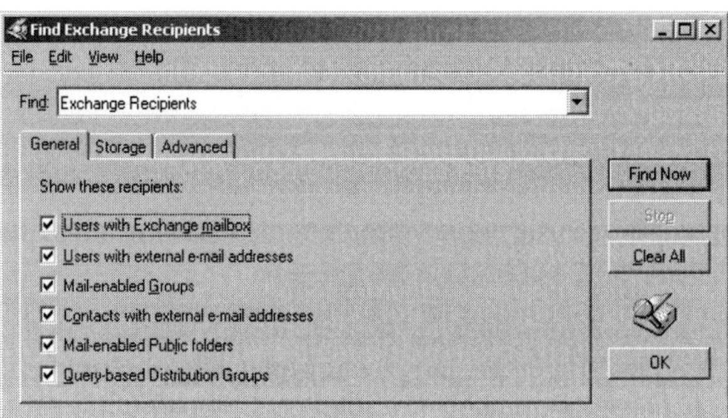

Offline Address Lists

Offline address lists are typically used by people who are not always connected to the Exchange network. Offline address lists are copies of online address lists that are stored on a user's local computer using an `.oab` extension. By default, the Default Global Address List is used to generate a Default Offline Address List. You can also create custom offline address lists by right-clicking the Offline Address Lists container in System Manager (refer to Figure 5.15) and choosing New Offline Address List. When creating the new offline address list, you will specify the list's name, the server that will store the new list, and any address lists (default or custom) that will be used to generate the new offline address list.

Recipient Update Service

The Recipient Update Service (RUS) is a component of the System Attendant service that is responsible for building and maintaining address lists. RUS polls Active Directory for updated recipient information on a predefined schedule (every one minute, by default) and updates address lists based on any new information. The RUS is also responsible for updating the e-mail addresses of any recipients that are attached to a recipient policy. Recipient policies are covered in Chapter 10, "Administration and Maintenance."

The Recipient Update Services container in System Manager is shown in Figure 5.18.

By default, two RUS objects are created:

- The Recipient Update Service (Enterprise Configuration) object updates the e-mail addresses of objects in the configuration partition of Active Directory. This includes objects such as the Information Store, MTA, and System Attendant.
- One Recipient Update Service (installation Active Directory domain) object exists for each Active Directory domain that contains an Exchange server. This RUS object updates the e-mail addresses for recipients found in the domain partition of Active Directory, including users, groups, public folders, and contacts. This RUS object also updates address lists based on changes to recipient objects in a domain.

Even though the RUS runs automatically, you can also update address lists manually using one of the following two commands, which are available by right-clicking a specific address list:

- The Update Now command updates the address list with any new changes in recipient information.
- The Rebuild command rebuilds the entire membership of the address list.

In addition, you can modify the parameters of the RUS object itself by right-clicking it and choosing Properties. The following four properties are available:

- The domain serviced by the RUS. This is not directly modifiable.
- The server in the domain responsible for generating and updating address lists for the domain.
- The domain controller that the server connects to for updated Active Directory information.
- The update interval at which the RUS will run. The Run Always option sets the RUS to run at its default—every one minute.

FIGURE 5.18 Viewing RUS objects in System Manager

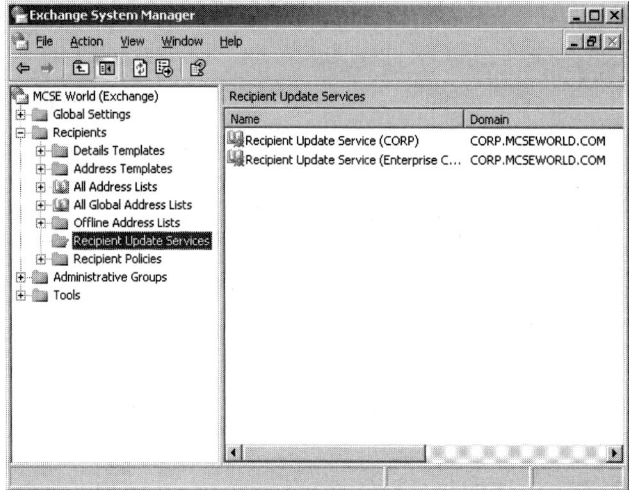

Summary

Recipients are Active Directory objects that are used to reference resources that can receive messages. The four main types of recipients are as follows:

- Users
- Groups
- Contacts
- Public folders

A user is an Active Directory object that usually represents a person with an Exchange mailbox. A mailbox-enabled user has an associated mailbox in a Private Information Store on an Exchange server. Each user mailbox is a private storage area that allows an individual user to send, receive, and store messages. A mail-enabled user is one who has an e-mail address and can receive, but not send, messages.

A group is a container into which you can place other recipients. Recipients in a group automatically inherit that group's permissions and rights. Exchange uses mail-enabled groups to form distribution lists. Messages sent to a group are redirected and sent to each member of the group. These groups allow users to send messages to multiple recipients without having to address each recipient individually.

Query-based distribution groups are a new type of distribution group in Exchange Server 2003 that allows Exchange administrators to create distribution groups that maintain their group membership dynamically. Once the LDAP query has successfully been created for the query-based distribution group, the applicable objects (those that meet the filter query criteria) will automatically be members of the query-based distribution group. Every time an e-mail message is sent to a query-based distribution group, the LDAP query is performed to determine the current group membership to which the message should be expanded.

A contact is a pointer to an e-mail address for a non-Exchange recipient. Contacts are most often used for connecting your organization to foreign messaging systems, such as Microsoft Mail, Lotus Notes, or the Internet. As an administrator, you would create contacts so that frequently used e-mail addresses are available in the Global Address List as real names.

A public folder contains information that is shared among a group of people. Public folders can contain e-mail messages, forms, word-processing documents, spreadsheet files, and files of many other formats.

With the exception of public folders, all recipient objects are created and managed using the Active Directory Users and Computers utility. When you create a new user, you are automatically given the chance to create a mailbox for that user. You can also create mailboxes for existing users. Contacts and groups are usually made mail-enabled when they are created.

Recipient objects are generally configured with property pages, which are groups of attributes that pertain to the object. Other Exchange-related tasks can be accessed through the Exchange Tasks command in the Action menu of Active Directory Users and Computers.

Public folders are created and managed using either an Exchange client or the System Manager snap-in for Exchange.

Exam Essentials

Understand group types and scopes. It is important that you understand fully the different group types and group scopes that can exist within Active Directory. As well, you should understand how the use of a particular group scope can impact your Exchange organization by limiting who can determine group membership.

Understand the background of query-based distribution groups. Query-based distribution groups are a great new feature in Exchange Server 2003. Therefore, you should expect to be tested on what they are, what they do, and how they work. You must understand the processes involved in creating one and in sending an e-mail to one. Also, you should understand the drawbacks associated with using query-based distribution groups.

Know the difference between mail-enabled and mailbox-enabled. Although it is very simple in nature, many people get confused when it comes to remembering the difference between a mailbox-enabled object and a mail-enabled object. Mailbox-enabled objects can send and received e-mail messages using the Exchange organization and store their messages in an Exchange mailbox. Mail-enabled objects can send and receive e-mail messages but do not have an associated Exchange mailbox. Some mail-enabled objects, such as contacts, send and receive e-mail using an external ISP account. Other mail-enabled objects, such as distribution groups, use the Exchange organization to receive mail but have no mailbox themselves.

Understand the Recipient Update Service. Although we only briefly examined the Recipient Update Service (RUS) here, you should understand its basic purposes as well as how and when it might be used manually in your Exchange organization. Recall that only one instance of the Recipient Update Service (Enterprise Configuration) object exists for the entire Exchange organization, but that there will be one Recipient Update Service (installation Active Directory domain) object per domain that contains one or more Exchange servers. You will see more of the RUS in Chapter 10 when we discuss recipient policies.

Review Questions

1. A user named Aaron leaves your company. Management would like a user named Bobbi to assume Aaron's responsibilities. What could you do so that Bobbi can receive Aaron's e-mail messages? Select the best answer.

   A. Make Bobbi's mailbox an alternate recipient for Aaron's mailbox.

   B. Disable Aaron's user account, and give Bobbi profile permission to access Aaron's mailbox.

   C. Delete Aaron's mailbox, and forward all undeliverable messages to Bobbi.

   D. Create a rule in Aaron's mailbox so that all of Aaron's mail is forwarded to Bobbi.

2. You want to allow all of the personnel in the technical support group to send and receive messages from the same mailbox. What can you do to enable this?

   A. Create a distribution group, and designate the mailbox as the owner of the distribution group.

   B. Designate each technical support person as an owner of the mailbox by configuring the Full Mailbox Access right on the mailbox.

   C. Allow each technical support person to send messages on behalf of the mailbox.

   D. Configure delivery restrictions on the mailbox.

3. You have become aware that a few of your users have signed up for a daily newsletter published by a user in another department of your company that often includes large file attachments. You would like to prevent all messages from this newsletter from reaching these users. What is the best way to do this?

   A. Configure delivery restrictions for the users that allow all messages except those from the newsletter's email address.

   B. Configure delivery restrictions for the users that allow only messages from within the Exchange system and from select originators outside the system.

   C. Configure a size limit on messages that can be sent to these users.

   D. Configure a storage limit on these users' mailboxes.

4. You have configured a three-day deleted item retention for all deleted items in a particular user's mailbox. You perform a full backup on the server every Tuesday night. What can you do to allow the user to recover deleted e-mail messages after the retention period expires?

   A. Use the Delivery Options button on the Exchange General page for the user to configure items not to be deleted until the store has been backed up.

   B. Use the Storage Limits button on the Exchange General page for the user to configure items not to be deleted until the store has been backed up.

   C. Use the Storage Limits button on the Exchange Advanced page for the user to configure items not to be deleted until the store has been backed up.

   D. Use the Storage Options button on the Exchange Features page for the user to configure items not to be deleted until the store has been backed up.

5. What does the Delete Mailbox Storage right allow a person to do?

   A. Delete items from a mailbox.

   B. Delete a mailbox from a Private Information Store.

   C. Delete a Private Information Store from a storage group.

   D. Delete a storage group from a server.

6. You have a distribution group with a large number of members. Often when messages are sent to that distribution group, the server experiences high CPU utilization. What could you do to minimize the performance loss on your server?

   A. Remove all unnecessary address spaces from all recipients.

   B. Move all members into their own Recipients container.

   C. Specify another server as the expansion server.

   D. Move all recipients to another server.

7. On what user object property page would you find the option for configuring delivery restrictions?

   A. Exchange General

   B. Exchange Features

   C. Exchange Delivery

   D. Exchange Advanced

8. You need to move 10 mailboxes to another server. Each mailbox has five unique messages of 1 MB each. Each mailbox also has five single-instance messages of 1 MB each. After you move the mailboxes to the new server, how will the size of the Private Information Store on the new server change?

   A. The Private Information Store will increase by 55 MB.

   B. The Private Information Store will increase by 100 MB.

   C. The size will not increase.

   D. The size will decrease.

9. What is the default limit on the size of outgoing messages from a mailbox?
   A. 2 MB
   B. 8 MB
   C. 15 MB
   D. It is the same as the limit set at the Information Store level.
   E. There is no default limit.

10. Which of the following foreign e-mail address types are automatically generated for a user object? (Choose all that apply.)
    A. X.400
    B. SMTP
    C. Lotus Notes
    D. Novell GroupWise

11. Your Exchange organization consists of 15 Exchange Server 2003 computers that are located equally among five child domains of your Active Directory forest. How many total instances of the Recipient Update Service will you see in the Exchange System Manager?
    A. One
    B. Two
    C. Five
    D. Six

12. Your Exchange organization consists of 15 Exchange Server 2003 computers that are located equally among five child domains of your Active Directory forest. Users in one of the child domains are complaining that they cannot determine the group membership of a distribution group located in another domain. No other problems related to the network or Exchange have been reported. What do you suspect is the most likely reason for this?
    A. The network connection between the domains is not functioning properly.
    B. The group is configured as a security group.
    C. The group is configured as a domain local group.
    D. The group has no members.

13. You are the Exchange administrator for your organization. During the winter months, your company hires several hundred new employees to help out as business increases. A network administrator from the Active Directory group creates the user accounts for each new employee, assigns them to a specific department, and creates an Exchange mailbox for them. You need to ensure that all new employees always receive e-mail messages that are sent to their department. What type of group should you create?

    A. You should create a distribution group for each department. You should then place the members of the department in their respective distribution group.

    B. You should create a security group for each department. You should then place the members of the departments in their respective distribution group.

    C. You should create a query-based security group for each department that filters group membership based on the Exchange object's department attribute value.

    D. You should create a query-based distribution group for each department that filters group membership based on the Exchange object's department attribute value.

14. You are the Exchange administrator for your organization. During the summer months, your company hires several thousand temporary employees to help out as business increases. These temporary employees typically work for only two to four months and then are let go. Each of these employees needs to be able to receive company wide e-mail announcements that are sent on a fairly routine basis. These employees do not have any access to the network. What should you do to ensure that the temporary employees receive the required e-mail messages? (Choose two correct answers. Each answer is part of the overall solution.)

    A. Create a mail-enabled user account for each one of them and enter their external e-mail address. Configure the user account to be a member of the Temporary Employees department.

    B. Create a distribution group and add each of the temporary employees to it.

    C. Create a mail-enabled contact for each of them. Configure the contact to be a member of the Temporary Employees department.

    D. Create a query-based distribution group with a filter that adds each of the temporary employees to it.

15. Your company has hired an outside marketing agency to create marketing materials. Many of your employees often need to e-mail messages to people in this marketing agency. Since both the marketing agency and your network have Internet access, Internet e-mail seems the best method. However, you want to set it up so that the people in the marketing agency appear in the Exchange Global Address List. What type of recipient object would you configure to achieve this?

    A. Mailbox

    B. Mail-enabled user

    C. Contact

    D. A mailbox with a foreign owner

16. Which of the following permissions allows a user to read and send messages using a mailbox?
    A. Send As
    B. Full
    C. Full Mailbox Access
    D. Change
17. Your Exchange organization consists of three Exchange Server 2003 computers, each configured with two storage groups. Each storage group contains three mailbox store databases. You want to move your users' mailboxes around such that they are placed into mailbox stores by department. Where will you be allowed to move the mailboxes?
    A. Only to other databases in the same storage group
    B. Only to other storage groups on the same server
    C. Only to other servers in the same routing group
    D. To any server in the organization
18. Which of the following statements is true regarding security and distribution groups?
    A. Only a security group can be mail-enabled.
    B. Only a distribution group can be mail-enabled.
    C. Both types of groups can be mail-enabled.
    D. Neither type of group can be mail-enabled.
19. Which of the following types of objects can a distribution group contain? (Choose all that apply.)
    A. User
    B. Group
    C. Contact
    D. Public folder
20. Which of the following tools can you use to manage a public folder's properties? (Choose all that apply.)
    A. Office Outlook 2003
    B. Active Directory Users and Computers
    C. Public Folder Manager
    D. Exchange System Manager

Answers to Review Questions

1. A. Making Bobbi's mailbox an alternate recipient ensures that both mailboxes receive a copy of all messages sent to Aaron's mailbox. Creating a rule in Aaron's mailbox that forwarded mail to Bobbi would also work but would require more configuration on your part.

2. B. Only a user with Full Mailbox Access permissions can send and receive messages from a mailbox as if it were their own.

3. A. The default delivery restrictions are to accept messages from everyone and reject messages from nobody. You can enter specific originators from whom you would like to block messages for individual users. You could configure a size limit on inbound messages to these users, but this would likely still allow some messages from the newsletter to be delivered.

4. B. To prevent excessive build-up of deleted items, Exchange allows you to set a retention time for deleted items. That length of time can be configured on this page or at the Information Store (IS) object. The IS default value will be used, but you can configure a mailbox to override that setting by specifying the number of days for deleted item retention. You can also configure a mailbox to keep deleted items (i.e., not permanently deleted items) until the mailbox has been backed up. This is configured on the Exchange General page for a user via the Storage Limits button.

5. B. The Delete Mailbox Storage right allows a user to delete the actual mailbox from the Information Store. This right is given only to administrators by default.

6. C. Whenever a message is sent to a group, the group must be expanded so that the message can be sent to each member of the group. The Message Transfer Agent Service of a single Exchange server performs this expansion. The default choice is Any Server In The Organization. This choice means that the home server of the user sending the message always expands the group. You can also designate a specific server to handle the expansion of the group. The choice of specifying a dedicated expansion server is a good one if you have a large group.

7. A. Delivery restrictions, delivery options, and storage limits for an object are all configured through the object's Exchange General property page.

8. B. Each mailbox has five messages of 1 MB and a pointer to five single-instance messages of 1 MB. If those 10 mailboxes were moved to another server, the single-instance storage would be lost, and each mailbox would have 10 MB of storage. The Private Information Store on the new server would increase by 100 MB.

9. D. By default, all storage limits set at the Information Store level are used for individual mailboxes.

10. A, B. Microsoft Exchange automatically generates foreign addresses for SMTP and X.400.

11. D. There will be a total of six instances of the Recipient Update Service listed in the Exchange System Manager for your Exchange organization. Recall that only one instance of the Recipient Update Service (Enterprise Configuration) object exists for the entire Exchange organization, but that there will be one Recipient Update Service (installation Active Directory domain) object per domain that contains one or more Exchange servers.

12. C. The membership of domain local groups is not published to the global catalog servers in the organization, thus preventing Exchange users from being able to determine the group membership of mail-enabled domain local groups outside the domain in which their user account is located. In most cases, if your organization consists of multiple domains, then you may opt to not use domain local groups for Exchange distribution purposes.

13. D. The best solution to this situation is to create a query-based distribution group that uses an LDAP filter query based on the value of the department attribute to determine group membership. In this way, a group configured with a filter for all Exchange objects that belong to the Marketing department will dynamically place all of these objects in the group. In the same way, another group configured with a filter for all Exchange objects that belong to the Maintenance department would dynamically place these objects in the group. There is no such thing as a query-based security group.

14. C, D. You should create a mail-enabled contact object for each of the temporary employees and configure the Department attribute to be Temporary Employees. You should then create a query-based distribution group that uses a filter query based on the value of the Department attribute.

15. C. A contact is a pointer object that holds the address of a non-Exchange mail recipient. Contacts are made visible in the Global Address List and, therefore, permit Exchange clients to send messages to non-Exchange mail users.

16. C. Only a user with Full Mailbox Access permissions can send and receive messages from a mailbox as if it were their own.

17. D. Mailboxes and their contents reside physically on their home server. Mailboxes can be moved to other servers or to other mailbox stores on the same server. This is done through Active Directory Users and Computers.

18. C. Any type of group can be mail-enabled.

19. A, B, C, D. A distribution group can contain any other type of recipient object, including other distribution groups.

20. A, D. Both Outlook and the Exchange System Manager can be used to create public folders. Each utility can also be used to manage certain properties of public folders.

Using Public Folders

MICROSOFT EXAM OBJECTIVES COVERED IN THIS CHAPTER:

✓ **Manage and troubleshoot public folders**

Chapter 5, "Creating and Managing Exchange Recipients," covered the creation and management of three of the four basic types of recipients in Exchange Server 2003: users, groups, and contacts. This chapter explores the fourth type of recipient: public folders. *Public folders* are one of the most important objects in an Exchange environment. They are a key element in the creation of folder-based applications, such as bulletin boards, discussion groups, help desks, and many others. Public folders allow multiple users to share and collaborate on information. In this chapter, you will learn to do the following:

- Create public folders
- Configure public folders
- Use public folders
- Manage public folders

An Overview of Public Folders

Public folders provide centralized storage for almost any type of information, including mail messages, electronic forms, documents from other applications, and even web pages.

Thus, public folders can be used to provide a number of advantages to your users:

- A public folder can serve as a forum where users can participate in threaded discussion forums with other users, similar to Internet newsgroups. In fact, public folders can even be used to provide your organization with access to Internet newsgroups.
- Public folders can provide a centralized storage area for documents for different groups or projects in your organization.
- Public folders can store data for custom-designed workflow applications and, since public folders are exposed via Exchange's Installable File System (IFS), they can store data for standard applications, as well.
- Public folders can store web pages that are delivered to browsers via the Internet Information Services.

Public Folder Configuration

The configuration of public folders in Exchange Server 2003 happens in two places. Public folders can be created using either the Exchange System Manager or a *MAPI client* such as Office Outlook 2003. Exchange System Manager and Outlook are used in the following respects to manage public folders:

- Exchange System Manager is used to configure the public folder store of an Exchange server and server-related aspects of individual public folders.
- Outlook is used to configure aspects of public folders such as permissions and electronic forms associated with the folders.

The reason why much of the public folder creation and management occurs in the Outlook client is that public folders are often used for workflow applications, and because most users work solely in the Outlook client, the administration of public folders was developed to reflect the application with which a user works.

Public Folder Storage

When you first install Exchange, a single *public folder tree* named *All Public Folders* is created. In previous versions of Exchange Server, an organization was stuck with only this default tree. In Exchange Server 2003, you can create multiple public folder trees that appear alongside the All Public Folders tree. Each public folder tree uses a separate database on an Exchange server.

While having multiple public folder trees sounds great, there is a catch: MAPI clients such as Outlook can access only the default public folder tree. The following types of clients can access the default public folder tree, but they are also the only ones that can access any additional trees that may have been created:

- Applications such as Microsoft Word and Excel
- Web browsers
- Windows Explorer
- NNTP clients

The actual procedures for creating and using new public folder trees are covered later in this chapter.

An Exchange organization can host multiple public folder trees. A public folder tree is organized hierarchically, like a directory structure (see Figure 6.1). The root, or highest level, of a tree is called the top level, and folders created here are called *top-level folders*. By default, all users may create folders at this level, but the Exchange System Manager console can be used to modify the list of users who have permissions to create top-level folders. It is important to have this administrative control so that users don't clutter up the root of the tree and make it difficult to navigate.

FIGURE 6.1 Public folder hierarchy

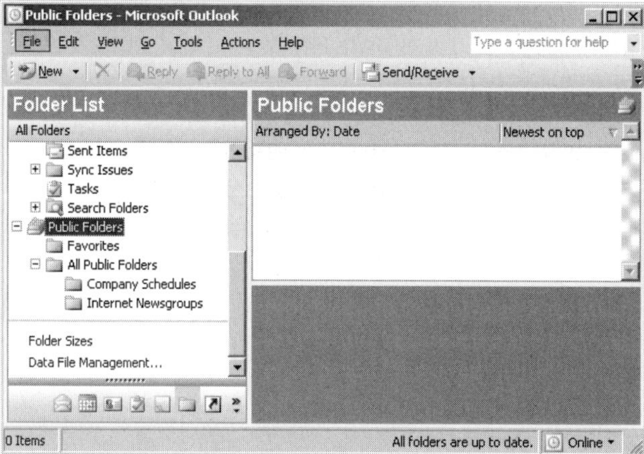

All public folders are created in the public folder store of a particular Exchange server. Any Exchange server that has a public folder store can host a public folder. In a typical organization, some folders exist on one server, others on another server, and so on.

When a user creates a top-level public folder, it is placed in the Public Information Store on that user's home server. When a user creates a lower-level public folder, it is placed in the Public Information Store of that new folder's parent folder. In addition, each individual public folder can be replicated to other servers in the organization. As you can see, this situation could get complicated. Public folders in the same tree may exist on different servers, and some public folders have instances on multiple servers.

A public folder is actually considered to have two parts. The first part is the public folder contents—the actual messages inside the public folder. The second part is that folder's place in the *public folder hierarchy*. The contents of a public folder exist on a single server, unless you specifically configure the contents to be replicated to other servers.

To ensure that information about public folders is distributed throughout the Exchange organization, Active Directory maintains a public folder hierarchy for each public folder tree, which is a single hierarchical structure that contains information about all the public folders in that tree. This hierarchy is automatically made available to every Exchange user in the organization.

Public Folder Web Access

Exchange dynamically creates a URL for each item in the Information Store. This means that users can access any piece of Exchange information, including mailboxes, messages, and public folders, from a standard web browser. You can access the contents of any public folder using a simple address such as `http://`*`servername`*`/public/`*`foldername`*, as seen in Figure 6.2.

FIGURE 6.2 Examining public folders using a web browser

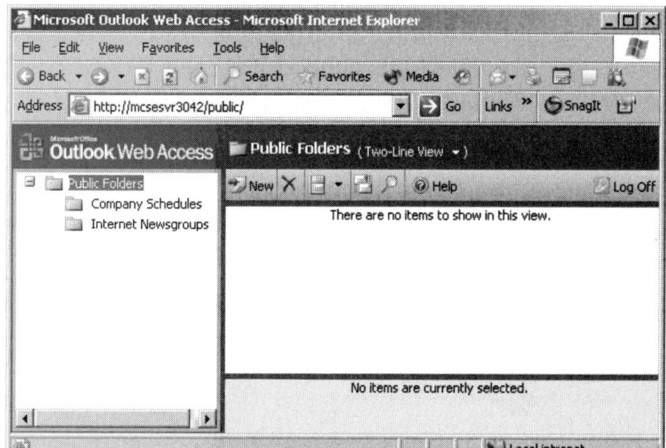

Each public folder also has an HTML page associated with it. When you create a folder, Exchange automatically creates a default HTML page. You can replace the automatically generated web page with a custom page, or you can change the URL to point to another website. You can gain access to all of the contents in a folder by accessing the folder container or by accessing a dynamically generated URL. This functionality is provided by Internet Information Services, whose integration with Exchange is discussed in detail in Chapter 2, "Microsoft Exchange Architecture."

Public Folders and Active Directory

Every public folder in a public folder store can appear as a mail recipient in the Global Address List. You can mail-enable a public folder by right-clicking it in Exchange System Manager, pointing to All Tasks, and selecting Mail Enable from the shortcut menu.

After a public folder is mail-enabled, the Exchange System Attendant service connects to Active Directory and creates an object for the public folder in a container named Microsoft Exchange System Objects in Active Directory Users and Computers.

System Folders

System folders are special public folders that are hidden by default and are accessible only through the System Manager snap-in (see Figure 6.3). You can view them by right-clicking the Public Folders container and selecting View Hidden Folders from the shortcut menu.

System folders contain items that facilitate the capabilities of many Exchange clients, such as collaborative scheduling in Outlook. For the most part, you will want to leave these folders alone. Much of their functionality is configured through other areas in the System Manager. Nonetheless, it may be helpful to know what a few of the folders are used for:

- Offline Address Book (OAB) contains a subset of the Global Address List that remote users can download and use for addressing mail when they are not connected to the Exchange server.
- Schedule+ Free/Busy contains objects that support the scheduling capabilities of Exchange clients.
- Schema-root contains objects related to the Active Directory Schema.
- StoreEvents contains objects for the configuration of event information that specifically relates to the Information Store service.

FIGURE 6.3 Viewing system folders

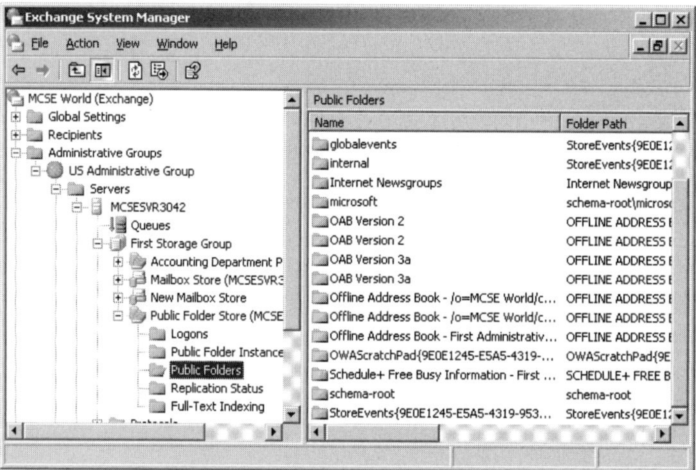

Managing Public Folders with Outlook

Office Outlook 2003 can be used to create public folders and perform a certain degree of public folder management. You can also use previous versions of Outlook, the Microsoft Exchange Client, and certain generic mail clients (specifically IMAP4 clients) to create public folders, but these applications may not provide the same level of management as Outlook 2003. Because the procedures for creation are fairly similar, this section focuses only on the use of Outlook 2003 in working with public folders.

Creating Public Folders in Outlook

Creating folders in Outlook 2003 is simple. Just make sure that the All Public Folders object (or the folder in which you want to create a new folder) is highlighted, and select the New Folder command from the File menu. The process for creating a new folder is outlined in Exercise 6.1.

EXERCISE 6.1

Creating a Public Folder in Outlook

1. Start Outlook.

2. Make sure that the public folder tree is showing by selecting the List command from the View menu.

3. In the List view, expand the Public Folders item.

4. To create a top-level folder, select the All Public Folders object. You can also select another folder in which you want to create a subfolder.

5. With a public folder selected, choose New Folder from Outlook's File menu. This opens the Create New Folder dialog box seen below.

6. Enter the name of the public folder you want to create and the type of items the folder should contain, and select the folder in which the new folder should be created. The default folder is the one that was selected when you issued the New Folder command.

7. Once everything is set, click OK to create the new folder.

EXERCISE 6.1 *(continued)*

8. Assuming you have the appropriate permissions to create a folder in the chosen location (and, by default, all users can create folders wherever they want), the folder is created and may be accessed by other users immediately. Keep in mind, though, that it may take some time for the public folder hierarchy to replicate itself throughout Active Directory, so it may take some time before all users can see the folder in their lists. The results of this exercise are displayed below.

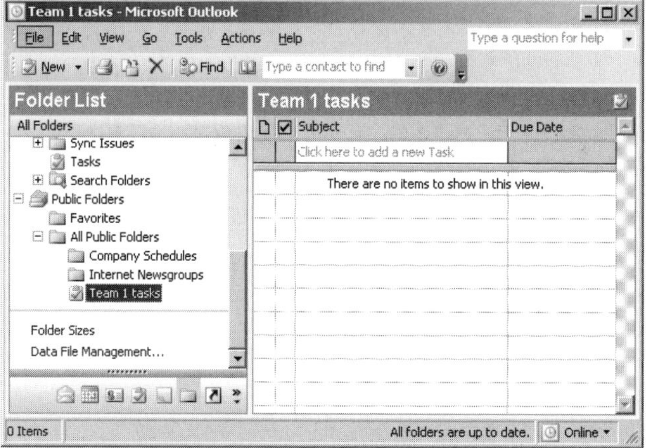

Configuring Public Folders from Outlook

After a public folder is created, it is managed using both Outlook and Exchange System Manager. Because users can create public folders with Outlook, it is advantageous to allow them certain managerial responsibilities, which is why part of the management occurs in the client.

When a user creates a public folder, that user automatically becomes the folder's owner. The owner is responsible for the folder's basic design, which includes access permissions, rules, and the association of electronic forms. To perform these management tasks, the user can simply open the property sheets for a particular public folder in Outlook. Public folders can also be managed to a degree from within Exchange System Manager (discussed later), but the Outlook option means that the user has only a single application with which to be concerned.

The key configuration elements of public folders in Outlook are as follows:

- Permissions
- Forms
- Rules
- Views

These elements are managed through a set of property pages that are used for configuration. There are two ways to display these property pages. One way is to highlight the public folder, click the right mouse button, and choose Properties from the pop-up menu that appears. Another way is to highlight the public folder and then choose Folders ➤ Properties For *<Public Folder Name>* from the File menu.

Permissions

By assigning permissions, a public folder owner can choose which users have access to the folder and what actions those users may perform. There are eight individual permissions and nine groupings of permissions, called *roles*, that can be assigned. Table 6.1 describes these permissions, descending from the permission with the most capabilities to the permission with the fewest capabilities. The word *items*, as used in this table, refers to the contents of the public folder, such as e-mail messages, forms, documents, and other files.

Table 6.2 lists the predefined groupings of permissions according to role.

TABLE 6.1 Public Folder Permissions

Permission	Description
Create Items	Can create new items in a folder.
Read Items	Can open and view items in a folder.
Create Subfolders	Can create subfolders within a folder.
Folder Owner	Can change permissions in a folder and perform administrative tasks, such as adding rules and installing forms on a folder.
Folder Contact	Receives e-mail notifications relating to a folder. Notifications include replication conflicts, folder design conflicts, and storage limit notifications.
Folder Visible	Determines whether the folder is visible to the user in the public folder hierarchy.
Edit Items	Can edit (modify) items in a folder.
Delete Items	Can delete items in a folder.

TABLE 6.2 Predefined Roles and Their Permissions

Role	Create Items	Read Items	Create Sub-folders	Folder Owner	Folder Contact	Folder Visible	Edit Items	Delete Items
Owner	Yes	Yes	Yes	Yes	Yes	Yes	All	All
Publishing Editor	Yes	All	Yes	No	No	Yes	All	All
Editor	Yes	All	No	No	No	Yes	All	All
Publishing Author	Yes	Yes	Yes	No	No	Yes	Own	Own
Author	Yes	Yes	No	No	No	Yes	Own	Own
Nonediting Author	Yes	Yes	No	No	No	Yes	None	None
Contributor	Yes	No	No	No	No	Yes	None	None
Reviewer	No	Yes	No	No	No	Yes	None	None
None	No	No	No	No	No	Yes	None	None

Custom roles consisting of any combination of individual permissions may also be assigned.

When a public folder is created, the following three users are included on the permissions list by default (see Figure 6.4):

The user who created the public folder This user is automatically assigned the Owner role. In Figure 6.4, the owner of the folder is the Administrator account. The owner of a folder may also grant other users this role.

A special user named Default This user represents all users who have access to the public folder store but aren't explicitly listed in the permissions list. In top-level folders, the Default user is automatically granted the Author role (this can be modified). Below the top-level folders, the Default user automatically inherits the permissions it has at its parent folder.

A special user named Anonymous The Anonymous user represents all users logged on with Anonymous access. For example, an Exchange server could contain public folders holding promotional information for public viewing. People without user accounts could use a web browser or newsreader program and the Anonymous account to access the Exchange server and read the promotional information. Any permissions assigned to the Anonymous account are applied to these users.

FIGURE 6.4 The Permissions property page of a public folder

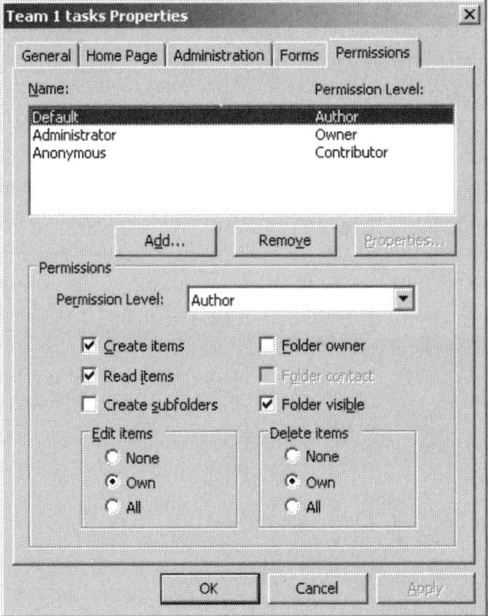

These three users cannot be removed from the permissions list of a public folder. However, the particular roles and permissions they have can be modified. All other users can be removed from the permissions list.

Exchange administrators can always designate themselves as the owners of public folders. This is especially important if the recipient who is the owner of a public folder (or all Active Directory accounts that are on the permissions list of that recipient) is deleted.

Exercise 6.2 outlines the steps to configure the permissions on a public folder.

EXERCISE 6.2

Configuring the Permissions on a Public Folder

1. In Outlook, highlight the public folder. Click the right mouse button, and choose Properties from the pop-up menu. The Properties dialog box for the folder appears.

2. Click the Permissions tab. Notice the permissions given to the Default user. The Default user is given the Author role by default for top-level folders and whatever permissions it has for the parent folder of all other folders. Notice also that the user who created this public folder has the Owner role.

3. Highlight the Default user, and then click the down-arrow in the Roles field. Choose the None role from the list.

EXERCISE 6.2 *(continued)*

4. Click Add, and highlight a new user from the list. Next, click Add, and then click OK. The user is added to the access list for the public folder with the role of None. This role was automatically assigned because the Default user's role is None, as you can see below.

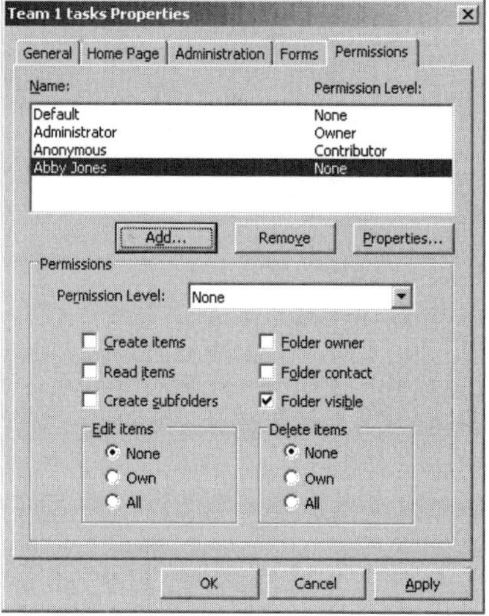

5. Change the new user's role to Author. Notice that the new user now has the Create Items and Read Items permissions. This role also allows the user to edit and delete the user's own items.

6. Click OK to save the configuration.

Forms

Forms can be associated with a public folder, allowing users to submit structured data into the folder. The list of forms associated with a public folder is found in the folder's property pages. Exercise 6.3 walks through the steps to associate a form with a public folder.

EXERCISE 6.3

Associating a Form with a New Public Folder

1. In Outlook, highlight the public folder. Click the right mouse button, and choose Properties from the pop-up menu. The Properties dialog box for the folder appears.

EXERCISE 6.3 *(continued)*

2. Click the Forms tab. Notice that there are currently no forms associated with this public folder but that the Allow These Forms In This Folder field is set to Any Form. You are going to associate a specific form with this folder and configure it as the only form to be used with this folder.

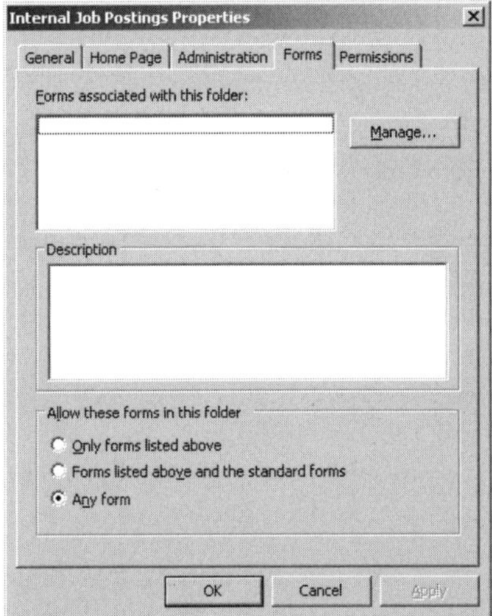

3. Click the Manage button. The Forms Manager appears, listing the forms published in the Organization Forms library.

4. Click a form, and then click Copy. If the form has already been installed, all you have to do now is click Close. Otherwise, you'll be walked through some extra steps for installing the form. Notice that the form is now associated with this public folder.

5. Under the Allow These Forms In This Folder field, choose Only Forms Listed Above, and then click OK. The form installation performed in this exercise will be tested in the upcoming section, "Using Public Folders."

Rules

Rules consisting of conditions and actions can be configured on public folders. Rules allow a public folder to automate certain procedures. The following is a list of some of the conditions (or *criteria*) that can be used in a rule:

From A message from specified recipients

Sent To A message sent to specified recipients

Subject Specified text in the Subject heading of a message

Message Body Specified text or phrase in the body of a message

Size A specified size of a message, "At least *x* size" or "At most *x* size"

Received A specified date range within which a message was received

The following actions can be triggered if the preceding conditions are met:

Delete Delete the message.

Reply With Reply to the message's sender with a specified message template.

Forward To Forward the message to specified recipients.

A rule could be used, for example, to keep postings separate from replies. If a company had a public folder named Company Events containing information on upcoming company events, users could be given permission to provide feedback on these events by sending replies to this folder. However, the number of replies in this folder could hinder users from finding the original events posting. To resolve this, the owner of this folder could create a subfolder called Discussions. The owner could then create a rule for Company Events that states that all replies to this folder should be forwarded to the Discussions folder. For this example to work, the preceding folders must be visible in the GAL.

Rules are added to public folders by clicking the Folder Assistant button on a folder's Administration property page. Clicking this button displays the Folder Assistant dialog box, which enables you to add, edit, delete, and order rules for a public folder. Exercise 6.4 outlines the steps involved in creating a rule on a public folder.

EXERCISE 6.4

Creating a Rule on a Public Folder

1. In Outlook, highlight the public folder. Click the right mouse button, and choose Properties from the pop-up menu. The Properties dialog box for the folder appears.

2. Click the Administration tab, seen below.

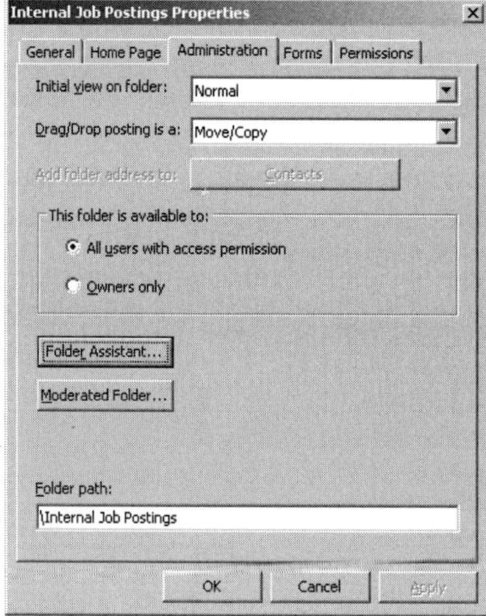

EXERCISE 6.4 *(continued)*

3. Click the Folder Assistant button. The Folder Assistant dialog box appears, as seen below.

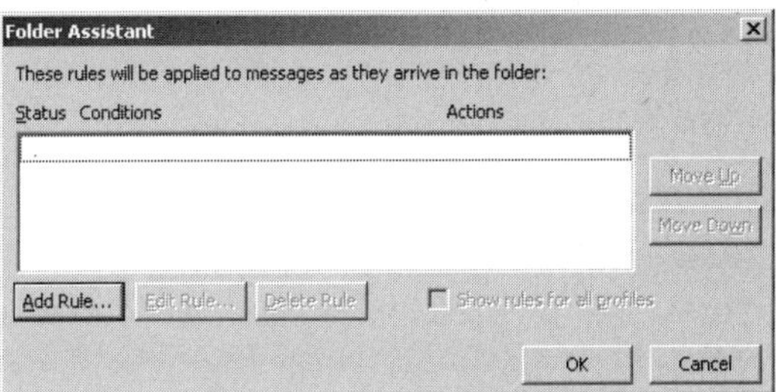

4. Click Add Rule. The Edit Rule dialog box appears. In the Subject field, type a word that should appear in the subject, and type the same word again in the Message Body field. This is the condition part of the rule and stipulates that any message that contains the chosen word in the subject or body of the message fits the criteria.

5. Now set the action part of the rule. Click the Forward check box, and then click To. The Choose Recipient dialog box appears. In the Show Names From The field, choose Global Address List.

6. Choose the user you want to automatically forward the message to, and then click the To button.

7. Click OK, and then click OK on the next three dialog boxes to close all open dialog boxes. The rule is now saved within the properties of the public folder.

Views

Outlook includes many powerful features to view items in a folder. Some of the features in Outlook are listed in Table 6.3.

TABLE 6.3 Outlook Features for Viewing Folder Items

Feature	Examples
Sort	Order items by sender, recipient, importance, subject text, sensitivity, or other properties.
Filter	Filter items by words or phrases contained in the subject text or message body, sender, recipient, what time they were sent, or other properties. Only items that pass through the filter are displayed in the Contents pane.
Group By	Group items by when they are due, sender, recipient, importance, subject text, sensitivity, or other properties.

Using Public Folders

This section and its exercises cover how to add content to a public folder. The two primary methods to add content to a public folder are as follows:

- Posting forms
- Sending e-mail messages

Posting

If a public folder is configured to accept postings, which is the default, users who have the necessary permissions can post data to the public folder. To post, a user must highlight the public folder and either click the New Post icon on the toolbar or choose New Post In This Folder from the Compose menu. Posting is an easy and efficient method of adding content to a public folder, because the user does not have to address the message as they do when sending a mail message to a public folder. Exercise 6.5 outlines the steps for this procedure.

EXERCISE 6.5

Posting Information to a Public Folder

1. In Outlook, select the public folder you want to post into.
2. Click the New Post icon on the Outlook toolbar to open a posting.
3. Enter the subject and body text, as seen below.

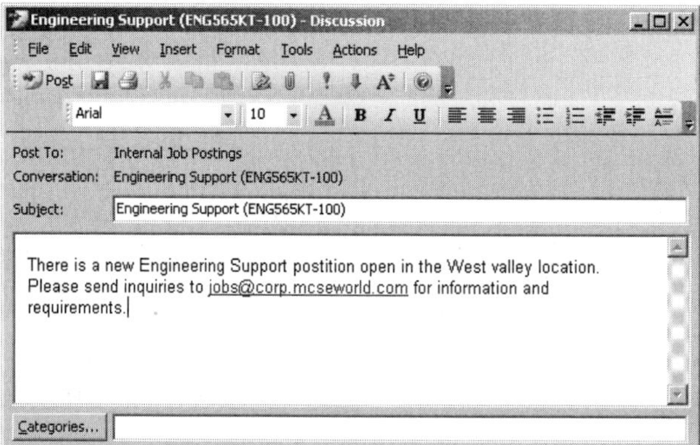

4. Post the message to the public folder.
5. The new posting appears in the public folder.

Mail Messages

A mail message can be sent to a public folder. As you may recall, a public folder is a recipient and, therefore, can receive and send messages. Exercise 6.6 outlines the steps to send a mail message to a public folder.

In order for someone to send a mail message to a public folder using their client's address book, the public folder must be visible in the address book. By default, public folders are visible in the address book. If you want to send a mail message to a public folder that is hidden, you will need to first unhide it.

EXERCISE 6.6

Sending a Mail Message to a Public Folder

1. In Outlook, choose Compose ➤ New Message. An untitled mail-message window appears.
2. Click To. In the Show Names From The field, choose Global Address List. Find the public folder in the Global Address List.
3. Select the public folder, click the To button, and then click OK.
4. Type an appropriate subject in the Subject field.
5. Type some information in the body of the message.
6. Click the Send icon in the toolbar.

Managing Public Folders with System Manager

The Exchange System Manager provides a second way to create public folders and also provides many configuration options that are different than those available from within Outlook.

Creating Public Folders in System Manager

In older versions of Exchange Server, you could create public folders only by using an Exchange client such as Outlook. Fortunately, Exchange Server 2003 allows you to perform this task from within the Exchange System Manager, offering Exchange administrators an easier way to create and manage public folders using only one tool. Exercise 6.7 outlines the steps for creating a public folder using System Manager.

EXERCISE 6.7

Creating a Public Folder in System Manager

1. Expand the public folder tree in which you want to create a new folder. If you have not created additional trees beyond the All Public Folders default tree, then expand that default tree.
2. If you want to make a top-level folder, select the tree object itself. Otherwise, navigate through the tree, and select the folder in which you want to create the new subfolder, as seen below.

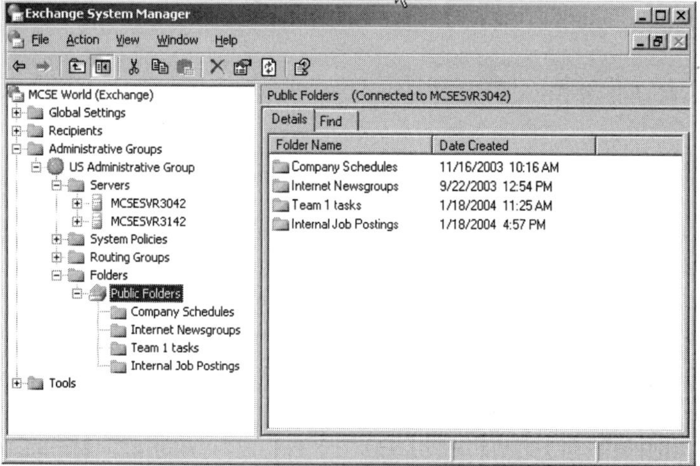

3. Right-click in the public folder tree where you want to create the new public folder and select New ➢ Public Folder.
4. In the Name field, enter a name for the new public folder.
5. Optionally, type a description for the public folder that will appear in the Global Address List.
6. Click the OK button to create the new public folder. The folder will immediately be available to users.

Mail-Enabling a Public Folder

Once you have created a new public folder, you will still need to mail-enable the folder and configure mail-related settings if you want the public folder to be able to receive e-mail messages. If you choose not to do this, users will be able to post messages only by using a MAPI client.

All public folders in the default tree and any *general-purpose trees* are not mail-enabled by default. If any folder in any tree is made mail-enabled, it becomes visible in the GAL by default.

To mail-enable a folder, select the folder in Exchange System Manager and choose All Tasks ➤ Mail Enable from the Action menu. The command should take effect immediately, although you will get no feedback from the Exchange System Manager after executing it. Once you have mail-enabled a folder, that folder's property sheet shows several extra mail-related property pages, including Exchange General, E-mail Addresses, and Exchange Advanced. These property pages work the same as the similar property pages for other recipients and allow you to perform such functions as setting delivery options and restrictions, changing the display name and alias, and setting custom attributes. Since Chapter 5 provided detailed coverage of performing these actions on other types of recipients, we refer you to that chapter for the specifics.

Hiding Public Folders

Public folders can be hidden from the GAL and the public folder hierarchy. Hiding public folders can be part of your security plan. By default, each public folder is not hidden from the GAL. A public folder can be hidden by selecting the Hide From Exchange Address Lists check box found on its Exchange Advanced property page, seen in Figure 6.5.

Before you can hide a public folder from the GAL, however, you will need to first mail-enable it from the Exchange System Manager, as discussed previously in the "Mail-Enabling a Public Folder" section.

FIGURE 6.5 Configuring a public folder to be hidden

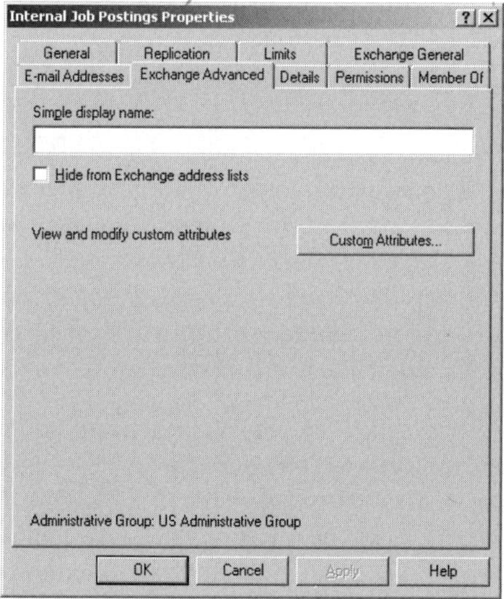

Latency Issues with Public Folder Hierarchy and Content

One Exchange service (the Public Folder Replication Agent) manages the replication of public folders, while another service (the System Attendant) manages the listing of public folders in the

Global Address List. Because of this segregated management, you may notice a number of latency issues, especially when working with large public folder trees. These issues include the following:

- Sometimes public folder trees appear differently when managed from two different servers. This is usually because changes to the public folder hierarchy have not yet been replicated to all servers.
- Users may see the public folder hierarchy in their MAPI client but not be able to see the individual public folders in their address book until both services have replicated their information.
- Certain properties may appear incorrectly (or not at all) in System Manager because the replication of the hierarchy has taken place faster than the directory information.

Configuring Public Folders in System Manager

No matter how you create a public folder, it becomes accessible to users almost immediately, using the default configurations. As you saw earlier in the chapter, a good bit of public folder configuration is available from within the Outlook client so that users can take on some of the administrative burden of creating and maintaining public folders. However, there is also a good bit of configuration available for public folders that can be accomplished only by using the Exchange System Manager.

Hiding a Public Folder from the Public Folder Hierarchy

By default, all public folders and their contents are visible in the public folder hierarchy to all other recipients. To hide the contents of a particular public folder, you must revoke the Read Items permission for the recipient or recipients at that particular folder. If you wanted to hide not merely the contents of a public folder but also its very listing in the hierarchy, you would revoke the Read Items permission for the parent folder of the folder you want hidden. Since a subfolder is considered part of the contents of its parent folder, revoking this permission at the parent folder would prevent the viewing of that subfolder in the hierarchy.

Many times, an organization will create a top level called Hidden Folders that will contain all the folders they want hidden from the majority of their users. The Default user will be assigned the None role for Hidden Folders, which will prevent them from viewing all subfolders. Even the top-level folder Hidden Folders could be made invisible by revoking the Folder Visible permission from the Default user. To enable the users who do need to access the subfolders under this root, you would create distribution lists and assign the relevant permissions at this root and any subfolders.

Within Exchange System Manager, public folders are managed at two distinct levels. The first is at the level of the public folder store, where you configure settings governing how the public folder store should handle public folders in general. The second is at the level of the public folder itself, where you configure properties that control certain aspects of the folder and often override settings made at the store level.

Configuring Public Folder Store Properties

The public folder properties managed at the level of a public folder store govern the default settings for all public folders in that store. As with most other objects, the settings for the public folder store are managed through property pages. Each public folder store exists on a specific server. The Public Folder Store object is found inside the container for that server in Exchange System Manager (see Figure 6.6). To access the store's property pages, right-click the Public Folder Store object, and select Properties from the shortcut menu.

Most of the property pages for the public folder store are used to control the replication of public folders to other Exchange servers. These pages, and replication itself, are discussed later in the chapter. The one property page that is important now is named Limits, shown in Figure 6.7.

When a user deletes a message from a folder, that message is marked as hidden and is actually kept on the server for a certain number of days before being permanently deleted. Within that period, called the *deleted-item retention time*, the user can recover the item. To do so, however, the user must be using Microsoft Outlook 8.03 or a later version. Outlook 2003 is considered to be version 11.0, Outlook XP is considered to be version 10.0, and so forth. Simply set the number of days that you want to keep deleted items on the server. The default setting is 0. In addition, you can specify that items not be permanently removed from the Information Store until at least one backup has occurred.

FIGURE 6.6 Viewing the public folder store

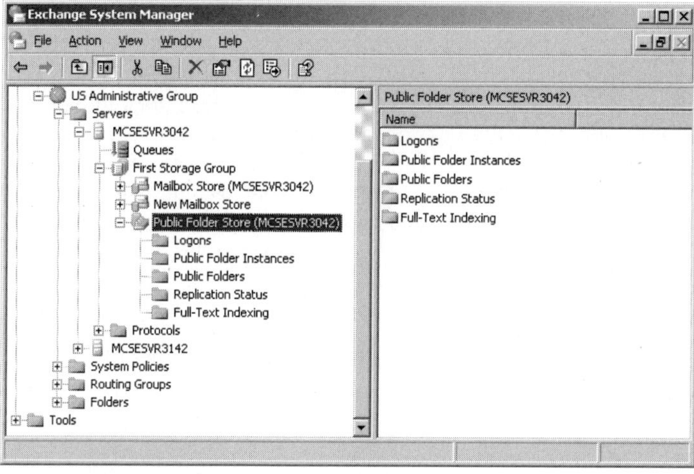

FIGURE 6.7 The Limits property page for the public folder store

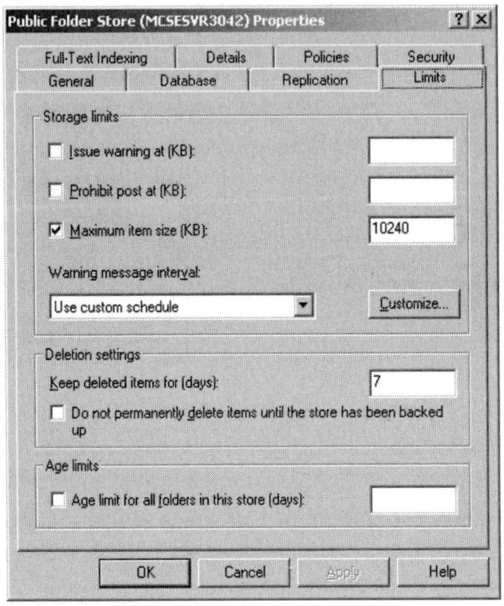

You can also use the Limits property page to set a default storage limit for public folders in a public folder store. This storage limit represents a size (in kilobytes) that the public folders can reach before a storage warning is issued to the folders' contacts. You can override this storage limit at the folder level for individual folders, as you'll see a bit later in the chapter.

The final limit that you can set on the Limits property page is the default number of days for which items are kept in the public folders for the public folder store. The default is no *age limit* at all.

Public folder age limits work in combination with deleted-item retention time. Suppose that you set a 10-day age limit on your public folders and a 6-day deleted-item retention period. An item is deleted on day 9—one day before it would automatically expire. The deleted-item retention period starts at this point. If the item is recovered within the deleted-item retention period, the age limit for the newly recovered item is reset to add 10 more days.

Examining Public Folder Store Subcontainers

The Public Folder Store container in System Manager (refer to Figure 6.6) has a number of subcontainers that offer valuable information about your public store and the folders inside:

- The Logons container provides information about who is logged on and using public folders.
- The Public Folder Instances container lets you view the folders in a public store, configure properties of a folder (discussed in the next section), and configure replication of a folder (discussed later in the chapter).

- The Public Folders container provides details such as the path, size, and number of items inside the public folders in the store.
- The Replication Status container lists all folders and the number of servers that contain a replica of each folder. It also lists the current replication state and the time of the last replication. Replication of public folders is discussed later in the chapter.
- The Full-Text Indexing container shows the current state of the indexing of public folders in the store. This is covered in Chapter 9, "Configuring the Information Store."

Configuring Public Folder Properties

Public folders are also managed at the individual folder level in the Exchange System Manager console. This management is performed using the property pages of the folders themselves. As with the public folder store property pages, a number of the property pages for the folder deal with replication, which is discussed later. The two pages that are important here are the General and Limits pages.

General Properties

The General property page, shown in Figure 6.8, lets you change the description of the folder that appears in the GAL. You'll also find an option named Maintain Per-User Read And Unread Information For This Folder. If you select this option, then the folder itself will keep track of and mark as read messages that each individual user of the folder has read. If a folder has been mail-enabled, as mentioned previously, another important setting is added to the General page. The Address List Name field governs whether you want the name that is visible in address books to be the same as the public folder name or a different name that you can enter.

FIGURE 6.8 Setting general properties for a public folder

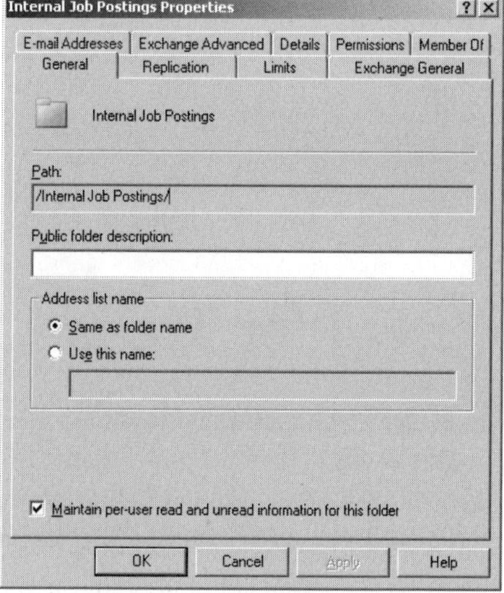

Limits Properties

The Limits property page, shown in Figure 6.9, defines messaging limits for the public folder. You can define the following limits on this property sheet:

- Storage Limits indicate the amount of disk space, in kilobytes, a folder can take up before a warning is issued to the folder's owner. This setting works the same way that the setting at the public folder store level works, as discussed previously. Any settings made at the public folder level override settings made for the server.
- Deletion Settings define the number of days that deleted messages are retained in the folder before being permanently removed. You can use the default defined for the public folder store level or override those settings for this particular folder.
- Age Limits set the maximum amount of time in days that a message remains in this public folder before it expires, or you can use the defaults set at the public folder store level.

FIGURE 6.9 Setting messaging limits for a public folder

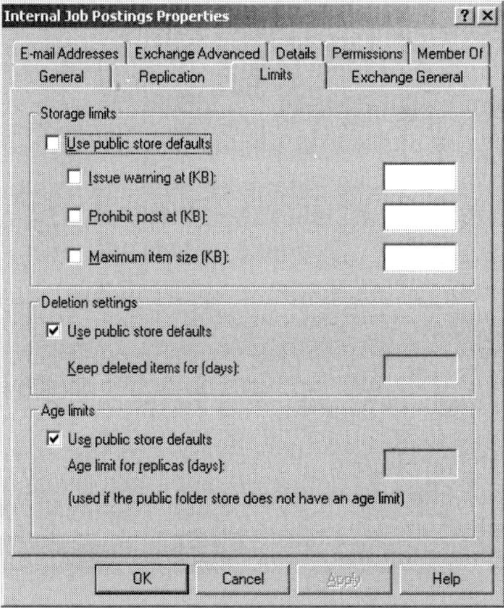

Creating New Public Folder Trees

Unlike older versions of Exchange, Exchange Server 2003 allows the creation of more than one public folder tree structure. You could, for example, create separate public folder tree structures for different departments of the company. You could also create a public tree for a specific project. This helps you to better organize your public folders and more efficiently delegate authority over those folders. Keep in mind, though, that MAPI clients such as Outlook will be able to view information only in the default tree for the organization. For users to see other trees, they must use clients such as web browsers or newsreaders.

There are three steps to creating a new public folder tree. First, you create a new top-level root folder that will house the new tree structure. Second, you create a new public folder store on the server to hold the new tree structure. Finally, you connect the new top-level folder to the new public folder store. This last step can be performed during the creation of the public folder store or later.

Creating a New Top-Level Root Folder

The first step in creating a new public folder tree is to create a new top-level root folder. Each top-level root folder exists on the same level as the public folder tree and uses its own database on each Exchange server that contains replicas of any of the folders in the tree's hierarchy. Exercise 6.8 outlines the steps for creating a new top-level root folder.

EXERCISE 6.8

Creating a New Top-Level Root Folder

1. Open the Exchange System Manager and select the Folders container for the administrative group in which you want to create the folder, as seen below. If you have only one administrative group, or if you have Exchange System Manager set to not display administrative groups, the Folders container should appear directly under the root node. Otherwise, you will need to drill down into the appropriate administrative group.

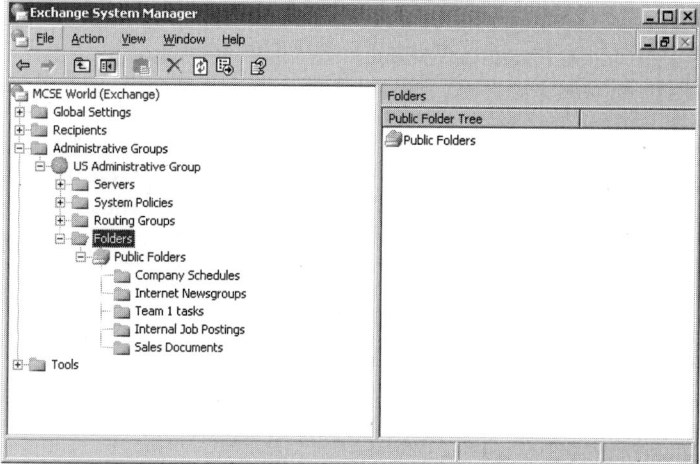

EXERCISE 6.8 *(continued)*

2. Right-click the Folders container and select New ➤ Public Folder Tree from the context menu. This opens the Properties dialog box for the new folder.

3. Enter a name for the new tree in the Name field of the General property page, as seen below.

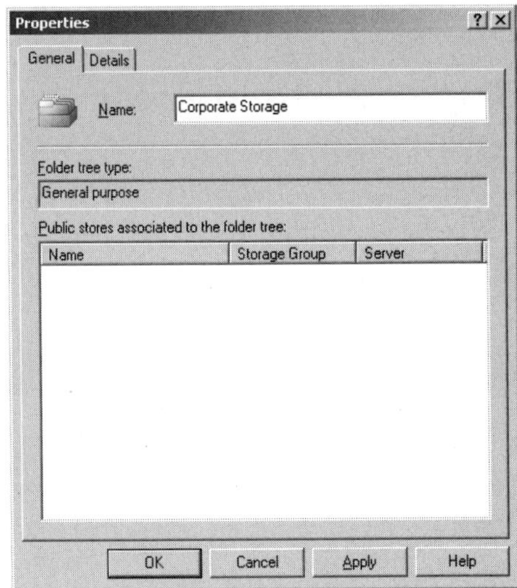

4. Once you have finished, click OK to close the property sheet and create the new public folder tree.

Creating a New Public Folder Store

Public folders reside in a Public Information Store. Each public folder tree uses its own database in the store. Once you create the new top-level root folder for a tree, you must then create a new public folder store to hold that tree. Exercise 6.9 outlines the steps for creating a new public folder store.

EXERCISE 6.9

Creating a New Public Folder Store

1. In the Exchange System Manager, locate and select the container for the storage group on the server on which you want to create the new tree. You will create the new public folder store in this storage group, as seen below.

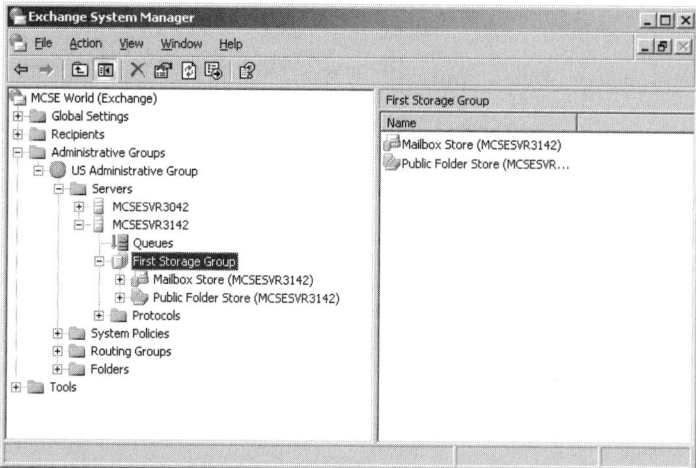

2. Right-click the selected storage group and select New ➢ Public Store from the context menu. This opens the Properties dialog box for the new store.

3. Enter a name for the new store in the Name field of the General property page, as seen below.

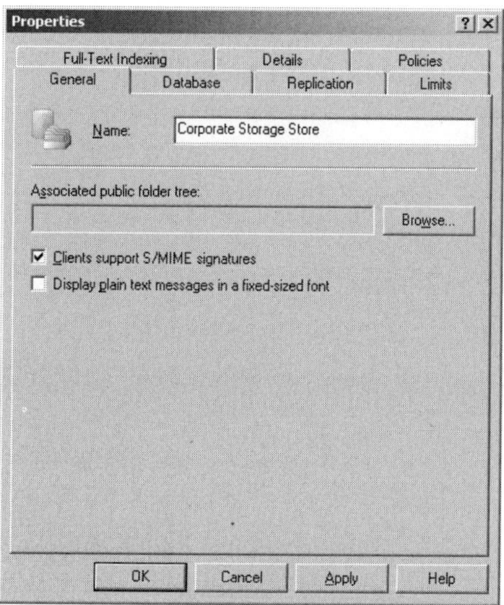

EXERCISE 6.9 *(continued)*

4. Click the Browse button to open a dialog that lets you associate the new store with a public folder tree. In the dialog, select the tree you created previously. If you choose not to do this now, you can connect the tree and the new store later following the procedure outlined in the next section.
5. Once you have finished, click OK to close the property sheet.
6. System Manager prompts you to mount the new store once it has been successfully created. Click Yes to mount the new store.

Creating Dedicated Public Folder Servers

A *dedicated public folder server* is an Exchange server that is used to store public folders and has no mailboxes. Dedicating a server for this purpose can increase client access to public folder data and can make for a more central backup strategy.

Implementing a dedicated public folder server involves the following steps:

1. Move public folders to the designated server. This can be done via replication, which is discussed later in the chapter.
2. If there are any mailboxes on the designated public folder server, they must be moved to another server or mail-disabled. Techniques for performing these actions are discussed in Chapter 5.
3. Remove any mailbox stores and unneeded storage groups from the server by right-clicking them and choosing Delete from the shortcut menu. For protection, you will not be allowed to delete any mailbox store that still has mail-enabled mailboxes in it.

Dedicated public folder servers can be an appropriate part of an Exchange environment when there are large amounts of public folder data and you need to offload processing and disperse the workload. Dedicated servers also provide for a more central backup strategy.

Public Folder Replication

Public folders can be copied to other Exchange servers. Each copy of a public folder is called a *replica*. Each replica contains the same information as the original public folder but resides on a different Exchange server. Replicas can reside in the same routing group as the home server of the original public folder, and they can reside on servers in different routing groups.

Reasons for using public folder replicas include the following:

Load balancing If a large number of users access a particular public folder, access times could be slow. A solution is to create public folder replicas and disperse user access to the various replicas.

Fault tolerance Having a public folder replicated eliminates a single point of failure.

Easier access for remote users If routing groups are geographically separated and users are accessing public folders in a remote group, it can make sense to distribute those public folders to the other routing groups through the use of replicas. This can be especially useful when users in one routing group are accessing public folders in another routing group over an unreliable network connection. Creating replicas in each remote group would allow users to access the public folders on their own local networks.

The following is a scenario that could warrant the use of public folder replicas. Suppose your organization has four routing groups, each group consisting of two Exchange servers and 500 users. The four routing groups are connected with a 256-KB wide area network (WAN). The available bandwidth during the workday is less than 64 KB, while at night the available bandwidth is 128 KB or more. You have created a public folder that contains 600 MB of data that is not time critical. Users access that folder approximately every 15 minutes, and the folder data is updated only twice a week. A good strategy would be to create a replica of that public folder on an Exchange server in each of the four routing groups.

Real World Scenario

Internet Newsgroups and Public Folder Servers

Your organization has six Exchange Server 2003 computers located in one routing group and one administrative group. Your entire network is located at one physical site in a building with 12 floors. Departments are organized on a floor-by-floor basis, and one Exchange server is configured to hold the mailbox for two departments. Each department has between 1,000 and 1,200 employees with the exception of the executives group, which has only around 100 employees total. In the past, you have used the Exchange server that hosts the executive mailboxes as your single public folder server. The public folder store within the organization is currently used only to post job openings that are to be announced to all employees.

You have been asked to investigate making several hundred Internet newsgroups available within your organization using a public folder. The newsgroups will be used by employees in various departments for various reasons. Although none of your current Exchange servers are overly taxed by their current configuration, you are concerned about the impact on performance if you place a large number of Internet newsgroups on the server that is currently hosting your public folder tree. As well, you would like to configure circular logging to occur in order to save disk space because the ability to restore items in this public folder is not required.

To solve all of your problems, you have asked for, and received, a seventh server to be installed into your Exchange organization. This server will be configured as a public folder store server only and will have the default mailbox store removed from it. On this server you will also be able to configure circular logging to occur for the public folder store to decrease disk space usage by the public folder store. As well, none of your current servers will be negatively impacted by the large volume of traffic that is likely to occur on the new public folder server (Internet newsgroups can be very busy and generate large amounts of messages).

Public folder replication follows the *multimaster replication model*, in which every replica of a public folder is considered a master copy. When you decide which folders you want to replicate, you manually create and configure those replicas. Any change made to a public folder is automatically replicated to other replicas of that folder by the Exchange *Public Folder Replication Agent (PFRA)* service based on settings you configure. Replication is a mail-based process that uses SMTP as its transport mechanism.

Creating Public Folder Replicas

The method for configuring replication involves pushing replicas from one public folder store to other public folder stores using the property pages of the public folder that you want to replicate. Exercise 6.10 outlines the steps for creating a replica of a public folder.

EXERCISE 6.10

Creating a Replica of a Public Folder

1. In Exchange System Manager, open the property page of the public folder for which you want to create replicas, and switch to the Replication property page.

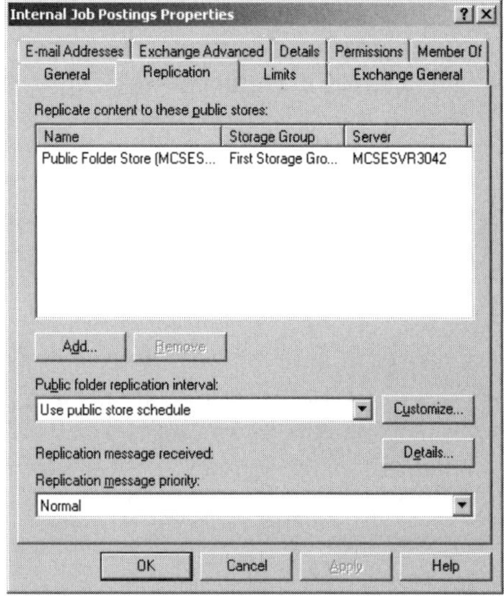

2. On this property page, you'll find a list of public stores that already contain a replica of the public folder. Click the Add button to open a dialog that contains a list of available public stores in your organization that do not already have replicas of the folder.

3. Select the store to which you want to replicate the folder, and click OK.

EXERCISE 6.10 *(continued)*

4. The public store is added to the list of stores that contain replicas. Below the list of public folder stores, you'll find a drop-down menu named Public Folder Replication Interval. Use this menu to schedule the replication of the public folder to the other public folder stores. You have several options here:

   - The Never Run option turns off replication of the public folder, which is handy if you want to stop the replication temporarily to do something like troubleshoot a bad connector.
   - The Always Run option essentially keeps replication going all of the time. Because this would cause excessive traffic, it is generally a poor option to choose. However, there is one time when it is a useful option. When you first configure a new replica and you want the public folder content of that new replica to be transferred as soon as possible, you can turn on the Always Run option to ensure that the content will be replicated quickly. Be sure that you set the schedule to something more reasonable afterward, however.
   - The Run Every 1, 2, Or 4 Hours options cause replication to occur at the defined intervals.
   - The Use Custom Schedule option allows you to click the Customize button to bring up a dialog with a calendar of hours that you can use to set up the replication schedule.
   - The Use Public Store Schedule option is the default setting and causes the folder to replicate according to the default replication schedule set for the public folder store to which the public folder belongs.

5. Click the Details button to bring up a dialog with information about the last replication message Exchange Server generated regarding the current public folder, as seen below.

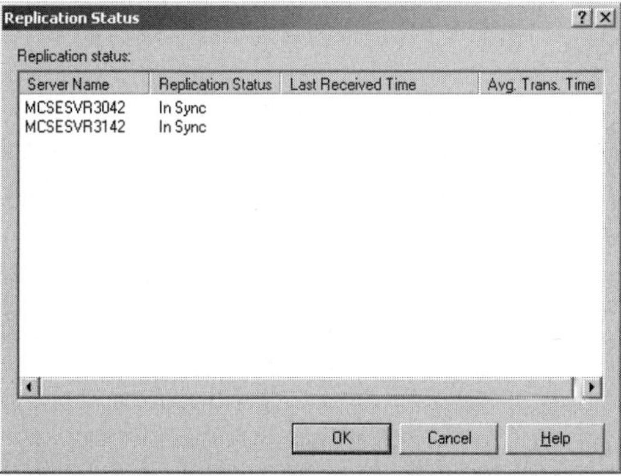

6. Use the Replication Message Priority drop-down list to set the priority that replication messages concerning this folder should take in your Exchange system.

FIGURE 6.10 Configuring replication for a public folder store

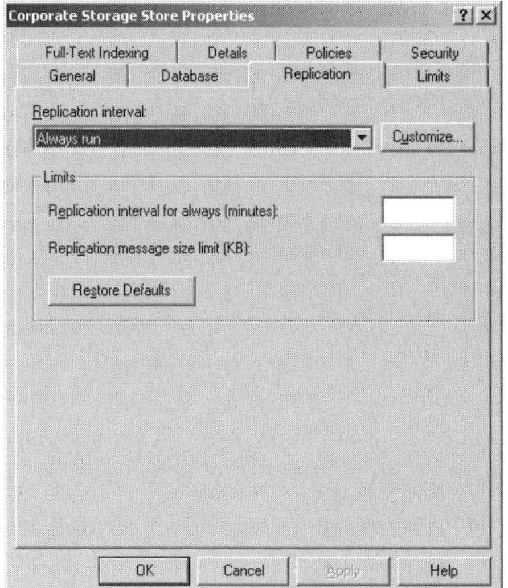

Once you have created replicas of a public folder and configured how replication should behave at the folder level, you can also configure how replication should behave at the public store level. To do this, open the property page for the Public Folder Store object, and switch to the Replication property page, shown in Figure 6.10.

The first action you can perform on this page is to configure replication defaults that apply to all of the folders in that store. Do this using the same type of drop-down menu that you used to configure a schedule for the individual folder. If you do not specifically set a schedule for an individual folder (if you leave it at its default setting), the folder will use the schedule set for the public folder store to which the folder belongs. If you set a schedule for an individual folder, that schedule overrides the public folder store schedule.

The second action you can perform on the Replication property page is to define limits for replication. By default, no limits are defined, but you can specify the maximum time, in minutes, that replication is allowed to go on when replication occurs. You can also define the maximum size, in kilobytes, that a single replication message may be.

Synchronizing Replicas

The Public Information Store uses three primary constructs to keep track of replication throughout an organization and to determine whether a public folder is synchronized. These constructs include the following:

- A *change number* is made up of a globally unique identifier for the Information Store and a change counter that is specific to the server on which a public folder resides. When a user modifies (or creates) a message in a public folder, the PFRA for that Information Store assigns a new change number to the message.

- The PFRA also assigns a *time stamp* to messages as soon as they arrive in a public folder and a new time stamp whenever a message is modified.
- The *predecessor change list* for a message is a list of all of the Information Stores that have made changes to a message and the most recent change number assigned by each Information Store on the list.

Together, these constructs are referred to as *message state information* and play a role in message creation, deletion, and modification.

Message Creation

When a new message is created in a folder, the Information Store receiving the message assigns a change number to the message and deposits it in the folder. The message is replicated to other replicas of the folder during the normal replication schedule.

Message Deletion

When a message is deleted from a folder, the Information Store running the replica in which the message is deleted sends a replication message to all other Information Stores that host a replica of the folder. When each Information Store receives the replication message, it removes the deleted message from its own replica.

Message Expiration

When a message expires (reaches the configured age limit for messages in the folder), the Information Store deletes the message from the folder but does not send a replication message to other Information Stores. Each Information Store removes expired messages from its own folders based on settings made for the store itself and for the folder. Thus, it is possible for different stores to expire a message at different times.

Message Modification

When a change is made to a message in one replica of a public folder, the PFRA for that Information Store updates the message state information for that message and sends a replication message to other Information Stores on which replicas of the folder exist. This replication message contains the modified message and all of its attachments.

When another Information Store receives such a replication message, the modified message inside is used to replace the original message in that store if the message state information determines that the message is indeed newer than the original, based on its time stamp.

While the PFRA sends out replication messages, there is no mechanism in place for ensuring that replication messages reach their destination. The logic behind this is that generating an extra confirmation message for each replication message would unnecessarily double the amount of traffic involved in replication. Thus, it is possible for a message in different replicas of a public folder to become out of sync. A process known as *backfill* is used to remedy this situation. During regular maintenance, status messages are sent between servers, and change numbers for messages on different replicas are compared. If a server is found to be out of sync, it then generates a backfill request for any changes that have not yet been received.

Public Folder Permissions

Public folders, like most objects in Active Directory, have permissions that can be configured on them. Also like other objects in Active Directory, public folders inherit their permissions from their parent objects. A top-level public folder inherits its default permissions from the administrative group to which it belongs. Child folders inherit their permissions from the parent folder under which they are created. Unlike most other objects in Active Directory, public folders have a somewhat complex—and confusing—permissions structure.

Changes that are made to the permissions on a public folder's parent object will not automatically be propagated down to that child object as with NTFS permissions. If you have changed the permissions on a parent object and you desire these changes to be propagated down to the child folder objects, you can do so manually. As you might expect, this action will cause any existing permissions on the child folder object to be overwritten by those being propagated from the parent object.

Public folders have three different sets of permissions that can be configured on them: client permissions, directory rights, and administrative rights. Permissions are configured from the Permissions tab of the public folder Properties dialog box, as seen in Figure 6.11. We've already examined the client permissions in the "Configuring Public Folders from Outlook" section of this chapter. We will examine the other two permission types here.

FIGURE 6.11 Public folders permissions

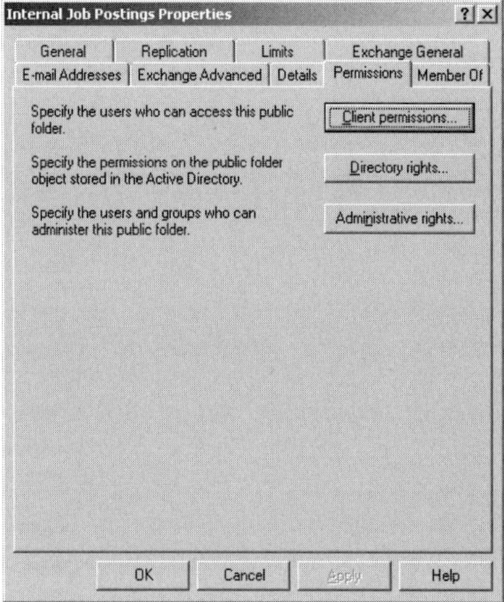

Directory Rights

Directory rights are used to configure the NTFS permissions that determine who can perform modifications on the public folder object that is stored in Active Directory. Clicking the Directory rights button on the Permissions tab opens the Permissions dialog box seen in Figure 6.12.

In most cases, you will not need to change any of the default permissions that have been configured here.

Administrative Rights

Administrative rights allow you to assign NTFS permissions to users and groups that determine who is actually allowed to perform administrative tasks on the public folder. For example, you might have five administrators within your organization, but only two of them are to be allowed to configure and manage replication properties on specific public folders. Clicking the Administrative rights button on the Permissions tab opens the Permissions dialog box seen in Figure 6.13.

As mentioned previously, you may find any number of reasons to configure custom settings for the administrative rights on a public folder depending on the needs of your organization.

FIGURE 6.12 Configuring directory rights

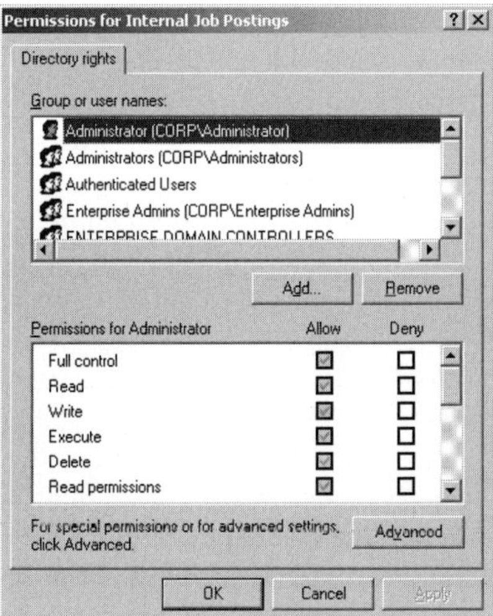

FIGURE 6.13 Configuring administrative rights

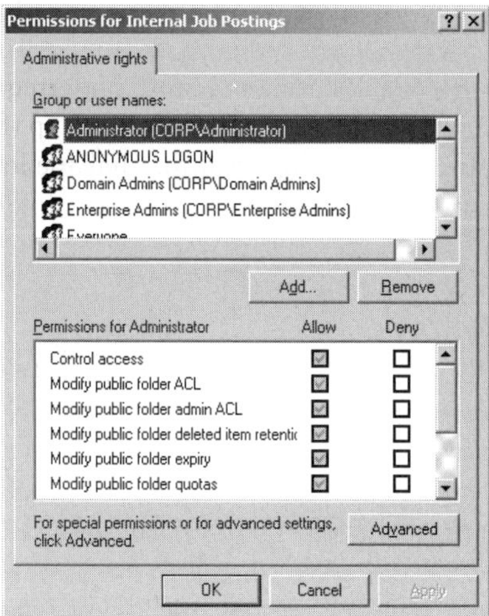

Public Folder Referrals

When a client attempts to connect to a public folder, the public folder might or might not be located in or have a replica in the same routing group as the user's Exchange mailbox. In addition, in any routing group there will likely be more than one public folder store. These factors combine to cause a *public folder referral* to be necessary to allow clients to successfully connect to the desired public folder. Two different, but related, scenarios exist with public folder referrals: one in which the public folder or a replica does exist within the same routing group as the user's mailbox and one in which the public folder or a replica does not exist within the same routing group as the user's mailbox.

When a user attempts to connect to any public folder, the connection is first attempted on the public folder store that is configured as the default public folder store for the mailbox store that houses their Exchange mailbox. If this public folder store does not contain the public folder in question or a replica of it, then the client will connect randomly to another public folder store in the same routing group. This process will continue until the desired public folder or its replica has been located or until all the public folder stores have been exhausted within the routing group. When this happens, a public folder referral must occur in order for the user to successfully connect to the desired public folder.

Although we will examine this in much more detail in Chapter 8, "Building Administrative and Routing Groups," we'll briefly mention here that routing groups are connected to each other using routing group connectors. Routing group connectors, much like a link between two routers, have a cost value associated with them. The cost value can range from a low value of 1 to a high value of 100, with lower values indicating the more preferred routes out of the routing group. When a client needs to connect to a remote routing group (for any reason, including public folder referral), the routing group connector that has the lowest cost value will be used if the routing group connector is configured to allow public folder referrals across it (see Figure 6.14). By default, all routing group connectors are configured to allow public folder referrals; however, this can be disabled by selecting the Do Not Allow Public Folder Referrals option. If a routing group connector allows public folder referrals across it, then the client will continue the process of attempting to locate the public folder or a replica of it in any routing group to which it can connect.

As an alternative to allowing "random" public folder referral, you can configure servers that contain public folder stores with a predefined list of referrals, thus forcing clients to use the configured list. The Public Folder Referrals tab of the server Properties dialog box, seen in Figure 6.15, allows you to change the default option of Use Routing Groups to Use Custom List. When you select the Use Custom List option, you can then configure specific servers and the cost values that are to be used for public folder referrals.

FIGURE 6.14 Allowing public folder referrals across a routing group connector

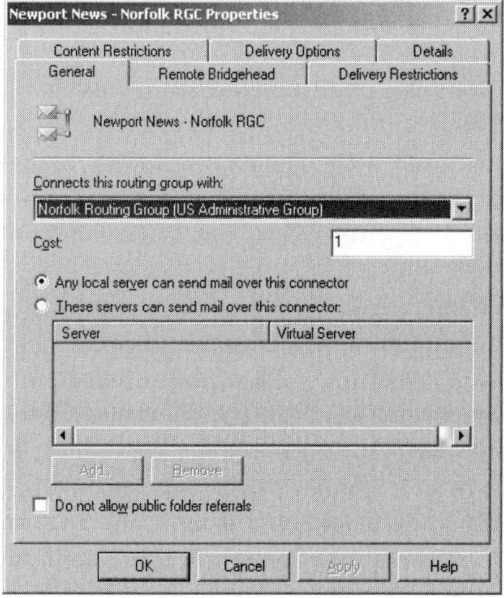

FIGURE 6.15 Configuring a custom referral list

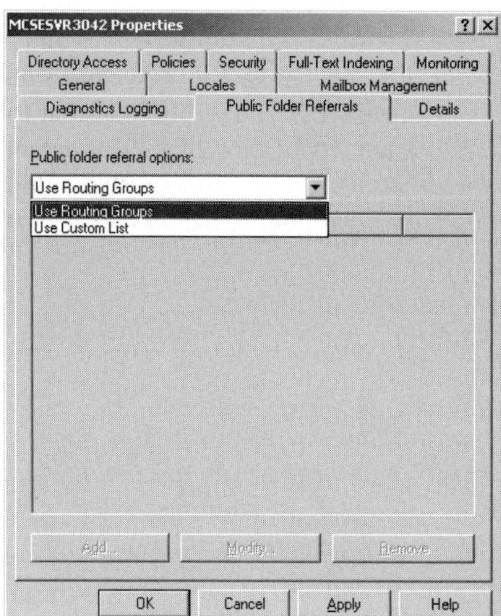

Summary

Public folders are an efficient and effective way to share data among several people. Permissions, forms, rules, and views can be configured on public folders to create folder-based applications. Users can easily create public folders and perform certain management functions using Outlook.

Permissions enable a folder owner to specify who can access a folder and what users can do in that folder. Associating a form with a public folder assists users in submitting structured information into the folder. Rules on public folders can perform automated actions when the appropriate conditions are met. Public folders can hold a large quantity and variety of information, so views can be leveraged to display the pertinent items in a desired way.

Adding content to public folders is very easy. It can be done by posting directly to a public folder or by sending the public folder regular e-mail messages.

Public folders can also be created using the Exchange System Manager. In addition, Exchange System Manager offers many more management options than are available in Outlook. You can configure public folder–related settings at the level of the Public Information Store for a server and at the level of the individual server. Settings made at the folder level typically override settings made at the Public Information Store level. As well, you can configure directory rights and administrative rights for public folders using the Exchange System Manager. Outlook allows the configuration of client permissions only on public folders.

Exchange Server 2003 offers the ability to use multiple public folder trees. The default tree in an organization, named All Public Folders, is also referred to as a MAPI top-level hierarchy. This public folder tree can be accessed by any type of client, including MAPI, NNTP, and HTTP. Additional public folder trees are referred to as general-purpose trees and may not be accessed by MAPI clients such as Outlook. They can be accessed by other types of clients.

Each public folder is created on a single Exchange server, but replicas of that folder can be created on other servers. Once replicas are created, replication of folder content happens according to a predetermined schedule. Public folder replication follows the multimaster replication model, in which every replica of a public folder is considered a master copy.

Exam Essentials

Understand public folder trees. When Exchange Server 2003 is installed, the Default public folder tree is created and can thereafter be accessed as All Public Folders in any MAPI, NNTP, or HTTP client. There can be only one default public folder tree within your Exchange organization. You can, however, create an unlimited number of general-purpose public folder trees that can then be accessed by only NNTP or HTTP clients. You can create public folder trees only from the Exchange System Manager, but you can create new public folders from within Outlook or the Exchange System Manager.

Understand how public folders acts as recipient objects. Like users and groups, public folders can be mail-enabled, allowing them to receive e-mail messages. As well, you can configure storage limits on public folders that are similar to those available for configuration on mailboxes. Store limits can be configured at the public folder level, the public folder store level, or through a public folder store policy (discussed later in Chapter 9.)

Know the different types of public folder permissions. Public folders, like most other objects in Active Directory, can be configured with permissions to determine access to the public folder itself. Public folders have three different sets of permissions that can be configured on them: client permissions, directory rights, and administrative rights. Permissions are configured from the Permissions tab of the public folder Properties dialog box. Client permissions determine which users are allowed to perform specific tasks in the public folder, such as posting new items and creating new child folders. Directory rights are used to configure the NTFS permissions that determine who can perform modifications on the public folder object that is stored in Active Directory. Administrative rights allow you to assign NTFS permissions to users and groups that determine who is actually allowed to perform administrative tasks on the public folder.

Review Questions

1. A user named Perry is the owner of a public folder named Research. Perry leaves your company, and another administrator deletes Perry's user account. What would you as an administrator have to do to modify the permissions on the Research folder?

   A. Create a new account with the same user information as the deleted account.

   B. Restore a backup tape of the server that was created before Perry was deleted.

   C. Designate your account as the owner of the Research folder.

   D. Create a new public folder and move the contents of the Research folder to it.

2. You want to create a public folder hierarchy that has both visible and hidden folders. You have created a distribution group named HR that contains the users who need to view the hidden folders. What would be an efficient way of providing the users who need to view the hidden folder hierarchy with the ability to do that?

   A. Give the List permission to the HR distribution group at each hidden folder.

   B. Give the Folder Contact permission to the HR distribution list at each hidden folder.

   C. Create a root folder that contains all the hidden folders. Revoke all permissions for the Default user. Give the Folder Visible permission to the HR distribution group at the root of the hidden folder hierarchy. Ensure that the HR distribution group has the Read Items permission on each of the root's subfolders either explicitly or through the Default entry.

   D. Give the Create Subfolders permission to the HR distribution group on each hidden folder.

3. You own a public folder named Company Events. Because of the large number of comments about the events sent as replies, users have a hard time distinguishing the original postings from the replies. You decide to create a subfolder named Discussions that you want to hold the replies to the Company Events postings. What is the most efficient way to ensure that all replies to Company Events go to the Discussions folder?

   A. Tell users to use the Discussions folder as a Cc recipient whenever they reply to Company Events.

   B. Configure a rule for Company Events that forwards everything to the Discussions folder except items from users who need to post company event items to the Company Events folder.

   C. Have all users add the Discussions folder to their Favorites folder.

   D. Configure Company Events to delete everything it receives.

4. Which of the following system folders contains Global Address List information that can be downloaded by remote clients?

   A. Offline Address Book

   B. Schedule+ Free/Busy

   C. Address Lists

   D. System Configuration

5. Your organization has four routing groups, each group consisting of two Exchange servers and 500 users. The four groups are connected with a 256-KB wide area network (WAN). The available bandwidth during the workday is less than 64 KB. At night, the available bandwidth is 128 KB or more. You have created a public folder that contains 600 MB of data that is not time critical. Users access that folder only every 15 minutes or so, and the folder data is updated only twice a week. On what servers should replicas be placed?

   A. On every server

   B. On one server in each routing group

   C. Only on the server where the public folder was originally created

   D. Only on domain controllers

6. Which of the following predefined public folder roles enable a user to delete items other than the items they created? (Choose all that apply.)

   A. Owner

   B. Reviewer

   C. Editor

   D. Publishing Author

7. You have replicas of a public folder configured on two servers in your organization. You configured the age limit of messages in the public folder store on the server hosting the original folder to be eight days before replicating the folder. One of the instances of the public folder seems to be expiring the messages right on schedule, but the other never does. You check the message logs on the server where the messages are being properly deleted but find no replication messages regarding the expired messages. What could be the problem and solution?

   A. The Public Folder Replication Agent service is not running properly. Check the Services Control Panel applet to restart it.

   B. Your server is not set to log replication messages. Set it to log replication messages, and check the logs later.

   C. Expiration of messages is not replicated between replicas. You need to check the age limit configured on each replica individually.

   D. Expiration of messages is not supported in multiple replicas of a public folder.

8. You have a public folder that is used by your executive staff. Certain executive assistants are also given access to the public folder, but there are two subfolders in that public folder that the assistants should not be able to view at all. What must you do to hide the subfolders from particular recipients?

   A. Revoke the Read Items permission from those recipients at the parent folder.

   B. Revoke the Read Items permission from those recipients at the subfolders.

   C. Remove the Folder Visible permission from the subfolders for those recipients.

   D. Hide the subfolders from the Global Address List.

   E. A subfolder cannot be hidden, only its contents.

9. Your Exchange organization has six public folders in it, two of which contain sensitive information used by employees in the Human Resources department. These public folders are located in a single public folder tree that has no replicas. You have three other administrators in your organization, none of whom are to be allowed to configure replication to occur for this public folder. How will you configure these permissions on the public folder?

   A. By configuring the client permissions in Outlook for the public folders

   B. By configuring the directory rights on the Permissions tab of the public folder Properties dialog box

   C. By configuring the administrative rights on the Permissions tab of the public folder Properties dialog box

   D. By configuring the client permissions on the Permissions tab of the public folder Properties dialog box

10. The age limit on your public folders is set to 14 days. The deleted-item retention time is set to 7 days. A user deletes an item 12 days after it was created. That same user then recovers the deleted item 7 days later. How long will it be until the item expires?

    A. The item will expire immediately.

    B. 2 days

    C. 5 days

    D. 14 days

11. In addition to a list of each of the Information Stores that have made changes to a message, which of the following items appear on a predecessor change list for a message? (Choose all that apply.)

    A. The last time stamp applied to the message by each Information Store on the list

    B. All of the time stamps applied to the message by each Information Store on the list

    C. The last change number applied to the message by each Information Store on the list

    D. All of the change numbers applied to the message by each Information Store on the list

12. Which of the following tools can you use to associate a form with a particular public folder? (Choose all that apply.)

    A. The property pages of the public folder in Outlook

    B. The property pages of the public folder in Exchange System Manager

    C. The property pages of the EFORMS System Folder in Exchange System Manager

    D. A separate utility called Electronic Forms Designer

13. Which three users are included by default on the permissions list of a new public folder?

    A. The user who created the folder

    B. The local Administrator account

    C. A special user account named Default

    D. A special user account named Anonymous

    E. The Exchange Administrator account

14. Several of your users routinely connect to your Exchange organization using Outlook Web Access. What URL will these users need to use in order to connect to your organization's public folders?

    A. `http://`*servername*`/exchange/`

    B. `http://`*servername*`/exchange/public/`

    C. `http:/`*servername*`/public/`

    D. `http://`*servername*`/folders/`

15. Your organization has a public folder named Safety Issues that employees use to post notices about safety hazards that have been located within your buildings and warehouses. You want all employees in the company to be able to post new items into this folder and read any existing items but perform no other actions. What role do you need to configure for the Default user on this public folder?

    A. Contributor

    B. Author

    C. Nonediting Author

    D. Editor

16. You recently created a public folder that employees of your company can use to post personal announcements, such as marriages and births. You have now become aware that a number of people are also posting large attachments to messages in the form of photos or other documents. This is causing the public folder to swell considerably in size. People enjoy the Announcements folder, and you would like to keep it available. However, you want to keep users from posting large messages or attachments. What is your best option?

    A. Set a limit on the size of messages that each user may send, using the property pages for that user.

    B. Set a limit on the size of messages that can be posted in the public folder, using the folder's property pages.

    C. Set a limit on the maximum size that a public folder can reach before new posts are prohibited, and then manually delete large posts.

    D. Set a limit on the maximum size that a public folder can reach before new posts are prohibited, and then create a script that deletes large posts automatically.

17. Where in System Manager would you go to find out the current replication state of public folders on a server?

    A. The property pages for that server

    B. The property pages for the public folder

    C. The property pages for the public folder store

    D. The Replication Status subcontainer of the public folder store

    E. The Public Folders subcontainer of the public folder store

18. Which of the following statements is true of public folder trees?

    A. Each public folder store may have only one public folder tree.

    B. Each public folder store may have only one default public folder tree but up to five general-purpose trees.

    C. Each public folder store may have only one default public folder tree but any number of general-purpose trees.

    D. Each public folder store may have any number of public folder trees.

19. When a public folder is mail-enabled, which Exchange service connects an object for the public folder to Active Directory?

    A. Microsoft Exchange Event Service

    B. Internet Information Server service

    C. System Attendant service

    D. Information Store service

    E. Public Folder Replication Agent (PFRA) service

20. You have just created a new public folder. Both the public folder and the public folder store use the default settings for age limits and deleted-item retention time. What would happen if a user deleted a message that was eight days old?

A. The user would have four days to recover the message before it was removed from the server.

B. The user would have seven days to recover the message before it was removed from the server.

C. The user could not recover the message.

D. The user could not delete the message because it would have already expired due to an age limit.

Answers to Review Questions

1. C. An administrator has the permission to change the owner of a folder. Once the administrator takes ownership of the folder, they can then perform administrative tasks, such as adding rules and installing forms.

2. C. The Folder Visible permission specifies whether the folder is visible to the user or group in the public folder hierarchy.

3. B. Rules consisting of conditions and actions can be configured on public folders. Rules allow a public folder to automate certain procedures.

4. A. The Offline Address Book folder contains a subset of the Global Address List that remote users can download and use for addressing mail when they are not connected to the Exchange server.

5. B. Since the folders are not accessed a great deal, there is really no need to have replicas configured on multiple servers in each routing group. However, because of the slow link speed during the day, it is important that at least one server in each routing group have a replica. Since there is more available bandwidth at night and since the public folder data is not time critical, you could also schedule replication to occur only at night.

6. A, C. Only the Owner, Editor, and Publishing Editor of a public folder can delete items other than their own. The Publishing Author, Author, and Nonediting Author can delete their own items only. All other roles cannot delete any items.

7. C. When a message expires (reaches the configured age limit for messages in the folder), the Information Store deletes the message from the folder but does not send a replication message to other Information Stores. Each Information Store removes expired messages from its own folders based on settings made for the store itself and for the folder. You relied on the public folder store's age limit setting on the original instance of the folder, but the age limit might be set differently for the public folder store on the other server.

8. C. The only way to hide a folder from recipients altogether is to remove the Folder Visible permission from those recipients. Revoking the Read Items permission from the parent folder would render all items in the folder unreadable. For better security, it would also be a good idea to revoke the Read Items permission from the recipients. To simply hide the folder, however, this action is not necessary.

9. C. Administrative rights allow you to assign NTFS permissions to users and groups that determine who is actually allowed to perform administrative tasks on the public folder, such as configuring replication for a specific public folder.

10. D. Since the item was recovered after the original expiration date, a new expiration date is set equal to the original expiration period. If the item had been recovered before the original expiration date, it would have then expired on the original expiration date.

11. C. A change number is made up of a globally unique identifier for the Information Store and a change counter that is specific to the server. When a message is modified, the Information Store updates the predecessor change list with the name of the Information Store and a change number. Only the last change number is listed in the predecessor change list.

12. A. You can associate electronic forms with a public folder only by using Outlook.

13. A, C, D. When a public folder is created, the user who created the folder is given the role of folder owner. The Default user represents all users who have access to the public folder store and aren't explicitly listed in the permissions list. The Anonymous user represents all users logged on with anonymous access.

14. C. Users connecting to a public folder using HTTP will need to connect to the URL `http://`*servername*`/public/` to access the public folders.

15. C. The Nonediting Author role will allow users to read existing items in the public folder and create new items but will not allow them any other permissions on the public folder.

16. B. The Limits property page for a public folder contains a number of settings that govern public folder limits. One setting allows you to specify the maximum size of messages that can be posted to the public folder. This is the best way to ensure that large posts are not made. Setting a limit on the size of the messages that users can send would also restrict the sending of regular e-mail messages. Deleting posts, whether done manually or automatically, might be considered intrusive and arbitrary by users.

17. D. The Replication Status subcontainer lists all folders and the number of servers that contain a replica of each folder. It also lists the current replication state and the time of the last replication.

18. A. Though a single server may host multiple public folder trees, a separate public folder store must be created for each tree.

19. C. The System Attendant is responsible for creating objects in the Active Directory for mail-enabled public folders.

20. C. No age limit or deleted-item retention time is set by default. This means that the age of the message in question would have no effect on deleting or recovering the item. Once the message was deleted, the user could not recover it because retention time is in effect.

Configuring Client Access

MICROSOFT EXAM OBJECTIVES COVERED IN THIS CHAPTER:

✓ Manage and troubleshoot connectivity

Microsoft Office Outlook 2003, a MAPI client, includes many powerful features and will likely be the primary Exchange client used in most organizations. In this chapter, you will learn about the installation and configuration of various Microsoft Exchange client programs. We discuss how to configure and take advantage of Outlook 2003, and we examine several important Internet protocols that can be used to access Exchange Server. Outlook Web Access provides a way for standard web browsers to access Exchange information. We also cover the POP3 and IMAP4 message retrieval protocols.

Specifically, this chapter covers the following topics:

- Client platforms for Microsoft Exchange
- The MAPI architecture
- Microsoft Outlook
- Virtual servers
- Outlook Web Access
- POP3 clients
- IMAP4 clients
- NNTP clients

Client Platforms for Microsoft Exchange

The very first order of business is to define what is meant by *clients* for Microsoft Exchange. The best way to do that is to compare and contrast an Exchange client with an Exchange correspondent (this term is the authors'). An Exchange client application has the ability to access an Exchange mailbox as the owner of that mailbox, whereas an Exchange correspondent has only the ability to send and receive mail to and from an Exchange user. If an Exchange mailbox were a physical mailbox at the post office, a client would have the key for accessing their mailbox, while a correspondent would only be able to send mail to that mailbox or receive mail sent from it.

An example of a client application is *Microsoft Outlook 2003*. An example of a correspondent might be a user on the Internet. This latter functionality is enabled through Microsoft Exchange connectors or gateways. Applications that can only correspond with Exchange are also referred to as *foreign mail clients*. The users of foreign mail applications are defined as contacts within the Active Directory, as you learned in Chapter 5, "Creating and Managing Exchange Recipients." This allows Exchange users to address mail to the foreign mail users (Exchange interoperability with foreign systems is covered in Chapter 13, "Connecting with Other Messaging Systems").

There are two main Exchange client application architectures:

MAPI (Messaging Application Programming Interface) *MAPI* is the Microsoft API used for messaging functions. Microsoft Outlook 2003 is a MAPI client, although it does not come bundled with Exchange Server 2003 as in previous versions of Exchange.

Following are examples of MAPI client applications that can still be used with Microsoft Exchange Server but are not necessarily supported:

- Microsoft Exchange Client (the version that shipped with previous versions of Exchange Server)
- Microsoft Schedule+ 7.5 (this product has been replaced by the Outlook Calendar function)
- Microsoft Outlook 97 version 8.03 (there are also versions of this product for Microsoft Windows 3.*x*, Windows 95, Windows NT, and Apple Macintosh)

Internet protocols Some Internet protocols can also be used by clients to access Microsoft Exchange. Examples are as follows:

Post Office Protocol version 3 (POP3) Retrieves mail from the Inbox folder of a mailbox on a remote server.

Internet Message Access Protocol version 4 (IMAP4) Retrieves mail from a mailbox on a remote server. Access includes personal and public folders, as well as the Inbox folder.

Hypertext Transfer Protocol (HTTP) Handles data transfer between World Wide Web servers and browsers.

Lightweight Directory Access Protocol (LDAP) Provides access to directory information. Clients and servers use LDAP to retrieve information from Active Directory. In previous versions of Exchange Server, clients used LDAP to access directories managed by Exchange.

Network News Transfer Protocol (NNTP) Transfers data between newsgroup servers and between newsgroup servers and newsgroup reader programs.

Figure 7.1 illustrates foreign mail users communicating with Exchange, and Figure 7.2 illustrates various types of Exchange clients communicating with Exchange.

FIGURE 7.1 Foreign mail user communication with Exchange

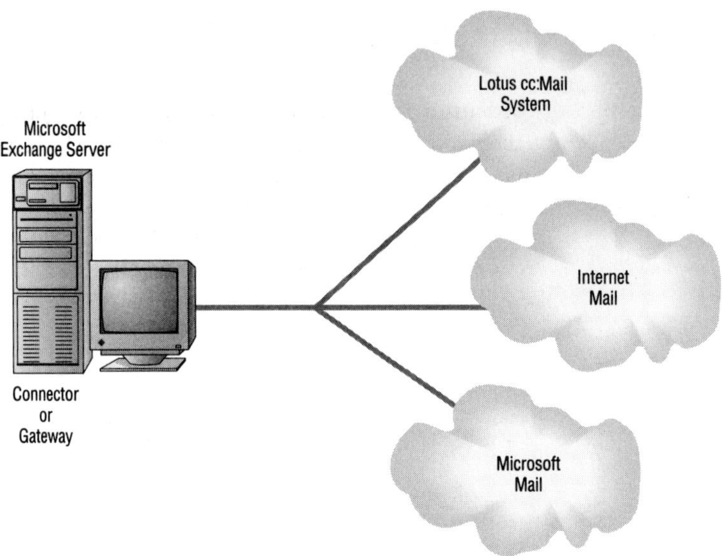

FIGURE 7.2 Exchange clients

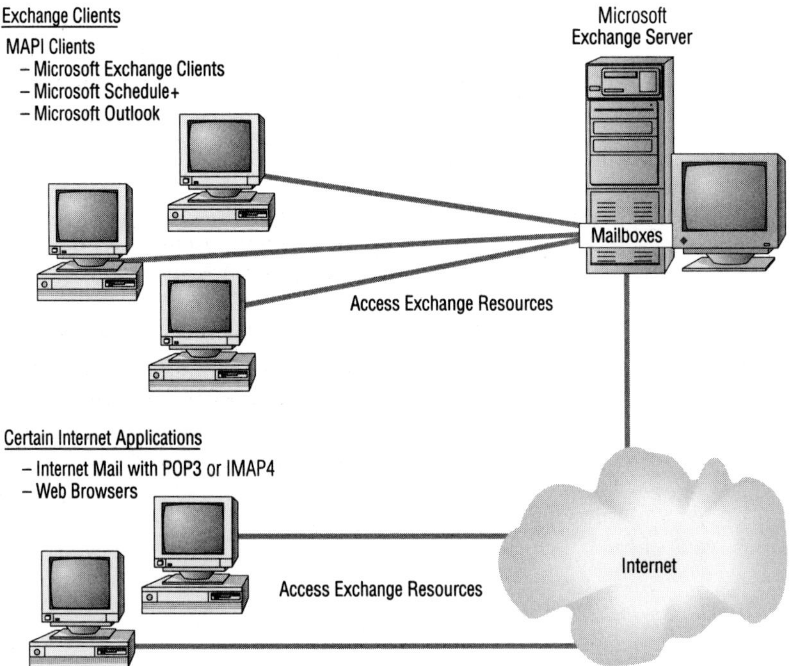

MAPI Architecture

Many messaging systems are divided into a client side and a server side. The client side provides an interface to users and permits them to read, save, create, and send mail. The server-side programs carry out the client requests. For example, if a client issues a read request for a certain message, the server responds by transmitting the message to the client. The client software is sometimes referred to as the *front end* to the server software, which can be referred to as the *back end*. The front-end programs can be thought of as consumers and the back-end programs as producers.

Do not confuse the front end and back end of a client/server system with the concept of front-end and back-end servers used in Exchange Server 2003. You can learn more about front-end and back-end servers in Chapter 4, "Creating and Managing Exchange Clusters," Chapter 9, "Configuring the Information Store," and Chapter 15, "Securing Exchange Server 2003."

Historically, messaging systems have been implemented using "closed" application programming interfaces (APIs). An API is a collection of instructions, also called function calls or services. When a user wants to read a message stored on the server, the client program issues the relevant API function call to the system interface, and the server responds accordingly.

The problem with the closed API model is that each model is proprietary, and thus each vendor has its own APIs. When someone wrote a client program to be used with one of these proprietary systems, it worked with only that system. With this architecture, multiple client programs were needed to connect to multiple messaging systems (see Figure 7.3).

Microsoft decided to remedy this situation by creating a standard messaging architecture known as MAPI. MAPI provides a way for client messaging applications to communicate with multiple messaging systems (see Figure 7.4). Although MAPI is an acronym for Messaging Application Programming Interface, it is much more than an API. It is an architecture that specifies components, how they should act, and how they should interface with each other.

Figure 7.5 illustrates the basic architecture of MAPI. The top layer, the client application layer, includes client applications that enable users to perform messaging activities. These client applications are the front-end programs that request services from the back-end server programs. Client applications can include different messaging services (such as e-mail, fax, voicemail, and paging), as long as they are written to the MAPI specification. The concept of having messages from multiple sources delivered to one place is referred to as the *universal inbox*.

FIGURE 7.3 Multiple client programs for multiple messaging systems

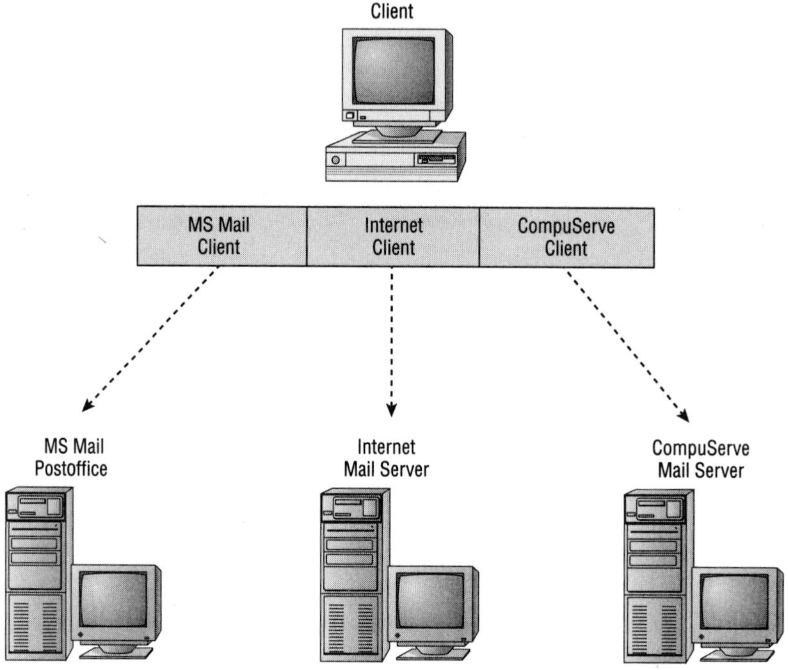

Previously, a single client program could not communicate with more than one server program, because the server programs all used different APIs. The MAPI architecture eliminates this limitation by providing a single layer through which the client programs and the server programs can communicate. This is the second layer and is called the MAPI subsystem (see Figure 7.6). The MAPI subsystem is referred to as *middleware* because it acts as a broker between two other layers.

Server programs can still use their own APIs on the back end. But the vendors of these programs must write a type of client component, called a *service provider*, that will interface their back-end system with the MAPI subsystem. Service providers constitute the third layer in the MAPI architecture (see Figure 7.7). Client software communicates with the MAPI subsystem, which communicates with a service provider, which communicates with the back-end message server. This is how a single client application, using multiple service providers, communicates with multiple back-end message servers.

The next sections provide additional details on the MAPI architecture.

FIGURE 7.4 A single MAPI application accessing multiple messaging systems

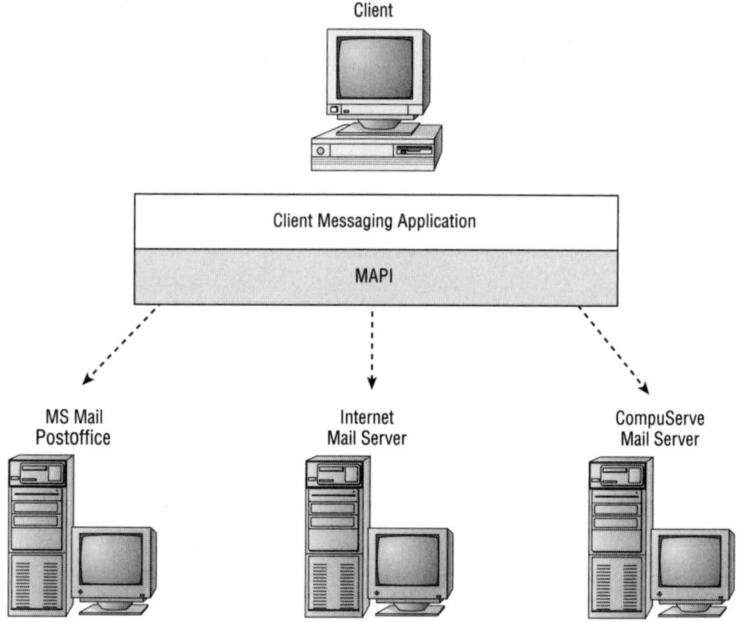

FIGURE 7.5 The basic MAPI architecture

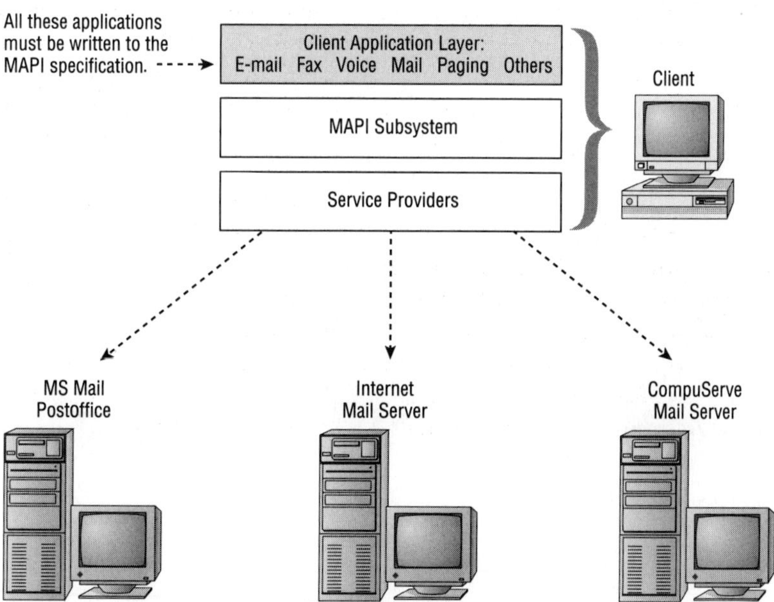

FIGURE 7.6 The MAPI subsystem

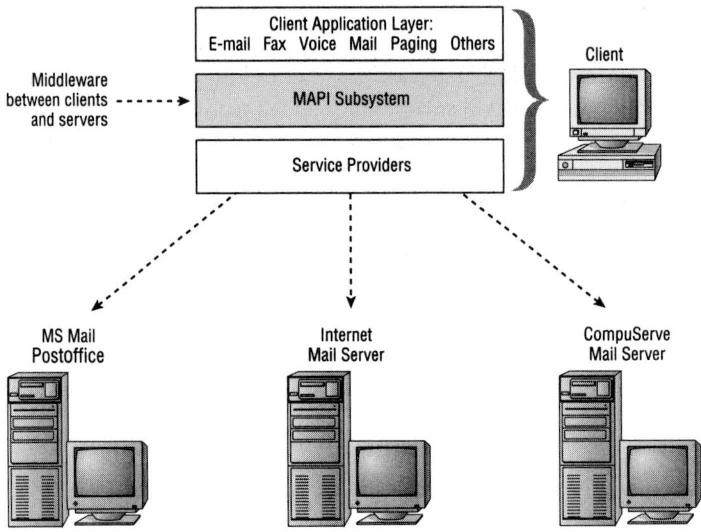

FIGURE 7.7 MAPI service providers

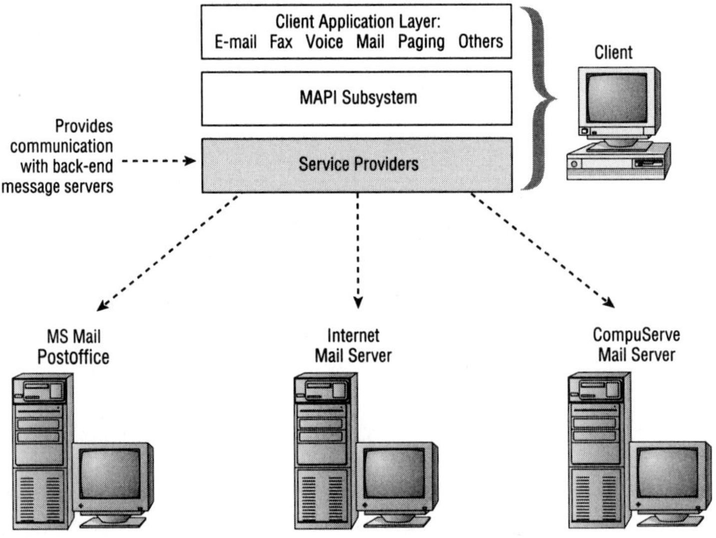

Client Application Layer

Client applications that need to perform messaging functions can have those functions implemented through the use of MAPI function calls. Examples of these calls are `MAPIReadMail`, `MAPISaveMail`, and `MAPISendMail`. When these instructions are executed in a client application, they initiate an action in the MAPI subsystem, which then interfaces with service providers, which interface with a server messaging system, such as Microsoft Exchange Server or CompuServe Mail.

MAPI encompasses three major API sets:

Simple MAPI This is a set of 12 straightforward messaging functions, such as reading (`MAPIReadMail`) and sending (`MAPISendMail`) messages. It is included in *messaging-aware* applications such as Microsoft Word.

Common Mail Call (CMC) This is a set of 10 messaging functions similar to Simple MAPI. CMC is geared for cross-platform, operating system–independent development. CMC was developed by the X.400 Application Programming Interface Association (XAPIA).

MAPI 1.*x* (also called Extended MAPI) This is the newer, more powerful MAPI standard. It includes the abilities of Simple MAPI but adds many other instructions for complex messaging functions, such as custom forms as the CDO Library API.

See Figure 7.8 for a depiction of these three APIs in the MAPI architecture.

These three API sets allow developers to create client messaging applications that fall into two broad categories:

Messaging-aware applications These are applications such as Microsoft Word that have some messaging functions included, such as a Send option on the File menu. Messaging is not essential to these applications. Simple MAPI or CMC is most conveniently used as the messaging API.

Messaging-based or messaging-enabled applications These are applications such as Microsoft Outlook that require messaging functionality. The comprehensive function call set of Extended MAPI is normally required to implement these applications.

MAPI Subsystem

The second layer of the MAPI architecture is the *MAPI subsystem* (see Figure 7.9). This component is shared by all applications that require its services and is therefore considered a *subsystem* of the operating system. Microsoft includes the MAPI subsystem with the 32-bit Windows 98, Me, NT, 2000, XP, and Server 2003 operating systems, and the file `MAPI32.DLL` is the primary function library for these operating systems. The MAPI subsystem for 16-bit Windows 3.*x* is loaded with the installation of the Exchange client, and the file `MAPI.DLL` is the primary function library.

FIGURE 7.8 The three MAPI API sets

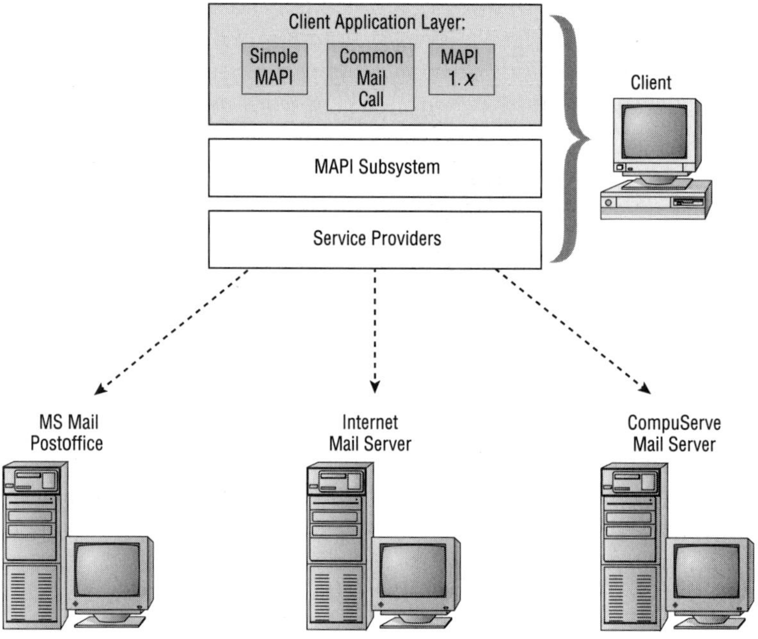

The MAPI subsystem is also referred to as the MAPI runtime.

The MAPI subsystem provides a single interface for client applications. Communication with all MAPI-compliant server messaging systems is facilitated by interfacing with the MAPI subsystem. It is the middleware, or broker, in the messaging environment. The subsystem manages memory, administers profiles, routes client requests to the relevant service provider, and returns results from servers via service providers.

The MAPI subsystem also presents a single, virtual address book and a single, virtual storage area to the user. As you will learn in the next section, multiple service providers can create multiple address books and multiple message stores. The MAPI subsystem presents all of these through a unified interface. Consequently, even though both an e-mail program and a fax program are being used, the user can view all addresses in one virtual address book. Because all data can be kept in the same virtual storage area, users can organize information based upon logical categories (e.g., all communication from Jane) rather than by application (e.g., e-mail directory, fax directory, etc.).

FIGURE 7.9 MAPI subsystem

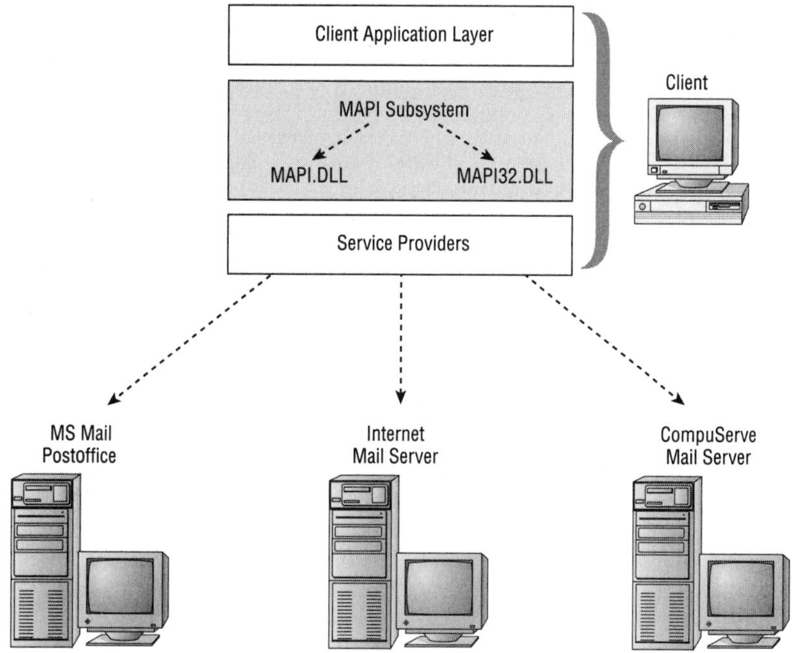

MAPI Service Providers

The MAPI architecture's third layer contains components called service providers. These replaceable components (manifested as DLL files) communicate with the messaging system back end. There are three main types of service providers:

- Address book providers
- Message store providers
- Message transport providers

The following three sections discuss these service providers.

A provider is sometimes called a driver.

Address Book Providers

An address book provider is a component that interacts with a database of message recipients. Some of these providers create their own address databases, called *personal address books*

(PABs); others can access address books on a server. Address book providers can be written for many kinds of back-end systems, and because they all interface with the MAPI subsystem, a user can still have a single, virtual address book.

The following are three examples of address book providers:

Global Address List (GAL) This provider enables a client application to view an Exchange server's Global Address List (GAL). The GAL is a database of all the recipients in an Exchange organization, such as mailboxes, distribution lists, custom recipients, and public folders. The file extension of this address book is usually `.gal`.

Personal Address Book This provider, also called the Local Address Book, enables the creation of a customized address book. Users can include frequently used e-mail addresses, as well as custom recipients and distribution lists that the user creates. Message recipients are not the only type of information that can be stored. Phone and fax numbers, postal addresses, and other information can be stored here. This address book can be stored on the user's machine or on a server. The file extension of this address book is usually `.pab`.

Offline Address Book (OAB) This address book provider permits an Exchange server's GAL to be downloaded to a user's machine. This can be useful when working offline. The file extension of this local database is usually `.oab`.

See Figure 7.10 for a depiction of the address book providers in the MAPI architecture.

FIGURE 7.10 Address book providers

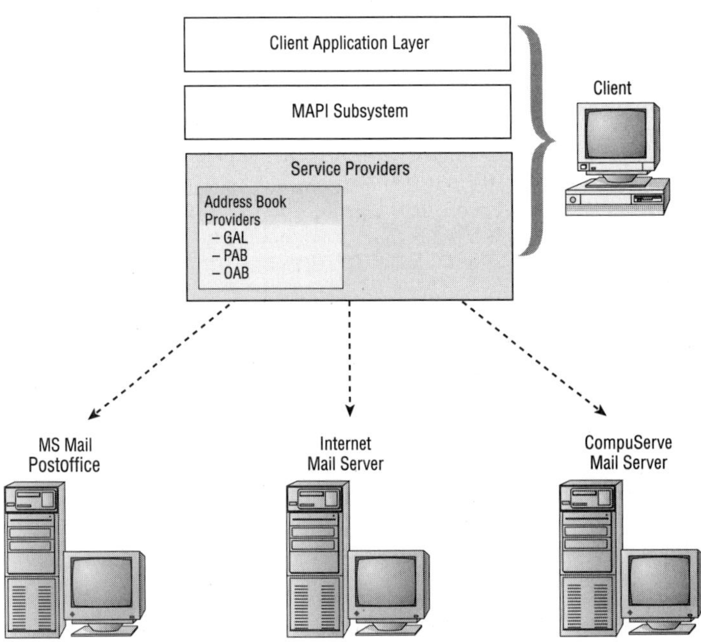

Message Store Providers

Message store providers are components that manage a database of messages. This entails client message storage, organization, and submission for sending and retrieving messages and attachments. Storage is organized in a hierarchical tree of folders. Views can be created to allow the user to see messages based on certain criteria, such as subject or date. Searches can also be conducted to retrieve specific information.

Message store providers can use server-based storage or client-based storage. Following are four examples of message store providers (see Figure 7.11):

Private folders This provider enables client access to an assigned mailbox on an Exchange server (i.e., the home server of the mailbox). The term *private folders* is another name for what are more commonly referred to as mailboxes. They are called "private" because, more often than not, they are associated with a single user (even though several users can be given permission to use a single mailbox). All private folders are stored on an Exchange server in the Private Information Store, which is managed by the Information Store service. The advantages of this type of storage are compression, security, and centralized backup.

Public folders Public folders are the groupware component of Exchange Server. This provider allows a client to access the hierarchical tree of public folder storage to which everyone in the Exchange organization has access. Public folders are stored on Exchange servers in the Public Information Store, which is managed by the Information Store service.

FIGURE 7.11 Message store providers

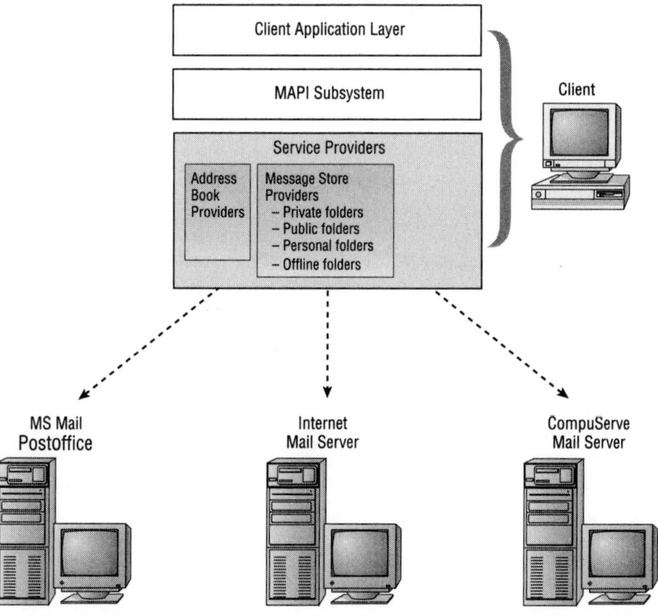

Personal folders (PST, Personal Store) A personal folder store is a file-based storage container independent of the Exchange Server back end. The file that is composed of a set of personal folders has the `.pst` extension. A PST file can be stored on the user's local machine or on a shared directory on a network server. As with private folders, a user can create a hierarchical tree of folders within a personal folder store. In previous versions of Outlook, you were limited to 2 GB in size for PST files and the PST files themselves were stored in the American National Standards Institute (ANSI) format. Outlook 2003 now uses the Unicode format by default, thus allowing for PST files that can grow to 20 GB and beyond in size. Versions of Outlook previous to Outlook 2003 cannot use these new, larger PST files, however.

Personal folder stores can be assigned a password for protection. Personal folders can also be designated as the location to where incoming mail messages are moved. Although all mail is always first sent to private folders on an Exchange server, users can configure their private folders to route messages to their personal folders. Because of storage technologies used in the Private Information Store, information moved from that location to a personal folder would take up more space in the personal folder. Note also that moving information to personal folders may make backing up more complicated than if everything were stored on a server. Of course, personal folders can also be stored on a server that is included in regular backups.

Passwords assigned to a personal folder cannot be viewed by the Exchange administrator. Therefore, if a user forgets this password, the information in that folder is inaccessible using tools provided in System Manager or Outlook. However, there are a number of third-party utilities that are usually able to crack personal folder and other application passwords.

Offline folders (OST, Offline Store) If mailbox storage is left in the default location (the Private Information Store) and offline access to that data is also needed, the user can utilize *offline folders*. An offline folder is a local copy of the user's private folders in the Private Information Store. The mailbox on the server remains the master copy. Offline folders have the `.ost` file extension.

Message Transport Providers

Message transport providers manage the physical transportation of messages between a MAPI client and a back-end system (see Figure 7.12). Like gateway components, they take a MAPI message, translate it to the format of the back-end system, and send it. They do the reverse for incoming messages. Message transport providers work with any of the Microsoft-supported network protocols, such as TCP/IP, IPX/SPX, and NetBEUI.

The following are examples of back-end systems that have message transport providers:

- Microsoft Exchange Server
- Microsoft Network online service (MSN)
- Microsoft Fax
- Microsoft Mail

- Internet Mail
- CompuServe Mail

Message Spooler

The message spooler (also referred to as the MAPI spooler) is an independent process that manages the flow of messages between the message store and the transport providers. It is like a queue where incoming and outgoing messages are sent and from there are routed to the necessary providers. When a message is marked for sending, a message store provider will send it to the message spooler. The message spooler then selects, based on the destination address, a message transport provider that can send the message to the relevant messaging system.

Messaging Profiles

A messaging profile is a collection of configuration parameters for MAPI operations. The first time a user starts a MAPI-based application, the Profile Wizard runs and prompts for various operational parameters related to messaging. For example, the user is prompted to choose the information services to be used, such as Microsoft Exchange Server, Microsoft Fax, Internet Mail, and others. Information services are collections of the various providers described earlier. The user is also prompted to configure his personal address book information service. Other information in the profile relates to message handling, such as saving sent mail or generating a delivery receipt. When the MAPI subsystem starts, it reads this profile to see which services to load and how to operate (see Figure 7.13).

FIGURE 7.12 Message transport providers

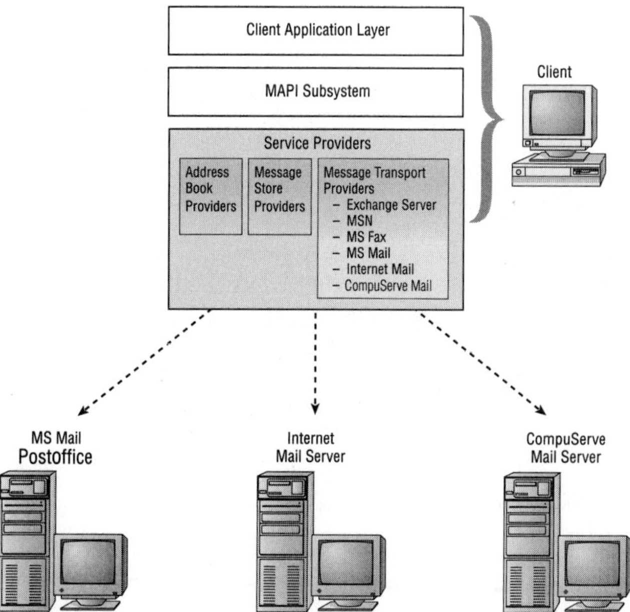

FIGURE 7.13 Messaging profile

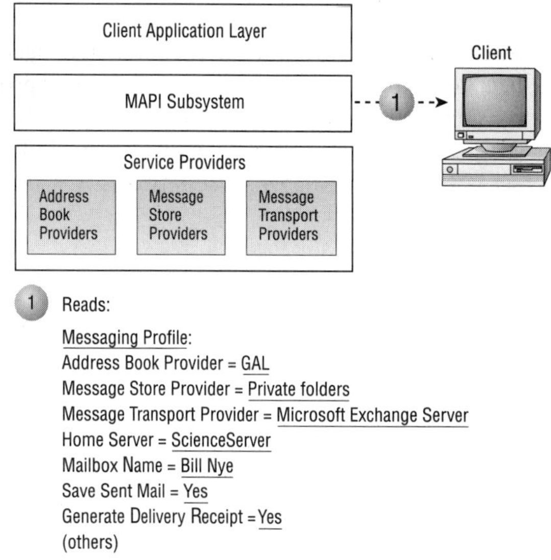

A user can have several profiles for one particular machine. For example, a user's computer might be a laptop that is used both at the office and on the road. When the user is at the office, the user profile connects the user to an Exchange server at the office. When the user is traveling, a different profile connects the laptop to the Internet. Multiple profiles for a particular machine are also useful when several people use the same machine.

Common Features of MAPI-Based Applications

Many common features are found in MAPI-based applications, including the following:

Universal Inbox Information from multiple sources (e.g., Exchange Server, Internet, etc.) and of varying types (e.g., e-mail, faxes, documents, and voicemail) is delivered to a single Inbox folder.

Single address book A standard user interface to the address book is provided. Information from all the address books configured in the current profile is consolidated in one place.

Hierarchical storage Messages and other items can be organized into a user-customizable hierarchical tree of folders. Four special folders are always present in the default store. They are the Inbox, Deleted Items, Sent Items, and Outbox folders.

Custom views Information stored in folders can be sorted and viewed using many types of criteria, such as author, date, keyword, or type of content.

Rich-text formatting Users can create message content that uses the rich-text format, which includes underlining, italic, bolding, bullet points, colors, fonts, different character sizes, and letter strikethrough.

Microsoft Outlook

Microsoft Outlook fits into several application categories. It is a personal information manager (PIM) because it functions as a personal calendar, scheduler, contact manager, and task manager. It is also a messaging application because it includes a powerful e-mail program and forms program. And finally, it is a groupware application because it can access Exchange Server public folders and enables calendars, schedules, contact information, and task information to be used in a group context. All of this functionality exists through a single, integrated, desktop environment.

Outlook 2003 is part of the Microsoft Office 2003 suite and as such is tightly integrated with the other Office applications, though it can also be purchased as a stand-alone product. Outlook is fully MAPI compliant.

Recall that each client, whether it be an Outlook client or any other client, will require a Microsoft Exchange Client Access License (CAL) to legally access Exchange Server. This CAL is over and above the server license you need to install Exchange Server 2003 in the first place.

Some of the improvements in Outlook 2003 over previous versions of the Outlook client include:

Cache mode operation When configured, allows Outlook 2003 to work from a local cache of the user's Exchange mailbox, which is stored in an OST file on the local computer. The Offline Address List is also made available. The local cache is refreshed periodically from the Exchange server.

RPC over HTTP Provides a means for Outlook 2003 users to make secure connections over the Internet to an Exchange organization without the need for a VPN.

Smart change synchronization Allows for changes to an item to require only synchronization of the changes, versus the entire item as with previous versions of Outlook.

Incremental Change Synchronization (ICS) check-pointing Using this method of synchronization prevents the resending of data that was successfully sent if network connectivity is interrupted during a synchronization event. In this event, Outlook 2003 will simply continue the synchronization event where it left off once connectivity is restored.

Skip Bad Items To prevent the failure of the synchronization process, as occurred in previous versions of Outlook, Outlook 2003 will skip and log all bad or malformed items that are found on the server during a synchronization event. Items that are marked as infected by a virus scanner that integrates with Exchange Server 2003 will also be skipped.

Pre-synchronization reporting MAPI compression Using MAPI compression allows for much faster communication between server and client. This compression is applied to the message header, message body, and any attachments.

PST/OST enhancements As mentioned previously, PST and OST files now use the Unicode format and can exceed the previous size limit of 2 GB.

Send/Receive groups improvements Additional configuration and customization options have been provided for users using Send/Receive groups to enhance their Outlook experience.

Architectural Design

Microsoft Outlook is designed to be a desktop information manager. This means it integrates personal and groupware tools, as well as their information, in a unified manner. This goal was achieved by including the following design features:

Single application, multiple functionality From a single interface, users can execute numerous programs such as e-mail, calendar, contact list, and task list.

Integrated user interface All the tools in Outlook are seamlessly integrated. For example, Outlook includes a feature called the Outlook Bar. This is a navigation tool that creates shortcuts to a user's e-mail Inbox, calendar, contacts, tasks, and folders. Outlook, as a MAPI program, provides a single address book that can be used for e-mail, phone dialing, faxing, and other functions. The Outlook interface permits users to access both local file folders and Exchange public folders.

Custom forms using Office 2003 One example of Outlook's tight integration with Office 2003 is its ability to create and send forms that include objects created in any of the Office 2003 applications. For instance, an expense report form that includes an Excel spreadsheet can be created. Because of Microsoft object technology (see note below), the spreadsheet contained in the form will not be merely rows and columns but will include the Excel code to execute the functions of the spreadsheet. The form's users can enter their numbers, have the spreadsheet calculate them, and then have the form automatically sent to a designated person. Outlook, along with Microsoft Office 2003, enables the creation of instant groupware applications.

ActiveX is an object technology developed by Microsoft. It is an extension of the earlier OLE technology. ActiveX allows programs to exchange objects that include both presentation data (i.e., what you see on the screen) and native data (i.e., the executable code to manipulate the presentation data).

Features of Microsoft Outlook

Microsoft Outlook includes some very powerful messaging, groupware, and personal productivity features. Tables 7.1, 7.2, and 7.3 describe many of those features.

TABLE 7.1 Messaging Features of Microsoft Outlook

Main Function	Features	Description
E-mail	AutoNameCheck	Outlook checks the name typed in message headers against the address book as soon as the user tabs out of the entry fields.
	Message recall	A user can recall a sent message, assuming the recipient has not already opened it.
	Voting	Users can create messages that include voting buttons in the message when received. Recipients can click one of the button choices and submit their choice back to the sender. The sender can automatically track responses to a question or issue.
	Delegate access	Users can grant other users the right to send and receive messages using their mailbox.
	Message tracking	All the information about delivery, receipt, recall, and voting notifications is tabulated on the original message in the sender's mailbox.
	AutoPreview	The first few lines of each message can be displayed without requiring the user to open the message in a separate window. This allows users to quickly view the contents of messages.
	MessageFlags	Users can place flags (i.e., notices) on messages to aid in sorting and prioritizing messages. Flags include reply, read, "for your information," or any custom text.
	Hyperlinks to URLs	If a message includes a web URL (Uniform Resource Locator) address, Outlook will recognize that address. If the user clicks the address, Outlook will start the user's web browser and connect to that location.
	Retrieve deleted items	Users can retrieve deleted items from their mailboxes through the Recover Deleted Items command. Recovered mailbox items are placed in the Deleted Items folder. This functionality is made possible by the Exchange Information Store and is configured through the private folder store and individual mailboxes.

TABLE 7.2 Groupware Features of Microsoft Outlook

Main Function	Features	Description
Group scheduling	Browsing free/busy information	Users can browse other users' free/busy schedule information.
	Meeting request processing	If a user sends another user a meeting request, that request is automatically copied from the Inbox to the calendar as a tentative meeting.
	Delegate access	Users can grant other users the right to read and modify their schedules.
Group calendars, contact lists, and task lists	Public folder use	Calendars, contact lists, and task lists can all be published to public folders to allow group access to that information.
Group task management	Task tracking	Users can send tasks to other users, and the status of those tasks can be automatically tracked.
	Status reports	An automatic status report on a task (containing details such as whether the task has been started, the percentage completed, the hours spent working on the task, and the task owner's name) can be sent as a mail message.
Forms and Office 2003 objects	Inclusion of Office 2003 objects	Microsoft Office 2003 applications can be used to create both presentation material and executable material for Outlook forms. For instance, Microsoft Word can compose the text of a form, and Microsoft Excel can add a spreadsheet to a form.

TABLE 7.3 PIM (Personal Information Manager) Features of Microsoft Outlook

Main Function	Features	Description
Functional integration within Outlook	Outlook Bar	This navigation tool permits the creation of shortcuts to a user's e-mail Inbox, calendar, contacts, tasks, and folders.
	AutoCreate	Outlook can automatically convert one Outlook item into another. For example, if an e-mail message represents a task a user needs to complete, the user can drag and drop the e-mail message into the Task folder, and Outlook will automatically convert it to a task.

TABLE 7.3 PIM (Personal Information Manager) Features of Microsoft Outlook *(continued)*

Main Function	Features	Description
Document browsing and retrieval	Outlook Journal	This feature maintains a log of users' actions, what they did, and when they did it. Users can then search for items based on when they were created, not just on what they are named or where they were saved.
	Outlook Views	Outlook comes with dozens of standard views of information, and users can create their own customized views.
Calendar/Schedule features	AutoDate	Outlook understands natural language input for dates and can convert loosely worded dates into discrete calendar dates. For example, if a user types "the third Wednesday of November at 5:00 p.m.," Outlook will automatically convert that to "Wednesday 11/17/04 5:00 PM."
Contact Manager features	Single address book	The lists of contacts in Contact Manager can be used to address e-mail or a fax and even jump to a website or dial a phone.
Functions for portable computer users	Local replication	Information that users enter into Outlook while on the road with the portable computer can later be replicated back to their Exchange server.
	Time switching	Outlook can change the system time and time zone as mobile users move from one location to another.
Microsoft Office 2003 integration	Office 2003 interface	Outlook shares many user interface elements with the other Office 2003 applications, such as command bars, menus, shortcut menus, tabbed dialog boxes, and toolbars.
	Single address book	The other Office 2003 applications can use the Outlook Contact Manager address book.
	Attachments	Users can attach any Office 2003 document to any Outlook item, such as an e-mail, contact, or task.
	Mail merge	Users can perform a mail merge between the Outlook Contact Manager and Microsoft Word.

TABLE 7.3 PIM (Personal Information Manager) Features of Microsoft Outlook *(continued)*

Main Function	Features	Description
	Word 2003 and e-mail	Word can be used as the text editor for creating e-mail content.
	Drag-and-drop	Users can drag and drop information between Office 2003 applications and Outlook modules.
	Outlook Journal	Office files can be located using Outlook Journal.
	Office 2003 objects and forms	As stated earlier, objects created in Office 2003 applications can be included in Outlook forms.
Importing and exporting data	Import and export of data	Microsoft Outlook can import and export data from and to all Microsoft calendar and mail products, as well as many third-party PIM and messaging products.
Visual Basic for Applications (VBA)	VBA integration	Outlook includes Microsoft object technology and therefore can be used with Microsoft's Visual Basic for Applications to create compound applications.

Installing and Configuring Outlook 2003

As with most other Windows programs, Outlook 2003 is installed using a fairly intuitive wizard that lets you choose the specific components of the program that you want installed (see Figure 7.14).

In addition to the new look that Outlook 2003 sports (seen in Figure 7.15), it has some nice new features that you will need to be aware of. First and foremost is the ability of Outlook 2003 to operation in a *cache mode*, where the Outlook client does not require constant connectivity to its Exchange server. While you may, at first, be tempted to think this is nothing new and is in fact just a new name for the familiar offline mode of operation, this is not the case. The plot thickens when you learn that both cache mode and offline mode use OST (offline storage files) to facilitate their operation.

The difference between the new cache mode and the existing offline mode is that users who are working in cache mode automatically have their OST file updated through a synchronization process to the user's mailbox server. As well, all standard Exchange features, such as mail, calendaring, free/busy information, and address lists, are available to a user when the user is using cache mode. A status indicator in the bottom of the Outlook window shows the current status of Outlook, as seen in Figure 7.15. By clicking on the status, you can configure the mode of operation that Outlook will use, as seen in Figure 7.16.

You must be using Outlook 2003 with Exchange Server 2003 in order to configure and use cache mode.

FIGURE 7.14 Choosing components in an Outlook 2003 installation

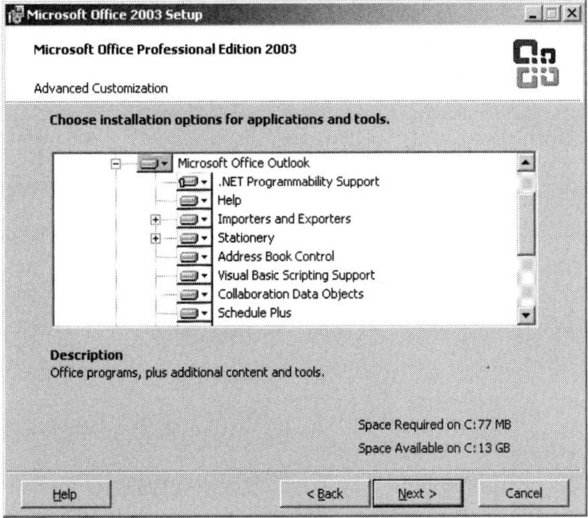

FIGURE 7.15 The new Outlook 2003 interface

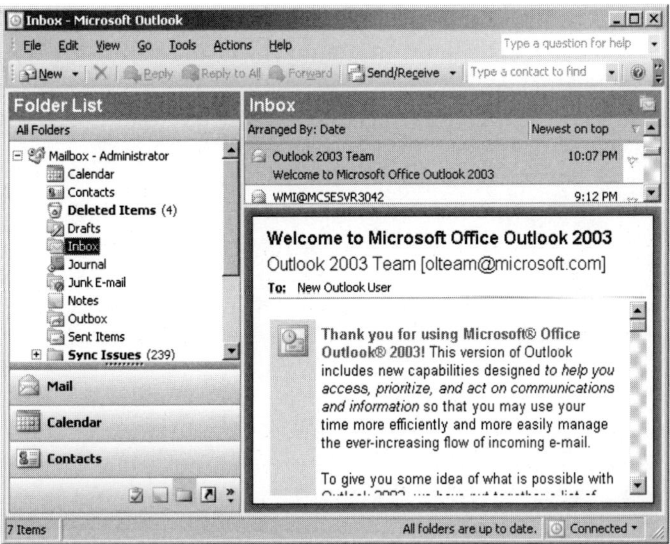

Because the cache mode of operation is new to Outlook 2003 when paired up with Exchange Server 2003, your users will likely want some help in getting it set up correctly on their client workstations. The default state for all newly created Outlook 2003 accounts is the cache mode of operation, thus improving the user's experience and reducing the load placed on the Exchange servers. Messages are still available on the Exchange server, but they are cached locally for the user. You do, however, when creating the account to connect to the Exchange server, have the option to configure how Outlook is initially configured, as seen in Figure 7.17.

The OST file used for the local cache is located in the `C:\Documents and Settings\%USER%\Local Settings\Application Data\Microsoft\Outlook` directory, assuming that your operating system is installed on Volume C.

The configuration options available when using Outlook 2003 in cache mode are explained in Table 7.4.

FIGURE 7.16 Configuring the Outlook operational mode

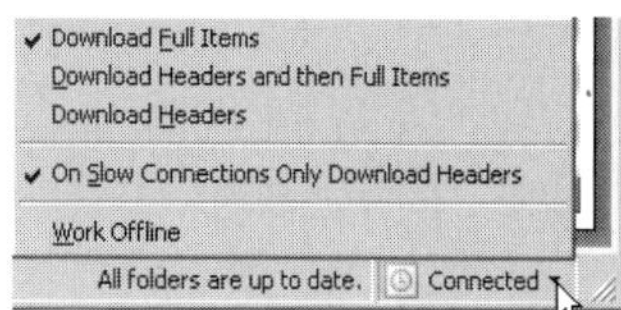

FIGURE 7.17 Configuring Outlook for cache mode during account creation

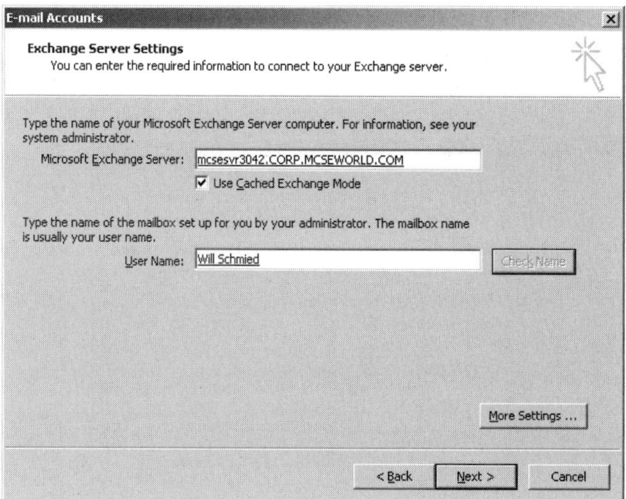

TABLE 7.4 The Outlook 2003 Cache Mode Settings

Option	Description
Download Headers And Then Full Items	When this option is selected, all message headers are downloaded first, followed by all message bodies and any attachments. This is the default selection when cache mode is used.
Download Full Items	When this option is selected, Outlook downloads the header, body, and any attachments of each message sequentially. This option is typically used when the client has a good connection to the Exchange server, such as when the client resides on the same internal network as the Exchange server.
Download Headers	When this option is selected, Outlook downloads only the headers for new messages. When a message is selected for viewing, Outlook then downloads the message body and any attachments to the message. Since this setting uses the least amount of bandwidth, it is typically recommended when connectivity between client and server is poor or slow.
On Slow Connections Download Headers Only	When this option is selected, Outlook controls its behavior depending on the network connection status it detects. This option causes the Offline Address List (OAL) *to not be* downloaded to the client.

Once Outlook is configured to use cache mode, you can change the way it operates at any time without needing to exit and restart Outlook.

Configuring RPC over HTTP

Another of the new features of Outlook 2003 when combined with Exchange Server 2003 is *RPC over HTTP*, which allows Outlook 2003 clients to connect securely to an Exchange Server 2003 organization over the Internet, which was previously impossible without the creation of a VPN tunnel before making the Outlook-to-Exchange connection. By configuring Outlook 2003 and Exchange Server 2003 to use RPC over HTTP, you allow users to connect to the Exchange organization over the Internet using Outlook instead of Outlook Web Access. As part of the configuration, you configure SSL for the HTTP connection to the front-end server. SSL is required because RPC over HTTP uses Basic authentication to authenticate users.

Although RPC over HTTP is a powerful new feature, it is not without cost and burden. Unlike most configurations in Exchange Server 2003, configuring RPC over HTTP is not necessarily a simple process, because you will need to configure both the Exchange servers and the Outlook clients to make it work properly. In order to use RPC over HTTP, you must meet the following requirements:

- Client computers must have Outlook 2003 installed.
- Client computers must be running Windows XP with Service Pack 1 and hot fix Q331320.
- Front-end servers must be running Exchange Server 2003 on Windows Server 2003.
- Back-end servers must be running Exchange Server 2003 on Windows Server 2003.
- Public folder servers must be running Exchange Server 2003 on Windows Server 2003.
- All Global Catalog servers must be running Windows Server 2003.

If your network meets these stringent requirements and you have a need for RPC over HTTP, you can configure it by performing the following basic steps:

1. Configure the Exchange computer to use RPC over HTTP.
2. Configure the RPC virtual directory in Internet Information Services.
3. Configure the RPC proxy server to use specific ports.
4. Configure the Outlook 2003 computer to use RPC over HTTP.
5. Verify that the connection can be made using RPC over HTTP.

Users will likely ask why it is necessary to create an additional Outlook profile to use RPC over HTTP. This is done so that users can quickly choose between connection methods when starting up Outlook, depending on how they will be connecting to the Exchange organization. By configuring the profile ahead of time, you can prevent users from making the complicated configuration changes in Outlook and save some calls to the help desk.

The process to configure and implement RPC over HTTP is not likely to be an exam item and is also very lengthy and complex. For these reasons it is not discussed in its entirety here. If you need the complete procedure to configure RPC over HTTP, be sure to see Knowledge Base article 833401, located at `http://support.microsoft.com/default.aspx?scid=kb;en-us;833401`.

The Office Custom Installation Wizard

As an administrator, you can customize the setup of Outlook in a few ways, including running the setup program with command-line options or using a settings file to answer various setup questions automatically instead of making the user answer them. However, the easiest and most powerful way to customize an installation of Outlook is with the *Office Custom Installation Wizard*, shown in Figure 7.18. This wizard is available as part of the Office 2003 Resource Kit, but it can also be freely downloaded from the Microsoft website as part of the Office 2003 Resource Kit Tools.

The Office Custom Installation Wizard works with Windows Installer to let you tweak almost every detail of the installation process. You can do the following:

- Define the path where Outlook is installed on client computers.
- Set the installation options (Run From Hard Drive, Install On First Use, Don't Install) for individual features of Outlook 2003.
- Define a list of network servers for Windows Installer to use if the primary installation server is unavailable.
- Specify other products to install or other programs to run on the user's computer when the Outlook installation is done.
- Hide selected options from users during setup.
- Add custom files and Windows Registry settings to the installation.
- Customize Desktop shortcuts for Outlook 2003.
- Set user default options.
- Use Office Profile settings created with the Profile Wizard for Office 2003 to preset user options.

FIGURE 7.18 Using the Office Custom Installation Wizard

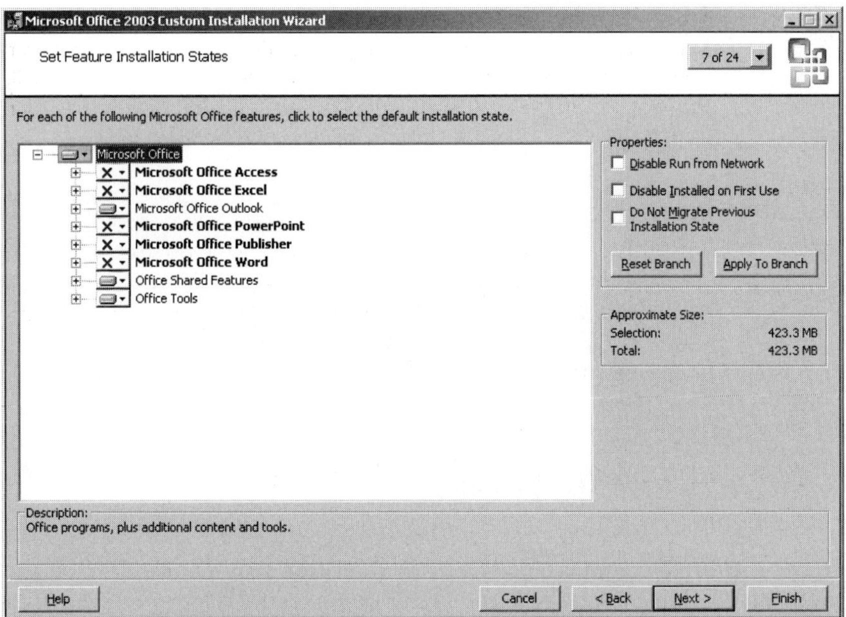

To accomplish all of this, the Windows Installer uses two types of files to install Outlook: an *installer package (MSI) file* and an *installer transform (MST) file*. The package contains a database that describes the configuration information. The transform file contains modifications that are to be made as Windows Installer installs Outlook. The package file never changes; it is essentially a database that helps Windows Installer relate various features to actual installation files. The transform file is what the Custom Installation Wizard helps you create. This means that you can create unique setup scenarios that all use the same installation files. In other words, you could create different installation routines for different departments but use only one network installation point for everyone to share.

Virtual Servers in Exchange Server 2003

As you learned in Chapter 2, "Microsoft Exchange Architecture," Exchange Server 2003 relies heavily on Internet Information Services (IIS) to support access via Internet protocols. This integration with IIS also provides Exchange with the ability to configure virtual servers for Internet protocols. A *virtual server* enables you to host different protocols on the same physical server. The use of virtual servers provides added functionality and scalability. From the client perspective, there is no difference in connecting to a physical server or a virtual server. From the administrative perspective, virtual servers allow much greater flexibility and control than do individual physical servers that have to be created to support Internet protocols.

When Exchange Server 2003 is installed, a virtual server is created by default for each Internet protocol, including SMTP, NNTP, HTTP, IMAP4, and POP3. Virtual servers are managed using the System Manager snap-in, as shown in Figure 7.19.

FIGURE 7.19 Viewing virtual protocol servers in System Manager

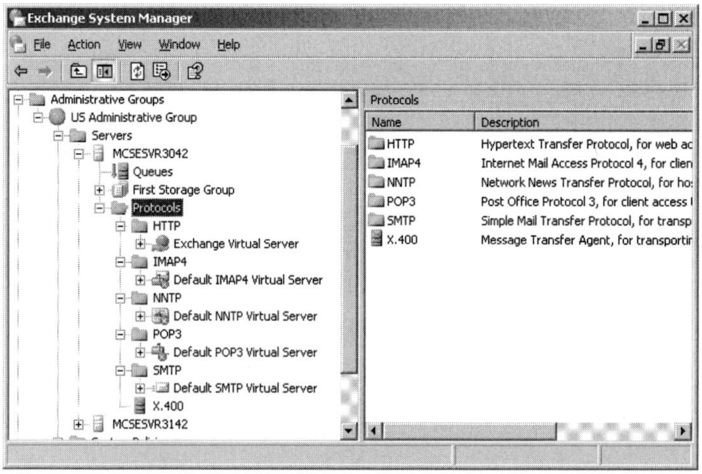

For the most part, the management of each type of virtual server is the same. You can right-click a virtual server and use the Pause, Stop, and Start commands to control the state of the service. Pausing a virtual server simply prevents new connections from being made to that server while the server itself remains running. Current connections are not disconnected. This is a graceful way of shutting down a virtual server that may be in use. When all users are finished, you can stop the server. Stopping the server will forcibly disconnect all connected users. If you want to disable certain protocols on a server-wide basis, stopping the virtual server for that protocol is usually the best way to go.

Aside from these basic commands, you can also open property pages for each kind of virtual server. These pages are covered in the sections later in this chapter that deal with the individual protocols themselves.

It is possible to configure virtual servers directly using IIS, but this is not recommended. When virtual servers are managed using the Exchange System Manager, the Exchange System Attendant writes the configuration information to Active Directory. From there, the information is written to the IIS metabase. If you configure virtual servers directly in IIS, it is possible that the information you configure will be overwritten by older information configured in the Exchange System Manager or Active Directory. The one exception to this rule is that the HTTP virtual server *must* be managed using the IIS Manager and cannot be accessed using the Exchange System Manager.

Microsoft Outlook Web Access

Outlook Web Access (OWA) was first introduced to Exchange Server in version 5 and provides a way to access Exchange-based folders using a web browser such as Internet Explorer. OWA can be used to access e-mail, public folders, contact information, and calendar information. Since its introduction, OWA has become very popular, and its architecture has once again been completely overhauled with the introduction of Exchange Server 2003 Server. It has been redesigned to provide improved performance and a streamlined user interface.

When using OWA, the only thing required on the client computers is Internet Explorer. This is also what makes OWA a good tool for cross-platform support, since versions of most web browsers exist for Windows, Macintosh, and Unix. In fact, OWA is the primary Exchange Server access method for users of Unix.

Outlook Web Access is designed to work with any browser that supports HTML version 3.2 and JavaScript. This includes the latest versions of Internet Explorer and Netscape Navigator, as well as many other browsers. However, OWA is also designed to take advantage of a number of features provided in Internet Explorer 5 and higher that are not supported by other browsers at this time, such as Dynamic HTML (DHTML) and Extensible Markup Language (XML). Such features help provide many advanced collaborative functions.

OWA Features and Restraints

OWA is installed by default when you install Exchange Server 2003. Taking advantage of the ASP.NET service of Windows Server 2003, an OWA user can access many of the functions available through Outlook, including functionality for e-mail, calendar and group scheduling, public folders, and collaborative applications (when the forms have been developed with Microsoft Visual InterDev). Although OWA in Exchange Server 2003 is an almost perfect replacement for Outlook 2003, the following are some of the items that are *not* available when using OWA:

- Personal address books (because they are stored on your workstation)
- Personal folders (PST files)
- WordMail and Microsoft Office integration
- Electronic forms creation
- Synchronizing local offline folders with server folders

Outlook Web Access simulates the look and feel of Outlook 2003, as shown in Figure 7.20. The ubiquity of the browser client makes OWA an attractive choice in environments that have a widespread mix of client platforms (such as Windows, Macintosh, and Unix) and that require shared client computers. Outlook Web Access is extremely useful for users who frequently move around among different workstations during the day and users who must access the Exchange server remotely via the Internet.

FIGURE 7.20 Accessing Exchange via OWA

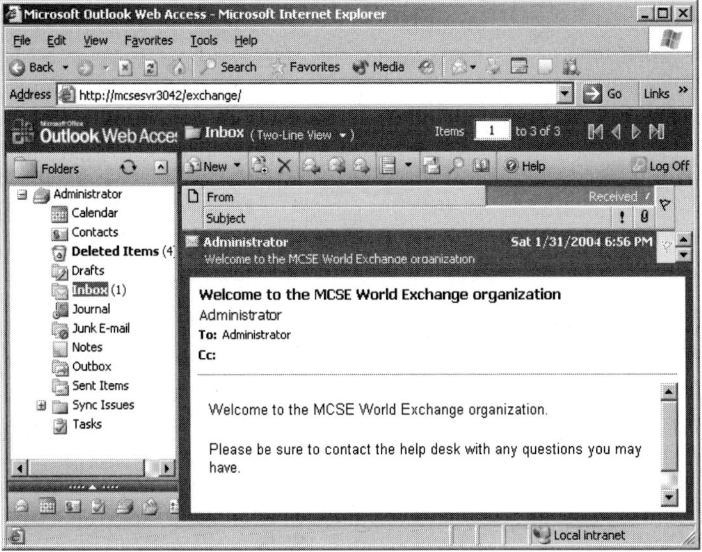

The OWA Process

The OWA process in Exchange Server 2003 is quite different from that of previous versions. OWA 5.*x* used *Active Server Pages (ASP)* to communicate with Exchange Server 5.5, which in turn used Collaboration Data Objects (CDO) 1.2 and MAPI. The effective number of users per server was limited by the overhead needed to support ASP and to run MAPI sessions within ASP. OWA was actually a part of IIS.

The new version of OWA does not use MAPI to communicate with the mailbox store and no longer uses ASP for client access. Instead, OWA is built into Exchange Server 2003's new web store and uses IIS only to receive requests and pass them to the web store. Thus, IIS acts as an intermediary between the browser and OWA. IIS receives a client request, looks at the URL, and passes the appropriate information for the URL back to the web browser. If the server houses the Exchange Server 2003 database, OWA uses a high-speed channel to access the mailbox store. If the server is a front-end server, OWA redirects the request to a back-end server using HTTP.

OWA is actually not a client itself but rather a set of Active Server Pages that run in the context of Microsoft's IIS. Client web browsers access IIS using HTTP over TCP port 80, by default, and in turn IIS accesses the OWA component on behalf of the clients using an extended version of HTTP known as HTTP-DAV. HTTP-DAV adds several features to HTTP such as file locking, namespace management, and document property access.

Many components play an important role in the OWA process, including the following:

- Active Directory
- Information Store
- The *Exchange DSAccess* component, which enables Exchange Server 2003 components to communicate with Active Directory (DSAccess uses the LDAP protocol to perform this communication)
- OLE DB Provider for Exchange (ExOLEDB), which acts as the interface between DAVEx and EXIPC (both discussed a bit later)
- Directory Service to the IIS metabase (DS2MB), which provides a one-way synchronization of configuration information from Active Directory to the IIS metabase
- EXIPC, a queuing engine that is used to pass information between the IIS and Information Store components
- *IIS metabase*, which is a Registry database for IIS configuration
- *W3svc*, the World Wide Web publishing service of IIS
- *DAVEx*, a component that passes client requests between W3svc and the Information Store
- ExProx, which acts as a protocol proxy on a front-end server if a front-end/back-end server configuration is being used
- *Forms Registry*, which stores the OWA forms rendered by IIS and passed to the client

As you can see, the OWA process is fairly complicated and involves a number of components. The complexity of the process is basically designed to ensure that each major tool in use does what it is good at and that the client needs no special configuration. Since the client needs to be able to access Exchange using a standard web browser, its only responsibility must be to request a simple URL, such as `http://owa.microsoft.com/exchange`, from a web server (in this case IIS) and display the results in its window. Everything else must happen on the server end. For example, to open a user's contacts, type the path to the user's mailbox followed by `/contacts`, as in `http://owa.microsoft.com/exchange/`*`user`*`/contacts`, where *`user`* is the user's mailbox name.

Here is the actual process that occurs when a client's browser requests information from an Exchange server:

1. W3svc in IIS receives the request and authenticates the user by querying Active Directory.
2. Once authentication is complete, W3svc relays the request to the DAVEx component.
3. DAVEx transfers the request through the EXIPC queue to the Information Store.
4. The Information Store retrieves the appropriate data and returns it to DAVEx.
5. DAVEx retrieves an appropriate form from the Forms Registry and merges it with the information from the Information Store, creating an HTML or XML document.
6. DAVEx sends the formatted document back to W3svc.
7. W3svc sends the information back the client, which displays it in the browser window.

Installing and Configuring OWA

OWA is installed as part of the default setup of Exchange Server 2003, and it is configured by default to allow access to users' mailboxes and the default public folder tree. However, you can configure the server to provide customized access for clients by specifying which users can access the server, which authentication method(s) to allow, and which public folders are exposed to users.

Since Outlook Web Access begins running when Exchange Server is installed, no special setup options are required other than a standard Exchange installation. The OWA client can offer your users much of the functionality offered by using Outlook 2003 from remote locations. Using a dedicated server for OWA can also increase network security by exposing only this dedicated server to the Internet.

When you install Exchange Server 2003, web access is installed and configured by default, and an Exchange virtual root and a Public virtual root are added to the IIS directory tree. These virtual roots point to their corresponding directories in Exchange Server 2003—the directories that hold the public store and the mailbox store.

To access mail folders from within the corporate intranet, users will need to enter the following address in their web browser: `http://`*`servername`*`/exchange/`*`user`*`/`, where *`servername`* is the name of the Exchange server, `exchange` is the default private web folder, and *`userid`* is the alias of the user. For connecting via the Internet, the above URL must be appended by the Fully Qualified Domain Name of the domain on which Exchange is running, for example, `http://`*`servername.domain`*`.com/exchange/`*`user`*`/`.

Web access to Exchange Server 2003 is enabled for all users by default. To change this configuration, use Active Directory Users and Computers. On the Exchange Features tab of the user Properties dialog box, seen in Figure 7.21, you can enable or disable HTTP, IMAP4, and POP3 access to the Exchange organization.

FIGURE 7.21 Modifying protocol settings for a user

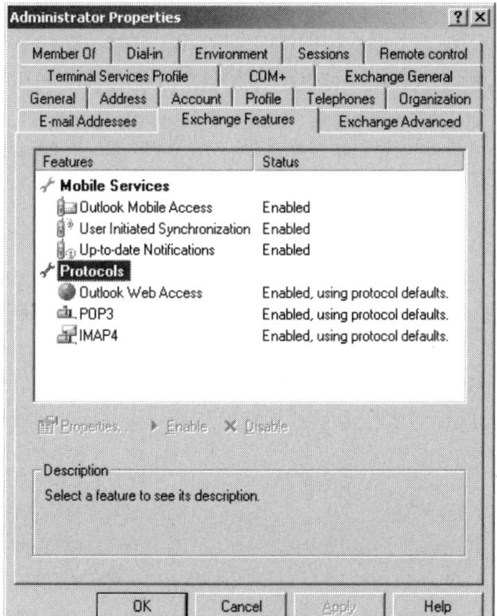

User Authentication in OWA

Users of OWA must be authenticated in some form before anything but Anonymous access is granted. A number of options are available for OWA authentication. Choosing the appropriate mechanism is usually a matter of the capabilities of the client operating system and specific security policies. In a single-server environment, the default authentication method for OWA is Anonymous authentication and Integrated Windows authentication (similar to NTLM). In a multi-server environment, the default authentication is Basic (clear-text) and NTLM. Authentication is set via the HTTP virtual servers configured for OWA. This configuration is actually set in Internet Information Server. Microsoft recommends configuring authentication on the back-end Exchange server only. The default authentication settings are the same on the front-end Exchange server, but securing the back-end server is much more important. In addition, authentication conflicts between the front end and back end could jeopardize user access. Exercise 7.1 outlines the steps for configuring OWA authentication. But first we must define the available types of authentication.

Basic authentication *Basic authentication*, also referred to as plain-text or clear-text, is commonly used on intranets. Unlike the NTLM protocol, which accepts established users' identification through the access token, Basic authentication relies on users to enter their username, domain, and password. Basic authentication is independent of the browser, which also makes it independent of the platform being used. Basic authentication results in the transmission of unencrypted passwords over the network, which makes it a relatively insecure method of authentication. Users must enter their username, domain, and password each time they log on.

Integrated Windows authentication *Integrated Windows authentication* works differently depending upon the situation. The optimal authentication takes place when the client is running Windows 2000 (or later) and Internet Explorer 5 (or later), in which case Kerberos provides the best security available. With other pre–Windows 2000 clients, Integrated Windows authentication uses the NTLM protocol instead of Kerberos. Integrated Windows authentication always encrypts the client's password, which provides excellent *security*. It also allows browser access without prompting the users for their user ID and password. Integrated Windows authentication does not work with browsers other than Internet Explorer 4 and 5, and it is not available in a front-end and back-end Exchange Server configuration.

Anonymous authentication *Anonymous authentication*, which IIS also allows, provides limited access to specific public folders and directory information. All browsers support Anonymous authentication, making it an easy way to provide insecure access to public folder data. A single point of configuration makes administration simple. Anonymous authentication does not identify users uniquely. Consequently, you cannot track usage by user.

Secure Sockets Layer authentication *Secure Sockets Layer (SSL)* provides the best level of security because the entire communications session is encrypted. SSL is not an authentication mechanism itself. Rather, SSL provides a secure channel for other authentication mechanisms. Although any *authentication* mechanism can be used with SSL, the most common implementation with SSL is Basic (clear-text). Most browsers support SSL communication. SSL creates a substantial amount of overhead in providing this security, so SSL communications tend to reduce the overall performance of an authenticating server and generate increased network traffic.

All in all, Outlook Web Access is a powerful means of providing cross-platform and remote access to your Exchange server. Authenticated users can log on to their personal accounts to access e-mail, public folders, and collaborative tools. Using web-based public folder access, an organization could even build private and public discussion forums on the Internet or on private intranets.

EXERCISE 7.1

Configuring Authentication for Outlook Web Access

1. Click Start ➢ Programs ➢ Administrative Tools ➢ Internet Information Services (IIS) Manager.
2. Expand the container for the server running OWA.
3. Expand the default website container.
4. Right-click the Exchweb object and select Properties from the shortcut menu.
5. Click the Directory Security tab.
6. Click the Edit button in the Authentication And Access Control section at the top of the page.
7. Select the forms of access that you want to allow.
8. Click OK twice to return to Internet Information Services (IIS) Manager.

Post Office Protocol (POP3) Clients

Post Office Protocol version 3 (POP3) enables a client to retrieve mail from a remote server mailbox. A user who is not always attached to their network can have their mailbox on a server that is permanently attached to the network. Mail sent to that user would be delivered to the server-based mailbox, and the server would act as a sort of mail drop. Clients can remotely connect to the server and download their mail to their computer. The protocol used both to store the mail on the server and to download the mail to the client is POP3. In this capacity, the server is referred to as a POP server and the client as a POP client. POP3 cannot be used to send mail; it is only a retrieval protocol. *Simple Mail Transfer Protocol (SMTP)* is still used to transfer mail between mailboxes.

The remainder of this section covers these POP-related topics:

- POP3 architecture
- An overview of Exchange Server POP3 (including server and mailbox configuration)
- POP3 client configuration

POP3 Architecture

POP works through a simple request-response mechanism. A POP client sends request commands, and a POP server sends responses back to the POP client. These client-server interactions can be divided into three main states:

- Authorization
- Transaction
- Update

Authorization, also called greeting, is the client logon to the POP server. The POP username and password are sent to the POP server. After a successful authorization, transactions can take place between the POP client and server. The POP client can request the number and size of messages in its mailbox, and messages can be downloaded and deleted. After the POP server has responded and the POP client is finished, the POP client issues a Quit command. This ends the POP session and causes the POP server to enter the update state for the user's mailbox. Messages can be deleted during the update state.

POP uses TCP/IP as its transport protocol. The session, or *conversation*, between the POP client and server takes place on TCP port 110. If Secure Sockets Layer (SSL) is being used to create an encrypted channel, port 995 is used instead. A *port* is a numeric identifier assigned to an application or protocol and is used to route incoming packets to the correct application. Although a packet has arrived at the correct computer, it still has to be delivered to the correct application on that computer. POP clients address the requests to port 110 on the POP server. The POP server listens to port 110 for those requests (this same principle is applicable to LDAP, HTTP, and other Internet protocols). The third revision of the POP standard, POP3, is documented in RFC 1939.

You may be familiar with Ethernet or Token Ring addresses, which are used to deliver a frame to a specific computer. You may even be familiar with network addresses, such as IP addresses, which are used to route packets to the correct networks and computers. Ports are yet another type of address that is used to route packets to the correct applications on a machine.

Real World Scenario

Connecting Clients to Exchange Server 2003

The decision of how you will allow remote and non-Windows clients to connect to your Exchange Server 2003 messaging infrastructure is not an easy one, nor is it one that you should take lightly or make without giving due consideration to the benefits and drawbacks of everything involved. Will you use Outlook, taking advantage of the new RPC over HTTP feature, will you use the improved Outlook Web Access in Exchange Server 2003, or will you force these users to use an industry standard POP3 or IMAP4 application?

Several factors should influence your decision:

- Which operating systems are in use by your clients?
- Which operating systems are in use by your Exchange servers, domain controllers, and global catalog servers?
- Are there existing means to securely connect users remotely over the Internet, such as VPN servers and so forth?
- What is the company's willingness to try new, cutting-edge features?

These questions are just a few of the many that you must take into consideration when determining how you will allow remote and non-Windows clients to connect to the Exchange organization. As an example of how you might solve this problem, consider the following:

- You have several Unix and Linux hosts on your network that will connect to the Exchange organization using Outlook Web Access.
- You have some traveling salespeople who use Windows XP Professional computers. These users require full Outlook functionality and will connect using RPC over HTTP.
- You have some other users who frequently travel and need access only to their Inboxes. When they travel, they keep all messages on their local computers in PST files. If needed, they move any messages back into their Exchange mailbox when they return to the company. These users connect to the Exchange organization using POP3 or IMAP4.

Exchange Server POP3 Overview

POP3 is integrated into the Internet Information Services (IIS) component of Windows Server 2003. Although it is not a separate service, the POP3 functionality is sometimes referred to as the POP3 Service. It permits any POP3-enabled e-mail program to connect to an Exchange server via IIS and retrieve mail (see Figure 7.22). Only messages in the Inbox folder of a mailbox can be accessed. The POP3 Service does not permit access to encrypted messages.

As mentioned previously, POP3 retrieves mail but does not send it. The Simple Mail Transfer Protocol (SMTP) is used to send mail. SMTP functionality is also provided by IIS and uses TCP port 25.

POP3 Server Configuration

The configuration options available for a POP3 virtual server in Exchange Server 2003 are described in Table 7.5.

POP3 Mailbox Configuration

An administrator can override server-level settings at the mailbox level using the Protocols button on the Exchange Advanced page of a mailbox object. A mailbox can independently have POP3 enabled or disabled or have unique POP3 settings. As mentioned earlier, if a protocol is disabled at the server level, the settings at the mailbox level have no effect.

FIGURE 7.22 Exchange and POP3

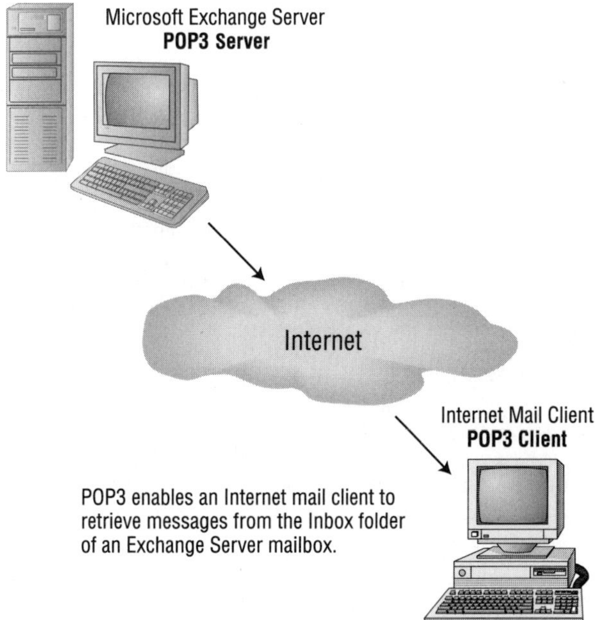
Microsoft Exchange Server
POP3 Server
Internet
Internet Mail Client
POP3 Client
POP3 enables an Internet mail client to retrieve messages from the Inbox folder of an Exchange Server mailbox.

TABLE 7.5 Property Pages for the Site and Server POP3 Objects

Property Page	Description
General	This page is used to assign an IP address to the virtual server. The default is for the server to have access to all IP interfaces configured on the server. You can select a specific IP address or use the Advanced button to configure IP address and TCP port information. This page is used to configure how long an idle POP3 connection will be held open before automatically closing and to limit the number of connections that the virtual server will allow.
Access	The Authentication section of this page is used to select the authentication protocols that POP3 clients must use to log on to the Exchange server with the POP protocol. The options are Basic, which works using an unencrypted username and password, and Windows Integrated Authentication, which works using Windows Server 2003 network security and an encrypted password.
	The Secure Communication section of the Access page is used to configure a certificate server to provide POP3 security. This type of security is discussed in Chapter 15.
	The Connection Control section of the Access page is used to grant or deny access to the POP3 virtual server based on computer names or IP addresses.
Message Format	This page sets the encoding method and character set used when converting Exchange messages for retrieval by POP3 clients. The encoding options include MIME and UUENCODE. Selecting UUENCODE makes available the option to use Binhex with Macintosh clients. The default character set used is US-ASCII, but you can choose from many international sets. You can also specify whether Microsoft Exchange rich-text format can be used in POP3 messages.
Calendaring	The options on this page are used to configure URL access to calendaring information by POP3 clients. This allows POP3 clients to use OWA as their calendaring client.

Configuring a POP3 Client

The following information must be configured on a POP3 client in order for it to connect to a POP3 server (in this case, the POP3 server is an Exchange server with the Exchange POP3 Service enabled):

POP3 server name The computer name of the home server of the Exchange mailbox.

SMTP server name The computer name of the Exchange server that is supporting SMTP.

Unless the client is connected to a server on the same network, you may need to indicate a Fully Qualified Domain Name for the POP3 and SMTP server names.

POP3 account name The name the POP3 client must use when being authorized by a POP3 server. The Exchange POP3 Service requires a Windows Server 2003 domain and user account that has read permissions on the Exchange mailbox, followed by the alias name of the mailbox in the format *domain\account\alias*. If the account name and alias are the same, the alias name can be left off.

POP3 account password The Exchange POP3 Service requires the password of the Windows Server 2003 user account that is specified in the POP3 Account Name field.

POP3 client e-mail address The SMTP address of the POP3 client. For an Exchange mailbox, this is the SMTP address found on the E-mail Addresses property page of the mailbox.

Table 7.6 provides sample information and shows how that information can be used to configure a POP3 client. Exercise 7.2 outlines the steps for configuring Outlook Express as a POP3 client. This exercise assumes that Outlook Express is already installed on your system.

TABLE 7.6 An Example of a POP3 Client Configuration

Sample Information	POP3 Client Configuration
Computer name running the POP3 Service=Education	POP3 server name=Education
Computer name running SMTP=Education	SMTP server name=Education
Window Server 2003 account with read permission on the mailbox=Domain\GeorgeW Alias name of mailbox=GeorgeW	POP3 account name=Domain\GeorgeW\GeorgeW or simply Domain\GeorgeW
Password of GeorgeW=woodenteeth	POP3 accountpassword=woodenteeth
Domain name=Chicago.com Alias name of mailbox=GeorgeW	POP3 client e-mail address=GeorgeW@Chicago.com

EXERCISE 7.2

Configuring Outlook Express As a POP3 Client

1. Click Start ➢ Programs ➢ Outlook Express.
2. Under the Tools menu, select the Accounts command.
3. Click the Add button and then click the menu's Mail command.
4. Enter a display name to appear in the From field of messages you send, and then click Next to continue.
5. Enter an e-mail address in the E-mail Address field and click Next.
6. Select the POP3 protocol from the drop-down menu.
7. In the Incoming Mail field, enter the name of the Exchange server that will service POP3 requests.
8. In the Outgoing Mail field, enter the name of the Exchange server that will service SMTP requests.
9. Click Next to go on.
10. In the Account Name field, enter the username of the mailbox to which you will connect.
11. Enter a password for the user, and then click Next.
12. Click Finish.

Internet Message Access Protocol Version 4 (IMAP4) Clients

As with POP3, IIS provides *Internet Message Access Protocol version 4 (IMAP4)* support to Exchange. This enables Internet e-mail applications using IMAP4 to retrieve data from an Exchange server. As with POP3, IMAP4 can only retrieve data and must use the SMTP functions of the Exchange Internet Mail Service (IMS) to send data.

One of the main differences between IMAP4 and POP3 is the Exchange folders they can access. As mentioned earlier, POP3 can access only the Inbox folder of a mailbox. IMAP4, however, can also access personal and public folders. IMAP4 also includes other advanced features (and non-POP3 features) such as search capabilities and selective downloading of messages or even only the attachment of a message.

The IMAP4 virtual server has many of the same properties as the POP3 virtual server, such as authentication, message format, and idle timeout. Some of the pages for these properties have additional attributes not present with POP3. IMAP4, for instance, also allows anonymous user access, meaning that an IMAP4 user without a Windows Server 2003 user account could access the server. Table 7.7 lists and describes the property pages and attributes of the IMAP4 object. Exercise 7.3 outlines the steps for configuring Outlook Express as an IMAP4 client.

TABLE 7.7 Property Pages of the IMAP4 Object

Property Page	Description
General	This page is used to assign an IP address to the virtual server. The default is for the server to have access to all IP interfaces configured on the server. You can select a specific IP address or use the Advanced button to configure IP address and TCP port information. This page is used to configure how long an idle IMAP4 connection will be held open before automatically closing and to limit the number of connections that the virtual server will allow. The Limit Number Of Connections To option allows you to specify a maximum number of simultaneous connections that can be made to the IMAP4 virtual server. The Include All Public Folders When A Folder List Is Requested option, which is enabled by default, permits a complete list of public folders to be sent to an IMAP4 client in response to the IMAP List command. Some IMAP4 client applications, however, encounter poor performance when downloading a large list of public folders. If that is the case, this field can be cleared (i.e., unchecked). The Enable Fast Message Retrieval option, which is enabled by default, permits an Exchange server to approximate the size of messages when reporting to an IMAP4 client application. Approximating message sizes increases the speed of message retrieval. Some IMAP4 client applications, however, require a server to report the exact message size. If that is the case, this field can be cleared (i.e., unchecked).
Access	An Exchange server can allow IMAP4 clients to be authenticated with the same protocols that are available with POP3. While the options are the same for both IMAP4 and POP3, each can be configured with a different set of authentication protocols. This is also true for any of the other attributes IMAP4 and POP3 have in common.
Message Format	This page is used to set the encoding method and character set used when converting Exchange messages for retrieval by IMAP4 clients. The encoding options are as follows: **MIME:** Both the message body and attachments will be encoded with MIME.

TABLE 7.7 Property Pages of the IMAP4 Object *(continued)*

Property Page	Description
	Provide Message Body As Plain Text: The message body will be placed in plain text and any attachments in MIME. **Provide Message Body As HTML:** The message body will be placed in HTML format and any attachments in MIME. If both this option and the Provide Message Body As Plain Text option are selected, Exchange will generate both plain-text and HTML versions of the message body.
Calendaring	The options on this page are used to configure URL access to calendaring information by IMAP4 clients. This allows IMAP4 clients to use OWA as their calendaring client.

EXERCISE 7.3

Configuring Outlook Express as an IMAP4 Client

1. Click Start ➢ Programs ➢ Outlook Express.
2. Click the Tools menu, and then choose the Accounts command.
3. Click the Add button, and then choose the Mail command.
4. Enter a display name to appear in the From field of messages you send, and click Next to continue.
5. Enter an e-mail address in the E-mail Address field, and click Next.
6. Select the IMAP protocol from the drop-down menu.
7. In the Incoming Mail field, enter the name of the Exchange server that will service IMAP4 requests.
8. In the Outgoing Mail field, enter the name of the Exchange server that will service SMTP requests, and click Next.
9. In the Account Name field, enter the username of the mailbox to which you will connect.
10. Enter a password for the user, and click Next to go on.
11. Click Finish.
12. Outlook Express displays a dialog asking you whether you would like to download folders from the mail server you just configured. Click Yes to retrieve information on private folders other than your Inbox and any available public folders.

Because of Exchange Server's support of IMAP4 and POP3, many Internet mail programs can be used as clients to Exchange Server.

Network News Transfer Protocol (NNTP)

As with the other Internet protocols, IIS provides support for the *Network News Transport Protocol (NNTP)*. Since the NNTP virtual server is installed and enabled by default when you install Exchange Server 2003, any NNTP-based newsreader application can be used to connect to and use public folders right away. Like the other protocols, the NNTP virtual server is configured using a number of property pages. Table 7.8 provides an overview of the property pages for this object.

TABLE 7.8 NNTP Property Pages

Property Page	Description
General	This page is used to assign an IP address to the virtual server. The default is for the server to have access to all IP interfaces configured on the server. You can select a specific IP address or use the Advanced button to configure IP address and TCP port information. This page is used to configure how long an idle NNTP connection will be held open before automatically closing and to limit the number of connections that the virtual server will allow. In addition, this page can be used to configure a path header, which is used by other Usenet servers to prevent a situation called "looping," which can happen when a Usenet server is connected to multiple providers. Finally, this page can be used to enable logging for the NNTP service for troubleshooting purposes.
Access	An Exchange server can allow NNTP clients to be authenticated with the same protocols that were options with POP3. But while the options are the same for both NNTP and POP3, each can be configured with a different set of authentication protocols.
Settings	The Settings page provides a number of options for configuring the NNTP protocol: The Allow Client Posting option controls whether users with NNTP-based newsreaders can post messages using the NNTP protocol. If this option is enabled, you can also control how large of a message, in kilobytes, can be posted and how much data, in megabytes, can be posted during a single user session.

TABLE 7.8 NNTP Property Pages *(continued)*

Property Page	Description
	The Allow Feed Posting option works the same way as the Allow Client Posting option, but it controls whether or not messages can be automatically posted by newsfeeds, which are discussed later in the chapter. The Allow Server To Pull News Articles From This Server option controls whether other Usenet servers can use the NNTP protocol to pull messages in a public folder to their own server. The Control Messages option is used to allow Usenet servers to govern the traffic between servers. The final three options control the domain and address of moderators for moderated newsgroups. In a moderated newsgroup, a designated moderator must approve messages before they are posted to a folder.

Creating Newsgroups

When NNTP is installed, two virtual directories are created by default:

- The default directory creates new newsgroups and stores them in the Newsgroups public folder.
- The control directory contains three folders for the three primary control commands, as seen in Figure 7.23: Remove Articles, Create Newsgroup, and Remove Newsgroup.

You can create new newsgroups using either a MAPI client or System Manager. The procedure for creating a newsgroup within a MAPI client varies, but it usually follows a pretty simple procedure of selecting a parent folder and creating a new folder inside of it. In System Manager, you can create a new newsgroup by expanding an NNTP virtual server, right-clicking the Newsgroups container inside it, and selecting the New Newsgroup command from the shortcut menu.

In addition to creating your own newsgroups, you can also configure Exchange to pull newsgroups and their contents from a Usenet server on the Internet. Before you learn to do that, however, a brief overview of Usenet itself is in order.

A Usenet Overview

Usenet is a network within the Internet that is composed of numerous servers containing information on a variety of topics. Each organized topic is called a newsgroup, which can be thought of as a discussion group or a bulletin board. The Usenet servers are also referred to as newsgroup servers. Users access these newsgroups to post information or to read other people's postings. Users interact with newsgroups through client applications referred to as newsgroup readers.

FIGURE 7.23 Viewing newsgroups in System Manager

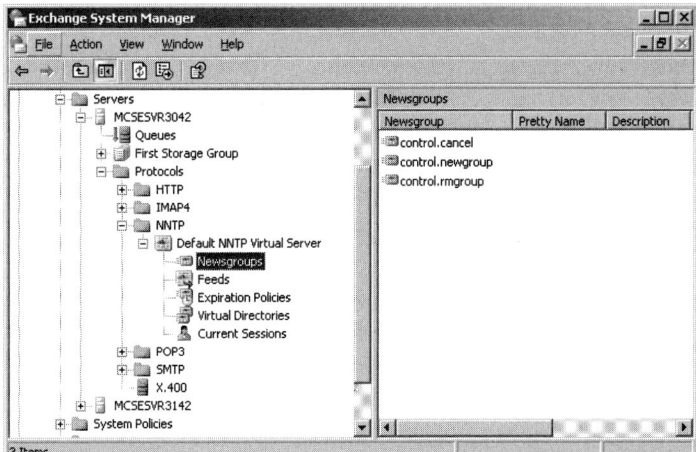

Clients and servers use the Network News Transfer Protocol (NNTP) to transfer information across Usenet. When a client reads or posts information to a newsgroup server, NNTP is used for this exchange.

NNTP is also used to transfer newsgroup content between servers. This function is referred to as a *newsfeed*. A newsgroup server can be configured to send all or some of its newsgroups to other servers. When one server actively sends information to another server, it is referred to as a *push feed* (it is also referred to as publishing). A server also can be configured to request that information be sent to it from another server. This is referred to as a *pull feed*. Push feeds are usually used with large newsfeeds. A pull feed allows a local administrator to specify which and when newsgroups are received.

Exchange Server 2003 can function as a full Usenet server and exchange newsgroup information with other Usenet servers on the Internet. This is done through the Newsfeed Configuration Wizard. The wizard prompts the installer for such information as the name of the Usenet host; the host's IP address; and the type of newsfeed, such as inbound (i.e., receiving data), outbound (i.e., publishing data), or inbound and outbound. Newsfeeds basically enable an Exchange server to function as a newsgroup server. It can publish public folder content as newsfeeds to other Usenet servers. It also can receive newsfeeds from the Usenet and place newsgroups in public folders. To receive newsfeeds, it can either pull a newsfeed or receive a push. See Figure 7.24 for an illustration of this process.

Once a newsfeed is configured, it is represented in the Feeds container of an NNTP virtual server as an object. The property pages of a Newsfeed object can be used to configure the newsfeed after its creation. Much of the information that was entered in the wizard can be later viewed and modified through the Newsfeed object. For example, if the IP address of the Usenet host changes, the new address can be entered in the properties of that newsfeed rather than creating a new newsfeed with the wizard.

FIGURE 7.24 Newsfeeds and the Usenet

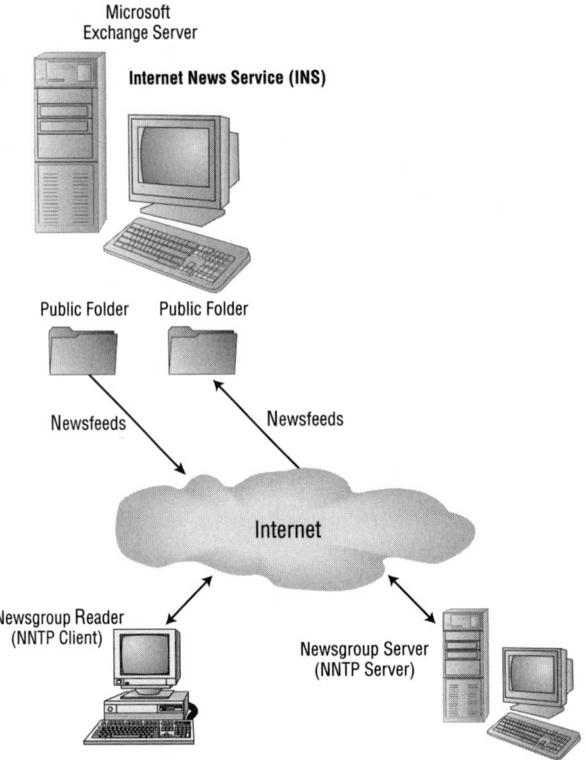

Summary

A messaging profile is the collection of configuration information used by a MAPI application, such as Microsoft Outlook. Some of the information contained in a profile indicates the information services to be used, such as Microsoft Exchange Server, Microsoft Fax, or Internet Mail. Other information in the profile relates to information storage, delegate access, and remote mail. Profiles can be created at the time of the client software installation. They can also be created and edited after the installation.

Outlook 2003 is the preferred client for use in an Exchange Server 2003 organization, although several older versions of Outlook can be used with slightly reduced functionality.

Exchange Server also extends support for the IMAP4, POP3, HTTP, and NNTP Internet protocols, thus expanding the number of client applications that can access Exchange.

IMAP4 and POP3 enable an e-mail program to retrieve messages from a remote server mailbox. Internet users who have Exchange mailboxes can use these protocols to retrieve mail.

HTTP is the primary protocol used for client-server interactions on the World Wide Web. Exchange Server supports HTTP using Outlook Web Access and IIS and thereby allows web users to access Exchange resources such as mailboxes, public folders, and calendars using a standard web browser.

Exchange Server supports NNTP and, therefore, can operate as part of the Usenet. Exchange can both publish public folders to the Usenet and receive newsfeeds from the Usenet. Newsgroups received from newsfeeds are published in public folders.

Exam Essentials

Understand Outlook's new features. While the list of new features in Outlook is long, two of the most important ones that you will want to understand are the cache mode of operation and RPC over HTTP. These represent two of the largest selling points of the new Outlook client over previous versions. As well, you should remember the requirements to use RPC over HTTP.

Understand the authentication mechanisms available. Although we will examine Exchange security again in Chapter 15, it is important for now that you understand the mechanisms available for user authentication on IIS servers. Recall that SSL combined with Basic authentication is the preferred method of authentication and encryption for both secure Outlook Web Access and Outlook RPC over HTTP connections.

Remember that Exchange is not just for MAPI clients. While you do get the best experience from Exchange Server 2003 when using a MAPI client such as Outlook 2003, you can still use other clients such as POP3 and IMAP4 clients to access Exchange Server 2003.

Review Questions

1. Jane uses Microsoft Outlook on both her office computer and her home computer. One night at home, Jane connects to her office server in order to read her mail. The next day at the office when Jane attempts to re-read the previous day's mail, there are no messages in her Inbox. What is the most likely cause of this situation?

   A. Jane's mail was delivered to an OST file on her home computer.

   B. Jane's home computer is still logged on to the server.

   C. Jane did not synchronize her mailbox with the server.

   D. Jane's mail was delivered to a PST file on her home computer.

2. Lou has a laptop computer for doing work away from the office and a desktop computer at the office. Microsoft Outlook is installed on both computers. Lou would like to see all of his messages while using either computer. The laptop computer does not have a continuous connection to the office server, but Lou would like to be able to read and compose messages while using the laptop offline. How should Lou configure his two computers?

   A. Configure the laptop computer with an OST file and the desktop computer to access his private folders in the Private Information Store.

   B. Configure both computers with PST files.

   C. Configure both computers to access his private folders in the Private Information Store.

   D. Configure the laptop computer with a PST file and the desktop computer to access his private folders in the Private Information Store.

3. Which of the following MAPI components manages memory, administers profiles, routes client requests to the relevant service provider, and returns results from servers via service providers?

   A. Client Application Layer

   B. MAPI subsystem

   C. Common Mail Call

   D. MAPI service provider

4. An IMAP4 client connects to your Exchange server and receives an error message stating that the message size is unknown. Which of the following should you do to fix this problem?

   A. Enable MCIS.

   B. Increase the Idle Timeout setting.

   C. Use plain-text authentication.

   D. Clear the Enable Fast Message Retrieval check box.

5. A user has come to you after forgetting the password she assigned to her personal folders. What can you do to retrieve the messages in those folders?

   A. Use the Inbox Repair Tool to assign a new password.

   B. Use System Manager to assign a new password.

   C. Use System Manager to create a new set of personal folders and then import messages from the old personal folders.

   D. Use Outlook to create a new set of personal folders and then import messages from the old personal folders.

   E. Nothing—you cannot retrieve the information.

6. You are creating a custom electronic form for a public folder using Outlook 2003. Which of the following components could you include on the form?

   A. A functioning Excel spreadsheet

   B. Voting buttons that let users vote on the usefulness of that spreadsheet

   C. A button that automatically routes the form to the next person on a routing list

   D. All of the above

7. Your company receives newsfeeds from your Internet Service Provider. You notice a folder within the newsgroup hierarchy that you do not want to receive. What must you do to permanently remove this folder from the hierarchy?

   A. Rename the folder.

   B. Exclude the folder from the newsfeed.

   C. Clear the folder's Folder Visible attribute.

   D. Delete the folder through Microsoft Outlook.

8. Management has decided to allow company access to various newsgroups. Your ISP can provide full newsgroup access, but they do not configure newsfeeds on a customer-by-customer basis. How would you configure the transfer of the newsfeeds?

   A. No transfer type is necessary.

   B. Configure it for both push and pull.

   C. Configure it for a push transfer only.

   D. Configure it for a pull transfer only.

9. You have just configured your Exchange server for POP3 client access. POP3 clients can be authenticated with Basic, Basic with SSL, or Integrated Windows authentication. The administrator of your firewall informs you that the firewall will allow traffic from SMTP (port 25), POP3 (port 110), and HTTP (port 80). For what additional traffic must the firewall be configured to allow your Exchange server POP3 configuration to be used?

   A. 995

   B. 443

   C. 137

   D. 135

10. An Outlook 2003 user has just sent a message to a recipient who is also using Outlook 2003, and he realizes that he has forgotten to attach an important document to the message. He can recall the message so long as what has not happened?

   A. The recipient has not received the message.

   B. The recipient has not opened the message.

   C. The recipient has not replied to or forwarded the message.

   D. The recipient has not moved the message from the Inbox.

   E. The recipient has not deleted the message.

11. Your organization consists of four back-end Exchange Server 2003 computers and two front-end Exchange Server 2003 computers. Only the back-end Exchange servers contain mailboxes. You want to configure and implement RPC over HTTP to allow your traveling sales force to use Outlook 2003 to connect securely to your Exchange organization. Which of the following are requirements that you must meet in order to be able to perform this task? (Choose all that apply.)

   A. The front-end servers must be running Exchange Server 2003 on Windows 2000 or better.

   B. The back-end servers must be running Exchange Server 2003 on Windows Server 2003.

   C. All client computers must be running Windows XP Service Pack 1.

   D. All Global Catalog servers must be running Windows 2000 Server Service Pack 4 or better.

12. You organization consists of three Exchange Server 2003 computers running on Windows Server 2003 servers. All employees in the company use Outlook 2003 as their standard messaging client. All employees have Outlook 2003 configured to use the cache mode of operation. If you want ensure that your users get a complete list of all new messages as quickly as possible, with message bodies and attachments being downloaded and synchronized after that, which option should you configure?

   A. Download Full Items

   B. Download Headers

   C. Download Headers And Then Full Items

   D. On Slow Connections Download Headers Only

13. If you wanted to prohibit certain IP addresses of web clients from accessing your Exchange server, what program would you use?

    A. Exchange System Manager

    B. Network applet in Control Panel

    C. Internet Information Services (IIS) Manager

    D. Network Monitor

14. Why can't POP3 clients see e-mail messages in subfolders of their Inbox?

    A. POP3 clients can access messages only in the Inbox, not subfolders of the Inbox.

    B. LDAP is not enabled at the mailbox object.

    C. NNTP is not enabled at the mailbox object.

    D. The IIS computer is down.

15. For POP3 clients to be able to send Internet mail from their mailbox, what other component must be operational?

    A. LDAP

    B. NNTP

    C. Active Server Components

    D. SMTP

16. What two types of files does the Windows Installer use to install Outlook?

    A. Installer package file

    B. Installer transform file

    C. Installer answer file

    D. Installer user file

17. You have made certain configuration changes to the POP3 protocol using Internet Information Services (IIS) Manager. However, soon after you make the changes, you find that the configuration has reverted to its previous state. You try again, but the same thing happens. What is the problem?

    A. You can make changes only using the Exchange System Manager.

    B. You must make the configuration changes in both the Exchange System Manager and Internet Information Services (IIS) Manager.

    C. You must make the configuration changes in both Active Directory Users and Computers and Internet Information Services (IIS) Manager.

    D. You must configure IIS to replicate changes to the Exchange System Manager.

18. Which of the following features are not available when accessing an Exchange server with a web browser via Outlook Web Access?

A. Personal folders

B. Public folders

C. Searching for messages

D. Group scheduling

19. Which of the following components is responsible for merging a form with information from the Information Store to create an HTML or XML page that is delivered to a web client?

A. W3svc

B. Information Store

C. DAVEx

D. Forms Registry

20. Which of the following components manages the flow of messages between a MAPI message store and MAPI transport providers?

A. MAPI client

B. Offline folder

C. Message spooler

D. Transport service

Answers to Review Questions

1. D. A personal folder store is a file-based storage container independent of the Exchange Server back end. A file that is composed of a set of personal folders has the `.pst` extension. A PST file can be stored on the user's local machine or on a shared directory on a network server.

2. A. If mailbox storage is left in the default location (the Private Information Store) and offline access to that data is also needed, the user can utilize an offline folder. An offline folder is a local copy of the user's private folders in the Private Information Store. The mailbox on the server remains the master copy.

3. B. The MAPI subsystem provides a single interface for client applications. Communication with all MAPI-compliant server messaging systems is facilitated by interfacing with the MAPI subsystem. It is the middleware, or broker, in the messaging environment.

4. D. The Enable Fast Message Retrieval option, which is enabled by default, permits an Exchange server to approximate the size of messages when reporting to an IMAP4 client application. Approximating message sizes increases the speed of message retrieval. Some IMAP4 client applications, however, require a server to report the exact message size. If that is the case, this field can be cleared (i.e., unchecked).

5. E. Passwords assigned to a personal folder can be neither viewed by the Exchange administrator nor retrieved without the password. Therefore, if a user forgets this password, the information in that folder is inaccessible. Several third-party utilities exist that can be used to try to break the password on a PST file, however.

6. D. Because of Microsoft object technology, a spreadsheet contained in a form would not be merely rows and columns but could include the Excel code to execute the functions of the spreadsheet. Voting buttons are a built-in function of Outlook 2003, and a routing function is an example of a simple custom code that could be placed into a form.

7. B. You can exclude the folder from the newsfeed using the Subscription page of the newsfeed's property pages.

8. D. When one server actively sends information to another server, it is referred to as a push feed (it is also referred to as publishing). A server can also be configured to request that information be sent to it from another server. This is referred to as a pull feed.

9. A. POP uses TCP/IP as its transport protocol. The session, or conversation, between the POP client and server takes place on TCP port 110. If Secure Sockets Layer (SSL) is being used to create an encrypted channel, port 995 is used instead.

10. B. An Outlook 2003 user can recall a sent message, assuming the recipient has not already opened it.

11. B, C. The requirements to configure and implement RPC over HTTP are as follows:

    - Client computers must have Outlook 2003 installed.
    - Client computers must be running Windows XP with Service Pack 1 and hot fix Q331320.

- Front-end servers must be running Exchange Server 2003 on Windows Server 2003.
- Back-end servers must be running Exchange Server 2003 on Windows Server 2003.
- Public folder servers must be running Exchange Server 2003 on Windows Server 2003.
- All Global Catalog servers must be running Windows Server 2003.

12. C. Leaving the default configuration, Download Headers And Then Full Items, in place results in the message list being built quickly because only the headers are downloaded initially. After all of the headers are downloaded, the message bodies and any attachments are then downloaded.

13. C. Internet Information Services (IIS) Manager is used to provide management of the HTTP protocol.

14. A. POP3 clients can be used to retrieve messages from the Inbox only.

15. D. POP3 is a protocol used for message retrieval only. In order to send messages, POP3 clients use the SMTP protocol.

16. A, B. Windows Installer uses two types of files to install Outlook: an installer package (MSI) file and an installer transform (MST) file. The package file contains a database that describes the configuration information. The transform file contains modifications that are to be made as Windows Installer installs Outlook. The package file never changes; it is essentially a database that helps Windows Installer relate various features to actual installation files. The transform file is what is modified using the Custom Installation Wizard.

17. A. When virtual servers are managed using the Exchange System Manager, the Exchange System Attendant writes the configuration information to the Active Directory. From there, the information is written to the IIS metabase. If you configure virtual servers directly in IIS, it is possible that the information you configure will be overwritten by older information configured in System Manager or Active Directory.

18. A. While OWA provides many advanced Exchange features, not all of the features available in a MAPI client such as Outlook are available through OWA.

19. C. DAVEx retrieves an appropriate form from the Forms Registry and merges it with the information from the Information Store, creating an HTML or XML document. DAVEx then sends the formatted document to the W3svc service for delivery to the client.

20. C. The message spooler is an independent process that manages the flow of messages between the message store and the transport providers. It is like a queue where incoming and outgoing messages are sent and from there are routed to the necessary provider. When a message is marked for sending, a message store provider will send it to the message spooler.

Building Administrative and Routing Groups

MICROSOFT EXAM OBJECTIVES COVERED IN THIS CHAPTER:

- ✓ Install, configure, and troubleshoot Exchange Server 2003
- ✓ Configure and troubleshoot Exchange Server 2003 for coexistence with other Exchange organizations
- ✓ Configure and troubleshoot Exchange Server 2003 for coexistence with other messaging systems
- ✓ Configure and troubleshoot Exchange Server 2003 for interoperability with other SMTP messaging systems

In Exchange Server 2003, there are two ways to organize servers: according to the physical routing needs of your organization and according to administrative needs. *Routing groups* are physical groupings of Exchange servers that have full-time, full-mesh, reliable connections between each server and every other server in the group. *Administrative groups* are Exchange servers and other Active Directory objects that are logically grouped together for the purposes of administration and permissions management.

In previous versions of Exchange Server 5.5, a single construct called the Exchange site was used to group servers for routing and administrative purposes. Routing groups are the closest to what these sites were in that they define a routing boundary for a physical group of servers. If you are coming from an Exchange 5.5 or earlier background, you can think of the routing group as the successor to the site and administrative groups, as a logical administrative layer imposed on top of the routing infrastructure.

This chapter covers the configuration and management of both administrative and routing groups. It begins by examining the different models for using multiple administrative groups and how using multiple groups is affected if you are running a mixed-mode organization—one in which previous versions of Exchange Server 5.5 coexist with Exchange Server 2003 (or Exchange 2000 Server). Next, this chapter looks at the process of creating and maintaining administrative groups. From there, the chapter turns to routing groups, examining the reasons an organization might benefit from using multiple routing groups and showing the actual process of creating new groups and linking them to one another using various types of connectors.

Creating and Configuring Administrative Groups

An *administrative group* is a collection of Active Directory objects that are grouped together for the purpose of permissions management. Administrative groups are logical, which means that you can design them to fit your needs—geographical boundaries, departmental divisions, different groups of Exchange administrators, or different Exchange functions. For example, one group of Exchange administrators might be responsible for managing the messaging and routing backbone of the organization, another might be responsible for managing public folders, and still another might be responsible for managing connectivity with a legacy messaging system. You could create an administrative group for each that contains only the objects the administrator needs.

The basic idea behind administrative groups is that they make it easier to assign permissions to groups of objects. Once you set permissions on an administrative group, any object moved to that group automatically inherits those permissions. You will learn more about assigning permissions in Chapter 10, "Administration and Maintenance."

An administrative group can hold the following types of objects:

- Servers
- Routing groups
- Public folder trees
- System policies

Mixed Mode versus Native Mode

Before you get started dividing up everything into administrative groups, it is important to understand that there are some differences in how they are handled, depending on whether the Exchange organization is running in mixed mode or native mode. *Mixed mode* allows Exchange Server 2003 and Exchange 2000 servers and servers running earlier versions of Exchange, such as Exchange Server 5.5, to coexist in the same organization. It allows this interoperability between versions by limiting functionality to features that the different versions share.

Limitations of mixed mode include the following:

- Each Exchange 5.5 site in the organization is mapped directly to a single administrative group and a single routing group, and vice versa. This limits your ability to use administrative and routing groups in the way that best fits the needs of your organization.
- You can move mailboxes only between servers that are in the same administrative group.
- Routing groups can contain only servers that are part of the administrative group that is defined with the routing group.

The Exchange Server 2003 native mode of operation is slightly different than the native mode of operation in Exchange 2000 Server. Native mode in Exchange Server 2003 allows for Exchange Server 2003 and Exchange 2000 Server to be used within the organization. Wherever you see native mode in Exchange Server 2003, this means that Exchange Server 2003 and Exchange 2000 Server computers can be used.

When you first install Exchange Server 2003, it defaults to running in mixed mode. If the entire organization will be running only Exchange Server 2003 servers and you do not plan to use any previous versions, you can switch to *native mode*. Native mode means you have a pure Exchange Server 2003 organization, which allows you to take full advantage of Exchange 2000 Server functionality. Be careful, though: If you change the operation mode of an Exchange Server 2003 organization from mixed mode to native mode, you cannot reverse this change, and the organization will no longer be interoperable with earlier versions of Exchange, such as Exchange Server 5.5.

Native mode offers the following benefits:

- A server can belong to an administrative group, but it does not have to belong to one of the routing groups within that administrative group.
- Administrative groups do not have to contain any routing groups.
- A single administrative group can contain all routing groups within the organization.
- You can move mailboxes between any servers in the organization.

You can learn more about mixed-mode operations and managing the coexistence of Exchange Server 2003 and Exchange 5.5 in Chapter 11, "Connecting to Exchange 5.5." From this point on, this chapter assumes that you are running Exchange Server 2003 in native mode and that all of the functionality of running in native mode is available.

Exercise 8.1 outlines the steps for switching an Exchange organization from mixed mode to native mode.

EXERCISE 8.1

Switching an Exchange Organization to Native Mode

1. Click Start ➢ Programs ➢ Microsoft Exchange, and then select System Manager.
2. In the left-hand pane, find the object for the organization that you want to switch to native mode. If you are running only one organization, this object is at the top of the pane.
3. Right-click the organization object and choose Properties from the context menu.
4. The Organization Mode field displays whether your organization is currently in mixed or native mode. Click the Change Mode button.
5. A warning appears stating that once you change to native mode, you cannot change back. Click OK to make the change.

EXERCISE 8.1 *(continued)*

6. You are returned to the organization object property pages, as seen below. Notice that the Organization Mode field now identifies the organization as being in native mode and that the Change Mode button is no longer available. Click OK to return to System Manager.

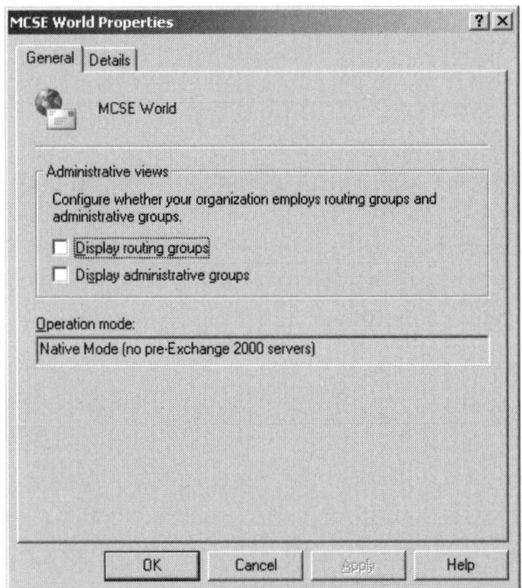

Using Multiple Administrative Groups

For most small to medium-size companies, where there is a single Exchange manager or a single management team, there is usually no reason to use more than one administrative group. In larger companies, it often makes sense to divide up the administration of the Exchange organization by location, department, or administrative duties.

There are three basic administrative models: centralized, decentralized, and mixed. It is important, both in the real world and for the exam, to know how these three models work.

Centralized Administrative Model

In the *centralized model*, one administrator or group of administrators maintains complete control over an entire Exchange organization. However, this does not necessarily mean that only one administrative group is defined. You might choose to create a few groups just to make it easier to assign permissions. Your routing topology does not need to match the administrative topology, of course. You may create many routing groups within a single administrative group.

Decentralized Administrative Model

The *decentralized model* is typically used to define administrative boundaries along real geographical or departmental boundaries. Each location would have its own administrators and its own administrative group. For example, a company with branch locations in three different cities would likely have administrators in each city. According to the decentralized model, an administrative group would be created for each location. Again, routing topology does not need to match administrative topology. You could create multiple routing groups within each administrative group. You could also have a routing group that spans multiple administrative groups or an administrative group that spans multiple routing groups.

Mixed Administrative Model

The *mixed model* is really a catchall model for any other ways you can think of to use administrative groups. It is useful for when you do not necessarily want the tight control of the centralized model and the strict geographic division of the decentralized model is not appropriate. Here are two examples of when the mixed administrative model is useful:

- You might want to keep most administration under the control of a single administrative group but restrict certain types of administration to certain administrators. For example, you might leave the default First Administrative Group intact for general Exchange management but create a special administrative group that holds all system policies. This way, only specific administrators could create and manage policies.
- You might want to combine geographic boundaries and functional boundaries. For example, assume that your company has its main location in one city and a branch location in another. You might want to leave the First Administrative Group intact for general management of the main location. You might then want to create an administrative group specifically for the branch location, another group for policy management, and another for public folder management.

Creating Administrative Groups

By default, Exchange Server 2003 is configured with a single administrative group named First Administrative Group. Also by default, this administrative group is hidden from view in System Manager, as shown in Figure 8.1. After all, why add a layer of complexity to the administration program by displaying administrative grouping when there is only one group?

To enable viewing of administrative groups, open the property pages for the organization object. Select the Display Routing Groups and Display Administrative Groups options on the General property page, and click OK to apply the new settings. You are informed that you must shut down and restart System Manager to see the changes. After you bring System Manager back up, it looks something like the view shown in Figure 8.2.

FIGURE 8.1 By default, administrative groups are not shown in System Manager.

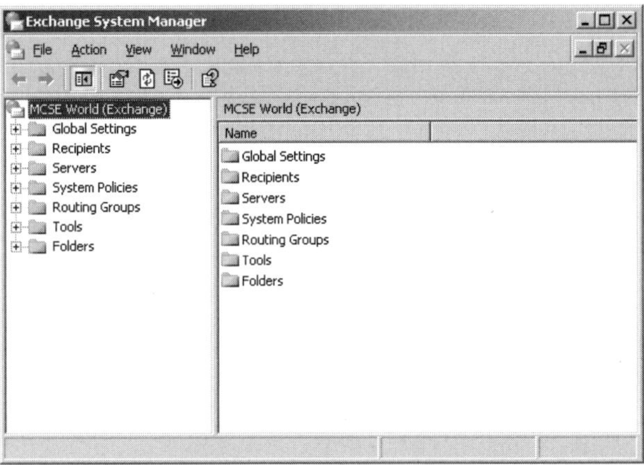

FIGURE 8.2 System Manager showing administrative and routing groups

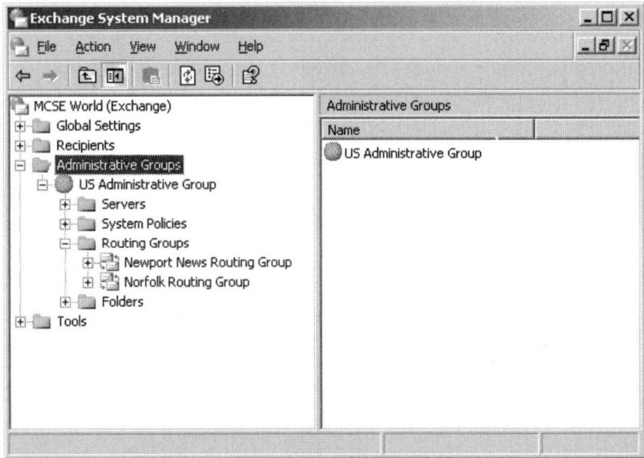

If you compare this view to the one shown in Figure 8.1, you'll notice that the Servers, Routing Groups, and Folders containers have all been moved to show which administrative group they belong to—in this case, the US Administrative Group. All functionality remains the same, except that now you can create new administrative groups and arrange most resources among them however you like. Exercise 8.2 outlines the steps for creating a new administrative group.

EXERCISE 8.2

Creating a New Administrative Group

1. Click Start ➤ Programs ➤ Microsoft Exchange, and then select System Manager.
2. Expand the organization object in which you want to create a new administrative group.
3. Right-click the Administrative Groups container and select the New Administrative Group command from the context menu. This opens the property pages for the new group.
4. On the General page, seen below, enter a name for the new administrative group that identifies its purpose.

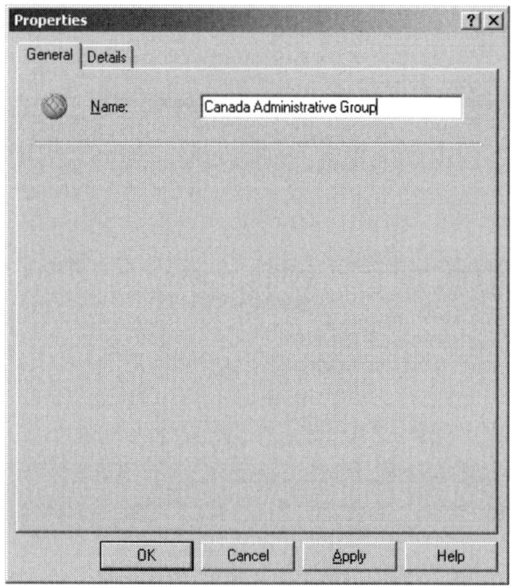

5. Optionally, you can switch to the Details page and enter some text that describes the purpose of the new group.
6. Click OK to return to System Manager. The new administrative group is displayed in the Administrative Groups container.

Once you have created a new administrative group, the first thing you'll want to do is assign the appropriate permissions to the group. By doing this first, you ensure that new objects created inside the group inherit those permissions. Permissions are covered in Chapter 10.

Once permissions have been assigned, it is time to structure the new administrative group. The first thing you must do is create one or more containers inside the group. Do this by right-clicking the group and selecting a new container type from the context menu. The types of containers you can create include the following:

- Routing Groups containers
- Public Folders containers
- Policy containers

Figure 8.3 shows the new administrative group we created previously, now populated with a Routing Groups container and a System Policies container.

Once you have created the subcontainers for the administrative group and defined the new group's structure, you then have two options for filling up that structure with objects:

- You can create new objects within those subcontainers using the methods discussed throughout this book. For example, you can create a new public folder tree in a Folders container; the method for this is covered in Chapter 6, "Using Public Folders." Creating new objects works in exactly the same way that creating objects in the default administrative group works. (Routing groups are discussed later in this chapter, and policies in Chapter 10.)
- You can drag objects from other administrative groups and drop them into the corresponding folders inside the new administrative group. For example, once you create a Routing Groups subcontainer in the new administrative group, you could drag routing groups from other administrative groups to the new administrative group. You can also drag the servers themselves between routing groups in the new administrative group. However, you cannot move servers between administrative groups.

There is one other item to be aware of regarding administrative groups. When you install Exchange servers into an organization after creating additional routing groups, the setup program lets you choose in which administrative group and routing group the server should be placed. This option never appears during setup if there is only one administrative group.

FIGURE 8.3 Creating containers inside a new administrative group

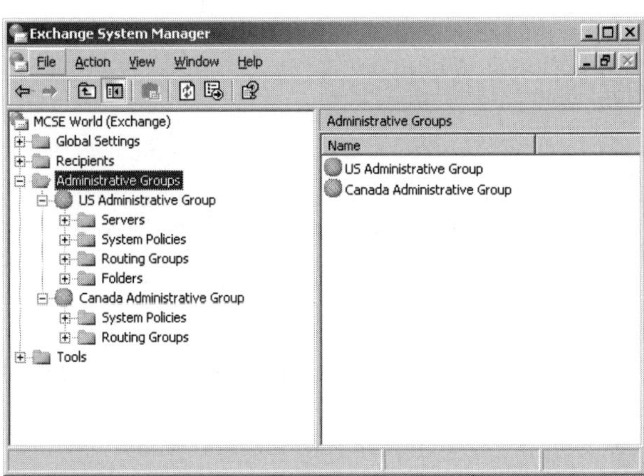

Creating and Configuring Routing Groups

A *routing group* is a collection of Exchange servers that have full-time, full-mesh, reliable connections between each and every server. Messages sent between any two servers within a routing group are delivered directly from the source server to the destination server. The message transport mechanism for this delivery is SMTP. Using SMTP as the native protocol provides several advantages. SMTP allows for a more flexible routing and administrative scheme because SMTP is more tolerant of low-bandwidth and high-latency topologies.

Ideally, you would be in a networking environment in which all servers were well connected. Of course, this is not always the case. For this reason, Exchange Server 2003 lets you define routing groups that collect well-connected servers into different groups and then connect those groups using several different kinds of connectors.

This chapter deals mainly with the actual process of creating and linking routing groups. Before you get started, it is important that you are familiar with the concepts discussed in the "Routing Architecture" and "Message Transport" sections of Chapter 2, "Microsoft Exchange Architecture." In particular, you should know the architectural concepts behind the use of routing groups and how messages flow when they are sent to recipients on the same server, within the same routing group, to a different routing group, or outside the Exchange organization.

Routing groups in Exchange Server 2003 should be planned similarly to sites in Exchange 5.5—according to available bandwidth and reliability of the connection. However, because Exchange Server 2003 uses SMTP, it is more tolerant of lower bandwidths and higher latency. This means you'll be able to group servers into the same routing group that may not have been possible with an Exchange 5.5 site.

The most important factor to consider when defining routing group boundaries is the stability of the network connection rather than the actual bandwidth of the connection. If the connection is prone to failure or is often too saturated with network traffic to be useful, then you should divide your servers into separate routing groups.

Be sure to have a Global Catalog server in each routing group and in each Windows site, if possible. This decreases traffic across slower WAN links when clients and servers need to look up information in the Global Access List (GAL).

In order for servers to exist in the same routing group, they must meet the following criteria:

- All servers running Exchange Server 2003 must have reliable, permanent, and direct network connectivity between them that supports SMTP.
- All servers must belong to the same Active Directory forest.
- All servers must be able to connect to the routing group master. The routing group master maintains data about all of the servers running Exchange Server 2003 in the routing group.

If your servers do not meet these criteria, or if you have a need to maintain greater control over the way messaging information flows on your network, you will need to create multiple routing groups.

Creating Routing Groups

You will need to create separate routing groups if you have any servers that are separated by slow or unreliable links. Creating a routing group is a very similar process to the one for creating an administrative group. Exercise 8.3 outlines the steps for creating a new routing group.

EXERCISE 8.3

Creating a New Routing Group

1. Click Start ➢ Programs ➢ Microsoft Exchange, and then select System Manager.
2. Expand the organization object in which you want to create a new routing group.
3. Expand the Administrative Groups folder.
4. Expand the administrative group in which you want to create a new routing group. If this administrative group does not already have a Routing Groups container in which to create a routing group, you will have to create one using the procedure discussed previously in this chapter.
5. Right-click the Routing Groups container and select the New Routing Group command from the context menu. This opens the property pages for the new routing group, as seen below.

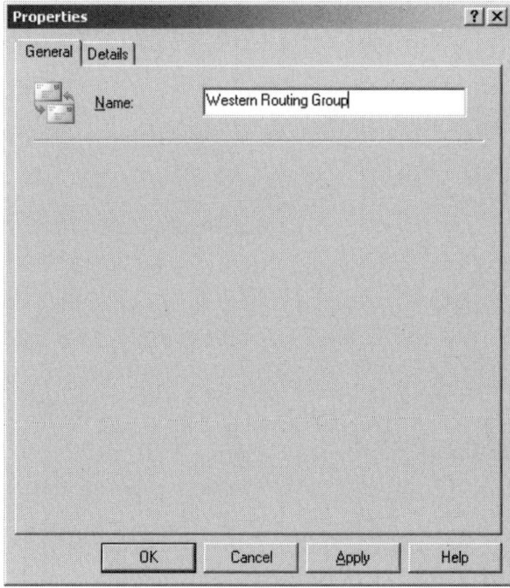

EXERCISE 8.3 *(continued)*

6. On the General page, enter a name for the new routing group that describes it.
7. Optionally, you can switch to the Details page and enter some text that describes the purpose of the new group.
8. Click OK to return to System Manager. The new routing group is displayed in the Routing Groups container.

The new routing group will hold two subcontainers, as shown in Figure 8.4. The Connectors container holds any connectors that you create to connect this routing group to other routing groups or to foreign messaging systems. These connectors are covered later in this chapter. The second object is a Members container, which holds the servers that are part of the routing group. Both of these containers are empty right after you create the new routing group.

Adding Servers to a Routing Group

Once a routing group is connected, there are two primary tasks you will need to take on to configure the new group. The first is moving or installing servers into the new group. The second, which is discussed a bit later in the chapter, is connecting the routing group to other routing groups.

There are two ways to make a server a member of a routing group. The first way is to drag a server from the Members container of an existing routing group and drop it into the Members container of the new routing group. It really is just that simple.

FIGURE 8.4 Viewing a new routing group

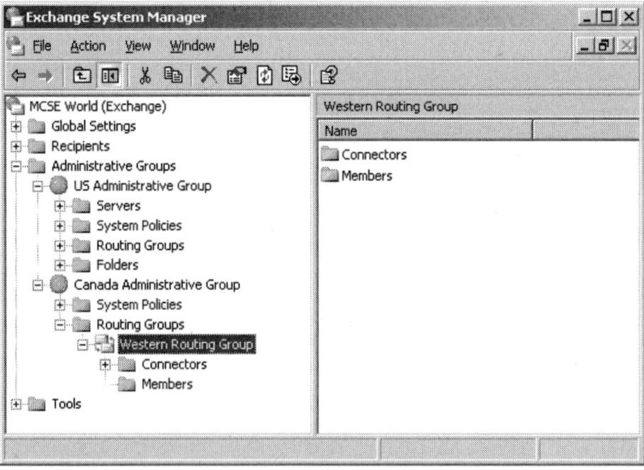

When you move a server from one routing group to another, you are actually removing the SMTP virtual server or the X.400 service through which the server communicates and re-creating the virtual server or service in the new routing group.

Real World Scenario

Using Multiple Routing Groups

In most small organizations, you will never have any reason to consider using more than one routing group. In these instances, it is fair to say that all of your Exchange servers will be located close to one another and have reliable, high-speed connectivity among them. But what will you do if your network happens to span multiple cities, states, countries, or even continents? Then you have a valid reason to start creating and using multiple routing groups.

A certain network, for example, has approximately 180 geographically distant sites within it that are located all over the globe. Of these approximately 180 remote sites, about 120 of them are located in the continental United States. The other 60 or so remote sites are located all over the globe in Germany, Korea, Japan, Italy, and several other countries. This network is split into five geographic regions based on network connectivity. Within each region, it can be reasonably said that reliable, high-speed IP connectivity exists between each and every host on the network. Between regions, often-unreliable WAN links exist, using a variety of technologies depending on where in the world they are located. Leased lines exist that are used to cross ocean expanses, with variable bandwidth available depending on the time of day.

In this network, it would be a good idea to create five different routing groups and place the servers from each of the five geographic regions into their respective routing groups. Within each routing group, several bridgehead servers could be configured from those that are available. In general, the bridgehead servers would usually be those that are located closest to the WAN Demarc point or points (the physical location in a network where external connections are made, such as to the Internet) for that region. If you're using Routing Group Connectors between these routing groups, you can assign different route costs to those bridgehead servers that are closest to a backup WAN link.

Even though this network is large and distributed, you can still conceivably use just one administrative group for the entire network if desired. When Exchange Server 2003 operates in native mode, you can organize your routing groups and administrative groups independently of one another.

The second way to get a server into a routing group is to put it there during Exchange installation. If your organization contains more than one routing group, the Exchange setup program will ask you into which routing group (and which administrative group, if applicable) you want to install the new server. After setup is finished, the new server is added to the chosen routing group. For more information on installing Exchange Server, see Chapter 3, "Installing Microsoft Exchange Server 2003."

Connecting Routing Groups

Once you have created multiple routing groups, you will need to connect them so that they can exchange messaging information. There are three types of connectors that you can create:

- The *Routing Group Connector (RGC)* is the main connector used to connect routing groups and is the simplest to configure. It used SMTP as its default transport mechanism, but it may also use a Remote Procedure Call (RPC) if the situation requires it.
- The *SMTP Connector* takes a bit more work to set up than the RGC and sports some different features. It is used mainly to connect routing groups where you want to force SMTP to be used for the transport mechanism. The SMTP Connector can also be used to connect an Exchange organization to a foreign messaging system using SMTP.
- The *X.400 Connector* can be used to connect routing groups and to connect to a foreign system. When used for connecting routing groups, its primary advantage is that it can be used over extremely low bandwidth and fairly unreliable connections.

The creation and configuration of each of these connectors are covered in the following sections.

In most cases, your best choice will be the Routing Group Connector because it is the simplest to configure and manage. However, your choice will depend on the purpose the connector will serve. In addition, multiple connectors, of differing types, can be created between the same two routing groups to provide a level of fault tolerance and load balancing.

Routing Group Connector

The RGC is the preferred method of connecting two routing groups in the same organization because it is fast, reliable, and the simplest to configure (has the fewest settings). SMTP is the native protocol used by the RGC, and the connector consults Exchange Server 2003's link-state table for routing information.

The RGC is a one-way connection from one server to another. Therefore, when you configure a connector in one routing group, you'll also need to create a connector in the other routing group to form a two-way connection. Fortunately, System Manager will automatically configure the other end of the link for you if you want it to.

A *bridgehead server* is one that is designated for passing messages from one routing group to another. The RGC offers a level of fault tolerance by allowing multiple source and destination bridgehead servers. Bridgehead servers can be used in one of three ways:

- No bridgehead server is designated, and all of the servers in the routing group function as bridgehead servers for message transmission.

- One bridgehead server is designated, and all mail destined for other routing groups flows through that one server. This gives the administrator great control over messaging configuration.
- Multiple bridgehead servers are used, and all mail flows over one of these designated servers. This configuration offers the advantages of load balancing and fault tolerance. Should one bridgehead server be unavailable for message transport, another will be available.

RGCs offer administrators the ability to control connection schedules, message priority, and message size limits.

Creating a Routing Group Connector

Creating a new RGC is a simple procedure. Exercise 8.4 outlines the steps involved.

EXERCISE 8.4

Creating a New Routing Group Connector

1. Click Start ➢ Programs ➢ Microsoft Exchange, and then select System Manager.
2. Expand the organization object, the Administrative Groups folder, the specific administrative group, and the Routing Groups folder in which you want to configure the connector.
3. Right-click the Connectors container and select the New Routing Group Connector command from the context menu.
4. This opens the property pages that you must configure for the new connector. Once you have configured these pages, which are described in the next section, System Manager offers to automatically create a connector for the other end of the link using the same properties you have just configured.

Configuring Routing Group Connector Properties

The RGC holds a number of property pages that can be configured. You have the option of configuring these pages when you first create the connector or later by opening the pages for the connector object, which is placed in the Connectors container for the particular routing group. All of these, and the parameters they hold, are covered in the next several sections.

GENERAL PROPERTIES

The General page, shown in Figure 8.5, lets you enter several settings regarding the connector. These include the following:

- The name of the connector can be entered only when you are creating the connector. This field is not editable after the connector is created.
- The Connects This Routing Group With drop-down box lists the routing group with which you want to connect. All routing groups in the organization should be listed here.
- The Cost field indicates the *cost value* of using the connector relative to any other connectors that may connect the two routing groups. This value can range from 1 to 100, and

lower cost links are always preferred over higher cost links. This provides you with a way of assigning preference when there are multiple connectors configured between routing groups. For example, you might want to configure two connectors to share the main messaging load between two sites and assign both of them a cost of 1. Then you might configure a backup connector with a cost of 5 that is used when the two main connectors are unavailable. As a general rule, the lower the bandwidth or reliability of the connection, the higher the cost value associated with the connector should be.

- While the option labeled Any Local Server Can Send Mail Over This Connector is enabled (which it is by default), all servers in the local routing group function as bridgehead servers and can route messages over the connector. You can specify that only particular servers be used as bridgehead servers by selecting the These Servers Can Send Mail Over This Connector option and then using the Add button to add servers to the list.
- The Do Not Allow Public Folder Referrals option specifies that clients may not access public folder content using this connector. When a client tries to access public folder content that does not exist on a server in that client's own routing group, it must try to find the content in other routing groups. This option gives you a way to govern the connections that can be used for this task.

REMOTE BRIDGEHEAD PROPERTIES

The Remote Bridgehead page, shown in Figure 8.6, allows you to specify one or more servers in the remote routing group as the bridgehead server(s) with which this connector will attempt to establish connections before sending messages. The servers are contacted in order, starting at the top of the list. Also, if the destination server has more than one *SMTP virtual server* configured, you'll need to select the appropriate virtual server that will allow messages to be sent across the connector you are setting up.

DELIVERY RESTRICTIONS PROPERTIES

The Delivery Restrictions page, shown in Figure 8.7, lets you specify who can use this connector, either by specifying that all messages are rejected except for specified users or that all messages are accepted except for specified users. You can add mailbox-enabled or mail-enabled users and contacts to this list, but you cannot add groups.

CONTENT RESTRICTIONS PROPERTIES

The Content Restrictions page, shown in Figure 8.8, lets you configure several parameters:

- The Allowed Priorities section lets you select what priority messages are allowed over the connection. This is a great way to establish connectors dedicated, for example, to passing high-priority messages.
- The Allowed Types section lets you specify whether system messages and non-system messages are allowed over the connector. System messages would include any non–user-generated message, including directory replication, public folder replication, network monitoring, and delivery and non-delivery report messages.
- The Allowed Sizes section lets you restrict the size of messages that can be sent over the connector.

FIGURE 8.5 Remote Bridgehead properties of an RGC

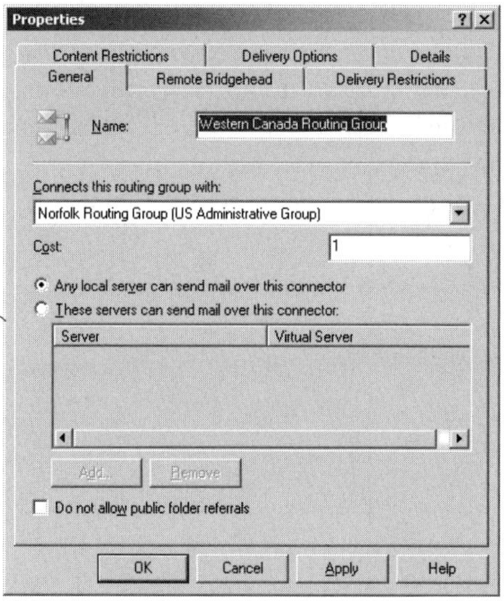

Properties
Content Restrictions
Delivery Options
Details
General
Remote Bridgehead
Delivery Restrictions
Name:
Western Canada Routing Group
Connects this routing group with:
Norfolk Routing Group (US Administrative Group)
Cost:
1
Any local server can send mail over this connector
These servers can send mail over this connector:
Server
Virtual Server
Add...
Remove
Do not allow public folder referrals
OK
Cancel
Apply
Help

FIGURE 8.6 Delivery Restrictions properties of an RGC

Western Canada Routing Group Properties
Content Restrictions
Delivery Options
Details
General
Remote Bridgehead
Delivery Restrictions
Remote bridgeheads:
Server
Virtual Server
MCSESVR3142
Default SMTP Virtual Server
Add...
Remove
Override connection credentials for Exchange 5.x
Domain:
Account:
Modify...
OK
Cancel
Apply
Help

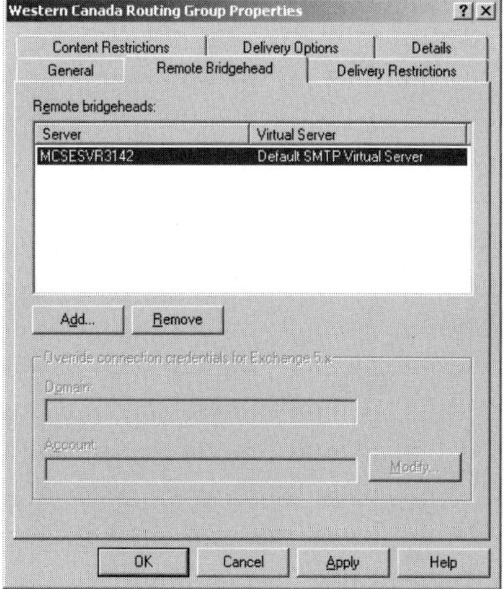

FIGURE 8.7 General properties of an RGC

Western Canada Routing Group Properties
Content Restrictions
Delivery Options
Details
General
Remote Bridgehead
Delivery Restrictions
By default, messages from everyone are:
Accepted
Rejected
Accept messages from:
Add...
Remove
Reject messages from:
Add...
Remove
OK
Cancel
Apply
Help

FIGURE 8.8 Content Restrictions properties of an RGC

Western Canada Routing Group Properties
General
Remote Bridgehead
Delivery Restrictions
Content Restrictions
Delivery Options
Details
Select which message types will be delivered through this connector.
Allowed priorities
High
Normal
Low
Allowed types
System messages
Non-system messages
Allowed sizes
Only messages less than (KB):
OK
Cancel
Apply
Help

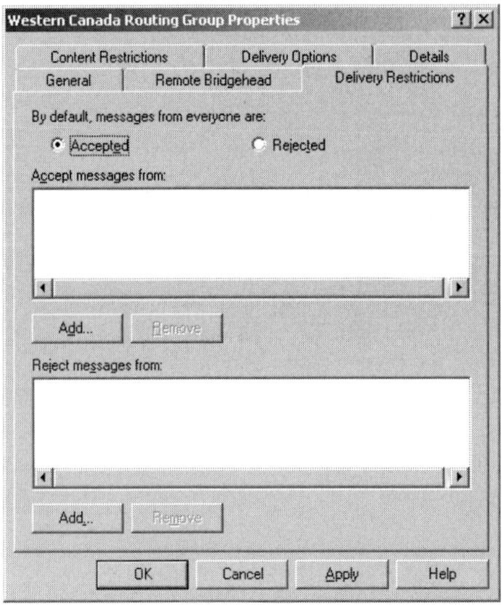

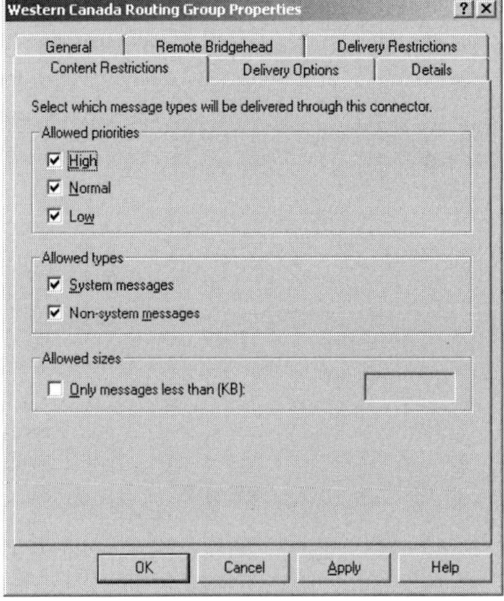

FIGURE 8.9 Delivery Options properties of an RGC

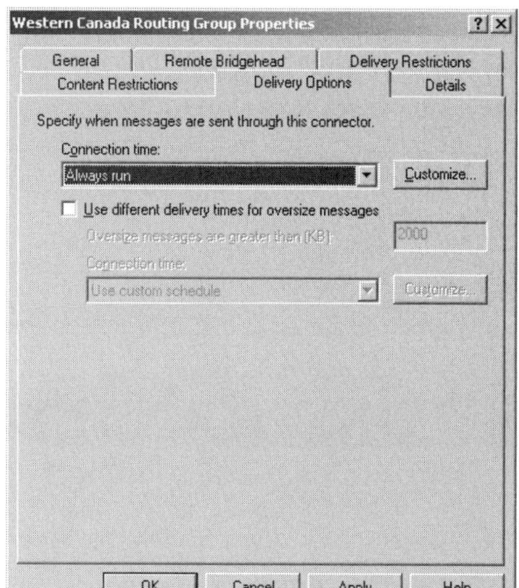

DELIVERY OPTIONS PROPERTIES

The Delivery Options page, shown in Figure 8.9, lets you specify when messages can flow through the connector. This is especially helpful if the connector uses a slow or unreliable WAN link. Click the Customize button to set up a schedule using a simple calendar interface. By selecting the Use Different Delivery Times For Oversize Messages option, you can channel larger messages to transfer at the times you configure, presumably when the connector would be experiencing little traffic.

SMTP Connector

Although the RGC uses SMTP as its native transport mechanism, Exchange Server 2003 also provides an SMTP Connector that can be used to link routing groups. There are three reasons why you might want to use an SMTP Connector instead of an RGC:

- The SMTP Connector is more configurable than the RGC and offers a greater ability to fine-tune the connection. The SMTP Connector also offers the ability to issue authentication before sending mail, specifying *TLS encryption*, and removing mail from queues on remote servers.
- The SMTP Connector always has to use SMTP. When you are connecting an Exchange 2000 Server with an Exchange 5.5 server, the RGC uses Remote Procedure Calls (RPCs) to communicate because it has no way of knowing whether the Exchange 5.5 server is configured to use SMTP, which was provided through the Internet Mail Service in previous versions of Exchange. There is no way to force the RGC to use SMTP, so an SMTP Connector can be used instead.

- The SMTP Connector is also capable of connecting independent Exchange forests within an organization so that messages can be transferred.

Another advantage of the SMTP Connector is that it can be used to connect an Exchange organization to the Internet or to a foreign (non-Exchange) messaging system that uses SMTP.

When connected to the Internet, the SMTP Connector uses a smart host or mail exchange (MX) records in DNS for next-hop routing. When configured internally between two routing groups, this connector will relay link-state information between routing groups but will still depend on the MX records in DNS for next-hop information.

Creating an SMTP Connector

Creating a new SMTP Connector is a simple procedure. Exercise 8.5 outlines the steps involved.

EXERCISE 8.5

Creating a New SMTP Connector

1. Click Start ➤ Programs ➤ Microsoft Exchange, and then select System Manager.
2. Expand the organization object, the Administrative Groups folder, the specific administrative group, and the Routing Groups folder in which you want to configure the connector.
3. Right-click the Connectors container and select the New SMTP Connector command from the context menu.
4. This opens the property pages that you must configure for the new connector. After you have configured these pages, which are described in the next section, System Manager does not offer to automatically create a connector for the other end of the link. You must do this manually.

Configuring SMTP Connector Properties

The SMTP Connector holds a number of property pages that can be configured. You have the option of configuring these pages when you first create the connector or later by opening the pages for the connector object, which is placed in the Connectors container for the particular routing group. Two of these property pages, Content Restrictions and Delivery Restrictions, are identical to the RGC property pages of the same name. The rest are discussed in the following sections.

GENERAL PROPERTIES

The General page, shown in Figure 8.10, lets you configure the following options:

- The name of the connector can be entered only when you are creating the connector. This field is not editable after the connector is created.

- The Use DNS To Route To Each Address Space On This Connector option makes the connector work with DNS to make direct connections to the destination SMTP server based on MX records. To forward mail upstream to another SMTP server instead, select the Forward All Mail Through This Connector To The Following Smart Hosts option. For this option, enter either the Fully Qualified Domain Name (FQDN) or IP address of the server.
- The Local Bridgeheads area allows you to configure the servers that are to act as the local bridgehead servers for this connector.
- The Do Not Allow Public Folder Referrals option works the same way as the option for the RGC, and it is covered in that section.

DELIVERY OPTIONS PROPERTIES

The Delivery Options page, shown in Figure 8.11, lets you specify when messages can flow through the connector. For the most part, this page works the same as the Delivery Options page for the RGC, except that one feature has been added. The Queue Mail For Remote Triggered Delivery option allows clients to periodically connect to the Exchange Server 2003 computer and download messages using a special command. You can select which Active Directory user accounts can download mail.

FIGURE 8.10 General properties of the SMTP Connector

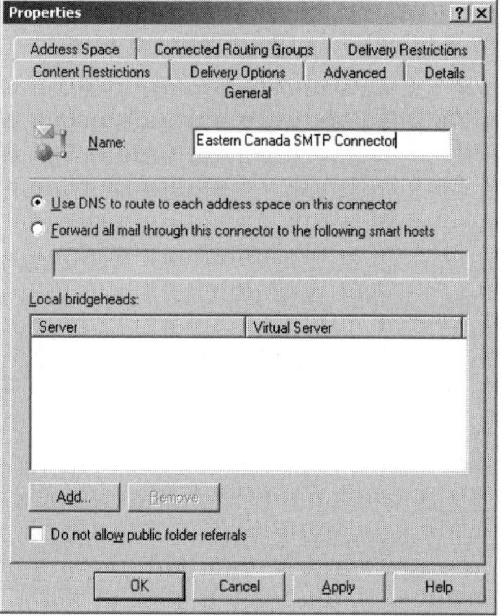

FIGURE 8.11 Delivery Options properties of the SMTP Connector

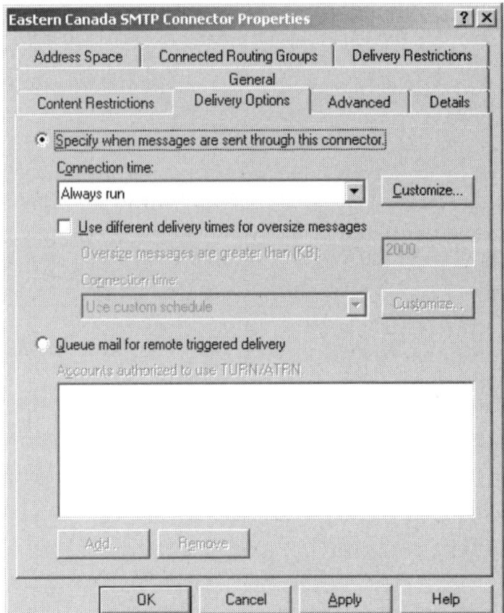

ADVANCED PROPERTIES

The Advanced page, shown in Figure 8.12, has a number of important configuration points. These include the following:

- Normally, an SMTP client connects to an SMTP server using a command named *HELO*, which signals the start of a session between two SMTP servers and identifies the sender of the coming message. By default, Exchange Server 2003 sends the *EHLO* command, another start command, which indicates that the Exchange Server 2003 computer can use the Extended SMTP (ESMTP) commands. Not all SMTP servers are capable of dialogue using the extended commands, but you really have to worry about this only when connecting to non-Exchange servers.
- The Outbound Security button can be used to provide authentication credentials to the remote domain.
- The Do Not Send ETRN/TURN option prevents this connector from processing requests for remote servers to process mail sitting in their queues. This is selected by default.
- The Request ETRN/TURN When Sending Messages option is used to request that the server deliver queued mail to the client via a new ESMTP connection at certain times. Do this by selecting the Additionally Request Mail At Specified Times option and then scheduling the dequeuing time using the Connection Time drop-down list.

- Use the Request ETRN/TURN From Different Server option and type the server's name to request dequeuing from a server other than the one to which the message was sent.
- To specify either the *ETRN* or the *TURN* command for dequeuing, select either the Issue ETRN or Issue TURN option. The ETRN command can be issued on a per-domain basis by clicking the Domains button and adding the domain names.

ADDRESS SPACE PROPERTIES

Whenever a message is sent that is not addressed to a recipient on the same server, that message is handed off for delivery to a remote server. To decide how to route that message to its destination, the routing engine uses an *address space*. An address space is the addressing information associated with a connector. Typically, an address space is a subset of a complete address. The Address Space property page, seen in Figure 8.13, lets you configure the default address spaces used for different types of messages, including SMTP, X.400, and many others. For the most part, this page is used when you are configuring the SMTP Connector to be used with a foreign system. This aspect is covered in detail in Chapter 13, "Connecting with Other Messaging Systems." The Connected Routing Groups page is used instead when you are connecting two routing groups together.

CONNECTED ROUTING GROUPS PROPERTIES

If you do not configure an address space on the Address Space tab, you must configure which routing groups are connected to the local routing group using the Connected Routing Groups page (shown in Figure 8.14). This is a much better (and easier) way of handling routing between routing groups than using the Address Space page. The purpose of specifying connected routing groups is to inform the connector which routing groups are adjacent to it in order to enable internal routing of messages.

FIGURE 8.12 Advanced properties of the SMTP Connector

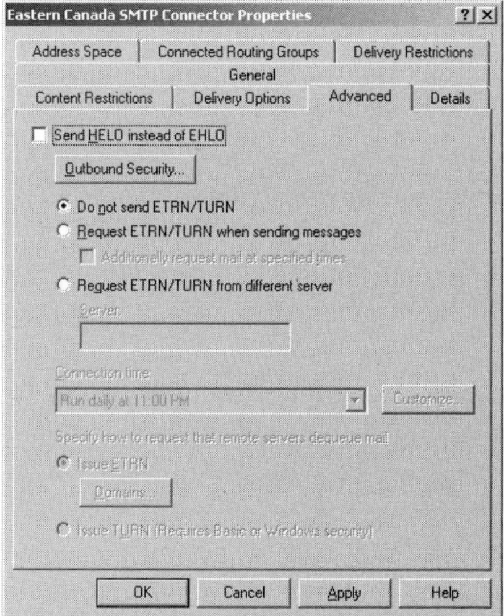

FIGURE 8.13 Address Space properties of the SMTP Connector

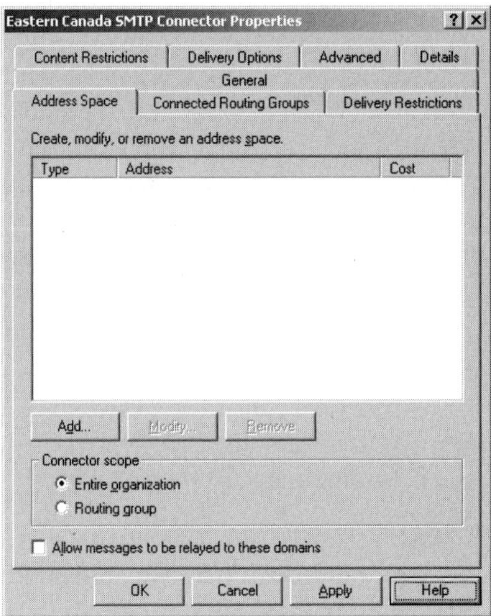

FIGURE 8.14 Connected Routing Groups properties of the SMTP Connector

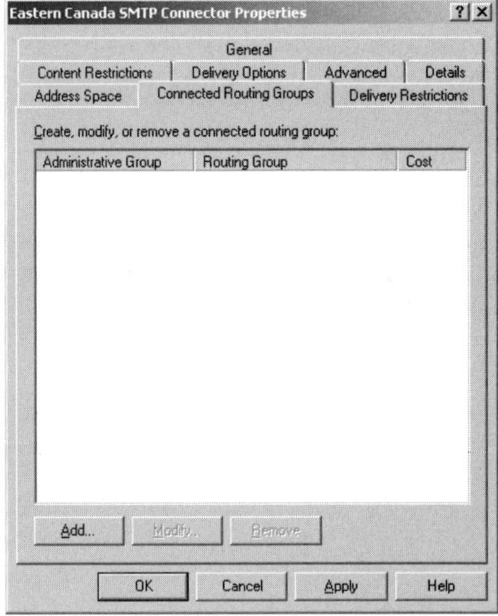

X.400 Connector

The X.400 Connector can be used to link Exchange routing groups and also to link an Exchange organization to a foreign, X.400-based messaging system. X.400 Connectors are useful for linking routing groups when there is very little bandwidth (less than 16 KB) available between servers or when X.400 is the only connectivity available. When linking routing groups with the X.400 Connector, you must designate a single server in each group as the bridgehead server. You must set up multiple X.400 Connectors between multiple servers in each routing group to gain a load-balancing feature.

Each end of an X.400 connection must be configured with the name of one remote Message Transfer Agent (MTA) to which it will connect. The local MTA name is assigned when an MTA Transport Stack is installed.

For details on the architecture of X.400, see Chapter 1, "Introduction to Microsoft Exchange."

Creating a Service Transport Stack

Creating an X.400 Connector to link routing groups is not too difficult. The one thing you must remember is that each end of an X.400 Connector must be configured separately and, unlike with the RGC, System Manager does not offer to do this for you automatically. To configure the X.400 Connector in Exchange Server 2003, you first must create an MTA *Service Transport Stack*. This transport stack is configured on a particular Exchange server and is basically a set of information about the software and hardware making up the underlying network. The use of the transport stack allows for a layer of abstraction between the X.400 Connector and the network itself.

Transport stacks exist at the server level and are associated with a particular Exchange server. This setup differs from the connector or connectors that will use the transport stack. Connectors exist at the routing group level. What this means to you is that multiple MTA Transport Stacks and X.400 Connectors can be configured within a routing group, giving you the ability to balance the load placed on servers by messaging connectors.

Exchange supports two different types of MTA Transport Stacks, each defined by the type of network hardware or software you have configured. The two types are as follows:

TCP/IP This type defines specifications for running OSI software, such as X.400 messaging systems, over a TCP/IP-based network. Microsoft Exchange Server 2003 uses Windows Server 2003 TCP/IP services.

TP0/X.25 This type uses an Eicon port adapter to provide both dial-up and direct communication in compliance with the OSI X.25 recommendation.

No matter which type of MTA Transport Stack you use, the configuration is nearly identical. Because it is easily the most-commonly installed, we cover the creation of a TCP/IP MTA Transport Stack in this chapter. Exercise 8.6 outlines the steps for creating a TCP/IP MTA Transport Stack.

EXERCISE 8.6

Creating a TCP/IP MTA Transport Stack

1. Click Start ➢ Programs ➢ Microsoft Exchange, and then select System Manager.
2. Expand the organization object in which you want to create a new administrative group.
3. Expand the Administrative Groups folder, the administrative group, and then the server on which you want to create the stack.
4. Expand the Protocols container, right-click the X.400 Container, and choose New TCP/IP X.400 Service Transport Stack from the context menu.
5. Use the property pages to configure the new transport stack.

Once the stack is created, you will manage it using two property pages: General and Connectors.

GENERAL PROPERTIES

The General property page, seen in Figure 8.15, is used to change the display name for the TCP Transport Stack and to configure OSI addressing information. Unless you plan to allow other applications besides Exchange Server 2003 to use the MTA Transport Stack, you do not need to worry about the OSI addressing values.

FIGURE 8.15 Examining the General properties of the TCP Transport Stack

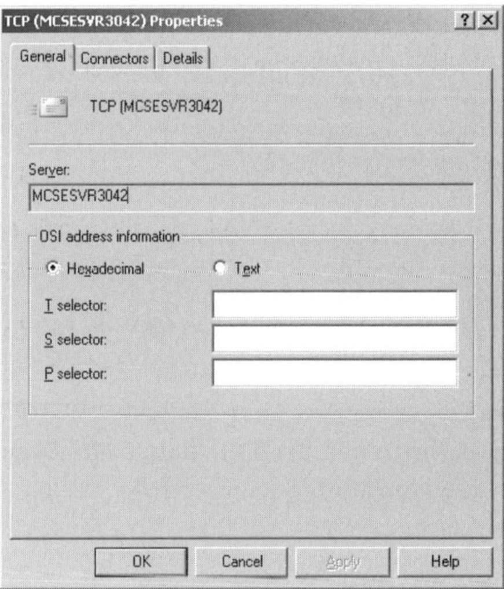

FIGURE 8.16 Viewing connectors for an MTA Transport Stack

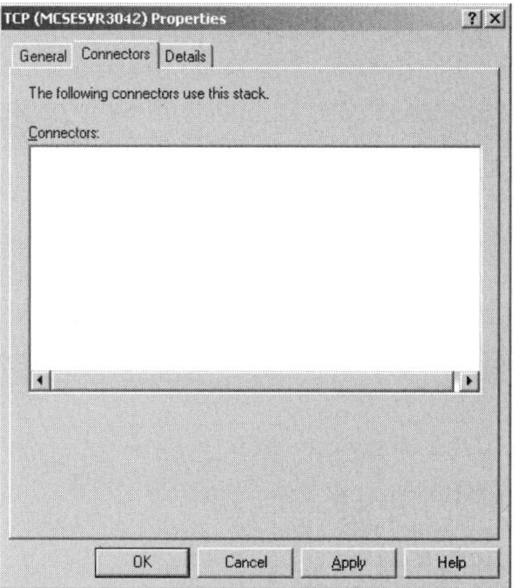

CONNECTORS PROPERTIES

The Connectors property page, shown in Figure 8.16, lists all of the messaging connectors in the routing group that are configured to use the current MTA Transport Stack. When you first create a stack, this list is blank. As new connectors are created that use the MTA Transport Stack, the connectors will be added to the list.

Creating an X.400 Connector

After you create an MTA Transport Stack, you must create the X.400 Connector itself. Exercise 8.7 outlines the steps involved.

EXERCISE 8.7

Creating a TCP/IP X.400 Connector

1. Click Start ➢ Programs ➢ Microsoft Exchange, and then select System Manager.
2. Expand the organization object, the Administrative Groups Folder, the specific administrative group, and the routing group for which you want to create the connector.
3. Right-click the Connectors container and choose the New TCP X.400 Connector command from the context menu.
4. This opens the property pages that you must configure for the new connector. After you have configured these pages, which are described in the next section, System Manager does not offer to automatically create a connector for the other end of the link. You must do this manually.

Configuring X.400 Connector Properties

Many of the property pages that you see for the X.400 Connector are used only when you are connecting your Exchange organization to a foreign X.400 messaging system, and they do not pertain to connecting two routing groups to one another. This section examines only the property pages and parameters that are relevant to connecting routing groups. Also, the Delivery Restrictions and Content Restrictions pages are identical to the pages of the same names for the Routing Group Connector.

GENERAL PROPERTIES

For the most part, the General property page, shown in Figure 8.17, does not hold any parameters that are useful when connecting routing groups. The exceptions are the following:

- You can enter the name of the connector only when you are creating the connector. This field is not editable after the connector is created.
- The X.400 Transport Stack setting lets you change the MTA Transport Stack that the X.400 Connector is currently configured to use. You can change the MTA Transport Stack at any time.
- The Do Not Allow Public Folder Referrals option works the same way as for the Routing Group Connector and the SMTP Connector.

FIGURE 8.17 The General properties of the X.400 TCP connector

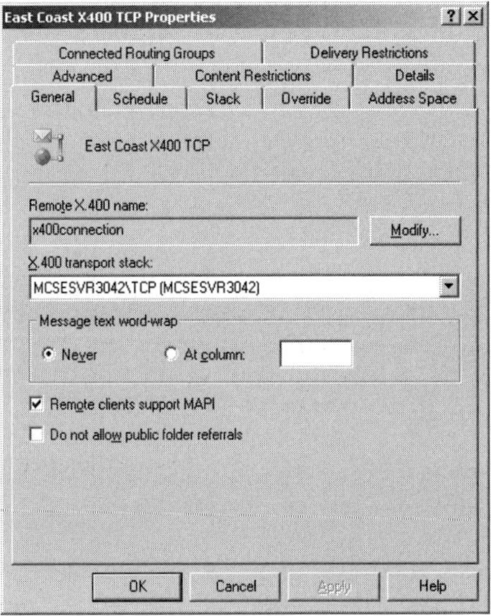

FIGURE 8.18 The Schedule properties of the X.400 TCP connector

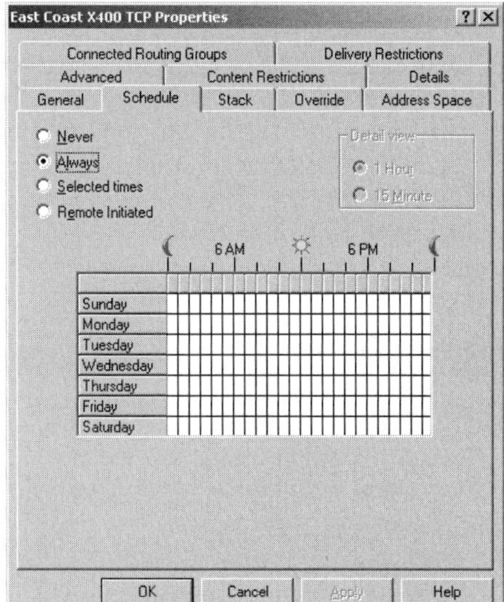

SCHEDULE PROPERTIES

The Schedule property page, shown in Figure 8.18, lets you restrict the times at which the X.400 Connector can be used. By default, the X.400 Connector can be used always and, for the most part, you will want to leave this value alone. There are times, however, when you may wish to limit connectivity, such as on a very busy network, or when you need to bring a network down for maintenance.

You can set an X.400 Connector schedule to one of four values:

- The Never option disables the connector altogether. It is useful for bringing down the connector while performing maintenance.
- The Always option allows connections to be made to and from the server at any time.
- The Selected Times option defines specific times at which the X.400 Connector is available. This can be useful on a busy network. If immediate messaging is not a concern, you can schedule messages to be sent only at specific periods during the day, when network traffic is otherwise low.
- The Remote Initiated setting allows remote servers to connect to the current server but does not allow the local server to initiate a connection.

FIGURE 8.19 Stack properties for an X.400 Connector

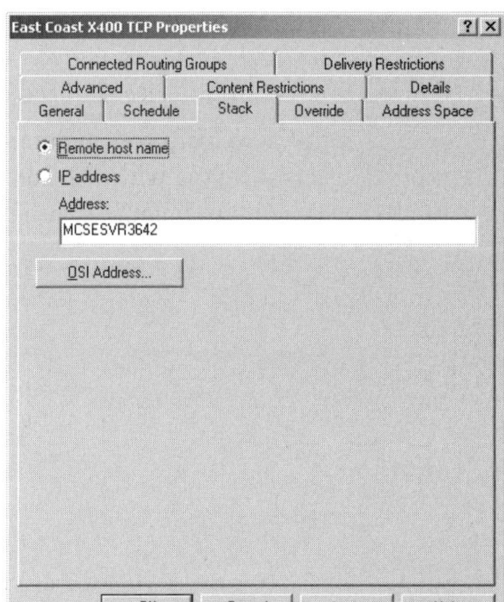

STACK PROPERTIES

The Stack property page, shown in Figure 8.19, is used to specify transport address information about the server in the other routing group. If you input an IP address instead of a host name, be sure to enclose it in brackets, such as [192.168.2.200].

CONNECTED ROUTING GROUPS PROPERTIES

Just as with the SMTP Connector, the purpose of specifying connected routing groups is to inform the connector which routing groups are adjacent to it in order to enable internal routing of messages. If you were not connecting routing groups, you would use the Address Space page to configure actual address spaces.

Summary

In previous versions of Exchange Server, the concept of a site was used to define both the physical routing boundaries of a group of well-connected servers and the administrative boundaries within an organization. In Exchange Server 2003, sites have been replaced by administrative groups, which are objects logically grouped together for permissions management, and routing groups, which are physical groupings of Exchange servers used to define routing boundaries.

The use of both types of groups depends on whether your organization is running in mixed mode or native mode. Mixed mode allows Exchange Server 2003 servers and servers running earlier versions of Exchange to coexist in the same organization. It allows this interoperability between versions by limiting functionality to features that both products share.

Microsoft defines three basic administrative models: centralized, decentralized, and mixed.

- In the centralized model, one administrator or group of administrators maintains complete control over an entire Exchange organization. This can be done with one administrative group or a few administrative groups created to make certain functions earlier.
- The decentralized model is typically used to define administrative boundaries along real geographical or departmental boundaries. Each location would have its own administrators and its own administrative group.
- The mixed model is really a catchall model for any other ways you can think of to use administrative groups. It is useful for when you do not necessarily want the tight control of the centralized model and the strict geographic division of the decentralized model is not appropriate.

By default, Exchange Server 2003 is configured with a single administrative group that is named First Administrative Group. You can add new administrative groups, name them what you want, and then create Public Folder, Routing Group, and Policy containers inside the new group. Once these are created, you can move resources from other groups into the new group.

A routing group is a collection of Exchange servers that have full-time, full-mesh, reliable connections between each and every server. Exchange servers in the same routing group must also belong to the same Active Directory forest.

You create routing groups in System Manager in much the same way as you create administrative groups. When created, they are simple containers waiting for you to fill them with servers.

Once your routing groups are defined, you must connect them together using one or more of three types of connectors. The Routing Group Connector (RGC) is the main connector used to connect routing groups and is the simplest to configure. It uses SMTP as its default transport mechanism but may also use a Remote Procedure Call (RPC) if the situation requires it. The SMTP Connector is a bit more involved to set up than the RGC and sports some different features. It is mainly used to connect routing groups where you want to force SMTP to be used for the transport mechanism. The X.400 Connector can be used to connect routing groups and to connect to a foreign system.

Exam Essentials

Understand the pros and cons of the various connectors. It is important to understand what is good and bad about each of the three types of connectors available in Exchange Server 2003. The Routing Group Connector (RGC) is the simplest to configure and manage and offers the ability to have Exchange create the other end of the connection automatically. RGCs work with both Exchange Server 2003 routing groups and Exchange Server 5.5 sites, using SMTP for the former and RPC for the latter—regardless of whether or not the Exchange Server 5.5 computers have SMTP installed. SMTP Connectors can be used to force an SMTP connection between routing groups and Exchange Server 5.5 sites and are also useful for establishing connectivity with foreign and Internet-based mail systems. SMTP Connectors also offer a wide array of configuration and security options that are not present in RGCs; this comes at the cost of more advanced skills required to configure and manage them as well as the fact the SMTP Connectors must be manually created for both ends of the connection. X.400 Connectors are useful in low-bandwidth situations, but like SMTP Connectors, they must be manually configured and managed on both ends of the connection. As well, X.400 Connectors require the presence of the X.400 stack before they can be created.

Know how operating in native mode changes the Exchange organization. At the cost of not allowing the coexistence with Exchange Server 5.5 computers, operating your Exchange Server 2003 organization in native mode is the best course of action. You gain the following capabilities when operating in native mode:

- A server can belong to an administrative group, but it does not have to belong to one of the routing groups within that administrative group.
- Administrative groups do not have to contain any routing groups.
- A single administrative group can contain all routing groups within the organization.
- You can move mailboxes between any servers in the organization.

Review Questions

1. You are configuring a connector between two routing groups that are in different buildings on your corporate campus. You have a dedicated, high-speed link between the buildings, but you have decided to create a routing group for each building anyway. You would like to use a connector that is fairly easy to set up and configure. What type of connector would you choose?

   A. Routing Group Connector

   B. Site Connector

   C. X.400 Connector

   D. SMTP Connector

2. Lou is managing mailboxes in an Exchange organization and needs to move several mailboxes to a server in a different administrative group. When he tries to move the mailboxes, System Manager returns an error. What is the cause of the problem?

   A. You can move mailboxes only between servers that are in the same administrative group.

   B. The organization is running in mixed mode.

   C. You cannot move mailboxes between servers, only between storage groups.

   D. You can move mailboxes only between servers that are in the same routing group.

3. Which of the following protocols can you use to create an MTA Transport Stack for an X.400 Connector? (Choose all that apply.)

   A. TCP/IP

   B. IPX

   C. X.25

   D. SMTP

4. Which of the following objects can an administrative group hold? (Choose all that apply.)

   A. Server container

   B. Recipients container

   C. System policy container

   D. Organization container

5. Which of the following connectors can be used to connect an Exchange organization to a foreign messaging system? (Choose all that apply.)

   A. Routing Group Connector

   B. SMTP Connector

   C. Active Directory Connector

   D. X.400 Connector

6. You are planning a large Exchange Server 2003 deployment. Your company has networks in four locations: New York, Toronto, London, and Madrid. Each of the locations has been configured as a Windows Active Directory domain in the same Active Directory forest. Each of the networks in the four locations is maintained within a central building and all computers within the buildings enjoy a high-bandwidth, full-time connection. There is a high-speed T1 line connecting New York with Toronto. There is a switched 256-KB connection between New York and London. The connection between Toronto and Madrid uses a low-bandwidth X.25 connection. Your design must group the servers in these various locations into routing groups, using the fewest routing groups possible. It is also desired, but not required, that your solution use the connectors that are the simplest to configure and maintain. You propose to perform the following actions:

   - Create a single routing group for each location: New York, Toronto, London, and Madrid.
   - Connect the New York and Toronto routing groups with a Routing Group Connector.
   - Connect the New York and London groups with an SMTP Connector. Connect the Toronto and Madrid groups with an X.25-based X.400 Connector.

   If you complete the proposed actions, will you have achieved the required and/or desired results?

   A. You will achieve both the required result and the desired result.

   B. You will achieve only the required result.

   C. You will achieve only the desired result.

   D. You will not achieve either the required result or the desired result.

7. You are planning a large Exchange Server 2003 deployment. Your company has networks in four locations: New York, Toronto, London, and Madrid. Each of the locations has been configured as a Windows Active Directory domain in the same Active Directory forest. Each of the networks in the four locations is maintained within a central building, and all computers within the buildings enjoy a high-bandwidth, full-time connection. There is a high-speed T1 line connecting New York with Toronto. There is a switched 256-KB connection between New York and London. The connection between Toronto and Madrid uses a low-bandwidth X.25 connection.

   Your design must group the servers in these various locations into routing groups, using the fewest routing groups possible. It is also desired, but not required, that your solution use the connectors that are the simplest to configure and maintain. You propose to perform the following actions:

   - Create a single routing group for the New York and Toronto locations. Create one routing group for the London location and one for the Madrid location.
   - Connect the New York/Toronto routing group to the London routing group with a Routing Group Connector.
   - Connect the New York/Toronto routing group to the Madrid routing group with an X.25-based X.400 Connector.

If you complete the proposed actions, will you have achieved the required and/or desired results?

A. You will achieve both the required result and the desired result.

B. You will achieve only the required result.

C. You will achieve only the desired result.

D. You will not achieve either the required result or the desired result.

8. You are planning a large Exchange Server 2003 deployment. Your company has networks in four locations: New York, Toronto, London, and Madrid. Each of the locations has been configured as a Windows Active Directory domain in the same Active Directory forest. Each of the networks in the four locations is maintained within a central building, and all computers within the buildings enjoy a high-bandwidth, full-time connection. There is a high-speed T1 line connecting New York with Toronto. There is a switched 256-KB connection between New York and London. The connection between Toronto and Madrid uses a low-bandwidth X.25 connection.

Your design must group the servers in these various locations into routing groups, using the fewest routing groups possible. It is also desired, but not required, that your solution use the connectors that are the simplest to configure and maintain. You propose to perform the following actions:

- Create a single routing group for the New York and Toronto locations.
- Create one routing group for the London location and one for the Madrid location.
- Connect the New York/Toronto routing group to the London routing group with an SMTP Connector.
- Connect the New York/Toronto routing group to the Madrid routing group with an X.25-based X.400 Connector.

If you complete the proposed actions, will you have achieved the required and/or desired results?

A. You will achieve both the required result and the desired result.

B. You will achieve only the required result.

C. You will achieve only the desired result.

D. You will not achieve either the required result or the desired result.

9. You have an organization that consists of three routing groups: RG1, RG2, and RG3. Two Routing Group Connectors are configured between RG1 and RG2. RGConnector1 is configured with a cost of 5. RGConnector2 is configured with a cost of 10. One Routing Group Connector, RGConnector3, is configured between RG2 and RG3. Its cost is 5. One SMTP Connector, SMTPConnector1, is also configured between RG2 and RG3. Its cost is 9. Which of the following preferred routes will a message take from RG1 to RG3?

A. RGConnector1, SMTPConnector1

B. RGConnector1, RGConnector3

C. RGConnector2, RGConnector3

D. RGConnector2, SMTPConnector1

10. You have a large network that is located in a single building in downtown Dallas. You also have a smaller network in a branch office in Houston. You have created two routing groups in the Dallas location to help direct the flow of messaging traffic and a single routing group in Houston. Four Exchange administrators work in Dallas, and one works in Houston. You want to create one administrative group for Houston and let that administrator handle all Exchange administration for that network. You would like one administrative group in Dallas, as well. However, you find that you must create another administrative group in Dallas to handle system policies since you want only the lead Exchange administrator to create system policies. Which of the following administrative models does this plan fall under?

A. Centralized

B. Decentralized

C. Mixed

11. Servers must meet which of the following criteria to be in the same routing group? (Choose all that apply.)

A. They must belong to the same Active Directory forest.

B. They must belong to the same Active Directory domain.

C. They must be capable of supporting SMTP connectivity.

D. They must all be in the same administrative group.

12. You are configuring a routing group to connect to a server in an Exchange 5.5 site. You want to ensure that the connector you use will definitely use SMTP and no other protocol to pass messages. Which of the following options is valid?

A. Configure a Routing Group Connector and specify that SMTP be used on the Protocols property page.

B. Configure a Routing Group Connector and specify that SMTP be used on the General property page.

C. Configure a Routing Group Connector and specify that SMTP be used on the Address Spaces property page.

D. Configure an SMTP Connector.

E. Configure an X.400 Connector.

13. You are currently running your Exchange organization in mixed mode and are considering making the switch to native mode. Which of the following would be valid concerns to take into account before making the switch? (Choose all that apply.)

A. The switch to native mode is irreversible.

B. Configuration and management of the Exchange organization is more complex when operating in native mode.

C. Exchange Server 5.5 cannot be run in a native-mode environment.

D. Exchange 2000 Server cannot be run in a native-mode environment.

14. You are configuring a connector between two routing groups and want to have servers issue authentication before sending any mail. Which connector allows this?

    A. Routing Group Connector

    B. SMTP Connector

    C. X.400 Connector

    D. Active Directory Connector

15. You are configuring an SMTP Connector. You do not want to allow the connector to use a DNS server to make direct connections to other SMTP servers. Instead, you want the connector to route mail to a specific SMTP server that will handle the messages. How would you do this?

    A. Configure a smart host on the connector's General property page.

    B. Configure a smart host on the connector's Hosts property page.

    C. Configure an MX Record on the connector's Delivery Options page.

    D. Use the connector's Delivery Restrictions page to reject messages from all except a specified server.

16. You are creating a series of connectors between two routing groups that have a fairly low-bandwidth connection. You want the connection to be available all the time, but you would like for messages over 5 MB to be sent only at specific times during the day. For which of the following connectors can you schedule the delivery of messages based on the size of the message?

    A. Routing Group Connector

    B. X.400 Connector

    C. SMTP Connector

17. You are running an Exchange organization in mixed mode. Previously, the organization consisted of four sites running Exchange Server 5.5. Now that you have installed Exchange Server 2003 into the organization, how many administrative groups can you configure?

    A. None

    B. One

    C. Four

    D. As many as you want

18. Which of the following connector types can use multiple bridgehead servers? (Choose all that apply.)

    A. Routing Group Connector

    B. SMTP Connector

    C. X.400 Connector

    D. TCP Connector

19. Which of the following is an extended SMTP command that is used to initiate an SMTP connection?

A. HELLO

B. HELO

C. EHLO

D. ELHO

20. What primary advantage does SMTP offer over RPCs for connectivity between servers within a routing group?

A. SMTP is faster.

B. SMTP does not require full-time connectivity.

C. SMTP does not require high-speed connectivity.

D. SMTP does not require reliable connectivity.

Answers to Review Questions

1. A. The Routing Group Connector is the fastest and simplest to set up. It also offers the ability to automatically configure the other end of a link once one end is set up.

2. B. When running in mixed mode, you can move mailboxes only between servers that are in the same administrative group.

3. A, C. Before creating an X.400 Connector, you must create an MTA Transport Stack. Both TCP/IP and X.25 Transport Stacks are available.

4. A, C. Administrative groups can contain servers, routing groups, public folder trees, and system policies.

5. B, D. Both the SMTP and X.400 Connectors can be used to connect routing groups together and to connect to foreign messaging systems. The Routing Group Connector can be used only to connect routing groups. The Active Directory Connector is used to connect an Exchange 5.5 site to Active Directory.

6. D. Since New York and Toronto enjoy a permanent, high-speed T1 connection between them, it is possible to configure them to be part of the same routing group; thus the required result of using the fewest groups possible is not met. The connector used between the New York/Toronto routing group and the London routing group should be a Routing Group Connector because it meets the optional result of using a connector that is the simplest to configure and maintain. The connector between the New York/Toronto routing group and the Madrid routing group should be an X.25-based X.400 Connector that supports both X.25 networks and the low-bandwidth connection.

7. A. Since New York and Toronto enjoy a permanent, high-speed T1 connection between them, it is possible to configure them to be part of the same routing group; thus the required result of using the fewest groups possible is met. The connector used between the New York/Toronto routing group and the London routing group should be a Routing Group Connector because it meets the optional result of using a connector that is the simplest to configure and maintain. The connector between the New York/Toronto routing group and the Madrid routing group should be an X.25-based X.400 Connector that supports both X.25 networks and the low-bandwidth connection.

8. B. Since New York and Toronto enjoy a permanent, high-speed T1 connection between them, it is possible to configure them to be part of the same routing group, so the required result of using the fewest possible groups is met. London and Madrid should be configured as individual routing groups. The connector used between the New York/Toronto routing group and the London routing group should be a Routing Group Connector because it meets the optional result of using a connector that is the simplest to configure and maintain.

9. B. Messages are sent over the preferred connectors when possible, and the preferred connectors are those with the lowest costs, regardless of what type of connector they are.

10. C. A centralized model is one where there is one administrative group or a tightly controlled set of groups used for functional purposes. A decentralized model is one where an administrative group is created for each of a set of geographical or departmental entities. A mixed model is one where both techniques are used. Since a group is being created for Houston and a main group is being created for Dallas, that makes the example at least partially decentralized. However, since another group is being created in Dallas for purely functional reasons, that makes it a mixed model.

11. A, C. In order to be in the same routing group, all servers must have reliable, permanent, and direct network connectivity that supports SMTP. They must also belong to the same Active Directory forest and be able to connect to a routing group master.

12. D. The only connector that you can force to use SMTP is the SMTP Connector. Actually, you don't force it; it's the only protocol it supports. This makes it ideal when you need to configure a connector to use SMTP between a routing group and an Exchange 5.5 site because the Routing Group Connector will default to RPC in this situation when an SMTP connection cannot be established.

13. A, C. The switch to native mode is a one-time, one-way switch and is irreversible. When your Exchange organization is configured for native mode, only Exchange Server 2003 and Exchange 2000 Server computers can be used in the organization.

14. B. The SMTP Connector is more configurable than the Routing Group Connector, offering the ability for more fine-tuning of the connection. The SMTP Connector offers the ability to issue authentication before sending mail, specifying TLS encryption, and removing mail from queues on remote servers.

15. A. To forward mail upstream to another SMTP server instead, select the Forward All Mail Through This Connector To The Following Smart Host option on the General property page for the connector. Also, you might want to specify the IP address instead of the name for the smart host so that no DNS query is required to resolve the name.

16. A. Although you can schedule delivery times on each of the connectors, only the Routing Group Connector also allows you to create a special schedule based on message size.

17. C. Each Exchange 5.5 site in the organization is mapped directly to a single administrative group and a single routing group, and vice versa.

18. A, B. Both the Routing Group Connector and the SMTP Connector can be configured to use multiple source and destination bridgehead servers. The X.400 Connector can support only one bridgehead server. There is no such thing as a TCP Connector.

19. C. Normally, an SMTP client connects to an SMTP server using a command named HELO, which signals the start of a session between two SMTP servers and identifies the sender of the coming message. By default, Exchange Server 2003 sends the EHLO command, another start command that indicates the Exchange Server 2003 computer can use the Extended SMTP (ESMTP) commands.

20. C. The primary advantage of SMTP over RPCs to transfer messages between servers in a routing group is its ability to transfer messages over slower connections than RPCs allow.

Configuring the Information Store

MICROSOFT EXAM OBJECTIVES COVERED IN THIS CHAPTER:

- ✓ **Manage, monitor, and troubleshoot data storage**

In Exchange Server 2003, the Information Store is the service responsible for storing data in the proper places and maintaining the integrity of that data once stored. Unlike Exchange Server 5.5, which supported only one private storage database and one public storage database per server, Exchange Server 2003 allows for the creation of multiple stores of each type on a server and the grouping of those stores into storage groups. It is these changes to the storage architecture that provide Exchange Server 2003 with much greater scalability and flexibility than previous versions. Also, these changes make new methods of accessing data—such as from standard Windows applications—possible.

This chapter provides a brief overview of how storage groups and stores interact and what you can do with them. It then looks at the creation, configuration, and management of both storage groups and stores. Finally, it examines a form of content indexing known as full-text indexing, which Exchange uses to provide greater search capabilities within the Information Store.

Overview of Storage Groups and Stores

Exchange Server 2003 Enterprise Edition supports up to four storage groups on a server and up to five stores in each storage group, providing great flexibility in the storage design and planning. Before we get started with the actual process of creating and managing storage groups and stores, though, it is important to become familiar with the major components in the Exchange storage system and the method Exchange uses to store data.

This chapter deals mainly with the procedures for creating and managing storage groups and stores. Although this overview provides a brief look at how Exchange storage works, it is also important that you are familiar with the architectural concepts discussed in the "Information Storage" section of Chapter 2, "Microsoft Exchange Architecture."

Main Storage Components

The *Information Store* is a Windows service that provides storage management on an Exchange Server 2003 server. It is an actual process, named *Store.exe*, that runs on the server. The Information Store is responsible for making sure that data is placed into transaction logs, that transaction log entries are committed to actual Exchange database files, and that routing maintenance is performed on those files.

A *store* is a logical database that is actually made up of two database files: a *rich-text file* (`*.edb`) and a *streaming media file* (`*.stm`). You learned about these files in Chapter 2, so we won't go into too much detail about them here; in short, the rich-text file is used for holding standard Exchange content (such as messages), and the streaming media file is used for holding other types of content in its native format so that Exchange does not have to spend time converting it.

There are two types of stores that you can create on an Exchange server: public and private. *Public stores* are used to hold public folders that are generally accessible by multiple users. *Private stores* are used to hold mailboxes that are normally accessible only by a specified user. Unlike previous versions of Exchange, Exchange Server 2003 allows you to create multiple stores of each type on a single server.

This ability to create multiple stores leads to several benefits:

- User downtime in the event of a failure is decreased because a failure in one store does not affect users of another store.
- Backup and restore routines are typically faster and more flexible because you can back up or restore a single store at a time without affecting other stores. For example, backing up one out of four 10-GB stores at different times of the day is often better than backing up a single 40-GB store.
- You can assign different general settings to different stores. For example, you might configure one private store for general use and another for use only by executives. The general store might have certain limitations placed on it that the executive store would not.

Exchange Server 2003 Enterprise Edition supports multiple mailbox stores and multiple private stores on a single server. Exchange Server 2003 Standard Edition supports only two databases in a single storage group. In addition, the single mailbox store allowed in the Standard edition is limited to 16 GB in size, while the Enterprise edition allows mailbox stores of any size.

A *storage group* is a logical grouping of stores that share the same set of transaction log files, as shown in Figure 9.1. You can create up to four storage groups on a single server, and each storage group can hold up to five stores. The primary reason behind the use of storage groups is to reduce the amount of server overhead that would be caused if every store had its own set of transaction logs, resulting in greater scalability. There are some additional advantages to using multiple storage groups:

- You can manage the stores in a storage group as a group or individually.
- You can configure different properties for the transaction logs of different groups. For example, suppose you have one storage group that contains only public folders that would not be impacted too much by the use of circular logging. You could then configure another storage group to hold more critical mailbox stores for which circular logging would be disabled.

FIGURE 9.1 Storage groups hold stores that share a single set of transaction logs.

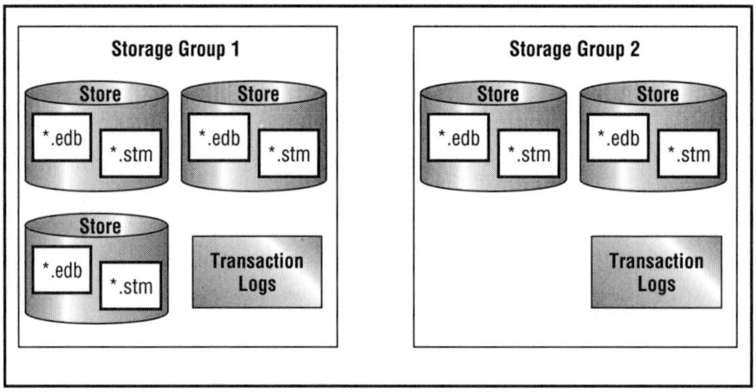

Exchange Storage Methods

When data is to be written to one of the Exchange databases, the database engine does not write the data to the database file immediately. The data is first *committed* (or written) to a *transaction log file* and then later committed to the database through a background process. This method has two advantages, one of which is performance. When data is written to a transaction log file, it is entered sequentially, always at the end of the file. This can be done very fast. When data is committed to a database file, however, the database engine must search for the appropriate location to place the data. This is much slower than the simple sequential method. The second advantage is fault tolerance. If a database file becomes corrupt, a transaction log file can be used to re-create the database file.

As transactions in transaction log files are committed to the database files, a *checkpoint file* (EDB.CHK) is updated. The checkpoint file keeps track of which transactions in the sequential list still need to be committed to a database by maintaining a pointer to the last information that was committed. This tells the engine that everything after that point still needs to be committed to a database. If a server shuts down abnormally, Exchange can read the checkpoint file to learn where in the transaction logs it needs to start recovering data. Thus the checkpoint file assists in the fault tolerance of Exchange.

Transaction log files can contain up to 5 MB of transactions, and they are always 5 MB in size no matter how many transactions they contain. This is because the engine creates them as 5 MB files and then proceeds to fill them with transactions. The current log file being written to is named EDB.LOG. When it is filled with 5 MB of transactions, it is renamed to EDB*nnnnn*.LOG (where *nnnnn* is a hexadecimal number), and a new, empty EDB.LOG file is created. Therefore, the log files will accumulate on the hard disk. A way to minimize this is to perform regular full or incremental backups of the databases. During a full or incremental backup, fully committed log files are automatically flushed (deleted) because the data in them is backed up. This prevents the number of log files from growing until they take up the entire disk.

Circular Logging

Transaction log files can also be configured to recycle themselves to prevent constant accumulation on the hard disk. This process is called *circular logging*. Instead of continually creating new log files and storing the old ones, the database engine "circles back" to the oldest log file that has been fully committed and overwrites that file. Circular logging minimizes the number of transaction log files on the disk at any given time. The downside is that these logs cannot be used to re-create a database, because the logs do not have a complete set of data. They have only the data not yet committed. Another disadvantage of circular logging is that it does not permit a differential or incremental backup of the databases.

Circular logging is disabled by default and can be enabled or disabled on a store's General property page (discussed later in the chapter). Table 9.1 presents a summary and comparison of when circular logging is enabled and disabled.

Reserve Log Files

One other feature of the transaction-based databases is the use of *reserve log files*. Exchange creates two reserve log files (`RES1.LOG` and `RES2.LOG`) for each database. They are used if the system runs out of disk space. If that happens, Exchange shuts down the database service, logs an event to the Event Log, and writes any outstanding transaction information into these reserve log files. These two files reserve an area of disk space that can be used after the rest of the disk space is used.

TABLE 9.1 Circular Logging Enabled vs. Disabled

Circular Logging Enabled	Circular Logging Disabled (default)
Transaction log files are recycled.	Old transaction log files are stored.
The re-creation of a database is not permitted.	The re-creation of a database is permitted.
Differential or incremental backups are not permitted.	Differential and incremental backups are permitted.
	A full or incremental backup automatically deletes old transaction log files.

Using Storage Groups

Since storage groups are basically containers that hold stores, they are fairly simple to create, and there is not much to manage about them other than a few simple details. This section describes the creation, configuration, and management of storage groups.

Creating a Storage Group

By default, a single storage group is created on each server and is named First Storage Group. Since every storage group is created on and associated with a single server, you will always find storage group containers inside a server container in the System Manager snap-in, as shown in Figure 9.2.

FIGURE 9.2 Storage groups always belong to a specific server.

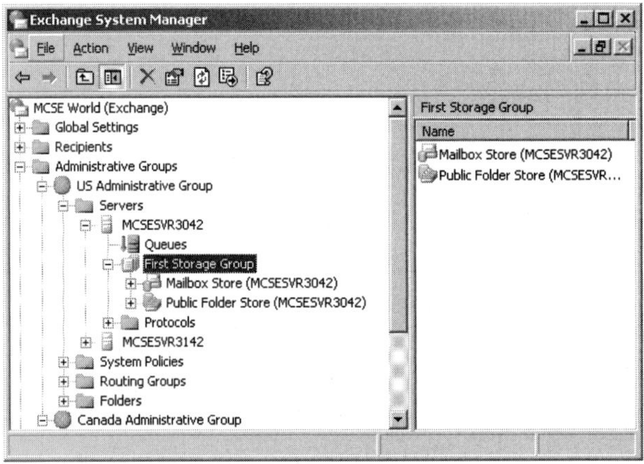

Exercise 9.1 outlines the steps for creating a new storage group.

EXERCISE 9.1

Creating a New Storage Group

1. Click Start ➤ Programs ➤ Microsoft Exchange, and then select System Manager.
2. Expand the organization object, the Administrative Groups folder, the specific administrative group, and the server on which you want to add a storage group.
3. Right-click the server object and select the New Storage Group command from the context menu. This opens the property pages for the new storage group.
4. Type a name for the new storage group in the Name field and click OK. This creates the storage group using the default properties suggested by System Manager.

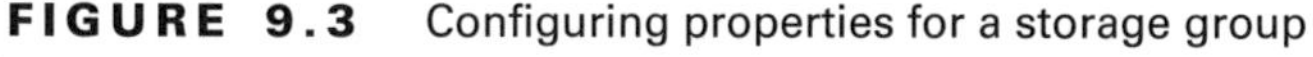

FIGURE 9.3 Configuring properties for a storage group

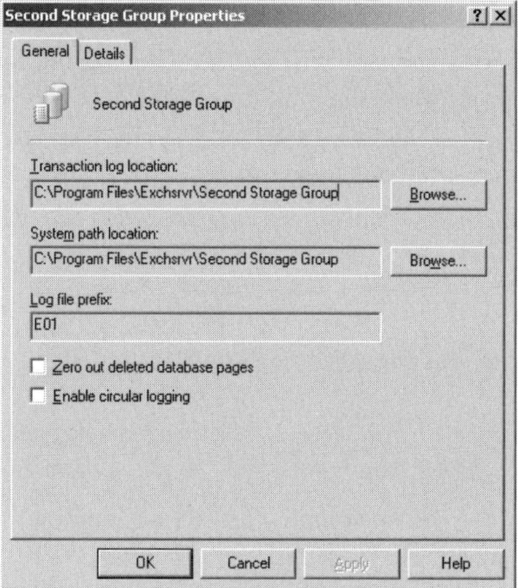

Configuring Storage Group Properties

There is only one property page that has useful configuration options on it for a storage group—the General page, shown in Figure 9.3. You are given the chance to configure it when you first create the storage group, and you can change the properties later by right-clicking the storage group object and choosing Properties from the context menu.

On the General page for a storage group, you can configure the following parameters:

- You can name the storage group during its creation. If the organization is running in native mode, you can change the name of the storage group at any time. If the organization is running in mixed mode, you cannot change the name after creation.
- The transaction log location is the directory in which the transaction log file for the storage group resides. By default, a location is created for the log file based on the name you give the storage group. You can change this location during creation of the storage group or any time after creation.
- The system path location is where any temporary database files (named `TMP.EDB`) and checkpoint files (named `EDB.CHK`) are stored. You can change this location during or after creation.
- The log file prefix is chosen by the system and cannot be altered. It designates the prefix attached to the log file for the group.
- The Zero Out Deleted Database Pages option is used to remove all 4-KB pages of data for items when they are deleted from a database. This option automatically writes zeros to these pages within all stores of the storage group. This process occurs after an online backup is performed. This means that the database pages on the backup are not zeroed

until the next backup. Be careful using this option, though, because it can significantly reduce your server performance.

- As mentioned earlier, circular logging enables Exchange to conserve disk space by maintaining a fixed number of transaction logs and overwriting those logs as needed. Without circular logging, Exchange creates new log files when old ones fill up. Circular logging is disabled by default, and it is generally recommended that you leave it disabled except possibly for storage groups that contain only public stores with noncritical data, such as Internet newsgroups.

Using Stores

The default storage group, named First Storage Group, is created during Exchange installation. Two stores are also created within that storage group:

- A public store named Public Folder Store *(servername)*. This store is made up of two databases, `pub1.edb` and `pub1.stm`, which are stored in the `\Program Files\Exchsrvr\Mdbdata` folder.
- A mailbox store named Mailbox Store *(servername)*. This store is made up of two databases, `priv1.edb` and `priv1.stm`, which are also stored in the `\Program Files\Exchsrvr\Mdbdata` folder.

You can create up to three new stores in the First Storage Group (unless you first delete the default stores), and you can create new stores in other storage groups, as well. The process for creating a private store and a mailbox store is identical and, for the most part, so is the configuration of the two different types of stores. In the sections that follow, we cover the creation, configuration, and management of a new mailbox store. When configuring a public store, many of the properties you will configure and much of the management are identical. Some differences in the configuration, such as the replication of public folders, were discussed earlier in Chapter 6, "Using Public Folders."

Creating a Store

Creating a new store is a straightforward process. You need only make sure that you are creating the store in a storage group with room for another store. Exercise 9.2 outlines the steps for creating a new mailbox store.

EXERCISE 9.2

Creating a New Mailbox Store

1. Click Start > Programs > Microsoft Exchange, and then select System Manager.
2. Expand the organization object, the Administrative Groups folder, the specific administrative group, and the server on which you want to add a store.

EXERCISE 9.2 *(continued)*

3. Right-click the storage group object in which you want to create the store and select the New Mailbox Store command from the context menu. This opens the property pages for the new store.

4. Type a name for the new mailbox store in the Name field of the General page and click OK. This creates the store using the default properties suggested by System Manager.

Configuring Store Properties

There are a number of property pages used to configure a mailbox store. You are given the chance to configure these pages when you first create the store and can change the properties later by right-clicking the store object and choosing Properties from the context menu. The following sections detail the parameters found on many of these property pages. For information on configuring the Policies and Security pages, see Chapter 10, "Administration and Maintenance."

General Properties

A mailbox store's General page, shown in Figure 9.4, is used to configure the following properties:

- You can name the store during its creation. As with storage groups, you can change the name of a store after creation only if the organization is running in native mode.
- Every Exchange user must have a default public store that is used for public folder access. This does not limit access to only the chosen public store but rather provides an entry point—the first place the client will look for public folder content. Click the Browse button to open a list of available public stores from which to choose.
- The Offline Address List field specifies the default offline address list that users of this mailbox store will download when synchronizing the Offline Address List on their client. Like the public folder setting, this is simply a default value and does not prevent other available offline address lists from being used.
- You have the option to Archive All Messages Sent Or Received By Mailboxes On This Store to a public folder. While this does increase the use of server resources and possibly increase network traffic, it also provides a way of logging e-mail sent in your organization—something your lawyers will love and your users will hate.
- *Secure/Multipurpose Internet Mail Extensions (S/MIME)* is a secure version of the MIME protocol that supports encryption of messages. It is expected that S/MIME will be widely implemented, which will make it possible for people to send secure e-mail messages to one another, even if they are using different e-mail clients.
- The final option, Display Plain Text Messages In A Fixed-Size Font, displays all messages sent using plain text in the 10-pt. Courier font, which makes reading many e-mail clients a bit easier.

FIGURE 9.4 General properties of a mailbox store

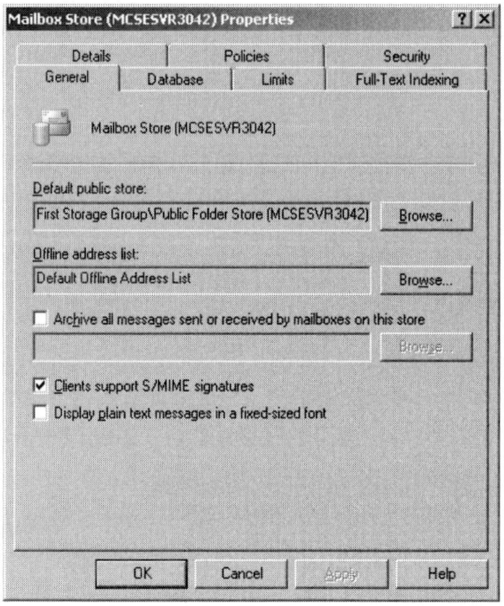

Database Properties

The mailbox store's Database page, shown in Figure 9.5, has controls that govern how Exchange handles the databases for the store. You can change the location and name of both the rich-text database and the streaming file database. One caveat, though: In order to move a database, you must be running System Manager on the server that holds the database you want to move.

You can also use the Database page to specify the times at which you want the automatic store maintenance routines to run. Select from several preset values using the drop-down list, or click Customize to bring up a calendar-style interface. Finally, you can set options for whether to mount the store when the Exchange server starts up (if it doesn't, you'll have to do it manually) and whether the store can be overwritten during a restore from backup. Check out Chapter 14, "Backup and Recovery," for more on backup and recovery.

Limits Properties

The Limits page, shown in Figure 9.6, should look familiar to you. It is used to configure the same types of limits that you can set on individual mailboxes, as discussed in Chapter 5, "Creating and Managing Recipients." At the mailbox level, you can set values that override any values you configure on this page, or you can elect to use the store defaults.

This page lets you set two parameters: storage limits and deletion settings. Storage limits refer to the limits (in kilobytes) placed on the size that mailboxes in the store can grow to and what happens when that limit is crossed. By default, no limits are set. You can set limits for when a warning is issued, when sending is prohibited, and when sending and receiving are prohibited. You can also configure the interval at which the Information Store checks these values and issues warnings.

FIGURE 9.5 Database properties of a mailbox store

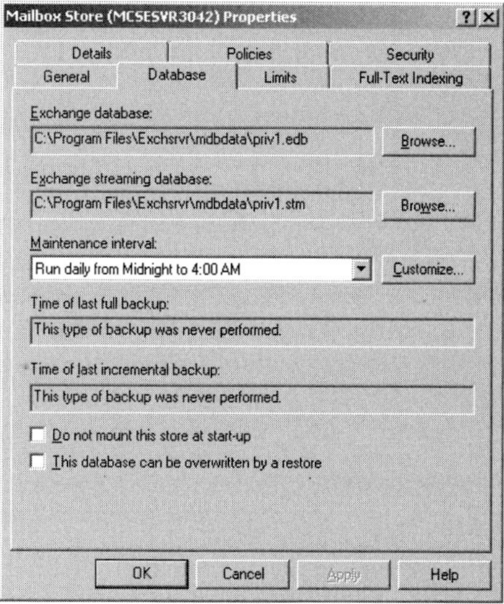

Deletion settings refer to how long (in days) deleted items in a mailbox and deleted mailboxes are retained on a server after a user or administrator deletes them. You can also configure the store to keep deleted items and mailboxes until the store has been backed up, regardless of the actual values entered.

FIGURE 9.6 Limits properties of a mailbox store

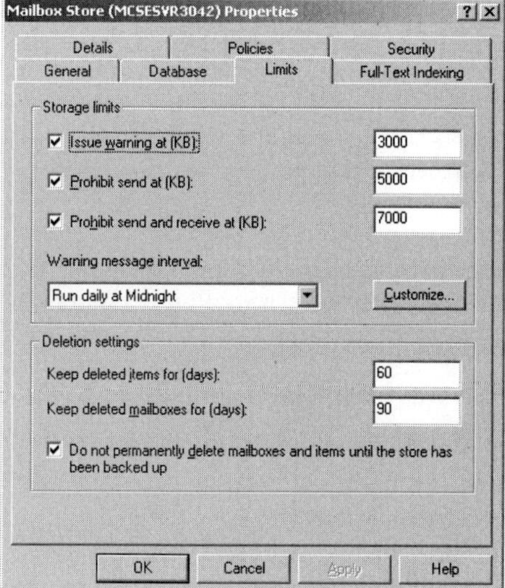

FIGURE 9.7 Full-text indexing properties of a mailbox store

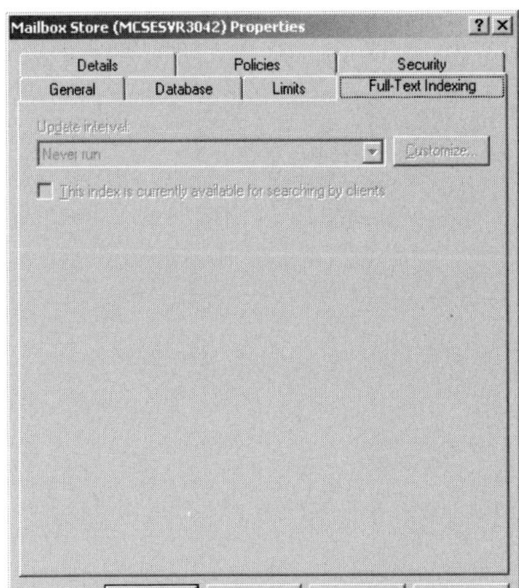

Full-Text Indexing Properties

The Full-Text Indexing page, shown in Figure 9.7, is unavailable for configuration until you create a full-text index on the store. We will examine full-text indexing later in this chapter.

Managing Stores and Storage Groups

Once created and properly configured, both storage groups and stores require proper management to keep everything running smoothly. Much of this management is covered elsewhere in this book:

- Backing up and restoring (Chapter 14)
- Managing public folders and replication (Chapter 6, "Using Public Folders")
- Managing individual users and their mailboxes (Chapter 6)
- Tracking messages and monitoring the status of message flow (Chapter 10)
- Configuring client access to the store data (Chapter 7, "Configuring Client Access")

FIGURE 9.8 Viewing logon information for a store

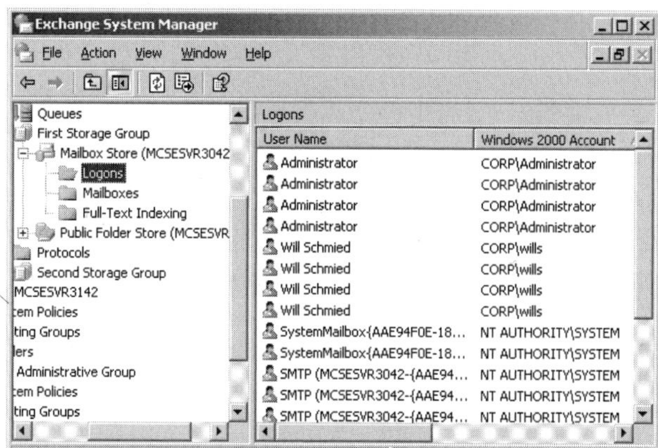

Viewing Logon Information

In the store container itself, a number of objects provide some management and monitoring ability over the store. The Logons container, shown in Figure 9.8, shows information regarding who has logged on to the mailbox store. Among other things, this information includes the username, the logon time, the logoff time, and the type of client used to connect.

Aside from these major administrative functions, other administrative tidbits regarding stores and storage groups are covered in the next few sections.

Viewing and Managing Mailbox Information

The Mailboxes container for a store, shown in Figure 9.9, shows all of the mailboxes configured in the store. Along with the actual mailbox name, you can see who last logged on to the mailbox, how much space the mailbox takes up on the server, how many actual items are in the mailbox, and the last logon/logoff times for the mailbox.

You cannot manage these mailboxes the same way you could in previous versions of Exchange. In fact, there are not even property pages to open. Almost all mailbox administration is performed using the Active Directory Users and Computers tool and the techniques described in Chapter 5.

However, there are two things that you can do to a mailbox from within System Manager. The first is to delete it, though this is called *purging* within the context of System Manager. To do this, right-click the mailbox and select Purge from the context menu.

FIGURE 9.9 Viewing mailbox information for a store

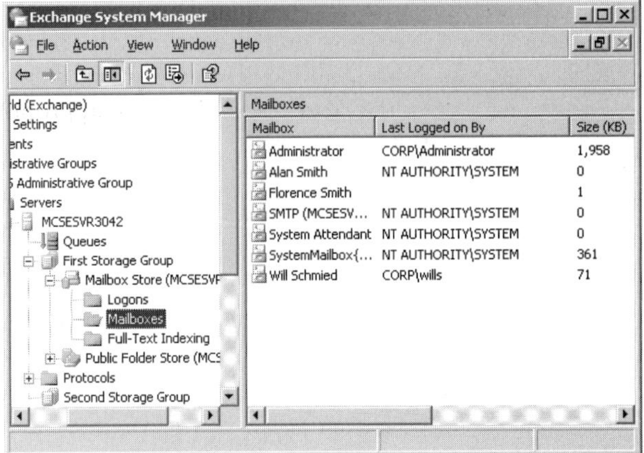

Once a mailbox is purged, it cannot be recovered.

Mailboxes can also be deleted from within Active Directory Users and Computers, although mailboxes deleted in this manner are not really deleted; they are simply disconnected from the user. This leads us to the second function that you can perform on mailboxes in System Manager, which is to reconnect a disconnected mailbox. Do this by right-clicking the mailbox and selecting Reconnect from the context menu.

This business with purging, deleting, disconnecting, and reconnecting brings up not only an interesting interface design point but something to be careful with on the exam. Why didn't Microsoft simply choose to call it deleting a mailbox in System Manager and disconnecting a mailbox in Active Directory Users and Computers? After all, purging a mailbox makes it sound like you are removing all the messages inside the mailbox. Whatever the reasons, this kind of confusing language and inconsistency can trip you up in real life and on the exam. On the exam, pay particular attention to the context of questions. For example, if an exam questions asks whether you can recover a deleted mailbox, paying close attention may clue you in to whether they really mean a deleted (purged) mailbox or a disconnected (deleted) mailbox.

Mounting and Dismounting Stores

One of the great advantages of having multiple stores is that individual stores can be taken down for maintenance without affecting other stores on the server. Taking a store offline is referred to as *dismounting*, and bringing it back online is referred to as *mounting*. To mount or dismount a store, simply right-click the store and choose the appropriate option from the context menu.

Deleting Mailbox Stores

To delete a mailbox store, just right-click it and choose Delete from the context menu. Before you can do this, however, you must either delete or move all mailboxes within that store. System Manager will not let you delete a store that contains mailboxes. In addition, if the store being deleted has any messages currently queued for outbound delivery, you will be informed that these messages will be lost if you proceed. If you choose to delete the store anyway, you will be asked to select a new store to be used for any messages in the inbound queue.

Deleting Public Folder Stores

Deleting public stores is a little more complicated than deleting mailbox stores. To begin with, the actual command is the same; right-click the store and choose the Delete command. However, there are several restrictions governing the process:

- The store cannot be the only store that contains a public folder tree.
- The store must not be the default public store for any mailbox stores or users.
- Before you can remove a public store that contains system folders, you must select a new public store for those folders.
- If the public store holds the only available replica of a public folder, you will be warned that all data in that folder will be lost.

When you delete a store, Exchange will not delete the actual database files for you. You will need to manually do this in order to reclaim that disk space.

Deleting a Storage Group

You can delete any storage group by right-clicking it and choosing Delete from the context menu. However, the storage group must not have any stores associated with it. This means you must first remove all stores in the storage group before you can delete the group itself.

Using Stores and Storage Groups

Many different theories abound on how you should configure your Exchange organization's storage groups and stores. We'll examine some cold hard facts here and then let you make the determination that provides the best solution for your organization's needs.

A storage group, no matter how many stores are in it, uses only one set of transaction logs. This is a good thing until you need to configure circular logging for any reason. Circular logging is configured at the storage group level and thus applies equally to all stores inside that storage group. This can become a large problem should that storage group happen to contain critical e-mail stores. In reality, is there such a thing anymore as a noncritical e-mail store? For your stores on which you wish to configure circular logging—think public folder stores, especially those housing Internet newsgroups—you should consider creating a storage group just to hold them. Public folders were discussed at length previously in Chapter 6.

When it comes to performing backups of the Exchange organization, you should be aware that backups can be configured only at the storage group level. Thus, you have the option to back up only an entire storage group and its stores, not individual stores within the storage group. However, when performing a restoration, you can opt to restore only specific stores within the storage group. The fact that storage groups are backed up as a whole can have an impact on the length of time required to perform your backups, especially when performing full (normal) backups. We will examine the topic of Exchange backup and restoration more in Chapter 14.

The combination of storage groups and stores that you ultimately configure will depend on the needs of your network.

Full-Text Indexing

Any client can search the Exchange databases for information by default. However, Exchange Server 2003 also provides a feature called *full-text indexing*, in which every word in a store (including those in attachments) is indexed for much faster search results.

Some of the key benefits provided by full-text indexing include:

- Indexing is configured on a store-by-store basis, allowing you control which stores get indexed and which do not. As well, you can individually configure how often the index is updated and where the index is to be kept for each store configured for indexing.
- Searches are faster because they are performed against a prepopulated index instead of the raw database itself.
- Searching is done for related words as well, increasing the chance of locating the desired information.

- Searching of many common document types is provided for those documents contained in the store, such as e-mail attachments and documents located within a public folder. The following file formats are indexed: ASP, DOC, EML, HTM, HTML, PPT, TXT, and XLS.

While full-text indexing does provide significant advantages, there are a few considerations you must make before you decide to use it:

- Building and updating the index consumes server resources. For large stores, the CPU usage and time involved in creating the index can be considerable.
- An indexed store requires about 20 percent more disk space than a nonindexed store.
- During the time that a store is being indexed or updated, clients may receive incomplete search results. Also, in general, search results are accurate only up to the time the store was last indexed.

Creating a Full-Text Index

Exercise 9.3 outlines the steps for creating a full-text index for a mailbox store.

EXERCISE 9.3

Creating a Full-Text Index for a Mailbox Store

1. Click Start ➢ Programs ➢ Microsoft Exchange, and then select System Manager.
2. Expand the organization object, the Administrative Groups folder, the specific administrative group, the server, and the storage group that contains the store you want to index.
3. Right-click the store and select the Create Full-Text Index command from the context menu.
4. In the dialog that opens, either type a path for the location of the index catalog or accept the default location, and then click OK.

Configuring Properties for a Full-Text Index

Once the full-text index is created (and this can take some time, depending on the size of the store being indexed), you can configure indexing properties by opening the property pages for the store and switching to the Full-Text Indexing page, shown in Figure 9.10. This page holds two parameters you can configure:

- The Update Interval option is used to schedule the interval at which changes in the store are added to the index.
- The This Index Is Currently Available For Searching By Clients option opens the index for searching. It is recommended that you disable this during the initial creation of the index and also during complete rebuilds of the index. This helps prevent incomplete searches being returned to clients who perform searches while the index is being built.

FIGURE 9.10 Viewing full-text indexing information for a store

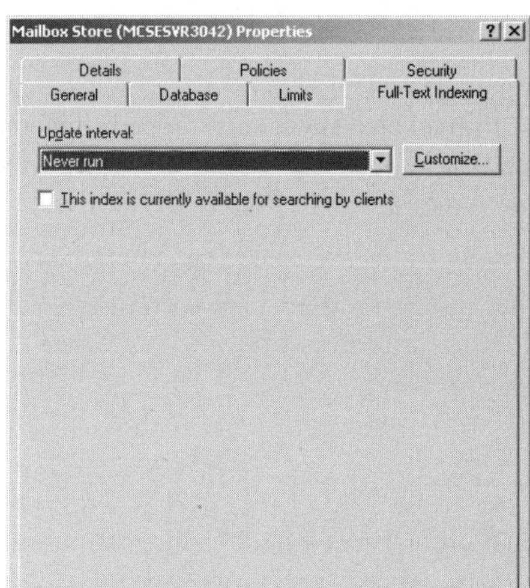

Managing a Full-Text Index

When you right-click a store for which full-text indexing has been enabled, several management tasks are available to you on the context menu that opens. These tasks include the following:

- Start Incremental Population, which finds any changed information in the store and adds it to the index.
- Start Full Population, which rebuilds the entire index. During this process, Exchange purges the index one document at a time instead of purging the entire index and then rebuilding it. This helps speed up the rebuilding process.
- Pause Population, which stops any population process that is currently happening without causing any loss of indexing.
- Stop Population, which halts any population process that is currently happening and causes any updates to be lost.
- Delete Full-Text Index, which deletes the index catalog associated with the store.

Troubleshooting Full-Text Indexing

Two tools will be helpful to you in troubleshooting problems with full-text indexing: Gather files and Application Logs.

Gather files Gather files are created whenever a full-text index is built and contain a record of errors encountered during indexing. These files are located in the `\ProgramFiles\Exchsrvr`

\ExchangeServer\GatherLogs folder by default and have the extension .gthr. These files identify all documents that were not successfully indexed. For the exam, it's really only important that you know what these files are and where to find them. You can learn more about using them from the Exchange documentation.

Application Log If indexing cannot be performed on an item or is stopped altogether for some reason, a search error is logged in the Windows Application Log. If the service is experiencing problems, you can also find errors relating to the Microsoft Search Service itself.

Summary

Each Exchange server can have from one to four storage groups. Each of those storage groups contains from one to five stores and a set of transaction logs associated with those stores. Transaction logs are used as the intermediary storage area for transactions that are committed to the actual Exchange databases later. A store is a logical database represented by two files, a rich-text file and a streaming media file. There are two types of stores found on an Exchange server: Public stores hold public folders meant for multiple users, and mailbox stores hold the mailboxes that store messages for individual users.

This assembly of databases, stores, and storage groups provides a great deal of scalability to Exchange Server 2003 and flexibility in the way that you configure storage in your organization.

The default storage group created when you first install Exchange Server 2003 is named First Storage Group. It contains one public store and one private store when created, though if you wish, you can delete these and/or create more stores. You can also create more storage groups on the server. Once created, stores and storage groups are configured just like any other object in the Exchange System Manager—using a series of property pages. The store objects also contain subcontainers, such as the Logons and Mailboxes containers, that let you monitor the status of the store. You can also mount, dismount, and delete individual stores using the object's context menu.

Full-text indexing is a form of content indexing available to all stores on an Exchange server. As an administrator, you can enable or disable full-text indexing on a store-by-store basis. Once a store is indexed, a client can search for items in the store much faster and more accurately than without indexing. Every word of every item in the store, including attachments, is made part of the index. Updating indexes happens automatically, and you can configure the scheduling of this using the Full-Text Indexing property page of the store object. You can also use the context menu for a store to manually control indexing at any time. Two tools are used in troubleshooting problems with full-text indexing. Gather files are created whenever a full-text index is built and contain a record of errors encountered during indexing. The Windows Application Log records any errors logged by the Microsoft Search Service.

Exam Essentials

Understand the difference between a storage group and a store. Storage groups contain stores, plain and simple. In Exchange Server 2003 Enterprise Edition, you can have up to four storage groups, each of which can contain up to five mailbox or public folder stores. Recall that some items are configured at the storage group level, while others are configured at the store level. A storage group, regardless of how many stores it contains, uses only one set of transaction logs.

Understand the benefits and costs of full-text indexing. Full-text indexing can make it quicker and easier for clients to search your stores, but it does come with a cost. Expect that the disk space required for any full-text index will be approximately 20 percent of that required for the associated store. As the store size increases over time, so does that of the full-text index. Remember that the following common file types are indexed as well: ASP, DOC, EML, HTM, HTML, PPT, TXT, and XLS.

Review Questions

1. You have configured three storage groups on your Exchange server. One group holds five mailbox stores and no public stores. The other two groups are configured with two public stores each and no mailbox stores. How many transaction logs are maintained on the system?

   A. One

   B. Three

   C. Five

   D. Nine

2. You have just installed a new drive on your Exchange server and would like to move the transaction logs for one of your storage groups to that drive. Where would you go to do this?

   A. The Logging property page of the server object that holds the storage group.

   B. The Database property page for the storage group object.

   C. The General property page for the storage group object.

   D. You cannot do this. Once a transaction log is created, it cannot be moved.

3. Which of the following does the Standard Edition of Exchange Server 2003 support? (Choose all that apply.)

   A. Multiple public stores

   B. Multiple mailbox stores

   C. Multiple storage groups

   D. Databases up to 16 GB

   E. Databases of any size

4. You are an assistant Exchange administrator for a large network. Your supervisor asks you to check a set of mailboxes to determine the last time the user logged on. How would you do this?

   A. Use the Advanced General page of the user's profile in Active Directory Users and Computers.

   B. View the Tools container in System Manager.

   C. View the Mailboxes container in System Manager.

   D. View the Logons container in System Manager.

5. For security reasons, you have decided to configure your mailbox storage group to zero out deleted databases. You realize that this process does not occur until after an online backup is performed, but you have decided that is secure enough for your purposes. What other concern does using this feature raise?

   A. The performance of the server will suffer.

   B. Online backups will take considerably longer.

   C. Users will no longer be able to recover deleted items from their client application.

   D. Multiple log files will be created that must be included in a backup routine.

6. You are planning storage on an Exchange server. You need to create two mailbox stores, one for general use and one for executive use. You also need to create one public store. All three stores will be created in a single storage group. As a required part of this process, you must ensure that the database for the executive mailbox store can be re-created from uncommitted log files. This requirement does not exist for the general mailbox store or the public folder store. In addition, it is desired (but not required) that you be able to perform both full and incremental backup jobs on all three stores located on this server. As well, it is desired (but not required) to minimize the amount of disk space that the general mailbox and public stores use by limiting the creation of new log files.

   To achieve these results, you propose to perform the following actions:

   - Create a single storage group.
   - Configure the executive mailbox store to use circular logging and to zero out deleted database pages.

   If you complete the proposed actions, will you have achieved the required and/or desired results?

   A. You will achieve both the required result and the two desired results.

   B. You will achieve the required result and only one of the desired results.

   C. You will achieve only the required result.

   D. You will not achieve the required result.

7. You are planning storage on an Exchange server. You need to create two mailbox stores, one for general use and one for executive use. You also need to create one public store. As a required part of this process, you must ensure that the database for the executive mailbox store can be re-created from uncommitted log files. This requirement does not exist for the general mailbox store or the public folder store. In addition, it is desired (but not required) that you be able to perform both full and incremental backup jobs on all three stores located on this server. As well, it is desired (but not required) to minimize the amount of disk space that the general mailbox and public stores use by limiting the creation of new log files.

   To achieve these results, you propose to perform the following actions:

   - Create three storage groups.
   - Put the storage mailbox store in one group, and disable circular logging on that group.

- Put the general mailbox store in another group, and configure that group to zero out deleted pages.
- Put the public store in the remaining group, and configure that group to zero out deleted pages.

If you complete the proposed actions, will you have achieved the required and/or desired results?

A. You will achieve both the required result and the two desired results.

B. You will achieve the required result and only one of the desired results.

C. You will achieve only the required result.

D. You will not achieve the required result.

8. You are planning storage on an Exchange server. You need to create two mailbox stores, one for general use and one for executive use. You also need to create one public store. As a required part of this process, you must ensure that the database for the executive mailbox store can be re-created from uncommitted log files. This requirement does not exist for the general mailbox store or the public folder store. In addition, it is desired (but not required) that you be able to perform both full and incremental backup jobs on all three stores located on this server. As well, it is desired (but not required) to minimize the amount of disk space that the general mailbox and public stores use by limiting the creation of new log files.

To achieve these results, you propose to perform the following actions:

- Create two storage groups.
- Put the executive mailbox store in one group, and configure that group not to use circular logging.
- Put the general mailbox store and the public folder store in the other group, and configure that group to use circular logging.

If you complete the proposed actions, will you have achieved the required and/or desired results?

A. You will achieve both the required result and the two desired results.

B. You will achieve the required result and only one of the desired results.

C. You will achieve only the required result.

D. You will not achieve the required result.

9. You have an organization that consists of three servers: Server1, Server2, and Server3. Server1 and Server2 contain only the default storage groups named First Storage Group, and each of those storage groups contain the default public store and mailbox store. The same is true of Server3, but here you have also configured a storage group named Executive that holds a single mailbox store for executive mail and another storage group named Jupiter that contains a public store for a new public folder tree. Server1 and Server2 are in one routing group, and Server3 is in another. Server1 is a member of one Windows Server 2003 domain, and Server2 and Server3 belong to a second Windows Server 2003 domain. Your organization is running in native mode. Which of the following statements are true? (Choose all that apply.)

   A. You could move a mailbox from the mailbox store on Server1 to the mailbox store on Server2.

   B. You could move a mailbox from the mailbox store on Server1 to the mailbox store on Server3.

   C. You could move a mailbox from the mailbox store on Server1 to the Executive store on Server3.

   D. You could move a mailbox from the mailbox store on Server2 to the mailbox store on Server3.

   E. You could move a mailbox from the mailbox store on Server2 to the Executive store on Server3.

10. You are planning to index a large public store. You are concerned that during the time it takes to index the store, users will submit reports of incomplete or inaccurate searches. How can you solve this problem?

   A. Dismount the store while the indexing takes place.

   B. Use the Full-Text Indexing property page of the store object to disallow searching while the indexing takes place.

   C. Use the General property page of the index to disallow searching while the indexing takes place.

   D. E-mail your users and let them know that search functions will be unavailable for a certain amount of time.

11. Which of the following files is used to keep track of the information in a transaction log that has already been committed to the database?

   A. `EDB.LOG`

   B. `CHECK.LOG`

   C. `EDB.CHK`

   D. `RES1.LOG`

12. In which of the following directories would you find the database files for the default public and mailbox stores created during Exchange Server 2003 installation?

    A. `\Program Files\Exchsrvr\Mdbdata`

    B. `\Program Files\Exchange\Mdbdata`

    C. `\WINNT\Exchsrvr\Mdbdata`

    D. `\WINNT\Exchange\Mdbdata`

13. You have an Exchange server that contains three storage groups. The first storage group contains a single mailbox store that consumes 10 GB of disk space. The second storage group contains two mailbox stores, each consuming 4 GB of disk space. The third storage group holds a single public store that consumes 5 GB of disk space. You want to enable full-text indexing on all of these stores. How much total disk space should the stores consume after indexing is complete?

    A. 23 GB

    B. 25.3 GB

    C. 27.6 GB

    D. 34.5 GB

    E. 46 GB

14. One of your Exchange servers has unexpectedly shut down its Information Store service. You check the Event Log and discover that the disk containing the log files for the Information Store has run out of space. What has happened to any transactions that were outstanding when the problem occurred?

    A. The transactions are stored in memory and must be committed before shutting down the computer.

    B. The transactions are written to reserve logs and will be committed when the IS comes back online.

    C. Circular logging is turned on, and the oldest committed transaction log is overwritten.

    D. The transactions are lost.

15. Which of the following statements is true of working in a mixed-mode organization?

    A. You cannot rename a storage group after its creation.

    B. You can rename a storage group at any time.

    C. You can rename a storage group, but you must dismount all stores in the group first.

    D. You can rename a storage group but only if all transaction logs are fully committed.

16. You recently created a mailbox store for use by executives in your company. You would like to create a public folder and have copies of all messages sent to users in that mailbox store sent to the folder as well. How could you do this?

    A. Configure the store to archive messages using the store's General property page.

    B. Configure the store to archive messages using the store's Advanced property page.

    C. Make regular backups of the mailbox store, and then restore those messages to the public store where the folder is kept.

    D. You cannot do this except by creating a custom program.

17. One of your assistant administrators has mistakenly purged a user's mailbox, thinking that the command was used to empty all messages from the mailbox. Instead, the mailbox has been deleted. How can you recover the mailbox?

    A. Purged mailboxes are disabled only for a specified period of time before being deleted. During this time, you can recover them from System Manager.

    B. Purged mailboxes are disabled only for a specified period of time before being deleted. During this time, you can recover them from Active Directory Users and Computers.

    C. You cannot recover the mailbox. You must create a new one for the user.

18. You are helping a small-business owner install Exchange Server on his network. He plans to use only one Exchange server and does not plan to use public folders. To save some system resources, you decide to remove the public folder store from the server. When you try to delete the store, however, System Manager will not let you. What could be the problem?

    A. You must remove all public folders from the store before deleting the store.

    B. You can delete a store only after dismounting it.

    C. You cannot delete the only store in an organization that contains a public folder tree.

    D. You cannot delete a public store from an Exchange server at all.

19. Which of the following statements is correct?

    A. You can create a full-text index for an individual store.

    B. You can create full-text indexes only for entire storage groups.

    C. You can create full-text indexes only for entire servers.

    D. Full-text indexing is either on or off for a whole organization.

20. Your users are complaining that the search results they get when looking for messages in certain public folders are always outdated by several days. You recognize that all of the folders are part of the same public store and that full-text indexing is turned on for the store. What is the best way to make the searches better for the users?

   A. Decrease the Update Interval option on the Full-Text Indexing property page of the public store.

   B. Decrease the Update Interval option on the Interval property page of the full-text index.

   C. Adjust the schedule at which updating occurs using the Schedule property page of the public store.

   D. Adjust the schedule at which updating occurs using the Schedule property page of the full-text index.

Answers to Review Questions

1. B. Only one transaction log is maintained for each storage group. Note that there may be multiple transaction log files that represent old transactions not yet committed to the database, but only one current log is used for each storage group.

2. C. The transaction log location is the directory in which the transaction log file for the storage group resides. By default, a location is created for the log file based on the name you give the storage group. You can change this location during creation of the storage group or any time after creation using the General property page for the storage group object.

3. D. Exchange Server 2003 Enterprise Edition supports multiple public stores and multiple private stores on a single server. Exchange 2000 Standard Server supports only two stores in a single storage group. In addition, the maximum store in the Standard Edition is limited to 16 GB in size, while the Enterprise Edition allows stores of any size.

4. C. The Mailboxes container displays a list of mailboxes and some related information, such as the size of the mailbox, how many items it contains, and the time of the last logon and logoff. The Logons container shows logons to the mailbox store itself.

5. A. The Zero Out Deleted Database Pages option is used to remove all 4-KB pages of data for items when they are deleted from a database by writing zeros to these pages within all stores of the storage group. This process occurs after an online backup is performed. This option can significantly reduce server performance, though, because of the additional overhead of writing to all the pages.

6. D. When circular logging is enabled, the database engine "circles back" to the oldest log file that has been fully committed and overwrites that file instead of creating a new one. This means that the log files cannot be used to re-create the database in the event of failure. In addition, incremental and differential backups cannot be used when circular logging is turned on. Finally, circular logging can be enabled only at the storage group level, since all the stores in a group share a common set of logs. The best thing to do in this scenario is to create two storage groups. Place the executive mail store into one group, and make sure that circular logging is turned off. Place the general mailbox and public store into the other storage group. You will be able to achieve only one of the optional results. If you turn off circular logging, you can use incremental backups on those stores, but you cannot limit the disk space used by the creation of new logs.

7. B. When circular logging is enabled, the database engine "circles back" to the oldest log file that has been fully committed and overwrites that file instead of creating a new one. This means that the log files cannot be used to re-create the database in the event of failure. In addition, incremental and differential backups cannot be used when circular logging is turned on. Finally, circular logging can be enabled only at the storage group level, since all the stores in a group share a common set of logs. The best thing to do in this scenario is to create two storage groups. Place the executive mail store into one group, and make sure that circular logging is turned off. Place the general mailbox and public store into the other storage group. You will be able to achieve only one of the optional results. If you turn off circular logging, you can use incremental backups on those stores, but you cannot limit the disk space used by the creation of new logs.

8. B. When circular logging is enabled, the database engine "circles back" to the oldest log file that has been fully committed and overwrites that file instead of creating a new one. This means that the log files cannot be used to re-create the database in the event of failure. In addition, incremental and differential backups cannot be used when circular logging is turned on. Finally, circular logging can be enabled only at the storage group level, since all the stores in a group share a common set of logs. The best thing to do in this scenario is to create two storage groups. Place the executive mail store into one group, and make sure that circular logging is turned off. Place the general mailbox and public store into the other storage group. You will be able to achieve only one of the optional results. If you turn off circular logging, you can use incremental backups on those stores, but you cannot limit the disk space used by the creation of new logs.

9. A, B, C, D, E. Assuming you are running in native mode, you can move a mailbox to any other store in the same organization.

10. B. The This Index Is Currently Available For Searching By Clients option on the Full-Text Indexing page for a store opens the index for searching. It is recommended that you disable this during the initial creation of the index and also during complete rebuilds of the index. Not only should you not dismount the store during indexing, but you cannot index a dismounted store. Also, there are no property pages for an index.

11. C. As transactions in transaction log files are committed to the database files, a checkpoint file (`EDB.CHK`) is updated. The checkpoint file keeps track of which transactions in the sequential list still need to be committed to a database by maintaining a pointer to the last information that was committed. This tells the engine that everything after that point still needs to be committed to a database.

12. A. By default, the databases making up the mailbox and public stores are created in `\Program Files\Exchsrvr\Mdbdata`.

13. C. An indexed store requires about 20 percent more disk space than a nonindexed store. Before indexing, the combined space consumed by the stores was 23 GB. Following indexing, this would increase by 20 percent, making the combined space consumed 27.6 GB.

14. B. Exchange creates two reserve log files (`RES1.LOG` and `RES2.LOG`) for each database. They are used if the system runs out of disk space. If that happens, Exchange shuts down the database service, logs an event to the Event Log, and writes any outstanding transaction information into these reserve log files. These two files reserve an area of disk space that can be used after the rest of the disk space is used.

15. A. In a mixed-mode organization, you can name the storage group only during its creation. Once it is created, you cannot change the name later.

16. A. You have the option of archiving all messages sent or received by users in the mailbox store to a public folder. While this does increase the use of server resources and possibly increase network traffic, it also provides a way of logging e-mail sent in your organization.

17. C. Mailboxes can be purged from the Mailboxes container in System Manager. Once a mailbox is purged, it cannot be recovered.

18. C. You can delete public stores from System Manager. However, the store cannot be the only store in an organization with a public folder tree. Also, the store must not be the default public store for any users. If the store contains any system folders, you must select a new store to hold those folders. Finally, if the store holds the only available replica of a public folder, you can still delete the store, but System Manager will warn you that the folder will be deleted as well.

19. A. Full-text indexing is enabled at the store level.

20. A. To begin with, there are no property pages for an index. The Update interval is the interval at which changes in the store are committed to the index. Decreasing this option would provide more current search results for your users. The option can be found on the Full-Text Indexing property page of the store object.

Chapter 10

Administration and Maintenance

MICROSOFT EXAM OBJECTIVES COVERED IN THIS CHAPTER:

- ✓ **Monitor, manage, and troubleshoot infrastructure performance**
- ✓ **Manage and troubleshoot permissions**
- ✓ **Manage recipient policies**
- ✓ **Manage, monitor, and troubleshoot server health**

Even after an Exchange environment is operational, it still requires a lot of work to keep everything running smoothly. As an administrator, it is your responsibility to monitor the status of the various components of your organization, perform a variety of daily administrative tasks, quickly spot problems in the system when they occur (or even before they occur), and fix those problems. It is also your responsibility to understand the tools used in performing all these tasks. Fortunately, Exchange Server 2003 handles a lot of monitoring, reporting, and repairing automatically. However, you still have the ability to control many of the parameters by which those automatic tasks function and, if the situation warrants, to perform various manual and offline management tasks.

This chapter covers a lot of ground. In previous chapters, you have been using System Manager to perform many of the tasks in Exchange. In this chapter, you'll take a closer look at this powerful utility. You will also learn about the following topics:

- Running snap-ins in the Microsoft Management Console
- Using various Windows and Exchange tools to monitor an Exchange server
- Managing message queues and tracking messages
- Using system and recipient policies
- Troubleshooting clients and servers

Administering a Server with System Manager

Most of the chapters in this book discuss some element of administering an Exchange server, group, or organization. Much of this management happens inside the *System Manager* snap-in and, if you've been following along with the exercises in this book so far, you're probably already pretty comfortable with the tool. This section offers a closer look at using System Manager.

Microsoft Management Console

Microsoft Management Console (MMC) provides a common environment for the management of system and network resources. MMC is a framework application in which modules called *snap-ins* are run. (System Manager is the snap-in used for managing Exchange Server 2003.) Snap-ins provide all the real functionality of MMC, and you can run multiple snap-ins inside a single instance of MMC, often called a *console*. This allows administrators to create custom management consoles that are geared toward a specific administrative function or administrator. For example, you might have an administrator who manages an Exchange server and is also responsible for various other aspects of management on that server. You could create a custom console that contains the System Manager snap-in and any other snap-ins that this administrator might need.

Figure 10.1 shows MMC with the System Manager snap-in loaded.

MMC menu bar The primary MMC menu bar always holds certain menu items, regardless of any snap-ins that are loaded: File, Action, View, Favorites, Window, and Help.

MMC toolbar The MMC toolbar appears below the MMC menu bar and provides quick access to common commands.

Snap-in action bar The snap-in action bar merges with the MMC menu bar and holds menus that pertain to the snap-in loaded in the console. If a console window contains multiple snap-ins, the action bar changes according to whatever snap-in you are viewing. Most action bars sport three menus: Action, View, and Favorites. The Action menu contains commands that apply to whatever object you have selected in the console. This means that many of the commands found on that menu will change as you select different objects. The View menu is used to control how information is displayed in the console. The Favorites menu lets you add items to a list of favorites and organize that list into categories. The Favorites list can include shortcuts to tools, items in the console, or tasks. The Favorites tab in the Scope pane lets you view items on your Favorites list.

Scope pane The Scope pane (not present in all consoles) is on the left-hand side of the main MMC window. It shows a hierarchy of containers referred to as a console tree. Some containers are displayed as unique icons that graphically represent the type of items that they contain. Others are displayed as folders, simply indicating that other objects are held inside.

FIGURE 10.1 The main MMC window with the System Manager loaded

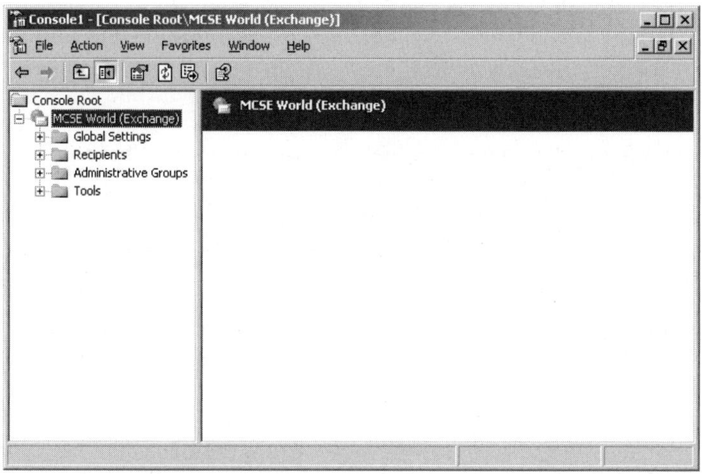

Results pane The Results pane is on the right-hand side of the console. This pane changes to show the contents of whatever container is selected in the Scope pane. In other words, the Results pane shows the results of the currently selected scope. The Results pane can display information in a number of different views. The standard views—large or small icon, list, and detail—are accessed through the View menu.

Containers and objects All of the items you see in both panes of the console window are called objects. These objects are the primary management tools of a snap-in, and you will use them by opening their property pages, selecting them to view data in the Results pane, or right-clicking them to access pertinent commands. Objects come in two types. *Container objects* hold other objects, even other container objects. They are used to arrange objects into an administrative hierarchy. All container objects form the expandable tree that you see in the Scope pane of a console. *Leaf objects* differ from container objects only in that they cannot hold other objects.

Using the System Manager Snap-In

In previous chapters, you have seen how the System Manager snap-in is used to create and manage recipients; build routing, administrative, and storage groups; and configure protocol usage. This section discusses how it can be used to manage other Exchange activities relating to organization and server management.

When System Manager is started, its default action is to try to connect to a domain controller that exists on the same subnet as the computer running System Manager. If no domain controller exists on the same subnet, System Manager tries to find one in the same Windows site. Once System Manager finds a domain controller, it queries Active Directory to fill the console with the current Exchange organization objects.

You can direct System Manager to connect to a specific computer by adding the snap-in to a blank MMC console rather than starting System Manager from the Microsoft Exchange folder. To do this, select the Run command from the Start menu and type MMC into the Run box. When the blank console opens, use the File menu to add a snap-in, and choose the Exchange System Manager snap-in from the list of available snap-ins. When you add the snap-in, you will be prompted to supply the name of a specific domain controller. You can save the console at this point so that you don't lose any selections.

Figure 10.2 shows the now familiar System Manager.

Organization The Organization container appears at the top of the hierarchy and is named for the organization itself (MCSE World in Figure 10.2). The property pages for this object hold options for displaying administrative and routing groups and for changing your organization from mixed mode to native mode. These properties were discussed in detail in Chapter 8, "Building Administrative and Routing Groups."

FIGURE 10.2 The hierarchy of an Exchange organization

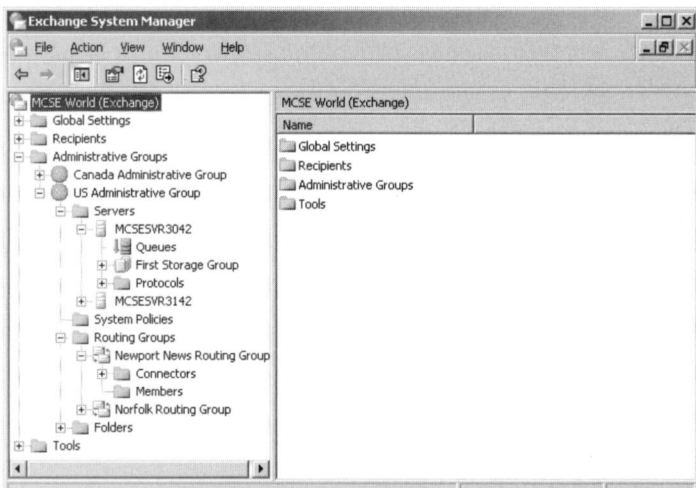

Global Settings The Global Settings container holds objects governing settings that apply to your entire organization. The container itself has no property pages associated with it, but inside the container you will find three objects. The first, Internet Message Formats, defines the formatting for SMTP messages sent over the Internet. The second object in the Global Settings container, Message Delivery, is used to configure message defaults for your organization. Open the property pages for this object (shown in Figure 10.3) to set message limit defaults that filter down to the information stores on your servers and to configure filters for handling messages from particular SMTP addresses. The final object in the Global Settings container, Mobile Services, is used to control the default settings for Outlook Mobile Access.

Recipients The Recipients container is used to manage server settings that apply to recipients in your organization. You can define recipient policies, manage address lists, and even modify address templates. Recipient policies are covered later in this chapter. You can find information on managing address lists in Chapter 5, "Creating and Managing Recipients."

Administrative Groups The Administrative Groups container holds all configured administrative groups. Each Administrative Groups container holds the following containers: Servers, System Policies, Routing Groups, and Folders.

Servers Servers containers hold configuration objects for managing the protocols, connectors, and storage groups configured on a server. You can find information on configuring these specific objects throughout this book.

System Policies The System Policies container holds the system policies that you have configured for mailbox stores, public folder stores, and servers.

Routing Groups The Routing Groups container holds all routing groups that exist within the selected administrative group. Within each individual Routing Groups container exist the Connectors and Members containers. The Connectors container holds configuration items for each of the connectors available within the routing group. The objects within the Connectors container represent connectors between routing groups in your organization and to foreign messaging systems. The Members container simply lists all members of the specific routing group.

Folders The Folders container holds the public folders hierarchy and properties but not their contents. It also contains the system folders, a list of folders that Exchange users do not see. The system folders hold the Offline Address Book and other system configuration objects.

Tools The Tools container holds objects that help you manage your Exchange organization. You'll find three containers within the Tools container. The Site Replication Services container lets you configure replication with existing Exchange 5.5 sites using the Active Directory Connector. This is covered in Chapter 12, "Coexisting with and Upgrading from Exchange 2000 Server." The Message Tracking Center object is actually a shortcut for opening the *Message Tracking Center (MTC)*, which lets you track specific messages in your organization. The MTC is discussed in detail later in this chapter. The Monitors container holds objects that let you monitor the status of servers and connections in your organization. Both of these are covered later in this chapter.

FIGURE 10.3 Configuring Message Delivery settings for an organization

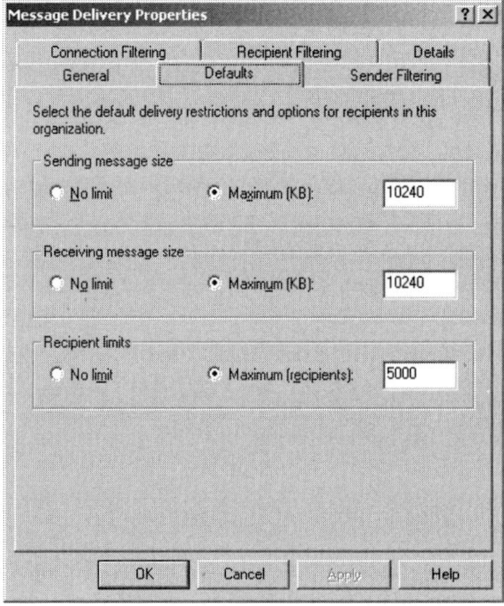

Customizing a Console

System Manager is actually a saved console file that connects to a Windows Server 2003 domain controller in order to get configuration information regarding your Exchange organization. While all Exchange administrative functionality can be controlled from the System Manager, there are reasons why you might want to create a custom console.

For example, you could create a custom System Manager console that provides specialized taskpad views for helping new Exchange administrators get used to the system or that always connects to a specific server in another organization.

In addition to the full System Manager snap-in, there is one additional Exchange-related snap-in you can use to create a custom console:

- The *Exchange Message Tracking Center snap-in* creates a console that displays only the message-tracking features.

Managing Administrative Security

Administrative access to Exchange objects can be configured. An administrator can assign permissions to specific users or groups at different levels of the Exchange hierarchy in order to determine who has what type of access to what information. To understand how permissions are assigned, you must understand the types of permissions available and the way that permissions are inherited by objects from their parent objects.

Types of Permissions

Exchange Server 2003 uses the Windows Server 2003 security model to manage access to objects. All Exchange objects are secured with a *discretionary access control list (DACL)* and individual *Access Control Entries (ACEs)* that give users and groups specific permissions on an object. In System Manager, you will configure permissions for an object using the Security property page for that object (see Figure 10.4).

For the most part, the Security page is common across all objects. You select a user or group from the list (you can add more by clicking the Add button) and then either allow or deny each permission for that user or group.

If you do not specifically allow or deny a permission, the state of the permission is inherited from the parent container. Read on for more on permissions inheritance.

There are two types of permissions available to you. *Standard permissions* are part of the default permissions that come with Windows Server 2003. *Extended permissions* are added when Exchange Server 2003 is installed. Extended permissions change depending on the object you are viewing. For example, many recipient objects have the extended permissions Send As and Receive As. Server objects have an Administer Information Store permission that is used to specify the users and groups that can administer stores on the server.

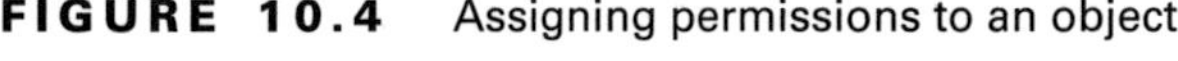

FIGURE 10.4 Assigning permissions to an object

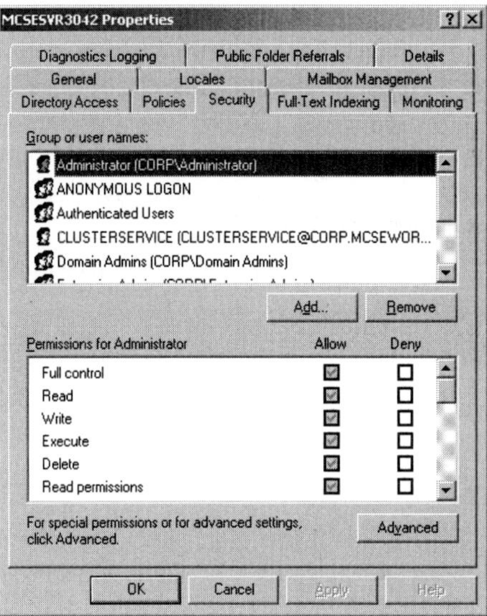

Table 10.1 lists the standard permissions available to you. These are the permissions you should really be familiar with on the job—and on the exam.

TABLE 10.1 Standard Permissions for Administrative Objects

Permission	Description
Full Control	Give full permissions on the object.
Read	View the object in System Manager.
Write	Make changes to the object.
Delete	Delete the object.
Read Permissions	View the Security page for the object.
Change Permissions	Modify the permissions for the object.
Take Ownership	Take ownership of the object.
Create Children	Create child objects inside the object.

TABLE 10.1 Standard Permissions for Administrative Objects *(continued)*

Permission	Description
Delete Children	Delete child objects from the object.
List Contents	View the contents of a container object.
Read Properties	View the properties of the object.
Write Properties	Modify the properties of the object.
List Object	View the objects in a container object.

Permissions Inheritance

By default, child objects in System Manager always *inherit* permissions from their parent objects. For the most part, this is a good thing, because it eliminates the need to manually assign permissions to every object, letting System Manager do much of the work for you. However, there will be times when you want to override this functionality. You can do so in two ways:

- Modify the permissions by specifically allowing or denying the permission to the appropriate user or group.
- Disable the Allow Inheritable Permissions From Parent To Propagate To This Object option from the Advanced Security Settings dialog.

You can also prevent permissions from being inherited in the first place by visiting the parent object's Security page and clicking the Advanced button. In the Advanced dialog that opens, you can specify whether the permissions for each access control setting should or should not propagate to child objects.

Exercise 10.1 outlines the steps for assigning permissions to an object and preventing that object from propagating permissions to any of its child objects.

For safety's sake do not perform Exercise 10.1 on a production server. As well, you might want to undo your changes after completing the exercise.

EXERCISE 10.1

Modifying Permissions on an Object in System Manager

1. Click Start ➤ Programs ➤ Exchange ➤ System Manager.
2. Double-click the Servers container to expand it.

EXERCISE 10.1 *(continued)*

3. Right-click a server object and select the Properties command.
4. Click the Security tab.
5. Select the Domain Admins group from the list.
6. Click the Deny option for the Full Control permission.
7. Click the Advanced button.
8. Select the Deny Domain Admins Full Control entry from the list.
9. Click the View/Edit button.
10. From the drop-down list, select This Object Only.
11. Click OK three times to return to System Manager.

The Exchange Administration Delegation Wizard

All users who will function as Exchange administrators must be granted the appropriate permissions on objects they will need to administer. Fortunately, System Manager provides a tool that makes the task of delegating administrative permissions in Exchange a good bit easier than having to assign them manually.

The *Exchange Administration Delegation Wizard* lets you select a user or group and assign them a specific administrative role. You can start the wizard either from the organization object (right-click and choose the Delegate Control command) or from a specific administrative group. Where you start the wizard defines the scope of permissions that are assigned to the user or group. For example, if you start the wizard from the organization object, the permissions assigned propagate all the way down through the hierarchy of objects. If you start the wizard from a specific administrative group, permissions propagate down through that group only. However, read-only permissions also propagate upward along the hierarchy so that the administrators can view, at least, the objects in the full hierarchy.

The Exchange Administration Delegation Wizard is a separate utility from the Delegation of Control Wizard available in Active Directory Users and Computers.

In addition, to start the wizard, you must have full administrative control yourself. Full administrative control is granted to the user who installed the first Exchange server in an organization.

There are three roles that you can assign using the Exchange Administration Delegation Wizard:

- The *Exchange Full Administrator role* gives full administrative capability. Administrators can add, delete, and rename objects as well as modify permissions on objects.
- The *Exchange Administrator role* gives the same full administrative capability as the Exchange Full Administrator role but does not give administrators permission to modify permissions for objects.
- The *Exchange View-Only Administrator role* lets administrators view Exchange configuration information but not modify it in any way. This role is often useful to assign to administrators who might need to see the way an organization is structured but do not perform any actual administration.

Monitoring a Server

By keeping close watch over your organization and its components, you can spot potential problems before they occur and quickly respond to the problems that do occur. Monitoring also allows you to identify trends in network use that signal opportunities for optimization and future planning. This section covers many of the Windows Server 2003 and Exchange Server 2003 tools that you will use to monitor your servers.

Windows Server 2003 Tools

Exchange Server 2003 is tightly integrated into Windows Server 2003 and leverages the management tools built into the operating system. In this section, we discuss these tools:

- Control Panel ➢ Administrative Tools ➢ Services
- Event Viewer
- System Monitor
- Registry Editor
- Computer Management
- Task Manager

Monitoring Services

Selecting Control Panel ➢ Administrative Tools ➢ Services (shown in Figure 10.5) can be used to check the status of the Exchange Server services. You can start, stop, and pause a service by selecting it and using the appropriate buttons on the toolbar. You can also configure the startup parameters of a service by double-clicking it to open the service's property pages.

FIGURE 10.5 Monitoring services in Windows Server 2003

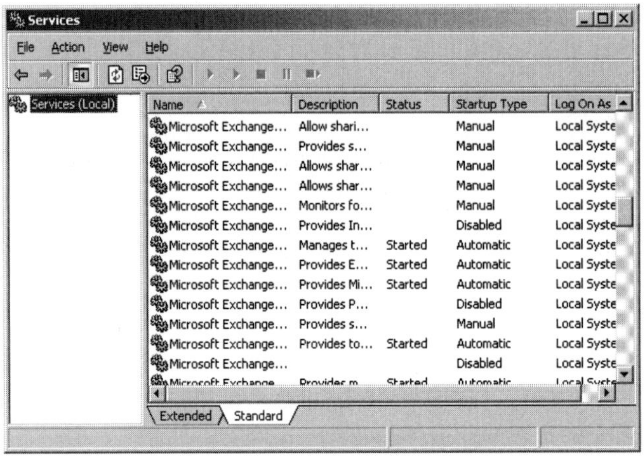

There are a number of Exchange-related services that you should be aware of, including the following:

- The Microsoft Exchange Information Store service manages the store databases.
- The Microsoft Exchange Routing Engine service processes the routing information for a server.
- The Microsoft Exchange System Attendant provides system-related services such as server maintenance.

There will be a number of other services listed depending on the components you have installed on the server.

Using Event Viewer

All Exchange services write event information to the *Windows Event Log*. Administrators should regularly (daily is recommended) view the Event Log for management and troubleshooting purposes using the Event Viewer application. Exchange services can be configured to log different amounts and types of events for diagnostics logging. Windows Server 2003 maintains three distinct logs:

- The Application log is a record of events generated by applications. All Exchange Server 2003 services write their status information to this log. If you enable diagnostics logging for any Exchange Server 2003 component, that information is also recorded in the Application log. This log is the most valuable log for monitoring the general health of an Exchange server.
- The Security log is a record of events based on the auditing settings specified in the Active Directory Users and Computers utility.
- The System log is a record of events that concern components of the system itself, including such events as device driver and network failures.

The vast majority of Exchange information is written to the Application log. The administrator may want to increase the maximum size of this log (the default is 512 KB) if logging levels are turned up for troubleshooting or just to maintain the events that have occurred over a longer period. Event Viewer can also be used to view the Event Logs of a remote server.

Using the Performance Snap-In

The Exchange Server setup program adds Exchange-related counters to Windows Server 2003's *Performance snap-in*, also called System Monitor, making it possible to view the performance of various Exchange activities. System Monitor graphically charts the performance of hundreds of individual system parameters on a Microsoft Windows Server 2003 computer and can also be used to log those parameters over time. When Exchange Server 2003 is installed on a Windows Server 2003 computer, several Exchange-specific counters can be charted as well.

This book uses the terms System Monitor and Performance Monitor interchangeably.

Table 10.2 shows a few of the performance objects added by Exchange and the counters for those objects.

TABLE 10.2 Exchange-Related Performance Objects and Counters

Object	Counter	Description
MSExchangeIS	User Count	Displays the number of users who are currently using the Information Store.
MSExchangeIS Mailbox and MSExchangeIS Public	Send Queue Size	Displays the queue of messages outbound from the Information Store.
	Receive Queue Size	Displays the queue of messages inbound to the Information Store.
	Message Sent/min	Shows the rate (per minute) at which messages are sent to the routing engine.
	Messages Delivered/min	Shows the rate (per minute) at which messages are delivered to all recipients.
SMTP Server	Local Queue Length	Indicates the number of messages in the local queue. A normal reading is 0. If the reading exceeds 0, the server is receiving messages faster than it can process them.

TABLE 10.2 Exchange-Related Performance Objects and Counters *(continued)*

Object	Counter	Description
	Categorizer Queue Length	Displays the number of messages waiting for advanced address resolution to occur.
	Inbound Connections Current	Measures the number of connections that are currently inbound.
	Message Bytes Received/sec	Measures the rate (per second) at which inbound messages are being received.
	Message Bytes Sent/sec	Measures the rate (per second) at which inbound messages are being sent.
MSExchangeMTA	Messages/sec	The number of messages the MTA sends and receives per second.
	Work Queue Length	The number of messages queued in the MTA.
MSExchangeMTA Connections	Queue Length	Displays MTA counters on a connection-by-connection basis.
MSExchangeSRS	Replication Updates/sec	Measures the rate (per second) at which replication updates are applied to local site replication services. This object is used to monitor integration of Exchange 5.5 with Exchange 2000 Server.
	Remaining Replication Updates	Measures how many messages in the current replication update message have yet to be processed.

Don't underestimate the benefit of using the Performance snap-in in your Exchange environment. The Performance snap-in can be used to collect and analyze data, perform a baseline of your Exchange servers, detect problems and provide the proper notification, as well as analyze the problems when they occur.

In addition to the Exchange-specific counters represented in the preceding table, there are several critical areas in which you should use the Performance snap-in to monitor an Exchange server's performance. These areas include the following:

Central Processing Unit (CPU) The Processor object has several counters you can use to monitor the CPU for potential bottleneck issues.

Network The Network Segment, Redirector, Server, and Server Work Queue objects hold counters that can help identify network subsystem bottlenecks.

Disk Input/Output (I/O) You should monitor both the logical and physical disk counters to help identify disk subsystem bottlenecks.

Memory The Memory object has several counters useful in determining the scope of memory-related bottlenecks.

System Monitor can also be used to warn you of a situation and therefore help you prevent a particular problem. For example, if all available disk space is used, your IS will stop. You could configure System Monitor to send you an e-mail message when the available disk space reaches a specified low level. You could then take steps to prevent all disk space from being used and therefore prevent the IS from being stopped.

Using System Monitor to Check Exchange

Here is a case study of using the Performance snap-in to monitor Exchange Server. An administrator is receiving reports from users that the Exchange server response time is slow. A quick examination shows that the server's disk is almost constantly active. The administrator decides to take a deeper look and, using System Monitor, collects the following information about that particular Exchange server:

%Processor time = 70

%Disk free space = 60

Pages/sec = 40

Avg. Disk sec/Transfer = 0.02

The administrator then compares these statistics to the "rule of thumb" thresholds that their organization has determined. The following are those thresholds, which when exceeded have been associated with performance problems:

%Processor time > 80%

%Disk free space < 10%

Pages/sec > 5

Avg. Disk sec/Transfer > .3

Comparing the current statistics with the thresholds, the administrator sees that the Pages/sec number is over the threshold. This suggests that there is not enough memory to cache information, therefore leading the system to page data to the disk. The administrator decides to add memory to this server and continue to monitor the situation.

Using Registry Editor

Like all Windows applications, Exchange Server stores some configuration information in the Registry. This information can be read and modified using the Registry Editor application (`regedit.exe`). All the Registry settings for Exchange Server are stored under the keys `HKEY_LOCAL_MACHINE\SOFTWARE` and `HKEY_LOCAL_MACHINE\SYSTEM`. Normally, you will not need to edit the Registry directly (which can be dangerous, because there are no safeguards to prevent mistakes). Most configurations are made through the Exchange Administrator program and are written to the Registry automatically.

Computer Management

The *Computer Management snap-in* (available in Control Panel ➢ Administrative Tools) holds a variety of management utilities, including the following:

- Event Viewer
- Disk Management Tools, which allows you to partition and format hard disks
- Various pieces of information about services and applications running on the server

Using Task Manager

Task Manager displays the programs and processes running on a computer. It also displays various performance information, such as CPU and memory usage. An Exchange administrator can use this tool to view the overall health of a server. You access Task Manager by right-clicking the taskbar and choosing Task Manager from the drop-down menu.

Exchange Tools

In addition to the Windows Server 2003 tools used for monitoring and managing a server, Exchange Server 2003 provides a number of its own tools, as well.

Configuring Diagnostics Logging

All Exchange services log certain critical events to the Windows Application Log. For certain services, however, you can configure additional levels of logging. *Diagnostics logging* is one of the most useful tools for troubleshooting problems in Exchange Server 2003.

You can modify the levels of diagnostics logging for all services on a particular Exchange server by using the Diagnostics Logging property page for the server object in System Manager (see Figure 10.6).

Do not leave a production server configured for diagnostics logging. Once you have completed troubleshooting using diagnostics logging, remember to turn it off because it uses a large amount of resources.

FIGURE 10.6 Configuring diagnostics logging

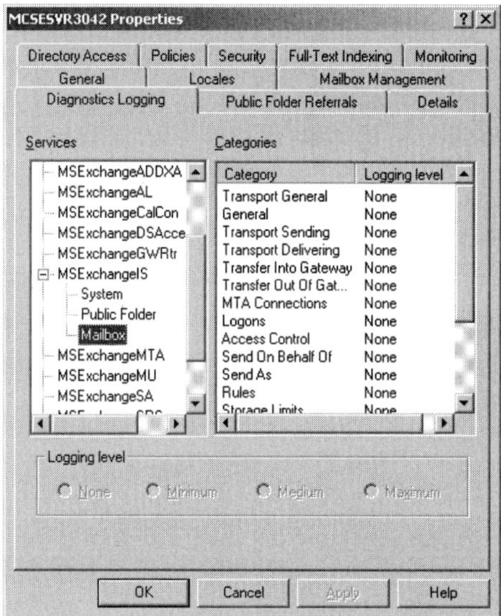

On the left side of this page, you'll find a hierarchical view of all the major services on the server for which you can enable advanced diagnostics logging. These services include many items, such as the following:

MSExchangeIS (Microsoft Exchange Information Store Service) You do not actually enable logging for the Information Store service as a whole. The MSExchangeIS item expands, allowing you to enable diagnostics logging individually for the Public and Private Information Stores and for the various Internet protocols.

MSExchangeMTA (Microsoft Exchange Message Transfer Agent) Use diagnostics logging on this service to troubleshoot problems with message delivery and gateway connectivity.

On the right side of the Diagnostics Logging page, you'll find a list of categories that can be logged for the selected service. You can enable four distinct levels of logging by using the radio buttons on the bottom of the page. All events that occur in Exchange Server 2003 are given an event level of 0, 1, 3, or 5. The logging level you set will determine which levels of events are logged:

- When the None option is selected, only events with a logging level of 0 are logged. These events include application and system failures.
- When the Minimum option is selected, all events with a logging level of 1 or lower are logged.
- When the Medium option is selected, all events with a logging level of 3 or lower are logged.
- When the Maximum option is selected, all events with a logging level of 5 or lower are logged. All events concerning a particular service are logged. This level can fill an Event Log quickly and is used mainly when working on an issue with Microsoft Product Support.

Monitoring Messages

Ensuring the efficient delivery of messages is paramount to an administrator's job. To accomplish this task, you need to first understand how messaging works within the Exchange system. Messaging architecture is covered in detail in Chapter 2, "Microsoft Exchange Architecture." Chapter 8, "Building Administrative and Routing Groups," also shows you how to construct and link routing groups and the role they play in the flow of messages in an Exchange organization. In this section, you will learn about managing message queues and tracking messages in the organization.

Managing Message Queues

Should you suspect a problem with a particular queue (such as in the case of messages not being delivered in a timely fashion), System Manager provides a tool called the *Queue Viewer* that can help you troubleshoot it. In the Queues container of each server in System Manager, you will find a list of queues on the server, as seen in Figure 10.7.

Selecting any particular queue within the Queues container allows you to search for messages in that queue. You can also freeze messages so that the Message Tracking Agent (MTA) does not attempt to send them while you troubleshoot the queue and then unfreeze them to let the MTA go ahead with the send. You can also delete messages from the queue altogether.

Tracking Messages

Message tracking is enabled at the server level using the General property page for the server object, as seen in Figure 10.8. You can also enable it using system policies, which are covered later in the chapter. Once message tracking is enabled, Exchange Server keeps a log of all messages transferred to and from the server. Log files are maintained by the System Attendant service on each server.

When message tracking has been enabled, you can track individual messages by using the Message Tracking Center (MTC), a component of System Manager. You can use the MTC to trace the route of test messages you send through the system or to help diagnose the cause of undelivered messages for which users have received non-delivery reports.

FIGURE 10.7 Viewing the Queues container

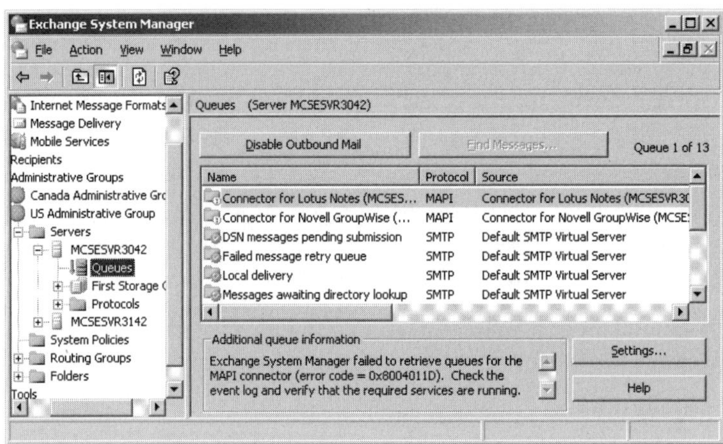

To use the MTC, open it by first navigating to and selecting the Message Tracking Center container in System Manager, as shown in Figure 10.9.

Click the buttons next to the Sender or Recipients boxes to open a standard address book, from which you can choose the originator or recipient of the message that you want to track in the MTC. You can also browse for the server(s) on which you would like to search for the messages. After you enter your criteria, click Find Now to perform the search.

FIGURE 10.8 Enabling message tracking

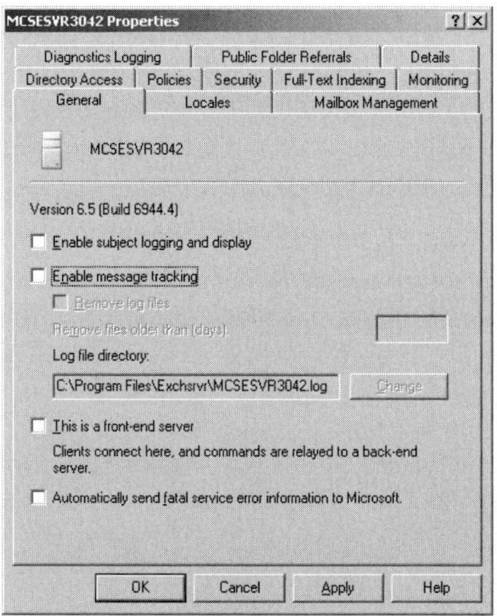

FIGURE 10.9 Using the Message Tracking Center

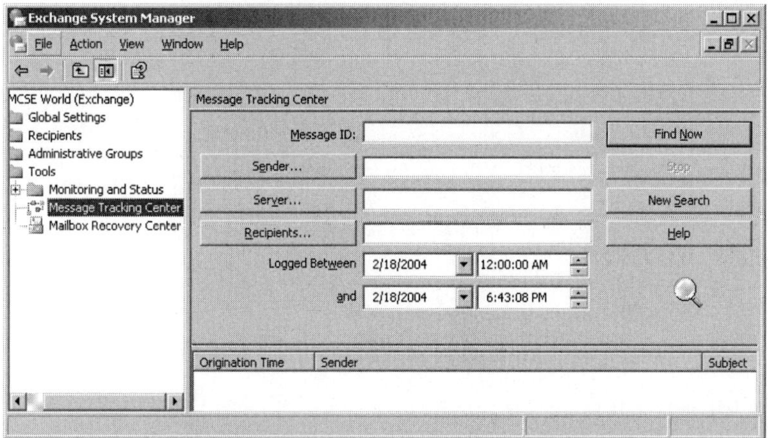

When the messages that meet your criteria are displayed in the bottom of the MTC window, you can open the property sheet of any message by selecting it and then clicking the Details button. Use this method to find the actual message that you want to track. When you find that message, select it and then click the Message History button to start the MTC tracking the history of the message. The results are displayed in the Message History window, shown in Figure 10.10. As you can see, the Message History window displays basic information about the message and a history of the message that shows each service the message has been through.

Using Exchange Monitors

By default, Exchange Server 2003 monitors the status of all connectors and a group of default services on every Exchange server. You can change the default services monitored, configure Exchange to monitor other services, and set up notification events to occur when problems arise. You do all of this using the *Monitoring and Status tool* (shown in Figure 10.11), which is actually a container in System Manager.

Monitoring Status

Status monitoring is configured using the Status container. Selecting the Status container in the System Manager snap-in, as shown in Figure 10.12, displays the basic status of all connectors and servers in the right-hand pane. This display gives you a quick overview of the names of the connectors and servers, the administrative group they belong to, and whether they are available or not.

Right-clicking the Status container provides access to two commands. The first is a filtering command that lets you filter the view of connectors and servers in the status window—useful for large organizations. The second command lets you connect to a specific Exchange server in the organization.

FIGURE 10.10 Viewing the tracking history for a message

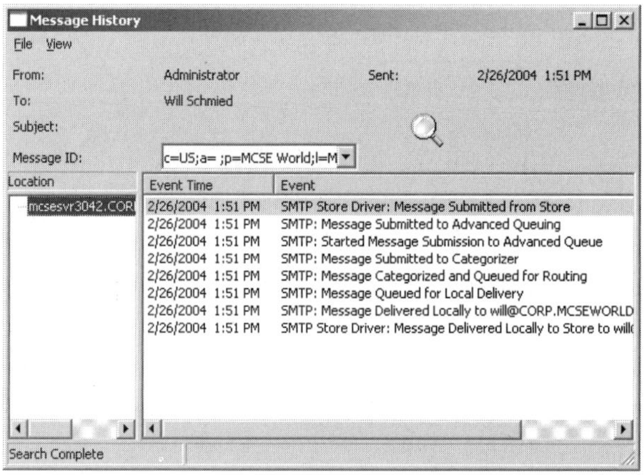

FIGURE 10.11 Accessing the Monitoring and Status tool

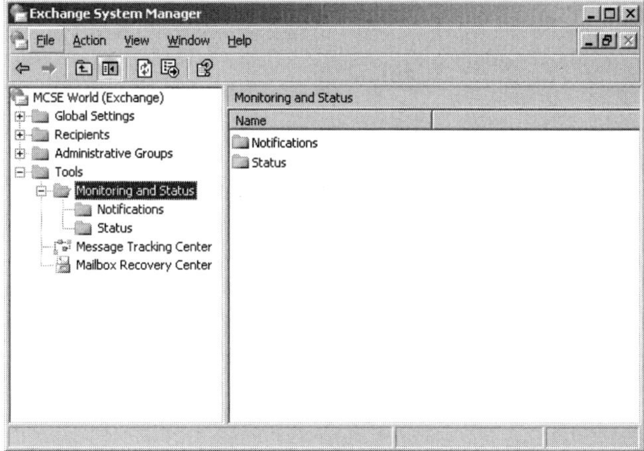

FIGURE 10.12 Using the Status container

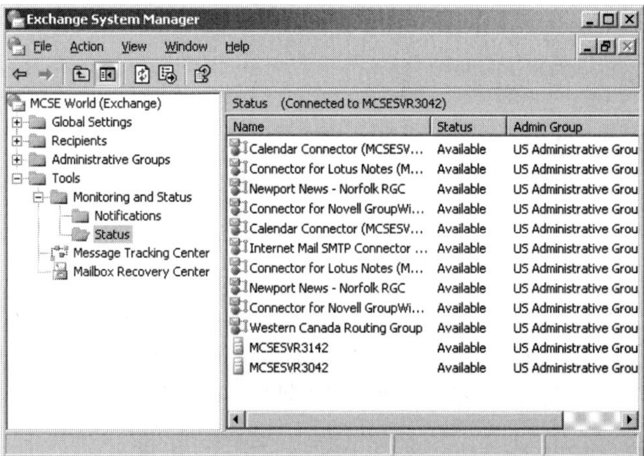

There are two types of objects that appear in the Status container: connectors and servers. For the connector objects, you really can't do much more than see whether the connector is available or not. Connector objects don't have property pages, so they are not configurable at this location. Server objects, on the other hand, are quite configurable. Right-click any server and choose Properties to open the property page shown in Figure 10.13.

FIGURE 10.13 Configuring properties for a server monitor

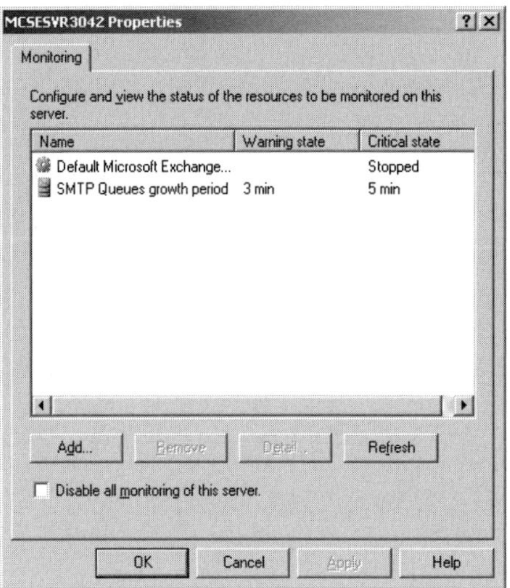

By default, Exchange Server 2003 monitors the following services on every Exchange server and logs a critical or warning state whenever any of the services stops:

- Microsoft Exchange Information Store service
- Microsoft Exchange MTA Stacks
- Microsoft Exchange Routing Engine
- Microsoft Exchange System Attendant
- Simple Mail Transfer Protocol (SMTP)
- World Wide Web Publishing service

You can add a new default service to be monitored by selecting the Default Microsoft Exchange Services entry and clicking the Detail button. This brings up a dialog box that lists the services currently being monitored. Use the controls on this dialog to add and remove services from the list. Note that you are not restricted to monitoring only Exchange-related services. You can add any service on the computer to be one of the default monitored services.

In addition to monitoring services, a server monitor can be configured to monitor other resources, as well. By clicking the Add button on the Monitoring tab, you can add any of the following resources to the list to be monitored:

- Available virtual memory
- CPU utilization

- Free disk space
- SMTP queue growth
- Any Windows service
- X.400 queue growth

For each of these resources, you will need to configure what threshold must be crossed to send the monitor into a warning state or a critical state. For example, you might want the monitor to enter a warning state when the amount of free disk space on a server reaches 500 MB and to enter a critical state when it reaches 100 MB.

Exercise 10.2 outlines the process for configuring a server to monitor the free disk space and enter a critical state when space falls below 250 MB.

EXERCISE 10.2

Setting Up a Monitor

1. Click Start ➢ Programs ➢ Microsoft Exchange ➢ System Manager.
2. Expand the Tools container and the Monitoring and Status container inside it, and then select the Status container.
3. Right-click the server you want to monitor, and select Properties from the shortcut menu.
4. Click Add.
5. In the dialog box that opens, select the Free Disk Space entry, and then click OK.
6. In the Disk Space Thresholds dialog, select the Critical State (MB) option and type **250**.
7. Click OK twice to return to System Manager.

SETTING UP NOTIFICATIONS

As the previous section just described, the Status container is used to configure whether stopped services or certain resource thresholds trigger a warning state or a critical state. A *notification* defines what happens when those states are entered. By default, the Notifications container is empty. This means that the only way you really have of noticing that a server or connector has entered a warning or critical state is by checking out the Status container yourself. The Notifications container lets you set up a notification that can either send you an e-mail or run an executable script when something goes amiss.

Figure 10.14 shows the property page for an e-mail notification. A script notification is quite similar but has parameters for running a script instead of sending an e-mail.

FIGURE 10.14 Setting up an e-mail notification

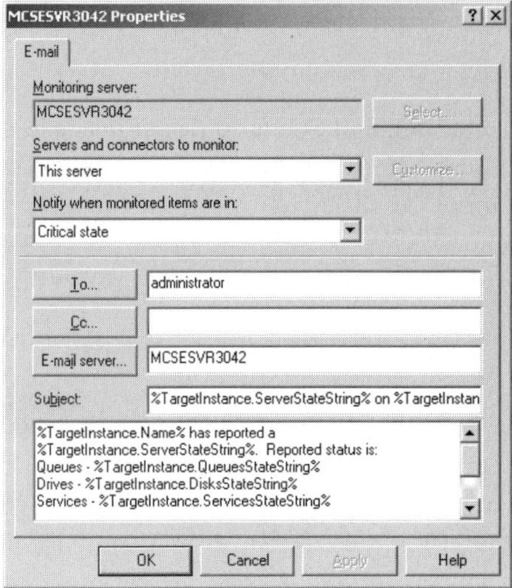

For each notification, you must set up the following in its property page:

- The monitoring server is the server that actually performs the monitoring and triggers the notification.

It is often good to put one server in charge of monitoring another, because a server sometimes can't send out a notification when one of its own services goes down.

- Select an individual server, all servers or connectors, a routing group, or a customized list of servers and connectors to which the notification will apply.
- Choose whether the notification should occur when the monitored resource enters a warning or critical state. For example, you could set an e-mail notification to inform you when a warning state is entered and a script notification to run a script that pages you when a critical state is entered.
- For e-mail notifications, you must configure the e-mail address and server to which the notification is to be sent.
- For script notifications, you must enter the path to the executable file and any command-line parameters.

Exercise 10.3 outlines the steps for setting up an e-mail notification to warn you when a server enters a critical state.

EXERCISE 10.3

Setting Up an E-mail Notification

1. Click Start ➢ Programs ➢ Microsoft Exchange ➢ System Manager.
2. Expand the Tools container and the Monitoring and Status container inside it.
3. Right-click the Notifications container and select New E-Mail Notification from the shortcut menu.
4. Click the Select button.
5. In the Select Exchange Server dialog box, select the Exchange server that you want to perform the monitoring and to send the notification, and click OK.
6. Click the To button.
7. In the Select Recipient dialog box, select the user to whom the notification should be sent, and click OK.
8. Click OK to create the notification and return to System Manager.

Using SNMP and the MADMAN MIB

Simple Network Management Protocol (SNMP) is used to collect information from devices on a TCP/IP network. SNMP was developed in the Internet community to monitor activity on network devices such as routers and bridges. Since then, SNMP acceptance and support have grown. Many devices, including computers running Windows Server 2003, can now be monitored with SNMP.

SNMP has a small command set and maintains a centralized database of management information. An SNMP system has three parts:

- The SNMP Agent is the device on a network that is being monitored. This device is typically a computer that has the SNMP Agent software installed. Windows Server 2003 includes SNMP Agent software in the form of the Microsoft SNMP Service, which you install by using the Windows Component Wizard in the Add or Remove Programs applet of the Control Panel.
- The SNMP Management System is the component that does the actual monitoring in an SNMP environment. Windows Server 2003 does not provide an SNMP Management System; third-party SNMP Management Systems include Hewlett-Packard's OpenView and IBM's NetView.
- The *Management Information Base (MIB)* is a centralized database of all the values that can be monitored for all the devices in an SNMP system. Different MIBs are provided for monitoring various types of devices and systems. Windows Server 2003 comes with four MIBs: Internet MIB II, LAN Manager MIB II, DHCP MIB, and WINS MIB. These four MIBs allow the remote monitoring and management of most components of Windows Server 2003.

Exchange Server 2003 includes a special MIB that you can use to enable an SNMP Management System that manages many Exchange 2000 Server functions. This MIB is based on a standardized MIB named the *Mail and Directory Management (MADMAN) MIB*, which is detailed in Internet Request for Comments (RFC) 1566.

Using Policies

Policies are a feature of Exchange Server 2003 that allows an administrator to create collections of configuration settings that can be easily applied to large numbers of objects at once. For example, you might configure a policy that configures a group of server-related settings. You could then apply those settings across a group of servers without having to manually configure each server.

There are two types of policies in Exchange Server 2003:

- *System policies* affect servers, mailbox stores, and public stores. These policies appear in the System Policies container in System Manager.
- *Recipient policies* are applied to mail-enabled Exchange objects to generate e-mail addresses. These appear in the Recipient Policies container inside the Recipients container in System Manager.

If you do not see a System Policies container in System Manager, you will need to create one. In order to do this, System Manager must be configured to display administrative groups, even if you have only one administrative group. To display administrative groups, open the property pages for the organization object and enable the administrative groups display. To create a System Policies container, right-click a specific administrative group and choose the New Server Policy Container command. Once the container is created, you can disable the viewing of multiple administrative groups if you want to.

System Policies

As mentioned, system policies can be created for and applied to servers, mailbox stores, or public stores. Once you define a policy, you can apply it to a set of objects throughout the organization. In addition, once a policy is associated with a group of objects, changing a setting in the policy changes that setting in all associated objects.

Creating a Policy

To create a new policy, right-click the policy container, point to New, and select the type of policy you want to create: Server, Mailbox Store, or Public Store. A set of property pages opens immediately for you to configure the policy. Each policy has a General page that lets you name the policy and a number of other pages that correspond to pages of the object for the type of policy you are creating. For example, the Server policy has only one extra page that represents the General property page of a server object.

Table 10.3 lists the pages available for each type of policy.

TABLE 10.3 Property Pages Available for System Policies

Type of Policy	Page	Description of Parameters
Server	General	Configuration of message tracking and log file maintenance
Public Store (see Chapter 6 for more information on specific settings)	General	General settings, such as support for S/MIME signatures and formatting of plain text messages
	Database	Maintenance interval for public store
	Replication	Replication interval and limits
	Limits	Storage and age limits and deletion settings
	Full-Text Indexing	Update and rebuild intervals
Mailbox Store (see Chapter 9 for more information on specific settings)	General	General settings, such as default public folder and offline folder settings
	Database	Maintenance interval for mailbox store
	Limits	Storage and age limits and deletion settings
	Full-Text Indexing	Update and rebuild intervals

Managing Policies

You can adjust the settings for a policy by opening its property pages. Selecting the policy in the left-hand pane displays all the objects attached to the policy in the right-hand pane. You can right-click an object to remove it from the policy.

You can also right-click a policy to find three useful commands:

- Delete: This command also dissociates the policy from any objects to which it is currently applied. However, the settings made by the policy remain in effect on objects unless otherwise modified. You can, however, change these settings if desired either manually or via another policy.
- Copy: Once a copy is made, you can make only the necessary adjustments to create a similar policy.
- Rename

Applying Policies

After creating and configuring a policy, you can apply it to objects throughout the organization. Exercise 10.4 outlines the steps for applying a server policy. The procedures for adding objects to the other types of system policies are almost identical.

EXERCISE 10.4

Applying a Server Policy

1. Start System Manager.
2. Expand the System Policies container.
3. Right-click the policy to which you want to add objects, and select the Add Server command from the shortcut menu.
4. Select a server from the list in the dialog that appears, and click the Add button to add it to the list of servers to add.
5. If a dialog box opens asking you to verify that you want to add the server to the policy, click Yes to proceed.
6. If the server is under the control of another policy, another dialog will appear asking you whether you want to change to the new policy. Click Yes to proceed.
7. Repeat Steps 4–6 to add as many servers to the policy as you want.
8. Once you have finished, click OK to return to System Manager.

Recipient Policies

Recipient policies work somewhat like system policies but are applied to groups of mail-enabled recipients instead of server objects. Recipient policies are used to generate e-mail addresses for recipients. By default, Exchange includes a single recipient policy that is used to generate SMTP and X.400 e-mail addresses for various mail-enabled recipients. You can create additional policies for other types of e-mail addresses.

Recipient policies use what is known as a background apply method, in which policies are defined and associated with recipients but are not immediately applied to recipients upon association (system policies are immediately applied). Instead, recipient policies are actually applied during regular maintenance intervals when the Recipient Update Service updates address lists within the Exchange organization. Alternatively, you can force an update by issuing the Update Now command to the applicable Recipient Update Service as discussed in Chapter 5, "Creating and Managing Exchange Recipients"

Client Troubleshooting Tools

One last tool bears mentioning in this chapter for client troubleshooting. The Inbox Repair Tool checks and repairs personal storage folders and may be useful to you if clients keep their mail on a local computer instead of the Exchange server for any reason.

Inbox Repair Tool The *Inbox Repair Tool* (`SCANPST.EXE`) tests and repairs a personal folder store (`*.pst`). It scans for bad blocks and attempts to rebuild them. If a PST file is corrupted beyond repair, this program will try to evacuate the good blocks of data and remove the corrupted blocks. This program does not need to be run unless there are operational problems with personal folders. On rare occasions, if an Exchange client application is abnormally terminated, a personal folder can become corrupted. You will be notified of the corruption on the next startup of the client application. The Inbox Repair Tool is installed with any installation of Outlook and can be found in the `Program Files\Common Files\System\Mapi\1033` directory.

It's worth noting that another tool, the OST Integrity Checker (`SCANOST.EXE`), also exists in this location, and it can be used to solve problems with synchronizing OST files with an Exchange server.

Summary

Many tools are included with Exchange Server to help manage an Exchange organization. An Exchange administrator can use various Windows Server 2003 tools, such as Event Viewer. The main tool in an administrator's arsenal is the System Manager snap-in, which manages objects throughout the Exchange hierarchy.

System Manager is actually a saved console file that connects to a Windows domain controller in order to get configuration information regarding your Exchange organization. You can customize the console to your use or create custom consoles for other administrators.

Administrative access to Exchange objects can be configured. An administrator can assign permissions to specific users or groups at different levels of the Exchange hierarchy in order to determine who has what type of access to what information. The Exchange Administration

Delegation Wizard lets you select a user or group and assign them a specific administrative role. Roles include the Exchange Full Administrator, Exchange Administrator, and Exchange View Only Administrator.

Many Windows tools are useful in monitoring an Exchange server. These include:

- Control Panel ➢ Administrative Tools ➢ Services
- Event Viewer
- System Monitor
- Registry Editor
- Computer Management
- Task Manager

In addition, Exchange provides a number of tools useful for monitoring system performance and troubleshooting. These include the Monitoring and Status utility, the Queue Viewer, and the Message Tracking Center.

System and recipient policies allow an administrator to create collections of configuration settings that can be easily applied to large numbers of objects at once. For example, you might create a policy that configures storage limits and deletion times for mailbox stores. You could then apply those settings across a group of stores without having to manually configure each store.

Exam Essentials

Understand the value of system policies. Much the same as you would configure a group policy in Active Directory, system policies in Exchange Server 2003 can be used to save you time when configuring changes across multiple servers and stores in the Exchange organization. Only one policy may be applied to any one tab of the properties for a mailbox store, public folder store, or server, so you will likely want to create one policy for each tab as required.

Know what you have available to work with. One thing Exchange Server 2003 is not short on is tools and utilities to help you get your job done. It is important that you be able to remember the tools we've discussed in this chapter as well as use them properly—both on test day and every day as you administer your Exchange organization.

Review Questions

1. You have installed Microsoft Exchange Server on a server that is heavily utilized. After installation, you notice that response times are slow and that the hard disk is constantly active. You use Windows NT System Monitor to collect the following statistics:

   %Processor time = 70

   %Disk free space = 60

   Pages/sec = 40

   Avg. Disk sec/Transfer = 0.02

   What should you do to reduce disk activity and improve server response time?

   A. Install more RAM.

   B. Install a faster CPU.

   C. Create additional swap files.

   D. Install an additional hard disk.

   E. Replace the hard disk with a faster hard disk.

2. A user receives a message stating that their OST file is damaged. What should you tell them so they can access their messages without losing the unsynchronized changes in that file?

   A. Move the OST file to the server and run ISINTEG.

   B. Use the Migration tool to import the OST into a new mailbox.

   C. Rename the OST file with a `.pst` extension and run SCANPST on the PST file.

   D. Run SCANOST on the OST file.

3. Your company has had problems with Exchange disk drives becoming full and stopping the IS service. What could you do to receive a warning before the IS reaches its limit again?

   A. Configure the Performance snap-in to send you an e-mail message when the Push Notification Cache Size has reached 100 percent.

   B. Configure an Exchange notification to send you an alert before the IS service stops.

   C. Configure an Exchange notification to send you an e-mail message when the IS service stops.

   D. Configure an Exchange notification to send you an e-mail message when disk space runs low.

4. You are an assistant Exchange administrator for a large network. Your supervisor asks you to send a test message to a recipient configured on a foreign messaging system and then determine the exact path that message took to get through the Exchange system. How would you do this?

   A. Use the Queue Viewer to monitor the message as it makes its way through the Exchange messaging queues.

   B. Use the Message Tracking Center to search for the message and see its history.

   C. Use the Monitoring and Status tool to send a test message that will automatically reply with a message that includes a trace.

   D. Use the Windows Event Viewer to trace the message's route.

5. Which of the following permissions would you assign to an object if you wanted a user to be able to view the object in System Manager but not access the object's properties?

   A. Read

   B. Read Permissions

   C. Execute

   D. Visible

6. Recently, users have been complaining that it seems to be taking longer and longer to connect to their Exchange server to get their e-mail. You have determined that all of the users have mailboxes on the same server. You want to find out what is slowing down the server by creating a performance log using the Performance snap-in. Which of the following would be important objects to monitor to determine the bottleneck in the system? (Choose all that apply.)

   A. The Pages/sec counter of the Memory object

   B. The Messages/sec counter of the MSExchangeMTA object

   C. The Local Queue Length counter of the SMTP Server object

   D. The %Disk free space counter of the Physical Disk object

7. You have 15 servers in your Exchange organization. Ten of those servers contain at least one mailbox store. Due to recent misuse of server-based storage, you have decided to limit the storage capacity of individual mailboxes. A store limit of 30 MB must be implemented for all mailboxes. As well, it is desired that you would be able to implement this storage limit without configuring each store manually. In addition, it is desired that you would be able to assign the Change Permissions permission on all of the mailbox stores to the Domain Admins security group.

   To achieve these results, you propose to perform the following actions:

   - Create a new server policy.
   - On the Limits page of the policy, assign the limits you want for all stores on the server.
   - On the Security page of the policy, assign the Change Permissions permission to the Domain Admins group.
   - Add all the servers that contain mailbox stores to the new policy.

If you complete the proposed actions, will you have achieved the required and/or desired results?

A. You will achieve both the required result and the two desired results.

B. You will achieve the required result and only one of the desired results.

C. You will achieve only the required result.

D. You will not achieve the required result or the desired results.

8. You have 15 servers in your Exchange organization. Ten of those servers contain at least one mailbox store. Due to recent misuse of server-based storage, you have decided to limit the storage capacity of individual mailboxes. A store limit of 30 MB must be implemented for all mailboxes. As well, it is desired that you would be able to implement this storage limit without configuring each store manually. In addition, it is desired that you would be able to assign the Change Permissions permission on all of the mailbox stores to the Domain Admins security group.

To achieve these results, you propose to perform the following actions:

- Create a new mailbox store policy.
- On the Limits page of the policy, assign the limits you want for all stores on the server.
- On the Security page of the policy, assign the Change Permissions permission to the Domain Admins group.
- Add all the mailbox stores to the new policy.

If you complete the proposed actions, will you have achieved the required and/or desired results?

A. You will achieve both the required result and the two desired results.

B. You will achieve the required result and only one of the desired results.

C. You will achieve only the required result.

D. You will not achieve the required result or the desired results.

9. When configuring permissions on Exchange objects, such as administrative groups or servers, what is the effect of not specifically granting or denying a permission on an object?

A. The user is granted access to the object but not to its child objects.

B. The user is denied all access to the object and its child objects.

C. The state of the permission is inherited from the parent container.

D. The state of the permission is inherited from the child container.

10. Which of the following permissions would you assign to a user if you wanted the user to be able to modify the properties of an object in System Manager?

A. Read Properties

B. Write Properties

C. Change Properties

D. Modify Properties

11. Which of the following tools represents the easiest way to get real-time information on items such as CPU and memory usage?
   A. Performance snap-in
   B. Computer Management
   C. Monitoring and Status
   D. Task Manager

12. Which of the following services does the Monitoring and Status tool monitor by default? (Choose all that apply.)
   A. Microsoft Exchange Information Store service
   B. Microsoft Exchange Event
   C. Microsoft Exchange Routing Engine
   D. Microsoft Exchange MTA Stacks
   E. Microsoft Exchange POP3

13. You have configured one of the servers in your organization with an X.400 connector so that users in the organization can exchange messages with users of a foreign X.400 system. Once it was configured, though, you noticed that the X.400 traffic tends to stack up in the queue once in a while, and you would like an easy way to know when this happens without having to constantly monitor the server yourself. What would be the best way to do this?
   A. Configure the Queue Viewer to log messages to the Windows Event Log when messages stack up in the queue.
   B. Set up the Performance snap-in to monitor the queue and send an alert when messages stack up.
   C. Configure a server monitor to monitor the X.400 queue and configure a notification to e-mail you when the threshold is reached.
   D. You must monitor the queue manually using the Queue Viewer.

14. Which of the following is not a component of an SNMP system?
   A. SNMP Agent
   B. SNMP Management System
   C. SNMP Alerter
   D. Management Information Base

15. Which of the following properties can be configured with a public store system policy? (Choose all that apply.)

A. The public folder tree associated with the store

B. Support for S/MIME signatures

C. The database associated with a store

D. Storage limits

E. Replication intervals

16. By default, what types of addresses are generated automatically for all recipients by the default recipient policy? (Choose all that apply.)

A. X.400

B. Microsoft Mail

C. SMTP

D. cc:Mail

17. You just hired two assistant administrators and want to provide them with the permissions necessary to administer the Exchange organization. However, you do not want them to be able to modify the permissions on any object. What should you do?

A. Assign them the Full Control permission at the organization level, but explicitly deny them the Write Permissions permission, and then propagate those permissions down throughout the hierarchy.

B. Assign them the Full Control permission for each administrative group, and then propagate those permissions down throughout the hierarchy.

C. Use the Exchange Administration Delegation Wizard to assign them the Exchange Administrator role at the organization level.

D. Use the Exchange Administration Delegation Wizard to assign them the Exchange Administrator role at each administrative group.

18. Your organization has three Exchange servers. All servers belong to a single administrative group and a single routing group. One server has an SMTP connector configured so that your organization can exchange mail with users on the Internet. You would like to be able to log the number of messages sent and received by your users to help establish a baseline of messaging activity to help with future troubleshooting efforts. Which tool would be best suited for this use?

A. System Monitor

B. Window Event Log

C. Diagnostics logging

D. Computer Management

E. Monitoring and Status

19. A user has been granted the permission to modify permissions on objects at the organization level. That same user has been denied the permission to modify permissions on objects at the server level but has been granted the permission on a specific server. The organization is set up to use the default inheritance settings. What effective permissions does the user have on the specific server?

A. The user can modify permissions.

B. The user cannot modify permissions.

C. Permissions cannot be set for individual servers.

D. Permissions cannot be set at the organization level.

20. Which of the following pieces of data regarding the Information Store service can you track with System Monitor? (Choose all that apply.)

A. The number of users currently using the service

B. The number of queries the service receives

C. The amount of processor time the service consumes

D. The numbered of messages queued in the service

Answers to Review Questions

1. A. Pages/sec is the key item here. This value indicates a high level of pages being written from memory to disk and means that RAM is the likely bottleneck. Even though the disk and CPU usage is also high, these values are likely a secondary effect of the memory bottleneck.

2. D. An OST file is a set of folders used for offline storage and uses the same format as the PST files used for personal folders. The OST Integrity Checker (`SCANOST.EXE`) should be able to fix the problem.

3. D. The Exchange Monitoring and Status tool can be set up to monitor for certain resource thresholds, such as low disk space, and to send e-mail notifications when thresholds are crossed.

4. B. The Message Tracking Center lets you search for specific messages sent within your organization and track those messages' progress through any server that has message tracking enabled.

5. A. The Read permission makes an object visible, but it does not allow a user to modify the object or even to view its property pages.

6. A, D. It would be best to start by logging the physical aspects of your computer, such as memory, networking, disk space, and CPU performance. The trouble with monitoring Exchange-specific counters and objects in relation to a noticeable slowdown in server performance is that most Exchange-related performance is going to be slowed down by a physical component bottleneck. Of course, if you determine that a physical bottleneck is not the likely culprit, you should move on to explore other areas.

7. D. Server policies can be used only to set message tracking and logging parameters for a server. They cannot be used to set security or limits for the stores on the servers. Mailbox store policies can be used to assign both age and storage limits to mailbox stores. However, no policies can be used to assign permissions to an object.

8. B. Server policies can be used only to set message tracking and logging parameters for a server. They cannot be used to set security or limits for the stores on the servers. Mailbox store policies can be used to assign both age and storage limits to mailbox stores. However, no policies can be used to assign permissions to an object.

9. C. When permissions are not specifically configured for a user or group on an object, they will be inherited from the parent object.

10. B. The Write Properties permission allows a user to change the properties of an object.

11. D. Task Manager displays the programs and processes running on a computer. It also displays various performance information, such as CPU and memory usage. An Exchange administrator can use this tool to view the overall health of a server. Access Task Manager by right-clicking the taskbar and choosing the Task Manager menu option.

12. A, C, D. By default, the Monitoring and Status tool monitors the Information Store service, MTA Stacks, Routing Engine, System Attendant, Simple Mail Transfer Protocol (SMTP), and World Wide Web Publishing services on every server. You can change these defaults or add services to any server.

13. C. Among other resources, a server monitor can be configured to monitor X.400 queue growth, and a notification can be set up to e-mail you when a threshold is reached. This is the best way to receive notification without having to monitor the system manually.

14. C. The SNMP Agent is the device on a network that is being monitored. The SNMP Management System is the component that does the actual monitoring in an SNMP environment. The Management Information Base (MIB) is a centralized database of all the values that can be monitored for all the devices in an SNMP system. There is no such thing as an SNMP Alerter component.

15. B, D, E. The General, Database, Replication, Limits, and Full-Text Indexing pages of a public store are available for configuration, but not all of the properties on those pages are available. You cannot configure a public folder tree or the database associated with a store because these are parameters that apply only to a specific store and cannot be applied to multiple stores using a policy.

16. A, C. Recipient policies are used to generate e-mail addresses for recipients. Exchange includes a single recipient policy by default that is used to generate SMTP and X.400 e-mail addresses for various mail-enabled recipients. In previous versions of Exchange Server, Microsoft Mail and cc:Mail addresses were also generated by default, but not in Exchange Server 2003.

17. C. The Exchange Administrator role gives users the same full administrative capability as the Exchange Full Administrator role but does not give them permission to modify permissions for objects. Running the wizard at the organization level would provide these permissions throughout the organization.

18. A. System Monitor graphically charts the performance of hundreds of individual system parameters on a Microsoft Windows Server 2003 computer and can also be used to log those parameters over time. Specifically, you would want to log the Messages Sent/min and Messages Delivered/min counters of the MSExchangeIS Mailbox object.

19. A. A specific permission granted or denied always takes precedence over any inherited permissions, no matter from where those permissions are inherited.

20. A. The MSExchangeIS System Monitor object includes only the User Count counter, which displays the number of users who are currently using the Information Store.

Coexisting with and Migrating from Exchange 5.5

MICROSOFT EXAM OBJECTIVES COVERED IN THIS CHAPTER:

- ✓ **Upgrade from Exchange Server 5.5 to Exchange Server 2003**
- ✓ **Migrate from other messaging systems to Exchange Server 2003**
  - Use the Migration Wizard to migrate from other messaging systems
  - Migrate from other Exchange organizations
- ✓ **Configure and troubleshoot Exchange Server 2003 for coexistence with other Exchange organizations**

Many companies that are installing Exchange Server 2003 will likely already have an existing messaging system in place. Many of those will be using a previous version of Exchange Server. Unless you are planning a full upgrade of all previous Exchange servers to Exchange Server 2003 and do not plan for users to access the system during the upgrade, there will be a time when Exchange Server 2003 servers and Exchange servers of previous versions need to coexist on the same network. You might choose to install an Exchange Server 2003 computer into an existing Exchange 5.5 organization, or you might choose to create a new organization for the Exchange Server 2003 computer that runs alongside the previous organization. Either way, you will have to manage the communications and the synchronization of directory information between Exchange Server 2003 and previous versions. That is what this chapter is all about.

Coexisting with Exchange Server 5.5

For any number of reasons, an organization may choose to leave existing Exchange Server 5.5 computers in operation and install new Exchange Server 2003 computers next to them. One of the most common scenarios for this type of deployment is to allow a smooth and planned out migration from Exchange Server 5.5 to Exchange Server 2003 while keeping user disruption to a minimum. In this section we will examine the benefits and drawbacks associated with coexisting with Exchange Server 5.5 as well as the benefits and drawbacks you can realize by removing all Exchange Server 5.5 computers from the Exchange organization. As well, we will examine the steps that you must complete to ensure that your new Exchange Server 2003 computers interact correctly with the Exchange Server 5.5 computers.

Nowhere in this chapter will we examine the first and most important part of any migration from a Windows NT environment—the moving of user accounts into Active Directory. If your Exchange Server 5.5 servers are still running on Windows NT, you will need to take the time to properly install and configure your new Windows Server 2003 Active Directory forest and then migrate user accounts and other resources into it before you even think about migrating from or coexisting with Exchange Server 5.5. For more information on making this critical migration, see the whitepaper "Migrating from Windows NT Server 4.0 to Windows Server 2003" on the Microsoft website or *Migrating from Microsoft Windows NT Server 4.0 to Windows Server 2003*, ISBN 0735619409.

Mixed-Mode Operations

An Exchange Server 2003 organization can operate in two modes: native and mixed. In *native mode*, only Exchange Server 2003 or Exchange 2000 Server is running, and the full Exchange Server 2003 functionality is present. No other previous versions of Exchange Server can communicate with the native-mode organization, except possibly via a connector or gateway as if it were a foreign system.

In *mixed mode*, Exchange Server 2003 can coexist and communicate with previous versions of Exchange Server in the same organization. When you first install an Exchange Server 2003 computer, it operates in mixed mode by default—even if you have no previous versions running on your network. Once you switch to native mode (described later in the chapter), you cannot go back, and direct interoperability with previous Exchange versions is permanently lost.

There are two big changes between all previous versions of Exchange Server and Exchange Server 2003 (and Exchange 2000 Server):

- In previous versions, Exchange Server managed its own directory of configuration and user objects. For example, mailboxes were objects in the Exchange directory that were associated with Windows NT 4.0 user accounts. In Exchange Server 2003, all directory functions have passed to Active Directory.
- In previous versions, Exchange sites were used to provide routing, administrative, and namespace boundaries. In Exchange Server 2003, routing groups provide routing boundaries, administrative groups provide administrative boundaries, and Active Directory provides namespace boundaries.

In this section, we discuss the benefits and limitations of running an organization in mixed mode, provide an overview of how Exchange 5.*x* directories and Active Directory can coexist, and examine the interaction of Exchange 5.*x* sites with Exchange Server 2003 routing groups and administrative groups.

Benefits and Limitations of Mixed Mode

Before we get too deep into the mechanics of mixed-mode operations, it is helpful to examine some of the benefits and limitations of working in mixed mode. Working in mixed mode provides the following benefits:

- There is interoperability between Exchange Server 2003 servers and servers running previous versions.
- Exchange 5.*x* directory objects are replicated to Active Directory and may be managed using System Manager and Active Directory Users and Computers.
- Exchange Server 2003 imports information from Exchange 5.*x* Gateway Address Routing Tables into its own link-state tables and thus provides access to Exchange 5.*x* connectors and gateways.
- You can continue to install Exchange 5.*x* servers, should you need to do so.
- Public folders can be replicated between Exchange Server 2003 and Exchange 5.*x* servers.

There are also a number of limitations imposed by working in mixed mode. These limitations include the following:

- Exchange 5.*x* sites are mapped directly to Exchange Server 2003 administrative groups and vice versa. This gives you less flexibility in setting up administrative groups than when working in native mode.
- You can move mailboxes only between servers that are in the same administrative group. In native mode, you can move mailboxes between servers in different administrative groups. In short, this prevents you from moving mailboxes between Exchange Server 5.5 and Exchange Server 2003 computers—except by using the Migration Wizard, which is discussed later.
- You can divide servers in an administrative group into different routing groups. However, these servers must all belong to the administrative group. In native mode, routing group boundaries and administrative group boundaries can cross.

Directory Interactions

Although many components and features are upgraded in Exchange Server 2003, one of the most important aspects of coexistence is the synchronization between the Exchange 5.*x* Directory Service and Active Directory. In order to successfully manage directory interactions, it is important that you understand the following:

- How the Exchange 5.*x* Directory Service works. This includes how it is structured, how it is replicated among Exchange 5.*x* servers, and how it is managed. We provide a brief overview below, but for more information check out your Exchange 5.*x* documentation or, better yet, pick up a copy of the previous edition of this book.
- How Active Directory works in relation to Exchange Server 2003. This includes how Exchange configuration objects are stored in Active Directory and how Active Directory is replicated among domain controllers. For more information on this, see Chapter 2, "Microsoft Exchange Architecture," and refer to your Windows Server 2003 documentation.
- The components that are used to allow Exchange 5.*x* servers to synchronize directory information with Exchange Server 2003 servers that use Active Directory. These components include the Site Replication Service (SRS) and the Active Directory Connector (ADC).

A Brief Review of the Exchange 5.*x* Directory Service

In Exchange 5.*x*, the *Directory Service (DS)* creates and manages the storage of all information about Exchange objects, such as the organization, site, servers, mailboxes, distribution lists, and public folders. The characteristics of these objects are called properties or attributes. The DS organizes all this information into a hierarchical database called the Directory, which is contained in a database file named `DIR.EDB`. The Directory hierarchy is patterned after the X.500 standard.

All Exchange servers in a site contain a complete copy of the Directory information. This is accomplished by automatic directory replication between servers of a site via *Remote Procedure Call (RPC)*. When an Exchange object, such as a mailbox, is created on a particular Exchange server, that object's information is automatically copied to all the other servers in that site.

There can also be directory replication between sites. This is not an automatic process, and it must be configured by an administrator. Directory replication between sites occurs using SMTP messages over whatever connectors are used to connect the sites. This ability allows administrators to decide which resources to share with other sites. Directory replication between sites can be used to create an enterprise messaging environment.

The DS component supports directory access through the MAPI interface and through the LDAP (Lightweight Directory Access Protocol) interface. This enables both MAPI client software (such as Outlook) and Internet LDAP-enabled applications (such as Outlook Express) to access the Exchange Directory. Administrators access the Directory through Microsoft Exchange Administrator, which is a MAPI program.

Supporting Directory Coexistence

Two main components facilitate coexistence between the Exchange 5.*x* Directory and the Active Directory in mixed-mode organizations: the *Site Replication Service (SRS)* and the *Active Directory Connector (ADC)*.

SITE REPLICATION SERVICE

The SRS runs on an Exchange Server 2003 computer and actually simulates an Exchange 5.*x* system from the viewpoint of the Exchange 5.*x* servers in a site. In fact, the SRS is really the same service as the Directory Service from Exchange 5.*x*; it has just been disabled in a few critical areas so that clients cannot connect to it and so that it does not interfere with operations on the Exchange Server 2003 computer. Within a site, Exchange 5.*x* servers treat SRS as if it were just another Exchange 5.*x* server running the Directory Service and replicate information with it freely. The information collected by SRS is then synchronized with Active Directory via the Active Directory Connector. SRS actually provides two functions:

- SRS provides a pathway for replicating configuration information between Active Directory and Exchange 5.*x* servers. As you'll learn in the next section, the ADC synchronizes directory information with Exchange 5.*x* servers directly but must go through SRS for configuration information.
- SRS provides Exchange 5.*x* servers in the site with a means of accessing directory information concerning the Exchange Server 2003 computer on which SRS is running.

ACTIVE DIRECTORY CONNECTOR

The ADC runs on an Exchange Server 2003 computer and synchronizes directory information between Active Directory and Exchange 5.*x* servers in the site. ADC also synchronizes configuration information with those servers using the SRS as an intermediary (see Figure 11.1).

There is a good reason why the SRS is used as the synchronization endpoint for configuration information instead of allowing a direct connection between Active Directory and the Directory Service. Different parts of the Exchange 5.*x* Directory are replicated to different areas within the Active Directory:

- Configuration information, such as the configuration of servers and connectors, is replicated to the configuration-naming partition of Active Directory.

- Recipient information is replicated to the domain-naming partition of Active Directory.
- Namespace information is replicated to the schema-naming partition of Active Directory.

Only one instance of the ADC can run on a single Exchange server, but you can configure multiple connection agreements for an ADC. A *connection agreement (CA)* is something like a virtual connector that runs over the ADC. Each connection agreement is defined to replicate certain directory objects to certain parts of the Active Directory and can even be configured to replicate at certain times. Having the SRS perform as the endpoint of communication for the ADC means that you don't have to reconfigure the connection agreements each time the status of an Exchange 5.*x* server in your site changes (for example, when you upgrade it to Exchange Server 2003). You can configure connection agreements between Active Directory and multiple sites, and you can configure multiple agreements to a single site.

There are two basic types of connection agreements:

- User connection agreements replicate recipient objects and their data between the SRS and Active Directory.
- Configuration connection agreements replicate Exchange-specific configuration information, such as connectors and site information.

You'll learn how to configure the SRS, ADC, and connection agreements later in this chapter.

FIGURE 11.1 Active Directory Connector and Site Replication Service

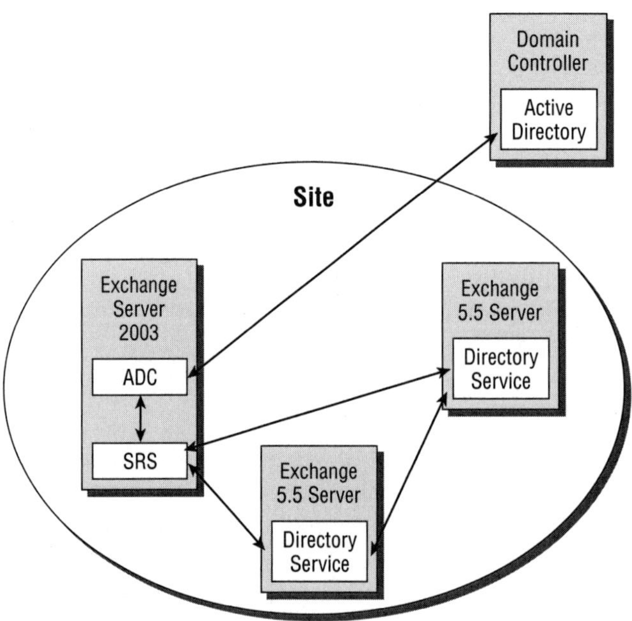

There are actually two versions of the Active Directory Connector: one that ships with Windows Server 2003 and one that ships with Exchange Server 2003. The ADC for Windows does replicate directory information between Exchange 5.*x* directories and Active Directory. It is intended for people who want to prepare Active Directory for Exchange during Windows deployment but before installing Exchange Server 2003. The ADC for Exchange has all the features of the ADC for Windows, but it is enhanced so that it can replicate not only the actual Exchange objects but also the configuration information about those objects. Because it includes all the features of the ADC for Windows and more, we always recommend upgrading to the ADC for Exchange.

Site and Administrative Group Interactions

In order to make Exchange 5.*x* and Exchange Server 2003 coexist, certain restrictions are placed on how you can configure Exchange Server 2003. When an organization is running in mixed mode, Exchange Server 2003 must follow the rules laid out by previous versions of Exchange. This means that administrative groups and routing groups must be mapped directly to Exchange 5.*x* sites so that, in essence, Exchange Server 2003 simulates the functionality of an Exchange 5.*x* site.

In an Exchange 5.*x* site, messages flow between Exchange 5.*x* Message Transfer Agents (MTAs) using RPC. When you add an Exchange Server 2003 server to the site, messages flow between the Exchange 5.*x* MTAs and the Exchange Server 2003 MTA using RPC. When multiple Exchange Server 2003 servers exist in the site, messages flow between Exchange 5.*x* and Exchange Server 2003 using RPC, but using SMTP, they flow between the Exchange Server 2003 servers.

Between Exchange 5.*x* sites, messages move across connectors in much the same way that connectors are used in Exchange Server 2003. The primary connector used between Exchange 5.*x* sites is the *Site Connector*, which makes use of RPC to transmit messages. In Exchange Server 2003 the *Routing Group Connector (RGC)* replaces the Site Connector used in previous versions. The RGC uses SMTP rather than RPC to transport messages between Exchange Server 2003 servers. For coexistence, however, the RGC uses RPC to transport messages to Exchange 5.*x* sites that use the Site Connector. This means you can target Exchange Server 2003 servers as bridgehead servers for Exchange 5.*x* sites that use the Site Connector. For all other connectors (such as X.400), Exchange Server 2003 uses its equivalent connector to communicate with Exchange 5.*x* sites.

Site Replication Service

As you learned earlier in the chapter, SRS is used to make Exchange Server 2003 servers appear as Exchange 5.*x* servers to other Exchange 5.*x* servers in a site. It is also used by ADC to synchronize configuration information. SRS is installed automatically when the first Exchange

Server 2003 server is introduced to an Exchange 5.*x* site. When it is installed, a connection agreement is also created so that the ADC can manage the synchronization of configuration information.

There is really not much for you to manage about the SRS; Exchange Server 2003 handles the configuration and maintenance of SRS pretty much automatically. However, there are a few points about SRS of which you should be aware.

SRS and LDAP SRS runs the *Lightweight Directory Access Protocol (LDAP)* in order to communicate with Active Directory. Because Windows Server 2003 also uses LDAP and locks the well-known port 389 for its own use, SRS defaults to using port 379 for its LDAP communications. No special configuration is needed for SRS to communicate with Active Directory, but on occasion, you may need to configure special firewall access for the port. You can learn more about configuring ports for LDAP in Chapter 15, "Securing and Troubleshooting Exchange Server 2003."

Site Consistency Checker The *Site Consistency Checker (SCC)* is an updated version of the Knowledge Consistency Checker from Exchange 5.*x*. The SCC ensures that knowledge consistency is maintained for sites and administrative groups when operating in mixed mode. It does this by dynamically configuring multiple connection agreements to establish the most efficient replication.

SRS database SRS uses the same ESE database technology that the Information Store uses and that the Exchange 5.*x* Directory Service uses. When SRS is installed, a set of databases and transactions logs much like those for a storage group is installed in the `\Program Files\Exchsrvr\srsdata` folder. Unlike the stores in a storage group, the SRS database cannot be mounted or dismounted. However, you can stop and start SRS manually using the Services tool provided with Windows.

Creating an additional SRS for a site Only one instance of SRS can run on a single Exchange Server 2003 server, and normally only the first Exchange Server 2003 server installed into an Exchange 5.*x* site is configured with SRS. Additional Exchange Server 2003 servers installed into the site do not really need the service because they can simply rely on Active Directory for their directory information. However, it is sometimes useful to have another instance of SRS running in a site; for example, it may help to balance the replication load in a busy site. You can install an additional instance of the service in System Manager by expanding the Tools container, right-clicking the Site Replication Service object, and selecting the New Site Replication Service command from the shortcut menu. Each additional instance of SRS requires an additional Exchange Server 2003 server in the site.

Active Directory Connector

The Active Directory Connector is installed automatically when you install Exchange Server 2003 into an existing Exchange 5.*x* site. You can also install the ADC before installing Exchange Server 2003 if you want to set up a replication model first. In this section, we discuss the installation of ADC and the creation and configuration of connection agreements.

The following discussion does not address the installation, configuration, or management of Exchange Server 5.5. It is assumed that you already have this knowledge and have the Exchange 5.5 organization in place.

Installing ADC

You will install the ADC from the `Active Directory Connector` folder on the Exchange Server 2003 CD-ROM in the `ADC\I386` directory or by using the Exchange Server Deployment Tools dialogs (recall from Chapter 3, "Installing Microsoft Exchange Server 2003," that the Exchange Server Deployment Tools provide step-by-step instructions on how to successfully install an Exchange Server 2003 computer). You will see later when we install the first Exchange Server 2003 computer into the Exchange 5.5 site where the installation of the ADC comes, regardless of which method you use or when you do it—the Setup Wizard or from the splash screen that appears when you insert the disc. During the installation, the Setup Wizard prompts you to install two components:

- The Active Directory Connector Service component is the actual connector itself. If you are installing the first ADC in a forest, you will need to have the appropriate permissions to modify the Active Directory schema. If an ADC or an instance of Exchange 2000 is already installed in the forest, you will not need these permissions, because the schema will already have been modified. You can find more information on how the installation routine modifies the schema in Chapter 3.
- The Active Directory Connector Management component is a snap-in that lets you manage the ADC outside the System Manager snap-in, which is useful if you want to install the ADC before installing the first Exchange Server 2003 server into an organization. You can install the snap-in on any computer from which you would want to manage the ADC.

If ADC is already installed on the computer on which you run Setup, you are given the option of removing the ADC from the computer—which is useful when you have decommissioned all of your Exchange 5.*x* servers. Before you can uninstall the ADC, however, you must first use System Manager to remove all of the connection agreements.

Exercise 11.1 outlines the steps for installing the ADC.

EXERCISE 11.1

Installing the Active Directory Connector

1. On the server that will have Exchange Server 2003 installed, insert the Exchange Server 2003 CD-ROM into the drive.

EXERCISE 11.1 *(continued)*

2. On the CD-ROM, open the ADC folder, and then open the I386 folder.

3. Double-click `setup.exe`.

4. The Microsoft Active Directory Connector Setup dialog opens. Click Next to go on.

5. Accept the End User License Agreement (EULA) and click Next.

6. On the Component Selection page, select the Microsoft Active Directory Connector Service Component and Microsoft Active Directory Connector Management Components options, and click Next to go on.

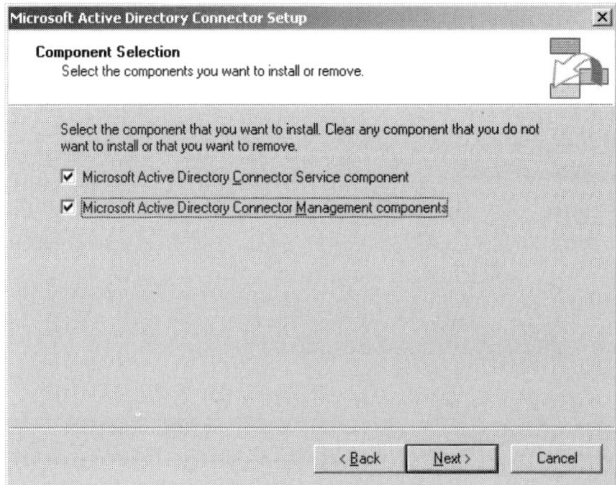

EXERCISE 11.1 *(continued)*

7. Leave the installation location at its default directory, and click Next to go on.

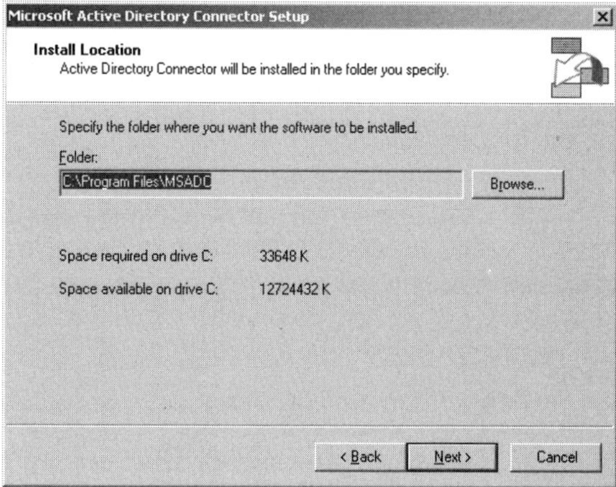

8. Exchange 5.*x* uses a special user account named the Site Service Account that lets other Exchange 5.*x* computers log on to the local computer to perform their functions. The SRS service on your Exchange Server 2003 server needs one, too. Enter the name of the account you would like to use as well as the password, and click Next to go on.

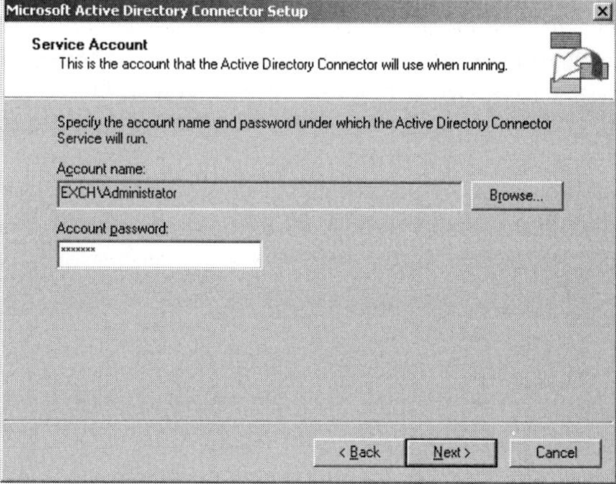

9. On the summary page, click Finish.

In a production environment you will likely create a special service account for use by the ADC.

Once you have installed the ADC, you can open its property pages to reveal general details and to enable diagnostic logging for the connector, but not much else. Most of the management of the ADC actually happens by creating and managing connection agreements.

Regardless of when or how you initiate the ADC installation, it must be done before you can successfully install Exchange Server 2003 into the Exchange 5.5 site.

Using the ADC Tools

The first thing you should do (and the next step in the installation process that we will discuss later) is to configure the Active Directory Connector properly so that it will help you create connection agreements correctly. Exercise 11.2 walks you through the process of using the ADC Tools.

Recall that if your Exchange 5.5 server is installed on a Windows 2000 Server Domain Controller, Active Directory will lock out all other applications from using LDAP over port 389 (the default). You will need to change the LDAP port for both your Exchange 5.5 sites and servers to something else, such as port 390. After this change has been made, you will need to stop and restart the Microsoft Exchange Directory Service. Note that three other services depend on this service and will also have to be restarted: Microsoft Exchange Message Transfer Agent, Microsoft Exchange Event Service, and Microsoft Exchange Information Store. Be sure you restart all four services.

SRS gets around the port 389 issue by using port 379 for its LDAP communications.

EXERCISE 11.2

Using the ADC Tools

1. Click Start ➢ Programs ➢ Microsoft Exchange ➢ Active Directory Connector. The Active Directory Connector Services console opens.

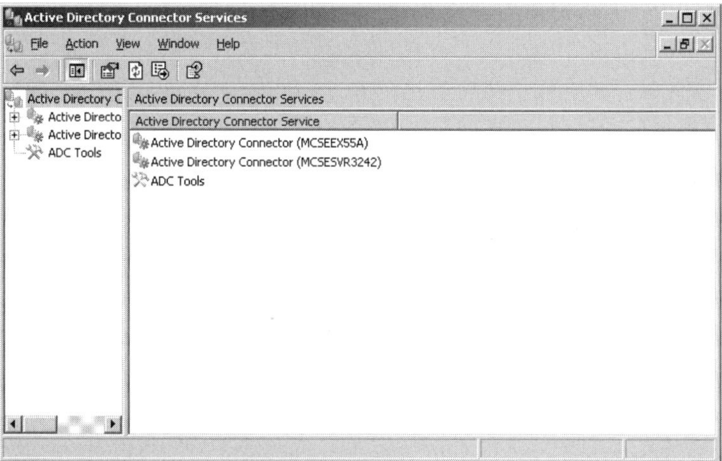

2. Click the ADC Tools node, as seen below.

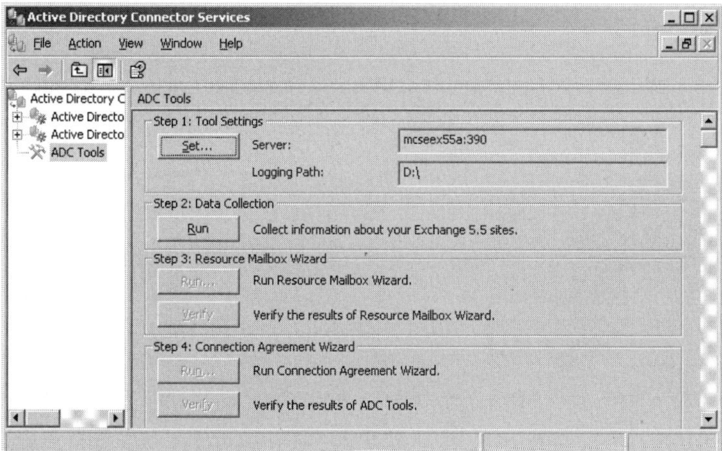

EXERCISE 11.2 *(continued)*

3. Under Step 1, click the Set button to enter the required information about the Exchange 5.5 server that is to be analyzed. Note that it can be any server in the site. Click OK after entering the information.

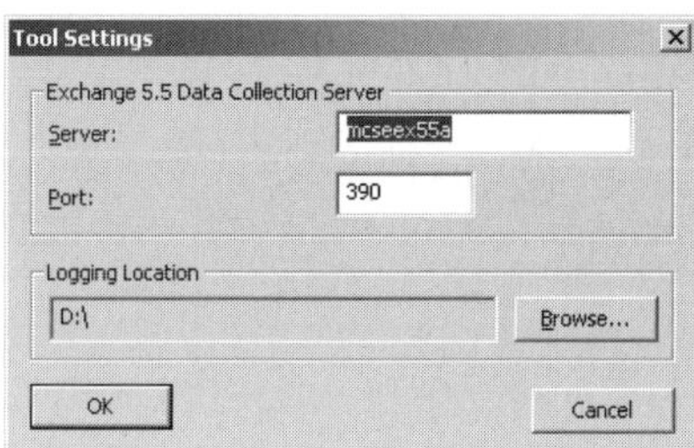

4. Click the Run button under Step 2. If you have entered the information correctly and an Exchange 5.5 server is found, you will be able to proceed to Step 3 and Step 4. The most common problems at this point are LDAP ports (see the tip above) and incorrect server names.

5. Step 3 is optional and really needed only if you have resource mailboxes.

6. Click Run under Step 4 to start the Connection Agreement Wizard—this is the easiest way to create properly configured connection agreements.

7. Click Next to dismiss the opening page of the Connection Agreement Wizard.

EXERCISE 11.2 *(continued)*

8. On the Staging Area page you will need to select the Active Directory container into which Exchange 5.5 recipients are replicated by default.

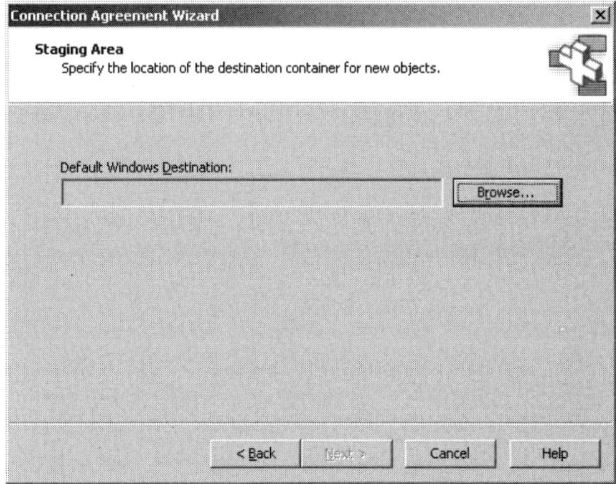

9. Click the Browse button to locate the container you wish to use. Click OK to close the Choose A Container dialog. Click Next to continue.

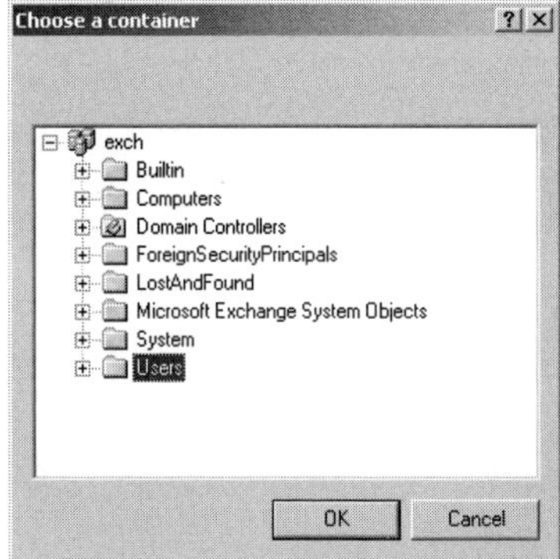

EXERCISE 11.2 *(continued)*

10. On the Site Connections page, you will be presented with the recommended connection agreement. In most cases, you will want to leave this as is, although you can change it to a one-way agreement if desired. Click Next to continue.

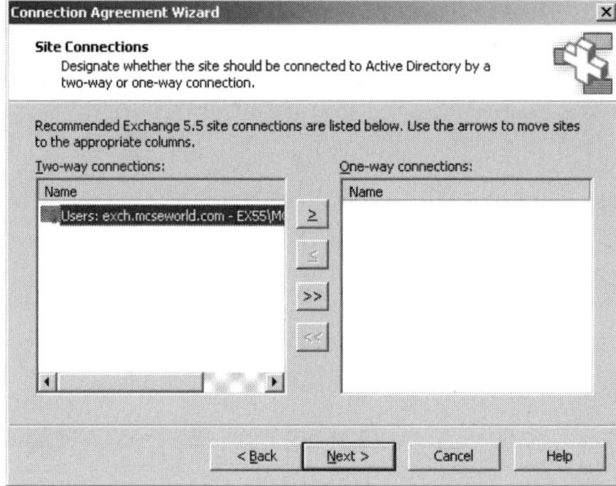

11. On the Site Credentials page you will be required to enter your Exchange 5.5 site account credentials.

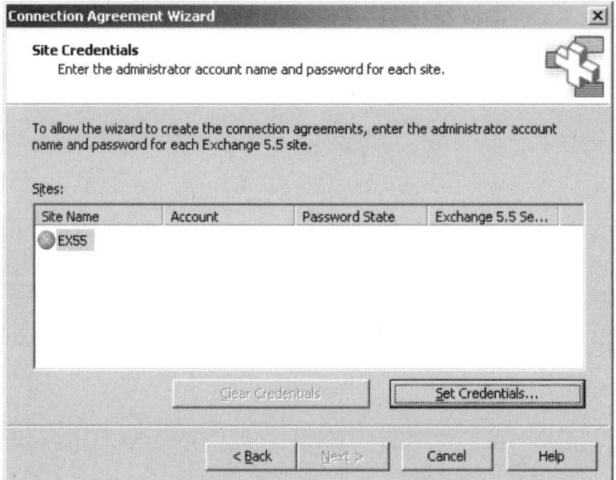

EXERCISE 11.2 *(continued)*

12. Click the Set Credentials button to open the Set Credentials dialog box. Enter your Exchange 5.5 credentials and click OK.

13. If your credentials are correct, they will be validated and you will be able to continue by clicking Next.

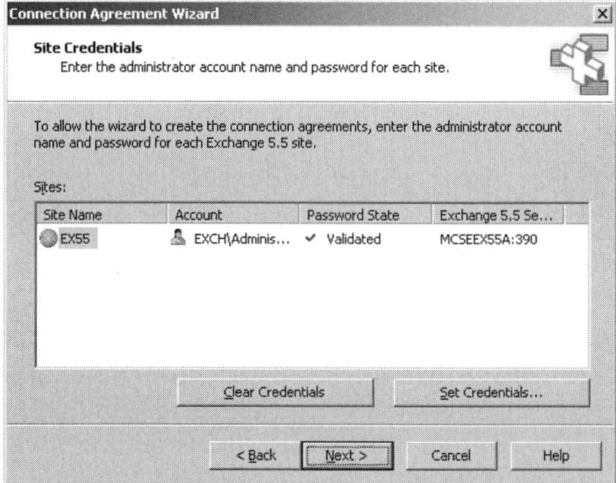

EXERCISE 11.2 *(continued)*

14. On the Domain Credentials page, you will be required to enter your Windows domain account credentials.

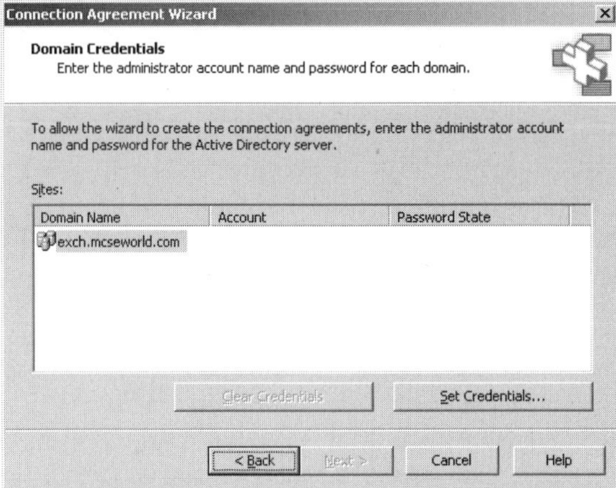

15. Click the Set Credentials button to open the Set Credentials dialog box. Enter your Windows domain credentials and click OK.

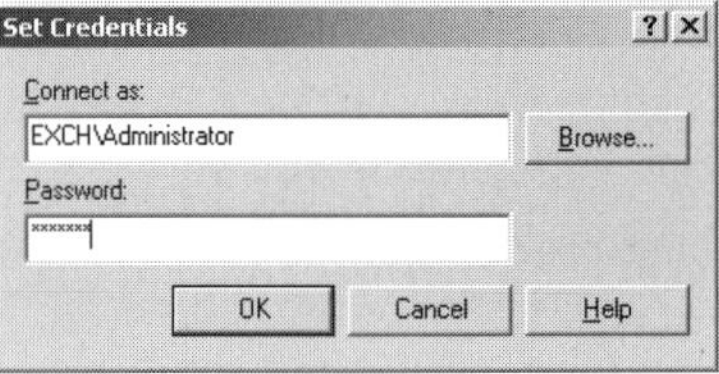

EXERCISE 11.2 *(continued)*

16. If your credentials are correct, they will be validated and you will be able to continue by clicking Next.

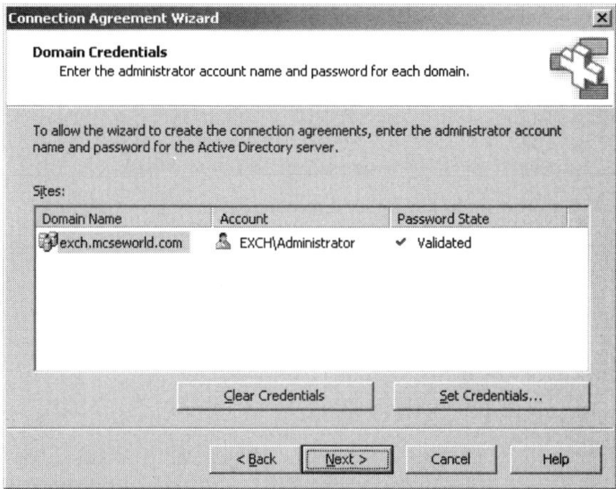

17. On the Connection Agreement Selection page, you will be presented with the recommended connection agreements. In most cases, you can use the recommended agreements. You can change them if you need, however. Click Next to continue.

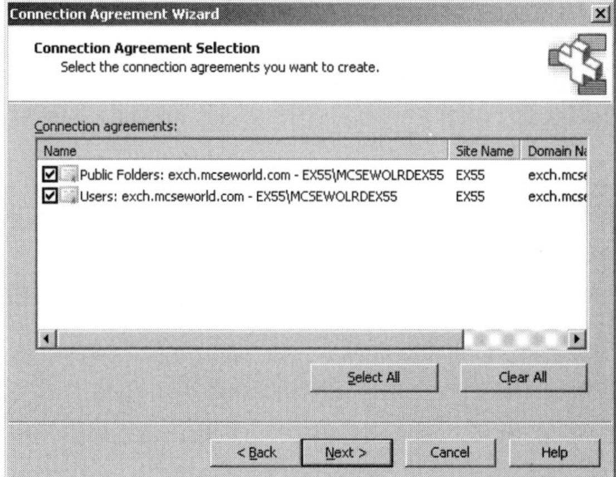

EXERCISE 11.2 *(continued)*

18. The Summary page appears, giving the opportunity to review your configuration. Click Next to continue and create the connection agreements you've configured.

19. You can click the Verify button under Step 4 to verify that things are in order if desired; however, you should give objects time to replicate.

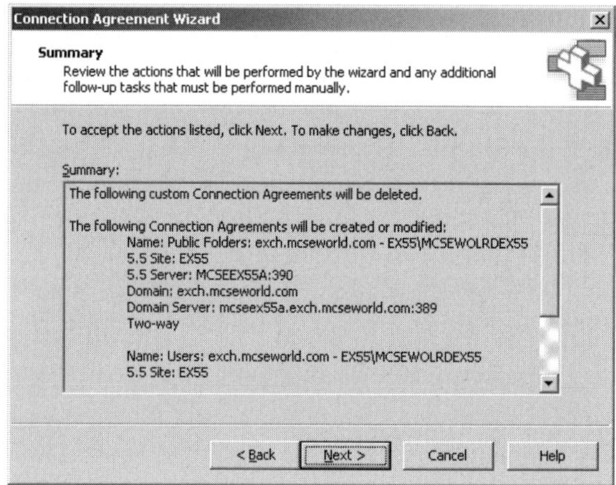

20. After the connection agreements are created, you can view them in the Active Directory Connector Services console.

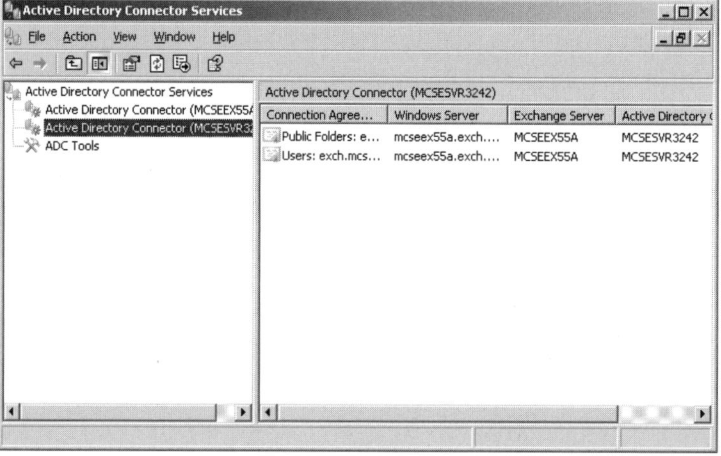

Installing Exchange Server 2003 into an Exchange Server 5.5 Site

The basic process to install Exchange Server 2003 into an Exchange Server 5.5 site is really not much different than it is to install into a new Exchange Server 2003 organization or an existing Exchange 2000 Server organization. The biggest difference, as we've already discussed at length in this chapter, is that you must synchronize Active Directory and the Exchange Directory Service. The Exchange Server Deployment Tools recommends the following steps for deploying the first Exchange Server 2003 in an Exchange Server 5.5 site:

1. Install the operating system on the future Exchange Server 2003 computer.
2. Ensure that the NNTP, SMTP, WWW, and ASP.NET services are running on the computer.
3. Run the DSScopeScan tool to help determine the scope of your deployment.
4. Install the Windows Support Tools on the new server, dependent on the version of Windows that was installed.
5. Run the DCDiag tool to check network connectivity and DNS.
6. Run the NetDiag tool to check network connectivity.
7. Review the logs created by the DSScopeScan, DCDiag, and NetDiag tools.
8. Run ForestPrep and DomainPrep to prepare the forest and domain for the installation of Exchange Server 2003.
9. Run the OrgPrepCheck tool to verify that the schema was properly extended.
10. Review the logs again for errors.
11. Install the Active Directory Connector (refer back to Exercise 11.1).
12. Use the ADC Tools to analyze the Exchange 5.5 site and then create the desired connection agreements (refer back to Exercise 11.2).
13. Run the SetupPrep tool to check one last time that the installation of Exchange Server 2003 will occur correctly.
14. Review the logs again for errors.
15. Install the first Exchange Server 2003 computer into the Exchange 5.5 site (discussed later in Exercise 11.3).
16. Change the connection agreements to the new server running Exchange Server 2003 to prevent replication problems and GAL viewing problems.
17. Validate the installation using the ADCConfigCheck, ConfigDSInteg, RecipientDSInteg, and PrivFoldCheck tools.

If your Exchange Server 5.5 servers are running on a Windows 2000 Server domain controller, don't forget to use the correct LDAP port when running the deployment tools.

The best way to go about this process is to have at least one Windows Server 2003 domain controller and global catalog server already in your organization. Recall that Exchange Server 5.5 will not run on Windows Server 2003, so you'll likely be faced with an existing Windows 2000 Server Active Directory forest that will need upgrading with the ADPrep tool. You should also have Windows Server 2003 member servers installed and joined to the domain for the Exchange Server 2003 installation. While you can install Exchange Server 2003 on a domain controller, it's not going to give you the best in performance from either Active Directory or Exchange. There are not any set rules for how to configure your organization, but you will at a minimum want to install one Windows Server 2003 domain controller and global catalog server as discussed above. See Microsoft Knowledge Base Article 309628 at `http://support.microsoft.com/default.aspx?scid=kb;en-us;309628` for information on using ADPrep.

Installing Exchange Server 2003

It's a long path to take to finally get to the point of being able to install Exchange Server 2003 into your Exchange 5.5 site, but you've made it—the end is now in sight. The installation process is similar in some ways but distinctly different in others because you will be joining an existing Exchange 5.5 site. Exercise 11.3 outlines the process to install the first Exchange Server 2003 computer into an Exchange 5.5 site.

EXERCISE 11.3

Installing Exchange Server 2003

1. Start the Exchange Server 2003 Setup routine by double-clicking `setup.exe` in the `SETUP\I386` directory of your CD or by letting it auto-play.

EXERCISE 11.3 *(continued)*

2. On the Welcome to Exchange Server 2003 Setup page that opens, click the Exchange Deployment Tools link.

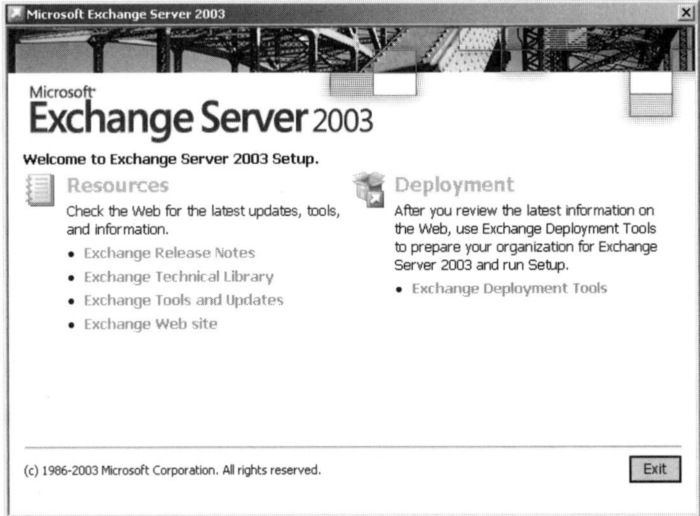

3. Click the Deploy The First Exchange Server 2003 link.

EXERCISE 11.3 *(continued)*

4. Click the Coexistence With Exchange 5.5 link.

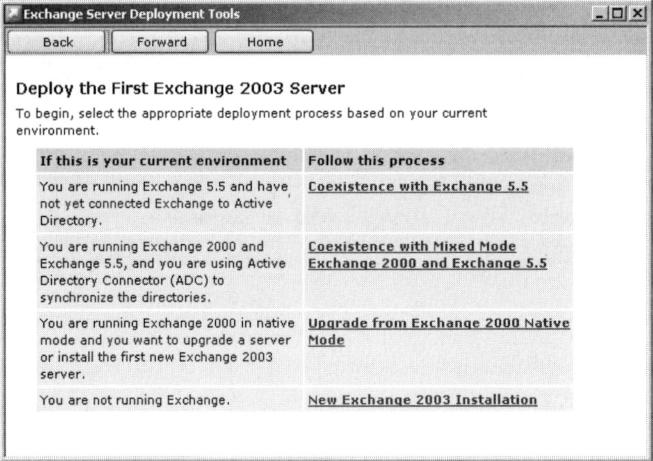

5. The Microsoft Exchange Installation Wizard appears. Click Next to dismiss its opening page and continue.

6. Accept the License Agreement and click Next to continue.

7. Enter your Product Key and click Next to continue.

8. Select the components you want installed from the Component Selection page, and click Next to continue.

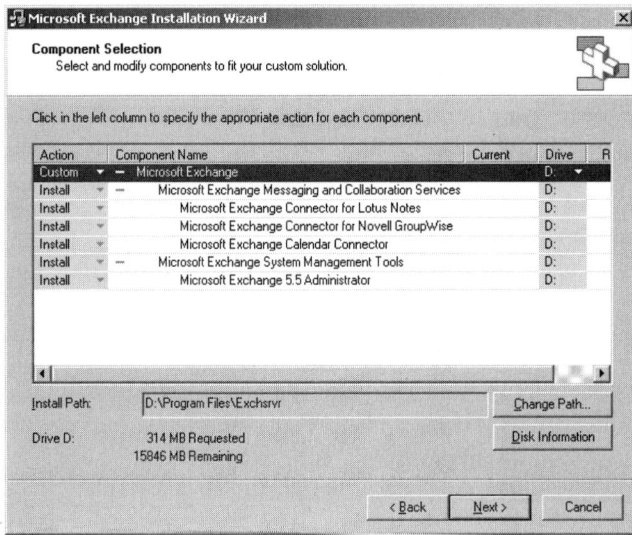

EXERCISE 11.3 *(continued)*

9. On the Installation Type page, select Join Or Upgrade An Existing Exchange 5.5 Organization, and click Next to continue.

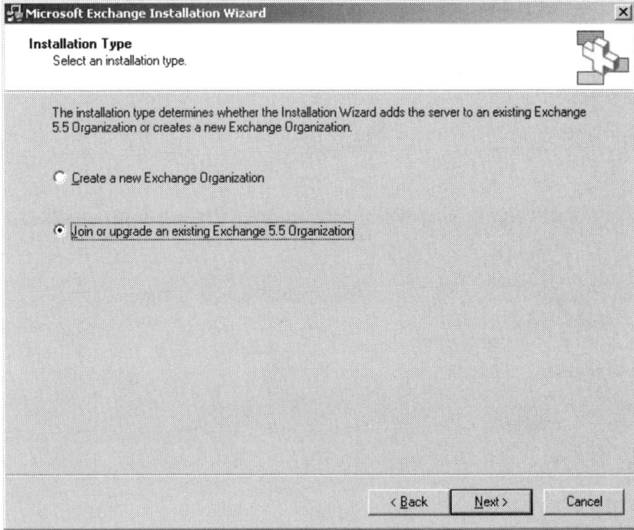

10. On the Select a Server in an Exchange 5.5 Organization page, enter the name of one server in the Exchange 5.5 organization you want to join, and click Next to continue.

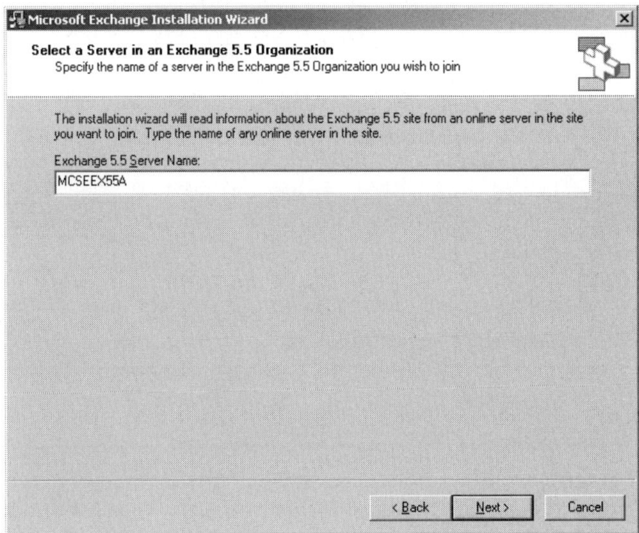

EXERCISE 11.3 *(continued)*

11. If prompted that Setup must verify prerequisite conditions, click OK.

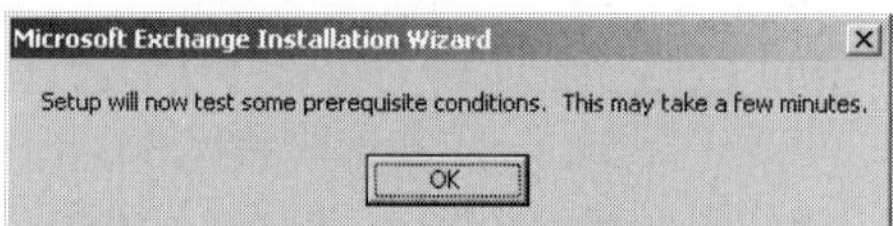

12. You will be required to acknowledge the server licensing mode under which Exchange operates. Be sure to acquire enough CALs for your clients. Click Next to continue.

13. On the Service Account page, you will need to enter the credentials for the Exchange 5.5 service account. Click Next to continue.

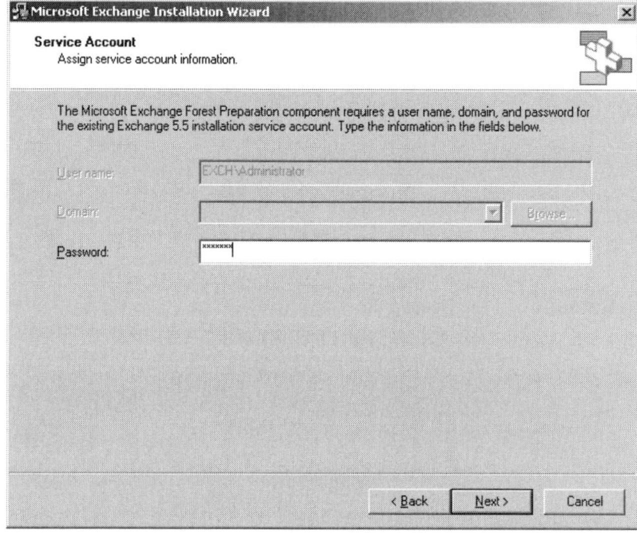

14. You will have the chance to review your installation options on the Installation Summary page. Click Next to continue.

15. The installation will begin and will likely take some time to complete. Click Finish to close the Microsoft Exchange Installation Wizard.

For best results you should have one or more Windows Server 2003 global catalog servers in your forest. If you do not, you will likely be unable to change the connection agreements to point toward the Exchange Server 2003 computer on the Windows end. For more information on creating Windows Server 2003 global catalogs, see MS Knowledge Base article 816105 at `http://support.microsoft.com/default.aspx?scid=kb;en-us;816105`.

As discussed previously, the next step you will need to perform is to retarget your connection agreements (created previously by ADC Tools) so that the Windows server is configured as the new Exchange Server 2003 server. Figure 11.2 shows the change being made to one of the connection agreements, and Figure 11.3 shows what you should see after you've changed them both. It's important to note that the inability to locate a Windows Server 2003 global catalog at this point will likely prevent you from making this critical change.

FIGURE 11.2 Changing the target on the connection agreement

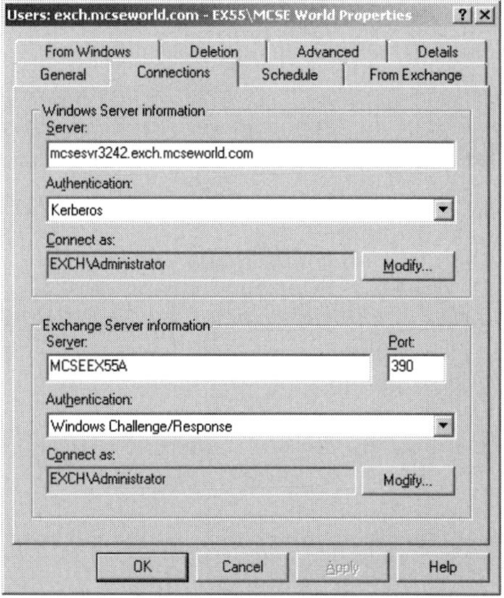

FIGURE 11.3 Viewing the changes

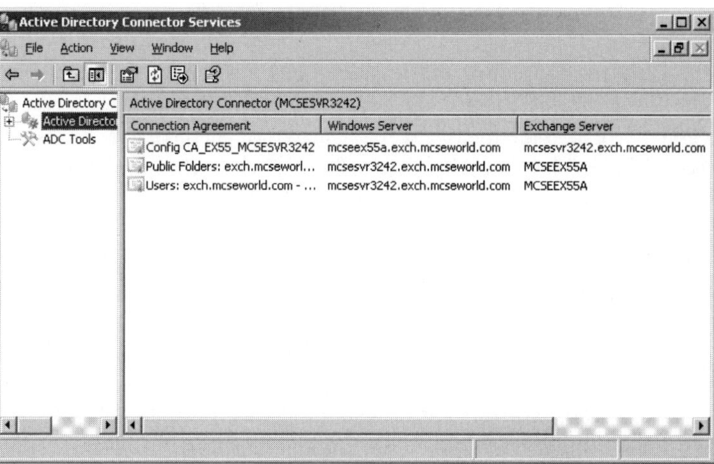

Creating Connection Agreements

If you've followed along with the exercises up to now, you really don't need to create any connection agreements manually. However, situations can change and you may later want to create a connection agreement for some reason. Should this be the case, it's helpful to understand the various properties pages that make up a connection agreement as well as the basic process to go about creating one.

Whether you are creating a recipient or public folder connection agreement, the creation process is basically the same. Exercise 11.4 outlines the steps for creating a recipient connection agreement.

EXERCISE 11.4

Creating a Recipient Connection Agreement

1. Click Start ➢ Programs ➢ Microsoft Exchange ➢ Active Directory Connector.
2. Right-click the Active Directory Connector (*computername*) object and select New ➢ Recipient Connection Agreement. This opens the property pages for the new connection agreement, which are discussed in detail in the next section.
3. Enter a name for the connection agreement on the General page. Try to make the name one that suggests the use of the CA.
4. Enter the name of the Exchange 5.*x* server to which you want to connect on the Connections page.
5. All of the other properties throughout the property pages are optional. When you have finished configuring the connection agreement, click OK.

Configuring Connection Agreement Properties

Whether you are creating a recipient or public folder connection agreement, the property pages you use to configure the agreements are identical. The property pages for a configuration connection agreement are also identical, except that two of the property pages, Deletion and Advanced, are not present. The following sections detail all of the available property pages for a CA.

General Properties

The General page, shown in Figure 11.4, is used to name the CA, to specify whether the CA is two-way or one-way, and to designate a server to run the CA.

FIGURE 11.4 General properties of a CA

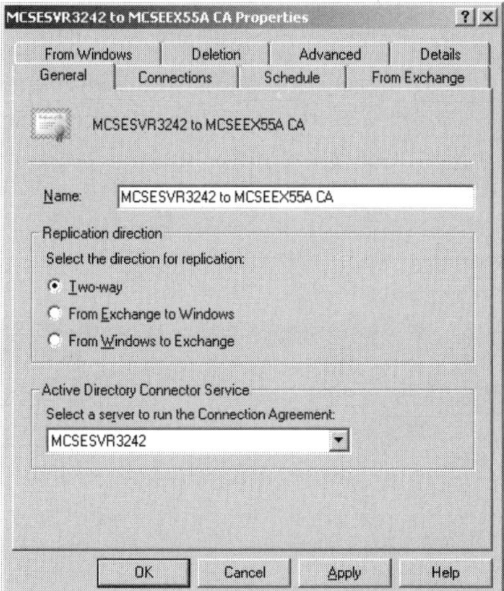

Connections Properties

The Connections page, shown in Figure 11.5, is used to enter connection information for the bridgehead servers of the connection: the Windows server (the Active Directory server) and the Exchange server (the server running Exchange 5.*x*). The Windows server must be running at least Windows 2000 with Windows Service Pack 3 (the minimum requirements to install Exchange Server 2003) and Active Directory. The Exchange server must be running Exchange Server 5.5 with at least Service Pack 3 applied, even though the rest of the servers in the site do not need to run this recent a version of Exchange.

You use the Connections page to specify the authentication method to use for each end of the connection agreement. For more information on authentication methods, see Chapter 15. Also, you use the Connections page to enter the authentication credentials for each server. The account you enter allows each server to connect to the directories on the other end of the connection. The permissions account defined for each server requires only write permissions for its directory.

Finally, you use the Connections page to specify the LDAP port number used by the Exchange 5.*x* server. Unless Exchange 5.*x* is running on a Windows 2000 domain controller, this option is not important. However, Active Directory locks port 389 for its own use and renders the Exchange 5.*x* server unable to accept LDAP connections. A common alternative port number is 390.

FIGURE 11.5 Connections properties of a CA

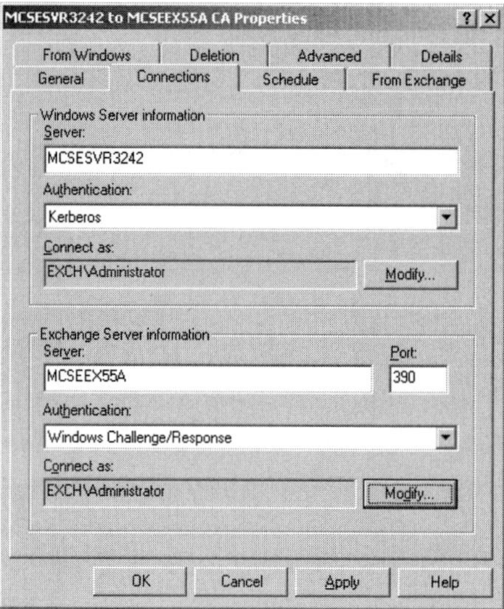

Schedule Properties

The Schedule page, shown in Figure 11.6, is like all the other Schedule property pages you've seen in this book and throughout Windows Server 2003. It allows you to specify the times during which replication can take place.

FIGURE 11.6 Schedule properties of a CA

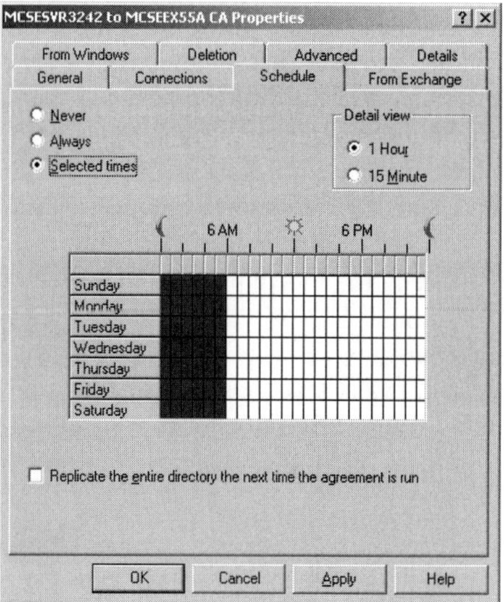

FIGURE 11.7 From Exchange properties of a CA

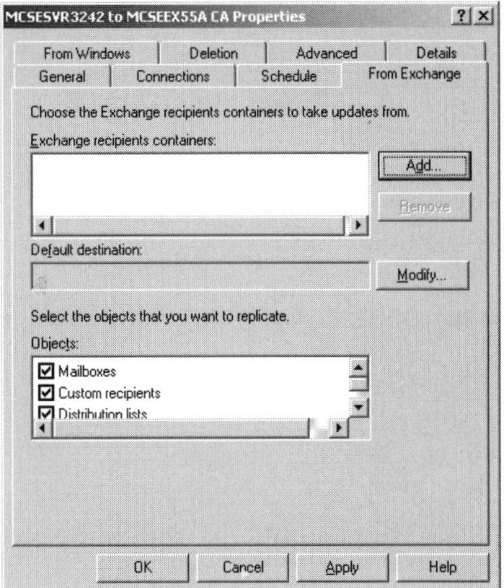

You can also start an unscheduled replication at any time by right-clicking a connection agreement and choosing the Replicate Now command from the All Tasks submenu.

From Exchange Properties

The From Exchange page, shown in Figure 11.7, lets you specify the location of the Exchange Directory container or containers that will be replicated, the location in Active Directory to which they will be replicated, and the specific objects that will be replicated. For public folder connection agreements, these options are already set, and you can't change them. For recipient connection agreements, you can fine-tune the options to meet your needs. For example, you might want to configure one connection agreement to replicate all of the mailboxes from a specific recipients container throughout the day and another agreement to replicate all other types of objects only at night.

From Windows Properties

The From Windows page, shown in Figure 11.8, is basically the opposite of the From Exchange page. It lets you configure the organizational units in Active Directory that should be replicated, the destination container they should be replicated to on the Exchange 5.*x* end, and the types of objects to replicate.

FIGURE 11.8 From Windows properties of a CA

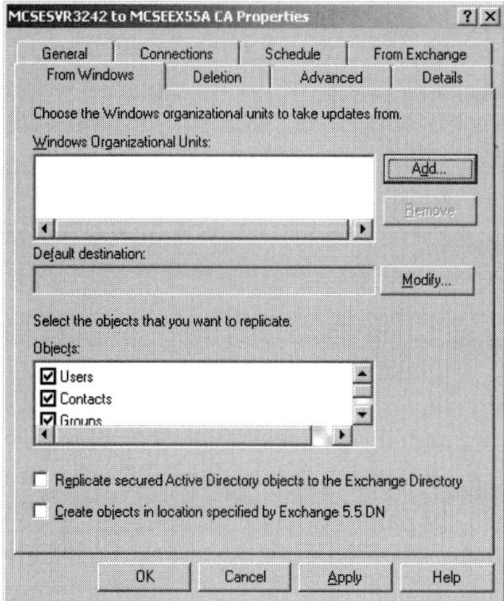

Deletion Properties

By default, objects deleted in one directory are not deleted in the other directory. Instead, a record of the deletion is stored in a file on the server running ADC in the `MSADC\MSADC\` *`<connection agreement name>`* folder. The Deletion page, shown in Figure 11.9, lets you change this behavior. For each direction of replication, you can choose whether objects deleted in the source directory are deleted in the target directory or not. Note that in a one-way connection agreement, one section of this page will be unavailable, as in Figure 11.9.

Advanced Properties

The Advanced page, shown in Figure 11.10, lets you configure a number of properties. These include the following:

- The Paged Results section lets you specify the number of entries that are paged together to be replicated as a single action. Paging helps improve replication performance, because a separate replication message does not have to be generated for each entry.
- A primary connection agreement is able to create new entries in the target directory. A CA that is not a primary agreement can replicate properties only to existing objects in the target directory. There are two primary agreement options on this page, one for each direction of the agreement.
- Use the This Is An Inter-Organizational Connection Agreement option if you are replicating information between two different Exchange organizations. Note that this option is not available for public folder connection agreements.
- Use the final setting on the page to specify the direction in which replication should occur first if you are configuring a two-way connection agreement.

- The When Replicating A Mailbox Whose Primary Windows Account Does Not Exist In The Domain menu lets you specify what should happen when a mailbox being replicated does not have a primary Windows account in the domain. This setting applies only to primary CAs, because many of the options call for creating new accounts in the target directory.

FIGURE 11.9 Deletion properties of a CA

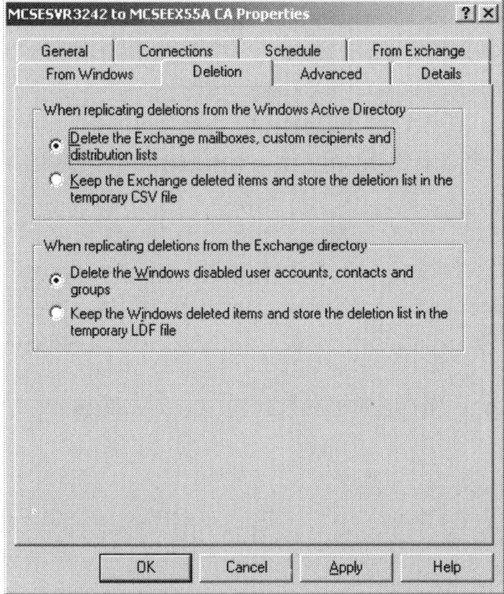

FIGURE 11.10 Advanced properties of a CA

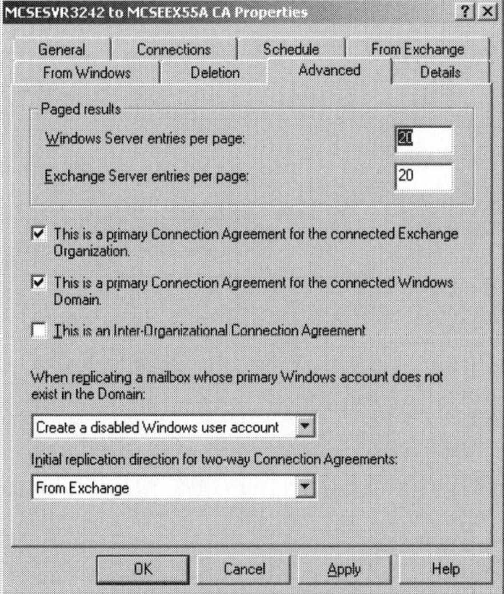

Managing a Mixed-Mode Organization

For the most part, managing a mixed-mode organization is not too difficult. You will just have to keep in mind the distinction between your Exchange Server 2003 servers and Exchange 5.*x* servers.

Managing Servers

Once an Exchange Server 2003 computer is added to an Exchange 5.*x* site, the Exchange 5.*x* servers become visible in System Manager as semitransparent icons, as seen in Figure 11.11. This is really just to let you know that those servers exist. Even though all configuration information for Exchange 5.*x* servers is replicated to Active Directory with the ADC, you cannot manage Exchange 5.*x* servers from System Manager. To manage the queues, connectors, address book views, and other configuration details for Exchange 5.*x* servers, you will have to use the *System Administrator* tool. System Administrator comes with previous versions of Exchange Server, and you can also install it as a custom option during the installation of Exchange Server 2003.

FIGURE 11.11 Viewing the Exchange site in Exchange System Manager

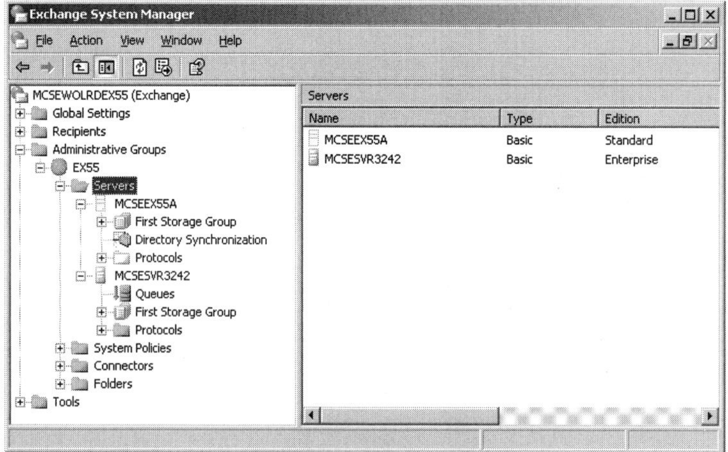

Managing Users

Assuming that the ADC is in place and that replication has occurred between Exchange 5.*x* and Active Directory, you can manage all users from both Exchange Server 2003 servers and Exchange 5.*x* servers with Active Directory Users and Computers. The property pages of a user object in Active Directory Users and Computers contain all of the same properties that you can find on the property pages of an Exchange 5.*x* mailbox in System Administrator. This offers the advantage of performing user management from a single location.

Moving Users

Moving users from an Exchange 5.*x* server to an Exchange Server 2003 server is an important step in migrating to Exchange Server 2003. Two tools are provided for your use in moving mailboxes to the Exchange Server 2003 mailbox stores: Exchange Task Wizard and the ExMerge utility. We will examine the simple process to move mailboxes using the Move Mailbox Wizard in Exercise 11.5.

EXERCISE 11.5

Moving Mailboxes from Exchange 5.*x* Server to Exchange Server 2003

1. Click Start ➢ Programs ➢ Administrative Tools ➢ Active Directory Users And Computers.

2. Expand the container for the appropriate domain.

3. Expand the user container that contains the Exchange 5.*x* user you want to move to Exchange Server 2003.

4. Right-click the user or users and select the Exchange Tasks command from the short cut menu.

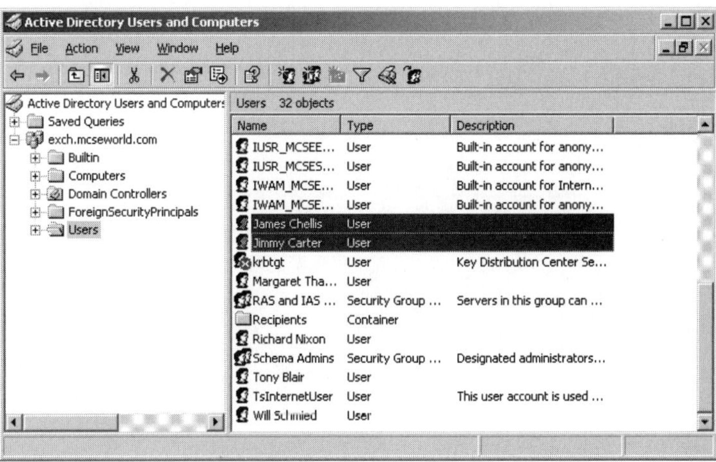

5. On the welcome page of the wizard that opens, click Next.

EXERCISE 11.5 *(continued)*

6. Select the Move Mailbox option, and then click Next.

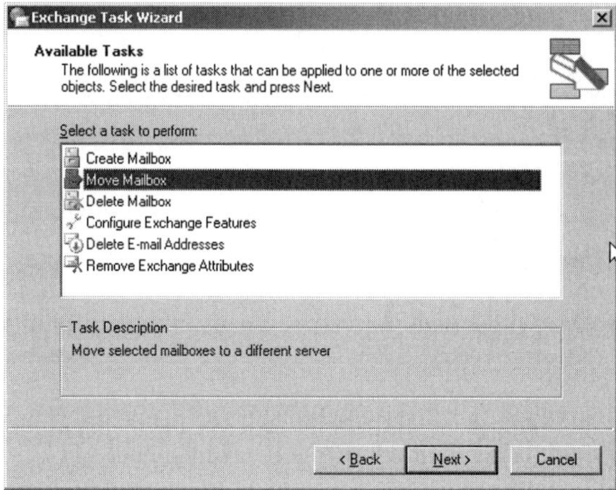

7. Select the server and mailbox store to which you want to move the user, and then click Next.

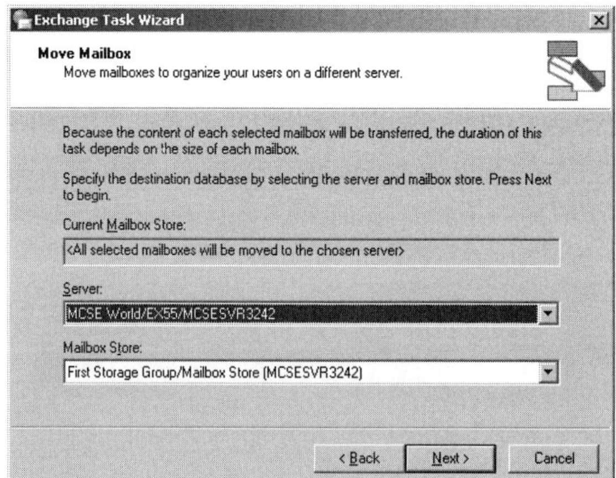

EXERCISE 11.5 *(continued)*

8. One of the new features of the Exchange Task Wizard in Exchange Server 2003 is that you can continue to process mailboxes even if errors should occur. Choose the option you want and click Next.

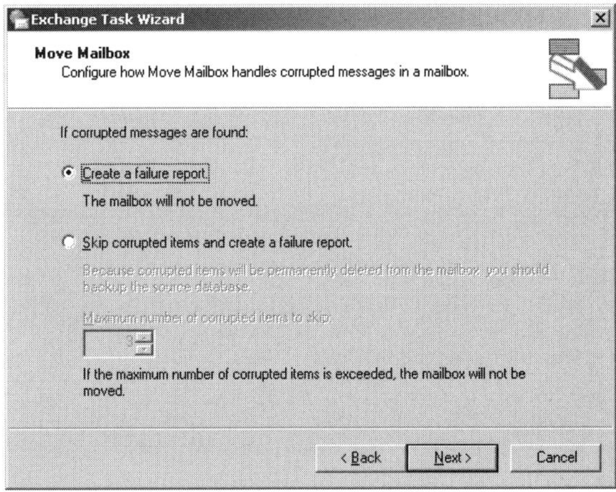

9. Another new feature is the ability to schedule the move process to occur as desired. This is useful in production environments where you cannot disturb a user's mailbox during working hours. Configure the desired time and click Next.

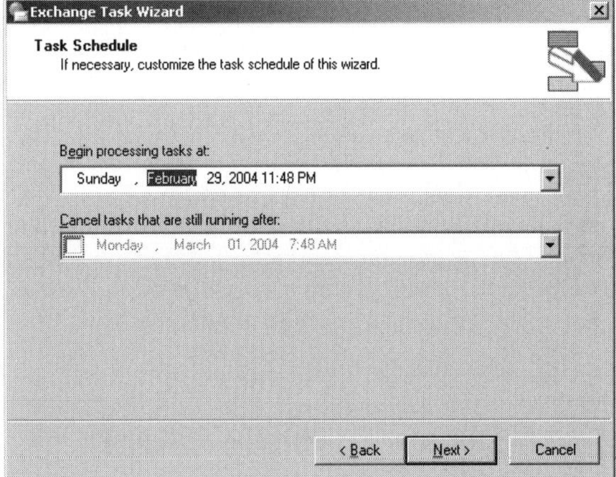

EXERCISE 11.5 *(continued)*

10. A status report will inform you as to the current progress of the move, which may take some time to complete depending on the size of the mailboxes.

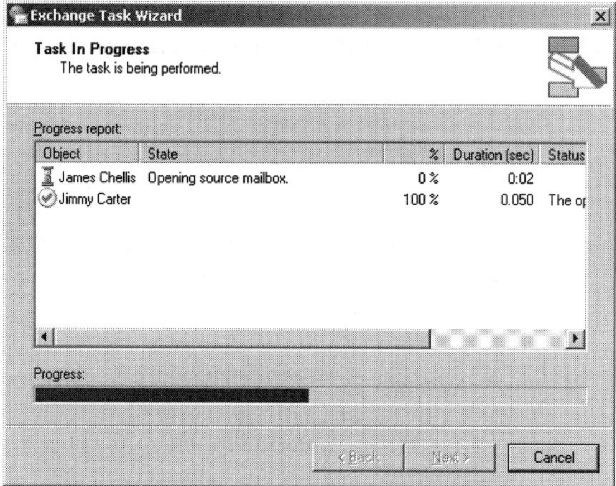

11. On the summary page, click Finish.

If you need to move a large number of mailboxes or want to explore more complex and perhaps scripted migrations, you will want to look into the ExMerge utility. The Exchange Mailbox Merge Program is part of the Exchange Deployment Tools and can be downloaded for Exchange Server 2003 by clicking the Exchange Tools And Updates link on the Welcome to Exchange Server 2003 Setup page that appears when you start the Exchange deployment process.

If a user's mailbox has not been initialized yet, either by receiving at least one message or by the user connecting to it at least one time, it will not be available for moving with ExMerge. You can, however, move the mailbox using the Exchange Task Wizard as outlined in Exercise 11.4.

Active Directory Account Cleanup Wizard

The *Active Directory Account Cleanup Wizard* is designed to merge duplicate accounts that may be created when multiple directories are migrated to Active Directory. This tool can be used to clean up after upgrading from Windows NT, migrating user accounts from another operating system, synchronizing with a foreign messaging system, or, as we are most concerned with here, synchronizing with Exchange 5.*x* directories.

The wizard searches for two types of criteria when performing its cleanup routines:

- It attempts to match active user accounts and disabled user accounts that represent the same object.
- It attempts to match active user accounts with contact accounts representing the same object.

Exercise 11.6 outlines the steps for using the Active Directory Account Cleanup Wizard to automatically search for duplicated accounts.

EXERCISE 11.6

Using the Active Directory Account Cleanup Wizard

1. Click Start ➢ Programs ➢ Microsoft Exchange ➢ Active Directory Account Cleanup Wizard.
2. On the welcome page of the Wizard, click Next to go on.
3. On the Identify Merging Accounts page, select the containers and subcontainers that you want to search by clicking Add and browsing for directories. By default, the wizard searches the entire Active Directory forest.
4. Make sure that the Search Based On Exchange Mailboxes Only option is enabled so that only objects created by the ADC are included in the search results.
5. Begin the search by clicking Next.
6. When the search is complete, you can review the list of suggested merge operations on the Review Merging Accounts page. We strongly recommend reviewing the operations. Just double-click any merge operation to review the details of the source and target accounts. If you see that a merge is missing, you can add a merge operation to the list using the Add button. You can also remove operations using the Remove button. Once you've finished with the review, click Next to go on.
7. On the Begin Merging Accounts screen, click Begin The Merge Process Now.
8. The wizard will warn you that merge operations cannot be undone once they are performed. Click Yes to go on.
9. To begin the merge process, click Next.
10. You can cancel the merge process at any time, but any operations that have already been completed are irreversible. Once the process is done, an Account Merge Results screen is displayed, where you can review the results of the merge operations.

Real World Scenario

Real-World Migration from Exchange Server 5.5 to Exchange Server 2003

This is a common scenario that many organizations are having to cope with right now—how to safely and efficiently migrate away from their Exchange Server 5.5 organization to an Exchange Server 2003 organization. What makes this migration so difficult for many is that there is no standard answer or set process that must be followed, because each organization has different needs. There are, however, some basic groups of processes that you should be aware of. How you put them together to reach the final solution will ultimately depend on what you are starting with.

If you are still running Windows NT PDC and BDCs, you should first make the move to Active Directory to upgrade all user accounts. You can go about this in one of two ways: either upgrade the domain controllers (or upgrade/replace them) to Windows 2000 Server or use the Active Directory Migration Tool to clone the NT user accounts into the new Active Directory format. If you opt for ADMT, you can, and should, just jump straight to Windows Server 2003. Be aware that you will be configuring and using a trust relationship between your old NT domain and your new Active Directory domain.

Once your user accounts are solely in Active Directory, you can then move forward and start to migrate from Exchange Server 5.5 to Exchange Server 2003. Remember that Exchange Server 5.5 will not run on Windows Server 2003 but runs just fine on Windows 2000 Server. You'll want any Windows 2000 Server machines hosting Exchange Server 5.5 to be at SP3 or better and any Windows NT 4.0 machines hosting Exchange Server 5.5 to be at SP6A. Exchange Server 5.5 itself needs to be at SP3 or better before you can migrate. Don't forget to change the LDAP port on all of your Exchange Server 5.5 computers to something other than 389 if they are running on a Windows 2000 domain controller.

The best possible scenario has you operating with no Windows 2000 Server global catalog servers, although you can still have Windows 2000 Server domain controllers without any issues. Note that you will need to run ADPrep to update an existing Windows 2000 Active Directory schema before you can promote any Windows Server 2003 computers to a domain controller. In this scenario you will need at least two Windows Server 2003 servers in order to get started: one acting as a DC/GC (Domain Controller/Global Catalog) and one as a member server in the domain onto which the first Exchange Server 2003 will be installed. Obviously, you will need to make sure you have an adequate number of Exchange Server 2003 servers to handle the number of users in your organization.

At this point, you've migrated user accounts and are using Active Directory for change and configuration management. The servers to host the Exchange Server 2003 installations are available and joined to your Windows Server 2003 Active Directory domain as member servers. At least one Windows Server 2003 global catalog server is also available. All you have left to do now is complete the steps discussed in this chapter and you're on your way. One final note of caution, though: Exchange Server 5.5 allowed a user to have multiple mailboxes. You will need to normalize your Exchange Server 5.5 mailboxes before attempting the migration. In other words, you need a one-to-one relationship between Active Directory user accounts and Exchange Server 5.5 mailboxes. The Exchange Server 2003 Deployment Guide from Microsoft will be a great asset to you during this process. You can get it at `www.microsoft.com/exchange/techinfo/deployment/2003.asp`.

Going Native

Once you switch an Exchange organization to native mode (see Chapter 8, "Building Administrative and Routing Groups," for details on the process), the organization is no longer directly interoperable with Exchange 5.*x* servers. Native-mode organizations can contain only Exchange Server 2003 or Exchange 2000 Server computers.

You must also be aware that the switch is one-way. Once you switch an organization to native mode, you cannot switch back to mixed mode. Therefore, it is important that your organization be ready for the switch. Here are a few guidelines to help you decide if switching to native mode is the right action to take:

- You no longer have any Exchange 5.*x* servers in your organization.
- You do not plan to add any Exchange 5.*x* servers at a later date.
- You have re-created all connectors on the Exchange Server 2003 servers that existed on the Exchange Server 5.*x* servers.
- If you do have Exchange 5.*x* servers still running on your network, you do not require interoperability between them and the Exchange Server 2003 organization (i.e., you are maintaining separate organizations).

Troubleshooting

Because you are relying on the Exchange 5.*x* Directory Service, the Active Directory, and the components that tie the two together, ADC and SRS, troubleshooting coexistence problems can be tricky. This section provides some troubleshooting tips and places to start looking when things go wrong.

The first action to take when troubleshooting is to check the more obvious sources of potential error. These include the following:

- Are all your servers running?
- Are the ADC and SRS services actually running on the Exchange Server 2003 server? Is the Directory Service running on any Exchange 5.*x* servers? Use the Services tool or Task Manager to make sure.
- Is a connection agreement configured between the Active Directory and the appropriate Exchange 5.*x* server? If so, is it properly configured?
- Is the container to which you want an entry replicated displayed in the Export Containers list? If not, you'll need to add it.
- Do you have sufficient permissions on the target directory to which you are trying to replicate?
- Have you checked the Windows Application Log for any error messages?
- Can you connect to the SRS port (379 by default) on the Exchange Server 2003 server?
- Is the correct port being specified for the Active Directory Connector's LDAP communications? Recall that Active Directory locks the default LDAP port 389 for its own usage.

Once you have exhausted these possibilities, there are a few situations you should be aware of in which an object would not replicate between an Exchange 5.*x* Directory and Active Directory. These are outlined in Table 11.1.

TABLE 11.1 Causes for an Object Not to Replicate When Using ADC

Active Directory to Exchange 5.*x*	Exchange 5.*x* to Active Directory
The Active Directory and Exchange objects being replicated match, but the Exchange object was deleted.	The Exchange and Active Directory objects being replicated match, but the Active Directory object was deleted.
The Active Directory and Exchange objects being replicated match, but the Exchange object is not in the same site as the Exchange 5.*x* server specified in the connection agreement.	The Exchange and Active Directory objects being replicated match, but the Active Directory object is not in a domain to which the ADC can write.
The connection agreement is not the primary connection agreement for the organization.	ADC is attempting to match an Exchange 5.*x* mailbox to a mail-enabled user instead of a mailbox-enabled user.
The object in Active Directory does not contain e-mail information.	ADC is attempting to match an Exchange 5.*x* custom recipient or distribution list to a mailbox-enabled user.
	The object could not be matched.

Summary

In this chapter, you learned how to use the tools that enable Exchange Server 2003 and previous versions of Exchange Server to coexist in the same organization. An organization running multiple versions of Exchange Server is referred to as running in mixed mode. An organization running only Exchange Server 2003 is referred to as running in native mode. Exchange Server 2003 operates in mixed mode by default, even if you have no previous versions running on your network. Once you switch to native mode, you cannot go back, and direct interoperability with previous Exchange versions is lost.

The primary advantage of running in mixed mode is that you can continue to use previous versions of Exchange (and any connectors and software specific to those versions) while upgrading your organization to Exchange Server 2003. There are also some limitations imposed by running in mixed mode. Exchange 5.*x* sites are mapped directly to Exchange Server 2003 administrative groups, meaning that administrative groups lose some of their flexibility. You also cannot move mailboxes between administrative groups when running a mixed-mode organization.

The primary components used in supporting mixed-mode operations are the Site Replication Service (SRS) and the Active Directory Connector (ADC). The SRS runs on an Exchange Server 2003 server and actually simulates an Exchange 5.*x* system from the viewpoint of the Exchange 5.*x* servers in a site. The ADC runs on an Exchange Server 2003 server and synchronizes directory information between Active Directory and Exchange 5.*x* servers in the site. ADC also synchronizes configuration information with those servers using the SRS as an intermediary. Only one instance of the ADC can run on a single Exchange server, but you can configure multiple connection agreements for an ADC. Each connection agreement is defined to replicate certain directory objects to certain parts of the Active Directory.

Once replication of directories is established, management of a mixed-mode organization is fairly straightforward. You can use Active Directory Users and Computers to manage all users from both Exchange Server 2003 and Exchange 5.*x*, although you can continue to manage users from System Administrator should you choose. Exchange Server 2003 servers and other Exchange Server 2003–specific configuration are managed through System Manager. Exchange 5.*x*–specific configuration must be managed using System Administrator.

Exam Essentials

Understand that coexistence is not your only solution. You do have another way to get from Exchange Server 5.5 to Exchange Server 2003; coexistence as we've discussed here is not the only way. A more advanced solution calls for you to install a new Exchange Server 2003 organization, most likely in a new domain, and then migrate mailboxes using the Exchange Migration Wizard. What we've examined in this chapter is the most common and easiest method for most organizations.

Know the limitations of mixed-mode operations. Mixed-mode operations are a requirement in order to perform the migration process outlined in this chapter. However, when the opportunity arises for you to make the change to native mode, you should jump at it. When operating in native mode, you will have increased administrative flexibility to use administrative and routing groups as desired. As well, you will rid yourself of the need for the Active Directory Connector and the Site Replication Service, making your Exchange organization simpler to manage and maintain. The standard recommendation is, after you've migrated 100 percent of your mailboxes from Exchange Server 5.5 to Exchange Server 2003, to take the Exchange Server 5.5 servers offline for a week (perhaps less in smaller organizations) and observe whether messaging occurs correctly. Once you have confirmed this, you can begin the process of permanently removing these legacy Exchange servers and getting into native mode.

Review Questions

1. You have an Exchange organization that consists of a single site with four servers running Exchange Server 5.5 with Service Pack 3. You have upgraded all of these servers to run Windows 2000 Advanced Server with Service Pack 3 and have designated two of them as domain controllers. You have just installed an Exchange Server 2003 server into the site. Users who have mailboxes on the two domain controllers complain that they are having problems accessing their address book. You check the Application Log on your Exchange servers and notice that a lot of errors have been generated by servers attempting to contact the domain controllers. What steps should you take to remedy the situation? (Choose all that apply.)

   A. Reapply Windows Service Pack 3 to the domain controllers.

   B. Apply Exchange Server 5.5 Service Pack 4 to all Exchange 5.5 servers.

   C. Change the LDAP port for the Exchange service on the domain controllers.

   D. Change the LDAP port used by the ADC connection agreements to connect to the domain controllers.

   E. Relocate the Exchange 5.5 servers so that they are not on domain controllers.

2. To which of the following Active Directory partitions is recipient information replicated?

   A. Configuration-naming partition

   B. Domain-naming partition

   C. Schema-naming partition

   D. Organization-naming partition

3. Which of the following is a limitation of working in a mixed-mode organization?

   A. You can move mailboxes only within the same storage group.

   B. You can move mailboxes only within the same administrative group.

   C. You cannot move mailboxes from an Exchange 5.*x* server to an Exchange Server 2003 server.

   D. You cannot move mailboxes from an Exchange Server 2003 server to an Exchange 5.*x* server.

4. You are the administrator of a mixed-mode organization and are responsible for monitoring the queues on all servers. You receive an alert that one of the connectors on a server running Exchange Server 5.5 is down. What program could you use to check the status of the queue?

   A. System Manager

   B. Exchange Administrator

   C. Active Directory Users and Computers

   D. Task Manager

5. When an Exchange Server 2003 server is installed into an existing Exchange 5.*x* site, with what services on the Exchange Server 2003 server do the Exchange 5.*x* servers directly interact? (Choose all that apply.)

   A. SRS

   B. ADC

   C. MTA

   D. Active Directory

6. You are the Exchange administrator for a large mixed-mode organization. You are about to decommission one of your Exchange 5.5 servers and need to move all of the mailboxes on that server to a single mailbox store on one of your Exchange Server 2003 servers. Which of the following tools could you use?

   A. Exchange Task Wizard

   B. System Manager

   C. Exchange Administrator

   D. Active Directory Account Cleanup Wizard

7. After using the ADC Tools to create the initial connection agreements between the Exchange Directory Service and Active Directory, where will the Exchange end of the connection agreements point?

   A. The Exchange 5.5 server

   B. The Exchange Server 2003 server

   C. The Windows Server 2003 domain controller

   D. The Windows Server 2003 member server

8. You are attempting to install an Exchange Server 2003 computer into an Exchange Server 5.5 site. Your three Exchange Server 5.5 servers are at SP3 and are running on Windows 2000 Server SP3 servers that are domain controllers. When you run the DSScopeScan tool, you get the following error reported in the `gcvercheck.log` file:

```
#*** GC Version Check began: 02/29/2004 20:57:48 ***#
Current Site (Default-First-Site-Name)
   Global catalog servers that could not be contacted:
      EXSVR55A
EXSVR55B
EXSVR55C
#*** GC Version Check finished: 02/29/2004 20:57:48 ***#
```

Users report no problems sending or receiving mail with these servers. What is the most likely reason for this problem?

A. You have not changed the LDAP port in the Exchange Server 5.5 properties.

B. You specified the wrong LDAP port for the Exchange Server 5.5 servers.

C. You specified the wrong LDAP port for the global catalog server.

D. You will need to upgrade your Exchange Server 5.5 servers to SP4.

9. You are attempting to install an Exchange Server 2003 computer into an Exchange Server 5.5 site. Your three Exchange Server 5.5 servers are at SP3 and are running on Windows 2000 Server SP3 servers that are domain controllers. When you run the DSScopeScan tool, you get the following error reported in the `ExDeploy.log` file:

```
Error: Could not connect to the Exchange 5.5 server EXSVR55A. Tools that
require an Exchange 5.5 server will not run.
```

Users report no problems sending or receiving mail with these servers. What is the most likely reason for this problem?

A. You have not changed the LDAP port in the Exchange Server 5.5 properties.

B. You specified the wrong LDAP port for the Exchange Server 5.5 servers.

C. You specified the wrong LDAP port for the global catalog server.

D. You will need to upgrade your Exchange Server 5.5 servers to SP4.

10. To which of the following Active Directory partitions is namespace information replicated?

A. Configuration-naming partition

B. Domain-naming partition

C. Schema-naming partition

D. Organization-naming partition

11. Which of the following actions are taken by the Active Directory Account Cleanup Wizard? (Choose all that apply.)

A. It attempts to match active user accounts and disabled user accounts that represent the same object.

B. It attempts to match active user accounts and contact accounts that represent the same object.

C. It attempts to match active groups and contact accounts that represent the same object.

D. It attempts to match active user accounts and mail-enabled accounts that represent the same object.

12. Which of the following statements is true?

A. Exchange Server 2003 servers in a mixed-mode organization can use connectors installed on Exchange 5.*x* servers in the same organization.

B. Exchange Server 2003 servers in a mixed-mode organization can use connectors installed on Exchange 5.*x* servers in other organizations.

C. Exchange Server 2003 servers in a mixed-mode organization cannot use connectors installed on Exchange 5.*x* servers.

D. Exchange 5.*x* servers can use connectors installed on Exchange Server 2003 servers in a mixed-mode organization.

13. You are running a mixed-mode organization that contains a number of Exchange Server 2003 and Exchange 5.5 servers in a single site. How do Exchange 5.*x* servers in that site exchange directory information?

A. Using SMTP

B. Using MAPI

C. Using RPCs

D. Using LDAP

14. Which of the following statements is true about public folders in mixed-mode organizations?

A. Public folders can not be replicated.

B. Public folders can be replicated from Exchange 5.*x* servers to Exchange Server 2003 servers only.

C. Public folders can be replicated from Exchange Server 2003 servers to Exchange 5.*x* servers only.

D. Public folders can be replicated in both directions.

15. You are the administrator of an Exchange 5.*x* organization consisting of a single site. You create a new site containing a single Exchange 5.*x* server and then install an Exchange Server 2003 server into that new site. Which of the following statements is true about directory replication in the organization?

A. Directory replication happens automatically between all servers in the organization.

B. Directory replication happens automatically between all Exchange 5.*x* servers in the organization but must be manually configured to the Exchange Server 2003 server.

C. Directory replication happens automatically between all servers in the same site but must be configured to happen between sites.

D. Directory replication cannot happen between the Exchange Server 2003 server and the Exchange 5.*x* servers in the other site.

16. Which of the following types of connection agreements would be used to replicate the information about a legacy Microsoft Mail connector configured on an Exchange 5.*x* server?

    A. Recipient connection agreement

    B. Configuration connection agreement

    C. Connector connection agreement

    D. Link-state connection agreement

17. What protocol does the Routing Group Connector use to transport messages to Exchange 5.*x* sites that are connected using Exchange 5.*x* Site Connectors?

    A. SMTP

    B. X.400

    C. RPC

    D. LDAP

18. What is the default port number used by SRS for LDAP communications?

    A. 369

    B. 379

    C. 389

    D. 399

19. Which of the following statements about the Active Directory Connector are true? (Choose all that apply.)

    A. The ADC must run on the same computer as Active Directory.

    B. The ADC must run on an Exchange 5.*x* server.

    C. Only one ADC can run in any given site.

    D. Multiple ADCs can run in a given site.

    E. Only one ADC can run on a single server.

    F. Multiple ADCs can run on a single server.

20. You are configuring a recipient connection agreement in a mixed-mode site. What two requirements exist for the bridgehead servers on either end of the agreement?

    A. One end of the connection must be a computer running Exchange Server 2003.

    B. One end of the connection must be a computer running Active Directory.

    C. One end of the connection must be a computer running Exchange 5.5 with Service Pack 3.

    D. One end of the connection must be a computer running Exchange 5.5 with Service Pack 3 on a Windows 2000 Server.

Answers to Review Questions

1. C, D. Windows Server 2003 and Windows 2000 Server domain controllers lock LDAP port 389 for their own use. This renders Exchange Server 5.5 unable to accept LDAP connections when running on a domain controller, since the default LDAP port is 389. You must change the LDAP port that the Exchange servers use and then change the LDAP port that the ADC uses to connect to the servers.

2. B. Configuration information, such as the configuration of servers and connectors, is replicated to the configuration-naming partition of Active Directory. Recipient information is replicated to the domain-naming partition. Namespace information is replicated to the schema-naming partition of Active Directory. There is no such thing as an organization-naming partition.

3. B. When operating in mixed mode, you can move mailboxes only between servers in the same administrative group. You can always move mailboxes between servers of different versions.

4. B. Even though all configuration information for Exchange 5.*x* servers is replicated to Active Directory with the ADC, you cannot manage Exchange 5.*x* servers from System Manager. To manage the queues, connectors, address book views, and other configuration details for Exchange 5.*x* servers, you will have to use the Exchange Administrator. Active Directory Users and Computers can be used for managing users on both Exchange 2000 and Exchange 5.*x* servers.

5. A, B. The SRS behaves like an Exchange 5.*x* Directory Service running on the Exchange Server 2003 server. SRS provides Exchange 5.*x* servers in the site with a means of accessing configuration information concerning the Exchange Server 2003 server on which SRS is running. The ADC is used to replicate directory information between the Active Directory and the Exchange 5.*x* servers. Exchange 5.*x* servers communicate with the Exchange Server 2003 server in the same site using RPCs. If the servers were in different sites, the MTA would be used.

6. A. From the list of available tools, you will need to use the Exchange Task Wizard in order to move mailboxes from Exchange 5.*x* to Exchange Server 2003.

7. A. The Exchange end of the connection agreements will point to the Exchange Server 5.5 computer and should always be configured this way. Initially, the Windows end of the connection agreements will also point to the same server, but you must change this after the first Exchange Server 2003 computer has been installed so that the connection agreements point to the new Exchange Server 2003 computer on the Windows end. Making this change will prevent problems with replication and the Global Address List.

8. C. The most likely problem in this scenario is that you specified the wrong port for the global catalog server. In this instance, you would need to specify the LDAP port in use by the Exchange Server 5.5 servers but not one for the global catalog server because it will be using the default port of 389.

9. B. In this instance, you did not specify the correct (or any port) for LDAP for the Exchange Server 5.5 computers. You attempted the scan using the default port of 389, and it failed because you already needed to change it since your Exchange Server 5.5 servers are running on Windows 2000 Server domain controllers.

10. C. Configuration information, such as the configuration of servers and connectors, is replicated to the configuration-naming partition of Active Directory. Recipient information is replicated to the domain-naming partition. Namespace information is replicated to the schema-naming partition of Active Directory. There is no such thing as an organization-naming partition.

11. A, B. The Active Directory Account Cleanup Wizard is designed to merge duplicate accounts that may be created when multiple directories are migrated to Active Directory. It works by searching for user accounts that match either disabled accounts or contacts and then allowing you to merge those accounts.

12. A. The configuration connection agreement of the ADC imports information from Exchange 5.*x* Gateway Address Routing Tables into Exchange Server 2003 server link-state tables and thus provides access to Exchange 5.*x* connectors and gateways.

13. C. All Exchange 5.*x* servers in the same site automatically replicate directory information using RPCs. Replication of directory information between Exchange 5.*x* servers in different sites must be configured manually and occurs by sending e-mail messages over whatever connector is used to connect the sites.

14. D. Public folders can be replicated freely between Exchange Server 2003 and Exchange 5.*x* servers.

15. C. The SRS on the Exchange Server 2003 server makes the server appear as an Exchange 5.*x* server to other 5.*x* servers. Directory replication between Exchange 5.*x* sites is not an automatic process and must be configured by an administrator. Directory replication between sites occurs using e-mail messages over whatever connectors are used to connect the sites. This ability allows administrators to decide which resources to share with other sites.

16. B. There are two basic types of connection agreements: user agreements (which come in the form of recipient and public folder agreements) and configuration agreements. Configuration agreements replicate Exchange-specific configuration information, such as connectors and site information.

17. C. The primary connector used between Exchange 5.*x* sites is the Site Connector, which makes use of RPC to transmit messages. In Exchange Server 2003, the Routing Group Connector (RGC) replaces the Site Connector used in previous versions. The RGC uses SMTP rather than RPC to transport messages between Exchange Server 2003 servers. For coexistence, however, the RGC uses RPC to transport messages to Exchange 5.*x* sites that use the Site Connector.

18. B. Because Active Directory also uses LDAP and locks the well-known port 389 for its own use, SRS defaults to using port 379 for its LDAP communications.

19. D, E. The ADC runs on an Exchange Server 2003 server. Only one instance of the ADC can run on a single Exchange server, but you can configure multiple connection agreements for an ADC. An instance of ADC can run on each server in a site that is running Exchange Server 2003.

20. B, C. The computer running the ADC service will have Exchange Server 2003 installed. The Windows server at one end of the connection agreement must be a computer running Active Directory. The Exchange server must be running Exchange Server 5.5 with at least Service Pack 3 applied, even though the rest of the servers in the site do not need to run this recent a version of Exchange.

Coexisting with and Upgrading from Exchange 2000 Server

MICROSOFT EXAM OBJECTIVES COVERED IN THIS CHAPTER:

✓ **Migrate from other messaging systems to Exchange Server 2003**

- Migrate from other Exchange organizations

✓ **Configure and troubleshoot Exchange Server 2003 for coexistence with other Exchange organizations**

We examined in Chapter 11, "Coexisting with and Migrating from Exchange 5.5," the difficulties and problems that go along with coexisting and migrating from Exchange Server 5.5 to Exchange Server 2003. Fortunately, the road from Exchange 2000 Server to Exchange Server 2003 is not nearly as bumpy. The existence of user objects within *Active Directory* and the familiar Exchange organization greatly help in making this scenario a much easier one to deal with, even for the relatively inexperienced Exchange administrator. In this chapter will examine the coexistence with and upgrading from Exchange 2000 Server to Exchange Server 2003. It's not as easy as simply upgrading Exchange in place, but it's not too difficult either.

Improvements in Exchange Server 2003

Although we've been discussing the improvements and changes in Exchange Server 2003 all through the book up to this point, it's important to review and summarize them again. These are likely some of the answers that you will provide when asked the question, "Why should we upgrade to Exchange Server 2003?"

Increased availability Exchange Server 2003 supports up to eight-node active/passive clusters when running on Windows Server 2003. Exchange 2000 Server supported only four-node active/passive clusters, while Exchange Server 5.5 could support only two-node clusters. As well, the failover response times in Exchange Server 2003 and Windows Server 2003 have been greatly improved to provide the best possible fault-tolerant, highly available solution.

Enhanced backup and recovery Exchange Server 2003 takes advantage of the new *volume shadow copy* feature of Windows Server 2003's `ntbackup.exe`, which allows for open files to be backed up as if they were closed at the time of the backup operation. In addition, Exchange Server 2003 provides new recovery functionality in the Mailbox Recovery Center and the Recovery Storage Group.

Performance Exchange Server 2003 provides enhanced public folder replication, distribution list caching, and the ability to suppress Out of Office messages from being sent to distribution lists. When used with Outlook 2003, Exchange Server 2003 offers many improvements in messaging, including cache mode of operation and improved synchronization.

Security Exchange Server 2003 supports many security enhancements, including using IPSec between front- and back-end servers, Kerberos authentication between front- and back-end servers, and improvements in the security stance of IIS 6.0, to name a few. Exchange Server 2003 also offers security enhancements over previous versions by restricting the ability to send messages to distribution lists to authenticated users, providing real-time safe and block lists for inbound messages, inbound recipient filtering, and attachment blocking in Outlook and OWA.

User experience Exchange Server 2003 Outlook Web Access offers many feature and security improvements over all previous versions and almost mirrors Outlook 2003 feature by feature. When used with Exchange Server 2003, Outlook 2003 provides for MAPI compression for faster synchronization. Exchange Server 2003 also provides support for cHTML, xHTML, and HTML for mobile phones and PDAs.

Management and deployment Exchange Server 2003 provides 1,700 events for use with Microsoft Operations Manager (MOM) for superior enterprisewide monitoring and management. As well, the new *Internet Mail Connection Wizard* greatly simplifies the daunting task of enabling your Exchange organization to send and receive mail from the Internet. The Exchange Task Wizard provides a quick and easy way to move multiple mailboxes at the same time and offers the ability to schedule the move for a later time.

Coexistence with Exchange 2000 Server

In a most situations where Exchange 2000 Server is already in place in an organization, you will be coexisting with it for at least a short period of time—perhaps indefinitely if no upgrade plans currently exist. Coexisting with Exchange 2000 Server is very easy as compared to coexisting with Exchange Server 5.5. You'll really need only to run *ForestPrep* and *DomainPrep* to prepare Active Directory for the new Exchange Server 2003 installations. Note that Exchange Server 2003 does not support several components, and thus you will need to keep them running on your Exchange 2000 Servers until they are no longer needed:

- Microsoft Mobile Information Server—Not needed in Exchange Server 2003 because this functionality has been built in.
- Instant Messaging—Replaced by the *Live Communications Server*, a separate add-on product for your network.
- Exchange Chat—Not supported.
- Exchange 2000 Conferencing Server—Not supported.
- Key Management Service (KMS)—Not needed in Exchange Server 2003 because the Windows Server 2003 PKI handles this responsibility.
- The cc:Mail connector—Not supported.
- The MS Mail connector—Not supported.

As you'll see later in this chapter, you will need to remove these components before attempting to upgrade an Exchange 2000 Server to Exchange Server 2003.

Before you attempt to install the first Exchange Server 2003 into your Exchange 2000 Server organization, you should first ensure that all your servers are at Windows 2000 Service Pack 3 or later and Exchange 2000 Server Service Pack 3 or later. Being at these SP levels will ensure that your organization is best prepared for both the coexistence and the eventual upgrade/migration to follow.

The high-level process to install the first Exchange Server 2003 server into an existing Exchange 2000 Server organization is composed of the following steps:

1. Install Windows Server 2003 on the server and join it to the domain in which the Exchange 2000 Server is located.
2. Ensure that .NET Framework, ASP.NET, the World Wide Web Publishing Service, the Simple Mail Transfer (SMTP) service, and the Network News Transfer Protocol (NNTP) service are installed and running on the server. Exercise 3.1 previously discussed installing these services.
3. Install the Windows Server 2003 Support Tools on the server.
4. Run the DCDiag utility.
5. Run the NetDiag utility.
6. Run Exchange Server 2003 `setup /forestprep` as discussed in Exercise 3.2.
7. Run Exchange Server 2003 `setup /domainprep` as discussed in Exercise 3.3.
8. Install Exchange Server 2003 as outlined below in Exercise 12.1.

If your plans call for an upgrade to Windows Server 2003, you will want to give some serious consideration to installing at least one Windows Server 2003 domain controller and configuring it as a global catalog server at this time. Doing so can prevent some problems that might occur during upgrades to Exchange Server 2003.

If you get an error telling you that the schema master could not be contacted when you attempt to run ForestPrep, ensure that the server is joined to the Active Directory domain and has the correct TCP/IP settings applied. Over 95 percent of these errors can be eliminated by checking and correcting these commonly overlooked issues.

EXERCISE 12.1

Installing the First Exchange Server into the Exchange 2000 Server Organization

1. Insert the Microsoft Exchange Server CD into the server's CD-ROM drive. If your CD-ROM drive is set to automatically run CDs, this will automatically open the Welcome to Exchange Server 2003 Setup page. If not, browse to the location of your CD-ROM and double-click the `setup.exe` file.
2. Click the Exchange Deployment Tools link.
3. On the Welcome to the Exchange Server Deployment Tools page, click the Deploy The First Exchange 2003 Server link.
4. On the Deploy the First Exchange Server 2003 page, click the Upgrade From Exchange 2000 Server Native Mode link.
5. Ensure that you've completed all of the preliminary actions in Steps 1 through 7 discussed previously.
6. Scroll down the Exchange Server Deployment Tools page until you locate Item 8, Install Exchange Server 2003. Click the Run Setup Now link.
7. When prompted, agree to the EULA, and click Next to continue.
8. Enter your 25-digit CD-key, and click Next to continue.
9. The Component Selection page lists the installation options, as well as the option to choose the directory into which Exchange Server will be installed. This latter option is accessed through the Change Path button. For this exercise, we will assume that the installation directory is the default, `C:\Program Files\Exchsrvr`. The installation option we will use for this exercise is Typical, which includes the messaging components and management tools. If you would like to see the individual components that can be selected, choose the Custom option from the drop-down menu to the left of the first item in the list, Microsoft Exchange. You can then choose whether to install each individual option using that option's drop-down menu. Once you've made all of your decisions, click Next to go on.
10. A Licensing screen appears, explaining the need for you to purchase Client Access Licenses before clients can access this Exchange server. Exchange Server 2003 supports only the per-seat licensing mode. Once you have read and agreed to this licensing, click the I Agree That I Have Read And Will Be Bound By The License Agreements For This Product option, and then click Next.

EXERCISE 12.1 *(continued)*

11. The Installation Summary dialog box appears, asking you to confirm your installation choices. You can use the Back button to change any settings you have made. When you are satisfied with your choices, click Next to install Exchange Server 2003.

12. The installation process can take some time. When it is done, a Congratulations screen appears, informing you that the installation is complete. Click the Finish button.

After the installation is complete, you might want to explore the *Exchange System Manager* (ESM) on both the Exchange 2000 Server and the newly installed Exchange Server 2003 server to see the small differences. Figure 12.1 shows the Exchange 2000 Server version, while Figure 12.2 shows the Exchange Server 2003 version.

While you will be able to perform common management tasks using the Exchange Server 2003 ESM, should you need to configure Exchange 2000 Server–specific items, such as the Key Management Service, Instant Messaging, IRC, or Chat, you will need to use the Exchange 2000 Server ESM. Likewise, if you need to work with Recovery Storage Groups or the Mailbox Recovery Center, you'll need to work with the Exchange Server 2003 ESM.

FIGURE 12.1 The Exchange organization via the Exchange 2000 Server ESM

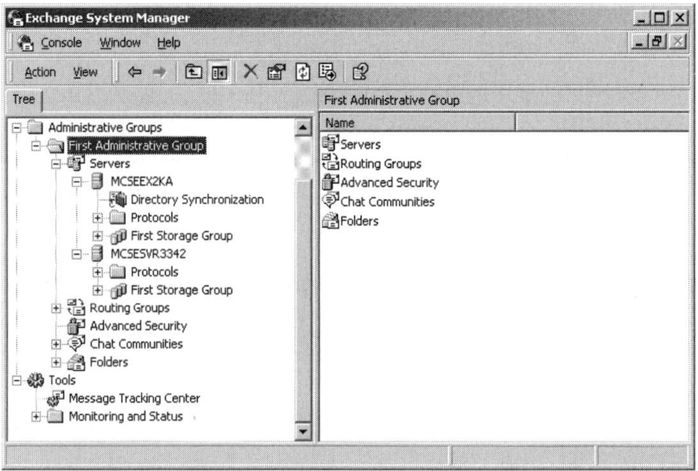

FIGURE 12.2 The Exchange organization via the Exchange Server 2003 ESM

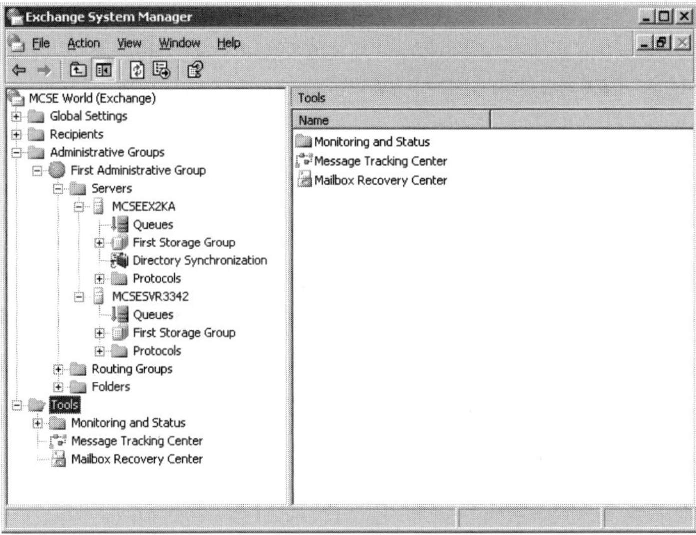

Upgrading from Exchange 2000 Server

The upgrade path from Exchange 2000 Server to Exchange Server 2003 is a simple one. In most cases, your hardware will be up to par with the requirements for Exchange Server 2003 and Windows Server 2003, but it's always good practice to verify this before starting any upgrades. The minimum and recommended hardware requirements for installing Exchange are detailed in Table 12.1. For more detailed information about the requirements to install Exchange Server 2003 on a computer, refer back to Chapter 3, "Installing Microsoft Exchange Server 2003."

The Microsoft Exchange Server software comes on a CD. If the machine intended to be the Exchange server has no CD-ROM drive, the administrator can copy the necessary files from the CD to a shared hard disk or share a CD-ROM drive on another machine.

TABLE 12.1 Exchange Server 2003 Hardware Requirements

Item	Minimum	Recommended
CPU	133 MHz Pentium or comparable	733 MHz Pentium or comparable
RAM	256 MB	512 MB
Disk space	500 MB available on the Exchange drive; 200 MB available on the system drive	Space as required, with the databases kept on fault-tolerant drive sets
Drives	CD-ROM for installation	CD-ROM for installation
Video display	VGA or better	VGA or better

Upgrade Considerations

As discussed previously, several Exchange 2000 Server components are not supported in Exchange Server 2003, so ensure that these items are removed before starting the upgrade:

- Microsoft Mobile Information Server
- Instant Messaging
- Exchange Chat
- Exchange 2000 Conferencing Server
- Key Management Service
- The cc:Mail connector
- The MS Mail connector

If you require connectivity to a cc:Mail system or an MS Mail system and migration from that system is not in your plans, you have two choices: Keep at least one Exchange 2000 Server in the organization or procure third-party connectors for these messaging systems.

Front-end and back-end servers If your organization uses Exchange 2000 Server in a front-end/back-end configuration, you must upgrade all front-end servers to Exchange Server 2003 before upgrading the first back-end server to Exchange Server 2003.

Tuning parameters If you've configured any tuning parameters on your Exchange 2000 Servers per the Microsoft Exchange 2000 Internals: Quick Tuning Guide, you will need to remove them before performing the upgrade process. These tuning configurations are no longer needed in

Exchange Server 2003 and, in most cases, will result in problems with Exchange Server 2003. The Microsoft Exchange 2000 Internals: Quick Tuning Guide can be found at `www.microsoft.com/technet/prodtechnol/exchange/2000/maintain/exchtune.mspx`. As well, Chapter 6 of the Exchange Server 2003 Deployment Guide contains guidance on removing these tuning parameters. You can find the Deployment Guide at `www.microsoft.com/technet/prodtechnol/exchange/2003/library/depguide.mspx`.

Upgrading to Exchange Server 2003

The high-level process to upgrade an Exchange 2000 Server to Exchange Server 2003 is composed of the following steps:

1. Ensure that Windows 2000 Server Service Pack 3 or later is installed.
2. Ensure that Exchange 2000 Server Service Pack 3 or later is installed.
3. Remove the unsupported components as discussed previously.
4. Ensure that the World Wide Web Publishing Service, the Simple Mail Transfer (SMTP) service, and the Network News Transfer Protocol (NNTP) service are installed and running on the server.
5. Install the Windows 2000 Server SP3 Support Tools on the server.
6. Run the DCDiag utility.
7. Run the NetDiag utility.
8. If this is the first Exchange Server 2003 server, run Exchange Server 2003 `setup /forestprep` as discussed in Exercise 3.2.
9. If this is the first Exchange Server 2003 server, run Exchange Server 2003 `setup /domainprep` as discussed in Exercise 3.3.
10. Upgrade the server to Exchange Server 2003 as outlined below in Exercise 12.2.

When upgrading an Exchange 2000 Server, the Exchange Server 2003 setup routine will automatically install the .NET framework and ASP.NET during the installation process.

After the upgrade has been completed, you can upgrade the server to Windows Server 2003 by completing these steps:

1. Run Windows Server 2003 `adprep /forestprep`.
2. Run Windows Server 2003 `adprep /domainprep`.
3. Upgrade the server to Windows Server 2003.

Exercise 12.2 presents the procedure to upgrade an Exchange 2000 Server, assuming that you've already completed the prerequisite steps.

EXERCISE 12.2

Upgrading from Exchange 2000 Server to Exchange Server 2003

1. Insert the Microsoft Exchange Server CD into the server's CD-ROM drive. If your CD-ROM drive is set to automatically run CDs, this will automatically open the Welcome to Exchange Server 2003 Setup page. If not, browse to the location of your CD-ROM and double-click the `setup.exe` file.

2. Click the Exchange Deployment Tools link.

3. On the Welcome to the Exchange Server Deployment Tools page, click the Deploy The First Exchange 2003 Server link.

4. On the Deploy the First Exchange Server 2003 page, click the Upgrade From Exchange 2000 Server Native Mode link.

5. Ensure that you've completed all of the preliminary actions in Steps 1 through 7 shown above.

6. Scroll down the Exchange Server Deployment Tools page until you locate Item 8, Install Exchange Server 2003. Click the Run Setup Now link.

7. When prompted, agree to the EULA, and click Next to continue.

8. Enter your 25-digit CD-key, and click Next to continue.

9. The Component Selection page lists the installation options, as well as the option to choose the directory into which Exchange Server will be installed. This latter option is accessed through the Change Path button. For this exercise, we will assume that the installation directory is the default, `C:\Program Files\Exchsrvr`. The installation option we will use for this exercise is Typical, which includes the messaging components and management tools. If you would like to see the individual components that can be selected, choose the Custom option from the drop-down menu to the left of the first item in the list, Microsoft Exchange. You can then choose whether to install each individual option using that option's drop-down menu. Once you've made all of your decisions, click Next to go on.

10. A Licensing screen appears, explaining the need for you to purchase Client Access Licenses before clients can access this Exchange server. Exchange Server 2003 supports only the per-seat licensing mode. Once you have read and agreed to this licensing, click the I Agree That I Have Read And Will Be Bound By The License Agreements For This Product option, and then click Next.

11. The Installation Summary dialog box appears, asking you to confirm your installation choices. You can use the Back button to change any settings you have made. When you are satisfied with your choices, click Next to install Exchange Server 2003.

12. The installation process can take some time. When it is done, a Congratulations screen appears, informing you that the installation is complete. Click the Finish button.

Remember that when you perform a clean installation of Exchange Server 2003 or when you upgrade to Exchange Server 2003 from Exchange 2000 Server, the Installable File System (IFS) is no longer mapped to the M: drive as in Exchange 2000 Server. This change is a direct result of significant data-corruption issues that may occur when the M: drive is accessed directly, such as by virus scanners or backup-and-restore operations.

Getting Back the M: Drive

Although many people consider the doing away with the M: drive in Exchange Server 2003 a good thing, that feeling is likely not universal among all organizations that are upgrading from Exchange 2000 Server. Again, in most situations, there is really no need to have the M: drive available, and having it gone is far more worthwhile because of the serious potential for database corruption due to file-level virus scanning or backup-and-restore operations performed directly against the M: drive.

Despite Microsoft's attempts to look out for your Exchange organization by removing the M: drive, you do have the final say in the matter. Situations when you might have a valid need to enable the M: drive under Exchange Server 2003 include:

- You are using the Microsoft Front Page extensions and the Microsoft Web Storage System.
- You have developed an application that makes use of the M: drive instead of using the UNC path of `\.\BackOfficeStorage`.

The procedure to get your M: drive back in Exchange Server 2003 is basically the same as it was if you wanted to change the drive letter in Exchange 2000 Server to something other than M: (just because you could). The following procedure requires direct editing of the Registry, so be careful—this is not recommended for the weak at heart or the inexperienced.

1. Open the Registry by selecting Start ➢ Run and then entering **regedit**. Click OK.
2. Locate the following key: `HKEY_LOCAL_MACHINE\SYSTEM\CurrentControlSet\Services\EXIFS\Parameters`
3. Click Edit ➢ New and select String Value.
4. Type **DriveLetter** and press Enter.
5. Click Edit ➢ Modify. In the Value entry area, type **M** and click OK.
6. Exit the Registry Editor.
7. Restart the Exchange Information Store service from the Services console.

Summary

This chapter discussed the processes to follow to coexist with and upgrade from Exchange 2000 Server to Exchange Server 2003. Unlike the complicated path and procedures involved when coexisting with and migrating from Exchange Server 5.5, the coexistence with Exchange 2000 Server is made easy by the familiar interface, similar services, and the fact that user accounts already exist as Active Directory objects.

Before you can install an Exchange Server 2003 server into an existing Exchange 2000 Server organization, all Windows 2000 Servers and Exchange 2000 Servers should be at Service Pack 3 or later. This requirement is also true when upgrading an Exchange 2000 Server computer directly to Exchange Server 2003. Exchange 2000 Server does not run on Windows Server 2003, so you must perform an upgrade to Exchange Server 2003 first and then to Windows Server 2003.

Several components that you may have gotten used to using in Exchange 2000 Server are no longer supported in Exchange Server 2003. Before you upgrade or decommission the last Exchange 2000 Server, ensure that you no longer need the following components in your Exchange organization:

- Microsoft Mobile Information Server
- Instant Messaging
- Exchange Chat
- Exchange 2000 Conferencing Server
- Key Management Service
- The cc:Mail connector
- The MS Mail connector

Exam Essentials

Know the operating system requirements for Exchange Server 2003. Exchange Server 2003 can be installed on Windows 2000 Server SP3 or later or on Windows Server 2003, although it's recommended that you perform new installations onto Windows Server 2003 computers to take advantage of the improved security features and other usability features offered by Windows Server 2003. On the other hand, Exchange 2000 Server cannot be installed on Windows Server 2003, so an upgrade from Exchange 2000 Server to Exchange Server 2003 must be completed before that server can be upgraded to Windows Server 2003.

Understand the relationship between front-end and back-end servers. You must upgrade all front-end servers to Exchange Server 2003 before you can upgrade any of the back-end servers to Exchange Server 2003. When upgrading front-end and back-end servers, it's recommended that you upgrade the entire front end in as short a time as you can and then move onto the back-end servers. Be sure that Windows 2000 Server and Exchange 2000 Server are both at Service Pack 3 before attempting the upgrade.

Know which components are not supported in Exchange Server 2003. Nothing will spoil your upgrade plan faster than not taking time to consider those components that you will not be able to use in an Exchange Server 2003 organization with no Exchange 2000 Servers. If you still need to use any of the unsupported components, you will need to keep at least one Exchange 2000 Server in the organization.

Review Questions

1. You are preparing to upgrade three Exchange 2000 Server SP 3 computers to Exchange Server 2003. Which of the following connectors must you remove before you can perform the upgrade to Exchange Server 2003? (Choose all that apply.)

   A. Lotus Notes

   B. cc:Mail

   C. Novell GroupWise

   D. MS Mail

2. Your organization has three Exchange 2000 Server SP 3 servers running on Windows 2000 Advanced Server SP 3 computers. You have just installed a new Exchange Server 2003 server into the existing Exchange organization. Where will you be able to configure and manage the IRC settings for your organization?

   A. The Exchange System Manager from any of the four Exchange servers

   B. The Exchange System Manager from any of the three Exchange 2000 servers

   C. The Exchange System Manager from the Exchange Server 2003 server

   D. The IRC MMC snap-in

3. Your organization has three Exchange 2000 Server SP 3 servers running on Windows 2000 Advanced Server SP 3 computers. You have just installed a new Exchange Server 2003 server into the existing Exchange organization. You organization currently uses Instant Messaging services provided by the Exchange 2000 Servers. If your company is to continue providing Instant Messaging internally after all Exchange 2000 Servers are removed, what product will you need to install?

   A. Microsoft One Note

   B. Microsoft Live Communications Server

   C. Microsoft Mobile Information Server

   D. Microsoft Exchange 2000 Conferencing Server

4. You are preparing to upgrade three Exchange 2000 Server SP 2 computers to Exchange Server 2003. The Exchange 2000 Servers are running on Windows 2000 Advanced Server SP 2 computers. Which of the following actions must you perform before you can upgrade the first server to Exchange Server 2003? (Choose all that apply.)

   A. Upgrade the domain controllers to Windows Server 2003.

   B. Upgrade the Exchange 2000 Servers to Service Pack 3.

   C. Upgrade the Windows 2000 Servers to Service Pack 3.

   D. Run the Exchange Server 2003 `setup /forestprep` command.

   E. Run the Windows Server 2003 `adprep /domainprep` command.

5. While attempting to run ForestPrep on a new Exchange Server 2003 computer, you get an error telling you that the schema master for the domain could not be reached. You've checked your TCP/IP settings and they are correct. What is the most likely reason for this error?

   A. The LAN is saturated with network traffic.

   B. You must upgrade the schema master to Windows Server 2003 before installing Exchange Server 2003.

   C. The server is joined to the Active Directory domain.

   D. The server is not joined to the Active Directory domain.

6. Which Windows services must you ensure are running on a server before installing Exchange Server 2003? (Choose all that apply.)

   A. World Wide Web Publishing Service

   B. Simple Mail Transfer Protocol (SMTP) service

   C. Simple Network Management Protocol (SNMP) service

   D. File Transfer Protocol (FTP) service

   E. Network News Transfer Protocol (NNTP) service

7. Your organization has a four-node Network Load Balancing cluster installed as front-end servers for Outlook Web Access. These servers communicate with a four-node active/passive back-end cluster. All servers run Exchange 2000 Server SP 3 on Windows 2000 Advanced Server SP 3. How many back-end servers must you upgrade to Exchange Server 2003 before you can upgrade the front-end servers?

   A. None

   B. One

   C. Two

   D. Three

   E. Four

8. You are upgrading three Exchange 2000 Server SP 3 computers to Exchange Server 2003. After the upgrade is complete, what will be status of the M: drive?

   A. No change.

   B. It will be replaced by the S: (store) drive.

   C. It will be removed.

   D. It will be replaced by the X: (Exchange drive).

9. Your organization currently has three Exchange 2000 Servers installed, one of which is hosting the MS Mail connector to a legacy MS Mail post office. You have been directed to upgrade all servers to Exchange Server 2003. What options do you have? (Choose all that apply.)

   A. Migrate the MS Mail system to Exchange Server 2003.

   B. Leave one Exchange 2000 Server in place.

   C. Upgrade all Exchange 2000 Servers and install the MS Mail connector on one of the upgraded servers.

   D. Upgrade the MS Mail server to Exchange Server 2003.

10. You are preparing to upgrade three Exchange 2000 Server SP 3 computers to Exchange Server 2003. Which of the following components must you remove before you can perform the upgrade to Exchange Server 2003? (Choose all that apply.)

   A. Routing Group Connectors

   B. SMTP connectors

   C. Key Management Service

   D. Lotus Notes connector

11. When you attempt to run the ForestPrep utility in preparation for installing the first Exchange Server 2003 server into an existing Exchange 2000 Server organization, it is not available under the Action area on the Component Selection page of the Exchange Installation Wizard. What is the most likely reason for this problem?

   A. You specified an invalid Product ID.

   B. Your installation of Windows Server 2003 is not licensed.

   C. The schema master could not be contacted.

   D. ForestPrep has already been run.

12. You are preparing to upgrade three Exchange 2000 Server SP 3 computers to Exchange Server 2003. All of the servers have Pentium II 400-MHz CPUs with 256 MB of RAM and 440 MB of free space on the Exchange drive. Which of these parameters, if any, will prevent the installation of Exchange Server 2003?

   A. The CPU

   B. The RAM

   C. The free disk space

   D. The Service Pack level

13. Your organization has a four-node Network Load Balancing cluster installed as front-end servers for Outlook Web Access. These servers communicate with a four-node active/passive back-end cluster. All servers run Exchange 2000 Server SP 3 on Windows 2000 Advanced Server SP 3. You are planning to upgrade all servers to Exchange Server 2003 Enterprise Edition. After the upgrade to Exchange Server 2003 is complete, you plan on upgrading all servers to Windows Server 2003 Enterprise Edition. Which of the following commands will you need to run in order to completely perform these actions? (Choose all that apply.)

   A. `eseutil`

   B. `setup /forestprep`

   C. `setup /disasterrecovery`

   D. `adprep /forestprep`

14. You are preparing to upgrade three Exchange 2000 Server SP 1 computers and five Exchange 2000 Server SP 3 computers to Exchange Server 2003. The Exchange 2000 Servers are running on Windows 2000 Advanced Server SP 3 computers. Which of the following actions must you perform before you can upgrade the first server to Exchange Server 2003? (Choose all that apply.)

   A. Upgrade the domain controllers to Windows Server 2003.

   B. Upgrade the three Exchange 2000 Server SP 1 servers to Exchange Server 2000 SP 3.

   C. Upgrade the three Windows 2000 Advanced Servers hosting the Exchange 2000 Server SP 1 servers to Windows 2000 Server SP 4.

   D. Run the Exchange Server 2003 `setup /forestprep` command.

   E. Upgrade.

15. What new feature in Windows Server 2003's version of `ntbackup.exe` allows for open files to be backed up as if they were closed at the time of the backup operation?

   A. Recovery Storage Group

   B. Automated System Recovery

   C. Mailbox Recovery Center

   D. Volume shadow copy

16. In addition to removing unsupported components used in Exchange 2000 Server, what else must you do before upgrading an Exchange 2000 Server to Exchange Server 2003?

   A. Move all mailboxes to another server.

   B. Remove any tuning parameters that you have configured on the Exchange 2000 Server.

   C. Move all public folders to another server.

   D. Install Exchange 2000 Server Service Pack 1 on the server.

17. Your organization has a four-node Network Load Balancing cluster installed as front-end servers for Outlook Web Access. These servers communicate with a four-node active/passive back-end cluster. All servers run Exchange 2000 Server SP3 on Windows 2000 Advanced Server SP3. You are planning to upgrade all servers to Exchange Server 2003 Enterprise Edition. After the upgrade to Exchange Server 2003 is complete, you plan on upgrading all servers to Windows Server 2003 Enterprise Edition. How many nodes will you be able to have in the back-end cluster after all upgrades are completed?

    A. Four

    B. Six

    C. Eight

    D. Sixteen

    E. Thirty-two

18. You are preparing to upgrade three Exchange 2000 Server SP 2 computers to Exchange Server 2003. All of the servers have Pentium II 400-MHz CPUs with 256 MB of RAM and 940 MB of free space on the Exchange drive. Which of these parameters, if any, will prevent the installation of Exchange Server 2003?

    A. The CPU

    B. The RAM

    C. The free disk space

    D. The Service Pack level

19. Your organization has a four-node Network Load Balancing cluster installed as front-end servers for Outlook Web Access. These servers communicate with a four-node active/passive back-end cluster. All servers run Exchange 2000 Server SP 3 on Windows 2000 Advanced Server SP 3. How many front-end servers must you upgrade to Exchange Server 2003 before you can upgrade the back-end servers?

    A. None

    B. One

    C. Two

    D. Three

    E. Four

20. You are preparing to upgrade three Exchange 2000 Server SP 3 computers to Exchange Server 2003. Which required items not present in Windows 2000 Server will the Exchange Server 2003 setup process install? (Choose all that apply.)

    A. Simple Network Management Protocol (SNMP) service

    B. ASP.NET

    C. .NET Framework

    D. World Wide Web Publishing Service

    E. Simple Mail Transfer Protocol (SMTP) service

Answers to Review Questions

1. B, D. Exchange Server 2003 does not support the cc:Mail and MS Mail connectors. You can migrate these systems using the Exchange Migration Wizard or maintain an Exchange 2000 Server to host these connectors until they are no longer needed.

2. B. If you use components that are unsupported by Exchange Server 2003 on your Exchange 2000 Servers, you must configure and manage them from the Exchange 2000 Server System Manager console.

3. B. Live Communications Server is an add-on product that replaces and provides more functionality than the Exchange 2000 Server Instant Messaging service.

4. B, C, D. All Exchange 2000 Servers must be upgraded to Exchange 2000 Server SP 3 and Windows 2000 Server SP 3 before the upgrade can occur. You must also run Exchange Server 2003's ForestPrep and DomainPrep utilities to prepare the schema and the domains for the installations of Exchange Server 2003. You do not need to upgrade the domain controllers to Windows Server 2003, but it won't hurt.

5. D. If the TCP/IP settings are correct, then the next most likely cause of this problem is that you did not join this server to the domain. Exchange Server 2003 (and Exchange 2000 Server, for that matter) can be installed only on servers that are part of an Active Directory domain.

6. A, B, E. Before you can install an Exchange Server 2003 computer, it must have the .NET Framework, ASP.NET, the World Wide Web Publishing Service, the Simple Mail Transfer Protocol (SMTP) service, and the Network News Transfer Protocol (NNTP) service installed and running.

7. A. You must upgrade all front-end servers to Exchange Server 2003 before you start the upgrade on the back-end servers.

8. C. Due to multiple problems arising from direct file-level access to the M: drive, it does not exist in Exchange Server 2003 by default. The share is still accessible by using its UNC path. You can, if desired, edit the Registry to restore the M: drive to use.

9. A, B. You will need to either leave the one Exchange 2000 Server hosting the MS Mail connector in place or migrate the MS Mail post office to Exchange Server 2003. The MS Mail connector is not supported in Exchange Server 2003, nor is an upgrade path from MS Mail.

10. C. The Exchange 2000 Server Key Management Service (KMS) is not supported in Exchange Server 2003 because its functionality has been replaced by that of the Windows Server 2003 PKI.

11. C. If the schema master cannot be contacted, ForestPrep will not run. You will likely receive a warning dialog informing you of this problem.

12. C. At the minimum you must have 500 MB of free space on the Exchange drive and 200 MB of free space on the system drive. Ideally, you'll have much more free space than this—you'll likely want to upgrade the hardware in these servers or retire them from service.

13. B, D. Before you can install the first Exchange Server 2003 computer, you must issue the Exchange Server 2003 `forestprep` and `domainprep` commands to extend the Active Directory schema for Exchange Server 2003 and to prepare domains for the Exchange Server 2003 servers. Before you can install the first Windows Server 2003 domain controller, you must run the Windows Server 2003 Active Directory `forestprep` and `domainprep` commands to extend the Active Directory schema for Windows Server 2003 and to prepare domains for the Windows Server 2003 domain controllers. The `eseutil` command is used only for low-level database checking and defragmentation. The DisasterRecovery switch of Exchange Server 2003 setup is used during a reinstallation of an Exchange server following its failure.

14. B, D. All Exchange 2000 Servers must be upgraded (at a minimum) to Exchange 2000 Server SP 3 and Windows 2000 Server SP 3 before the upgrade can occur. In this case, no Windows 2000 Server Service Pack updates are required because all servers are running at Windows 2000 Server SP 3. As well, you must run Exchange Server 2003's `forestprep` and `domainprep` commands to prepare the schema and the domains for the installations of Exchange Server 2003. You do not need to upgrade the domain controllers to Windows Server 2003, but it won't hurt.

15. D. The volume shadow copy, new in `ntbackup.exe` for Windows Server 2003, allows for open files to backed up as if they were closed at the time of the backup. These files will be written to the backup media in a closed state.

16. B. You must remove any custom-configured tuning parameters from the Exchange 2000 Server before attempting the upgrade to prevent problems with the Exchange Server 2003 installation. Mailboxes and public folders need not be moved but should be backed up as a precautionary measure. Exchange 2000 Server Service Pack 3 is required to be installed before the upgrade.

17. C. Exchange Server 2003 Enterprise Edition on Windows Server 2003 Enterprise Edition can support up to eight nodes in an active/passive clustering configuration.

18. D. Exchange 2000 Servers must be at Service Pack 3 or later on Windows 2000 Server Service Pack 3 or later before they can be upgraded to Exchange Server 2003.

19. E. You must upgrade all front-end servers to Exchange Server 2003 before you start the upgrade on the back-end servers.

20. B, C. Exchange Server 2003 setup will install ASP.NET and the .NET Framework when upgrading from Exchange 2000 Server.

Connecting with Other Messaging Systems

MICROSOFT EXAM OBJECTIVES COVERED IN THIS CHAPTER:

- ✓ **Migrate from other messaging systems to Exchange Server 2003**
  - Use the Migration Wizard to migrate from other messaging systems
- ✓ **Configure and troubleshoot Exchange Server 2003 for coexistence with other messaging systems**
- ✓ **Configure and troubleshoot Exchange Server 2003 for interoperability with other SMTP messaging systems**

As you learned in Chapter 8, "Building Administrative and Routing Groups," Exchange Server 2003 relies on various connectors to provide messaging links between routing groups in an organization. Connectors are also used to provide messaging links between Exchange organizations and external messaging systems. The external messaging system could be a legacy system you have in place on your own network, a messaging system (even another Exchange organization) on someone else's network, or the Internet itself. Exchange Server 2003 comes with a few general-use connectors, such as the X.400 and SMTP Connectors, which are used to establish communications with other systems capable of using these same protocols. In addition, Exchange Server 2003 comes with several specialized connectors used to establish communications with the Novell GroupWise and Lotus Notes messaging systems.

This chapter begins with a look at two of the general-purpose connectors: the X.400 Connector and the SMTP Connector. Since the basic configuration of these was covered when we discussed linking routing groups together in Chapter 8, we will look at the differences in configuring the connectors to be used with external systems. We will also look at the details of using the SMTP Connector to enable communications with the Internet. From there, we will turn our attention to the Novell GroupWise and Lotus Notes connectors.

Connecting to X.400 Systems

If you recall from Chapter 8, the *X.400 Connector* can be used to link Exchange routing groups in the same organization and also to link an Exchange organization to a foreign, X.400-based messaging system. When you create an X.400 Connector, the computer on which the connector is configured becomes a bridgehead server to the foreign system.

It is important to note that you can also configure the X.400 Connector between Exchange Server 2003 routing groups when connectivity between them is poor. The X.400 Connector uses standard messaging-based data transfer from one end of the connection to the other, while the routing group connector uses Remote Procedure Calls (RPCs). RPCs require reliable connectivity to function properly.

Unlike the Routing Group Connector, which can automatically create a connector at the opposite end of the connection for you, X.400 connectors will need to be configured manually on both ends to ensure proper communications occur.

To configure the X.400 Connector in Exchange Server 2003, you first must create a *Message Transfer Agent (MTA) Service Transport Stack*. This Transport Stack is configured on a particular Exchange server and is basically a set of information about the software and hardware making up the underlying network. The use of the Transport Stack allows for a layer of abstraction between the X.400 Connector and the network itself. You can configure Transport Stacks that support either the TCP/IP or X.25 protocols.

After creating the Transport Stack, you must create the connector. Exercise 13.1 outlines the basic steps for creating a new TCP/IP Transport Stack and an X.400 Connector to use that stack.

Many of the property pages used to configure an X.400 Connector were previously discussed in detail in Chapter 8. However, three of the pages are relevant only to configuring external X.400 connections. Those pages are covered in the next few sections.

EXERCISE 13.1

Creating a TCP/IP Transport Stack and an X.400 Connector

1. Click Start ➤ Programs ➤ Microsoft Exchange ➤ System Manager.
2. Expand the Administrative Groups folder, the administrative group, and then the server on which you want to create the stack.
3. Expand the Protocols container, right-click the X.400 container, and choose New TCP/IP X.400 Service Transport Stack from the context menu.
4. Use the property pages that open to configure the new stack, and click OK when you have finished.
5. Locate the routing group for which you want to create the connector.
6. Right-click the Connectors container and choose the New TCP X.400 Connector option from the context menu.
7. This opens the property pages that you must configure for the new connector. After you have configured these pages, you must get the administrator of the external X.400 system to create the corresponding connector to your system.

Override Properties

The Override page, shown in Figure 13.1, lets you configure settings that override the local MTA settings when messages are sent over the X.400 Connector. For the most part, you can leave these advanced settings alone. When connecting to a foreign X.400 system, that system's administrator will be able to tell you the settings that need to be adjusted.

You can also override the name and password of your local MTA. This is used mainly when the name and password of the local MTA are too long or use characters or spaces that MTAs on foreign systems cannot accept. The overriding values are used only for the X.400 connection.

FIGURE 13.1 Configuring override properties for an X.400 Connector

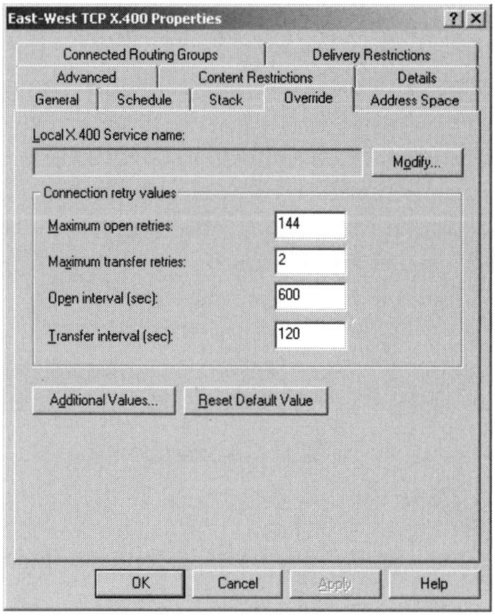

Address Space Properties

Foreign systems do not necessarily use the same addressing scheme as Exchange Server 2003. For this reason, the Exchange MTA relies on address spaces to choose foreign gateways over which messages should be sent. An *address space* is the part of an address that designates the system that should receive the message. For example, look at a typical Internet address: `user@company.com`. Everything after the @ sign is the address space. The format of the address space is enough to tell the MTA that the message should be sent via SMTP.

The Address Space property sheet, shown in Figure 13.2, lets you configure an address space for the foreign X.400 system to which you are connecting. The Exchange MTA compares the destination address of outgoing messages with this address space to determine whether the outgoing messages should be sent over the X.400 Connector.

Clicking the Add button opens an Add Address Space dialog box, shown in Figure 13.3, which allows you to specify the type of address space that you want to add. Because you are connecting to a foreign X.400 system, you want to configure an X.400 address space.

After you choose the X.400 address space type and click OK, the X.400 Address Space Properties dialog box appears, as shown in Figure 13.4. The particular addressing information that needs to be configured for the foreign system should be provided by the administrator of the foreign system. X.400 addresses are case-sensitive and need to be typed in exactly the same format as provided.

FIGURE 13.2 Configuring address spaces for an X.400 Connector

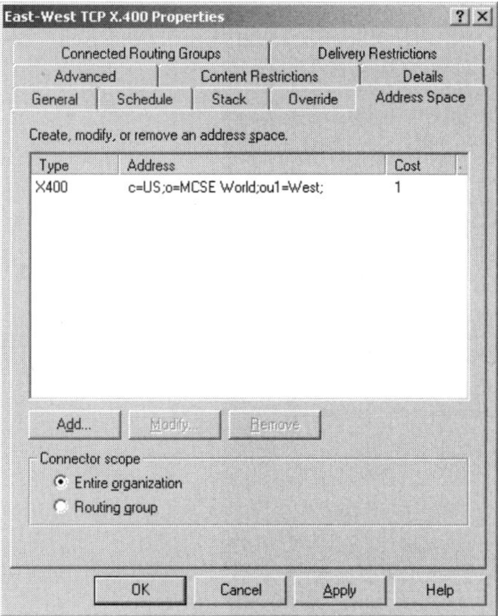

FIGURE 13.3 Choosing an address space type

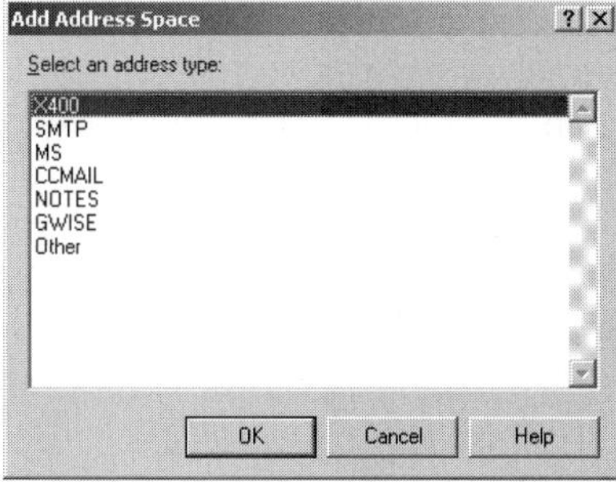

Advanced Properties

The Advanced page, shown in Figure 13.5, is used to specify options for MTA conformance, links, and message attributes. The settings depend mostly on the specifications of the foreign system to which you are connecting.

FIGURE 13.4 Configuring the address space

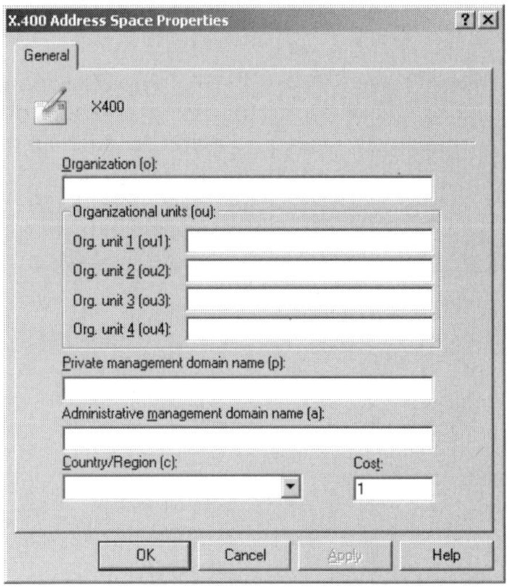

FIGURE 13.5 Configuring Advanced properties for an X.400 Connector

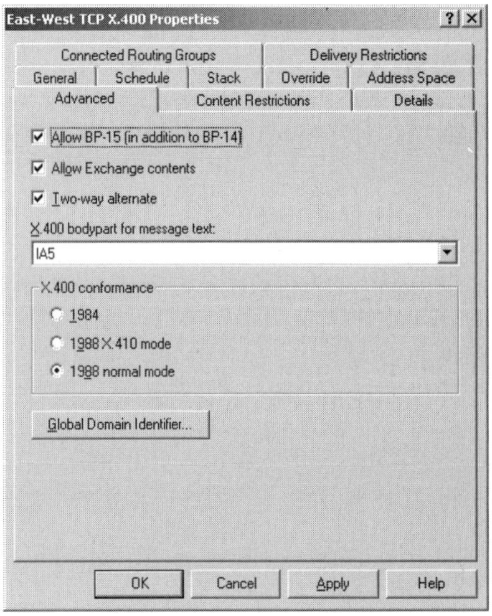

Table 13.1 lists the properties available on the Advanced page.

TABLE 13.1 Advanced Properties for an X.400 Connector

Property	Description
Allow BP-15 (in addition to BP-14)	The Body Part 15 (BP-15) standard is part of the 1988 X.400 recommendation and supports several advanced messaging features, such as the encoding of binary attachments. The Body Part 14 (BP-14) standard is part of the older 1984 X.400 recommendation, which supports fewer features. If you do not select the Allow BP-15 option, only the BP-14 standard will be used.
Allow Exchange Contents	Microsoft Exchange supports the use of Extended MAPI-compliant clients, which in turn support such features as rich-text format. Make sure that any foreign X.400 system to which you are connecting supports such features before you allow them to be transferred.
Two-Way Alternate	The Two-Way Alternate specification is an X.400 standard in which two connected X.400 systems take turns transmitting and receiving information. If the foreign system to which you are connecting supports this option, enabling it can greatly improve transmission speed.
X.400 Bodypart For Message Text	This option specifies how message text should be formatted. Unless you are communicating with foreign systems that use foreign-language applications, leave this value at its default setting, International Alphabet 5 (IA5).
X.400 Conformance	X.400 standards are periodically published as recommendations. Exchange Server 2003 supports the two primary recommendations: those issued in 1984 and those from 1988. New updates have been made to the standard since 1988, but they don't really form a new recommendation. The 1988 recommendation itself has two versions: normal mode and X.410 mode. The default setting is 1988 normal mode, and you can expect it to work with most foreign X.400 systems.
Global Domain Identifier	The global domain identifier (GDI) is a section of the X.400 address space of the target system. The GDI is used to prevent message loops that can occur with outgoing messages. The administrator of the foreign X.400 system will let you know if you need to modify these values.

SMTP and Internet Connectivity

In Chapter 8, you saw how the *SMTP Connector* could be used to connect routing groups in the same organization and to connect an Exchange Server 2003 routing group to an Exchange 5.5 server site. You can also use SMTP Connectors to connect an Exchange organization to the Internet or to a foreign messaging system that uses SMTP.

SMTP Overview

The *Simple Mail Transfer Protocol (SMTP)* defines the methods for exchanging mail messages between applications. The protocol addresses mail transfer between an SMTP client and an SMTP server (the client may itself be another SMTP server). This section discusses SMTP and outlines how it works.

SMTP Process

The SMTP process involves a TCP connection, a series of client/server commands and replies, and the use of spooling. We will discuss each of these in the following sections.

TCP Connection

When an SMTP client application sends mail to an SMTP server, it uses TCP to establish a connection with port 25 on the SMTP server. Port 25 is the application doorway on the SMTP server for mail activity. Once that connection is established, a series of commands and replies is exchanged between the client and the server. The connection is similar to a telephone connection, and the commands and responses are similar to verbal communication over a telephone connection.

SMTP Commands and Replies

Now we will examine the steps in the SMTP process (including the TCP connection). In this example, we will send a message. You do not need to remember the reply code numbers. They are included here merely to provide a complete picture.

1. A client establishes a connection with the server at port 25.
2. The server confirms the connection by replying with a 220 reply code, which means "ready for mail."
3. The client computer identifies itself to the server by sending the HELO command with the computer's identity (for example, `HELO server1.acme.com`).
4. The server confirms the HELO by responding with the 250 reply code (which means "all is well") and its identity. The server may also require a password or some other form of authentication.
5. The client sends the MAIL FROM command that contains the identification of the sender.
6. The server responds with the 250 reply code ("all is well").

7. The sender then sends the RCPT TO (Recipient To) command with the identity of a recipient of the mail message.
8. The server responds with either a 250 reply code or a 550 reply code (which means "no such user here").
9. After all the RCPT TO commands are sent (one command is sent per recipient), the client sends the DATA command indicating that it is ready to send the actual mail message.
10. The server responds with a 354 reply code (which means "start mail input").
11. Upon receiving the 354 reply, the client sends its outgoing mail messages line by line. The data must be in 7-bit ASCII format. If the data is in 8-bit format, it must be translated into 7-bit format using either Multipurpose Internet Mail Extension (MIME) or UUENCODE (UNIX-to-UNIX encode).
12. After the data has been sent, the sender sends a special sequence of control characters (e.g., CRLF.CRLF) to signal the end of the transfer.
13. The client sends a QUIT command to end the session.
14. The server responds with the 221 reply code (which means that it "agrees with the termination"). Both sides of the communication close the TCP connection.

SMTP and Spooling

The word *spooling* in this context means *queuing*. SMTP uses *spooling* to delay message delivery. For example, when a client sends a message addressed to another user, that message is spooled on the sender's SMTP server. The SMTP server will periodically check its spooled messages and try to deliver them to the relevant users. If it cannot deliver a message, the SMTP server will keep the message spooled and try to deliver it at a later time. When the recipient's server comes online, the SMTP server can deliver the message. If a message cannot be delivered within a time period set by the administrator, the spooled message is returned to the sender with a non-delivery message.

The advantage of the spool mechanism is that the message sender does not have to establish a connection with a recipient's computer in order to send a message. After sending a message, the sender can proceed with other computing activities because she does not need to wait online for the message to reach the recipient. The recipient also does not have to be online in order for mail to be sent to him.

DNS and SMTP

Transferring messages between SMTP hosts is dependent on the Domain Name Service (DNS). When an SMTP host sends an e-mail message to another SMTP host, DNS must resolve the domain name of the receiving host to an IP address. DNS does this by storing special records named *Mail Exchanger (MX) records* in the DNS database. Each MX record in a DNS database represents an SMTP host to which mail can be forwarded. You can also assign each MX record a preference relative to the other MX records in the database.

A sending SMTP host retrieves all MX records for the receiving domain from DNS, resolves the IP address for the SMTP host with the lowest preference number, and attempts to send its message to that host. If that host is unavailable, the sender tries the host with the next higher preference number. If you have three mail servers in your organization that can send and receive mail across your network boundaries, the MX record entries in your DNS forward lookup zone might look like this:

```
mcseworld.com        MX    10    mcsesvr3042.corp.mcseworld.com.
mcseworld.com        MX    30    mcsesvr3142.corp.mcseworld.com.
mcseworld.com        MX    50    mcsesvr3242.corp.mcseworld.com.
```

Each entry is composed of several different fields. The first field specifies the name of the domain that the MX record is responsible for, in this case the mcseworld.com domain. The second field specifies the record type, in this case an MX record. The third field specifies the preference number for that mail server. The last field specifies the fully qualified domain name (FQDN) or IP address of the mail server that the MX record entry is pointing to.

SMTP Folders in Exchange Server 2003

SMTP uses three file system folders to manage messages on an Exchange Server 2003. By default, all of these folders are created in the `C:\Program Files\Exchsrvr\Mailroot\vsi` *x* folder. The three folders are as follows:

- The *Pickup folder* is used for outbound messages on some SMTP hosts. Exchange Server 2003 creates, but does not normally use, this folder.
- The *Queue folder* is where SMTP stores inbound messages as they are received. Once received, Internet Information Server (IIS) processes them for delivery.
- The *Bad Mail folder* is where undeliverable messages that cannot be returned to the sender are stored.

Configuring Multiple SMTP Domain Names

SMTP can be configured in a number of different ways. For example, you might provide your users with one or multiple SMTP addresses. You might also segregate users into virtual organizations, each with their own SMTP address spaces. For example, you might configure some of your users to receive mail using the @widgets.com address space, while others receive mail using the @cooltools.com address space. To do this, you must configure separate SMTP virtual servers for these users and configure MX records to resolve the IP address associated with those virtual servers.

The SMTP Virtual Server

With Exchange Server 2003, you can create multiple virtual servers for every supported Internet protocol, including SMTP. Creating multiple *SMTP virtual servers* allows you to segment SMTP traffic to use different IP addresses or TCP ports, each with its own configuration. This allows you a good bit of leeway in your SMTP configuration. For example, you might configure one SMTP virtual server with stricter authentication policies than another. Or, you might configure one virtual server to send and receive SMTP messages between all Exchange Server 2003 servers inside an organization and configure another virtual server to send and receive SMTP messages from the Internet.

As with most other objects, you'll configure the SMTP virtual server using its property pages. Just expand the Protocols container under the Exchange server on which the virtual server is configured, and then expand the SMTP container, as shown in Figure 13.6.

To start with, only the Default SMTP Virtual Server exists. You can add new virtual servers by right-clicking the SMTP container and selecting the New SMTP Virtual Server command. This command opens the property pages for configuring the new server. Each of the available pages is discussed in the upcoming sections.

General Properties

The General page, shown in Figure 13.7, is used to set several general parameters, including the following:

- The IP address assigned to the virtual server (this is unassigned by default)
- The number of concurrent connections the server is allowed to support (no limit is set by default)
- The maximum amount of time a connection may be idle before being timed out (again, no default is set)
- Whether logging is enabled (disabled by default)

Access Properties

The Access properties page, seen in Figure 13.8, provides access to a number of separate dialog boxes used to control access to the virtual server.

FIGURE 13.6 Viewing SMTP virtual servers

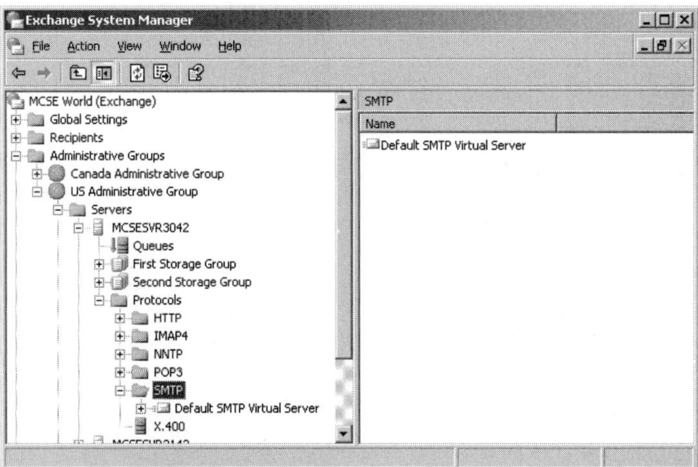

FIGURE 13.7 General properties of an SMTP virtual server

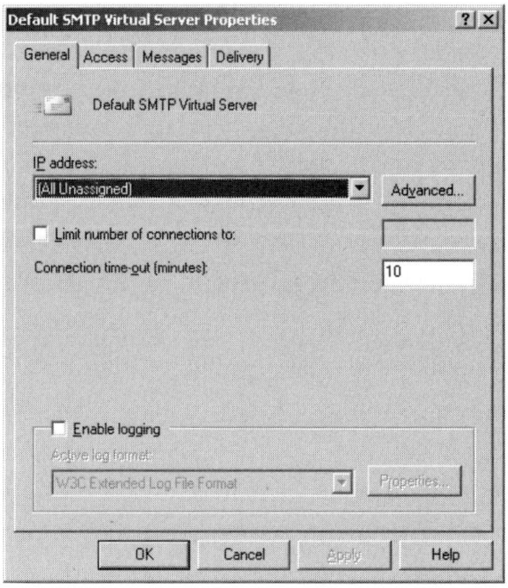

FIGURE 13.8 Access properties of an SMTP virtual server

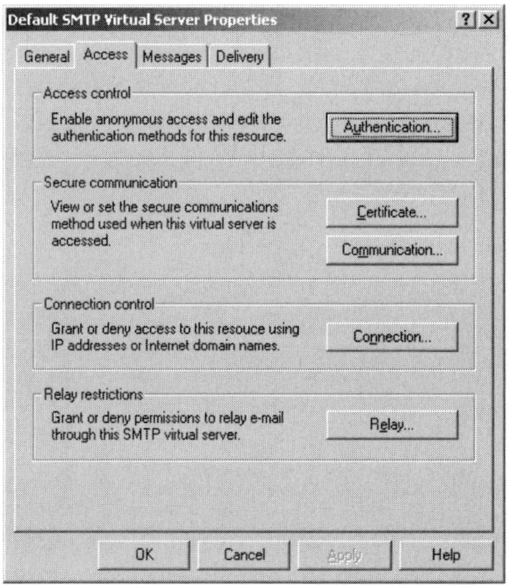

Table 13.2 describes the parameters you can configure using the buttons on this page.

Messages Properties

The Messages page, shown in Figure 13.9, lets you configure how messages are handled by the SMTP virtual server. You can place several limits on messages, including the message size, the cumulative size of messages that can be transferred during a single session, the number of messages that may be sent per connection, and the number of recipients a single message can name. You can also use this page to designate a recipient to receive Non-Delivery Reports (NDRs) and change the directory in which bad mail is stored.

The final field on this page, Forward All Mail With Unresolved Recipients To Host, is probably not featured prominently enough in the list of options. This field lets you name a *smart host* to which messages are forwarded when they cannot be resolved within your domain. This offers the powerful ability to configure a single host to which all external mail (such as to the Internet) should go. For example, you could configure your SMTP virtual server to forward all unresolved messages (those not to recipients in your own organization) to an SMTP host at your ISP or to a smart host of your own that you have placed outside the company firewall. This allows you the ability to specify how messages are to be routed outside of your organization, such as by using a specific link that has a lower cost.

TABLE 13.2 Setting Access Properties for an SMTP Virtual Server

Button	Settings
Authentication	It is often useful to require an SMTP host or client to authenticate before allowing message transfer. You can use this button to choose from Anonymous, Basic, or Integrated Windows authentication methods. This dialog also lets you configure TLS encryption. Authentication and encryption are covered in Chapter 15.
Certificate	This button launches a wizard for creating and configuring web server certificates (also discussed in Chapter 15).
Communication	This button lets you configure whether a secure channel is required to transfer messages using the SMTP virtual server and whether that secure channel should use 128-bit encryption.
Connection	This button opens a dialog that lets you configure a specific list of hosts to grant or deny access to.
Relay	By default, an SMTP virtual server will accept messages from any host but will relay only messages sent from authorized clients. This allows clients in your domain using POP3 or IMAP4 clients to send SMTP messages using the SMTP virtual host. If you want to configure your SMTP virtual server to act as a smart host for relay messages coming in from other domains, you can configure the specific clients for whom to relay messages using this button. Note that this is used to configure only inbound relay restrictions. Outbound restrictions are configured using the SMTP Connector.

Delivery Properties

The Delivery page, seen in Figure 13.10, lets you set several options governing how the SMTP virtual server tries to deliver mail and some parameters governing the security and configuration of outbound connections.

FIGURE 13.9 Configuring message properties

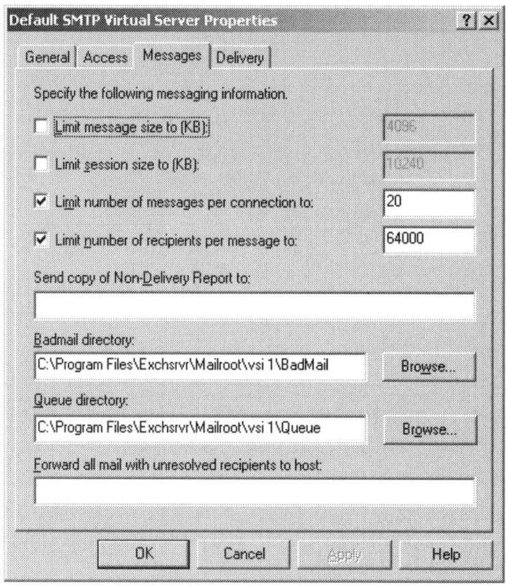

FIGURE 13.10 Delivery properties of an SMTP virtual server

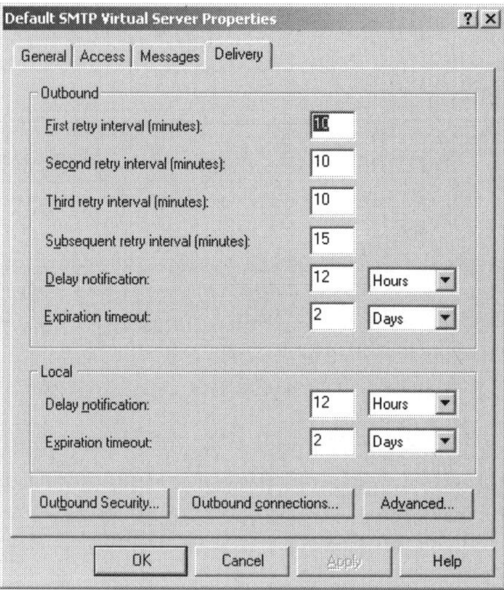

The parameters you can configure on this page are shown in Table 13.3.

TABLE 13.3 Setting Delivery Properties for an SMTP Virtual Server

Property	Description
Retry Intervals	By default, each virtual server tries to deliver messages as they arrive. When delivery fails for some reason, the virtual server queues the message for retries. The First through Third and Subsequent Retry Interval settings let you configure how long it takes the server to attempt to send a message after a failure.
Delay Notification	If a message has been queued for 12 hours (the default setting), the sender is notified that the message has not been delivered yet.
Expiration Timeout	After two days (again, the default setting), the message is returned to the sender with an NDR.
Local	The Delay Notification and Expiration Timeout settings in the Local section work the same as those in the Outbound section but apply only to recipients within the organization.
Outbound Security	As you saw in the previous section, inbound security is set using the Authentication button on the Access page. Outbound security is configured using this button. Usually, you should configure outbound security to use the same authentication protocols that you require for inbound security.
Outbound Connections	Use this button to assign limits on the allowable number of outbound connections.
Advanced	One common security problem with Internet mail occurs when the person sending the message misrepresents their identity. This is referred to as spoofing. To help prevent spoofing, you can configure an SMTP virtual server to perform a reverse DNS lookup on people who send messages. This confirms that the IP address of the sender is from the same network as is registered in DNS. Use the Advanced button to enable Reverse DNS lookup. One caution, however: Using reverse DNS lookup can significantly decrease performance.

Managing SMTP Virtual Server Queues

SMTP maintains four queues in which messages are held for various stages of processing. These queues are:

- local_domain_name (Local Delivery), which contains messages waiting for delivery to a local mailbox. If this queue backs up, look for problems within IIS or the Information Store.
- Messages awaiting directory lookup, which contains messages waiting for recipient addresses to be resolved. If this queue backs up, look for problems between Exchange Server 2003 and Active Directory.
- Messages waiting to be routed, which contains messages waiting for Exchange Server 2003 to determine the best route along which to send them. Once the route is determined, messages are moved to various temporary link queues for delivery. If this queue backs up, look for problems with connectors.
- Final destination unreachable, which contains messages the SMTP virtual server was unable to deliver. If this queue backs up, look for problems with the SMTP virtual server, the destination SMTP server, or improper addressing.

For more information on managing queues, see Chapter 10, "Administration and Maintenance."

When creating additional virtual servers, you will need to specify a single IP address/port number combination. You cannot use the IP address selection of (All Unassigned) for more than one virtual server on a specific port number.

Follow along with Exercise 13.2 as we create an SMTP virtual server.

EXERCISE 13.2

Creating an SMTP Virtual Server

1. Click Start ➢ Programs ➢ Microsoft Exchange ➢ System Manager.
2. Expand the Administrative Groups folder, the administrative group, and the server on which you want to create the new virtual server, and then expand the Protocols container.
3. Right-click the SMTP container and select New SMTP Virtual Server from the context menu.
4. On the first page of the wizard that appears, enter the name for the new SMTP virtual server and click Next to continue.

EXERCISE 13.2 *(continued)*

5. Select the specific IP address configured on your server to be the new SMTP virtual server. Note that the IP address and port number combination you configure must be separate from any that are already in use on your server.

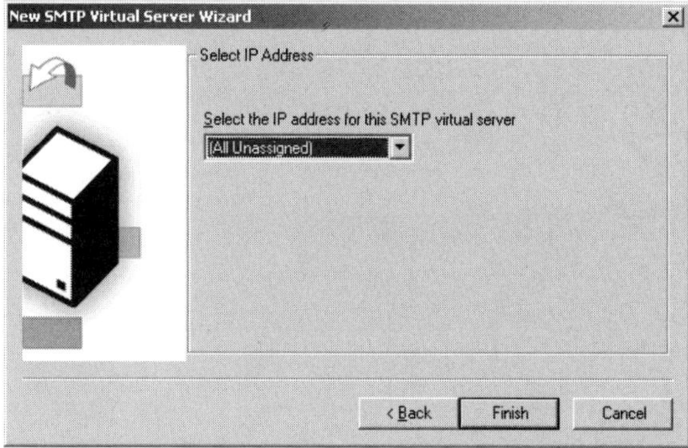

6. Click Finish to create the new connector and return to System Manager.
7. In System Manager, expand the SMTP container.
8. Right-click the new SMTP virtual server, and select Properties from the shortcut menu.
9. Click the Access tab.
10. Click the Authentication button.
11. Remove the checkmarks next to the Anonymous Access and Basic Authentication options and click OK.

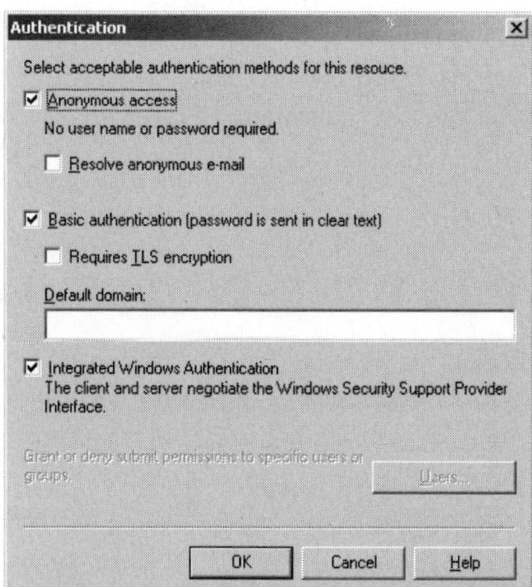

EXERCISE 13.2 *(continued)*

12. Click the Messages tab.
13. Select the Limit Message Size To (KB) option, and enter a maximum message size into the corresponding field.

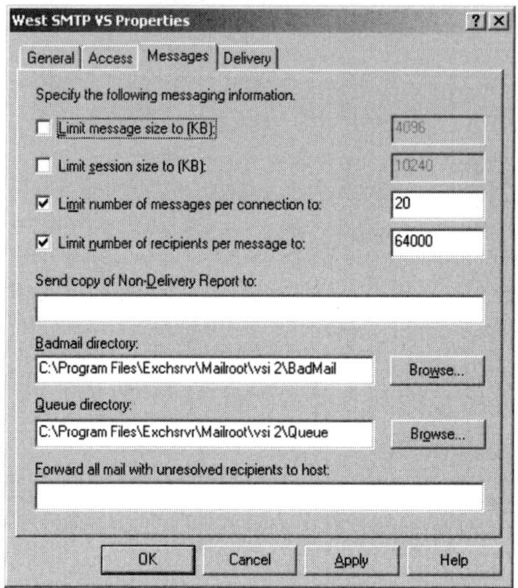

14. Click OK to set the new properties and return to System Manager.

The SMTP Connector

While an SMTP virtual server is used to define basic SMTP transport properties, an SMTP Connector is used to define properties for a specific address space. In Chapter 8, we covered the creation and configuration of SMTP Connectors in detail. Even though that discussion was aimed primarily at using the SMTP Connector to connect routing groups, the process of setting up the SMTP Connector for other uses is almost identical, so we refer you to Chapter 8 for specifics.

Connecting to Lotus Notes

If your organization uses a Lotus Notes messaging system, and you cannot migrate from it to Exchange Server 2003, you are not completely out of luck. Exchange Server 2003 does provide a *Lotus Notes connector* that can be used to connect the two messaging systems so that your organization can function smoothly, with messages flowing between both systems invisibly to the end user.

The Lotus Notes connector also works with Domino servers.

To configure the Lotus Notes connector, you need only locate it in the routing group of your choice, right-click it, and select Properties from the context menu. We will examine each of the pertinent property pages in the following sections.

General The General page, seen in Figure 13.11, allows you to configure the Notes server name, the location of the `notes.ini` file, the location of the import container (where imported objects will be placed), the connector mailbox name, how often to poll the Notes server, the Notes server language, and what to do with Notes DocLinks.

Address Space The Address Space page, seen in Figure 13.12, allows you to configure the common e-mail address space that both the Exchange organization and the Notes organization will use. In addition, you can specify that this connector applies to the entire Exchange organization or just this specific routing group, which is very useful when you have Notes servers distributed geographically in the same pattern as your Exchange servers.

To create an address space entry, click the Add button to open the Add Address Space dialog box seen in Figure 3.13.

FIGURE 13.11 General properties of the Notes connector

FIGURE 13.12 Address Space properties of the Notes connector

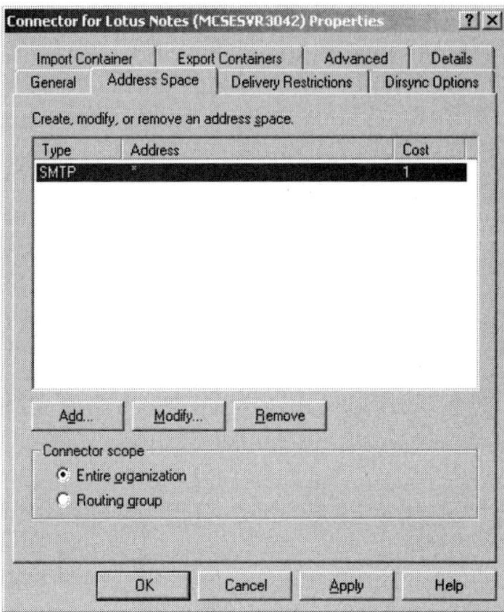

FIGURE 13.13 Adding an address space to the Notes connector

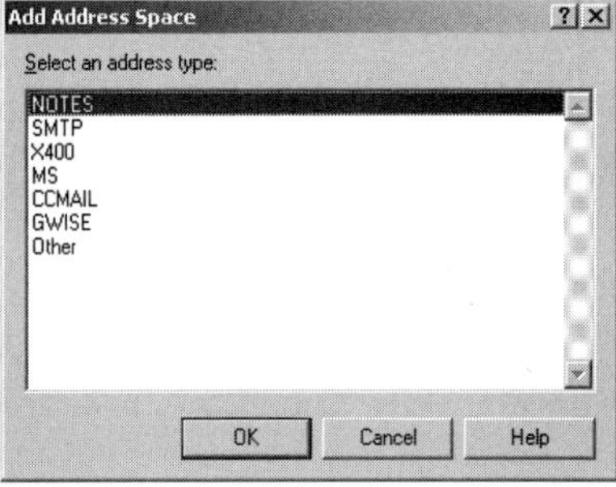

Delivery Restrictions On the Delivery Restrictions page, seen in Figure 13.14, you can configure permissions to pass messages over this connector. You can leave the default setting of allowing everyone to send messages or you can modify an accept list or reject list as desired.

Dirsync Options The Dirsync Options page, seen in Figure 13.15, allows you to configure multiple synchronization options, such as when the synchronization event should take place and settings for Address Book synchronization. It also lets you force an immediate Exchange or Notes synchronization event to occur.

FIGURE 13.14 Delivery Restrictions properties of the Notes connector

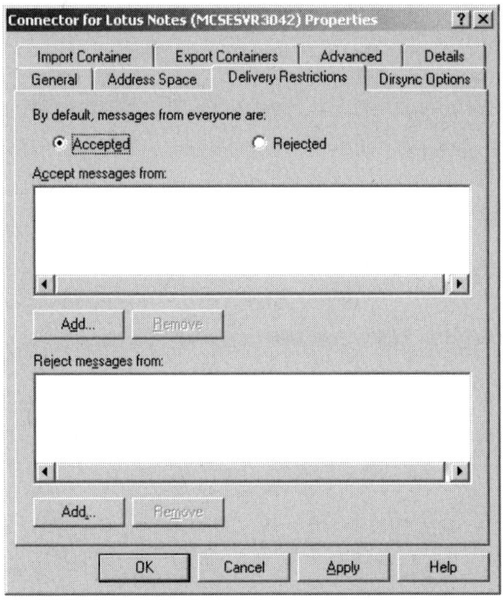

FIGURE 13.15 Dirsync Options properties of the Notes connector

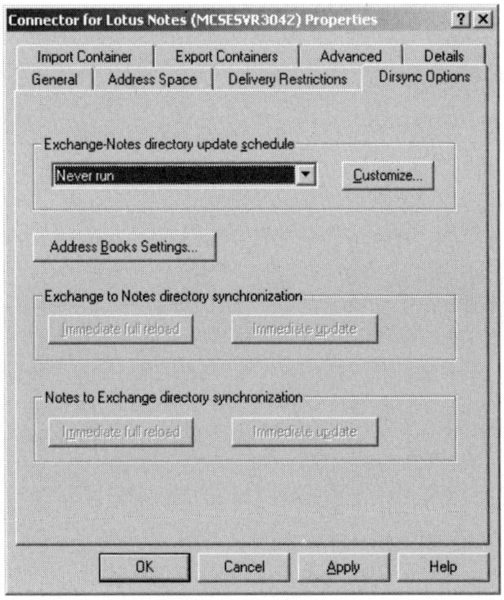

Import Container The Import Container page, seen in Figure 13.16, allows you to select the Active Directory container that will be used when synchronizing items into Active Directory from Notes. You also have the option to specify what action should take place when a Notes mailbox that does not have a Windows account is synchronized.

Export Containers The Export Containers page, seen in Figure 13.17, allows you to select the Active Directory container or containers that will be synchronized to the Notes server. As well, you have the option to enable or disable synchronization of contacts and groups to Notes.

Advanced The Advanced page, seen in Figure 13.18, contains all those settings for the Notes connector that didn't fit in anywhere else. Options on this page include the type of letterhead to use (the appearance of messages), which mailbox is used to route messages, how messages should be delivered, which domains are routable between the organizations, and the maximum message size that can cross the connector.

FIGURE 13.16 Import Container properties of the Notes connector

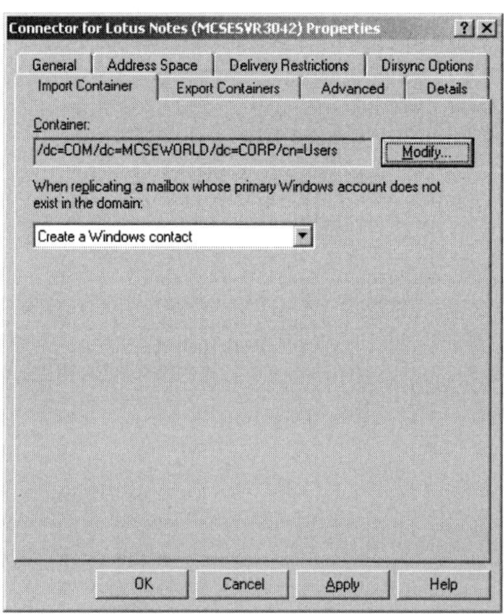

FIGURE 13.17 Export Container properties of the Notes connector

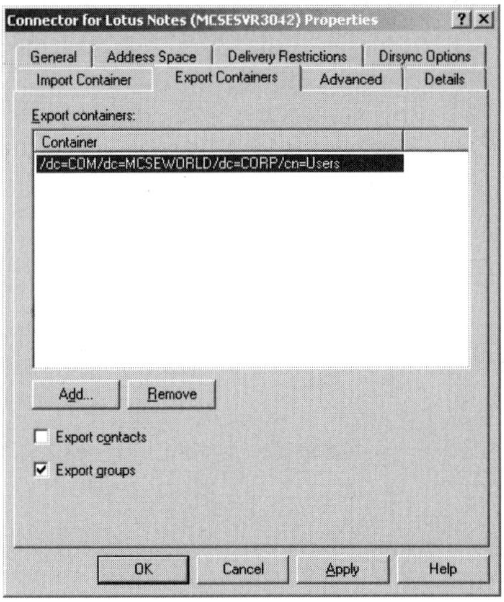

FIGURE 13.18 Advanced properties of the Notes connector

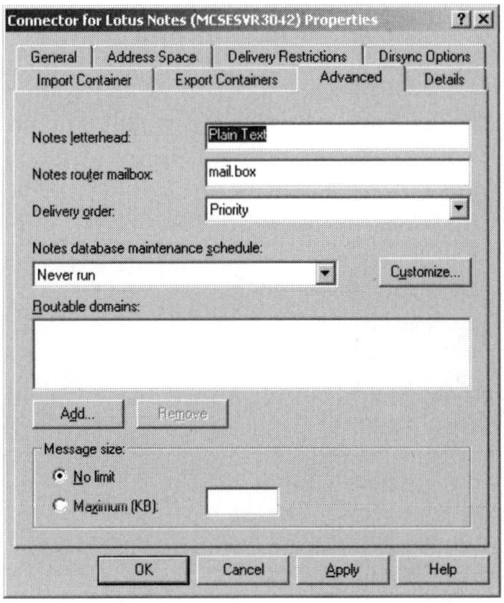

The Calendar Connector

Unfortunately, the Lotus Notes connector does not synchronize calendaring information between Exchange and Notes. To that end, you will need to configure the Calendar connector after you've completed configuring the Notes connector. To configure the Calendar connector, you need to locate it in the same routing group as the configured Notes connector, right-click it, and select Properties from the context menu. We will examine each of the pertinent Properties pages in the following sections.

General The General page, seen in Figure 13.19, allows you to configure options that control how the calendar synchronization will occur. Also, you will need to associate the Calendar connector with the connector that is importing users, such as the Notes connector.

Calendar Connections The Calendar Connections page, seen in Figure 13.20, requires you to configure a calendar type to be synchronized.

Clicking the New button causes the Calendar Type dialog box, seen in Figure 13.21, to open, allowing you to select the calendar type. When you click OK, the Notes Calendar Connections dialog box, seen in Figure 13.22, opens, requiring you to enter the server information.

Schedule The Schedule page, seen in Figure 13.23, looks pretty much like any other Schedule page you might have seen up to now. From here you can configure when calendaring information should be synchronized across the Calendar connector.

FIGURE 13.19 General properties of the Calendar connector

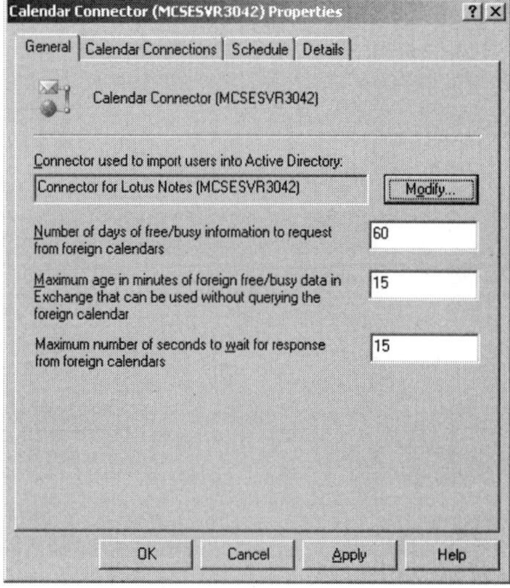

FIGURE 13.20 Calendar Connections properties of the Calendar connector

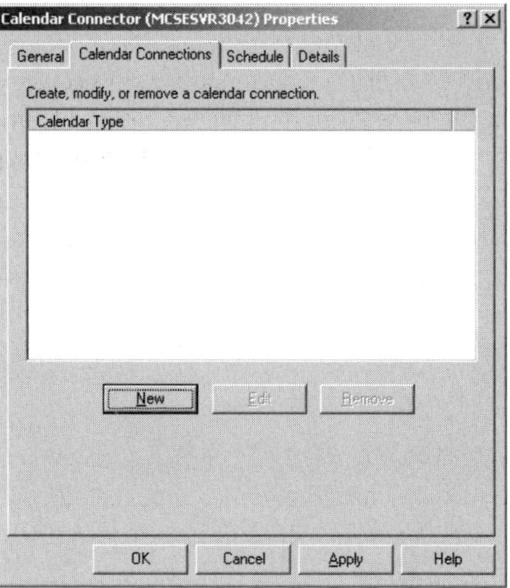

FIGURE 13.21 Choosing the calendar type for the Calendar connector

FIGURE 13.22 Specifying Notes server information for the Calendar connector

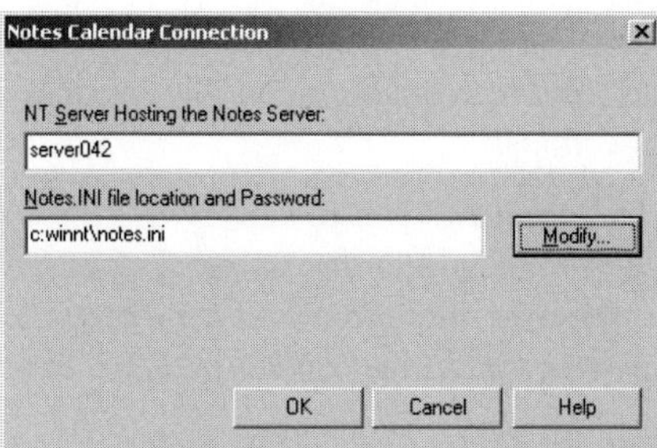

FIGURE 13.23 Schedule properties of the Calendar connector

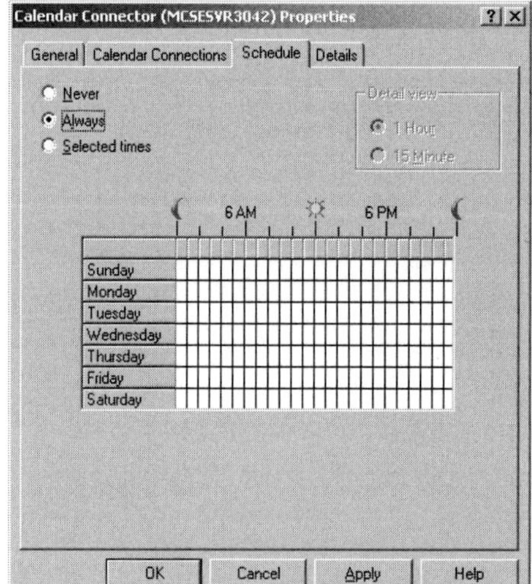

Connecting to Novell GroupWise

If your organization uses a Novell GroupWise messaging system, and you cannot migrate from it to Exchange Server 2003, you are not completely out of luck. Exchange Server 2003 does provide a Novell GroupWise connector that can be used to connect the two messaging systems so that your organization can function smoothly, with messages flowing between both systems invisibly to the end user.

The GroupWise connector has been tested for GroupWise versions 4.*x* and 5.*x*, but it should work with 6.*x* since the APIs have not been changed.

To configure the Novell GroupWise connector, you need only locate it in the routing group of your choice, right-click it, and select Properties from the context menu. We will examine each of the pertinent property pages in the following sections.

General The General page, seen in Figure 13.24, allows you to specify the UNC path to the API Gateway, the GroupWise server, and the user account and password of a NetWare user with administrative rights on the GroupWise server configured on the connector. You can also specify the maximum message size that is allowed to cross the connector as well as the message delivery order.

FIGURE 13.24 General properties of the GroupWise connector

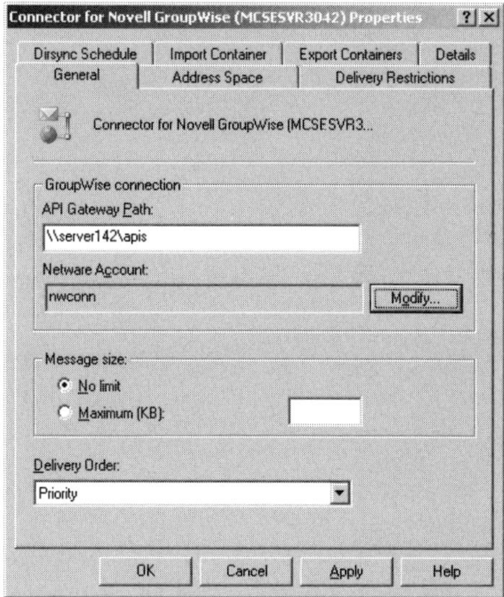

Address Space The Address Space page for the GroupWise connector has the same options as for the Notes connector.

Delivery Restrictions The Delivery Restrictions page for the GroupWise connector has the same options as for the Notes connector.

Dirsync Schedule The Dirsync Schedule page, seen in Figure 13.25, allows you to configure multiple synchronization options, such as when the synchronization event should take place, and it also lets you force an immediate Exchange or GroupWise synchronization event to occur.

Import Container The Import Container page, seen in Figure 13.26, allows you to select the Active Directory container that will be used when synchronizing items into Active Directory from GroupWise. You also have the option to specify what action should take place when a GroupWise mailbox that does not have a Windows account is synchronized. In addition, you can configure several Filtering options that will affect which items are synchronized.

Export Container The Export Container page for the GroupWise connector has the same options as for the Notes connector.

After you've completed configuring the GroupWise connector, you will need to configure the Calendar connector.

FIGURE 13.25 Import Container properties of the GroupWise connector

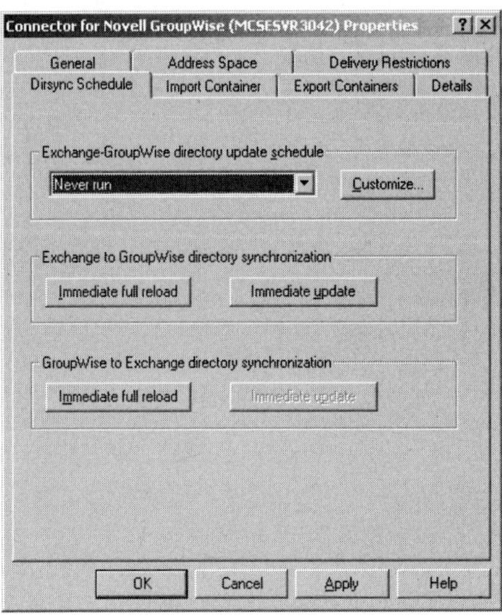

FIGURE 13.26 General properties of the GroupWise connector

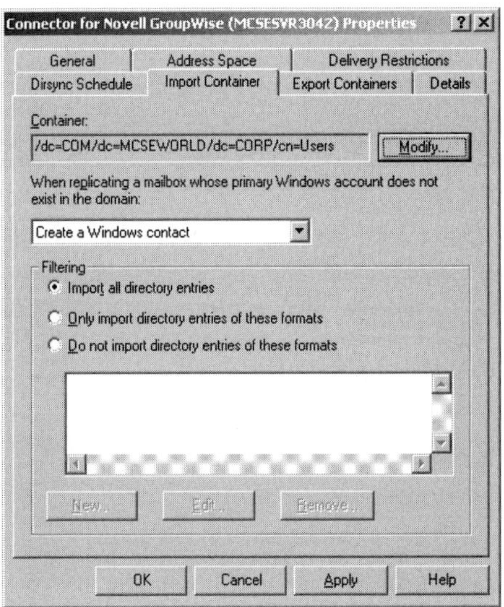

Coexisting with Multiple Foreign Systems

So what does your organization do when you have the unlucky task of configuring connectivity to both Lotus Notes and Novell GroupWise at the same time? No problem as long as you've enough Exchange Server 2003 servers installed to go around!

Since each installation of Exchange Server 2003 includes only one instance of the Notes connector, the GroupWise connector, and the Calendar connector, you will need to configure one Exchange server with the Notes connector and its associated Calendar connector. You would then need to configure a separate Exchange server to host the GroupWise connector and its associated Calendar connector. Routing group connectors, X.400 Connectors, and SMTP Connectors are not limited to one per server.

Depending on the amount of message and calendar traffic that is crossing your Notes or GroupWise connectors, having one server that hosts each one is likely to be a more reliable and effective solution. On the other hand, if you have a small organization and you don't mind not being able to synchronize calendaring information between both foreign e-mail systems and Exchange at the same time, you could create both the Notes and the GroupWise connector on the same server.

Summary

Exchange Server 2003 relies on connectors to communicate with external messaging systems. Two protocol-based connectors, the X.400 Connector and the SMTP Connector, can be used either to connect two Exchange routing groups together or to connect an Exchange organization to an external messaging system that uses the same protocol.

SMTP is also used to provide messaging connectivity with the Internet. Creating multiple SMTP virtual servers allows you to segment SMTP traffic to use different IP addresses or TCP ports, each with its own configuration. Virtual servers are used to define basic SMTP transport properties. SMTP Connectors are configured on virtual servers to define properties for a specific address space.

In previous versions of Exchange, coexistence via connectors was supported for MS Mail and Lotus cc:Mail. As the times have changed, so has the support for foreign and legacy messaging systems in Exchange. Exchange Server 2003 provides connectors that allow Exchange Server 2003 organizations to coexist with Lotus Notes and Novell GroupWise messaging systems.

Exam Essentials

Know the various methods you have available to connect to foreign messaging systems. Exchange Server 2003 continues to offer superior support for foreign and legacy messaging systems by providing the X.400, SMTP, Lotus Notes, and Novell GroupWise connectors. Should you need to connect to older systems, such as Lotus cc:Mail or MS Mail, you will need to maintain at least one Exchange 2000 Server for the immediate future.

Understand the SMTP messaging transfer process. As an administrator responsible for an Exchange server organization, you must understand how SMTP works, especially when messages cross the outside edge of your organizational network. Understanding the interrelationships between SMTP and DNS will go a long way toward keeping mail flowing into and out of your organization efficiently and securely.

Review Questions

1. You have configured SMTP on your network to allow users to exchange messages with the Internet. Exchange recipients can send mail to Internet users, but Internet users cannot send mail to the Exchange recipients. You verify that your SMTP virtual server is accessible from the Internet. What is the most likely cause of the problem?

   A. Your firewall is not open to port 110 (POP3).

   B. Your firewall is not open to port 25 (SMTP).

   C. Your client computers are not configured with TCP/IP.

   D. Your client computers are not directly connected to the Internet.

   E. Your domain has no MX record in DNS.

2. Which of the following SMTP folders is not normally used by Exchange Server 2003?

   A. Pickup folder

   B. Queue folder

   C. Bad Mail folder

   D. DNS folder

3. How would you set the maximum size of messages allowed over an X.400 Connector?

   A. Using the General property page of the connector.

   B. Using the Limits property page of the connector.

   C. Using the Content Restrictions property page of the connector.

   D. You cannot set this limit on an X.400 Connector.

4. Your Exchange environment uses SMTP to exchange mail with a company named Sockets & Wrenches, which uses a host-based SMTP mail system. When users on your system send mail to the name of the host at Sockets & Wrenches, it is not delivered. But if those users use an IP address for addressing, the mail is delivered. You are informed that other systems can send mail to Sockets & Wrenches using a host name in the addressing. What should you do to enable your users to be able to send mail to Sockets & Wrenches using a host name in the addressing? (Select the best answer.)

   A. Configure a mapping on the DNS server on your network.

   B. Configure a HOSTS file on each client.

   C. Configure an LMHOSTS file on each client.

   D. Configure SMTP to forward all mail to Sockets & Wrenches.

5. As administrator of an Exchange organization, you have been asked to have all outgoing SMTP mail sent to a single SMTP server. How should you configure this?

   A. Enter the SMTP server as an MX record in the DNS.

   B. Enter the SMTP server as a CN record in the DNS.

   C. Enter the SMTP server in the SMTP virtual server properties.

   D. Enter the SMTP server in the SMTP Connector properties.

   E. Make the SMTP server the default gateway in the TCP/IP settings of your IMS computer.

6. SMTP relies on which of the following components to resolve addresses of Exchange recipients on inbound messages?

   A. DNS

   B. SMTP

   C. Resolver program

   D. Active Directory

7. Your DNS forward lookup zone contains the following MX record entries:

```
mycompany.com        MX   100   mail1.mycompany.com.
mycompany.com        MX   50    mail2.mycompany.com.
mycompany.com        MX   150   mail3.mycompany.com.
```

   On which server, by default, is a connection attempted to route SMTP messages?

   A. The server listed first.

   B. The server with the lowest preference value.

   C. The server with the highest preference value.

   D. The servers will be randomly connected to.

8. In the MX record

```
mycompany.com        MX   150    mail3.mycompany.com.
```

   what does the `mycompany.com` entry specify?

   A. The domain for which the MX record will handle inbound mail.

   B. The domain for which the MX record will handle outbound mail.

   C. The domain that is authorized to send mail to the organization in which the MX record is configured.

   D. The domain that is not authorized to send mail to the organization in which the MX record is configured.

9. You have recently completed the configuration of an X.400 connection between your Exchange Server 2003 organization and a foreign X.400 organization that is using a Unix-based messaging system. The administrator in the other organization reports to you that inbound messages from your organization are garbled. Messages inbound to your organization are not affected. What is the most likely problem?

   A. You have not selected the Allow BP-15 option.

   B. You have selected the Allow Exchange Contents option.

   C. You have selected the Two-Way Alternate option.

   D. You have not set the Global Domain Identifier.

10. You are attempting to configure a new TCP X.400 connector so that your Exchange Server 2003 organization can interact with a Unix-based X.400 messaging system. When you attempt to create the TCP X.400 connector in the desired routing group, you receive an error dialog. What is the most likely reason for this occurrence?

    A. You did not install the X.400 connector item during Exchange setup.

    B. You do not have a DNS server in your network.

    C. You did not first create a TCP X.400 transport stack service.

    D. The schema master could not be reached.

11. You are the Exchange administrator for your organization. You have five Exchange Server 2003 servers all located in one administrative group and one routing group. A recent virus outbreak on your network caused a large number of messages to be sent using fake and spoofed source addresses. Many of the messages were sent to incorrect e-mail addresses and thus could not be delivered. Where could you go to look for these messages?

    A. Pickup folder

    B. Queue folder

    C. Bad Mail folder

    D. DNS folder

12. In the basic SMTP process, what command does the client computer use after the server has confirmed the HELO command with the 250 reply code?

    A. EHLO

    B. HELO

    C. MAIL FROM

    D. REQ

13. You are the Exchange administrator for a company that has five geographically distant sites in North America. Although all sites have full T-1 connectivity between them, circuit reliability has been very poor over the past few months. In many cases, the links have dropped altogether, causing message transfer problems for your Exchange Server 2003 routing groups. What type of connector could you create between these routing groups that would work best in this situation?

   A. Routing group connector

   B. X.400 Connector

   C. Lotus Notes connector

   D. Active Directory connector

14. When sending SMTP data, what format must the data be in?

   A. 32-bit

   B. 16-bit

   C. 8-bit

   D. 7-bit

15. You have recently completed the configuration of the Lotus Notes connector, allowing your Exchange Server 2003 organization to coexist with your Lotus Notes organization. Users report no problems sending or receiving messages but complain that the schedule information for Notes users is not up-to-date. What is the most likely reason for this problem?

   A. The Active Directory connector is not configured completely.

   B. The Microsoft Exchange MTA stacks service has stopped.

   C. The Calendar connector is not configured for the Notes organization.

   D. The Recipient Update Service has not run recently.

16. After how many hours, by default, will a message that has not been delivered by the SMTP virtual server be returned to the sender with an NDR?

   A. 12

   B. 24

   C. 36

   D. 48

17. After how many hours, by default, will an undelivered message cause a delay notification to be sent to the sender of the message?

   A. 12

   B. 24

   C. 36

   D. 48

18. The administrator of an X.400 messaging system with which your Exchange organization is connected tells you that the speed of the connection could be enhanced if you were to turn on the Two-Way Alternate option. Where would you go to do this?

A. The Connection property page of the MTA Transport Stack used by the X.400 Connector

B. The Connection property page of the X.400 Connector

C. The Override property page of the X.400 Connector

D. The Advanced property page of the X.400 Connector

19. In the basic SMTP process, what command does the client computer use to identify itself to the SMTP server?

A. EHLO

B. HELO

C. MAIL FROM

D. REQ

20. You would like to require SMTP hosts and clients to authenticate themselves before allowing messages to be transferred using your Exchange server. What forms of user authentication does the SMTP virtual server support? (Choose all that apply.)

A. Anonymous

B. Basic

C. Digest

D. Secure Sockets Layer

E. Integrated Windows

Answers to Review Questions

1. E. Transferring messages between SMTP hosts is dependent on the Domain Name Service (DNS). When an SMTP host sends an e-mail message to another SMTP host, DNS must resolve the domain name of the receiving host to an IP address. DNS does this by storing special records named Mail Exchanger (MX) records in the DNS database. Each MX record in a DNS database represents an SMTP host to which mail can be forwarded.

2. A. SMTP creates three file system folders to manage messages on an Exchange 2000 Server: Pickup, Queue, and Bad Mail. However, the Pickup folder is not used. By default, all of these folders are created in the `C:\Program Files\Exchsrvr\Mailroot\vsi` *x* folder.

3. C. As with most connectors, the X.400 Connector allows you to set limits on message sizes. You do this using the Content Restrictions property page of the connector.

4. A. Since your users cannot connect to the remote host by name but can connect by IP address, it is apparent that there is a problem resolving the server name through DNS. Since other hosts can resolve the name, it is also apparent that the problem is local.

5. C. You would need to configure the name of the SMTP server on the Message property page of the SMTP virtual server. This page lets you name a smart host to which messages are forwarded when they cannot be resolved within your domain. This offers the powerful ability to configure a single host to which all external mail should go (such as to the Internet).

6. D. All information about users, including their addresses, is stored in the Active Directory.

7. B. The MX record that has the lowest preference value will be the first server that a connection attempt is made to, which is the

   ```
   mycompany.com          MX     50     mail2.mycompany.com
   ```

   record.

8. A. The first field in this MX record specifies the domain namespace to which the MX record will apply. Thus, all mail sent to the `mycompany.com` namespace will use this (and possibly other similarly configured) MX record(s).

9. B. The most likely cause for this problem is that you have selected the Allow Exchange Contents option, which enables features that are likely not compatible with the foreign X.400 messaging system, such as Rich Text formatting.

10. C. You cannot create the TCP X.400 connector until you have created the TCP X.400 transport stack service.

11. C. The Bad Mail folder is where undeliverable messages that cannot be returned to the sender are stored.

12. C. After the server returns the HELO command with the 250 status code, the client next sends the MAIL FROM command with the identification of the sender. The server then replies to this with another 250 status code.

13. B. The X.400 system of data transfer is designed for low-reliability, low-bandwidth connections. By using the X.400 Connector between your routing groups, you can increase message transfer reliability.

14. D. SMTP data is sent in 7-bit format. If the outgoing data is in 8-bit format, it will be converted to 7-bit using either the MIME extensions or UUENCODE.

15. C. The Lotus Notes connector synchronizes only mailboxes between the organizations, not calendaring information. You must properly configure the Calendar connector to run along with the Notes connector in order to synchronize calendar information.

16. D. If the message cannot be delivered in two days (48 hours), it will be returned to the sender with an NDR explaining such.

17. A. If the message has not been delivered after 12 hours, the sender of the message will receive a delay status notification informing them that the message has not yet been sent, but attempts to send the message are continuing.

18. D. The Two-Way Alternate specification is an X.400 standard in which two connected X.400 systems take turns transmitting and receiving information. If the foreign system to which you are connecting supports this option, enabling it can greatly improve transmission speed.

19. B. The client computer identifies itself to the server by sending the HELO command with the computer's identity (for example, `HELO server1.widgets.com`).

20. A, B, E. It is often useful to require an SMTP host or client to authenticate before allowing messages transfer. You can choose from the Anonymous, Basic, or Integrated Windows authentication methods. You can also configure TLS encryption for the virtual server.

Backup and Recovery

MICROSOFT EXAM OBJECTIVES COVERED IN THIS CHAPTER:

- ✓ **Perform and troubleshoot backups and recovery**
- ✓ **Manage, monitor, and troubleshoot data storage**
- ✓ **Remove an Exchange Server computer from the organization**

Because of the importance of the Exchange databases and transaction logs, backing up those components is essential. There are also a number of other components that you will want to include when backing up an Exchange server. When Exchange Server 2003 is installed, an Exchange-aware version of Windows Backup replaces the existing version that comes with Windows Server 2003. This chapter begins with an overview of backup technologies and strategies and then looks at using Windows Backup to back up and restore an Exchange server.

Understanding Backups

Before you fire up your backup program and start backing things up, it's important to have a clear understanding of the technologies involved and to create a good backup plan. This section looks at the various components of Exchange and Windows that you should back up, the types of backups available to you, and several backup strategies.

What's New with Windows Backup

The Windows Backup utility in Windows Server 2003 has undergone two dramatic improvements since its last release in Windows 2000 Server. The Emergency Repair Disk (ERD) has been replaced by the new (and much improved over ERD) *Automatic System Recovery (ASR)* functionality. In addition, Windows Server 2003 includes *Volume Shadow Copy (VSC)* support.

VSC is implemented in two ways in Windows Server 2003. When used in Windows Backup it allows a backup process to create an instant and exact copy of the data to be backed up at the time the backup is initiated. This snapshot is then written to the backup media instead of the original files being referenced while writing to the backup media. When VSC is used in this way, it allows a safe and effective mechanism to back up files that are open at the time of the backup. These files, which would normally be skipped, are backed up in a closed state as of the time the snapshot is taken and thus appear closed on the backup media. Running applications are not affected by this process and continue to run unaffected by the backup. In order to use VSC, the volume must be using NTFS (New Technology Filesystem). VSC can also be disabled during the creation of a backup job if desired.

What to Back Up

An Exchange server is composed of a great deal of information, including the Exchange databases of user messages and public messages and the transaction logs associated with those databases. Configuration information is stored in the Microsoft Windows Registry, in various places in the Exchange Server installation path, in Active Directory, and even on some users' computers. This section covers the information that you should include when backing up an Exchange server.

Much of the information in this section is a recap of how the Information Stores in Exchange Server 2003 work. You can learn more about the Exchange storage architecture in Chapter 2, "Microsoft Exchange Architecture."

Databases

Much of the information in Exchange Server 2003, including private and public user messages, is stored in two databases: `PRIVx.EDB` and `PUBx.EDB`.

PRIV*x*.EDB Each mailbox store database on an Exchange server is named using the format `PRIVx.EDB`, where `x` ranges from 1 to the number of databases on the server. The private store databases hold user mailboxes and messages. By default, these databases are located in `Program Files\Exchsrvr\Mdbdata\`.

PUB*x*.EDB Each public store database on an Exchange Server is named using the format `PUBx.EDB`, where `x` ranges from 1 to the number of databases on the server. The public store databases hold messages and documents stored in public folders. By default, these databases are also located in `Program Files\Exchsrvr\Mdbdata\`.

In addition to these core databases, a streaming database with the extension `.STM` is associated with each mailbox and public database. Several optional databases might also be available on any given Exchange server. These optional databases represent various services that may be installed on a server, such as a *Site Replication Services (SRS) database*.

Transaction Logs

Whenever a transaction occurs on an Exchange server, that transaction is first recorded in a *transaction log*. Transactions are written to the database later during idle time. Transaction logs are the primary storage areas for new transactions. One set of transaction logs exists for each storage group on a server. A set is composed of a current log, any number of previous logs, reserve logs, and a checkpoint file. The current transaction log file, named `EDB.LOG`, resides in the `\Exchsrvr\Mdbdata` directory by default.

Data is written to log files sequentially as transactions occur. Regular database maintenance routines commit changes in the logs to the actual databases later. The most current state of an

Exchange service, therefore, is the .EDB database and .STM database, *plus* the current log files (including the checkpoint file) that have not yet been committed to the database. Thus, transaction logs are an essential part of the backup routine.

Checkpoint files are used to keep track of transactions that are committed to the database from a transaction log. Using checkpoint files ensures that transactions cannot be committed to a database more than once. Checkpoint files are named `EDB.CHK` and reside in the same directories as their log files and databases.

Log files are always given 5 MB of reserved disk space. When a log file fills, it is renamed, and a new log file is created. Old, renamed log files are called *previous logs*. Previous logs are named sequentially, using the format `EDBxxxxx.LOG`, in which each `x` represents a hexadecimal number. Previous logs are stored in the same directories as their current-log-file counterparts.

During an online backup of an Exchange server, previous log files that are fully committed are purged. Previous log files can still consume a good deal of disk space. Exchange Server 2003 provides a feature called *circular logging* that can help prevent that waste of disk space. When circular logging is enabled, only previous log files with uncommitted changes are maintained for each storage group. This can significantly reduce the amount of hard disk space that is required for your Exchange server, compared with keeping all transaction logs until a backup is completed. Circular logging is disabled by default, but you can enable it on the General property sheet of a storage group container in System Manager.

You can find more information on using circular logging in Chapter 9, "Configuring the Information Store."

In addition to all of the current and previous transaction logs, the online backup process also creates *patch files* that serve as temporary logs to store transactions while the backup is taking place. Transactions in these logs are committed when the backup is finished.

Other Items to Back Up

In addition to Exchange databases and transaction log files (all of which are included automatically in a regular online backup of Exchange), you will want to consider several other items:

EXCHSRVR subdirectories Many valuable pieces of information, including message-tracking data, are located in various subfolders of `Program Files\Exchsrvr`.

Site Replication Service (SRS) database The SRS database is used in mixed Exchange Server 5.5 and Exchange 2000 Server/Exchange Server 2003 environments. You can learn more about the SRS database itself in Chapter 11, "Coexisting with and Migrating from Exchange 5.5."

User information Many administrators allow the storage of users' personal folders (PST files) and address books on the Exchange server or another network server. Always make sure that information of this sort is included in your backup strategy. When users store personal folders on their local workstations, you will need to involve the users in the backup procedure.

Backing Up System State Information

A *System State backup* is used to back up configuration information critical to a Windows Server 2003 computer. You'll learn how to create a System State backup later in the chapter. System State information includes the following:

Windows 2003 Registry The Windows Registry contains a great deal of configuration information relating to Exchange Server 2003, especially information relating to the coexistence of Exchange Server 2003 with previous versions. You should perform regular System State backups on Exchange servers to include the Windows Registry.

Internet Information Services metabase Since Exchange Server 2003 relies so heavily on IIS for protocol support, it is only natural that IIS be a part of any good backup plan. The IIS metabase, a database of configuration information, is included in a System State backup. Running regular System State backups on the Exchange server also backs up the IIS metabase.

Active Directory While Active Directory is not really a part of Exchange, most of the configuration information for Exchange Server 2003 is stored in Active Directory. Recipient objects are also kept in Active Directory. You should run regular System State backups of domain controllers to capture Active Directory information. You should back up Active Directory and Exchange Server 2003 databases at the same time to avoid losing configuration of user objects on the domain controllers or in global catalogs.

Preparing a System for Backup and Disaster Recovery

When your Exchange server has only one hard disk, system information, databases, and log files are all stored on that disk. More often, however, an Exchange server is configured with more than one local hard disk. This is because Exchange offers flexibility in partitioning data across multiple locations to help with performance and for purposes of restoration.

In general, we recommend the following practices to optimize performance and disaster recovery:

Keep log files on separate hard disks. The speed of an Exchange Server 2003 database depends a good deal on how quickly transactions are copied from memory to the transaction log. For this reason, we recommend that you place the log files for each storage group on a dedicated hard disk so that the transaction logs do not compete with any other read/write operations. The best performance is usually obtained from a mirrored disk device. Also, it is a good idea to keep transaction logs on a separate disk from the Information Store to ensure recoverability.

Keep storage groups on separate disks. We also like to keep storage groups on separate disks from other storage groups. This decreases the damage that a single drive failure can do. However, it is more important to have the transaction logs on a separate disk than to separate the storage groups themselves. Storing log files on separate disks dramatically increases your odds of successful recovery in the event of failure. For example, if you had three free hard disks (aside from the hard disk holding system information) and two storage groups, it would be better to put the two storage groups on one disk and then to put the transaction logs for each storage group onto their own disks than to try to separate the storage groups. In Figure 14.1, storage groups 1 and 2 are placed on a single disk array (F:). The logs for each storage group are placed on their own volumes (D: and E:).

Keep databases small. Within a storage group, data can be partitioned into multiple databases. We recommend that you keep these databases smaller rather than larger. If you have a particularly large database, dividing it into multiple databases improves recovery for two reasons:

- Users can begin accessing a database as soon as it is restored.
- If you use multiple backup media, you can actually restore the multiple databases in parallel. Restoring a smaller database takes less time than restoring a larger database.

Turn off circular logging for all storage groups. The disadvantage of using circular logging is that it prevents you from using differential or incremental backups (discussed later in this chapter). Also, because some log files are discarded before backup, you may not be able to fully restore a server by replaying the log files, a potentially serious situation. For this reason, we generally recommend that you leave circular logging disabled for all your Exchange servers.

You may want to turn on circular logging when importing a large amount of data. However, you must remember to disable it afterward and do a full backup. You may also want to turn on circular logging for servers where recovery is not so important, such as for front-end servers that do not contain mailboxes or public folders.

FIGURE 14.1 Separating log files is more important than separating storage groups.

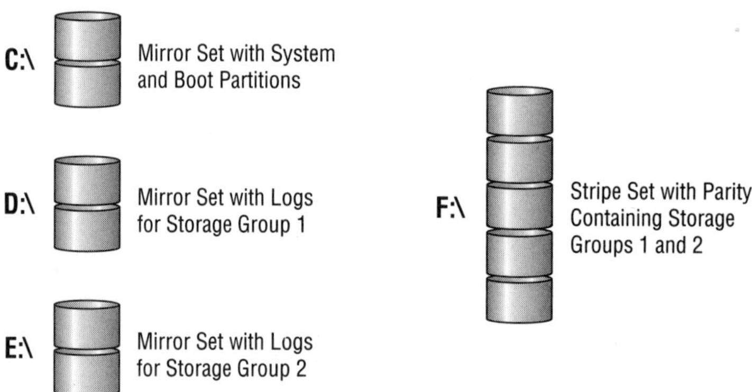

Back up whole storage groups at once. We recommended that you back up an entire storage group at the same time. This makes the backup process easier to manage because the databases within the storage group share the same set of log files. The log files can be truncated only after all databases have been backed up.

Back up storage groups to different media. To prepare for a failure of all storage related to a server, you could partition data into separate storage groups and back up these storage groups to different media. As long as you initiate separate restore sessions for each storage group, Exchange can restore multiple storage groups at the same time. The storage groups should also be hosted on separate physical disks and RAID disk arrays so the physical disk media do not become a bottleneck for the restore. This is known as a *parallel restore*.

Backup Methods

Exchange Server 2003 supports two methods of performing backups on your databases: online and offline. When possible, you should always strive to perform online backups because service to your users is not disrupted during the backup when databases are left online. Users will continue to have access to mailbox and public folder stores with little to no difference in performance.

Online backups An online backup, as discussed below in Exercise 14.1, backs up the EDB, STM, and LOG files that constitute the database. Each of these files is checked for corruption at the file level during the backup process by verifying that the checksums on each 4-KB page in the database are correct. Should a checksum failure occur, the online backup will fail and you will receive a report from both the Windows Backup utility and one or more Application Log entries related to the event, indicating that the backup could not completed. The failure of a checksum is indicative of larger database corruption issues.

Offline backups An offline backup, as you might expect, requires that you first dismount the database to be backed up, thus making it unavailable for user access. Should online backups fail because of checksum errors, an offline backup may be performed. You may also find yourself needing to do offline backups if you are using a third-party backup application that does not support the Exchange online backup APIs (Application Programming Interfaces).

Besides taking the database out of use, offline backups do not purge committed transaction logs after the backup has completed. In addition, no automatic checksum error checking is performed during an offline backup. You will need to use the `eesutil` utility to check the offline backup for corruption after it has been completed.

Types of Backups

You can perform five basic types of backups using the Windows Backup utility (and most other backup programs). The key difference between these backup types is how each one handles the archive bit in every file. When a file is created or modified, the archive bit is set to on. When some types of backups run, the archive bit is set to off, which indicates that the file has been backed up.

The five backup types are as follows:

Normal During a *normal backup*, all selected files are backed up, regardless of how their archive bit is set. After the backup, the archive bit is set to off for all files, indicating that those files have been backed up. Upon the completion of the normal backup, any transaction logs that have already been committed to the Exchange database are purged from the server.

Copy During a *copy backup*, all selected files are backed up, regardless of how their archive bit is set. After the backup, the archive bit is not changed in any file. Copy backups do not purge committed transaction logs from the server.

Incremental During an *incremental backup*, all files for which the archive bit is on are backed up. After the backup, the archive bit is set to off for all files that were backed up. Upon the completion of the incremental backup, any transaction logs that have already been committed to the Exchange database are purged from the server.

Differential During a *differential backup*, all files for which the archive bit is on are backed up. After the backup, the archive bit is not changed in any file. Differential backups do not purge committed transaction logs from the server.

Daily During a *daily backup*, all files that changed on the day of the backup are backed up, and the archive bit is not changed in any file. Daily backups are not a sensible Exchange server backup method and thus are not recommended or discussed any further.

Backup Strategies

Although there are many backup strategies, three basic strategies serve most purposes. Table 14.1 describes these three basic strategies, along with some of their advantages and disadvantages. A five-day workweek is assumed.

TABLE 14.1 Three Basic Backup Strategies

Backup Strategy	Description	Advantages	Disadvantages
Full daily (also called normal)	A full (i.e., complete) backup is performed every day. Given the storage capacity and speed of modern backup devices and that the Windows Backup utility allows you to back up to any available drive, daily full backups are the choice of most Exchange administrators, and we recommend them.	Only one tape is needed to perform a restoration. This strategy requires the least amount of time to restore (assuming an entire backup fits onto one tape).	This strategy requires the longest amount of time to perform the backup.

TABLE 14.1 Three Basic Backup Strategies *(continued)*

Backup Strategy	Description	Advantages	Disadvantages
A full backup once per week and an incremental backup every other day	A full backup is done on day one. An incremental backup (using a new tape every day) is performed every day for the next four days. This procedure backs up only the new and changed data since the last full or incremental backup (whichever is more recent).	This strategy takes the least amount of time to back up.	This strategy could require up to five tapes to perform a restoration. This strategy takes the most time to restore.
A full backup once per week and a differential backup every other day	A full backup is done on day one. A differential backup (using a single new tape) is performed every day for the next four days. This procedure backs up only the new and changed data since the last full backup.	No more than two tapes (the full and the last differential) are required to perform a restoration, making restoration faster than with the incremental method.	This strategy takes progressively longer to back up each day.

Restoration Strategies

Having a backup plan is only one part of a disaster recovery plan. You must also plan for restoration (among other items not discussed here, such as media storage and rotation patterns). There are three basic means you can employ to restore an Exchange database: restore in place directly to the storage group, restore using an alternate recovery forest, or restore using the new *recovery storage group*. Exercise 14.2 illustrates the very straightforward restoration directly to the affected storage group; this method is not discussed any further here.

As mentioned previously, the recovery storage group is a new feature in Exchange Server 2003 that provides an easy-to-use storage group for the restoration of databases and the recovery of mailboxes only—you cannot use it to hold production databases. In order to use the recovery storage group to recover a mailbox store, you must keep the following limitations in mind:

- Public folder stores cannot be restored using the recovery storage group.
- The storage group was backed up from an Exchange Server 2003 computer or an Exchange 2000 Server SP3 (or later) server.
- You can restore only one storage group at a time, but this storage group can contain multiple mailbox stores.
- The Exchange server holding the recovery storage group must be located in the same administrative group as the server from which the storage group was backed up.
- Only one backup set can be used to perform the restoration.

- Adequate disk space must exist on the recovery storage group server to hold the temporary data.
- Volume Shadow Copy backups cannot be restored using the recovery storage group method.
- The Exchange server hosting the recovery storage group must be running exactly the same version of Exchange as the server from which the storage group was backed up. This requirement is due to the different log file formats that exist between Exchange 2000 Server and Exchange Server 2003.
- When using the recovery storage group to recover a single mailbox, the mailbox owner must still be in Active Directory and must have a mailbox.

Creating the Disaster Recovery Plan

Determining your backup methodology and your restoration methodology is just the beginning of a complete disaster recovery plan. Several other important issues must be considered. The following are a partial list of these items, but the list should not be considered full and complete by any means:

- What sort of media rotation scheme will be used? Using the same backup media each day will quickly deteriorate the physical condition of the backup media. A well-planned media rotation scheme can provide a backup history of weeks, months, or even years, depending on the scheme used.
- Where will the backup media be stored? Storing your backup tapes in the file cabinet in your office does little good if your building is flooded or catches fire. Several companies exist today that will pick up and store your backup media in a secure location. They also offer the ability to have backup media returned to you in the event you need it for restoration. Note that these companies can also help with a media rotation scheme.
- Who will be responsible for maintaining, testing, and validating the disaster recovery plan? If no one is responsible for making sure the plan works, then you'll likely have an unpleasant surprise when it comes time to perform a restoration for real.
- Who will be part of the disaster recovery team? Depending on the size of your organization, you may need to group several employees into a disaster recovery team. It may also be useful to include representatives from outside the IT department. These are the people who will want to know when their data is coming back.
- Realize that Exchange is not the only critical item that needs to be backed up. While e-mail is more mission-critical now than it has ever been in the past, your company likely has many other vital pieces of data that need to be treated with the same concern as the Exchange databases. SQL databases, file shares, and Active Directory data all have a direct impact on your company's ability to function properly.

So far, it may seem like using the recovery storage group is not a very useful option—nothing could be further from the truth. When you use the recovery storage group to restore a database, you achieve significantly reduced mailbox store downtime. When you use the recovery storage group method, the store must be dismounted only when the data is moved into place.

The last restoration method, the alternate recovery forest, is the most complex restoration method, but it has some significant advantages, which we'll examine momentarily. To perform restorations using this method, you must first create another Active Directory forest that supports an Exchange server installation. This forest must have the exact same names as the production forest you're restoring from. In most cases, you can use a single server to create the forest and host the Exchange installation, thereby reducing hardware and software expenses. This server, however, does become a dedicated restoration server and cannot typically be used for any other network purpose. The alternate recovery forest provides the following benefits:

- Restorations can be performed and tested in a nonproduction environment.
- Public folder stores can be restored.
- Backups made using Volume Shadow Copies can be restored.
- Purged mailboxes can be removed after the mailbox-deletion retention period has passed.

As mentioned previously, the only real drawbacks to this method are the complexities involved with creating and maintaining this environment and the hardware and software investment that must be made.

Using Windows Backup

When you install Exchange Server 2003, an enhanced version of Windows Backup is installed that supports online Exchange server backups. This section briefly explains how to use Windows Backup to perform an online backup of an Exchange server.

If you have a dedicated backup server, as many organizations do these days, you do not need to install Exchange Server onto it to get the updates to the Windows Backup utility. Simply installing the Exchange System Manager onto that server will update the Windows Backup utility to work with Exchange Server 2003.

Performing a Backup

You can find Windows Backup in the System Tools program group. When the program starts, you can run the Backup or Restore Wizard (seen in Figure 14.2) or go right to the Backup tab and configure everything yourself. In this section, we look at how to use the Backup tab. If you choose to use the Backup or Restore Wizard, you make all of the same selections that are shown in this section but in a different fashion.

FIGURE 14.2 The Backup Or Restore Wizard

To go directly to the Backup tab, click the Advanced Mode link on the Welcome to the Backup Or Restore Wizard page. The Backup tab is shown in Figure 14.3 with the System State option selected and the Microsoft Exchange Server container expanded.

The Backup tab shows a hierarchical directory of the entire system. You can back up anything on your server that you like, including Microsoft Exchange Server. You can choose as much or as little of your Exchange organization to back up as you like—a single database on one server or even multiple servers from different routing groups. You can even back up one database on one server and one on another, should you wish.

If you choose to back up System State information, you must back up all of it. You cannot select individual components within the System State container.

Once you have selected all of the components you wish to back up, you must specify where to back them up. Use the Backup Destination drop-down list to specify whether you want to back up to tape or to file. Then, use the Backup Media Or Filename field to specify the tape drive or the drive and filename to which you want to back up. When you're satisfied with your choices, click Start Backup. This opens the Backup Job Information dialog box, shown in Figure 14.4.

The basic information you need to supply is the name of the backup set and whether or not media should be overwritten or appended if there is already a backup present on the media. When you are ready to go, click Start Backup, and the backup will begin. You are shown the backup progress and a summary when the backup is finished.

FIGURE 14.3 Configuring a backup

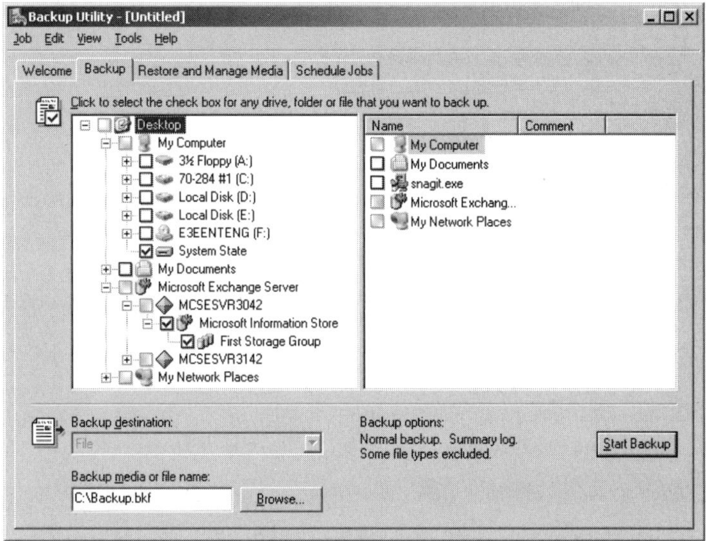

FIGURE 14.4 Setting backup information

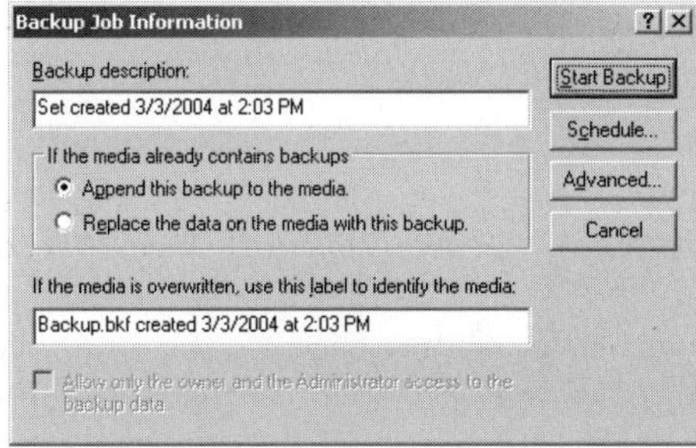

If you wish to perform a backup type other than normal, click the Advanced button to open the Advanced Backup Options dialog box. From the Backup Type drop-down list, you can choose to perform a normal, incremental, differential, copy, or daily backup. You can also use the Advanced Backup Options dialog to set additional options, such as verifying and compressing data. The complete steps for performing a backup are outlined in Exercise 14.1.

EXERCISE 14.1

Backing Up an Exchange Server

1. Click Start ➢ Programs ➢ Accessories ➢ System Tools ➢ Backup.
2. Click the Advanced Mode link on the Welcome to the Backup or Restore Wizard page.
3. Select the Backup tab.
4. Select the check box next to the System State container.
5. Expand the Microsoft Exchange Server container.
6. Expand the server that contains the databases you want to back up.
7. Expand the Microsoft Information Store container.
8. Select the check boxes next to the stores you want to back up. If you want to back up individual databases, expand the store containers and select the check boxes next to the databases.

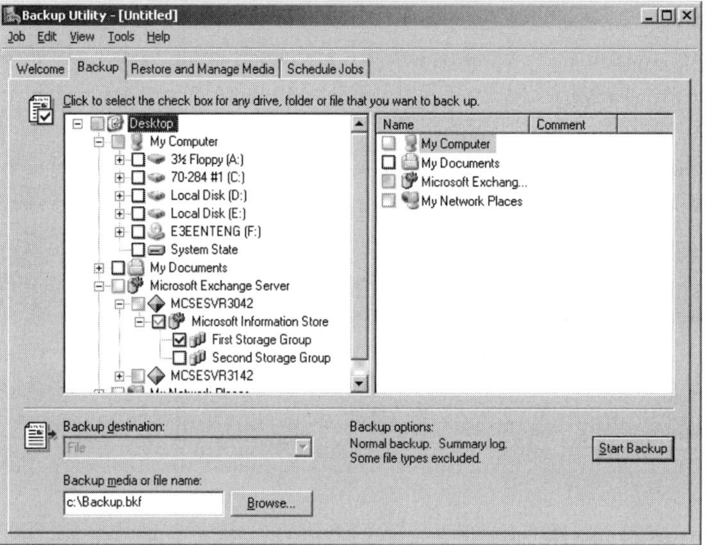

9. Click the Browse button and select a location to hold the backup.
10. Click the Start Backup button.
11. Enter a backup description and choose whether to append the backup to any backups already on the media or to overwrite information on the backup media.
12. Click the Advanced button.
13. On the Advanced Backup Options dialog box, make sure that the normal backup type is selected.

EXERCISE 14.1 *(continued)*

14. Click OK.
15. Click Start Backup. The Backup Progress dialog will keep you informed as to the status of the backup.

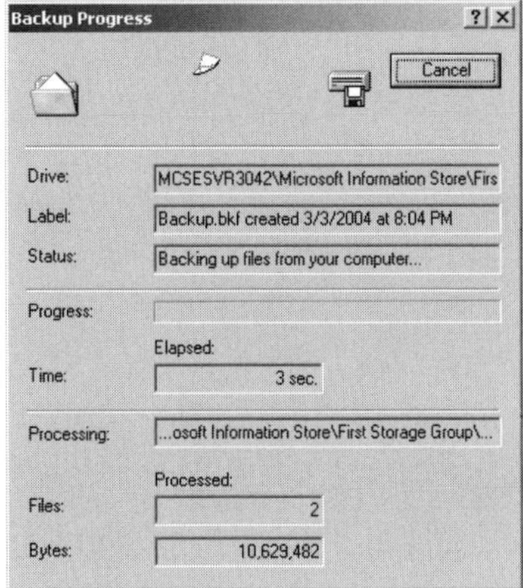

16. When the backup is finished and the summary dialog box is displayed, click OK.

If you have Exchange Server 2003 databases on the same volume as the Windows Server 2003 OS, you will have backup problems when you attempt to back up the System State information and databases at the same time. This is due to a limitation in the `ntbackup.exe` application. See Microsoft Knowledge Base Article 820272 at `http://support.microsoft.com/default.aspx?scid=kb;en-us;820272` for workarounds to this issue.

Performing a Restore

Restoring from an online backup is basically the reverse process of performing the backup, with one caveat: You must configure the specific databases you want to restore to allow the restoration to occur. Failure to select the This Database Can Be Overwritten By A Restore option on the Database tab (seen in Figure 14.5) of the store properties page will prevent the restoration from occurring, oftentimes with little to no useful information in the Application log. Also, if you will not be taking advantage of the Recovery Storage Group feature of Exchange Server 2003 (discussed in the next section of this chapter), then you will need to dismount the store before attempting the restoration process.

FIGURE 14.5 Configuring the store to allow a restoration

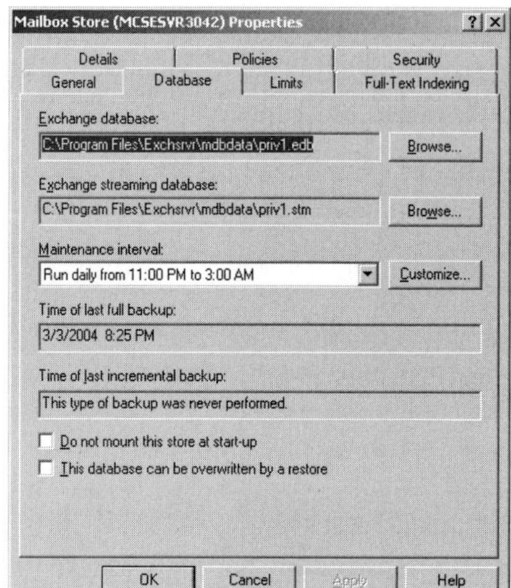

With the store configured to allow restoration, you can get back to work in the Windows Backup utility. First, you have to specify which backup set you want to restore. In Windows Backup, click the Restore and Manage Media tab (see Figure 14.6). All available backup jobs are displayed, and you simply drill down and select which backup job and which components of that job you want to restore.

In the bottom-left corner of the Restore and Manage Media tab, you need to specify whether to restore files to their original location, to an alternate location, or to an individual folder. If you are restoring an Exchange server, you will use the first option. If you are using a backup to move items to another server or to a newly installed server, you will usually use the second option. Restoring to an individual folder is useful if you want to try to find some particular piece of data within the backup job.

The Start Restore button opens the Restoring Database Store dialog box shown in Figure 14.7. Here, you can redirect the restore to another Exchange server, if you want. Also, you need to enter a temporary folder to hold the backed up log and patch files during the restore. First, Exchange Server 2003 will apply the older transaction logs from the temporary location to the database, and then it will apply the more recent logs from the original location.

If the Last Restore Set option is specified, Exchange Server 2003 will begin replaying the log files to rebuild the database as soon as the backup set is restored. If you will be restoring multiple databases in the same storage group, you should not set this option until the final backup set is being restored. Click OK when you have finished, and the restore will start. When it is done, you are shown a summary of the job. If you selected the Mount Database After Restore option, the database is now mounted. Exercise 14.2 details the process of restoring a backup set.

FIGURE 14.6 Selecting a backup set to restore

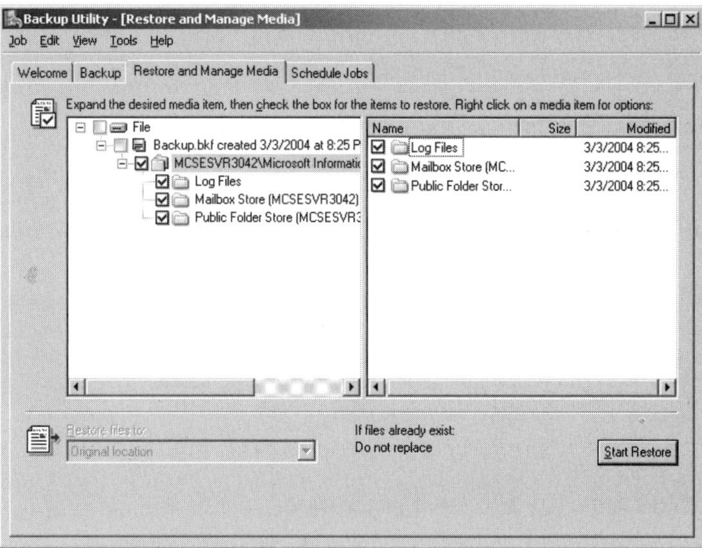

FIGURE 14.7 Setting restore options

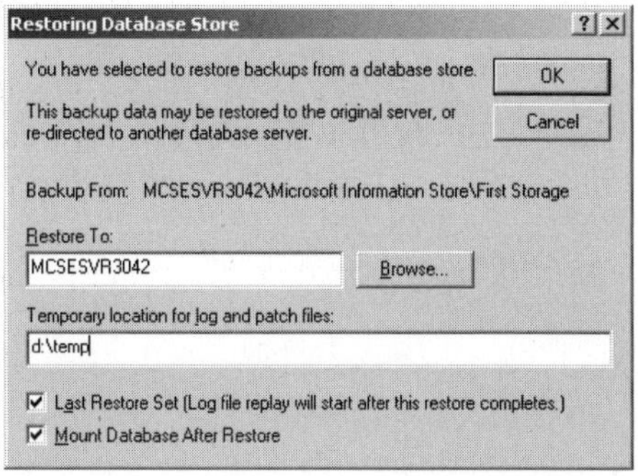

Restoring Database Store

You have selected to restore backups from a database store.

This backup data may be restored to the original server, or re-directed to another database server.

OK

Cancel

Backup From: MCSESVR3042\Microsoft Information Store\First Storage

Restore To:

MCSESVR3042

Browse...

Temporary location for log and patch files:

d:\temp

☑ Last Restore Set (Log file replay will start after this restore completes.)

☑ Mount Database After Restore

EXERCISE 14.2

Restoring a Backup Set

1. Click Start ➢ Programs ➢ Accessories ➢ System Tools ➢ Backup.
2. Click the Restore and Manage Media tab.

EXERCISE 14.2 *(continued)*

3. Expand the media hierarchy, and select the check boxes next to items you want to restore.
4. Choose whether to restore files to their original location or to an alternate location.
5. Click the Start Restore button.
6. Enter a temporary location for the log files.
7. Select the Last Restore Set (as applicable) and Mount Database After Restore options.
8. Click OK.
9. When the restore process is completed and the summary dialog box is displayed, click OK.
10. From the Exchange System Manager, be sure to mount the store if you did not select the Mount Database After Restore option previously.

Scenarios for Restoring Exchange Server

Now that you know the basics of using the Windows Backup tool to restore a backup set, it is helpful to examine a few scenarios in which restores may be used:

Restoring a database to the same server Restoring a mailbox or public folder store to the same server on which you perform the backup is useful if one of your databases becomes damaged. You must dismount the damaged database, replace it from the last successful backup, and then mount the database again.

Restoring multiple databases to the same server If you want to restore two databases from the same storage group during one operation, you must choose different directories in which to save the temporary logs. If you choose to use only one temporary location, you must ensure that the first restore is complete before starting a second restore of another database in the same storage group. To complete the first restore, you must choose the Last Restore Set option and then allow the log file replay to complete.

Restoring a database to a different server Restoring a database to an Exchange server that is different from the one on which you performed the backup provides one way to move a database to a different storage group. It also provides a way to recover individual items from a backup without restoring over a server that is in use.

Restoring after a complete server failure Performing a complete server restore involves several important steps:

Reinstalling Windows Server 2003 First, you must reinstall the same version of Windows Server 2003 that was on the failed computer. You must also install Windows on the same hard disk and using the same paths as the previous installation. Be sure that you use the same computer name and that you select all of the same components that were installed on the original computer. Do not rejoin the domain during installation.

Restoring the system drive Next, you should run Windows Backup to restore full backups of the system drive and any other drive on which application data was installed.

Restoring the System State information Next, run Windows Backup to restore the System State information for the computer. This returns the computer to its original domain and restores the IIS metabase and Windows Registry information. After restoring the System State information, you'll have to restart the computer. When it restarts, you may see a number of error messages relating to failed services. These are usually Exchange services that Windows expects to find but does not, because Exchange has not yet been restored.

Running Exchange Setup in Disaster Recovery mode Next, run Exchange Setup in *Disaster Recovery mode* using the command line `setup /DisasterRecovery`. For the most part, the Setup program works the same as when performing a normal installation. However, at the component selection screen, you must ensure that Exchange is installed to the same drive and path as the original installation and that the Disaster Recovery option is set for all components that were previously installed.

Restoring the Exchange databases Finally, you must run Windows Backup using the procedures you've learned in this chapter to restore the Exchange databases to the server.

Recovering deleted mailboxes If you set a deleted-item retention period on a mailbox or public store, users can restore messages after they have been deleted from their mailbox. By default, the deleted-item retention period is 0 days. If you do not set a deleted-item retention period, or if the retention period has expired for an item, you must restore deleted messages from backup. You do this by restoring the appropriate mailbox store to an alternate server, moving the messages to a PST file, and then making the PST file available to the user.

Using the Recovery Storage Group

If your organization cannot tolerate long unavailability periods for your mailbox stores, or you need to recover specific individual mailboxes, then you should give consideration to using the recovery storage group method of restoration. Recall that your backups must not have been created using the Volume Shadow Copy feature of Windows Backup in order to be restored via the recovery storage group. Exercise 14.3 details the process of restoring a backup set using the recovery storage group.

EXERCISE 14.3

Using the Recovery Storage Group

1. Click Start ➢ Programs ➢ Microsoft Exchange ➢ System Manager.
2. Locate a server in the same administrative group as the server from which the backup occurred.

EXERCISE 14.3 *(continued)*

3. Right-click the server object in the System Manager and select New ➤ Recovery Storage Group from the context menu.

4. Click OK to close the Recovery Storage Group Properties dialog box.

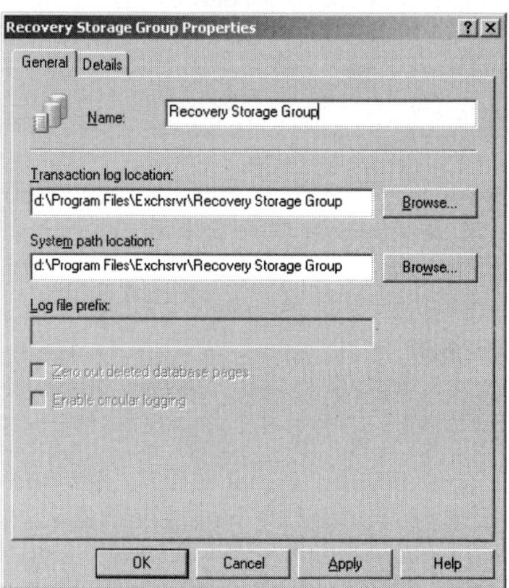

5. The Recovery Storage Group node appears under the selected server.

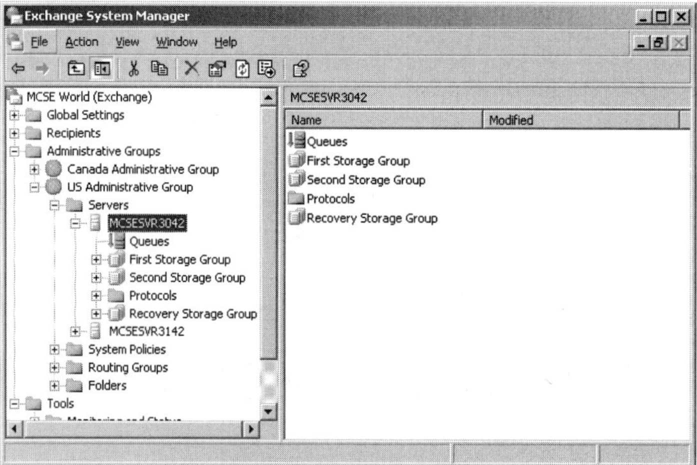

EXERCISE 14.3 *(continued)*

6. Right-click the recovery storage group you just created and select Add Database To Restore from the context menu. Locate the mailbox store that is to be restored using the Select Database To Recover dialog box, and click OK.

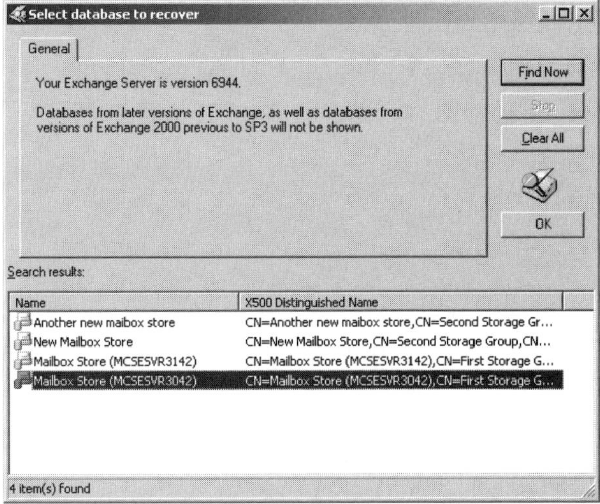

7. Click Start ➢ Programs ➢ Accessories ➢ System Tools ➢ Backup.
8. On the Welcome To The Backup Or Restore Wizard page, click Next to continue.
9. On the Backup Or Restore page, select Restore Files And Settings and click Next to continue.
10. On the What To Restore page, select the backup set that represents the one you want to restore. Expand the backup set to locate the mailbox store and database logs in question, and click Next to continue.

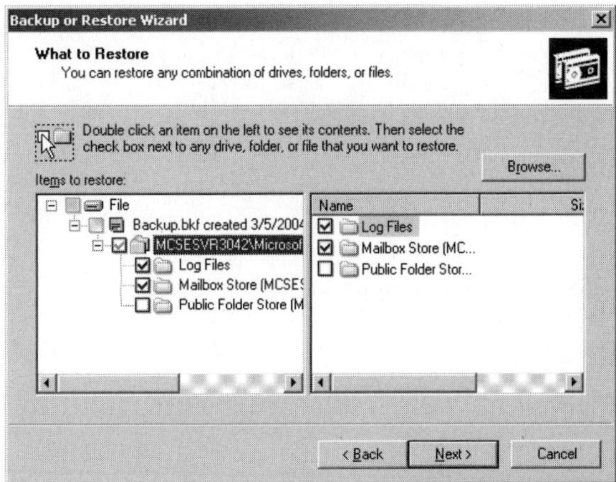

EXERCISE 14.3 *(continued)*

11. Enter a temporary location for the log files. Also select the Last Restore Set option. Do not select the option to mount the database after the restoration completes. Click Next.

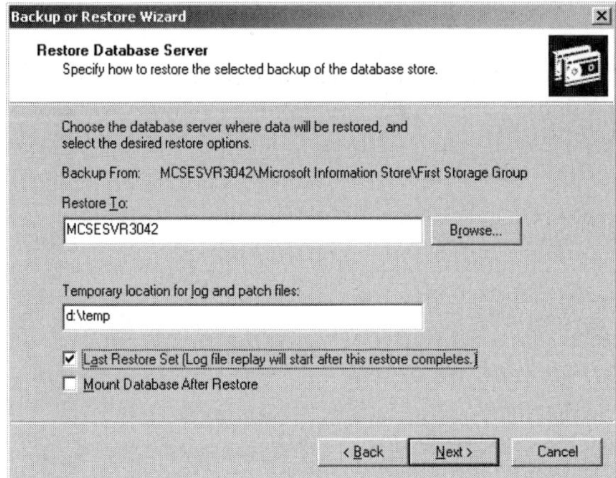

12. Click Finish to start the restoration action.

13. Wait for the restoration to be completed by Windows Backup. Click Close.

14. Open the Exchange System Manager if it is not already open.

15. In the Recovery Storage Group node, right-click the mailbox store that has been restored, and select Mount Store from the context menu. Should you receive an error, wait a few minutes and try again—you must wait for the transaction logs to complete the replay process. You will see a warning dialog either way informing that you should restore the store before mounting it; click Yes to acknowledge the warning.

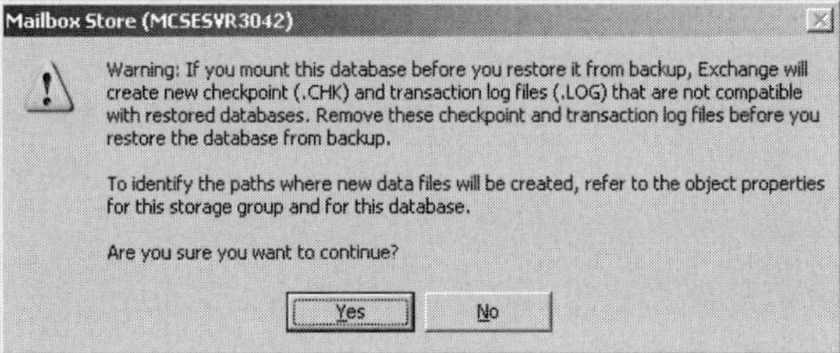

16. Click OK after the store has been mounted.

17. If desired, you can now delete the mailbox store from the recovery storage group and remove the recovery storage group from the server.

Being Prepared for Disaster

Performing regular backups is only part of a good disaster recovery plan. You must also test your plans and be prepared for when disaster does strike. We generally recommend the following practices:

Using recovery servers A computer that you have prepared to take the place of a failed Exchange server is called a *recovery server* (sometimes referred to as a *standby server* or *cold server*). A recovery server would have Windows Server 2003 and Exchange Server 2003 already installed. It should also have the Exchange database files loaded. At the least, the database files should be loaded on media that would facilitate loading on that server. Some organizations create a batch file that stops the Exchange services on the primary server and copies the relevant files to the standby server. These files could also be copied to removable media and then uploaded to the standby server when needed. Recovery servers are also useful for restoring single mailboxes.

Validating your backups It is important to validate that each backup occurs without errors. Check the Windows Backup Log and the Windows Event Log to ensure your backup has completed as scheduled.

Documenting backups It is important to document your backup strategy and provide step-by-step instructions describing how to use backups to restore data. You should also keep track of old backup logs in case you need to refer to them.

Running fire drills You should schedule regular fire drills in which administrators are required to restore a failed server from backup under different scenarios. This process accomplishes two things. First, it helps train administrators on how to perform restore procedures. Second, it helps verify that your backup media and plans really work.

Troubleshooting

Problems can occur when you back up or restore servers. Table 14.2 lists some problems (and possible causes and solutions) that you may encounter when you perform two common procedures.

You can also use the backup log file, `BACKUP.LOG`, which resides in your Windows directory (e.g., `\WINNT`), as a diagnostic tool when you troubleshoot.

TABLE 14.2 Backup and Restore Problems, Causes, and Solutions

Situation	Problem	Cause/Solution
The Information Store will not start after restoring from backup.	The Information Store may need to be patched before it can be operational.	The Information Store may be corrupted. Execute the following command line: `ISINTEG -PATCH`.
The Information Store was restored to a different server.	After the restore, users cannot access the Information Store.	The restore was performed on a server in a different Windows domain than the original server. Restore to a server in the same domain.

Removing Exchange Servers from the Organization

You may, over time, find any number of reasons to remove an active Exchange Server 2003 server from your Exchange organization. Common reasons include server maintenance, consolidation, or replacement, although the possibilities are virtually boundless. The process you must follow to safely remove the Exchange server is straightforward; however, it may take some time to perform depending on the number of mailbox or public folders located on the server. The basic, high-level steps that you must complete in order to remove the Exchange server from the organization are outlined here:

1. Synchronize public folders located on the Exchange server that need to be retained in the Exchange organization by creating a replica on another Exchange server.
2. Use the Exchange Task Wizard or the ExMerge utility to move all mailboxes to another mailbox store in the Exchange organization.
3. Create any required connection agreements and virtual servers on one or more Exchange servers that will be remaining in the Exchange organization.
4. Remove Exchange Server 2003 from the computer.
5. Remove the server from the Active Directory organization.

Summary

This chapter demonstrated how to back up and restore an Exchange server. The first step in backing up a server is deciding what you need to back up. This can include the main Exchange databases (PRIVx.EDB, PUBx.EDB, and their corresponding STM files) as well as transaction logs. You might also elect to back up items in the Exchange Server subdirectories, any server-stored user information, and System State information.

Once you have decided what to back up, you must decide how to perform the backup. There are five basic types of backups: normal, copy, incremental, differential, and daily. Exchange Server 2003 supports the use of the normal, incremental, and differential backup types. When you install Exchange Server 2003, you also install an enhanced version of Windows Backup that provides support for online backups.

Restoring a database from an online backup using Windows Backup is essentially the reverse process of performing the backup in the first place. If you are restoring multiple databases to the same server, you must choose different directories in which to save the temporary logs or you must restore one database at a time. When restoring after a complete system failure, you must first reinstall Windows Server 2003, restore the system drive and the System State backup information, reinstall Exchange Server 2003 using Disaster Recovery mode, and then restore the Exchange databases.

Performing regular backups is one part of a good disaster recovery plan. You should also verify and document your backups, perform practice restores, and have recovery servers standing by in case of emergency.

Exam Essentials

Understand the relationship between each backup type and the committed transaction logs. A properly configured and executed backup will cause committed transaction logs to be purged from the Exchange server. It's important that you understand each of the five backup types and how they interact with Exchange Server 2003.

Know what's new in Exchange Server 2003. New features are almost always popular exam questions; thus you should take the time to ensure that you understand the recovery storage group and Volume Shadow Copies.

Know which restoration methods you have available. In previous versions of Exchange, you had only two choices for restoration: restore in place or restore to the alternate recovery forest. In Exchange Server 2003, you have the ability to use the recovery storage group for restoration with decreased mailbox store downtime. Of course, the recovery storage group is not the perfect answer for every solution, so you will do well to understand the caveats associated with each of the three methods and use this knowledge to make your disaster recovery plans.

Review Questions

1. You are the Exchange administrator for your company. Your Exchange organization consists of five Exchange Server 2003 computers installed on Windows Server 2003 Enterprise Edition servers. Each Exchange server hosts two storage groups, each with two mailbox stores. No public folders are in use in your organization. Overnight one of your mailbox stores has become corrupted. A power outage occurred, and the UPS for that server did not keep the server running long enough to perform a safe shutdown. You do have a backup set for that mailbox store that is less than 24 hours old. What is the quickest way to restore this mailbox store so that users with mailboxes in that store can get back to work?

   A. Use the alternative recovery forest method.

   B. Use the recovery storage group method.

   C. Dismount the mailbox store, restore it, and then mount the mailbox store.

   D. Use the alternative recovery forest method, and extract each user's mailbox into a PST file for importing into the mailbox store on the production server.

2. You are an Exchange administrator for a large company. One of your Exchange servers recently suffered a complete failure. You have repaired the computer and now must rebuild the server before you can restore your Exchange backups. Which of the following actions should you take? (Choose all that apply.)

   A. Install the same version of Windows Server 2003 that was running before.

   B. Join the same domain of which the computer was originally a member.

   C. Use Windows Backup to restore the System State information.

   D. Run Exchange Setup in Disaster Recovery mode.

3. You are the backup administrator for a set of Exchange servers in your company's organization. Recently, you had to restore the mailbox stores on one of your servers. After the restore, the Information Store service would not restart. What should you do?

   A. Restore the databases to a different server and then move the stores to the proper server.

   B. Perform the restore again and choose the Last Restore Set option.

   C. Run the command-line utility `ISINTEG -PATCH`.

   D. Perform the restore again, and restore the System State information.

4. You are the backup administrator for a large Exchange organization. Recently, one of your users discovered that he had deleted an important file by mistake. Unfortunately, the deleted-item retention time on your server was set to zero, so the file is not recoverable from the user's client. What should you do?

   A. Use the mailbox object for the user in System Manager to recover the file.

   B. Restore the latest backup of the mailbox store to the production server.

   C. Restore the latest backup of the mailbox store to an alternate server and then move the user's mailbox to the production server.

   D. Restore the latest backup of the mailbox store to an alternate server and then copy the files in the user's mailbox to a PST file.

   E. Tell the user that you cannot recover the file.

5. Which of the following information is contained in a System State backup? (Choose all that apply.)

   A. The IIS metabase

   B. The Windows Registry

   C. Active Directory

   D. System Manager configuration information

6. An Exchange server is configured with the following volumes:

   - C: A two-disk mirror set with the system and root partitions
   - D: A five-disk RAID-5 array that holds SG1, SG2, and the transaction logs for SG1
   - E: A two-disk mirror set that is currently empty
   - F: A two-disk mirror set that holds the transaction logs for SG2

   The Exchange server holds two storage groups. The first storage group (SG1) contains four mailbox stores and one public store. The second storage group (SG2) contains one mailbox store. Which of the following actions would have the most beneficial effect on server performance?

   A. Move SG2 to the E: drive.

   B. Move the transaction logs for SG1 to the E: drive.

   C. Move the transaction logs for SG1 to the F: drive.

   D. Move the transaction logs for SG2 to the D: drive.

7. Which of the following would be the best backup scheduling strategy?
   - A. Back up Active Directory for a domain at the same time you back up the Exchange databases in the domain.
   - B. Separate the backup of Active Directory and the Exchange databases by at least an hour.
   - C. Separate the backup of Active Directory and the Exchange databases by at least a day.
   - D. Separate the backup of Active Directory and the Exchange databases by at least the amount of time it takes the Active Directory to replicate throughout the domain.
   - E. Separate the backup of Active Directory and the Exchange databases by no more than the amount of time it takes the Active Directory to replicate throughout the domain.

8. Which of the following backup types cause the archive bit for a file that is backed up to be set to the off position? (Choose all that apply.)
   - A. Normal
   - B. Copy
   - C. Incremental
   - D. Differential
   - E. Daily

9. You are the backup administrator for a large Exchange organization and are currently designing a backup plan. You have decided that the time it takes to restore after a failure is more critical than the time it takes to back up. Which of the following backup methods would be the best choice?
   - A. A full normal backup every day
   - B. A full normal backup once per week and an incremental backup every other day
   - C. A full normal backup once per week and a differential backup every other day
   - D. A daily backup every day

10. You have just finished repairing and rebuilding a server after a complete failure and are ready to restore the databases. You have three different backup sets—one for three mailbox stores in one storage group, one for two mailbox stores in another storage group, and one for a public store in yet another storage group. You plan to restore the backup sets in that order and to use only one temporary location during the restores. Which of the following should you do?
    - A. Enable the Last Restore Set option only when restoring the public store in the final storage group.
    - B. Enable the Last Restore Set option for each of the three backup sets.
    - C. Enable the Last Restore Set option only when restoring the public store in the final storage group, but enable the Mount Database After Restore option for all three backup sets.
    - D. Enable the Last Restore Set option and the Mount Database After Restore option for all three backup sets.
    - E. Restore each database individually, and enable the Last Restore Set option for each database.

11. Which of the following files would be useful in troubleshooting a failed backup?

    A. BACKUP.LOG

    B. BACKLOG.TXT

    C. NTBACK.TXT

    D. SYSTEM.BAK

12. You are the administrator of a small organization with a single Exchange server. You are preparing to restore a mailbox store on that server. Which of the following should you do first?

    A. Dismount the database you intend to restore.

    B. Dismount all databases in the same storage group as the database you intend to restore.

    C. Stop the Information Store service on the Exchange server.

    D. Nothing—Windows Backup will take care of dismounting the appropriate databases and stopping any services.

13. During an online backup, checksum errors were found in the database. How will this affect your backup?

    A. You will be able to complete the online backup; however, you should check the backup for integrity after it has completed.

    B. You will not be able to back up the database until the integrity has been restored.

    C. You will not be able to complete the online backup. You can use an offline backup if desired.

    D. You will be able to complete the online backup. During the restoration process, the data integrity will be checked.

14. Which of the following backup types purge committed transaction logs after successful completion of the backup process? (Choose all that apply.)

    A. Normal

    B. Copy

    C. Incremental

    D. Differential

    E. Daily

15. You are the Exchange administrator for your company. Your Exchange organization consists of five Exchange Server 2003 computers installed on Windows Server 2003 Enterprise Edition servers. Each Exchange server hosts two storage groups, each with two mailbox stores. No public folders are in use in your organization. The number of employees in your company has decreased over the past year, and you have been directed by the CIO to decommission one of the Exchange servers. Which of the following issues should you consider while removing this server from the Exchange organization? (Choose all that apply.)

A. You must first move all mailboxes to another mailbox store.

B. You must first move all mailbox stores to another storage group.

C. You must create any required connectors or virtual servers on another Exchange server.

D. You must remove the computer from Active Directory before removing Exchange Server 2003 from it.

16. One of your users has come to you complaining that she has forgotten the password she used for her personal folders (PST file). She needs to get something out of those folders. What can you do with the tools provided by Exchange Server 2003 and Outlook?

A. Use `scanpst.exe` to recover the personal folders.

B. Use System Manager to import the messages in the personal folders to the user's mailbox.

C. Use your administrative password to open the personal folders and assign a new password to the user.

D. Nothing—you cannot access the personal folders without the password.

17. Which of the following actions would generally offer the greatest performance enhancement on an Exchange server?

A. Turning off circular logging

B. Breaking large stores into smaller ones

C. Putting storage groups on separate disks from one another

D. Putting transaction logs on disks separate from their storage groups

18. Which of the following statements is true?

A. You must dismount a store before performing a backup.

B. You must dismount a store before performing a backup only if you are backing up multiple stores in the same backup set.

C. You must dismount a store before performing a restore unless you are using the recovery storage group.

D. You must dismount a store before performing a restore only if you are restoring multiple stores in the same backup set.

19. You are restoring two stores from the same storage group during the same restore operation. Which of the following should you do?

    A. Enable circular logging while the restore is being performed, and turn it off again afterward.

    B. Choose different directories for each store in which to store the temporary logs during the restore process.

    C. Restore both stores at once, and enable the Last Backup Set option.

    D. Restore both stores at once, and enable the System State option.

20. Which of the following statements is true of backing up Exchange Server 2003?

    A. A single backup set can include only stores within a single storage group.

    B. A single backup set can include only stores on a single server.

    C. A single backup set can include only stores within a single routing group.

    D. A single backup set can include only stores within a single administrative group.

    E. A single backup set can include stores throughout the organization.

Answers to Review Questions

1. B. In this scenario, there is no reason why you cannot use the recovery storage group method to restore the server. This is the fastest and most efficient method of restoring a mailbox store to the production Exchange server.

2. A, C, D. You should not rejoin the domain during or after installation of Windows Server 2003. When you restore the System State information, the computer will be made a member of the domain again.

3. C. The Information Store may need to be patched before it can be operational. The `ISINTEG` utility can be used to perform checks on the integrity of a database, and the `-PATCH` switch is used to patch the databases.

4. D. If you set a deleted-item retention period on a mailbox or public store, users can restore messages after they have been deleted from their mailbox. By default, the deleted-item retention period is 0 days. If you do not set a deleted-item retention period or if the retention period has expired for an item, you must restore deleted messages from backup. You do this by restoring the appropriate mailbox store to an alternate server, moving the messages to a PST file, and then making the PST file available to the user.

5. A, B, C. A System State backup includes the Windows Registry, the IIS metabase, and the Active Directory if the computer is a domain controller.

6. B. Storing log files on separate disks dramatically increases performance and your odds of successful recovery in the event of failure. Putting multiple storage groups on one disk and then putting the transaction logs for each storage group onto their own disks would be better than trying to separate the storage groups.

7. A. You should back up Active Directory and the Exchange Server 2003 databases at the same time to avoid losing the configuration of user objects on the domain controllers or in global catalogs.

8. A, C. When a file is created or modified, the archive bit is set to on. When some types of backups run, the archive bit is set to off, which indicates that the file has been backed up. The normal and incremental backup types set the archive bit to off so that the same files will not be backed up in subsequent backups unless the files change.

9. A. Given the speed of modern backup devices, there is really no reason to do anything other than a full normal backup every day. The actual backup does take the longest time of any backup method to perform, but it provides the easiest and fastest restore.

10. A. If the Last Restore Set option is specified, Exchange Server 2003 will begin replaying the log files to rebuild the database as soon as the backup set is restored. If you want to restore two databases from the same storage group during one operation, you must choose different directories in which to save the temporary logs. If you choose to use only one temporary location, you must ensure that the first restore is complete before starting a second restore of another database in the same storage group. To complete the first restore, you must choose the Last Restore Set option and then allow the log file replay to complete.

11. A. BACKUP.LOG resides in your Windows directory (e.g., \WINNT) and serves as a good diagnostic tool when you troubleshoot.

12. A. Restoring a mailbox or public folder store to the same server on which you perform the backup is useful if one of your databases becomes damaged. You must dismount the damaged database, replace it from the last successful backup, and then mount the database again.

13. B. A checksum error will prevent you from performing an online backup. You can, however, perform an offline backup. You will need to use the eesutil utility to check the offline backup for corruption after it has been completed.

14. A, C. Only normal and incremental backups purge committed transaction logs from the server after the completion of the backup process.

15. A, C. The basic high-level steps required to remove an Exchange Server 2003 server from the organization are as follows:

    1. Synchronize public folders located on the Exchange server that need to be retained in the Exchange organization by creating a replica on another Exchange server.
    2. Use the Exchange Task Wizard or the ExMerge utility to move all mailboxes to another mailbox store in the Exchange organization.
    3. Create any required connection agreements and virtual servers on one or more Exchange servers that will be remaining in the Exchange organization.
    4. Remove Exchange Server 2003 from the computer.
    5. Remove the server from the Active Directory organization.

16. D. Once the password to personal folders is forgotten, it cannot be recovered, nor can the folders be accessed. For this reason, it is important that you include personal folders in your backup plan.

17. D. Although each of these actions can increase the performance of an Exchange server, putting transaction logs on separate disks from their storage groups typically offers the greatest increase if you have to make a choice.

18. C. You do not need to dismount a store before performing a backup, even if you are backing up multiple stores. You do need to dismount a store before restoring it, however, unless you are using the new recovery storage group method.

19. B. If you want to restore two databases from the same storage group during one operation, you must choose different directories in which to save the temporary logs. If you choose to use only one temporary location, you must ensure that the first store is restored completely by choosing the Last Restore Set option before restoring another store in the same storage group.

20. E. You can back up as much or as little of your Exchange organization as you like—a single store on one server or multiple stores throughout the organization.

Chapter 15

Securing and Troubleshooting Exchange Server 2003

MICROSOFT EXAM OBJECTIVES COVERED IN THIS CHAPTER:

- ✓ Manage and troubleshoot connectivity across firewalls
- ✓ Manage audit settings and audit logs
- ✓ Manage and troubleshoot permissions
- ✓ Manage and troubleshoot encryption and digital signatures
- ✓ Detect and respond to security threats
- ✓ Diagnose problems arising from host resolution protocols
- ✓ Diagnose problems arising from Active Directory issues
- ✓ Diagnose network connectivity problems

As computer networking has become more pervasive, the information transported over networks has become more valuable. As a result, some unscrupulous people try to steal information and disrupt business affairs. E-mail messages are susceptible to eavesdropping, tampering, and forgery. Implementing the proper security measures can prevent these and other security threats.

This chapter covers three aspects of security that you must concern yourself with as an Exchange administrator. The first feature is the collection of basic security services built into Windows Server 2003, including permissions, policies, and auditing. The second is network security, which includes authentication, the configuration of firewalls and proxy servers, and the prevention of virus attacks. The final aspect (and the primary focus of the chapter) is messaging security, which includes the digital signature and encryption of messages using the Windows Server 2003 Certificate Services.

Of course, nothing ever works perfectly forever, Exchange Server 2003 included. Your ability to troubleshoot and quickly resolve problems affecting your Exchange organization will be critical to keeping your Exchange organization running smoothly and your users happy. To that end, we will briefly examine some common issues related to name resolution, network connectivity, and Active Directory that you may encounter.

Windows Server 2003 System Security

As you know, Exchange Server 2003 is heavily integrated with Windows Server 2003. Since much of the Exchange configuration lies in Active Directory, good Windows Server 2003 security practices are essential for good Exchange security. This section is intended to provide a brief overview of the security features in Windows Server 2003 that Exchange is designed to take advantage of. The integration of Windows Server 2003 and Exchange Server 2003 is covered in detail in Chapter 2, "Microsoft Exchange Architecture," and Exchange-specific permissions and groups are covered in Chapter 10, "Administration and Maintenance." You can also learn more about Windows Server 2003 security from your system documentation.

User Accounts and Authentication

Before users or services can access Exchange, they must log on to the Active Directory network by supplying a valid username and password. Windows Server 2003 must then authenticate the logon information, which it does using *Kerberos version 5 authentication*. Once a user is validated, that user is assigned a token that identifies the user whenever the user attempts to access resources during that logon session.

Each resource on an Active Directory network maintains an *Access Control List (ACL)*, a list of users and groups that are allowed access to the resource and the specific permissions they are assigned. A *permission* provides specific authorization to perform an action, such as deleting an object.

All objects in Exchange also maintain an ACL that defines the level of access users have to that object. You will grant users permissions on the various Exchange-related objects in Active Directory and in System Manager to create security for your organization. Check out Chapter 10 for details on the permissions available on most Exchange objects and the various administrative roles you can assign.

Administrative Groups

An *administrative group* is a collection of Active Directory objects that are grouped together for the purpose of permissions management. Administrative groups are logical, which means that you can design them to fit your needs—geographical boundaries, departmental divisions, different groups of Exchange administrators, or various Exchange functions. For example, one group of Exchange administrators might be responsible for managing the messaging and routing backbone of the organization, another might be responsible for managing public folders, and still another might be responsible for managing connectivity with a legacy messaging system. You could create an administrative group for each that contains only the objects the administrators need. You can find details on using administrative groups in Chapter 8, "Building Administrative and Routing Groups."

Policies

A *policy* is a collection of configuration settings that you can apply across any number of objects in the Active Directory at once. Making a change in a policy affects every object that is attached to that policy. *System policies* affect server objects such as servers, mailbox stores, and public stores, while *recipient policies* affect objects such as users and groups. Since you can use policies to make changes to such large numbers of objects, they are an important part of Exchange security. You can find detailed coverage of both types of policies in Chapter 10.

Auditing

Auditing is a feature in Windows Server 2003 that logs the actions of users and groups based on certain criteria. For example, a Windows Server 2003 server can audit successful and failed logon attempts or access to certain files. Because Exchange Server 2003 essentially works as a collection of Windows Server 2003 services, you can use auditing to track significant Exchange events, such as mailbox or server access. Auditing is a basic Windows administrative function and as such is not discussed any further in this chapter. You can find a wealth of information on auditing in the Windows Server 2003 Security Guide at `www.microsoft.com/technet/security/prodtech/win2003/w2003hg/sgch00.mspx`.

Networking Security

These days, Internet access for a company network is a vital asset. However, along with the benefits that Internet access can provide come the risks of having your network permanently connected to the outside world. Thus, it is essential that a network be secured from unauthorized access. This affects you as an Exchange administrator because the methods put in place to keep unwanted outsiders from connecting to your network must often allow connection by any Exchange users outside the network. For example, you may want traveling employees to be able to connect to their mailboxes over the Internet. This section describes several methods used for securing network access.

Authentication

If users are authenticated with a Windows Server 2003 domain controller using Kerberos v5, then those users are automatically granted the appropriate access to Exchange objects without having to be authenticated again. If users are not authenticated by a domain controller, they must be authenticated by another means. For example, a user connecting to an Exchange server over the Internet with a POP3 client would not necessarily be authenticated by a domain controller.

If authentication is not already granted to a user, a virtual server (such as the POP3 server) may authenticate the user instead. Each virtual server on an Exchange server can be configured to use different forms of authentication. With the exception of HTTP, you can configure the authentication method for all protocols by opening the property pages for the appropriate virtual server in System Manager and switching to the Authentication page.

Virtual servers support the following forms of authentication:

Anonymous *Anonymous authentication* allows any user to access the virtual server without providing a username or password.

Basic (Clear-Text) *Basic (Clear-Text) authentication* requires the user to submit a valid Windows username and password. The username and password are sent across the network as unencrypted clear text.

Basic over Secure Sockets Layer (SSL) *Basic over Secure Sockets Layer (SSL) authentication* extends the Basic authentication method by allowing an SSL server to encrypt the username and password before they are sent across the network.

Integrated Windows authentication *Integrated Windows authentication* also requires the user to provide a valid Windows username and password. However, the user's credentials are never sent across the network. If you are running a Windows Server 2003 network that is still at the Windows 2000 Server mixed domain functional level, this method uses the NTLM authentication protocol used by Windows NT 4.0. If your network is running at the Windows 2000 Server native domain functional level (or higher), this method uses Kerberos v5.

Firewalls

A *firewall* is a set of mechanisms that separates and protects your internal network from unauthorized external users and networks. Firewalls can restrict inbound and outbound traffic, as well as analyze all traffic between your network and the outside. Different criteria can be used by a firewall to analyze traffic, such as IP addresses and TCP/IP port numbers. The remainder of this section covers port numbers and example security scenarios that use a firewall.

Port Numbers

A *port number* is a numeric identifier used to route packets to the correct application on a computer. Just as Media Access Control (MAC) addresses are used to deliver frames to the correct physical computer (actually to the network adapter) and IP addresses are used to route packets to the correct logical computer (e.g., 147.4.56.76), port numbers are used to route a packet to the correct application after the packet has arrived at its destination computer. Multiple applications often run on a single server. When a packet arrives at that server, it cannot be delivered to just any application. For example, POP3 client requests are not going to be understood by an LDAP server application.

Port numbers range from 1 to over 65,000. Most established Internet protocols have assigned port numbers, referred to as *well-known port numbers*, somewhere below port 1024. Table 15.1 lists some of the protocols discussed in this book and their well-known port numbers.

One way a firewall can work is by prohibiting certain port numbers or allowing only designated port numbers to pass through the firewall. This functionality can be used to restrict the applications that can be used to access your network. For example, if a firewall were configured to prohibit port 80, HTTP clients would not be able to pass through the firewall and communicate with any internal virtual servers. Many firewalls are configured to prevent all but the most well-known port numbers (such as those for POP3, HTTP, and SMTP) from passing through. Often, you will have to open specific ports in order to let the proper traffic pass.

For an extra measure of security, you can usually change the port numbers that an application uses. For example, you might change your POP3 virtual server and all POP3 clients to use port 28,345 instead of the default 110. The downside of doing this is that you will have to manually change any application that will need to communicate with the server. Exercise 15.1 outlines the steps for changing the regular and SSL port numbers for the POP3 virtual server.

TABLE 15.1 Protocols and Their Well-Known Port Numbers

Protocol	Port Numbers
SMTP	25
DNS	53
HTTP	80
Kerberos v5	88, 750–754
MTA - X.400 over TCP/IP	102
POP3	110
NNTP	119
RPC	135
NetBIOS name service	137
IMAP4	143
IRC	194
LDAP	389
HTTP (over SSL)	443
SMTP (over SSL)	465
NNTP (over SSL)	563
LDAP (over SSL)	636
IMAP (over SSL)	993
POP3 (over SSL)	995
Instant Messaging	2890
Global Catalog lookup	3268

EXERCISE 15.1

Changing Port Numbers for a POP3 Virtual Server

1. Click Start ➢ Programs ➢ Microsoft Exchange ➢ System Manager.
2. Expand the administrative group and server that contain the virtual server you want to modify.
3. Expand the Protocols container and then the POP3 container.
4. Right-click the POP3 virtual server object you want to modify, and select Properties from the context menu.
5. On the General page, click the Advanced button.
6. Select the IP address for which you want to change the port number, or leave the default All Unassigned option selected.

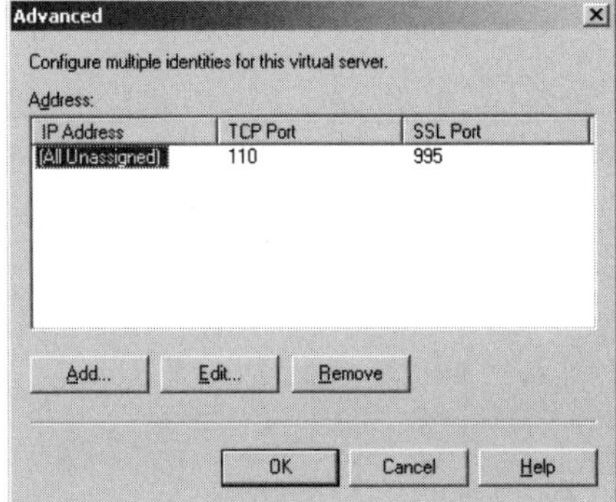

7. Click the Edit button.
8. In the TCP Port and SSL Port fields, type the new port numbers you want to use. Make sure that the new port numbers do not conflict with the port numbers in use by any other application.
9. Click OK three times to return to System Manager.

Security Scenarios Using a Basic Firewall

Firewalls are useful in a number of ways, some of which are illustrated in the following scenarios.

Scenario 1

You have just configured your Exchange server for IMAP4 client access. IMAP4 clients can be authenticated with either the Basic (Clear-Text) or Basic over SSL authentication method. The administrator of your firewall tells you that the firewall will allow traffic from SMTP (port 25),

IMAP4 (port 143), and HTTP (port 80). For what additional traffic must the firewall be configured to allow your Exchange server IMAP4 configuration to be used?

Because the Exchange server is using SSL as one of its authentication methods, IMAP over SSL (port 993) would also need to be opened on the firewall.

Scenario 2

A new Exchange server has been installed and configured for LDAP, HTTP, and POP3. The network project plan calls for allowing the following clients to access this server: LDAP, web software using Integrated Windows NT, POP3, and Microsoft Outlook using secure passwords. You refer to the current firewall configuration and see that it is open to DNS, HTTP, SMTP, and ports higher than 1023. What, if anything, must you do to enable the desired Exchange clients to pass through the firewall?

You must open LDAP (port 389), POP3 (port 110), and the RPC Endpoint Mapper Service (port 135). Without these changes, the firewall would not allow traffic from LDAP, POP3, or Exchange MAPI clients (which Outlook is).

Scenario 3

In each of the next three scenarios (including this one), you will see the same starting situation. But each scenario requires different mandatory and optional results, and it presents different possible courses of action.

CURRENT SITUATION

Your Exchange server is using TCP/IP and is configured with LDAP, HTTP, and POP3. A firewall sits between your network and the Internet. Your Exchange server has its name and IP address entered into a public DNS server on the Internet.

Your network's firewall prohibits traffic on all ports that are not explicitly allowed. The open ports are port 25 (SMTP), port 53 (DNS), port 80 (HTTP), and all ports greater than port 1023.

REQUIRED RESULTS

Management requires that users be able to connect over the Internet to your Exchange server using Microsoft Outlook and LDAP applications. Policy dictates that passwords be transmitted in a secure manner.

OPTIONAL RESULTS

While not required, management would like web clients that do not support Integrated Windows authentication to be able to connect to your Exchange server. Another preference is for POP3 clients to connect to the Exchange server and download their messages.

PROPOSED COURSE OF ACTION

One proposed course of action is to do the following:

- Assign port numbers to the Exchange Directory Service and Information Store. Then allow those ports through the firewall.
- Configure LDAP on the Exchange server to allow Anonymous access.

- Configure the Exchange protocols to use SSL as an authentication method.
- Allow SSL traffic through the firewall.
- Allow LDAP traffic (port 389) through the firewall.
- Allow RPC traffic (port 135) through the firewall.
- Allow POP3 traffic (port 110) through the firewall.

See Figure 15.1 for a depiction of this scenario.

RESULTS OF THE PROPOSED ACTIONS

This course of action would meet both required results and both optional results. The key actions were forcing Exchange to use fixed port numbers for the DS and IS, configuring SSL on the Exchange server, and enabling the firewall to allow LDAP, POP3, SSL ports, RPC, and the fixed port numbers for the DS and IS.

FIGURE 15.1 Scenario 3 illustrated

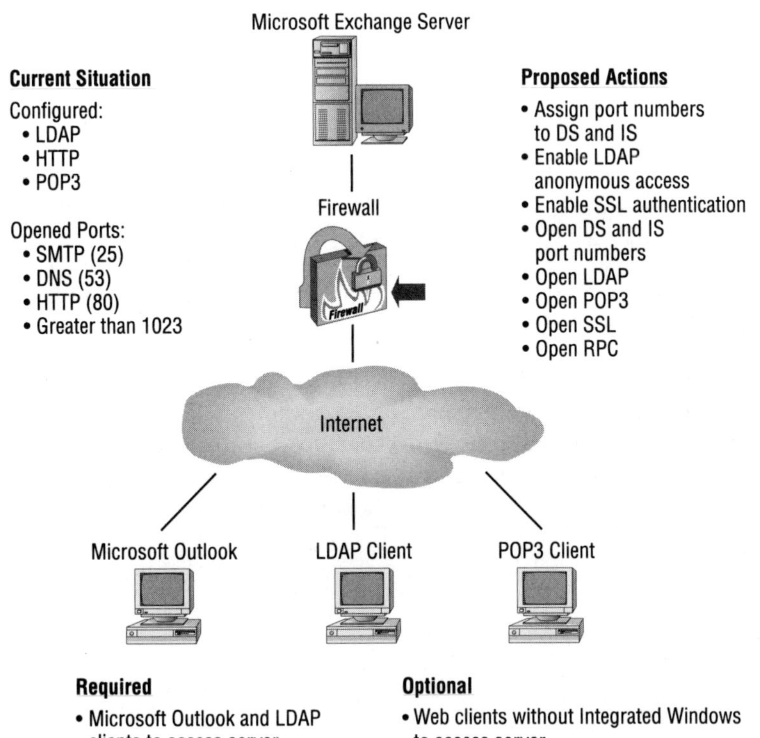
Microsoft Exchange Server
Current Situation
Configured:
• LDAP
• HTTP
• POP3
Opened Ports:
• SMTP (25)
• DNS (53)
• HTTP (80)
• Greater than 1023
Firewall
Proposed Actions
• Assign port numbers to DS and IS
• Enable LDAP anonymous access
• Enable SSL authentication
• Open DS and IS port numbers
• Open LDAP
• Open POP3
• Open SSL
• Open RPC
Internet
Microsoft Outlook
LDAP Client
POP3 Client
Required
• Microsoft Outlook and LDAP clients to access server
Optional
• Web clients without Integrated Windows to access server

Scenario 4

As mentioned, the following current situation, required results, and optional results are the same as above. The difference in this scenario is the proposed actions and, possibly, the results of those actions.

CURRENT SITUATION

Your Exchange server is using TCP/IP and is configured with LDAP, HTTP, and POP3. A firewall sits between your network and the Internet. Your Exchange server has its name and IP address entered into a public DNS server on the Internet.

Your network's firewall prohibits traffic on all ports that are not explicitly allowed. The open ports are port 25 (SMTP), port 53 (DNS), port 80 (HTTP), and all ports greater than port 1023.

REQUIRED RESULTS

Management requires that users be able to connect over the Internet to your Exchange server using Microsoft Outlook and LDAP applications. Policy dictates that passwords be transmitted in a secure manner.

OPTIONAL RESULTS

While it is not required, management would like web clients that do not support Integrated Windows authentication to be able to connect to your Exchange server. Another preference is for POP3 clients to be able to connect to the Exchange server and download their messages.

PROPOSED COURSE OF ACTION

One proposed course of action is to do the following:

- Assign port numbers to the Exchange Directory Service and Information Store. Then allow those ports through the firewall.
- Configure LDAP on the Exchange server to allow Anonymous access.
- Allow LDAP traffic (port 389) through the firewall.

RESULTS OF THE PROPOSED ACTIONS

This course of action would not meet the required results because port 135, used by the Mapper service, is not open on the firewall, and there is no capability to use secure passwords. Only one of the optional results is met, namely web access to your server (that ability was already inherent in the current situation). The POP3 optional result is not met because POP3 is not allowed through the firewall.

Scenario 5

The final scenario presents the same situation as the previous scenario but proposes a different course of action.

CURRENT SITUATION

Your Exchange server is using TCP/IP and is configured with LDAP, HTTP, and POP3. A firewall sits between your network and the Internet. Your Exchange server has its name and IP address entered into a public DNS server on the Internet.

Your network's firewall prohibits traffic on all ports that are not explicitly allowed. The open ports are port 25 (SMTP), port 53 (DNS), port 80 (HTTP), and all ports greater than port 1023.

REQUIRED RESULTS

Management requires that users be able to connect over the Internet to your Exchange server using Microsoft Outlook and LDAP applications. Policy dictates that passwords be transmitted in a secure manner.

OPTIONAL RESULTS

While it is not required, management would like web clients that do not support Integrated Windows NT authentication to be able to connect to your Exchange server. Another preference is for POP3 clients to be able to connect to the Exchange server and download their messages.

PROPOSED COURSE OF ACTION

One course of action would be to do the following:

- Assign port numbers to the Exchange Directory Service and Information Store. Then allow those ports through the firewall.
- Configure LDAP on the Exchange server to allow Anonymous access.
- Allow LDAP traffic (port 389) through the firewall.
- Allow RPC traffic (port 135) through the firewall.

RESULTS OF THE PROPOSED ACTIONS

This course of action would meet one of the required results, namely allowing Microsoft Outlook and LDAP clients to access the Exchange server. The second required result, secure passwords, is not met because an authentication method using SSL is not used. Only one of the optional results is met, namely web access to the server. The other optional result, POP3 client access, is not met because the firewall does not allow POP3.

Firewalls and Front-End/Back-End Servers

In addition to the basic use of firewalls outlined previously, the introduction of *front-end servers* and *back-end servers* in Exchange Server 2003 presents other possible configurations for the use of firewalls. There are three basic configurations that you can use, each offering a different level of security.

Using a Firewall between a Front-End Server and a Back-End Server

In this configuration, a front-end server sits outside the firewall for your network, as shown in Figure 15.2. This type of configuration can be useful for authenticating and then redirecting clients using different protocols to various back-end servers behind the firewall. Keep in mind, though, that no firewall protects the front-end server.

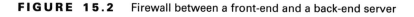

FIGURE 15.2 Firewall between a front-end and a back-end server

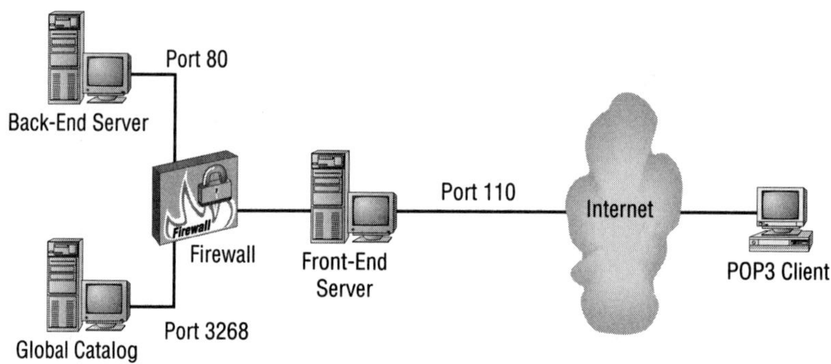

Figure 15.2 illustrates the following process:

1. A POP3 client connects to the front-end server using port 110.
2. The front-end server connects to the Global Catalog through the firewall over port 3268 and identifies the correct back-end server to receive the POP3 request.
3. The front-end and back-end servers communicate using HTTP over port 80.
4. The front-end server returns the information to the client using port 110.

Using a Firewall between a Client and a Front-End Server

In this configuration, the front-end server sits inside the network firewall, as shown in Figure 15.3. This method offers a higher level of security for the front-end server than placing it outside the firewall but also requires more configuration of the firewall. Instead of having to open just two ports (3268 for the Global Catalog and 80 for the HTTP communications between front and back-end servers), you must open a port for each type of communication that you want to allow. For example, to allow POP3, IMAP, and HTTP clients to connect, you would have to open ports 110, 143, and 80.

Placing the Front-End Server in a Perimeter Network

One highly secure firewall configuration calls for placing two firewalls between the outside world and your private network. A front-end server is then placed between the two firewalls, as shown in Figure 15.4. The area between the two firewalls is commonly referred to as a *perimeter network* or a *demilitarized zone (DMZ)*. When using this configuration, you must open all ports on the outside firewall for the clients that should be able to connect to the front-end server (i.e. POP3, IMAP, or HTTP) and then open ports 3268 and 80 on the interior firewall so that the front-end server can query the Global Catalog and pass information to the back-end server. Also, if you are using Kerberos V5 authentication, you must open port 88 on both firewalls.

FIGURE 15.3 Firewall between clients and a front-end server

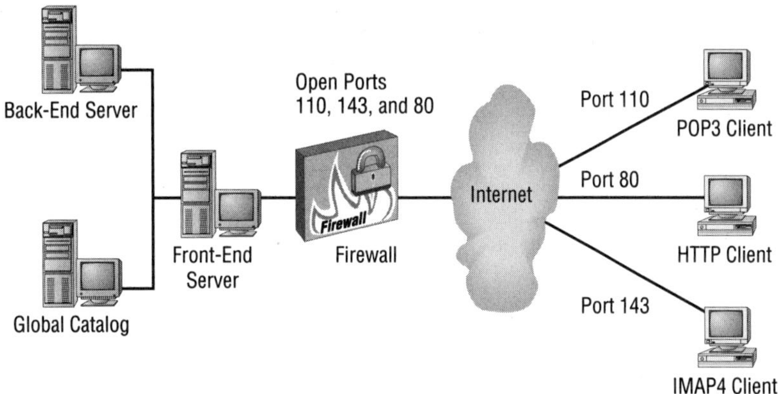

FIGURE 15.4 A perimeter network

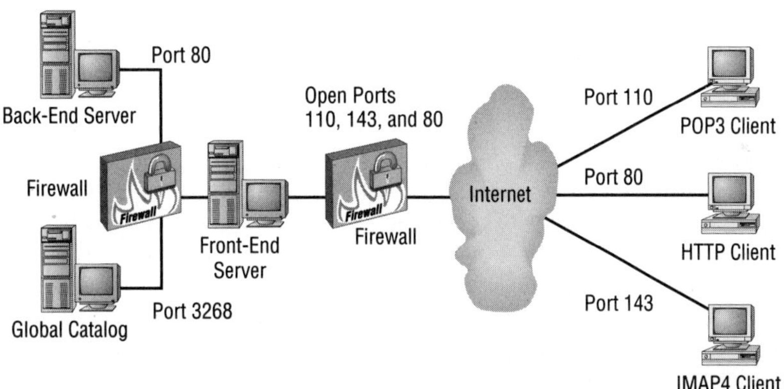

Viruses

Viruses can enter a system in a number of ways—through an infected file on a floppy disk that someone brings in, by downloading a file from the Internet, through e-mail, and even through shared documents. Most networks implement a number of virus protection schemes that work together to help prevent the problems viruses can cause. Some of these schemes are as follows:

- Virus protection built into the network firewall that tries to prevent viruses from entering the network in the first place.
- Virus software that works with Exchange Server 2003 to scan all messages transferred through Exchange.

- Virus scanning software on servers and clients that examines files as they are transferred or used and examines messages as they are received by a client application. However, messages that are encrypted for security cannot be effectively scanned for viruses, allowing those messages to slip through the firewall and Exchange Server virus scanners. One great advantage this scheme has over the others is that once a message is decrypted on the client computer, any virus protection on that computer can scan the contents of the message and any attachments.

Exchange Server 2003 provides a new and more robust version of the *Virus Scanning API (VSAPI)*, allowing antivirus products developed for Exchange Server 2003 to run on servers that do not typically host any mailboxes, such as gateway servers and bridgehead servers. As well, the new VSAPI allows antivirus products to automatically delete an infected message and send a notification, if desired, to the sender of that infected message.

Messaging Security

Even if you have the best system and network security in place, it is often important to secure the actual messages being transferred within your organization and to users outside the organization. To accomplish this, Exchange Server 2003 provides full integration and operability with Windows Server 2003 Certificate Services using X.509 digital certificates.

Real World Scenario

Sending Notifications of Infected Messages

In the not-so-recent past, it was considered good administrative practice to have an antivirus product generate and send a notification back to a message originator when a virus-infected item was found. However, with the recent outbreak of virus and worms that are both spoofers and mass-mailers, this is no longer considered a valuable practice. In fact, by configuring your antivirus product in this way, you are only adding to the effect caused by the infection since you are at least doubling the amount of e-mail messages generated when your servers reply back to the originator. Not only does this place extra stress on your servers (and the Internet as whole), more often than not the value of the originator e-mail address has been spoofed and is either invalid or internal to your own organization. Sending e-mail messages to invalid addresses further complicates the problem by placing additional loading on all servers that handle the invalid message.

It is recommended that you quarantine or delete all infected messages with no further action on the part of the antivirus product. Quarantined messages can be examined for possible cleaning either manually or automatically at a later time.

Overview of Certificate Services

Certificates and public key encryption were originally designed for use on the Internet. Encryption keys are handed out between web servers and from web servers to clients using certificates or cookies. These keys are used primarily to give the client some assurance that the server is a trusted source for data. However, the trend toward requiring increasing levels of security while at the same time requiring greater scalability and exposure to the Internet has led to the incorporation of certificate services on many private networks.

To answer these needs, Windows Server 2003 implements security using a technology called *public key infrastructure (PKI)*, which is a system of components working together to verify the identity of users who transfer data on a system and to encrypt that data if needed. PKI is still an emerging standard, so you'll likely find that many systems incorporate a rather loose version of it.

Encryption Methods

Theft, tampering, and forgery can be countered through cryptology, which is the study and implementation of hiding and revealing information. Cryptology provides for confidentiality by preventing stolen data from being read or altered, making it useless to the thief.

The word *cryptology* comes from two Greek words, *kryptos*, which means "hidden," and *logos*, which means "word." A cryptological method can take information in standard format, called plaintext or clear text, and hide it by scrambling it to make it unintelligible. This is called *encryption*. Encrypted information is sometimes called cipher text. Most methods of hiding information do so by rearranging patterns or substituting characters with other characters (see the following sidebar, "The Caesar Code"). The procedure used to unscramble the information back to plaintext, so that it can be read, is called *decryption*.

The terms *encryption* and *authentication* are sometimes substituted with the terms *sealing* and *signing*.

The Caesar Code

One early form of cryptology was the Caesar code:

```
a b c d e f g h i j k l m n o p q r s t u v w x y z
D E F G H I J K L M N O P Q R S T U V W X Y Z A B C
```

To encrypt a message, its letters are taken one by one and substituted with the letters appearing below them. The message "Send spears" would be encrypted as "VHQG VSHDUV." The substitution method used today is much more complicated.

Modern encryption methods scramble information by running a mathematical algorithm involving a number called a *key* on the data to be encrypted. The key is added to the algorithm by a user or by software. Because the algorithm can remain constant, and may even be published, the keys are what add the variations and secrecy to the encryption. For example, a sender encrypts data using an agreed-upon algorithm and a secret key. The recipient, using the same algorithm, must supply the same secret key for the algorithm to decrypt the data.

The length of a key determines the difficulty of breaking the encryption. Each bit in a key can be in one of two states, a one or a zero. A key of four bits would have only 16 (2^4) unique combinations. If the algorithm were known, it would be simple to try every possible key with the algorithm and decrypt any message. But a key of 56 bits would have 2^{56} unique combinations, which is 72 quadrillion possible keys. Keys do not make encryption unbreakable, but they make it costly, time-consuming, and impractical to break. With the computer hardware available in the 1970s, it would take over 2,000 years to decrypt a message encrypted with a 56-bit key. Recently, a network of computers working together was able to decrypt a message with 56-bit encryption in fewer than six months. Therefore, as computers get more powerful, more bits are needed to keep encryption strong. In the following sections, we discuss the two basic types of key mechanisms: public/private key pairs and secret keys.

Public/Private Key Pairs

Some encryption methods assign each user a key that is divided into two mathematically related halves, called a *key pair*. One half of the key is made public and is called the *public key*. The other half is known by only one user and is called the *private key*. Some encryption protocols have the sender encrypt a message using the recipient's public key. The only key that can be used to decrypt the message is the other half of the key, the private key, which is known only to the recipient. Because there are two different keys, this method is referred to as being *asymmetrical*.

Figure 15.5 illustrates the use of public/private key pairs. This technique is often called simply *public key encryption*.

FIGURE 15.5 Public key encryption

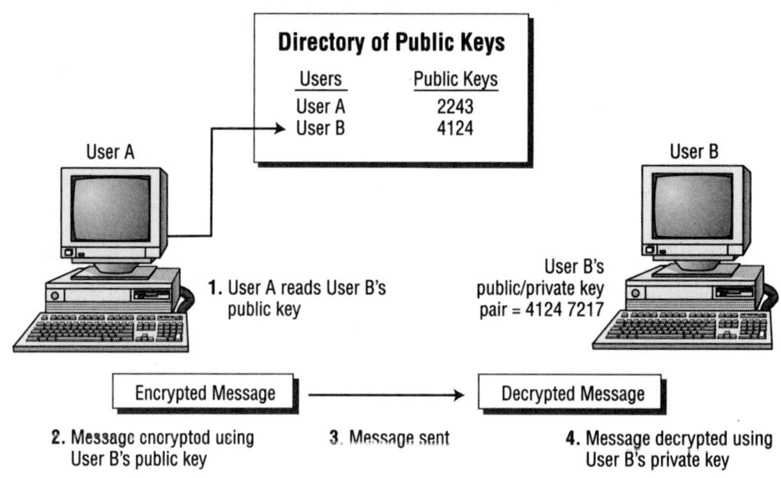
Directory of Public Keys
Users
Public Keys
User A
2243
User B
4124
User A
User B
1. User A reads User B's public key
User B's public/private key pair = 4124 7217
Encrypted Message
Decrypted Message
2. Message encrypted using User B's public key
3. Message sent
4. Message decrypted using User B's private key

One of the most frequently used public key algorithms is called *RSA*. The RSA algorithm was developed in the late 1970s by Ron Rivest, Adi Shamir, and Leonard Adleman. They used the first letters of their last names, RSA, to name the algorithm. The RSA algorithm is computationally intense and slower than other methods, so it is not usually used to encrypt large amounts of data. However, it is used for secure user authentication.

Just as a fingerprint or retinal pattern can be used to uniquely identify a person, a key pair can be used to identify a message sender. When keys are used in this manner, they help to create *digital signatures*. A sender adds a digital signature to a message. When the recipient receives the message, he uses the digital signature to authenticate (or prove) the sender's identity. Digital signatures help protect against message forgeries.

Thus, the public-key system provides two capabilities:

- Users can digitally sign data so that the recipient of the data can verify the authenticity of both the sender and the data. During this process, the sender of the data uses her own private signing key to sign the data. The data is not encrypted in any way during the signing process. The recipient of the data uses the sender's public signing key to verify the digital signature. The message is valid if the public and private signing keys correspond to one another.
- Users can encrypt data to be transferred securely. During this process, the sender uses the recipient's public key to encrypt the data, and the recipient uses his own private key to decrypt the data.

Secret Keys

A *secret key* mechanism uses the same key to both encrypt and decrypt information. When a message is encrypted, the key used by the algorithm is sent along with the message. The recipient uses the single secret key to decrypt the information. Because there is only one key, the secret-key scheme is a symmetrical method and is sometimes referred to as the *shared-secret method*. The *Data Encryption Standard (DES)* and *CAST* algorithms both use the secret-key method.

DATA ENCRYPTION STANDARD (DES)

DES was developed by IBM and in 1977 was accepted by the U.S. government as an official standard. DES is extremely secure and is used by many financial institutions for electronic fund transfers. DES uses a 64-bit key. The only method of cracking a DES-encrypted message is the brute-force approach of attempting every possible key.

Software-based DES encryption can be performed about 100 times faster than RSA encryption. Because of its speed, DES is suited for encrypting and decrypting large amounts of data.

When a message is encrypted in Exchange using DES, the secret key is encrypted with RSA and sent in a *lockbox* with the message. This type of hybrid system leverages the speed advantages of DES and the strength of 512-bit public-key RSA. When the message is received, the recipient's private key is used to decrypt the secret-key lockbox, and the secret key is used to decrypt the message. Figure 15.6 illustrates this type of hybrid system.

FIGURE 15.6 A hybrid encryption system using both RSA and DES

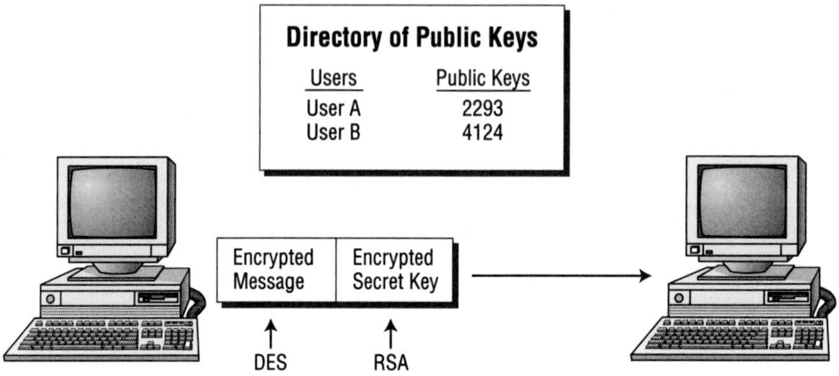

Certificates

While the public-key encryption method is a highly secure one, there is still a piece missing. How do you know that the public key being used is valid? The answer to this question comes in the form of a *certificate*, which you can think of as a message of authenticity associated with a public key and coming from a trusted source. Certificates allow verification of the claim that a given public key actually belongs to a given individual. This helps prevent someone from using a phony key to impersonate someone else.

The most widely used format for certificates is defined by the International Telecommunications Union (ITU) in Recommendation X.509. An *X.509 certificate* contains not only the public key but also information that identifies the user and the organization that issued the certificate. This information includes the certificate's serial number, validity period, issuer name, and issuer signature.

Certificate Authorities

The issuer of a certificate is called a *Certificate Authority (CA)*. The CA is any trusted source that is willing to verify the identities of the people to whom it issues certificates and to associate those people with certain public and private keys. Because anyone can become a CA, certificates are only as trustworthy as the CA that issues them.

A CA issues certificates in response to a request to do so and based on the CA's policy for issuance. CAs can issue certificates to end users, computers, and other CAs. A CA accepts a certificate request, verifies the requester's information according to the policy for the CA, and then uses its own private key to digitally sign the certificate. The CA then issues the certificate to the subject (end user, computer, or other CA) of the certificate.

A CA can be provided by a third party, such as VeriSign, or you can set up your own CA for use in your organization. Windows Server 2003 provides the Certificate Services component for setting up a CA internal to your network.

CA Classes

There are two different classes of CAs:

Enterprise CA The *Enterprise CA* acts as a CA for an enterprise, so it should come as no surprise that this type of CA requires access to the Active Directory. However, the Active Directory does not have to be installed on the same server functioning as the CA. Enterprise CAs have a number of special features:

- All users and computers in the same domain always trust the Enterprise CA.
- Certificates issued by an Enterprise CA can be used to log on to Windows Active Directory domains using smart cards.
- Enterprise CAs publish certificates and Certificate Revocation List (CRL) information to the Active Directory so that the information is available throughout the enterprise.
- Enterprise CAs use certificate types and templates stored in the Active Directory (discussed a bit later in the chapter) to construct the content of new certificates.
- Enterprise CAs always approve or reject a certificate request immediately and never mark a request as pending. The CA makes the decision based on the security permissions on the security template and on permissions and group memberships in the Active Directory.

Stand-alone CA The *stand-alone CA* is used to issue certificates to users outside the enterprise and does not require access to the Active Directory. For example, a stand-alone CA might be used to issue certificates to Internet users who access your company's website. Unlike Enterprise CAs, stand-alone CAs typically mark incoming certificate requests as pending, because the CA is not presumed to have access to the Active Directory to validate the request. Also, certificates generated by stand-alone CAs are not published if no Active Directory access is present—they must be manually distributed. Finally, certificates generated by stand-alone CAs cannot be used for smart card logons.

CA Roles

Within each class, a CA can operate in one of two roles:

Root CA A *root CA* is at the top of a CA hierarchy and is trusted unconditionally by a client. All certificate chains terminate at a root CA. The root CA must sign its own certificate because there is no higher authority in the certification hierarchy. Enterprise root CAs can issue certificates to end users but are more often used to issue certificates to subordinate CAs, which in turn issue certificates to end users.

Subordinate CA A *subordinate CA* is found underneath the root CA in the CA hierarchy and may be even under other subordinate CAs. Subordinate CAs are typically used to issue certificates to users and computers in the organization; an organization does not have to have its own root CA. For example, you may establish a subordinate CA that receives certificates from another CA that belongs to a third-party company such as VeriSign. That way, you can let a trusted third party take care of the security policy and use a subordinate CA mainly for convenience within your own network.

Certificate Trust List

The *Certificate Trust List (CTL)* for a domain holds the set of root CAs whose certificates can be trusted. You can designate CTLs for groups, users, or an entire domain. If a CA's certificate is not on the CTL, a client responds to the untrusted certificate depending on the client's configuration.

Trust in root CAs can be set by policy or by managing the CTL directly. In addition to establishing a root CA as trusted, you can set usage properties associated with the CA. If specified, these restrict the purposes for which the CA-issued certificates are valid.

Certificate Templates

You can configure Enterprise CAs to issue specific types of certificates to authorized users and computers. *Certificate templates* are stored in Active Directory and define the attributes for certificate types.

Certificate Store

The *Certificate Store* is a database created during the installation of a CA. If certificate services are installed on an Enterprise root CA, the store is created in the Active Directory. If services are installed on a stand-alone root CA, the store is created on the local server. The store is a repository of certificates issued by the CA, and each store can support up to 250,000 certificates.

Installing and Configuring Certificate Services

Before your messaging clients can begin using digital certificates to sign and encrypt their messages, you must first install at least one Certificate Authority on your network. The first CA you install is the Root CA, and since we're working in an Active Directory environment here, it will be an Enterprise root CA. Exercise 15.2 outlines the steps required to install and configure the Enterprise root CA.

Once you install Certificate Services on a server, you cannot rename it. As well, you cannot remove an Enterprise CA from the Active Directory domain. In either case, you will need to remove Certificate Services to make the change.

If you've already installed IIS on the server, you can skip Steps 4 and 5.

EXERCISE 15.2

Installing an Enterprise Root Certificate Authority

1. Click Start ➢ Settings ➢ Control Panel.
2. Double-click the Add or Remove Programs icon.
3. Click the Add/Remove Windows Components button.
4. On the list of components, double-click the Application Server option.

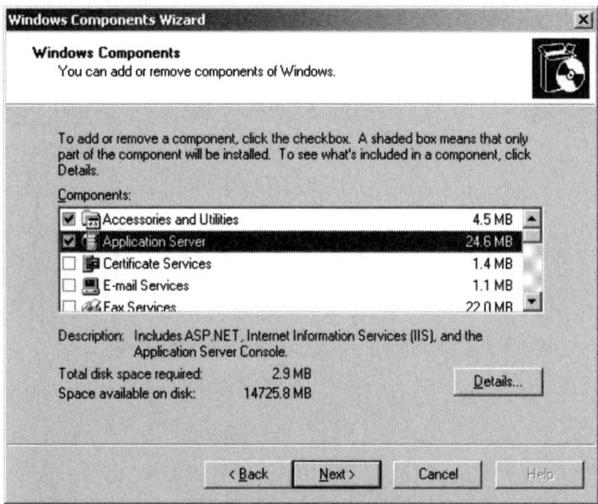

5. On the Application Server dialog box, select the Internet Information Services (IIS) option and click OK.

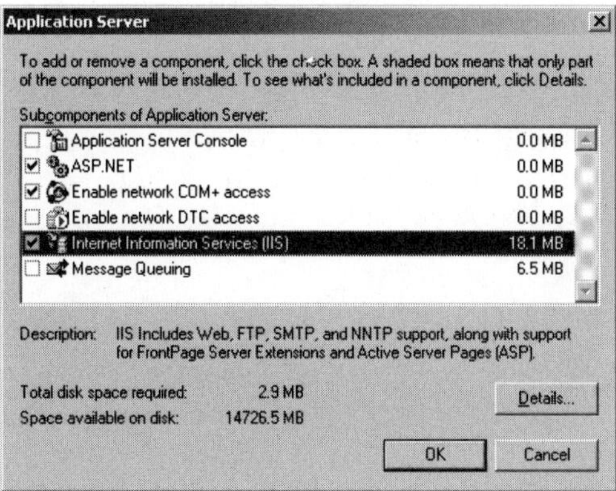

EXERCISE 15.2 *(continued)*

6. Back at the list of components, select the Certificate Services option.

7. A dialog box opens, warning you that once you install Certificate Services, you will not be able to change the name of the computer or change your domain status. Click Yes to go on.

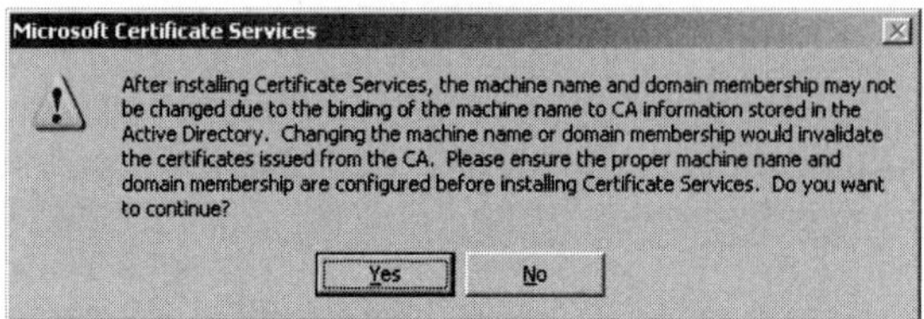

8. On the Certificate Services dialog box, click OK.

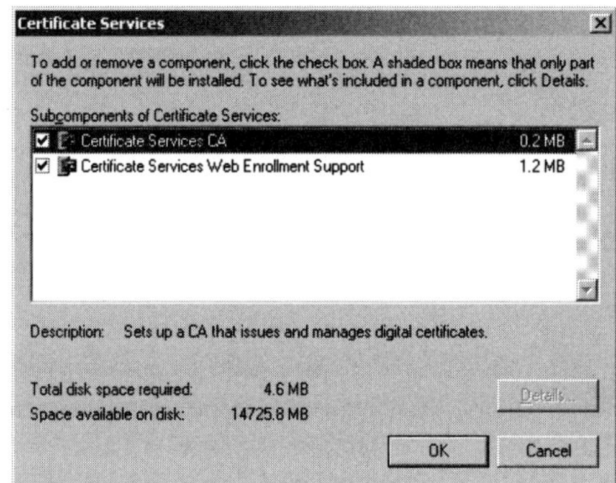

9. Back at the list of components, click Next to go on.

EXERCISE 15.2 *(continued)*

10. Select the appropriate type for your new CA. If this is the first CA you are installing in an organization, you will probably want to choose the Enterprise Root CA option.

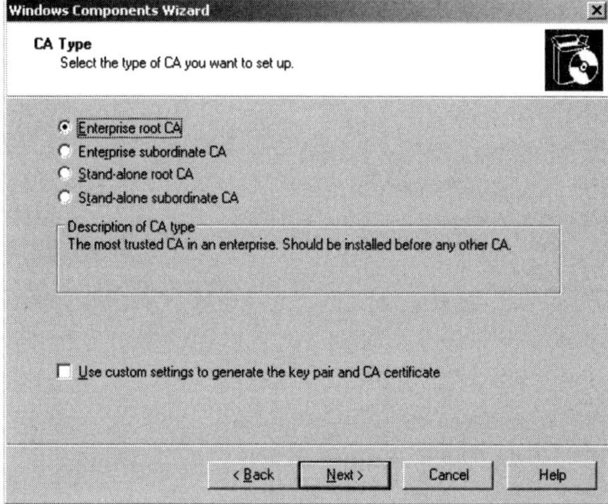

11. Click Next to go on.

12. Enter the identifying information for your CA. The CA name is required, and each CA in an organization must have a unique name. The country and expiration information is also required. All of the other information is optional and is used solely to help you identify the CA. Click Next to go on.

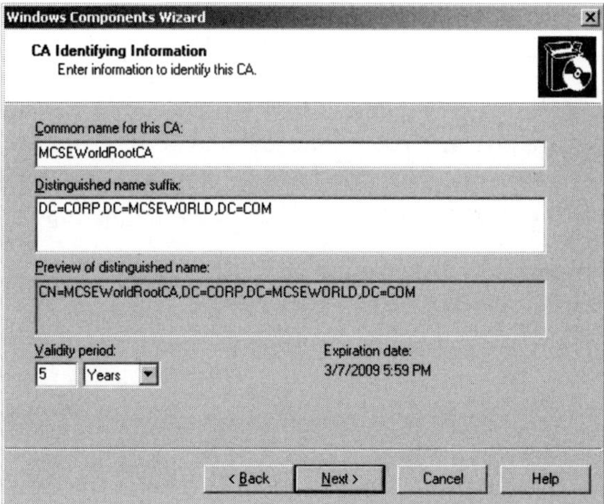

EXERCISE 15.2 *(continued)*

13. Confirm the location where the certificate database and certificate log should be stored. By default, these are both stored in the `C:\WINDOWS\System32\CertLog` folder. Click Next to go on.

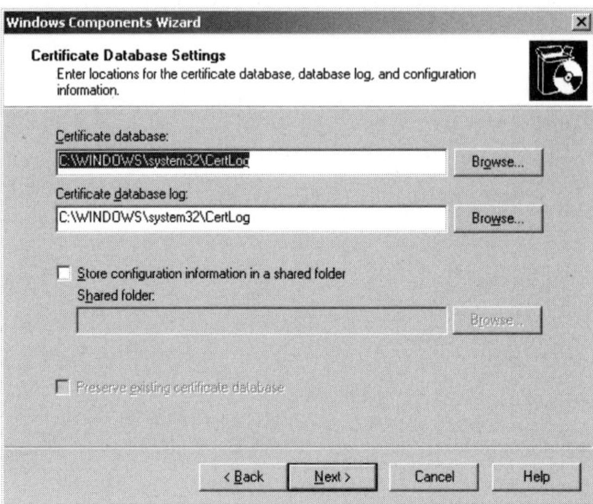

14. A dialog box appears, letting you know that the IIS services must be stopped for installation to continue. Click Yes to go on.

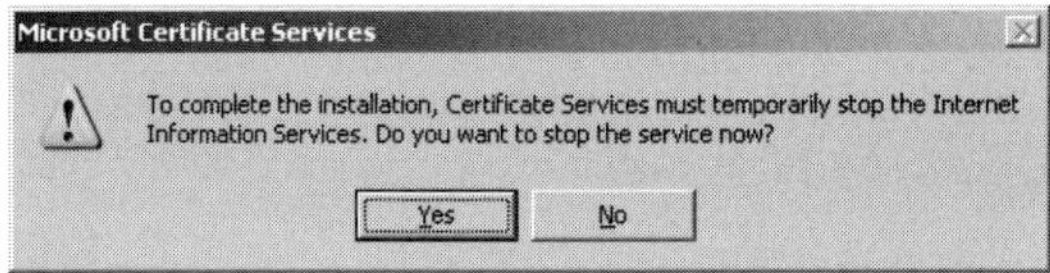

15. At this point, the wizard prompts you for the location of the Windows Server 2003 installation files and the files for the latest Windows Service Pack you have applied. Once you have directed the wizard to these locations, the wizard begins copying files.

16. When the summary screen is displayed, click Finish.

Requesting Certificates

Once the first Certificate Authority is installed on your network, users can begin to request digital certificates. Certificate requests can be submitted via the web enrollment pages or the Certificates MMC. In Exercise 15.3 we will complete the steps required to request a digital certificate using the web enrollment pages.

Using the web enrollment pages to request a certificate is the simpler of the two methods for the less-experienced users on your network.

EXERCISE 15.3

Requesting a Digital Certificate

1. Click Start ➤ Programs ➤ Internet Explorer.
2. In the Address box, enter the URL for your CA. The CA can be found at **http://** *ServerName*/**certsrv**.

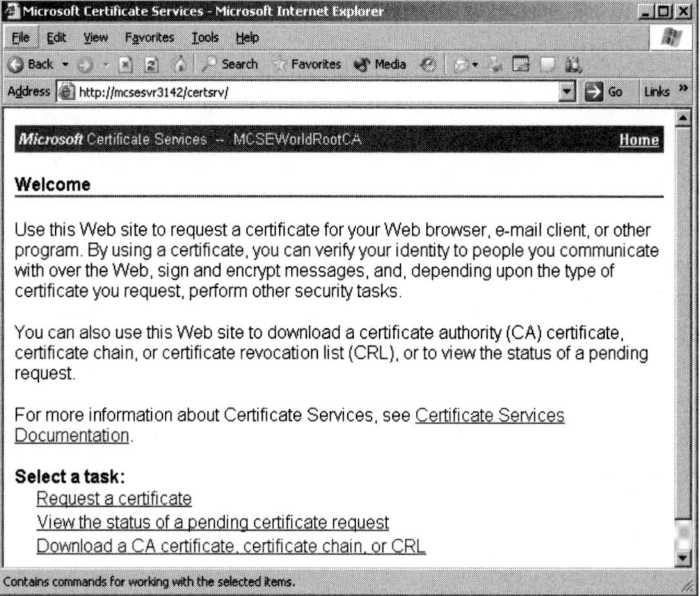

3. Click the Request A Certificate link.

EXERCISE 15.3 *(continued)*

4. Click the User Certificate link.

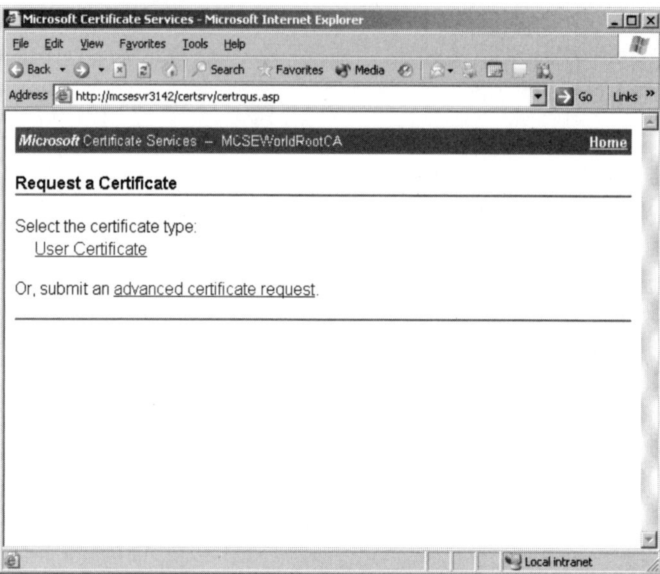

5. Click the Submit button.

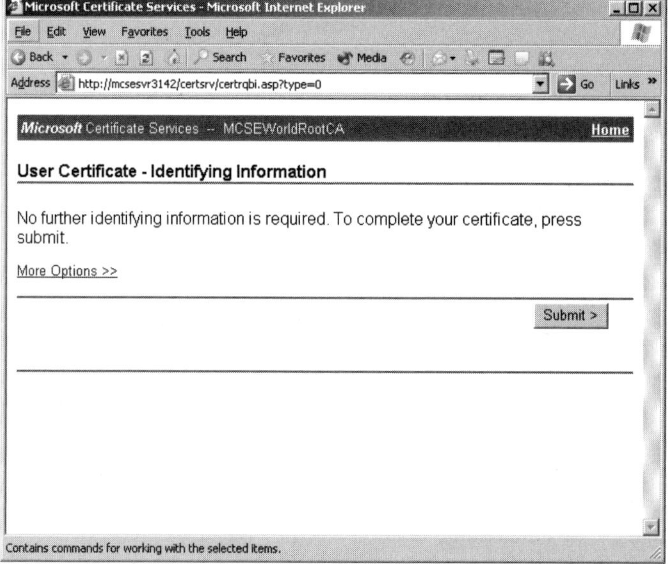

EXERCISE 15.3 *(continued)*

6. When prompted by the warning dialog, click the Yes button.

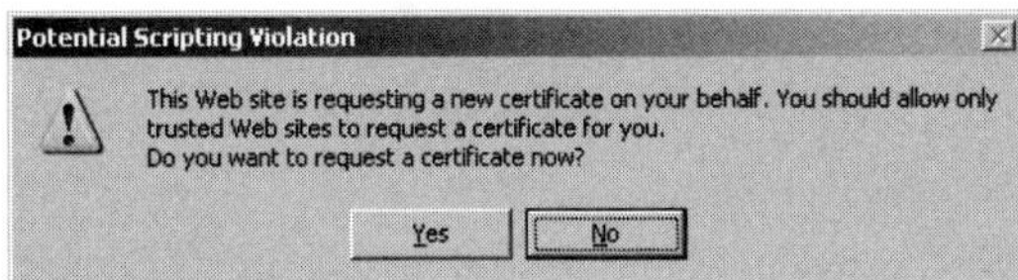

7. Click the Install This Certificate link.

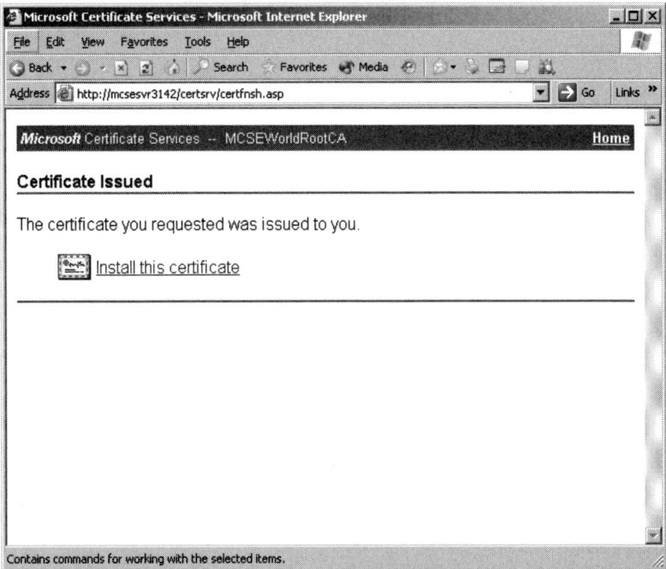

8. When prompted by the warning dialog, click the Yes button.

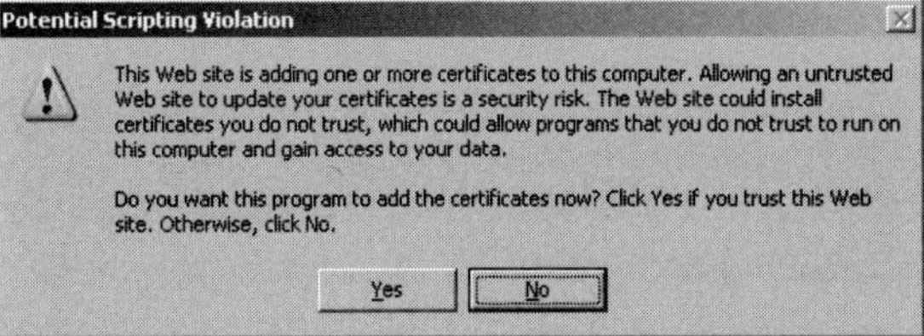

EXERCISE 15.3 *(continued)*

9. If prompted about installing a root certificate, click the Yes button.

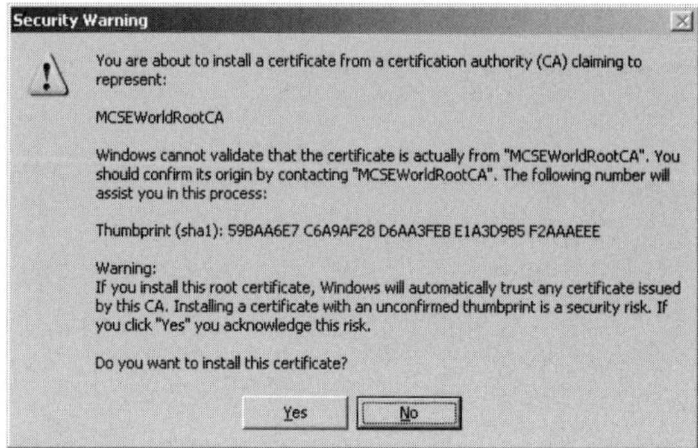

10. Close the Internet Explorer windows.

You can verify that the certificate has in fact been issued by viewing the Published Certificates tab, seen in Figure 15.7, of the user account property pages in Active Directory Users and Computers. You will need to have enabled the Advanced Features option under the View menu in ADUC beforehand.

FIGURE 15.7 Viewing the installed certificates for a user

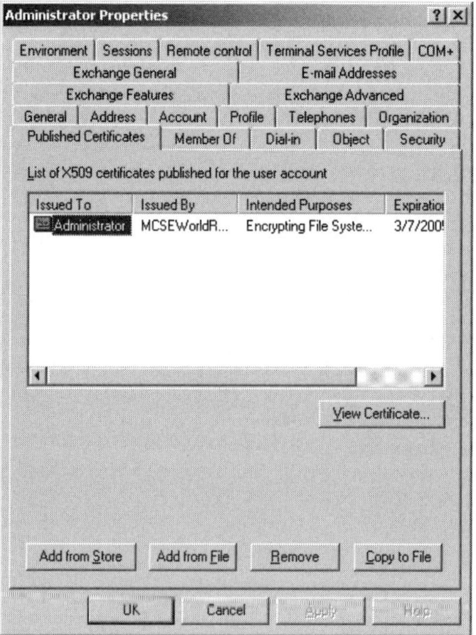

Double-clicking a certificate in the list opens the Certificate Information dialog, as seen in Figure 15.8.

FIGURE 15.8 Examining an installed certificate

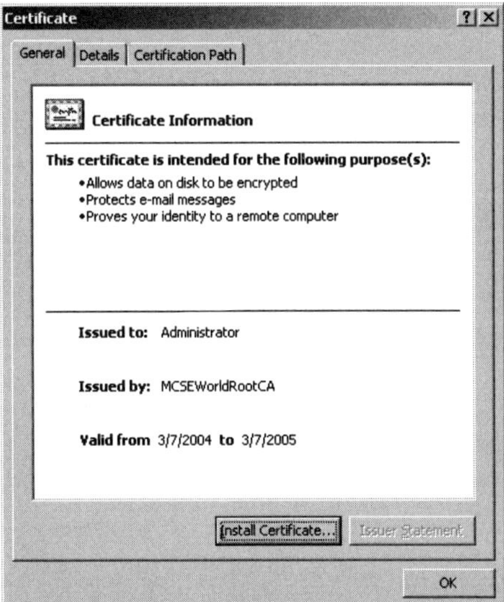

Preparing Exchange Server 2003 for S/MIME

With the CA installed and users having been issued certificates, your next step is to ensure that any mailbox stores that will have users using e-mail security have been configured properly. Open the Mailbox Store Properties page and ensure that the Clients Support S/MIME Signatures option is selected, as seen in Figure 15.9.

If any of your Outlook Web Access users will be using *S/MIME*, you will need to ensure that the S/MIME control for OWA has been downloaded to their computers. This is done by clicking the Go To Options button at the bottom of the OWA screen and then clicking Download in the E-mail Security area, as seen in Figure 15.10.

You will need to be logged into the local computer with an account having administrative credentials to perform this task.

FIGURE 15.9 Configuring the mailbox store for S/MIME

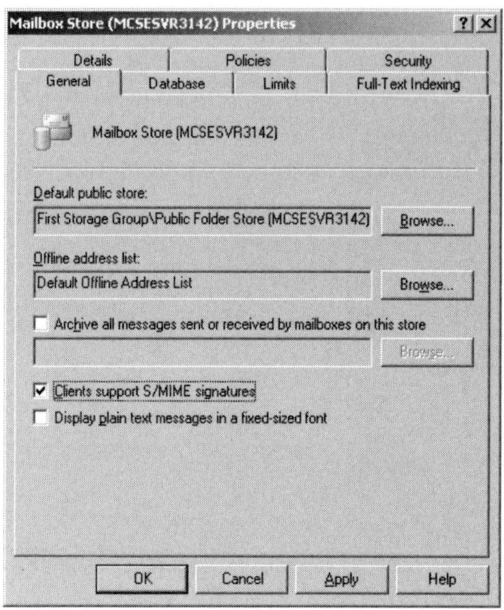

FIGURE 15.10 Configuring OWA for S/MIME

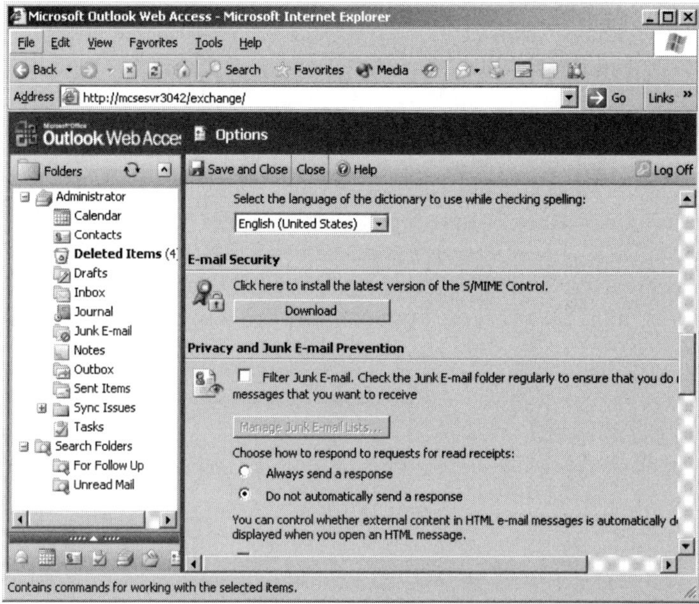

Sending Secure Messages

The last step in securing messages is to ensure that Outlook 2003 is configured properly and send a test message. Exercise 15.4 outlines the steps to perform these actions.

The process to configure and send secure messages in Outlook Express and Outlook Web Access is similar to that outlined here for Outlook 2003.

EXERCISE 15.4

Requesting a Digital Certificate

1. Click Start ➢ Programs ➢ Microsoft Office ➢ Microsoft Office Outlook 2003.
2. Click Tools ➢ Options to open the Options page. Click the Security tab.

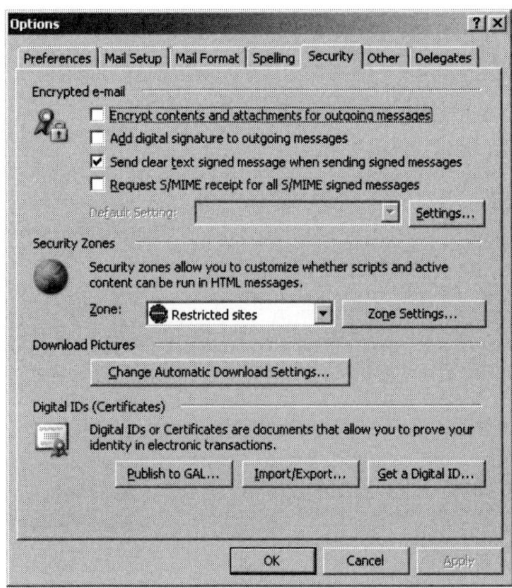

EXERCISE 15.4 *(continued)*

3. Click the Settings button. The Change Security Settings dialog box appears.

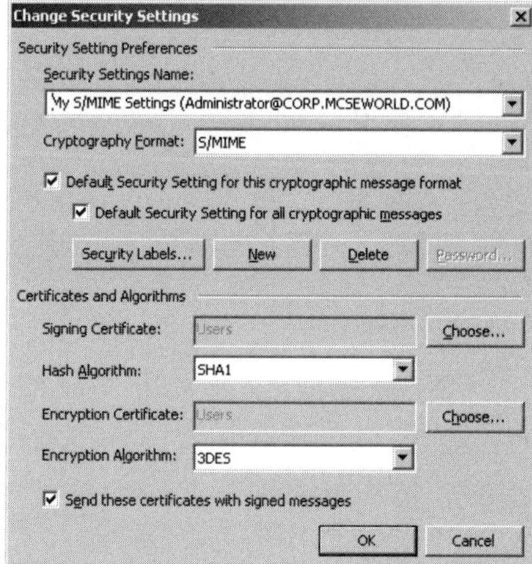

4. Ensure that the options are configured as shown above (the default configuration), and click OK twice.

5. Compose a new message. Note the location of the Signature and Encryption buttons on the right side of the toolbar. Send the message.

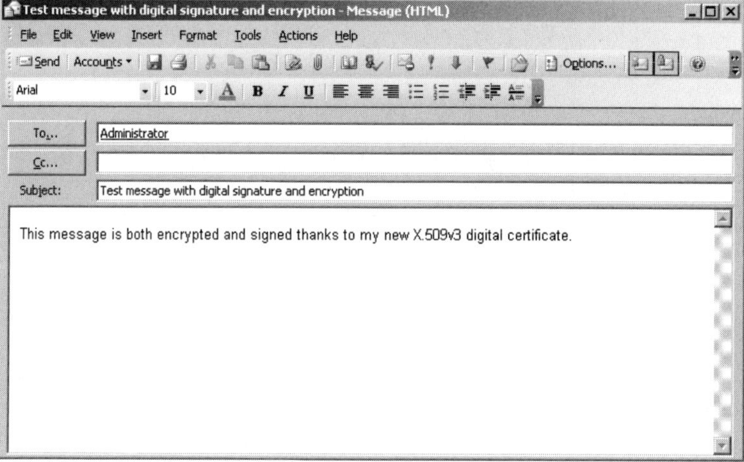

EXERCISE 15.4 *(continued)*

6. Upon receipt of an encrypted message, Outlook will not be able to display it in the reading pane. Double-click the message.

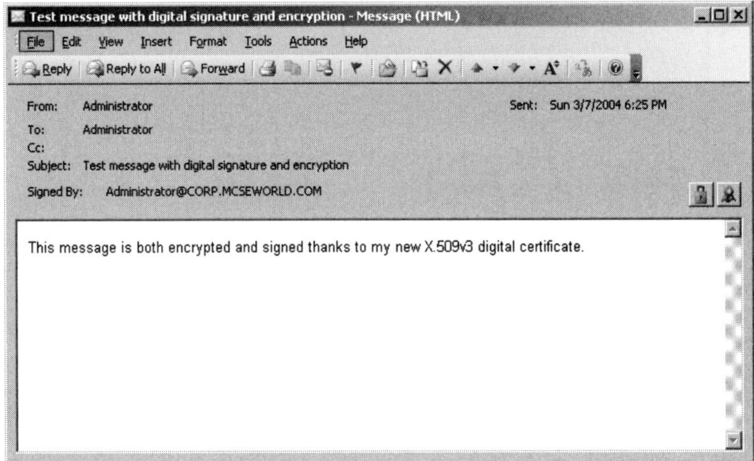

7. Click the Encryption button to view the encryption details.

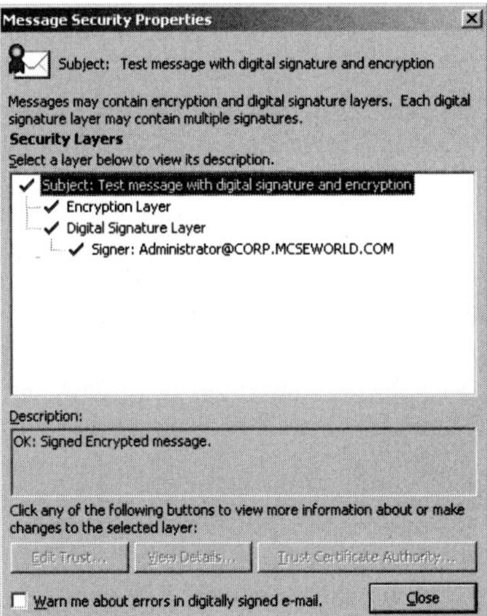

EXERCISE 15.4 ***(continued)***

8. Click the Signature button to view the signature details.

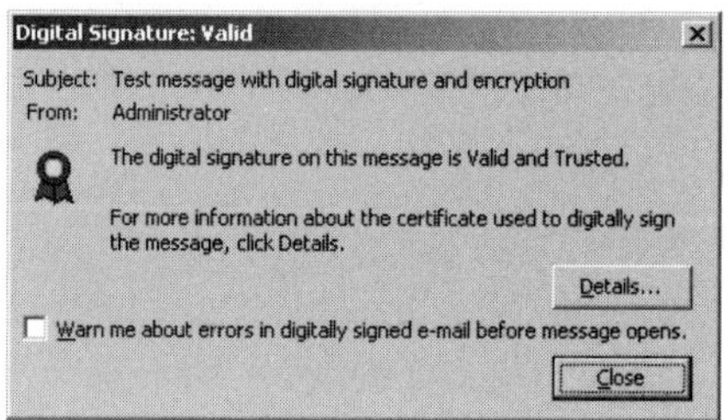

Troubleshooting Exchange Server 2003

In the Utopian world, nothing would ever go wrong with your Exchange Server 2003 organization. Unfortunately, we do not live in Utopia. In the following sections we will briefly examine some of the more common problem areas in Exchange Server 2003: network connectivity, Active Directory, and host name resolution.

Troubleshooting Network Connectivity Issues

Without network connectivity, there really is no Exchange organization. Network connectivity troubleshooting is part science, part art, and part luck. Those who do it well typically do it very well—luckily for the rest of us, several very useful tools exist that can be used to diagnose and troubleshoot network connectivity issues.

PING To start out with, you should conduct the simplest of all tests: Can you ping key servers on the network? The *ping* command works by sending a series of ICMP Echo Request datagrams to a destination and waiting for the corresponding ICMP Echo Reply datagrams to come back. The return packets are then used to determine how many datagrams are getting through, the response time, and the TTL (time to live). Try to ping other Exchange servers, the DNS servers, the DHCP servers, the domain controllers, and the global catalog servers. This simple test can quickly rule out problems with network connectivity.

Ipconfig The *ipconfig* command can be issued from the command line to quickly detail the TCP/IP configuration status of all network adapters in a server.

You'd be surprised at the number of network connectivity problems that can be traced back to incorrectly entered TCP/IP configuration information (since most servers have static TCP/IP configuration, this can be a real problem if values are entered without caution).

Nbtstat The *nbtstat* command is used to resolve NetBIOS names to IP addresses. If your network is still supporting WINS, then the `nbtstat` command can be useful in your troubleshooting efforts.

Netstat The *netstat* command is used to display TCP/IP connection information and protocol statistics for a computer. You can use `netstat` to quickly determine what other workstations and servers have open connections with a server.

Tracert The *tracert* command uses ICMP packets to determine the path that an IP datagram takes to reach its final destination. Along each hop of the path, information is returned to the requesting server (where the `tracert` command was issued). The `tracert` command is useful in determining that a specific link or router is not functioning properly.

Pathping The *pathping* command is a newer command that is a mix of both `ping` and `tracert`. The `pathping` command provides the ability to determine the packet loss along each link in the path and at each router in the path to the destination, which can be particularly helpful when troubleshooting problems where multiple routers and links are involved. When you are tempted to use the `ping` or `tracert` command to troubleshoot a problem, the `pathping` command should more often than not be your first choice.

Telnet The *telnet* command can be used to test basic responsiveness of a service on a port even if ICMP packets are being blocked at the firewall (a common configuration in these times). By successfully connecting to an Exchange server at port 25, you'd then know that SMTP was operating.

NetDiag and DCDiag More advanced network connectivity tools exist in the Windows Server 2003 Support Tools, which can be found in the `Support/Tools` directory on the Windows Server 2003 CD. You can use the *NetDiag* tool to troubleshoot and isolate network connectivity problems by performing a number of tests to determine the exact state of a server. You can even fix some simple problems directly with the NetDiag tool. The *DCDiag* tool is used to analyze the status of all domain controllers in a forest and provides very detailed output, which can then be used to identify problematic behaviors.

Troubleshooting Active Directory Issues

Exchange Server 2003 relies on Active Directory for virtually every operation that it performs. Therefore, should domain controllers and global catalogs be unable to be contacted, you should expect that problems will quickly appear in your Exchange organization. Common problems include users being unable to authenticate themselves, new objects (such as users) cannot be created, group membership changes cannot be made, or the schema cannot be extended for installation.

Users cannot authenticate In organizations that are still operating at the Windows 2000 Server mixed domain functional level and have non–Active Directory–aware clients, such as Windows NT 4.0 Workstation or Windows 95, difficulty contacting the *Primary Domain Controller (PDC) emulator* will result in authentication problems. In non-mixed domains, the failure to contact a global catalog server or domain controller will result in authentication problems.

New objects cannot be created New objects cannot be created without first contacting the *Relative Identity (RID) master*. When this problem occurs, you should check connectivity to the RID master and ensure that it is, in fact, still operating correctly.

Group membership cannot be changed The *Infrastructure master* must be contacted any time you need to change group membership. When group membership cannot be changed, you should check connectivity to the Infrastructure master and ensure that it is, in fact, still operating correctly.

Schema cannot be extended As discussed previously, a failure to contact the *Schema master* when attempting to run the `forestprep` command will prevent the schema from being extended. When this problem occurs, you should check connectivity to the Schema master and ensure that it is, in fact, still operating correctly. If your DNS settings in the TCP/IP configuration are incorrect, you will likely have this problem.

Troubleshooting Name Resolution Issues

Name resolution issues can sometimes be the most difficult to troubleshoot and correct because they can manifest themselves in a seemingly endless number of ways. The situation becomes even more complex when you still use and support WINS servers or legacy non–Active Directory–integrated DNS zones.

Most times, the complete failure of DNS in an Active Directory domain is highly unlikely—especially when Active Directory integrated zones are in use. More likely problems with name resolution include improper or no TCP/IP properties configured on the computer, negative cache entries in the local DNS resolver cache, or network problems that are preventing effective communications between DNS servers and DNS clients.

To clear the local resolver cache, issue the **`ipconfig /flushdns`** command from the command line. If the issue is that the DNS client has not properly registered its host records with DNS, then you can force the situation by issuing the **`ipconfig /registerdns`** command at the command line. You can also use the *nslookup* command to gather information about the DNS infrastructure inside and outside your organization and troubleshoot DNS-related problems. Note that for `nslookup` to function completely properly, there must be a reverse lookup zone configured on the DNS server that is authoritative for the DNS zone you are querying.

Summary

Three aspects of security were covered in this chapter. The first aspect is Exchange Server's basic reliance on Windows Server 2003's security services. These include user accounts and authentication, Exchange administrative groups, system and recipient policies, and auditing.

The second aspect concerns networking security. This includes the protection of virtual servers through authentication, as well as the use of firewalls to protect private network resources from unauthorized access. Firewalls provide protection by closing access to port numbers, except for those applications that are permitted to pass data through the firewall.

Exchange Server 2003 extends the use of firewalls with application of front-end and back-end servers.

The final aspect is messaging security. Advanced security facilitates the authentication of a message sender's identity and the privacy of message data. Authentication is accomplished using digital signatures, and message privacy is maintained using encryption. In Exchange terminology, *signing* refers to authentication, and *sealing* refers to encryption.

Using the native PKI available in Exchange Server 2003, you need only install and configure one or more Certificate Authorities, make some minor configurations to the Exchange organization, and issue your users digital certificates to allow them to digitally sign and encrypt e-mail messages. The complicated and difficult to work with KMS has gone the way of the dinosaur in Exchange Server 2003.

Problems with your Exchange organization are something that you never want to have to deal with. However, understanding some of the more common issues that you may face will give you a leg up when things are bad. Common issues with Exchange Server 2003 include name resolution–based problems, Active Directory problems, and network connectivity issues. Being able to recognize the signs of trouble and react correctly to the situation at hand will be instrumental in keeping your Exchange organization operating smoothly.

Exam Essentials

Understand how Certificate Services works. Exchange Server 2003 features full integration with the Windows Server 2003 PKI, eliminating the need to use the complex and complicated Key Management Service in Exchange 2000 Server. You should understand the basics of how public-key encryption works and how Exchange and the Outlook client work together once a user has a digital certificate to send and received secure messages.

Know the ports associated with common services. Knowing the ports that are associated with the common Exchange and Windows services is important not only for your exam experience but also for your daily routine as the Exchange administrator. There are some things that you should just commit to permanent memory, and the ports assigned to common services are one of those things.

Review Questions

1. You have installed and configured an Enterprise root CA for your network. At what URL can your user now request new certificates for use with Exchange Server 2003?

   A. `http://`*ServerName*`/exchange/certsrv`

   B. `http://`*ServerName*`/certsrv/exchange`

   C. `http://`*ServerName*`/exchange`

   D. `http://`*ServerName*`/certsrv`

2. This morning when you came to work, several dozen users on your network had called the help desk stating that they could not log in to the network. All of the users are using workstations that run Windows NT 4.0 Workstation or Windows 98. Users with Windows 2000 and Windows XP workstations report no problems. What do you suspect is the most likely problem?

   A. The RID master cannot be contacted.

   B. The Infrastructure master cannot be contacted.

   C. A DNS server cannot be contacted.

   D. A global catalog server cannot be contacted.

   E. The PDC emulator cannot be contacted.

3. You are troubleshooting a name resolution problem on your network. You suspect that some of your users' workstations have negative cache data in their local DNS resolver caches. What can you do about this problem?

   A. Issue the `ipconfig /registerdns` command.

   B. Issue the `ipconfig /flushdns` command.

   C. Issue the `ipconfig /release` command.

   D. Issue the `ipconfig /dropdns` command.

4. Which of the following types of Windows authentication can be used in a Windows Server 2003 network that is operating at the Windows 2000 mixed domain functional mode? (Choose all that apply.)

   A. Kerberos v3

   B. Kerberos v5

   C. NTLM

   D. Basic

   E. Basic over SSL

5. You have just configured your Exchange server for IMAP4 client access. IMAP4 clients can be authenticated with either Basic (Clear-Text) or Basic over SSL. The administrator of your firewall informs you that the firewall will allow traffic from SMTP (port 25), IMAP4 (port 143), and HTTP (port 80). What additional port must be opened on the firewall to allow your Exchange server IMAP4 configuration to be used?

   A. 993

   B. 443

   C. 137

   D. 135

6. Which of the following constructs is used to verify the identity of a person associated with a public key?

   A. Certificates

   B. Private key

   C. Trust

   D. Certificate Authority

7. Which of the following authentication protocols passes a person's username and password over the network? (Choose all that apply.)

   A. Basic

   B. Basic over SSL

   C. NTLM

   D. Kerberos v5

8. One of your network users has reported that he cannot log into the network. You have checked with two dozen other users on the same IP subnet and no one else has reported any problems. In this situation, what is the most likely cause of the problem?

   A. A domain controller could not be reached.

   B. A global catalog server could not be reached.

   C. The user's workstation has incorrect TCP/IP settings configured.

   D. The DNS server could not be reached.

9. A new Exchange server has been installed and configured for HTTP and POP3. The network project plan calls for allowing the following clients to access this server: HTTP using Windows Integrated authentication, and POP3 and Microsoft Outlook using secure passwords. You refer to the current firewall configuration and see that it is open to DNS, HTTP, SMTP, and ports higher than 1023. What ports, if any, must you open to enable the desired Exchange clients to pass through the firewall? (Choose all that apply.)

   A. 389

   B. 110

   C. 443

   D. 135

   E. All of the above

10. When a user digitally signs a message, which two keys are used in the process?

   A. The sender's public signing key

   B. The sender's private signing key

   C. The recipient's public signing key

   D. The recipient's private signing key

11. Your Exchange server is configured for anonymous HTTP clients, but those clients who are outside your firewall report that they cannot access the directory. What is the problem?

   A. The DS needs to be stopped and restarted.

   B. Windows Integrated authentication needs to be enabled.

   C. The HTTP port is not open on the firewall.

   D. Basic (Clear-Text) authentication is needed.

12. When a user encrypts a message, what keys are used in the process? (Choose all that apply.)

   A. The sender's public encryption key

   B. The sender's private encryption key

   C. The recipient's public encryption key

   D. The recipient's private encryption key

   E. A secret key

13. Your network is configured as shown below. Your company uses two firewalls to create a perimeter network. Your front-end server has its name and IP address entered into a public DNS server on the Internet. Both firewalls prohibit traffic on all ports that are not explicitly allowed. The ports that are currently open on both firewalls are port 25 (SMTP), port 53 (DNS), and port 80 (HTTP).

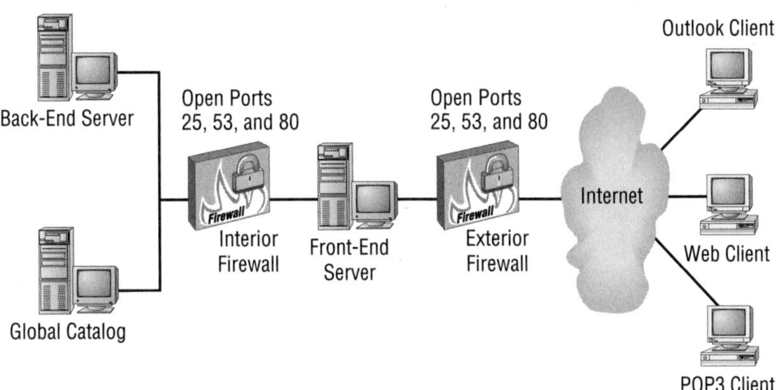

Management requires that users be able to connect over the Internet to your Exchange server using Microsoft Outlook. Policy dictates that passwords be transmitted in a secure manner. In addition, management would like web clients that do not support Windows Integrated authentication to be able to connect to your Exchange server but not transmit user information in clear text, and management would like POP3 clients to be able to connect to the Exchange server and download their messages. The last two items are desired, but not required, of your final solution.

You propose to perform the following actions:

- Open port 135 on the exterior firewall.
- Open port 110 on the exterior firewall.
- Open port 443 on the exterior firewall.

If you complete the proposed actions, will you have achieved the required and/or desired results?

A. You will achieve the required result and both of the desired results.

B. You will achieve the required result and one of the desired results.

C. You will achieve only the required result.

D. You will not achieve the required result.

14. Your network is configured as shown below. Your company uses two firewalls to create a perimeter network. Your front-end server has its name and IP address entered into a public DNS server on the Internet. Both firewalls prohibit traffic on all ports that are not explicitly allowed. The ports that are currently open on both firewalls are port 25 (SMTP), port 53 (DNS), and port 80 (HTTP).

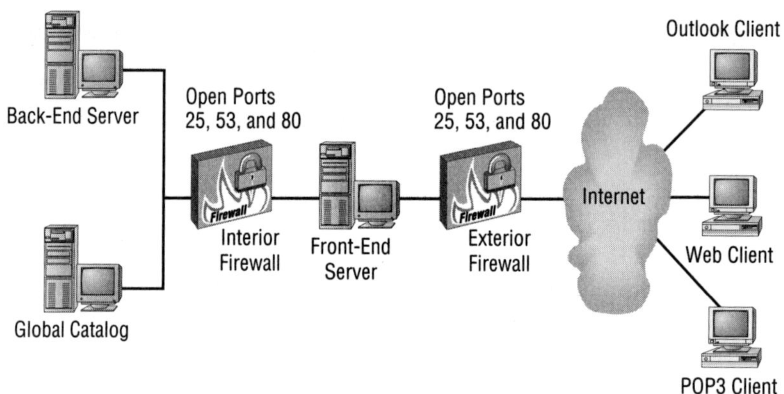

Management requires that users be able to connect over the Internet to your Exchange server using Microsoft Outlook. Policy dictates that passwords be transmitted in a secure manner. In addition, management would like web clients that do not support Windows Integrated authentication to be able to connect to your Exchange server but not transmit user information in clear text, and management would like POP3 clients to be able to connect to the Exchange server and download their messages. The last two items are desired, but not required, of your final solution.

You propose to perform the following actions:

- Open port 135 on the exterior firewall.
- Open port 110 on the exterior firewall.
- Open port 443 on the exterior firewall.
- Open port 3268 on the interior firewall.

If you complete the proposed actions, will you have achieved the required and/or desired results?

A. You will achieve the required result and both of the desired results.

B. You will achieve the required result and one of the desired results.

C. You will achieve only the required result.

D. You will not achieve the required result.

15. Your network is configured as shown below. Your company uses two firewalls to create a perimeter network. Your front-end server has its name and IP address entered into a public DNS server on the Internet. Both firewalls prohibit traffic on all ports that are not explicitly allowed. The ports that are currently open on both firewalls are port 25 (SMTP), port 53 (DNS), and port 80 (HTTP).

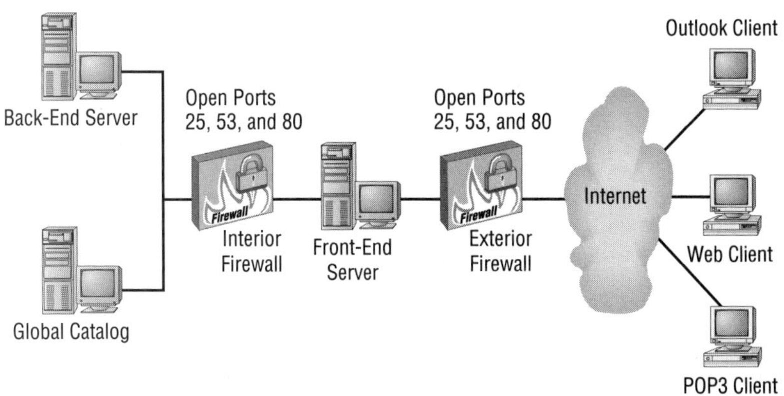

Management requires that users be able to connect over the Internet to your Exchange server using Microsoft Outlook. Policy dictates that passwords be transmitted in a secure manner. In addition, management would like web clients that do not support Windows Integrated authentication to be able to connect to your Exchange server but not transmit user information in clear text, and management would like POP3 clients to be able to connect to the Exchange server and download their messages. The last two items are desired, but not required, of your final solution.

You propose to perform the following actions:

- Open port 135 on the exterior firewall.
- Open port 110 on the exterior firewall.
- Open port 3268 on the interior firewall.

If you complete the proposed actions, will you have achieved the required and/or desired results?

A. You will achieve the required result and both of the desired results.

B. You will achieve the required result and one of the desired results.

C. You will achieve only the required result.

D. You will not achieve the required result.

16. What security feature of Windows Server 2003 lets you log the actions of users and groups based on certain criteria?

A. Auditing

B. Diagnostics logging

C. Accounting

D. Tracking

17. You have configured an X.400 Connector between your mixed-mode organization and a foreign messaging system. The ports that are currently open on your company's firewall are port 25 (SMTP), port 53 (DNS), and port 80 (HTTP). What additional port would you need to open to allow the traffic for the X.400 Connector to pass?

    A. 98

    B. 102

    C. 110

    D. 119

18. You are attempting to isolate and troubleshoot a problem with host name resolution on your network. You suspect that one of your Exchange Server 2003 servers is not properly registering its DNS information with your Active Directory DNS servers. What command can you use to examine the DNS zone data to determine whether the required DNS records exist?

    A. `telnet`

    B. `nslookup`

    C. `pathping`

    D. `netstat`

19. Which of the following types of Certificate Authority does not require access to the Active Directory?

    A. Enterprise CA

    B. Organization CA

    C. Stand-alone CA

    D. Domain CA

20. You are attempting to isolate and troubleshoot a problem with packet loss somewhere in your network. You suspect that one or more routers in your internal network may be dropping packets. What command should you use to gather the most complete information about the status of all links and routers between one host and another?

    A. `telnet`

    B. `nslookup`

    C. `pathping`

    D. `netstat`

Answers to Review Questions

1. D. The web enrollment pages of your CA are accessible at `http://`*ServerName*`/certsrv`.

2. E. The PDC emulator is required in order for users on legacy workstations that are not Active Directory–aware to successfully log in to the network. In this scenario where only these users are affected, the problem is most likely with connectivity to the PDC emulator or else the PDC emulator is not responding to client requests.

3. B. The `ipconfig /flushdns` command is used to clear the local DNS resolver cache. The `ipconfig /registerdns` command is used to manually force the host to register itself with dynamic DNS. The `ipconfig /release` command is used to release a DHCP lease from one or more network adapters.

4. C, D, E. The Basic (Clear-Text) and Basic over SSL authentication methods may be used on any type of network. The third method available is Integrated Windows authentication. When operating at the Windows 2000 mixed domain functional mode, Integrated Windows authentication uses the NTLM protocol supported by Windows NT 4.0. When running in native mode, Integrated Windows authentication uses Kerberos v5.

5. A. The standard IMAP4 protocol uses port 143. IMAP4 (SSL) uses port 993, which must be opened on the firewall to allow IMAP4 (SSL) traffic to pass.

6. A. Certificates allow verification of the claim that a given public key actually belongs to a given individual. This helps prevent someone from using a phony key to impersonate someone else.

7. A, B. Basic authentication passes the username and password over the network in unencrypted clear text. Basic over SSL still passes the information over the network but encrypts it using SSL. Neither NTLM nor Kerberos v5 passes the information over the network at all.

8. C. In the situation where only one or a very small number of users are affected, you should start your search by examining what could be the root of the issue. A broken or disconnected network cable would yield the same result as incorrect TCP/IP settings—the inability to contact the rest of the network as required.

9. B, D. Opening port 110 allows POP3 traffic to pass. Opening port 135 allows RPC traffic to pass and thus enables Microsoft Outlook clients. Since the HTTP port 80 and all ports over 1023 are already open, HTTP is already allowed using Windows Integrated authentication.

10. A, B. The sender's own private signing key is used to sign the data. The data is not encrypted in any way during the signing process. The recipient of the data uses the sender's public signing key to verify the digital signature. The message is valid if the public and private signing keys correspond to one another.

11. C. If outside users report that they are having trouble making a connection, one of the first things you should check is whether the firewall is configured to allow the traffic to pass. One way to verify that the problem is with the firewall is to determine whether an internal user can connect to the same server with the same protocol.

12. C, D, E. First, the sender's client generates a secret key to encrypt the actual message and any attachments. Next, the recipient's public encryption key to encrypt the secret key in a lockbox is sent to the recipient. The receiving client then uses the recipient's private encryption key to decrypt the secret key, which is then used to decrypt the message.

13. D. In order to let the appropriate clients access the front-end server, you must open port 135 (RPC) for Outlook, port 110 (POP3) for POP3 clients, and port 443 (HTTP over SSL) for web clients on the exterior firewall. The front-end and back-end servers communicate using port 80 (HTTP), which is already open on the interior firewall. However, the front-end server must also be able to look up information in the Global Catalog so that it knows the appropriate back-end server to use. Therefore, you must also open port 3268 on the interior firewall.

14. A. In order to let the appropriate clients access the front-end server, you must open port 135 (RPC) for Outlook, port 110 (POP3) for POP3 clients, and port 443 (HTTP over SSL) for web clients on the exterior firewall. The front-end and back-end servers communicate using port 80 (HTTP), which is already open on the interior firewall. However, the front-end server must also be able to look up information in the Global Catalog so that it knows the appropriate back-end server to use. Therefore, you must also open port 3268 on the interior firewall.

15. B. In order to let the appropriate clients access the front-end server, you must open port 135 (RPC) for Outlook, port 110 (POP3) for POP3 clients, and port 443 (HTTP over SSL) for web clients on the exterior firewall. The front-end and back-end servers communicate using port 80 (HTTP), which is already open on the interior firewall. However, the front-end server must also be able to look up information in the Global Catalog so that it knows the appropriate back-end server to use. Therefore, you must also open port 3268 on the interior firewall.

16. A. Auditing is a feature that logs the actions of users and groups based on certain criteria. For example, a Windows Server 2003 server can audit successful and failed logon attempts or access to certain files.

17. B. MTA traffic using X.400 over TCP/IP operates on port 102.

18. B. `Nslookup` is used to gather information about and troubleshoot DNS-related name resolution issues. The `pathping` command provides the ability to determine the packet loss along each link in the path and at each router in the path to the destination, which can be particularly helpful when troubleshooting problems where multiple routers and links are involved. `Telnet` can be used to perform basic troubleshooting by verifying that a service is running on a server in instances where ICMP packets are dropped by routers or firewalls. `Netstat` can be used to examine protocol information and also list which ports are currently open on a host.

19. C. Enterprise CAs are used as CAs for an enterprise and require Active Directory access. The stand-alone CA is used to issue certificates to users outside the enterprise and does not require access to the Active Directory. There is no such thing as an organization CA or a domain CA.

20. C. The `pathping` command is a mix of both `ping` and `tracert`. The `pathping` command provides the ability to determine the packet loss along each link in the path and at each router in the path to the destination, which can be particularly helpful when troubleshooting problems where multiple routers and links are involved. `Telnet` can be used to perform basic troubleshooting by verifying that a service is running on a server in instances where ICMP packets are dropped by routers or firewalls. `Nslookup` is used to gather information about and troubleshoot DNS-related name resolution issues. `Netstat` can be used to examine protocol information and also list which ports are currently open on a host.

Glossary

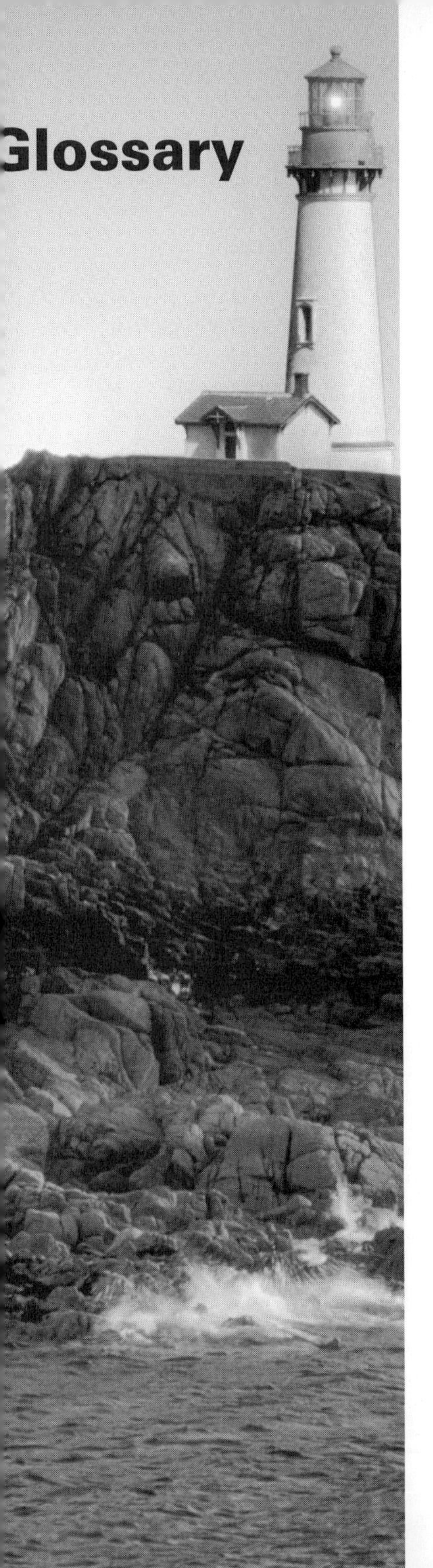

A

Access Control Entries (ACEs) Entries on an Access Control List (ACL) that define a user's permission for an object.

Access Control List (ACL) A list of users and groups allowed to access a resource and the particular permissions each user has been granted or denied.

Active/Active clustering A clustering mode in which a cluster can contain between two and eight nodes. At least one node must be active and at least one node must be passive.

Active/Passive clustering A clustering mode in which each node in the cluster runs one instance of the clustered service. Should a failure of the clustered service occur, that instance is transferred to the other active node.

Active Directory Stores information about objects in a Windows Server 2003 network and makes this information easy for administrators and users to find and use.

Active Directory Account Cleanup Wizard Designed to merge duplicate accounts that may be created when multiple directories are migrated to Active Directory.

Active Directory Connector (ADC) Runs on an Exchange Server 2003 and synchronizes directory information between Active Directory and Exchange 5.*x* servers in the site. ADC also synchronizes configuration information with those servers using the SRS as an intermediary.

Active Server Pages (ASP) A specification for a dynamically generated web page that uses ActiveX scripting. IIS uses ASP to generate many of the pages it displays.

address space The set of remote addresses that can be reached through a particular connector. Each connector must have at least one entry in its address space.

administrative group Used to define administrative boundaries within an Exchange environment.

administrative rights NTFS permissions that determine what administrative tasks a user or group is permitted to perform on a public folder.

age limit A property that specifies the length of time a unit of data may remain in its container (e.g., public folder).

alias An alternative name for an object. In Exchange Server 2003, an alias is normally generated for a user based on the user's name.

All Public Folders The name for the default public folder tree in an Exchange Server 2003 organization. This tree is accessible by all clients that can access public folders.

Anonymous access Accessing a server by logging in using a Windows account set up for general access.

Anonymous authentication *See* Anonymous access.

Application Programming Interface (API) A collection of programming classes and interfaces that provide services used by a program. Other programs can use a program's API to request services or communicate with that program. For example, Windows 98 contains an API referred to as the win32 API. For an application to request a service from Windows 98, it must issue that request using a win32 API.

architecture The description of the components of a product or system, what they are, what they do, and how they relate to each other.

attribute A characteristic of an object. For example, attributes of a mailbox-enabled user include display name and storage limits. The terms *attribute* and *property* are synonymous.

auditing Windows Server 2003 can be configured to monitor and record certain events. This can help diagnose security events. The audit information is written to the Windows Event Log.

authentication A process whereby the credentials of an object, such as a user, must be validated before the object is allowed to access or use another object, such as a server or a protocol. For instance, the Microsoft Exchange Server POP3 protocol can be configured to allow access only to POP3 clients that use the Integrated Windows authentication method.

B

back-end server Exchange Server 2003 allows the use of front-end servers, which accept incoming client requests for information and then forward those requests to back-end servers, which actually hold user information. This lets you balance the load between servers and provide a single namespace from your client's perspective.

backfill The process used in public folder replication to fill in messaging data that is missing from a replica.

Bad Mail folder The folder in which SMTP stores undeliverable messages that cannot be returned to the sender.

Basic (Clear-Text) authentication Requires the user to submit a valid Windows username and password. The username and password are sent across the network as unencrypted clear text.

Basic over Secure Sockets Layer (SSL) authentication Extends the Basic (Clear-Text) authentication method by allowing an SSL server to encrypt the username and password before they are sent across the network.

bridgehead server A server within one bounded area, such as a routing group, that is designated to deliver data or messages to another area.

C

cache mode A new feature in Outlook 2003 that allows clients to work disconnected from the Exchange server. Outlook will periodically reconnect to the Exchange server and synchronize any changes to the user's mailbox.

Categorizer A component of the Exchange Server 2003 routing engine used to resolve the sender and recipient for a message, expanding any distribution groups as needed. In previous versions of Exchange Server, this task was performed by the MTA.

centralized model An administrative model in which one administrator or group of administrators maintains complete control over an entire Exchange organization.

certificate Allows verification of the claim that a given public key actually belongs to a given individual. This helps prevent someone from using a phony key to impersonate someone else. A certificate is similar to a token.

Certificate Authority (CA) The central authority that distributes, publishes, and validates security keys. The Windows Server 2003 Certificates Services component performs this role. *See also* public key, private key.

Certificate Revocation List (CRL) A list containing all certificates in an organization that have been revoked.

Certificate Store A database created during the installation of a Certificate Authority (CA) that is a repository of certificates issued by the CA.

certificate templates Stored in Active Directory and define the attributes for certificates.

Certificate Trust List (CTL) Holds the set of root CAs whose certificates can be trusted. You can designate CTLs for groups, users, or an entire domain.

challenge/response A general term for a class of security mechanisms, including Microsoft authentication methods, that use Windows Server 2003 network security and an encrypted password.

change number One of the constructs used to keep track of public folder replication throughout an organization and to determine whether a public folder is synchronized. The change number is made up of a globally unique identifier for the Information Store and a change counter that is specific to the server on which a public folder resides.

checkpoint file The file (`EDB.CHK`) that contains the point in a transaction log that is the boundary between data that has been committed and data that has not yet been committed to an Exchange database.

child domain Any domain configured underneath another domain in a domain tree.

circular logging The process of writing new information in transaction log files over information that has already been committed. Instead of repeatedly creating new transaction logs, the Exchange database engine "circles back" and reuses log files that have been fully committed to the database. Circular logging keeps down the number of transaction logs on the disk. These logs cannot be used to re-create a database because the logs do not have a complete set of data. The logs contain only the most recent data not yet committed to a database. Circular logging is disabled by default.

Client Access License (CAL) Gives a user the legal right to access an Exchange server. Any client software that has the ability to be a client to Microsoft Exchange Server is legally required to have a CAL purchased for it.

client/server messaging A system in which tasks are divided between the client processes and server processes. Each side works to accomplish specific parts of the task.

cluster A group of servers (also called nodes) that function together as a single unit.

Clustering A Windows service that enables multiple physical servers to be logically grouped together for reasons of fault tolerance.

cluster resource A service or property, such as a storage device, an IP address, or the Exchange System Attendant service, that is defined, monitored, and managed by the cluster service.

coexistence When two different systems of any type are present on the same network. For example, Exchange Server 2003 can coexist with Lotus Notes or previous versions of Exchange.

committed When a transaction is transferred from a transaction log to an Exchange database, it has been committed.

Computer Management snap-in An administrative tool holding a variety of utilities, including Event Viewer and disk management tools.

connection agreement Defined for an Active Directory Connector to replicate specified directory objects on an Exchange 5.*x* server to the Active Directory and can even be configured to replicate at certain times.

connector Components that manage the transport of data between Exchange routing groups (e.g., the routing group connector) or between Exchange and a foreign messaging system (e.g., the X.400 Connector or Lotus Notes Connector).

contact A recipient object that represents a foreign message recipient. Contacts appear in the Global Address List (GAL) and allow Exchange clients to address messages to foreign mail users.

container object An object in the Exchange or Active Directory hierarchy that contains and groups together other objects. For example, the organization object in System Manager is a container object that contains all other objects in the organization.

contiguous namespace When multiple entities share a common namespace. For example, Windows Server 2003 domain trees share a contiguous namespace; domain forests do not.

convergence The process during which the active nodes in a cluster calculate a new, stable state among themselves after the failure of one or more cluster nodes.

copy backup During a copy backup, all selected files are backed up, regardless of how their archive bit is set. After the backup, the archive bit is not changed in any file.

cost value Connectors are assigned cost values that bias them relative to other connectors. For example, Exchange Server would route a message over a connector with a cost value of 1 before a connector with a cost value of 5.

Custom installation An installation type for which you choose the specific components that will be installed.

D

daily backup During this backup, all files that changed on the day of the backup are backed up, and the archive bit is not changed in any file.

Data Encryption Standard (DES) A secret-key encryption method that uses a 56-bit key.

DAVEx An IIS component that passes client requests between W3svc and the Information Store.

DCDiag A command-line utility that can be used to analyze the state of all domain controllers in a forest and report problems that were found.

decentralized model Typically used to define administrative boundaries along real geographical or departmental boundaries. Each location would have its own administrators and its own administrative group.

decryption Translating encrypted data back to plaintext.

dedicated public folder server An Exchange server whose primary purpose is to hold public folder stores and from which the mailbox stores have been removed.

deleted-item retention time The period that items in a public or private store deleted by users are actually retained on the Exchange server.

demilitarized zone (DMZ) *See* perimeter network.

Destination Message queue A temporary queue from which the SMTP service can read a message and pass it along.

diagnostics logging You can configure many Exchange services to log several different levels of events to the Windows Event Log for use in troubleshooting.

differential backup A method in which all files that have been changed since the last full backup are backed up. *See also* incremental backup.

digital signature A process of digitally signing data using public and private keys so that the recipient of the data can verify the authenticity of both the sender and the data.

directory A hierarchy that stores information about objects in a system. A Directory Service (DS) manages the directory and makes it available to users on the network.

directory replication The transferring of directory information from one server to another. In Active Directory, directory information is replicated between domain controllers. In previous versions of Exchange, directory information is replicated between Exchange servers.

directory replication bridgehead server In previous versions of Exchange, the Exchange server designated as the server that will send site directory information to another site. Only one server in a site can be assigned to replicate information with each remote site. There can be more than one directory replication bridgehead server in a site, but each must connect with a unique remote site. However, one server can perform directory replication with multiple remote sites.

directory rights Used to configure the NTFS permissions that determine who can perform modifications on the public folder object that is stored in Active Directory.

Directory Service (DS) In Exchange 5.*x*, creates and manages the storage of all information about Exchange objects, such as the organization, site, servers, mailboxes, distribution lists, and public folders. This functionality is assumed by Active Directory in Exchange Server 2003.

Disaster Recovery Mode A mode in which you can run Exchange Server 2003 setup that lets you recover an Exchange installation after a failure.

discretionary access control list (DACL) A list of Access Control Entries (ACEs) that give users and groups specific permissions on an object.

discussion thread A collection of postings to a public folder related to a single subject.

dismounting The process of taking a public or private store offline.

distribution group An Active Directory group formed so that a single e-mail message can be sent to the group and then sent automatically to all members of the group. Unlike security groups, distribution groups don't provide any security function.

domain A group of computers and other resources that are part of a Windows Server 2003 network and share a common directory database.

domain controller A computer running Windows Server 2003 that validates user network access and manages Active Directory.

domain forest A group of one or more domain trees that do not necessarily form a contiguous namespace but may share a common schema and Global Catalog.

Domain Name Service (DNS) The primary provider of name resolution within an organization.

DomainPrep An Exchange Server 2003 setup switch that is used to prepare an Active Directory domain prior to Exchange installation.

domain tree A hierarchical arrangement of one or more Windows Active Directory domains that share a common namespace.

DNS *See* Domain Name Service (DNS).

E

EHLO The ESMTP command used by one host to initiate communications with another host.

e-mail Electronic messages sent between users of different computers.

encryption The process of scrambling data to make it unreadable. The intended recipient will decrypt the data into plaintext in order to read it.

Enterprise CA Acts as a Certificate Authority for an enterprise and requires access to the Active Directory. *See also* Certificate Authority (CA).

Enterprise Edition Edition of Exchange Server 2003 that contains all the features of the Standard Edition as well as the ability to have four storage groups with five stores each and also allows stores to be over 16 GB in size.

Event Log A set of three logs (Application, Security, and System) maintained by Windows Server. The operating system and many applications, such as Exchange Server 2003, write software events to the Event Log.

Exchange Administration Delegation Wizard Tool in System Manager that lets you select a user or group and assign them a specific administrative role in an Exchange organization. *See also* Exchange Administrator role, Exchange Full Administrator role, Exchange View-Only Administrator role.

Exchange Administrator role Gives users the same full administrative capability as the Exchange Full Administrator role but does not give them permission to modify permissions for objects. *See also* Exchange Administration Delegation Wizard, Exchange Full Administrator role.

Exchange DSAccess A component that enables other Exchange Server 2003 components to communicate with Active Directory using the LDAP protocol.

Exchange Full Administrator role Gives users full administrative capability within an organization. They can add, delete, and rename objects, as well as modify permissions on objects. *See also* Exchange Administration Delegation Wizard.

Exchange Interprocess Communication Layer (ExIPC) The process that manages several queues used for communications between IIS and Exchange Server 2003.

Exchange System Manager A snap-in for the Microsoft Management Console used to manage an Exchange Server 2003 organization.

Exchange View-Only Administrator role Lets users view Exchange configuration information but not modify it in any way. *See also* Exchange Administration Delegation Wizard.

expanding a distribution group The process of determining the individual addresses contained within a distribution group. This process is performed by the home server of the user sending the message to the group unless an expansion server is specified for the group.

extended permissions Permissions added to the standard Windows Server 2003 permissions when Exchange Server 2003 is installed.

Extensible Storage Engine (ESE) The database engine used by Exchange Server 2003.

F

failback The process of cluster resources moving back to their preferred node after the preferred node has resumed active membership in the cluster.

failover The process of moving resources off a cluster node that has failed to another cluster node. If any of the cluster resources on an active node becomes unresponsive or unavailable for a period time exceeding the configured threshold, failover will occur.

failover pair In this cluster operation mode, resources are configured to failover between two specific cluster nodes. This is accomplished by listing only these two specific nodes in the possible owner list for the resources of concern. This mode of operation could be used in either Active/Active or Active/Passive clustering.

failover ring In this cluster operation mode, each node in the cluster running an instance of the application or resource being clustered. When one node fails, the clustered resource is moved to the next node in the sequence.

firewall A set of mechanisms that separate and protect your internal network from unauthorized external users and networks. Firewalls can restrict inbound and outbound traffic, as well as analyze all traffic between your network and the outside.

folder-based application An application built within a public folder by customizing properties of the folder, such as permissions, views, rules, and the folder forms library to store and present data to users.

foreign system A non-Exchange messaging system.

ForestPrep An Exchange Server 2003 setup switch that is used to prepare an Active Directory forest prior to Exchange installation.

forest root domain The first domain installed in a domain forest and the basis for the naming of all domains in the forest.

Forms Registry Stores the Outlook Web Access (OWA) forms rendered by Internet Information Services (IIS) and passed to the client.

frame The unit of information sent by a Data Link protocol, such as Ethernet or Token Ring.

free/busy Terminology used in the Microsoft Schedule+ application to denote an unscheduled period of time (free) or a scheduled period of time (busy).

front-end server *See* back-end server.

full-text indexing A feature that can be enabled for a store in which every word in the store (including those in attachments) is indexed for much faster search results.

Fully Qualified Domain Name (FQDN) The full DNS path of an Internet host. An example is `sales.dept4.widget.com`.

function call An instruction in a program that calls (invokes) a function. For example, MAPIReadMail is a MAPI function call.

G

GAL *See* Global Address List (GAL).

gateway Third-party software that permits Exchange to interoperate with a foreign message system. *See also* connector.

general-purpose trees Public folder trees added to an Exchange organization beyond the default public folder tree. General-purpose trees are not accessible by MAPI clients such as Microsoft Outlook.

Global Address List (GAL) A database of all the recipients in an Exchange organization, such as mailboxes, distribution lists, custom recipients, and public folders.

Global Catalog Used to hold information about all objects in a forest. The Global Catalog enables users and applications to find objects in an Active Directory domain tree if the user or application knows one or more attributes of the target object.

group A collection of users and other groups that may be assigned permissions or made part of an e-mail distribution list.

groupware Any application that allows groups of people to store and share information.

H

heartbeat A special communication among members of a cluster that keeps all members aware of one another's existence (and thus their operational state).

HELO The SMTP command used by one host to initiate communications with another host.

hierarchy Any structure or organization that uses class, grade, or rank to arrange objects.

hot standby In this cluster operation mode, a passive node can take on the resources of any failed active node.

HTML *See* HyperText Markup Language (HTML).

HTTP *See* HyperText Transfer Protocol (HTTP).

HTTP Digest authentication An Internet standard that allows authentication of clients to occur using a series of challenges and responses over HTTP.

HyperText Markup Language (HTML) The script language used to create content for the World Wide Web (WWW). HTML can create hyperlinks between objects on the Web.

HyperText Transfer Protocol (HTTP) The Internet protocol used to transfer information on the World Wide Web (WWW).

I

IIS metabase The Registry-like database of configuration information maintained by Internet Information Services.

Inbox The storage folder that receives new incoming messages.

Inbox Repair tool A utility (`Scanpst.exe`) that is used to repair corrupt personal folder (PST) files.

incremental backup Method in which all files that have changed since the last normal or incremental backup are backed up.

Information Store *See* `Store.exe`.

inheritance The process through which permissions are passed down from a parent container to objects inside that container (child objects).

Infrastructure master An operations master role server that is responsible for updating references from objects in its domain to objects in other domains.

Installable File System (IFS) Permits normal network client redirectors, such as Exchange, to share folders and items. This is a means of exposing the Exchange Information Store to users and applications on the network.

installer package (MSI file) One of the files generated by Windows Installer; used to control configuration information during installation. The installer package contains a database that describes the configuration information. *See also* installer transform (MST file).

installer transform (MST file) One of the files generated by Windows Installer; used to control configuration information during installation. The transform file contains modifications that are to be made as Windows Installer installs Outlook. *See also* installer package (MSI file).

Integrated Windows authentication Requires the user to provide a valid Windows username and password. However, the user's credentials are never sent across the network. If you are running in the Windows 2000 mixed domain functional level, this method uses the NTLM authentication protocol used by Windows NT 4.0. If your network is running at the Windows 2000 native domain functional level or the Windows Server 2003 domain functional level, this method uses Kerberos v5.

Internet Information Services (IIS) A built-in component of Windows Server 2003 that allows access to resources on the server through various Internet protocols, such as POP3, IMAP4, and HTTP.

Internet Mail Connection Wizard A new wizard in Exchange Server 2003 that makes it easy to create and configure an SMTP connector to send and receive Internet mail.

Internet Message Access Protocol version 4 (IMAP4) An Internet retrieval protocol that enables clients to access and manipulate messages in their mailbox on a remote server. IMAP4 provides additional functions over POP3, such as access to subfolders (not merely the Inbox folder), and selective downloading of messages.

ipconfig A command-line utility that can be used to display and modify TCP/IP information about all installed network adapters. Common uses include flushing the local DNS resolver cache and releasing and renewing DHCP leases.

K

Kerberos version 5 (v5) The primary form of user authentication used by Windows Server 2003.

key A randomly generated number used to implement advanced security, such as encryption or digital signatures. *See also* key pair, public key, private key.

key pair A key that is divided into two mathematically related halves. One half (the public key) is made public; the other half (the private key) is known by only one user.

L

leaf object An object in a Microsoft Management Console window that does not contain any other objects.

Lightweight Directory Access Protocol (LDAP) An Internet protocol used for client access to an X.500-based directory, such as Active Directory.

link Generic term referring to the connection between two systems. In Exchange, a link is generally synonymous with a connector.

Link State Algorithm The process used by Exchange Server 2003 to apply the information in the link state table when determining a route.

link state table A table maintained by Exchange Server 2003 that specifies the routes a message can pass over and whether any given link on the route is up or down.

Live Communications Server An enterprise-level real-time communications product that replaces the Exchange Instant Messaging feature in Exchange 2000 Server.

local delivery The delivery of a message to a recipient object that resides on the same server as the sender.

Local Procedure Call (LPC) When a program issues an instruction that is executed on the same computer as the program executing the instruction. *See also* Remote Procedure Call (RPC).

lockbox The process of using a secret key to encrypt a message and its attachments and then using a public key pair to encrypt and decrypt the secret key.

Lotus Notes Connector An Exchange Server 2003 connector that allows the exchange of messages and the synchronization of directories between an Exchange organization and a Lotus Notes system.

M

Mail and Directory Management (MADMAN) MIB A specialized version of the base Management Information Base that was created for monitoring messaging systems. *See also* Management Information Base (MIB).

mailbox The generic term referring to a container that holds messages, such as incoming and outgoing messages.

mailbox-enabled user A user who has been assigned an Exchange Server mailbox.

mailbox store A set of two databases (a rich-text file and a streaming media file) on an Exchange server that hold mailboxes. *See also* store.

mail-enabled user A user who has been given an e-mail address but no mailbox.

Mail Exchanger (MX) Record A record in a DNS database that indicates the SMTP mail host for an organization.

mainframe computing Consists of a powerful host computer, such as a mainframe computer or minicomputer, and numerous input-output devices attached to the host, such as terminals, printers, and personal computers running terminal emulation software.

majority node set cluster A new high-end clustering model first available in Windows Server 2003 that allows for two or more cluster nodes to be configured so that multiple storage devices can be used. The cluster configuration data is kept on all disks across the cluster, and the Microsoft Clustering Service is responsible for keeping this data up-to-date.

Management Information Base (MIB) A set of configurable objects defined for management by the SNMP protocol.

MAPI *See* Messaging Application Programming Interface (MAPI).

MAPI client A messaging client that uses the Messaging Application Programming Interface (MAPI) to connect to a messaging server. *See also* Messaging Application Programming Interface (MAPI).

MAPI subsystem The second layer of the MAPI architecture; this component is shared by all applications that require its services and is therefore considered a *subsystem* of the operating system.

message state information Information that identifies the state of a message in a public folder. Message state information is made up of a change number, a time stamp, and a predecessor change list.

Message Transfer Agent (MTA) X.400 component that is used to route messages in previous versions of Exchange Server and is still used with the X.400 Connector.

Message Transfer Agent (MTA) Service Transport Stack A set of information about the software and hardware making up the underlying network that is used by an X.400 Connector. The use of the transport stack allows for a layer of abstraction between the X.400 Connector and the network itself.

Message Tracking Center (MTC) An interface within System Manager used to search for messages sent within an Exchange organization and then track the route taken by those messages.

Messaging Application Programming Interface (MAPI) An object-oriented programming interface for messaging services, developed by Microsoft.

Microsoft Clustering Service (MSCS) A Windows service that provides for highly available server solutions through a process known as failover. An MSCS cluster consists of two more nodes (members) that are configured such that upon the failure of one node, any of the remaining cluster nodes can transfer the failed node's resources to itself, thus keeping the resources available for client access.

Minimum installation This installation type installs only the Exchange Server 2003 software and the basic Messaging and Collaboration components.

Microsoft Management Console (MMC) A framework application in which snap-ins are loaded to provide the management of various network resources. System Manager is an example of a snap-in.

Microsoft Office Outlook 2003 The premier client application for use with Exchange Server 2003.

Microsoft Search Service The service that performs full-text indexing of mailbox and public stores.

migration Moving resources, such as mailboxes, messages, etc., from one messaging system to another.

mixed mode In mixed mode, Exchange Server 2003 can coexist and communicate with previous versions of Exchange Server in the same organization.

Monitoring and Status tool A tool within System Manager used to set up the services monitored on a server and configure the notifications that are triggered when a monitored service fails.

mounting The process of bringing a private or public store online. *See also* dismounting.

Multipurpose Internet Mail Extensions (MIME) An Internet protocol that enables the encoding of binary content within mail messages. For example, MIME could be used to encode a graphics file or word processing document as an attachment to a text-based mail message. The recipient of the message would have to be using MIME also to decode the attachment. MIME is newer than UUENCODE and in many systems has replaced it. *See also* Secure/Multipurpose Internet Mail Extensions (S/MIME), UUENCODE.

multimaster replication model A model in which every replica of a public folder is considered a master copy.

MX *See* Mail Exchanger (MX).

N

name resolution The DNS process of mapping a domain name to its IP address.

namespace Any bounded area in which a given name can be resolved.

native mode In a native-mode organization, only Exchange Server 2003 or Exchange 2000 Server is running, and the full Exchange Server 2003 functionality is present.

nbtstat A command-line utility that is used to resolve NetBIOS names to IP addresses.

Network Load Balancing A service that is installed as a network interface driver on all participating members and that uses a mathematical algorithm to equally distribute incoming request to all members of NLB cluster. Incoming client requests are assigned to cluster members based on their current loading level but can be modified through the use of filtering and affinity for applications that require session state data to be maintained, such as an e-commerce application that uses cookies to place items in a shopping cart for purchase.

Network News Transfer Protocol (NNTP) An Internet protocol used to transfer newsgroup information between newsgroup servers and clients (newsreaders) and between newsgroup servers.

NetDiag A command-line utility that is used to troubleshoot and isolate network connectivity problems by performing a number of tests to determine the exact state of a server.

netstat A command-line utility that is used to display TCP/IP connection information and protocol statistics for a computer.

newsfeed The newsgroup data that is sent from one newsgroup server to other newsgroup servers.

NNTP *See* Network News Transfer Protocol (NNTP).

node In a Microsoft Management Console window, a node is any object that can be configured. In clustering, a node is one of the computers that is part of a cluster.

normal backup During this backup, all selected files are backed up, regardless of how their archive bit is set. After the backup, the archive bit is set to off for all files, indicating that those files have been backed up.

notification Defines the event that is triggered when a service or resource being watched by a server or link monitor fails. Notifications can send e-mail and alerts and even run custom scripts.

Novell GroupWise Connector An Exchange Server 2003 connector that allows the exchange of messages and the synchronization of directories between an Exchange organization and a Novell GroupWise organization.

nslookup A command-line utility that can be used to gather information about the DNS infrastructure inside and outside an organization and troubleshoot DNS-related problems.

O

object The representation, or abstraction, of an entity. As an object, it contains properties, also called attributes, that can be configured. For example, each Exchange server is represented as an object in System Manager. An Exchange server object can have properties that give certain administrators permission to configure that server.

Object Linking and Embedding version 2 (OLE 2) The Microsoft protocol that specifies how programs can share objects and therefore create compound documents.

Office Custom Installation Wizard Part of the Office Resource Kit that lets you customize and automate installations of Microsoft Office.

Offline Address Book (OAB) A copy stored on a client's computer of part or all of the server-based Global Address List (GAL). An OAB allows a client to address messages while not connected to their server.

offline folder *See* Offline Storage folder (OST).

Offline Storage folder (OST) Folders located on a client's computer that contain replicas of server-based folders. An OST allows a client to access and manipulate copies of server data while not connected to their server. When the client reconnects to their server, they can have their OST resynchronized with the master folders on the server.

OLE 2 *See* Object Linking and Embedding version 2 (OLE 2).

Open Shortest Path First (OSPF) A routing protocol developed for IP networks based on the Shortest Path First or Link State Algorithm.

Organization The highest-level object in the Microsoft Exchange hierarchy.

organizational unit An Active Directory container into which objects can be grouped for permissions management.

Originator/Recipient Address (O/R Address) An X.400 address scheme that uses a hierarchical method to denote where on an X.400 network a recipient resides. An example is: c=us;a= ;p =widgetnet;o=widget;s=wilson;g=jay;.

Outlook Web Access (OWA) A service that allows users to connect to Exchange Server and access mailboxes and public folders using a web browser.

P

patch files Temporary logs that store transactions while a backup is taking place. Transactions in these logs are committed when the backup is finished.

pathping A new command that is a mix of both `ping` and `tracert`. The `pathping` command provides the ability to determine the packet loss along each link in the path and at each router in the path to the destination, which can be particularly helpful when troubleshooting problems where multiple routers and links are involved.

Performance Monitor *See* Performance snap-in.

Performance snap-in A utility used to log and chart the performance of various hardware and software components of a system. In various documentation, the Performance snap-in is also referred to as Performance Monitor, Performance tool, and System Monitor.

Performance tool *See* Performance snap-in.

perimeter network A network formed by using two firewalls to separate an internal network from the Internet and then placing certain servers, such as an Exchange front-end server, between the two firewalls. This is also referred to as a demilitarized zone (DMZ).

permission Provides specific authorization or denial to a user to perform an action on an object.

Personal Address Book (PAB) An address book created by a user and stored on that user's computer or a server.

Personal STore (PST) folder Folder created by a user and used for message storage instead of using their mailbox in the private store. PSTs can be located on a user's computer or on a server.

Pickup folder Used for outbound messages on some SMTP hosts. Exchange Server 2003 creates, but does not normally use, this folder.

PING Packet Internet Groper. The basic network connectivity troubleshooting tool that works by sending a series of ICMP Echo Request datagrams to a destination and waiting for the corresponding ICMP Echo Reply datagrams to come back. The return packets are then used to determine how many datagrams are getting through, the response time, and the TTL (time to live).

plaintext Unencrypted data. Synonymous with clear text.

Point-to-Point Protocol (PPP) An Internet protocol used for direct communication between two nodes. Commonly used by Internet users and their Internet Service Provider on the serial line point-to-point connection over a modem.

policy A collection of configuration settings that you can apply across any number of objects in the Active Directory at once. System policies affect server objects such as servers, mailbox stores, and public stores. Recipient policies affect objects such as users and groups.

polling Process that queries a server-based mailbox for new mail.

POP3 *See* Post Office Protocol version 3 (POP3).

port number A numeric identifier assigned to an application. Transport protocols such as TCP and UDP use the port number to identify to which application to deliver a packet.

Post Office Protocol version 3 (POP3) An Internet protocol used for client retrieval of mail from a server-based mailbox.

predecessor change list A list of all of the Information Stores that have made changes to a message and the most recent change number assigned by each Information Store on the list.

previous logs A log file that has filled to its 5-MB limit and has been renamed so that a new current log file can be created. Previous logs may contain uncommitted transactions.

Primary Domain Controller (PDC) emulator An operations master role server that is responsible for authenticating non–Active Directory clients, such as Windows 95 or Windows 98 clients. The PDC emulator is responsible for processing password changes from these clients and is also the responsible server for time synchronization within the domain.

private folder *See* mailbox.

private key The half of a key pair that is known by only the pair's user and is used to decrypt data and to digitally sign messages.

private store A folder used to hold mailboxes on an Exchange server; normally accessible only by a specified user.

property A characteristic of an object. Properties of a mailbox include display name and storage limits. The terms *property* and *attribute* are synonymous.

public folder A folder stored in a public store on an Exchange server and accessible to multiple users.

public folder hierarchy The relative position of all of the folders in a public folder tree.

public folder replication The transferring of public folder data to replicas of that folder on other servers.

Public Folder Replication Agent (PFRA) The Exchange service that governs the public folder replication process.

public folder referral The process by which a client can locate a requested public folder outside of their home Exchange server.

public folder tree A hierarchy of public folders associated with a particular public store.

public key The half of a key pair that is published for anyone to read and is used when encrypting data and verifying digital signatures.

public-key encryption An encryption method that employs a key pair consisting of a public and a private key.

public key infrastructure (PKI) A system of components working together to verify the identity of users who transfer data on a system and to encrypt that data if needed.

public store A set of two databases that hold public folders on an Exchange server. *See also* store.

pull Procedure in which a user finds and retrieves information, such as when browsing a public folder. Users accessing a public folder containing a company's employee handbook is a type of pull communication.

pull feed Procedure in which a newsgroup server requests newsfeed information from another newsgroup server. The opposite of a push feed.

public folder A folder used to store data for a group of users. Some of the features of a public folder are permissions, views, and rules.

purging The process of deleting a user's mailbox in System Manager.

push Procedure in which information is sent (pushed) to users. Users do not need to find and retrieve (pull) the information. Exchange Server pushes incoming messages to MAPI-based Exchange clients.

push feed Procedure in which a newsgroup server sends information to another newsgroup server without requiring the receiving server to request it. The opposite of a pull feed.

Q

Queue folder A folder in which messages that have yet to be delivered are stored.

Queue Viewer A part of System Manager that lets you view and manipulate the messages in a queue.

query-based distribution group An e-mail enabled distribution group whose group membership is determined by the results of an LDAP query created when the group is configured. Query-based distribution groups are new in Exchange Server 2003.

quorum disk The disk set that contains definitive cluster configuration data. All members of an MSCS cluster must have continuous, reliable access to the data that is contained on a quorum disk. Information contained on the quorum disk includes data about the nodes that are participating in the cluster, the applications and resources that are defined within the cluster, and the current status of each member, application, and resource.

R

random failover In this cluster operation mode, the clustered resource will be randomly failed over to an available cluster node.

recipient An object that can receive a message. Recipient objects include users, contacts, groups, and public folders.

recipient policies *See* policy.

recovery server A server separate from the organization that is used as a dummy server for recovering individual mailboxes or messages from a backup.

Recovery Storage Group A new feature in Exchange Server 2003 that provides a special storage group on a server that can be used for performing restorations without the need to use an alternative recovery forest or the need to take the store offline for an extended period of time.

Relative Identity (RID) master An operations master role server that is responsible for maintaining the uniqueness of every object within its domain. When a new Active Directory object is created, it is assigned a unique security identifier (SID). The SID consists of a domain specific SID that is the same for all objects created in that domain and a relative identifier (RID), which is unique amongst all objects within that domain

replica A copy of a public folder located on an Exchange server.

replication The transferring of a copy of data to another location, such as another server or site. *See also* directory replication, public folder replication.

remote delivery The delivery of a message to a recipient that does not reside on the same server as the sender.

Remote Procedure Call (RPC) A set of protocols for issuing instructions that can be sent over a network for execution. A client computer makes a request to a server computer, and the results are sent to the client computer. The computer issuing the request and the computer performing the request are separated remotely over a network. RPCs are a key ingredient in distributed processing and client/server computing. *See also* Local Procedure Call (LPC).

reserve log files Two transaction log files created by Exchange Server that are reserved for use when the server runs out of disk space.

resolving an address The process of determining where (on which physical server) an object with a particular address resides.

resource group Functions in a cluster that are not bound to a specific computer and can fail over to another node.

rich-text (EBD) file The database used by Exchange Server to store general messages and attachments.

Rich-Text Format (RTF) A Microsoft format protocol that includes bolding, highlighting, italics, underlining, and many other format types.

role A group of permissions that define which activities a user or group can perform with regard to an object.

root CA Resides at the top of a Certificate Authority hierarchy; is trusted unconditionally by a client. All certificate chains terminate at a root CA. *See also* Certificate Authority (CA).

root domain The top domain in a domain tree.

routing group A collection of Exchange servers that have full-time, full-mesh, reliable connections between each and every server. Messages sent between any two servers within a routing group are delivered directly from the source server to the destination server.

Routing Group Connector (RGC) The primary connector used to connect routing groups in an organization. The RGC uses SMTP as its default transport mechanism.

Routing Group Master A server that maintains data about all of the servers running Exchange Server 2003 in the routing group.

RPC over HTTP A new mode of connecting remote Outlook 2003 clients to an Exchange Server 2003 organization without requiring the use of a Virtual Private Network (VPN) or Outlook Web Access (OWA). RPCs are passed over the HTTP connection and secured with SSL encryption. Basic authentication is used to authenticate the user and is also protected by the SSL.

rule A set of instructions that define how a message is handled when it reaches a folder.

S

scalable The ability of a system to grow to handle greater traffic, volume, usage, etc.

Schedule+ Free Busy public folder A system folder that contains calendaring and synchronization information for Exchange users.

schema The set of rules defining a directory's hierarchy, objects, attributes, etc.

Schema master An operations master role server that controls all updates and changes that are made to the schema.

secret key A security key that can be used to encrypt data and that is known only by the sender and the recipients whom the sender informs.

Secure/Multipurpose Internet Mail Extensions (S/MIME) An Internet protocol that enables mail messages to be digitally signed, encrypted, and decrypted.

Secure Sockets Layer (SSL) An Internet protocol that provides secure and authenticated TCP/IP connections. A client and server establish a "handshake" whereby they agree on a level of security they will use, such as authentication requirements and encryption. SSL can be used to encrypt sensitive data for transmission.

security group A group defined in Active Directory that can be assigned permissions. All members of the group gain the permissions given to the group.

Server License Provides the legal right to install and operate Microsoft Exchange Server 2003 (or another server product) on a single-server machine.

service provider A MAPI program that provides messaging-oriented services to a client. There are three main types of service providers: address book, message store, and message transport.

Service Transport Stack *See* Message Transfer Agent (MTA) Service Transport Stack.

shared-file messaging system A messaging system in which active clients deposit messages and poll for new messages in shared folders on a passive server.

signing The process of placing a digital signature on a message.

simple display name An alternate name for the mailbox that appears when, for some reason, the full display name cannot.

Simple Mail Transfer Protocol (SMTP) The Internet protocol used to transfer mail messages. It is now the default transport protocol for Exchange 2000 Server.

Simple Network Management Protocol (SNMP) Internet protocol used to manage heterogeneous computers, operating systems, and applications. Because of its wide acceptance and applicability, SNMP is well suited for enterprise-wide management.

single-instance storage Storing only one copy. A message that is sent to multiple recipients homed in the same storage group has only one copy (i.e., instance) stored on that server. Each recipient is given a pointer to that copy of the message.

single-node cluster A cluster model useful for testing and application development that has only one cluster node that uses either local storage or an external storage device.

single-quorum cluster The standard clustering model that comes to mind when most people think of clustering. In the single-quorum model, all nodes are attached to the external shared storage device. All cluster configuration data is kept on this storage device; thus, all cluster nodes have access to the quorum data.

site A logical grouping of servers in previous versions of Exchange (prior to Exchange 2000 Server) that are connected by a full mesh (every server is directly connected to every other server) and communicate using high-bandwidth RPC. All servers in a site can authenticate one another either because they are homed in the same Windows domain or because of trust relationships configured between separate Windows domains. A site is also a group of Windows servers that are connected with full-time, reliable connections.

Site Connector A connector used to connect Exchange 5.*x* sites. The Site Connector has been replaced by the Routing Group Connector (RGC) in Exchange Server 2003.

Site Consistency Checker (SCC) An updated version of the Knowledge Consistency Checker from Exchange 5.*x*. The SCC ensures that knowledge consistency is maintained for sites and administrative groups when operating in mixed mode.

Site Replication Service (SRS) Runs on an Exchange Server 2003 and simulates an Exchange 5.*x* system from the viewpoint of the Exchange 5.*x* servers in a site. SRS also provides a pathway for replicating configuration information between Active Directory and Exchange 5.*x* servers.

Site Replication Service (SRS) database Contains information maintained by the Site Replication Service (SRS).

smart host An SMTP host designated to receive all outgoing SMTP mail. The smart host then forwards the mail to the relevant destination.

S/MIME *See* Secure/Multipurpose Internet Mail Extensions (S/MIME).

SMTP *See* Simple Mail Transfer Protocol (SMTP).

SMTP Connector Using SMTP as its transport mechanism, the SMTP Connector can be used to connect routing groups to one another and to connect Exchange to a foreign SMTP system.

SMTP virtual server A logical representation of the SMTP protocol on a physical server.

SNMP *See* Simple Network Management Protocol (SNMP).

spooling The process used by SMTP to temporarily store messages that cannot be delivered immediately.

stand-alone CA Used to issue certificates to users who are outside the enterprise and who do not require access to the Active Directory. *See also* Certificate Authority (CA), Enterprise CA.

Standard Edition The basic edition of Exchange Server 2003 that includes support for only basic features. The Standard Edition is limited to having one storage group, and stores are limited to only 16 GB in size.

standard permissions Permissions that are defined in a standard installation of Windows Server 2003. Extended permissions are created when Exchange Server 2003 is installed.

storage group A collection of stores (up to four) that all share a common set of transaction logs.

storage limit A limit placed on the amount of data that can be stored in a mailbox or public folder. Limits can be assigned at the store level and at the folder or mailbox level.

store There are two types of stores in Exchange 2000 Server: public stores that hold public folders meant to be accessed by groups of users and private stores that hold user mailboxes. Each store is composed of two databases: a rich-text database and a streaming media database.

Store.exe The actual process that governs the use of stores on an Exchange server. Often referred to as the Information Store service.

store-and-forward A delivery method that does not require the sender and recipient to have simultaneous interaction. Instead, when a message is sent, it is transferred to the next appropriate location in the network, which temporarily stores it, makes a routing decision, and forwards the message to the next appropriate network location. This process occurs until the message is ultimately delivered to the intended recipient or an error condition causes the message to be returned to the sender.

streaming media (STM) file One of two files that compose every Exchange store, the streaming media file is used to hold content that does not need to be translated by Exchange Server before it is presented to the client.

subordinate CA A CA found underneath the root CA in the CA hierarchy and maybe even under other subordinate CAs. *See also* Certificate Authority (CA), root CA.

subsystem A software component that, when loaded, extends the operating system by providing additional services. The MAPI program, `MAPI32.DLL`, is an example of a subsystem. `MAPI32.DLL` loads on top of the Windows 98 or Windows XP operating system and provides messaging services.

system folders Special public folders that are hidden by default and are only accessible through System Manager. System folders contain items that facilitate the capabilities of many Exchange clients, such as collaborative scheduling in Outlook.

System Manager *See* Exchange System Manager.

System Monitor *See* Performance snap-in.

system policies *See* policy.

system state backup A form of backup that includes the Windows Registry, the IIS metabase, and the Active Directory (if run on a domain controller).

T

Task Manager Displays the programs and processes running on a computer. It also displays various performance information, such as CPU and memory usage.

telnet A text-based command-line tool that allows you to remotely communicate with a host.

template An object, such as a user or group, that contains configuration information that is applicable to multiple users. Objects for each user can be easily created by copying the template and filling in individual information.

time stamp The Information Store marks each message with the time and date the message was last modified.

TLS encryption Transport Layer Security (TLS) encryption is a generic security protocol similar to Secure Sockets Layer encryption.

token The packet of security information a Certificate Authority sends to a client during advanced security setup. Information in the packet includes the client's public key and its expiration. A token is similar to a certificate.

top-level folders The folders found in the root level of a public folder tree.

tracert A command-line utility that uses ICMP packets to determine the path that an IP datagram takes to reach its final destination.

transaction log A file used to quickly write data. That data is later written to the relevant Exchange database file. It is quicker to write to a transaction log file because the writes are done sequentially (i.e., one right after the other). Transaction log files can also be used to replay transactions from the log when rebuilding an Exchange database. All stores in a single storage group share the same set of transaction logs.

Triple Data Encryption Standard (3DES) A newer, more secure, variant of the DES standard that uses three 56-bit keys, one after another, to produce a 168-bit key.

Typical installation This option installs the Exchange Server software, the basic Messaging and Collaboration components, and the System Manager snap-in program. It does not include the additional connectors.

U

Uniform Resource Identifier (URI) A generic term for all types of addresses that refer to objects on the World Wide Web and private networks.

Uniform Resource Locator (URL) An addressing method used to identify Internet servers and documents.

universal Inbox A single folder or service that receives incoming items from all outside sources and of all types, such as e-mail, voice mail, faxes, pages, etc.

URL *See* Uniform Resource Locator (URL).

Usenet A network within the Internet that is composed of numerous servers containing information on a variety of topics. Each organized topic is called a newsgroup.

user object An object in Active Directory that is associated with a person on the network. Users can be mailbox-enabled or mail-enabled in Exchange Server 2003.

UUENCODE Stands for UNIX-to-UNIX Encode, and is a protocol used to encode binary information within mail messages. UUENCODE is older than MIME. *See also* Multipurpose Internet Mail Extensions (MIME.)

V

Virus Scanning API (VSAPI) An API provided in Exchange Server 2003 that allows antivirus vendors to develop products that more completely integrate with Exchange Server 2003. The VSAPI in Exchange Server 2003 allows antivirus products to run on Exchange Server 2003 servers that do not have any mailbox stores, such as gateway or bridgehead servers, in an attempt to catch viruses at the entry point into an organization.

virtual server A representation of a particular protocol (such as HTTP or SMTP) that is separately configurable from other virtual servers for the same protocol.

Volume Shadow Copy A new feature in the Windows Server 2003 Backup Utility to back up open files as if they were closed at the moment of the backup event.

W

W3svc The World Wide Web (WWW) publishing service of Internet Information Server (IIS).

Web The World Wide Web (WWW).

Web Storage System The name given to the Exchange Server 2003 storage system to emphasize the new web-enabled features that Exchange Server 2003 Server supports.

Web store A term used to refer to the Information Store in Exchange Server 2003, particularly to its web-enhanced capabilities.

well-known port numbers Numbers that are commonly used as the TCP port numbers for popular applications.

Windows 2000 mixed domain functional level The domain functional level that allows Windows NT 4.0 backup domain controllers to exist and function within a Windows 2003 domain.

Windows 2000 native domain functional level The domain functional level that requires all domain controllers to be Windows 2000 Server or Windows Server 2003 and does not provide support for Windows NT 4.0 backup domain controllers.

Windows Event Log *See* Event Log.

Windows site A group of computers that exist on one or more IP subnets. Computers within a site must be connected by a fast, reliable network connection.

Windows Internet Naming System (WINS) A name resolution service for resolving NetBIOS names on a Windows network.

Windows Server 2003 domain functional level The highest domain functional level in Windows 2003, which implements all the new features of Windows 2003 Active Directory.

World Wide Web (WWW) The collection of computers on the Internet using protocols such as HTML and HTTP.

WWW *See* World Wide Web (WWW).

X

X.400 An International Telecommunications Union (ITU) standard for message exchange.

X.400 Connector Using X.400 as its transport mechanism, the X.400 Connector can connect routing groups or connect Exchange to a foreign X.400 messaging system. An X.400 Connector requires the use of a TCP/IP or X.25 MTA Service Transport Stack.

X.500 An International Telecommunications Union (ITU) standard for directory services.

X.509 certificate The most widely used format for certificates, X.509 certificates contain not only the public key but also information that identifies the user and the organization that issued the certificate.

Index

Note to the Reader: Throughout this index **boldfaced** page numbers indicate primary discussions of a topic. *Italicized* page numbers indicate illustrations.

A

B

C

F

G

H

I

J

K

L

M

N

O

P

Q

R

S

T

U

V

W

X